# INTERNATIONAL POLITICS

*Introductory Readings*

# INTER-NATIONAL POLITICS

*Introductory Readings / Edited by*

### GEORGE S. MASANNAT
Western Kentucky University

### & GILBERT ABCARIAN
The Florida State University

NEW YORK

CHARLES SCRIBNER'S SONS

Printed in the United States of America
Library of Congress Catalog Card Number 75–94870

*To Janice
and Raisa*

# PREFACE

THE SPECIFIC PURPOSE of this volume is to present a set of scholarly, probing essays that will serve as a useful supplement to standard textbooks in courses on international relations and world politics. Since only a fraction of the large body of relevant literature can be reproduced in a collection of this type, we urge the student to explore his specific interests by reading some of the books and periodical literature noted at the end of each part of this text. Although the readings are hardly exhaustive, we have deliberately included selections that will sharpen the reader's curiosity, interest, and understanding in the field of international politics.

The readings are divided into six parts: 1) Perspectives in the Study of International Politics; 2) Determinants of Power; 3) Conflict and Coexistence; 4) Social Psychological Aspects of International Behavior; 5) The United States in the World Arena; and 6) World Order: Problems and Prospects of Transformation. Each part opens with a brief introduction that supplies the political and analytical context for the readings, and identifies their salient aspects. The selected bibliography and the study questions which conclude each part are intended to provoke further reading, class questions, and lively discussion.

Forging a book of this kind while immersed in the vast sea of literature on international politics led to difficult and sometimes painful decisions by the editors. Opinions may differ about the relevance and utility of the selections included, but this is to be expected. The range and quality of available literature did not allow us to make simple decisions about inclusion. We are hopeful that what we have assembled in this volume will meet the needs of both students and instructors, contributing to thought and inquiry in a crucial area of human affairs.

The editors express their sincere appreciation to these authors and publishers who were kind enough to grant permission for reproduction of their materials. We are also grateful to the Western Kentucky University for making its various facilities available in the preparation of the manuscript.

*George S. Masannat*
*Gilbert Abcarian*

# CONTRIBUTORS

ARON, RAYMOND

BRZEZINSKI, ZBIGNIEW

BUEHRIG, EDWARD H.

DAVIES, JOHN PATON JR.

DINERSTEIN, HERBERT S.

FENWICK, CHARLES G.

FRANKEL, CHARLES

FULBRIGHT, J. W.

GARDINER, ROBERT K. A.

HAMMARSKJÖLD, DAG

HOVET, THOMAS JR.

HOWARD, MICHAEL

KARPOV, VICTOR P.

KENNAN, GEORGE F.

KENNEDY, JOHN F.

KISSINGER, HENRY A.

LIPSON, LEON

MASTERS, ROGER D.

MORGENTHAU, HANS J.

NEEDLER, MARTIN C.

ROSECRANCE, R. N.

SINGER, J. DAVID

SPROUT, HAROLD & MARGARET

THOMPSON, KENNETH W.

VAN WAGENEN, RICHARD W.

VITAL, DAVID

WALLACE, A. F. C.

WILCOX, FRANCIS O.

WORCHEL, PHILIP

ZOPPO, CIRO ELLIOTT

# CONTENTS

PART SIX   WORLD ORDER: PROBLEMS AND PROSPECTS
           OF TRANSFORMATION

# PART ONE □ PERSPECTIVES IN THE STUDY OF INTERNATIONAL POLITICS

IN THE PAST decade, political science has entered a period of intensified self-reflection as evidenced by the growing volume of scholarly works dealing with the study of the study of politics. Among many reasons for the development of disciplinary evaluation of this type is recognition that at various stages in its continuous development, any science will feel the need to ask how its practitioners are dealing with their subject matter, in terms of governing analytical models and concepts, and whether prevailing intellectual goals, habits, and assumptions might not be improved. As a field of political science, international politics has been vitally affected by these developments of reevaluation and reorientation.

Unlike everyday events in the life of the individual, the sphere of international politics only rarely can be experienced directly, and never in its totality. The activities of our neighbors or civic groups or fellow students are near enough for direct, personal observation. Most of the activities in the international sphere, however, are not. As in other areas of crucial human concern, one must turn to scholars and their works in order to comprehend the nature and problems of international politics.

Today, two schools or approaches are dominant in the study of international politics. One seeks to identify "underlying" forces, motives, and patterns. The other concerns itself with historical dimensions. Both approaches are addressed to the problems at the very core of international politics study: explanation of the behavior of nations; methods of scientifically analyzing foreign policies; and utilizing analytical models that will maximize understanding of the vast and bewildering international arena. Expectedly, the search for answers to these problems has carried scholars into such related fields of study as psychology, economics, geography, law, sociology, and history, with the long-range intent of finding a general theory of international politics.

The search for such theory has precipitated debate between the

*1*

Behavioralists, the first school mentioned, and the Traditionalists. The first group demands analytic rigor, precision, and systematization, while the second seeks understanding through analytical emphasis upon the real, observable world in its historic manifestations.

Much, perhaps most, contemporary writing in international politics exemplifies the traditional approach in the sense of dealing with descriptive history, policy study, or structural analysis as opposed to emphasis upon testing hypotheses drawn from deductive models through the use of empirical procedures.

There is general agreement that the field of international politics remains weak in theory. This is attributed to its inability thus far to develop a distinct subject matter (a question of proper boundaries); agree on basic analytical models; define crucial concepts through a shared vocabulary containing precise definitions; and standardize analytic methods among scholars in order to permit and encourage retesting of initial studies. Harry Howe Ransom sums up the state of the field in the following terms:

The field possibly is inching towards more clarity with regard to levels of analysis; sharper conceptualization; more precisely defined variables; better identification of linkages among levels and units; more skillful adaptations from other disciplines; perhaps the beginnings of "islands of theory;" closer relations between theory construction and empirical research; and more careful attempts to build cumulatively and through additive testing. But if forward movement is indicated in these regards, this motion has not yet carried international relations toward any clearly marked goal-lines. And scientific rigor too often has been displayed at the expense of relevance to the real world.[1]

In part one of this book, there are five essays, each concerned with broad theoretical issues about the study, scope, and problems of international politics. These essays are heavily and deliberately normative; that is, each prescribes certain problems, directions, and analytical approaches that, in the authors' views, ought to command the attention of the student of international politics. These selections address themselves to five problems, respectively: theory, method, focus, values, and models.

*Theory*. The search for a single, encompassing theory of international relations continues unabated. Raymond Aron expresses skepticism that any "pure" theory explaining the behavior of nations can be found, for, he asserts, the types of relationships that would need inclusion in such a theory are impossible to specify in any systematic way since the international arena is in an inherent state of change. Hence the deficiencies of many current theories, he says, are attributable less to such theories than to the complexity of the subject matter. No theory, then,

[1] Harry Howe Ransom, "International Relations," *Journal of Politics*, XXX (May 1968), 369.

is able to incorporate the basic fact of change into its perspectives in a way that promises complete empirical and predictive reliability.

While a completed theory of international relations is not possible, the best approximation of one, Aron urges, is "praxeology," the theory of practice, since it takes all other theories into logical consideration. Understanding of the global international system at any given point in time must take all levels—and their corresponding theories—into account. To do this, it is necessary to realize that in studying international relations, the object of knowledge "is not only the logic of systems but also the logic of action."

*Method.* As we have noted, the search for a comprehensive theory of international relations has tended to divide international studies scholars into "classical" and "scientific" camps, sometimes resulting in strenuous debate over the fundamental question of "proper" methods for such inquiry. According to David Vital, the influence of the classicists has remained somewhat dominant.

After exploring each camp, he points out that neither is entirely adequate as an exclusive model for the study of contemporary international life, for there is no general agreement on "that sector of human experience and activity" that should be at the core of international research. Currently popular, the scientific approach is flawed because "method largely determines subject matter" and leads to concern with "peripheral" matters that promise but do not deliver understanding of central questions. The classical approach is strong on normative study, but weak on empirical insights.

Both approaches produce relevant pieces of study, yet fail to offer a "central, dominating topic" as a proper focal point.

Vital's basic thesis is that the proper unifying study is "governments in their foreign relations," an emphasis which, if accepted, presumably would render the study of international relations as "integrated discipline" by defining what is central to it.

*Focus.* In contrast with other social sciences, debate over the various possible levels of analysis in international relations has scarcely begun, according to David Singer. The purpose of his essay is to examine the significance of two such widely employed levels: the international system, and national sub-systems.

The international system as level of analysis tends to obscure the impact of specific "actors" (nations) on the total system and assumes a high degree of uniformity among the actors' foreign policy behavior. But that approach does have the advantage of depicting international behavior "in relatively gross and general terms." The national state as level of analysis permits significant differentiation among the actors, but may tend to distort reality by exaggerating differences, and also lead to ethnocentrism (a we-they orientation) in which the observer imputes virtue to his own nation and vice to others. That approach does justifiably focus attention on "the entire question of goals, motivation, and purpose in national policy." This level is likely to produce "richer description and . . . explanation of international relations . . ." but at the price of "considerable methodological complexity."

Singer concludes that there is no overriding case for the greater value of one level over the other. Rather, he warns that sensitivity to the conceptual issue of analytical level ought to precede and guide research of enduring value.

*Values*. According to Kenneth W. Thompson, the study of national policies and objectives cannot be separated from value questions, for the most salient questions of international relations, such as those of war and peace or ends and means, are grounded in normative assumptions.

While it is true that normative debate is currently avoided in favor of "factual" study, Thompson insists that the price paid is avoidance of "ultimate" questions. Normatively, international society is characterized by "certain broader principles of justice, freedom, and order" which the investigator must take into account if he wishes to deal with basic rather than peripheral matters.

Earlier in the history of the field of international relations, a crusading spirit was dominant; this has changed somewhat since, among normativists, "the spirit is more likely to be analytical and critical than crusading." Thompson urges that the need for "serious and exacting normative thinking" is greater than ever, referring to three qualities necessary to accomplish this task: 1) ability to explore international relations in the contexts of philosophy, history, and the social sciences; 2) capacity to improve the quality of normative thinking through a blending of old and new approaches; and 3) willingness to deal with ambiguities that resist complete understanding and analysis.

*Models*. Referring to the fact that many primitive peoples live in political situations that are analogous to the contemporary international political system, Roger D. Masters analyzes "stateless" types of primitive societies in order to determine what elements of primitive life may illuminate the "anarchy," or "state of nature" that characterizes present international relations. Both systems, he points out, lack a higher, authoritative agency of judgment in conflict situations and are in that sense stateless.

Masters notes that despite obvious differences, there are "some striking similarities" between primitive and contemporary political systems with respect to the role of violence in intergroup conflict. First, the range of social relationships is relatively exempt from self-perpetuating violence since there is a procedure for terminating conflict within "nuclear" (basic) groups, at least in theory. And second, in both there is a tendency to restrain violence between groups that consider themselves "near" each other.

Self-help and deterrence in primitive societies have their counterparts in the international sphere because "when there is no government, retaliation and the threat of violence serve to unite social groups and maintain legal or moral criteria of right and wrong." He suggests, further, that "reliance upon self-help and deterrence in international relations appears to be evidence that the world forms a political system that is in many respects similar to primitive systems." Therefore, "the comparison with stateless primitive peoples serves the useful purpose of identifying the characteristic properties of a political system in which law is sanctioned by self-help." In this sense, the study of stateless societies among primitive peoples may serve as a partial model for attaining a better understanding of our own international system and thereby suggest means for increasing its stability.

---

RAYMOND ARON

---

*What Is a Theory of International Relations?*

---

Few words are used as often by economists, sociologists, or political scientists as the word "theory." Few are as ambiguous. A recent book developing two ideas—the virtues of non-alignment and the influence that the priority of economic considerations in modern societies allegedly exerts in favor of peace—has as its subtitle "general theory."[1] A hypoth-

[1] J. W. Burton, *International Relations: A General Theory* (Cambridge: Cambridge University Press, 1965).

SOURCE: Raymond Aron, "What Is A Theory of International Relations?" *Journal of International Affairs*, XXI (1967), 185–206. Copyright by the Board of Editors of the *Journal of International Affairs*. Permission to reprint is gratefully acknowledged to the Editors of the *Journal*.

esis that alliances are founded on calculations of national interest and do not withstand a conflict of those interests is christened "theory" in the current language of political science.[2] As a matter of fact, the distinction is rarely explicitly made between related but distinct concepts such as "model," "ideal type," "conceptualization," and even an empirically observed regular occurrence. What authors call "theory" belongs more or less to one or the other of these categories, or may contain elements borrowed from one or the other in varying proportions.

This lack of rigor in the use of a key word can be explained and perhaps justified by the desire for progress. Political scientists feel that their discipline appears underdeveloped compared to economics, not to mention the natural sciences. This desire for progress has the unfortunate effect of making it seem more important to do than to know what one is doing. The accumulation of information matters more than the critical understanding of it.

However, the quarrel between proponents of the "classical" and "scientific" approaches to the study of international relations, a quarrel I deplore because it has increased the confusion, shows that scholars in the field are not indifferent to the theoretical basis of their discipline. Thus, perhaps it will not be entirely useless to pose the question: What is a theory of international relations?

## I

It seems to me that in the Western world the concept of theory has a double origin or, if you prefer, two meanings, each derived from a different tradition. Theory as contemplative knowledge, drawn from ideas or from the basic order of the world, can be the equivalent of philosophy. In that case, theory differs not only from practice or action, but from knowledge animated by the will to "know in order to predict and thus be able to act." The less practical a study is, the less it suggests or permits the handling of its object, the more theoretical it is. At most, it changes the one who has conceived it and those who are enlightened by it through his findings.

The other line of thought leads to authentically scientific theories, with those of physical science offering the perfect model. In this sense, a theory is a hypothetical, deductive system consisting of a group of hypotheses whose terms are strictly defined and whose relationships between terms (or variables) are most often given a mathematical form. The elaboration of this system starts with a conceptualization of perceived

[2] Raymond Dawson and Richard Rosecrance, "Theory and Reality in the Anglo-American Alliance," *World Politics*, Vol. XIX, No. 1 (Oct. 1966), pp. 21–51.

or observed reality; axioms or highly abstract relationships govern the system and allow the scientist to rediscover by deduction either appearances that are thereby fully explained, or facts that are perceptible through devices, if not through the senses, and that temporarily either confirm the theory or invalidate it. An invalidation necessitates a rectification; a confirmation never constitutes an absolute proof of the theory's truth.

We shall entirely discard the first meaning, i.e., theory as philosophy, and restrict ourselves to the second meaning, the meaning preferred by the "modernists" among sociologists and political scientists.

Aside from the special case of linguistics, probably economics, of all the social sciences, has developed theoretical elaboration to the greatest extent. Pure economics, in the style of Walras and Pareto, constitutes the equivalent of a hypothetical, deductive system; it is expressed in a set of equations. But it is well known, as Walras and Pareto were the first to point out, that pure economics sets up a simplified representation of reality. In place of actual economic life the economist substitutes an artificial market where men of flesh and bones are replaced by subjects with specially defined characteristics. They have perfect information at their disposal and a single objective, the maximization of a certain quantity (the intervention of money makes this calculation easy).

· · ·

Progress in economic science results from a ceaseless dialectic between theory and experiments. The theory in operation today has been profoundly marked by the influence of Keynes, whose "general theory" diverged sharply from classical theories in several respects: it was directly macroeconomic; it set up six variables, some independent and some dependent (at the same time, it suggested a technique of manipulation); it considered equilibrium at the level of full employment as a special case; it set up an entrepreneur different from the economic subject of traditional theory, an entrepreneur who would make investment decisions based upon expected profit (individual psychology, the psychological climate of the community, in other words social-psychological data, were thereby introduced into the system); and finally, it postulated, so to speak, the non-elasticity of nominal wages, thereby integrating additional social data into the system.

One could debate whether Keynesian theory is a general theory or just a model valid for explaining short-term fluctuations and their control for a historical period characterized by certain extra-economic factors. I shall not undertake this discussion, which would be an excessively long digression in view of the aims of this short essay. Indeed, the preceding discussion should suggest the following propositions that have implications for the study of international relations.

1) In order to elaborate the theory of a social sub-system, we need a definition of this sub-system that defines both its limits and its specificity. What are the true characteristics of the interconnected actions that constitute a relatively defined whole, whose implicit logic the theory tries to elaborate?

2) Scientific progress requires shuttling back and forth between simplified systems and renewed observations. Keynes' system involves actors who are less remote from actual actors than those in Walras' system. At the same time, Keynes postulates certain historical and social facts outside the specific field of economics (external variables).

3) Even the Keynesian system assumes the constancy of data that, in reality, are not constant; focusing on short-term fluctuations, Keynes does not take technical progress into consideration.

4) Progress in the economic field over the past thirty years has been largely due to empirical, statistical, and descriptive studies. Empirical and statistical studies have led to an awareness of essential phenomena, such as long-term growth and the transformation of price relationships among goods of different sectors owing to unequal rates of growth in productivity. National accounting, much more than theory, has given governments better control over economic fluctuations. Models of crisis —the configurations of variables considered as crisis indicators—have been misleading; indeed, it has not yet been proven that "crisis situations" are all alike. It is possible that each crisis is unique or, if you prefer, has its own particular story, and that the structure of the system itself contains possibilities of a crisis.

5) Progress in economic knowledge has not eliminated doctrinal conflicts, uncertainties in short- or middle-term forecasting, or the political (in other words partisan) dimension of the decisions taken by governments (decisions affecting the interests of various social classes in various ways). In short, neither theoretical knowledge nor empirical findings authorize the economist to dictate, in the name of science, a specific action to a ruler, although he can often advise the ruler on how to avoid evils dreaded by the whole community and sometimes predict the probable consequences of the ruler's actions. We cannot go directly from theory as a science to theory as a doctrine for action.

From these propositions emerge the problems I should like to raise about the theory of international relations.

1) Is it possible, and if so how, to define and delimit the sub-system of international relations?

2) What is the relation of this theory to empirical study, of the sub-system to the social context? Is this theory historical or meta-historical?

(This question was debated by the marginalist and historicist schools of economic thought at the end of the nineteenth century.)

3) What are the connections between theory and doctrine or, to use a word that shocked so many American readers, between theory and praxeology.[3]

Thus we rediscover the classical antitheses that define the meaning of theory: reality and theory, empiricism (historical and sociological) and theory, practice and theory.

II

We can determine the true field of international relations in two ways. Either we try to grasp what distinguishes this field from other social fields, what differentiates relationships among politically organized communities from all other social relationships, or we start with concepts that can be applied to areas other than international relations. This difference in approach in no way corresponds to that between traditionalists and modernists. Hans Morgenthau is a traditionalist and Kenneth Boulding is a modernist, yet both begin with general concepts not unique to international relations: *power* and *conflict*. International power politics or international conflicts are treated as species belonging to a genus, as illustrations or special cases of universally human phenomena. The first pages of that classic, *Politics Among Nations*,[4] offer an equally classic example of conceptual confusion arising from the use of a term such as "power," which, depending on the paragraph or even the sentence one is reading, means either the end or the means of politics and which, finally, is of no use. If "power" is defined in Weber's way, which is moreover the common way, as the ability of agent A to get agent B to submit to his will or to obey his orders (or, more precisely, the good fortune of agent A to achieve submission and obedience), then all social life is a question of power to some extent; power is obviously essential for collective action in any field whatsoever. Setting up power, thus defined, as the unique and highest goal of individuals, parties, or nations does not constitute a theory in the scientific sense, but instead amounts to a philosophy or an ideology. In any event, it is not a propo-

---

[3] May I say, without being impertinent, that the reaction of American critics to the word *praxeology*, including that of my friend Henry Kissinger, who was in other respects so kindly disposed, seems typically parochial to me. Recalling the awkward jargon found on every page of sociological studies, one is amazed that a correctly composed word (praxis-logos), which has no equivalent (the science of practice) and is in current use in Europe (Professor Kotarbinski, Professor of the Polish Academy of Sciences, wrote a well-known book bearing this title), should offend a linguistic purism so rarely in evidence.

[4] Hans J. Morgenthau, *Politics Among Nations* (New York: Alfred Knopf, 1949).

sition that can be proven false; thus it cannot even be considered a scientific hypothesis.

I chose the other alternative in my book *Paix et Guerre entre les Nations*.[5] I tried to determine what constituted the distinctive nature of international or interstate relations, and I concluded that it lay in the legitimacy or legality of the use of military force. In superior civilizations, these are the only social relationships in which violence is considered normal.

This conclusion was not at all original: it was obvious to the classical philosophers and to the jurists who developed European international law (*jus gentium*). It has been confirmed, if I may say so, by the experience of our century and by the failure of American statesmen. The latter, prisoners of the contradiction between a national ideology (that war is a crime and that the rule of law must prevail in the relations between nations) and the nature of international society, have appeared to others as cynical, naïve, or hypocritical. Never was the contradiction as glaring, and in a way both tragic and comic, as at the time of the double crisis in Hungary and Suez. To justify the stand taken against the British and French, President Eisenhower made the memorable remark, "There should not be two laws, one for friends, another for enemies" (the British and French were the friends), at the very time when he was passively witnessing the crushing of the Hungarian revolution by Soviet troops. American friends told me later that they had felt moral pride upon learning that President Eisenhower was joining the Soviets and the Third World against the British and French "in the name of law." They did not want to admit that President Eisenhower,[6] in allowing the Soviet Union to do as it pleased in Eastern Europe, was devaluating the legal or moral significance of the UN censure of the Anglo-French expedition and was applying the old rule of the international jungle: there are two laws, one for the strong, another for the weak. The strong have not yet found a better means of avoiding conflict and imposing something approaching order than by defining spheres of influence.

In short, neither the Kellogg-Briand Pact nor the United Nations has as yet eliminated the basic characteristic of the international system that philosophers and jurists of previous centuries designated the "state of nature." They contrasted it with the civil state, which possessed a tribu-

---

[5] Translated into English as *Peace and War: A Theory of International Relations* by Richard Howard and Annette Baker Fox (Garden City, N.Y.: Doubleday and Co., 1966).

[6] It goes without saying that these remarks are not meant as either an attack on or an approval of American policies in 1956. Maybe there was nothing better to do, but the moralizing speech, perhaps necessary for American public opinion, camouflaged a diplomacy that the European disciples of Machiavelli would not have repudiated.

nal and a police force. There is no equivalent of a tribunal in international society; and if the United Nations tried to compel one of the great powers to submit against its will, the police action would degenerate into a major war. Furthermore, the UN Charter explicitly recognizes the "sovereign equality" of states, and diplomats have never succeeded in defining the "international crime" *par excellence*—aggression.

The Cuban missile crisis of 1962 provides the same lesson. Frederick II gave his lawyers the task of justifying, ex post facto, the conquest of Silesia. President Kennedy found lawyers to formulate the "quarantine" of Cuba in apparently legal terms. But all the legal subtleties could not hide an undeniable fact: the United States itself has continuously applied the principle that every government has the right to request the stationing of armed forces of another state on its territory if it judges this outside assistance necessary to its security. According to this principle, Cuba had as much right to set up Soviet medium-range missile bases as Turkey had to set up American bases. Fortunately, President Kennedy was not dissuaded by legal considerations. As Frederick had done, he consulted his lawyers for the apparent legitimization of a necessity. And the whole world is grateful to him for having strengthened the effectiveness of deterrence more in a few days than hundreds of books or speeches would have done in a dozen years. At the same time, that crisis, settled without the loss of human lives, marked a turning point in the postwar era; it hastened the liquidation of the Berlin affair and gave a new content to "peaceful coexistence" between the two superpowers. World opinion was grateful for the priority given to the exigencies of the balance of nuclear forces over the sovereign rights of a small country. Wiser than the ideologists, it took into account the circumstances and intentions rather than the law.

Can that essential characteristic—the absence of a tribunal or police force, the right to resort to force, the plurality of autonomous centers of decision, the alternation and continual interplay between peace and war[7]—serve as a basis for a scientific theory, even though it is obvious to the actors themselves and belongs to their own intuitive "sociology" or "political science"? Should not science substitute for everyday notions those concepts that science itself elaborates? It seems easy for me to answer that nothing prevents us from translating the preceding idea into a word or a formula more satisfactory to the "scientists." As we know, Max Weber defined the state as a "monopoly of legitimate violence." Let us say that international society is characterized by "the absence of an entity that holds a monopoly of legitimate violence."

A theoretical definition of this kind cannot be proven in the same

---

[7] The formulas are not equivalent but can easily be deduced from each other.

way as an equation in theoretical physics: by showing its agreement with experimental data. Nor can it be invalidated. Even if a monopoly of legitimate violence in international society should be established in the future, we would merely say that the specific domain of interstate relations, as it had existed for a few thousand years, had disappeared as such. Yet a theoretical definition of this kind entails several direct and indirect confirmations. To simplify matters, I shall say that these confirmations will be brought forth by answering the following questions: (1) Does this definition permit the delimitation of the sub-system that is being considered? (2) Does it allow us to deduce or include other elements of the sub-system? (3) Does it permit us to rediscover (and to explain) the original data that served as a starting point for the theoretical elaboration?

The answer to the first question seems, on the whole, positive. I do not deny the difficulties involved. The real delimitation is often more difficult than the conceptual one. In primitive societies, it is sometimes hard to find the effective power that holds the highest authority. In the absence of politically and territorially organized entities, distinctions between various types of more or less violent conflict and between groups are vague. The collective actor that reserves for itself the right to use violence against other collective actors is more or less large: a village, a clan, or a tribe. But the difficulty in defining sub-systems in primitive societies by using concepts derived from complex societies exists in economics as well as in international relations. Why blame the theory for what can be imputed to the very nature of its subject matter? Likewise, it would be easy to object that feudal societies, owing to the dispersion of means of combat, make it difficult to distinguish between violence within the state and violence between states. Civil wars, such as the American Civil War, are also often hard to distinguish from foreign wars. Moreover, international law has taken these marginal cases into account. When a state loses the "monopoly of legitimate violence," and two parties have organized military forces at their disposal, the non-belligerents tend to treat the two camps as if each one formed a separate state. However, such marginal cases do not constitute a valid objection to the rigor of the initial definition.

I believe that the answer to the second question provides the best justification for our chosen point of departure. Indeed, by postulating a society without a monopoly of legitimate violence, composed of collective actors, each of which confers the monopoly of legitimate violence on an entity within itself, we also implicitly define the main variables necessary to explain the systems and the events. As a matter of fact, the plurality of collective actors implies geographical space in two respects: the area in which each of the collective actors is established, and the area within which the relations between the actors take place. Actors whose mutual relations are such that each one takes all the others into account in the calculations preceding its decisions belong to the same system. In the absence of a monopoly of legitimate violence, each actor is obliged to provide for its own security, either with its own forces or by joining forces with its allies. Consequently, the configuration of forces (bipolar or multipolar) is one of the main variables of any international system. Since each actor is controlled, in its relations with the other actors, by the entity that possesses a monopoly of legitimate violence, and thus by the handful of men who are responsible for it, the internal regimes of the collective actors constitute one of the variables of the international system: the homogeneity or heterogeneity of the system depends upon the kinship or opposition between the internal regimes of the different actors.

Should such an analysis be called a *theory* or a *conceptualization?* Is it an outline of a theory or an admission that a general theory is impossible? It all depends on what we expect of a theory, of the model of a theory (in physics or in economics) to which we refer. Such a conceptual analysis seems to me to fulfill some of the functions that we can expect from a theory: it defines the essential features of a sub-system; it provides a list of the main variables; it suggests certain hypotheses about the operation of the sub-system, depending on whether it is bipolar or multipolar, homogeneous or heterogeneous.

It has an additional value: it makes it easier to distinguish between theory and ideology or, if you prefer, between pseudo-theories and theories. For example, let us take the formula, sometimes presented as theoretical, according to which states act according to their "national interest." The formula is just as meaningless as that of La Rochefoucauld, who discerned selfishness behind behavior that was apparently the most unselfish. It is enough, indeed, to postulate that Meredith's character Beauchamp, who drowns while trying to save a child, finds more satisfaction in sacrificing his life than in saving it at the expense of someone else's death. Likewise, whatever the diplomacy of a state may be, nothing prevents one from asserting after the fact that it was dictated by considerations of "national interest," as long as "national interest" has not been strictly defined.

Indeed, the so-called theory of "national interest" either suggests an idea as undeniable as it is vague—that each actor thinks first of itself— or else tries to oppose itself to the other pseudo-theories, e.g., that the foreign policy of states is dictated by political ideology or moral principles. Each of these pseudo-theories means something only in connection with the other. To say that the Soviet Union conducts its foreign affairs on the basis of its "national interest" means that it is not exclusively guided by ideological considerations, by its ambition to spread Communism. Such a proposition is undeniable, but to conclude from it that the rulers of a non-Communist Russia would have had the same diplomatic policy between 1917 and 1967 is simply absurd. The purpose of the empirical study of international relations consists precisely in determining the historical perceptions that control the behavior of collective actors and the decisions of the rulers of these actors. The theoretical approach we have adopted throws light upon the diversity of the stakes involved in conflicts between collective actors, of the goals that they may have in view. The obsession with "space," characteristic of Japan's and Hitler's ambitions between the two world wars, has disappeared. The Marxist-Leninist ideology of an implacable conflict between the capitalist and socialist camps, which if it has not dictated the day-by-day decisions of the Kremlin leaders, has at least molded their thinking, is in the process of erosion. The Kremlin's diplomacy is being transformed at the same time as their image of the world.

This theory can be presented as a failure or as a limitation of theory. Indeed, if we refer to the pure economics of Walras and Pareto, there can be no "pure theory of international relations" any more than there can be a "pure theory of internal politics" because we cannot endow the actors, either through the centuries or within a given system, with a single aim: the conscious or unconscious desire for a certain maximum gain. Those who presuppose the will to "maximize power" are not even aware of the ambiguity of the term they use.

If we refer to the Keynesian model, the gap between economic theory and the theory of international relations is less wide, but it still exists. There is no equivalent in the international system either for accounting identities (investment = savings) or for the distinction between independent and dependent variables. The international system is even less homeostatic than the system conceived by Keynes: although the latter contains equilibria without full employment, automatic or manipulated mechanisms tend either to re-establish equilibria or to induce alternating movements of expansion and contraction. No international system, whether homogeneous or heterogeneous, bipolar or multipolar, has a mechanism guaranteed to restore equilibrium. Innumerable are the factors, within states or in their relations, that tend to modify the nature of the system or to bring about a shift from one system to another.

Only a halfway affirmative answer can be given to the last question, but this does not condemn our theoretical choice. Systems and social events are *undefined* in the epistemological sense of the term: as they are experienced by their subjects and observed by historians or sociologists, they neither parcel themselves out into neat and definite subsystems, nor can they be reduced to a small number of variables that could be organized into a body of interconnected propositions. The definition we have adopted allows us to set up such a body, but we could not deduce the systematic murder of millions of Jews by the Nazis as a necessary consequence of any theory. An analysis of the European state system of 1914 helps us understand the unlimited nature of the First World War. Indeed, a hypothesis to the effect that "a conflict between two alliance systems involving an entire international system, whose outcome will determine the hierarchical position of all the principal actors, will naturally tend to be carried on until its conclusion, that is, until the complete victory of one of the two camps" seems probable. But such a hypothesis, assuming that its wording is precise enough for it to be applied to many other cases, should be confirmed by historical studies. Besides, it could have been contradicted if the course of military events had been different in the summer of 1914. For that matter, the decisive factor between 1914 and 1918 seems to have been what I have elsewhere called "the technical surprise."[8] (None of the military high commands had been prepared for a long war and none had foreseen the relentless mobilization, which was the work of civilians on both sides.) On the other hand, the period of revolutionary wars between 1792 and 1815 can be attributed to the ideological factor much more than to other elements of the international situation. Clausewitz wrote that there is a theory of tactics but not of strategy, because the strategist must base his decisions on a particular situation, and each situation presents too many special features for us to be able to substitute deduction from certain generalizations for the intuition, common sense, or intelligence of the military leader. It is not always ignorance but sometimes the very nature of the subject matter that determines the limits of a theory.

On the other hand, from the theoretical definition we have adopted, one cannot deduce all of what I shall call "peaceful commerce between communities," whether it concerns relations between individuals (buyers and sellers belonging to two political entities) or relations between states (scientific, economic, intellectual, tourist, etc.). There is no prohibition against attempting to define international society on the basis of the state of peace instead of the risk of war, or against considering tests of strength and military competition as exceptional situations rather than essential features of international relations. It might be objected that we have confused international and interstate relations and that our definition can at most be applied only to the latter, and even then only during times of crisis. Transnational (or trans-state) society would thus be presented as the true international society, which supranational organizations would progressively regulate, military competition between states gradually losing its virulence and narrowing its scope.

[8] *The Century of Total War* (Boston: Beacon Press, 1955), Chap. 1.

I wish it would be so tomorrow. But considering the long history of complex societies, the theoretical definition I have chosen seems to me to be closer to reality, more in keeping with experience, more instructive, and more productive. Any definition that fails to take account of the basic characteristic of international relations, which is rooted in the legitimation of the resort to force, neglects both a constant factor in civilizations, one that has had tremendous effects on the course of history, and the human meaning of military activity. Statisticians such as Lewis Richardson who count acts of violence or homicide without differentiating between murderers and soldiers provide an opportune reminder that figures in themselves are meaningless. The theoretical definition offered here coincides with actual experience; statesmen, jurists, moralists, philosophers, and military men throughout the ages have perceived the essence of international relations to be just what I see as the starting point for a theory. Perhaps some modernists will condemn me for this. On this matter, I am a traditionalist.

III

•   •   •

The theory of international relations differs from economic theory in that the distinction between internal and external variables, even in the abstract, is impossible. Indeed, the distinctive feature of the behavior of actors in relation to one another is that, in the absence of a tribunal or police force, they are obliged to calculate forces, especially military forces, available in case of war. No actor can rule out the possibility that another is harboring aggressive designs against it. Each must therefore estimate which forces are reliable in view of what Clausewitz called the outcome of credit transactions: payment in cash, the test of strength.[9] This calculation of forces in itself requires a reference to the area controlled by each actor, to its population and economic resources, to its military system or mobilization coefficient, and to the types of weapons available. Military systems and weapons are in turn the expression of political and social systems. Every concrete study of international relations is thus a sociological and historical study, since the calculation of forces refers to a number, space, resources, and regimes (military, economic, political, and social); and these elements in turn constitute

[9] In the atomic age, "payment in cash" is perhaps no longer war but a crisis. At least it has been so up until now. I have analyzed this transformation in Chap. V of *The Great Debate: Theories of Nuclear Strategy* (Garden City, N.Y.: Doubleday and Co., 1965).

the stakes involved in conflicts between states. Once again, theoretical analysis itself reveals the limits of pure theory.

• • •

Any concrete study of international relations is sociological, as I see it, in the sense in which Pareto contrasted sociology with economics (i.e., it is not possible to isolate a system of international relations because the actors' conduct, controlled by calculations of force, is determined by economic, political, and social variables).

• • •

The historian's intention can be defined in four different ways. Either he is interested in the past and not in the present, or he is interested in events rather than in systems, or he narrates history rather than analyzing it, or he sticks to peculiarities rather than generalities. In the end, the first definition seems meaningless to me because the subject we are discussing already belongs to the past at the time we speak about it. The global system, as I described it, had already changed by the time my description was published. It is true that the historian of the present lacks the archives, the perspective that loosens the bonds between the observer and his object of study, and especially the knowledge of the consequences. A history of the present[10] will serve as a document for the historian of the future. Historical science proceeds by the accumulation of knowledge, yet also by a constant reinterpretation of preceding interpretations. From the history of the present written by a contemporary to the history of the same period written in the next century, the amount of reinterpretation will probably be greater than from Mommsen's *History of Rome* to a history of Rome written in the middle of the twentieth century. The difference appears to me as one of degree rather than of kind.

The second definition does not seem to me to be valid either. To be sure, the professional historian, because of his training and his tradition, pays more attention to accidents than the sociologist or the economist. But the present-day historian, who is interested in demographic, economic, or social data, also strives to reconstruct the meaningful wholes that have marked out the course of human development. If indeed the historian is more interested in events than the sociologist, it is to the extent that he relates what happened: he puts events or systems viewed as events into place, into their order of succession, and discerns a meaning immanent in this order, a meaning that would be lost in any other method of reconstruction.

Thus, we arrive at two legitimate definitions. The historian either

---

[10] A history of the cold war is already possible.

narrates events or tries to comprehend the uniqueness of a culture, a society, or an international system. Thucydides narrates the events of the Peloponnesian War, but Jacob Burckhardt, who tries to grasp and convey the unique whole of the century of Constantine or of the Italian Renaissance, is also a historian. My analysis of the global system in the thermonuclear age is historical, although it does not narrate events. After seeking generalities or peculiarities, it has a special aim: the extension to the whole globe, for the first time, of a single international system, a system distinguished by its heterogeneity and dominated by the thermonuclear duopoly of the United States and the Soviet Union.

I have wrongly given the impression in *Paix et Guerre entre les Nations* that sociological research did not lead to any result. But that was not my thought. I tried to refute the geographical, demographic, and economic single-cause explanations of peace and war; but taking space, numbers, and resources into account is obviously indispensable to any explanation of international relations, as is a consideration of the character of political regimes or of nations. Furthermore, by refuting the demographic or economic "theories" (in the sense of causal explanations) of wars, one makes a positive contribution to knowledge by shedding light on the constant data of international society, and even of human and social nature, which form the structural conditions for hostility. One dissipates the illusions of those who hope to put an end to the reign of wars by modifying a *single* variable (the number of men, the status of property, the political regime). Above all, one gains a deeper understanding of the historical diversity of international systems by discriminating between the variables that have a different meaning in each period and the variables that, at least temporarily, remain unchanged despite technological upheavals (e.g., the concern for autonomy and the desire for power on the part of collective actors who constantly vie with each other for their security, their glory, or their ideas, through alternately violent and non-violent means).

•  •  •

The theory of nuclear strategy is in certain respects more like economic theory than the general theory of international relations. Indeed, it relies on implicit axioms: that a "rational" Prince will not intentionally unleash a thermonuclear war, or will not even risk thermonuclear war except for a vital stake. The "rational" Prince of nuclear strategy resembles the economic man of game theory more than that of Walras. But it is not possible to make an exact calculation of either the stakes or the risk. The theory of nuclear strategy is nonetheless a theory, albeit restricted to a particular phase of history and a special problem. It could not arise before the weapons whose implications it seeks to explain. It applies to only a single aspect of the conduct of states in our time. Moreover, it takes account of its own limitations: the greater the stability at the higher level of nuclear weapons, the more the danger of escalation diminishes, and the less terrifying are the non-nuclear military conflicts. These hypotheses are theoretical because they do not take the whole reality into account. The United States and the Soviet Union, for many reasons, can either agree to impose *their* peace or clash here and there without fearing mutual destruction. For the time being, they seem to have chosen the first alternative. Rulers of other states are secretly pleased with this: it is good that the concern to avoid a thermonuclear war prevails over other considerations. This concern also dictated the United States' attitude during the simultaneous crises of Hungary and Suez. It could be expressed by the familiar saying: "Injustice is better than the risk of nuclear war."

Can the theorist approve or condemn? Certainly not. We thus arrive at our final antithesis: practice and theory.


IV

Many authors are severely critical of political science or of the science of international relations because it permits neither prediction nor manipulation.[11] A science that is not operational is not a science. Economic science is at least partially operational since it shows statesmen how to tax a definite portion of individual incomes without jeopardizing the growth of production; it teaches them to control economic fluctuations at all costs, and to limit the extent of deflationary and inflationary movements. It seems undeniable to me that, in this sense, political science or the science of international relations is not operational and will perhaps never be so, at least not until the time when politics per se, that is, the rivalry between individuals and the community to determine what is good in itself, will have disappeared.

Let us consider only the field of international relations. There is no lack of partial studies of a purely scientific character, in the strict sense of that term as used in physics or chemistry. How vulnerable are the silos in which nuclear missiles are stored? Given the explosive force of thermonuclear warheads, the average deviation in range, and the "hardness" of the sites, how many missiles are needed on an average to destroy an enemy device? The method of analysis, in such a case, is no different from that used in the natural sciences. The nature of the new weapons has given an unprecedented rigor and technical precision to the traditional calculation of the relations between forces. But these cal-

[11] Cf. Oscar Morgenstern, *The Question of National Defense* (New York: Random House, 1959).

culations are not yet sufficient to dictate a *scientific strategy*, whether it concerns a single decision (e.g., the "quarantine" of Cuba), or a whole political program (e.g., preventing the proliferation of nuclear weapons and refusing to assist allies anxious to develop their own nuclear industry), or a vision of the desirable international order. The science of international relations (and especially the analysis of the relations between nuclear powers) has had an effect upon the outlook of the Princes (the President of the United States and the men of the Kremlin) by turning strategists into the equivalent of what were called the Prince's counselors in Machiavelli's century. The theory of non-proliferation is not a scientific theory. It is a doctrine for action that coincides almost exactly with the interests of the United States and the Soviet Union, and perhaps with those of all states (which, for the time being, are not sure of this).

During the Cuban crisis, President Kennedy applied one of the lessons suggested by theoretical analysis: since the major danger, in case of a confrontation between two nuclear powers, is a total war that would be disastrous for everyone, wisdom compels the state that wants to impose its will upon the other to act gradually. It is advisable to begin at a lower degree of violence and, through actions that are messages and messages that are actions, to make known one's inflexible determination to go as far and as high as necessary to obtain satisfaction. Thus the duelists allow themselves time to reach a settlement without letting the irreparable take place. The winner—the one who has finally achieved his goal—will not cause his rival to lose his face, and will have left the path open for an honorable retreat. He will voluntarily create the illusion of a compromise even though he has won a victory.

On the whole, opinion in the United States, as in the world, approved of the conduct of the crisis, viewing it as the perfect expression of diplomatic skill or of the strategy of the nuclear age. Only a few cynics have stood apart. They have argued that even if President Kennedy had not taken so many precautions to spare the Kremlin leaders' pride, the latter would not have allowed themselves to be provoked. They would have adhered to Lenin's rule of taking two steps forward and one backward, a rule that takes on additional validity in the nuclear age. I am raising the argument of the cynics, not because I accept it myself, but in order to show that, even in such a critical situation, science proposes and the Prince disposes.

Another example will illustrate the limitations of a doctrine based only on the lessons of abstract analysis. Such analysis clearly shows that the more monstrous a total nuclear war is, the less plausible is a threat to unleash it. The doctrine of all or nothing, of massive retaliation, becomes more and more unreasonable and, in the end, ineffectual. The result is that deterrence by nuclear threat requires the existence of conventional forces sufficient to prevent a would-be aggressor from gaining easy victories at small cost, and to give the defender the means of increasing his stakes until the time when the use of nuclear weapons becomes plausible or even inevitable.

Passing from the doctrine of massive retaliation to the doctrine of flexible response is in keeping with the logic of strategic thinking. All countries possessing nuclear weapons will accept the abstract value of this reasoning as soon as they have the means to apply its conclusions, that is, when they will no longer be compelled, consciously or unconsciously, to pretend to be irrational because they lack the resources to adopt another strategy. But the doctrine of flexible response does not necessarily justify America's insistence, since 1961, on increasing NATO's conventional forces, on accumulating stockpiles for battles to be waged for ninety days without resorting to nuclear weapons, and on planning for a "pause" after a few days or a few weeks of combat before using nuclear weapons.

Finally, it remains true, according to abstract reasoning, that the reinforcement of conventional armaments adds to deterrence by giving the potential victim of aggression an additional margin of maneuver. But this freedom of maneuver belongs only to the holder of atomic weapons, i.e., in the West to the United States; moreover, restricting the battle to Europe and to conventional weapons would consequently spare the United States and the Soviet Union the horrors of war. Once this is realized, the objections or suspicions of Europeans, and of the Germans in particular, cannot be attributed solely to a lack of understanding, as American analysts want to believe. Depending on the language used, the interpretation suggested, and the extent of preparation, the accumulation of conventional forces will appear destined either to make the threat of escalation plausible (i.e., to maintain the threat of resorting to nuclear weapons) or to permit prolonged, costly combat on European soil (i.e., to delay, if not eliminate, the threat of resorting to nuclear weapons). In the latter case, the policy fosters European skepticism ("the United States will not sacrifice New York or Boston to save Frankfort, London, or Paris"); in the former, it dispels this skepticism. But if the Prince does not understand the various possible interpretations of his nuclear policy, if he goes too far in one direction, if he does not tailor his preparations to the extent and foreseeable duration of conventional battles, he will upset the alliance he wished to consolidate. That is what has been done since 1961 by American leaders, who started with sound ideas but became the victims of the capital sin of diplomats and strategists: single-mindedness.

The same is true of the doctrine of non-proliferation. Let us assume that the chiefs of state all agree that the avoidance of a nuclear war is their highest objective. Let us further assume that they all believe that the risk of that war increases with the number of states possessing those weapons. It still does not follow that they should rationally adhere to the doctrine of non-proliferation that the Russians and Americans preach and strive to put into practice. This doctrine implies a discrimination between states, with some deemed worthy and others unworthy of holding such weapons. This discrimination may endanger the security of non-nuclear states. At any rate, it subjects them to the status of protectorates, which Princes traditionally have considered incompatible with dignity and sovereignty. Not to have to depend on any protector is a value in itself, even if dependence does not jeopardize security.

Do not misunderstand me: I am not saying that the Russians and Americans are wrong to subscribe to the doctrine of non-proliferation. It is possible that an implicit or explicit agreement between the two major powers is desirable. But I want to show that the doctrine, drawn from a simplified model and presuming that all actors have a single or ultimate goal, has no claim to validity or scientific accuracy. Whether the doctrine is inspired by unselfish motives or by an unconscious desire for power, it appears to be cynical since it tends to sanctify the reign of the two superpowers. In any case, the doctrine conforms to the essential nature of the system of international relations I have analyzed: it endeavors to substitute the rule of the strongest for the still nonexistent tribunal and police force. Far from having modified the asocial nature of international relations, nuclear weapons have given rise to new expressions of that nature: solidarity of interests between ideological enemies, conflict of interests among allies. Because resort to force is still possible at any moment, the two superpowers subordinate their rivalry not to a rule of law but to a common concern for their security.

If we expect a theory of international relations to provide the equivalent of what a knowledge of construction materials provides the builder of bridges, then there is no theory and never will be. What the theory of action is able to offer, here as elsewhere, is an understanding of various ideologies—moralism, legalism, realism, and power politics—through which men and nations think out problems in international relations, establish their goals, or assign themselves duties. The theory of practice, or *praxeology*, differs from these ideologies insofar as it considers them all and determines the full implications of each one. As long as international society remains an asocial society whose law, in serious cases, is left to the interpretation of each actor, and which lacks an authority holding a monopoly of legitimate violence, the theory will be scientifically valid to the very extent that it does not provide the equivalent of what noble-hearted people and lightweight minds expect, that is, a simple ideology guaranteeing morality or efficiency.

This theory, as objective a study as possible of the conditions under which foreign policy develops, is not irrelevant to the morality or efficiency of action. For moralism, if it leads to Max Weber's *Gesinnungsethik*, by failing to take account of the probable or possible consequences of the decisions taken, turns out to be immoral. As for realism, it would be unrealistic if it considered the moral judgments men pass on the conduct of their rulers as negligible, if it disregarded the interest of all actors in maintaining a minimum of legal order in their reciprocal relations, or if it ignored the yearning of humanity, now capable of destroying itself, to reduce interstate violence. The more the theorist of practice bears in mind the multiplicity of aims pursued by actors in the international system, the less he will be a prisoner of an oversimplified representation of *homo diplomaticus*, and the chance he will have of understanding his allies and enemies by understanding the diversity of perceptions that govern their conduct. The *hic et nunc* decision, about Cuba or Vietnam, can never be dictated by the theorist. Nor will he be able to dictate, with assurance of scientific validity, the strategy that would lead humanity beyond "power politics" toward a monopoly of legitimate violence.

The course of international relations is eminently historical, in all senses of the term: its changes are incessant; its systems are diverse and fragile; it is affected by all economic, technical, and moral transformations; decisions made by one man or several men put millions of men into action and launch irreversible changes, whose consequences are carried out indefinitely; and the actors, citizens or rulers, are forever subjected to apparently contradictory obligations.

• • •

Is it a failure or a success for the theory of practice to rediscover the paradoxes of human existence as they have always appeared to philosophers, both ancient and modern, without resolving them? Failure or success, it is a fact that the scientist has not yet been given the means to transform man's historical condition.

## V

Perhaps after this itinerary we can again take up that meaning of the concept of theory we put aside: theory and philosophy as one and the same. Not that we have in some way found in conclusion what we decided not to seek at the outset, namely, a philosophical truth of a higher order than scientific knowledge. But the whole approach, which proceeds from the determination of the international system as a specific social system to the prudence of the statesman through the analysis of sociological regularities and historical peculiarities, constitutes the critical or questioning equivalent of a philosophy.

No technique of inquiry, no traditional or modern method, should be accepted or rejected *a priori* so long as the investigator remains aware of the whole into which his individual undertaking is placed or integrated. The different levels of conceptualization—a definition of the asocial society of sovereign states, a theory or pseudo-theory of the demographic or economic causes of wars, models of typical situations between nuclear powers, an enumeration of the main variables of all international systems—are distinguished from each other to suit the needs of clarity. Understanding of a single system—for example, the global system from 1949 to 1960—must take all levels into account; it calls for the simultaneous use of all available instruments. It is not even a paradox to suggest that theory alone makes it possible to incorporate the personal relationship between two men, Khrushchev and Kennedy, into an interpretation of the development of the Cuban crisis of 1962. In the opposite sense, this crisis adds something to our theoretical knowledge, reminding us that the historian has to be a philosopher and the philosopher has to be aware of what we shall never see a second time— at least when the object of knowledge is not only the logic of systems but also the logic of action.

DAVID VITAL

# On Approaches to the Study of International Relations: Or, Back to Machiavelli

## I

A heavy onslaught on the (predominantly American) "scientific" school of students of international relations has recently been delivered[1] to the

[1] Hedley Bull, "International Theory: The Case for a Classical Approach," *World Politics*, xviii (April 1966), 361–77.

SOURCE: David Vital, "On Approaches To The Study of International Relations Or, Back to Machiavelli," *World Politics*, xix (July 1967), 551–562. Reprinted by permission.

evident satisfaction and comfort of those who practice or respond most comfortably to the "classical approach." Still, the defeat of one school—if defeat there was[2]—need not, of course, necessarily redound to the honor of the other, and it is surely worth considering what positive case has been made out on this occasion, explicitly or by implication, in favor of "classicism." In fact, this article will argue, neither approach is entirely adequate. Neither provides a really firm basis on which to found a coherent and well-integrated field of study or—what is undoubtedly more important—a framework within which the facts of contemporary international life can be selected, compared, and interpreted in a thoroughly valid and enlightening manner.

The present article rests on the view that the study of international relations is and must be an empirical one and that, in consequence, problems in theory depend for their solution *before all else* on an agreed demarcation of that sector of human experience and activity with which we are principally concerned. An attempt will be made to show that much of the debate on the nature and limitations of theory in international relations and on the methodology appropriate to its study conceals uncertainty about the objects of both theory and investigation.

Mr. Hedley Bull describes and defines the classical approach under two main heads. First, method:

What I have in mind . . . is . . . the approach to theorizing that derives from philosophy, history, and law, and that is characterized above all by explicit reliance upon the exercise of judgment and by the assumptions that if we confine ourselves to strict standards of verification and proof there is very little of significance that can be said about international relations, that general propositions about this subject must therefore derive from a scientifically imperfect process of perception or intuition, and that these general propositions cannot be accorded anything more than the tentative and inconclusive status appropriate to their doubtful origin.[3]

Second, subject matter:

For example, does the collectivity of sovereign states constitute a political society or system, or does it not? If we can speak of a society of sovereign states, does it presuppose a common culture or civilization? And if it does, does such a common culture underlie the worldwide diplomatic framework in which we are attempting to operate now? What is the place of war in international society? Is all private use of force anathema to society's working, or are there just wars which it may tolerate and even require? Does a member

---

[2] Strenuously denied by a notable "scientist": see Morton A. Kaplan, "The New Great Debate: Traditionalism vs. Science in International Relations," *World Politics*, XIX (October 1966), 1–20.

[3] P. 361.

state of international society enjoy a right of intervention in the internal affairs of another, and if so in what circumstances? Are sovereign states the sole members of international society, or does it ultimately consist of individual human beings, whose rights and duties override those of the entities who act in their name? To what extent is the course of diplomatic events at any time determined or circumscribed by the general shape or structure of the international system; by the number, relative weight, and conservative or radical disposition of its constituent states, and by the instruments for getting their way that military technology or the distribution of wealth has put into their hands; by the particular set of rules of the game underlying diplomatic practice at the time? And so on.[4]

It is clear that if this is, indeed, the subject matter of international relations, then the suggested method of dealing with it is largely valid. In this respect Mr. Bull's view corresponds, broadly speaking, with Martin Wight's, namely, that the "disharmony between international theory and diplomatic practice, a kind of recalcitrance of international politics to being theorized about" must be recognized and that it follows from the fact "that the theorizing has to be done in the language of political theory and law."[5] But if the subject matter of international relations is, genuinely, *diplomatic practice*, it is worth seeing how well Mr. Bull's questions serve to specify and clarify what underlies an otherwise somewhat ambiguous phrase. Alternatively, are the answers to his questions what we really want to know?

The first observation must be that many of the terms that Mr. Bull employs (e.g., "What is the *place* of war in international society?") cry out for preliminary but exhaustive philosophical-logical analysis. There is certainly very little room here for empirical treatment, for reasonably rigorous standards of observation and verification.

But what is possibly more striking is the emphasis on moral and partly moral questions, or on questions having a strong legal content, or, again, on questions which are in the most ordinary sense of the term political—*without* its being in any way stressed or explained that such questions are and must remain distinct for all purposes from those of a factual character. "Does a member state of international society enjoy a right of intervention in the internal affairs of another, and if so in what circumstances?" is a teasing combination of the legal, the ethical, and (at least one hopes) the factual. So is a question dealing with the fine point whether society may ever properly tolerate a "just war."

Now, of course, if we are really supposed to concern ourselves with

4 P. 367.
5 "Why Is There No International Theory?" in Herbert Butterfield and Martin Wight, eds., *Diplomatic Investigations* (London 1966), 33.

such problems of indeterminate logical status to which no reasonably final, empirically based solution can conceivably be found, then the extreme form in which Mr. Bull has laid down the methods appropriate to theorizing about international relations (and, by implication, appropriate to its study as well) is only too valid, and the irrelevancy of any of the "scientific" approaches all too clear. On the other hand, those who are inclined to dismiss all such cogitations, however subtle and sophisticated, as so much wisdom literature may have a point. It is only odd that one of Mr. Bull's own most telling points against the "scientists" is that many of them pay far less attention to empirical evidence than they claim to do and that such evidence as they do adduce is often barely relevant to the issues they claim to be dealing with.

There can be no question that Mr. Bull's topics are, each in its own right, of great—one might truly say, of abiding—fascination. But their immediate value lies in their power to stimulate interest in the field as a whole, rather than in such answers as might be furnished in direct response to them. They bear much the same relation to "diplomatic practice" as, say, reasoned exhortations about the dangers of nuclear proliferation may be said to bear to analyses of the strategic considerations of the states concerned. At all events, the notable result of treating these topics as constituting the central subject matter of the study of international relations is to entrench the still common conviction that it is a field that cannot be unified, but must remain a congeries of disparate and disconnected studies, the logical and empirical ties between which we can dimly perceive, but cannot possibly formulate.

It would therefore seem pertinent to ask whether we ought not to pay much more attention to "diplomatic practice" in the raw, so to speak, and whether there is any room at all for a theory of international relations which is in any sense and to any degree incompatible with actual and observed diplomatic practice, and finally, by extension, whether any weight should be attached to studies—theoretical or otherwise—that do not in one way or another concern or illuminate it.

## II

The "scientists" vary so greatly in their techniques, purposes, and subjects of interest that it may be presumptuous to attempt to generalize about them. In any case, as will be indicated below, some of their work is founded on an approach that is substantially that which this article attempts to advance. However, much "scientific" work suffers from a characteristic flaw: method largely determines subject matter. Much "scientific" work seems to be justified in terms of the proposition that once the right analytical and investigatory techniques are evolved, the heart of the subject will stand revealed and duly lend itself to study and analysis.

Not unnaturally, one is therefore faced with a great range and variety of projects. At one extreme there may be found an exhaustive collation on such a topic at which states were represented in which capitals at certain given times and by what rank of mission. At the other extreme one finds the altogether impressive analytical studies of systems, of which Morton Kaplan's are among the best known. In the middle range there will be an examination of the effect of stress on policymakers, a study of the role of images, and so forth.

In the case of the first type of study, it is surely plain that, however meticulously executed, the forced attempt to find *something* in the political sphere of international relations which is amenable to quantification and statistical analysis only results, in practice, in the illumination (if that is the right word) of one, small, marginal point in almost total isolation from all others. Of the third type, a product of the general attempt to apply the content and methods of the behavioral sciences to the study of international politics, it may certainly be said that it represents an extremely valuable approach. But so long as the work is to all intents and purposes divorced from detailed and serious historical research (or, alternatively, from the careful and thoroughly informed study of contemporary cases) and is linked, as is only too often the case, to such "laboratory" techniques as simulation or is adapted from studies of the business world, the actual results are likely to be unhelpful and incapable of being clearly related to the problems with which most students of international relations are ostensibly concerned. It is simply not credible that study of the behavior of American (or any other) students of eighteen can reveal anything of proven or provable value that is not already known from other sources about Kaiser Wilhelm II or Patrice Lumumba or any other equivalent or lesser figure of whom it may be said with *prima facie* justification that their political behavior at some point must be at least partly explained in individual psychological terms if it is to be understood at all. However, the more general difficulty about this kind of work is that, while it can certainly reveal factors (such as stress) which, conceivably, may have been neglected in the past, the *verification* of any hypothesis concerning them must involve a return to historical (or contemporary) sources in what one may, perhaps, be forgiven for calling the ordinary way. And it is striking about much of this otherwise interesting work that it is precisely this verification that is very, very rarely performed.

Mr. Kaplan's work is in a different class. The conception that underlies it is, in his own words.

If the number, type, and behavior of nations differ over time, and if their military capabilities, their economic assets, and their information also vary over time, then there is some likely interconnection between these elements such that different structural and behavioral systems can be discerned to operate in different periods of history. This conception may turn out to be incorrect, but it does not seem an unreasonable basis for an investigation of the subject matter. To conduct such an investigation requires systematic hypotheses concerning the nature of the connections of the variables. Only after these are made can past history be examined in a way that illuminates the hypotheses. Otherwise the investigator has no criteria on the basis of which he can pick and choose among the infinite reservoir of facts available to him. These initial hypotheses indicate the *areas of facts* which have the greatest importance for this type of investigation; presumably if the hypotheses are wrong, this will become reasonably evident in the course of attempting to use them.[6]

All this is logically and procedurally impeccable. (It is only odd that for all his harsh criticism of E. H. Carr, Mr. Kaplan has failed to notice the striking parallel between his procedure and the one that Mr. Carr has outlined in *What is History?*)

But two closely connected observations may be made. The first is that Mr. Kaplan (unlike Mr. Carr) leaves to others the systematic verification on the ground, as it were, of his own hypotheses. The second is that, in his own words, "international systems theory is designed to investigate problems of macrosystem structure." And he readily goes on to admit, "It is not, for instance, easily adaptable to the investigation of microstructural problems of foreign policy."[7] However, if this is the case —and surely it is—then it immediately becomes clear that he and Mr. Bull have much more in common than they seem to think. For it is only in "microstructural" terms that any empirical verification of the "macrosystem" is possible, and such a verification Mr. Kaplan has refused to attempt. The major purpose of the systems analyst is to account for behavior by positing regularities. This raises two questions. Firstly, what or who *behaves* in international affairs? Secondly, are all the observerable or known facts accounted for or shown to be irrelevant? In this field, no less than in any other branch of social science, it is human behavior that we are concerned with, albeit in a particular context. Unless macrosystem analysis can be applied to human behavior (i.e., microsystems) or be shown to be advancing in that direction, we must, perforce, take it on trust. And so far no really convincing grounds for our doing so have been advanced.

The difficulty, in fact, goes far beyond the question of the "adapta-

[6] P. 8, italics added.
[7] P. 11.

bility" of international systems theory to "microstructural problems." It is questionable whether any effective and continuous tie between the two is practicable at all, any more than between, say, meteorology and physiology, despite the evident influence of the weather on the behavior of our muscles, sweat glands, and the rest. For all practical purposes, investigation of one field must proceed separately from investigation of the other. And it is this kind of practical discontinuity between what Mr. Kaplan is engaged in and what, say, Messrs. Snyder, Bruck, and Sapin[8] have concerned themselves with that raises the question of the precise relationship of such international systems study to the very much greater body of work being done on "microstructural" aspects of the subject. If formulators of international systems hypotheses feel no urge to test the validity of their structures themselves and are not over-troubled by the divide between their work and that of those who are concerned more directly with the rude and intractable facts of international life, it becomes difficult to avoid viewing their work as interesting, often intellectually impressive exercises in latterday scholasticism which are, and must remain, essentially peripheral to the subject as a whole. It is certainly remote from diplomatic practice.

In short, while one can sense and sympathize with the urgency of the desire of the "scientists" to introduce new techniques and new topics into the field, one remains unconvinced that the preferred combinations of topics and techniques are all of such weight as to contribute even indirectly to a substantially improved understanding of the matter in hand. It is not enough to state the simple belief that progress with the peripheral will ultimately lead to discovery of the central. A glance at any other field of empirical enquiry will surely reveal that it is enlightened consideration of central topics that leads to progress on all fronts and, ultimately, to better understanding of the peripheral, too. It is only if the seemingly peripheral topic is seriously thought to be, in fact, the truly central one that such vast labors on marginalia would seem justified. But so far, at any rate, no one seems to have made this claim outright.

## III

Much of the difficulty evidently derives from the familiar fact that the student of international relations lacks a traditionally accepted and commonly respected frame of conceptual and empirical reference for his work, even one which he may reject, but in terms of which he can operate with reasonable confidence that at least on the essentials of what

---

[8] Richard C. Snyder, H. W. Bruck, and Burton Sapin, *Foreign Policy Decision-Making* (New York 1962).

constitutes the subject he is in broad agreement with the majority of his fellows. A scholar who is dissatisfied with fashionable approaches or outlooks is, in a profound sense, a lonely man. To a degree that has hardly any contemporary parallel in other fields, he must create for himself the scheme in terms of which he will order his observations and analysis *before* proceeding to seek, let alone deal with, the evidence he will use to support that analysis and, ultimately, justify the chosen frame of reference itself. It is only natural that the most fruitful and original work is therefore precisely that which suggests new frameworks, new manners of ordering observations, and, by extension, new topics of investigation.

In retrospect it need hardly surprise us, then, that for many years the field as a whole was largely dominated by lawyers—for this much may be said about international law, that it is generally apparent what does and does not pertain to it and, moreover, that by adopting the necessary working principle that serious discussion of legal systems and practices must presuppose that whatever is law will be respected, it is possible for lawyers to operate quite rationally within a framework of some considerable internal rigor without having constantly to ask themselves how far it actually relates or corresponds to the facts of international life and which of its elements are fictions and which are not. However, for those who take international law as only one of the elements of the field, and by no means the most important—certainly not the lens through which the field as a whole is best surveyed—the major problems remain untouched by it. And if nothing better offers, one is then left with Mr. Bull's central questions.

It has already been suggested that the great value of these central questions is to stimulate interest in the subject. But the problem of pinpointing what topics should be investigated in practice is logically distinct, and his major questions cannot greatly assist us in solving it. The most cursory look at current "classical" literature consequently reveals, as does the "scientific," that a vast number and variety of topics ranging from statistically rigorous head-counting at the United Nations to a reinterpretation of Clausewitz in terms of twentieth-century military techniques are all thought, probably rightly, to pertain to the general field of "international relations." But what is not at all clear is how such disparate matters are to be related to one another, and, indeed, if the various specialists engaged in their study consider that such an interrelationship is genuinely rewarding or even possible, logically or otherwise. Above all, what is lacking is any sense of priority, any hierarchy of subjects, either empirical or conceptual, such as may be found in each of the physical sciences and, to some extent, within the class of physical sciences as a whole.

In political science in its municipal aspect such a hierarchy of topics does seem to be generally accepted. One justification (apart from the satisfaction of curiosity) for studying, say, the performance of the political press during a general election is, crudely, for the light that may be thrown on some aspects of the interaction between political institutions and organizations and the anonymous public itself. And this topic can be related in turn very closely and clearly to such central questions of political science as whose writ it is that runs within the given state, and how far, and in what manner and why. The great advantage of these latter questions, as opposed to the central questions of international relations put forward by Mr. Bull, is that it is possible both in principle and practice to proceed to the discovery of their answers. Furthermore, they provide both a key topic for investigation and analysis *and* a center for the field as a whole to which most, if not all, other topics relate centripetally.

It is this kind of central, dominating topic, broadly recognized as such, that we need. For reasons already suggested, it can be provided neither by the philosophically oriented, "classical" approach, nor by those approaches which owe their major origins and methods to econometrics or to the psychology of behavior or to studies in philosophy and logic. All are valuable, but because in the first case the insoluble problem of procedure cuts the student off from the facts of international life, while in the latter group procedure dominates to the extent of obscuring the subject, none, it would seem, can be accepted in unmodified form.

## IV

The thesis of the present article is that the key subject in the study of international relations, the one in terms of which all others are to be weighed for value, and the only one which can provide a natural and unifying center of investigation in respect of both method and topic is the study of *governments in their foreign relations* (alternatively, "foreign policy analysis" or the study of "decision-making," in the broadest possible sense of these terms). Of course, it is *not* suggested that this is by any means a neglected subject today, still less that it is the only one really worth bothering about. The argument is that the proliferation of disconnected topics of research and the variety of logically and factually incompatible methodologies are functions of the failure of all too many scholars to ask themselves at regular and decent intervals what it is they are about. Specifically, the thesis is that if the study of international relations is to become an integrated discipline it is necessary, as has been suggested, that we agree to distinguish clearly between what is and is not of *central* interest and to be absolutely clear in our minds as to how the investigation or discussion of any given topic is likely, if only in principle, to advance our understanding of a very few simple, but interconnected, questions. These are (and no doubt improved formulations are possible), How do governments (or other bodies of equivalent authority) deal in practice with affairs that pertain to the sphere that is beyond their domestic authority? What material and diplomatic options are available to them? What motivates them collectively and individually? Under what circumstances, with what instruments, and to what extent can they alter the external environment at will? and, How do the actions or inactions of one government affect the affairs of another?

In themselves these questions are as old as the hills. What is contended here is that the priority, their place in the hierarchy of topics that interest us, and, indeed, their own profound and intrinsic interest tend to be overlooked—above all by those who are the staunchest champions of a single favored approach—and that it is surely time that they were restored to their proper precedence over all others. There will then be some hope that the "classicists" will emerge from the despair that seems to have impelled so many of them to concern themselves overmuch with disconnected studies of institutions, or diplomatic history in the narrow sense, or the texts of ancient theorists, and that "scientists" will cease to bury themselves in marginalia in the hope that, ultimately, the light will dawn.

The arguments in favor of such an approach to the subject are, accordingly, of two kinds: (a) those which pertain to the coordination of the various streams within the field as a whole; and (b) those which are concerned with the general advance of scholarship toward improved understanding and knowledge of the subject matter.

Under the first head, this approach would provide us with clear criteria for distinguishing the relevant from the irrelevant and the central from the marginal by facilitating the constitution of tests for judging the significance of any given piece of research not just in terms of its own internal logic, as is necessary at present, but in the light of the contribution it may make to answering our major questions. In addition, it would serve to bring home the absolute requirement that work be empirically oriented and the fact, too, that elaborate discussion of hypotheses for which evidence is lacking and which may not be susceptible to empirical verification even in principle is in a profound sense, despite superficial attractiveness, unfruitful. This approach would also provide a clear meeting ground (or, at the very least, a middle ground) between those whose interest in the subject stems from their view of it as a contribution to the kind of problems found in Mr. Bull's list and those who are, quite rightly, at pains not to divorce international relations from the mainstream of political science. Finally, in this approach the bond between the science and the practice of international relations would be preserved and greatly strengthened, and the descent into scholastic endeavors arrested.

But the arguments for this approach under the second head are probably of greater importance. Some of these, it is submitted, are as follows: Firstly, concentration on the processes of government in the external sphere (diplomatic, military, institutional, intellectual, economic, personal, and so on) would cut to the heart of the subject and its central mystery, viz., the nexus between the domestic and external aspects of state affairs. In consequence, it would help to rework the traditional but misleading and confusing distinction between domestic and foreign politics. Eventually, it could be expected to help dissolve the myths associated with each of the two traditional categories and reduce the difficulty of relating one to the other—particularly where, as is so common today, the external activities of one state impinge directly on the internal affairs of another.

It may be noted, parenthetically, that international systems analysis, in contrast, tends to perpetuate the crude distinction between the foreign and the domestic and, more particularly, to reinforce the tendency to employ undifferentiated statehood as the key building block for general theories in international relations. There is surely at least a *prima facie* case for asserting that one of the notable characteristics of the modern international scene is the growing disparity in human and material resources to be found where important categories of states are compared—with the result that the only genuine common denominator left is the purely *legal* equality of states that carries with it only such tenuous advantages as membership in the United Nations. Even domestic authority varies so greatly in content and form that it is misleading to assume that it can serve, except very crudely, as a common denominator of "states."

Secondly, it is here (i.e., in the study of governments in their foreign policy-making role), if anywhere, that some solution is most likely to be found to the ancient problem of the interrelation between actors and environment, statesmen and states. For it is surely *through* the actor (statesman, diplomat, staff officer, intelligence analyst) that the environment—if comprehended—enters into the policy-making process or—where comprehension is absent or incomplete or erroneous—fails to enter into the process, with the result that the process itself is liable to fail in the sense that the ends of policy are not achieved.

Thirdly, by this approach the systematic study of international *institutions* would be kept firmly in its appropriate hierarchical place: matters to be understood primarily (but, of course, not exclusively) in terms of the policies of the participating governments. It is surely time that the last vestiges of neo-Wilsonian sentimentality and humbug about the

United Nations, for example, were banished from the textbooks, let alone from research papers.

Finally, such an approach would serve to make clearly apparent (as it is *not* in much or most of the literature) that generalizations and theories about states are liable to fail not only because of random dissimilarities between states, their resources, and their respective environments, but also because of random dissimilarities between leaders (and other policy-makers) and their views on, and attitudes toward, even such elementary questions as war, aggression, peace, deception, the value attaching to the status quo, and so on. It is surely much more important and instructive to bring out both the differences *and* such similarities (or common patterns) as may be uncovered, so as, ultimately, to make some progress toward a greater degree of understanding of the general processes involved and the beginnings of a real predictive capability, than to ponder about "just wars" (which question can be resolved only in terms of the ethos of a *single* society and political context), or to construct intricate theoretical models that cannot be relevant, even in principle, to more than a tiny unrepresentative sample of the some 140 members in the international state system in a limited number of artificial situations, or, again, to indulge in the study of marginalia in the pious hope that somehow, sometime, all will cohere.

It is only when we know enough about the processes of foreign policy-making in a very wide range of cases that we are likely to proceed to international systems-building with any reasonable hope of formulating substantially valid hypotheses. And it may also be worth observing that it would, in any case, and by these means, be desirable to break away from some of the provinciality that afflicts much international relations study, namely, the entirely natural, understandable, but, on the whole, harmful tendency to consider, in effect, the affairs of a very small number of very interesting and important states to the almost total exclusion of all others.

J .  D A V I D  S I N G E R

*The Level-of-Analysis Problem*
*in International Relations*

In any area of scholarly inquiry, there are always several ways in which
the phenomena under study may be sorted and arranged for purposes of
systemic analysis. Whether in the physical or social sciences, the observer may choose to focus upon the parts or upon the whole, upon the
components or upon the system. He may, for example, choose between
the flowers or the garden, the rocks or the quarry, the trees or the forest,
the houses or the neighborhood, the cars or the traffic jam, the delinquents or the gang, the legislators or the legislative, and so on.[1]
Whether he selects the micro- or macro-level of analysis is ostensibly a
mere matter of methodological or conceptual convenience. Yet the
choice often turns out to be quite difficult, and may well become a central issue within the discipline concerned. The complexity and significance of these level-of-analysis decisions are readily suggested by the
long-standing controversies between social psychology and sociology,
personality-oriented and culture-oriented anthropology, or micro- and
macro-economics, to mention but a few. In the vernacular of general
systems theory, the observer is always confronted with a system, its sub-
systems, and their respective environments, and while he may choose as
his system any cluster of phenomena from the most minute organism

[1] As Kurt Lewin observed in his classic contribution to the social sciences: "The first
prerequisite of a successful observation in any science is a definite understanding
about what size of unit one is going to observe at a given time." *Field Theory in
Social Science*, New York, 1951, p. 157.

SOURCE: J. David Singer, "The Level-Of-Analysis Problem In International Relations,"
in Klaus Knorr and Sidney Verba (eds.), *The International System* (Princeton:
Princeton University Press, 1961), pp. 77–92. Reprinted by permisssion of Princeton
University Press.

to the universe itself, such choice cannot be merely a function of whim or caprice, habit or familiarity.[2] The responsible scholar must be prepared to evaluate the relative utility—conceptual and methodological—of the various alternatives open to him, and to appraise the manifold implications of the level of analysis finally selected. So it is with international relations.

But whereas the pros and cons of the various possible levels of analysis have been debated exhaustively in many of the social sciences, the issue has scarcely been raised among students of our emerging discipline.[3] Such tranquillity may be seen by some as a reassuring indication that the issue is not germane to our field, and by others as evidence that it has already been resolved, but this writer perceives the quietude with a measure of concern. He is quite persuaded of its relevance and certain that it has yet to be resolved. Rather, it is contended that the issue has been ignored by scholars still steeped in the intuitive and artistic tradition of the humanities or enmeshed in the web of "practical" policy. We have, in our texts and elsewhere, roamed up and down the ladder of organizational complexity with remarkable abandon, focusing upon the total system, international organizations, regions, coalitions, extra-national associations, nations, domestic pressure groups, social classes, elites, and individuals as the needs of the moment required. And though most of us have tended to settle upon the nation as our most comfortable resting place, we have retained our propensity for vertical drift, failing to appreciate the value of a stable point of focus.[4] Whether this lack of concern is a function of the relative infancy of the discipline or the nature of the intellectual traditions from whence it springs, it nevertheless remains a significant variable in the general sluggishness which characterizes the development of theory in the study of relations among nations. It is the purpose of this paper to raise the issue, arti-

[2] For a useful introductory statement on the definitional and taxonomic problems in a general systems approach, see the papers by Ludwig von Bertalanffy, "General System Theory," and Kenneth Boulding, "General System Theory: The Skeleton of Science," in Society for the Advancement of General Systems Theory, *General Systems*, Ann Arbor, Mich., 1956, 1, part 1.

[3] An important pioneering attempt to deal with some of the implications of one's level of analysis, however, is Kenneth N. Waltz, *Man, the State, and War*, New York, 1959. But Waltz restricts himself to a consideration of these implications as they impinge on the question of the causes of war. See also this writer's review of Waltz, "International Conflict: Three Levels of Analysis," *World Politics*, XII (April 1960), pp. 453–61.

[4] Even during the debate between "realism" and "idealism" the analytical implications of the various levels of analysis received only the scantiest attention; rather the emphasis seems to have been at the two extremes of pragmatic policy and speculative metaphysics.

culate the alternatives, and examine the theoretical implications and consequences of two of the more widely employed levels of analysis: the international system and the national sub-systems.

## I. The Requirements of an Analytical Model

Prior to an examination of the theoretical implications of the level of analysis or orientation employed in our model, it might be worthwhile to discuss the uses to which any such model might be put, and the requirements which such uses might expect of it.

Obviously, we would demand that it offer a highly accurate *description* of the phenomena under consideration. Therefore the scheme must present as complete and undistorted a picture of these phenomena as is possible; it must correlate with objective reality and coincide with our empirical referents to the highest possible degree. Yet we know that such accurate representation of a complex and wide-ranging body of phenomena is extremely difficult. Perhaps a useful illustration may be borrowed from cartography; the oblate spheroid which the planet earth most closely represents is not transferable to the two-dimensional surface of a map without *some* distortion. Thus, the Mercator projection exaggerates distance and distorts direction at an increasing rate as we move north or south *from* the equator, while the polar gnomonic projection suffers from these same debilities as we move *toward* the equator. Neither offers therefore a wholly accurate presentation, yet each is true enough to reality to be quite useful for certain specific purposes. The same sort of tolerance is necessary in evaluating any analytical model for the study of international relations; if we must sacrifice total representational accuracy, the problem is to decide where distortion is least dysfunctional and where such accuracy is absolutely essential.

These decisions are, in turn, a function of the second requirement of any such model—a capacity to *explain* the relationships among the phenomena under investigation. Here our concern is not so much with accuracy of description as with validity of explanation. Our model must have such analytical capabilities as to treat the causal relationships in a fashion which is not only valid and thorough, but parsimonious; this latter requirement is often overlooked, yet its implications for research strategy are not inconsequential.[5] It should be asserted here that the primary purpose of theory is to explain, and when descriptive and explana-

---

[5] For example, one critic of the decision-making model formulated by Richard C. Snyder, H. W. Bruck, and Burton Sapin, in *Decision-Making as an Approach to the Study of International Politics* (Princeton, N.J., 1954), points out that no single re-

tory requirements are in conflict, the latter ought to be given priority, even at the cost of some representational inaccuracy.

Finally, we may legitimately demand that any analytical model offer the promise of reliable *prediction*. In mentioning this requirement last, there is no implication that it is the most demanding or difficult of the three. Despite the popular belief to the contrary, prediction demands less of one's model than does explanation or even description. For example, any informed layman can predict that pressure on the accelerator of a slowly moving car will increase its speed; that more or less of the moon will be visible tonight than last night; or that the normal human will flinch when confronted with an impending blow. These *predictions* do not require a particularly elegant or sophisticated model of the universe, but their *explanation* demands far more than most of us carry around in our minds. Likewise, we can predict with impressive reliability that any nation will respond to military attack in kind, but a description and understanding of the processes and factors leading to such a response are considerably more elusive, despite the gross simplicity of the acts themselves.

Having articulated rather briefly the requirements of an adequate analytical model, we might turn now to a consideration of the ways in which one's choice of analytical focus impinges upon such a model and affects its descriptive, explanatory, and predictive adequacy.

## II. The International System as Level of Analysis

Beginning with the systemic level of analysis, we find in the total international system a partially familiar and highly promising point of focus. First of all, it is the most comprehensive of the levels available, encompassing the totality of interactions which take place within the system and its environment. By focusing on the system, we are enabled to study the patterns of interaction which the system reveals, and to generalize about such phenomena as the creation and dissolution of coali-

---

searcher could deal with all the variables in that model and expect to complete more than a very few comparative studies in his lifetime. See Herbert McClosky, "Concerning Strategies for a Science of International Politics," *World Politics*, viii (January 1956), pp. 281–95. In defense, however, one might call attention to the relative ease with which many of Snyder's categories could be collapsed into more inclusive ones, as was apparently done in the subsequent case study (see note 11 below). Perhaps a more telling criticism of the monograph is McClosky's comment that "Until a greater measure of theory is introduced into the proposal and the relations among variables are specified more concretely, it is likely to remain little more than a setting-out of categories and, like any taxonomy, fairly limited in its utility" (p. 291).

tions, the frequency and duration of specific power configurations, modifications in its stability, its responsiveness to changes in formal political institutions, and the norms and folklore which it manifests as a societal system. In other words, the systemic level of analysis, and only this level, permits us to examine international relations in the whole, with a comprehensiveness that is of necessity lost when our focus is shifted to a lower, and more partial, level. For descriptive purposes, then, it offers both advantages and disadvantages; the former flow from its comprehensiveness, and the latter from the necessary dearth of detail.

As to explanatory capability, the system-oriented model poses some genuine difficulties. In the first place, it tends to lead the observer into a position which exaggerates the impact of the system upon the national actors and, conversely, discounts the impact of the actors on the system. This is, of course, by no means inevitable; one could conceivably look upon the system as a rather passive environment in which dynamic states act out their relationships rather than as a socio-political entity with a dynamic of its own. But there is a natural tendency to endow that upon which we focus our attention with somewhat greater potential than it might normally be expected to have. Thus, we tend to move, in a system-oriented model, away from notions implying much national autonomy and independence of choice and toward a more deterministic orientation.

Secondly, this particular level of analysis almost inevitably requires that we postulate a high degree of uniformity in the foreign policy operational codes of our national actors. By definition, we allow little room for divergence in the behavior of our parts when we focus upon the whole. It is no coincidence that our most prominent theoretician—and one of the very few text writers focusing upon the international system— should "assume that [all] statesmen think and act in terms of interest defined as power."[6] If this single-minded behavior be interpreted literally and narrowly, we have a simplistic image comparable to economic man or sexual man, and if it be defined broadly, we are no better off than the psychologist whose human model pursues "self-realization" or "maximization of gain"; all such gross models suffer from the same fatal weakness as the utilitarian's "pleasure-pain" principle. Just as individuals differ widely in what they deem to be pleasure and pain, or gain and loss, nations may differ widely in what they consider to be the national interest, and we end up having to break down and refine the larger category. Moreover, Professor Morgenthau finds himself compelled to go still further and disavow the relevance of both motives and ideological pref-

[6] Hans J. Morgenthau, *Politics Among Nations*, 3rd ed., New York, 1960, pp. 5–7. Obviously, his model does not preclude the use of power as a dimension for the differentiation of nations.

erences in national behavior, and these represent two of the more useful dimensions in differentiating among the several nations in our international system. By eschewing any empirical concern with the domestic and internal variations within the separate nations, the system-oriented approach tends to produce a sort of "black box" or "billiard ball" concept of the national actors.[7] By discounting—or denying—the differences among nations, or by positing the near-impossibility of observing many of these differences at work within them,[8] one concludes with a highly homogenized image of our nations in the international system. And though this may be an inadequate foundation upon which to base any *causal* statements, it offers a reasonably adequate basis for *correlative* statements. More specifically, it permits us to observe and measure correlations between certain forces or stimuli which seem to impinge upon the nation and the behavior patterns which are the apparent consequence of these stimuli. But one must stress the limitations implied in the word "apparent"; what is thought to be the consequence of a given stimulus may only be a coincidence or artifact, and until one investigates the major elements in the causal link—no matter how persuasive the deductive logic—one may speak only of correlation, not of consequence.

Moreover, by avoiding the multitudinous pitfalls of intra-nation observation, one emerges with a singularly manageable model, requiring as it does little of the methodological sophistication or onerous empiricism called for when one probes beneath the behavioral externalities of the actor. Finally, as has already been suggested in the introduction, the systemic orientation should prove to be reasonably satisfactory as a basis for prediction, even if such prediction is to extend beyond the characteristics of the system and attempt anticipatory statements regard-

---

[7] The "black box" figure comes from some of the simpler versions of S-R psychology, in which the observer more or less ignores what goes on within the individual and concentrates upon the correlation between stimulus and response; these are viewed as empirically verifiable, whereas cognition, perception, and other mental processes have to be imputed to the individual with a heavy reliance on these assumed "intervening variables." The "billiard ball" figure seems to carry the same sort of connotation, and is best employed by Arnold Wolfers in "The Actors in International Politics" in William T. R. Fox, ed., *Theoretical Aspects of International Relations*, Notre Dame, Ind., 1959, pp. 83–106. See also, in this context, Richard C. Snyder, "International Relations Theory—Continued," *World Politics*, XIII (January 1961), pp. 300–12; and J. David Singer, "Theorizing About Theory in International Politics," *Journal of Conflict Resolution*, IV (December 1960), pp. 431–42. Both are review articles dealing with the Fox anthology.

[8] Morgenthau observes, for example, that it is "futile" to search for motives because they are "the most illusive of psychological data, distorted as they are, frequently beyond recognition, by the interests and emotions of actor and observer alike" (*op.cit.*, p. 6).

ing the actors themselves; this assumes, of course, that the actors are characterized and their behavior predicted in relatively gross and general terms.

These, then, are some of the more significant implications of a model which focuses upon the international system as a whole. Let us turn now to the more familiar of our two orientations, the national state itself.


III. The National State as Level of Analysis

The other level of analysis to be considered in this paper is the national state—our primary actor in international relations. This is clearly the traditional focus among Western students, and is the one which dominates almost all of the texts employed in English-speaking colleges and universities.

Its most obvious advantage is that it permits significant differentiation among our actors in the international system. Because it does not require the attribution of great similarity to the national actors, it encourages the observer to examine them in greater detail. The favorable results of such intensive analysis cannot be overlooked, as it is only when the actors are studied in some depth that we are able to make really valid generalizations of a comparative nature. And though the systemic model does not necessarily preclude comparison and contrast among the national sub-systems, it usually eventuates in rather gross comparisons based on relatively crude dimensions and characteristics. On the other hand, there is no assurance that the nation-oriented approach will produce a sophisticated model for the comparative study of foreign policy; with perhaps the exception of the Haas and Whiting study,[9] none of our major texts makes a serious and successful effort to describe and explain national behavior in terms of most of the significant variables by which such behavior might be comparatively analyzed. But this would seem to be a function, not of the level of analysis employed, but of our general unfamiliarity with the other social sciences (in which comparison is a major preoccupation) and of the retarded state of comparative government and politics, a field in which most international relations specialists are likely to have had some experience.

But just as the nation-as-actor focus permits us to avoid the inaccurate homogenization which often flows from the systemic focus, it also may lead us into the opposite type of distortion—a marked exaggeration of the differences among our sub-systemic actors. While it is evident that neither of these extremes is conducive to the development of a sophisti-

[9] Ernst B. Haas and Allen S. Whiting, *Dynamics of International Relations*, New York, 1956.

cated comparison of foreign policies, and such comparison requires a balanced preoccupation with both similarity and difference, the danger seems to be greatest when we succumb to the tendency to overdifferentiate; comparison and contrast can proceed only from observed uniformities.[10]

One of the additional liabilities which flow in turn from the pressure to overdifferentiate is that of Ptolemaic parochialism. Thus, in overemphasizing the differences among the many national states, the observer is prone to attribute many of what he conceives to be virtues to his own nation and the vices to others, especially the adversaries of the moment. That this ethnocentrism is by no means an idle fear is borne out by perusal of the major international relations texts published in the United States since 1945. Not only is the world often perceived through the prism of the American national interest, but an inordinate degree of attention (if not spleen) is directed toward the Soviet Union; it would hardly be amiss to observe that most of these might qualify equally well as studies in American foreign policy. The scientific inadequacies of this sort of "we-they" orientation hardly require elaboration, yet they remain a potent danger in any utilization of the national actor model.

Another significant implication of the sub-systemic orientation is that it is only within its particular framework that we can expect any useful application of the decision-making approach.[11] Not all of us, of course, will find its inapplicability a major loss; considering the criticism which has been leveled at the decision-making approach, and the failure of most of us to attempt its application, one might conclude that it is no loss at all. But the important thing to note here is that a system-oriented model would not offer a hospitable framework for such a detailed and comparative approach to the study of international relations, no matter what our appraisal of the decision-making approach might be.

Another and perhaps more subtle implication of selecting the nation as our focus or level of analysis is that it raises the entire question of

[10] A frequent by-product of this tendency to overdifferentiate is what Waltz calls the "second-image fallacy," in which one explains the peaceful or bellicose nature of a nation's foreign policy exclusively in terms of its domestic economic, political, or social characteristics (*op.cit.*, chs. 4 and 5).

[11] Its most well-known and successful statement is found in Snyder *et al., op. cit.* Much of this model is utilized in the text which Snyder wrote with Edgar S. Furniss, Jr., *American Foreign Policy: Formulation, Principles, and Programs,* New York, 1954. A more specific application is found in Snyder and Glenn D. Paige, "The United States Decision to Resist Aggression in Korea: The Application of an Analytical Scheme," *Administrative Science Quarterly,* III (December 1958), pp. 341–78. For those interested in this approach, very useful is Paul Wasserman and Fred S. Silander, *Decision-Making: An Annotated Bibliography,* Ithaca, N.Y., 1958.

goals, motivation, and purpose in national policy.[12] Though it may well be a peculiarity of the Western philosophical tradition, we seem to exhibit, when confronted with the need to explain individual or collective behavior, a strong proclivity for a goal-seeking approach. The question of whether national behavior is purposive or not seems to require discussion in two distinct (but not always exclusive) dimensions.

Firstly, there is the more obvious issue of whether those who act on behalf of the nation in formulating and executing foreign policy consciously pursue rather concrete goals. And it would be difficult to deny, for example, that these role-fulfilling individuals envisage certain specific outcomes which they hope to realize by pursuing a particular strategy. In this sense, then, nations may be said to be goal-seeking organisms which exhibit purposive behavior.

However, purposiveness may be viewed in a somewhat different light, by asking whether it is not merely an intellectual construct that man imputes to himself by reason of his vain addiction to the free-will doctrine as he searches for characteristics which distinguish him from physical matter and the lower animals. And having attributed this conscious goal-pursuing behavior to himself as an individual, it may be argued that man then proceeds to project this attribute to the social organizations of which he is a member. The question would seem to distill down to whether man and his societies pursue goals of their own choosing or are moved toward those imposed upon them by forces which are primarily beyond their control.[13] Another way of stating the dilemma would be to ask whether we are concerned with the ends which men and nations strive for or the ends toward which they are impelled by the past and present characteristics of their social and physical milieu. Obviously, we are using the terms "ends," "goals," and "purpose" in two rather distinct ways; one refers to those which are consciously envisaged and more or less rationally pursued, and the other to those of which the actor has little knowledge but toward which he is nevertheless propelled.

Taking a middle ground in what is essentially a specific case of the free will vs. determinism debate, one can agree that nations move to-

---

[12] And if the decision-making version of this model is employed, the issue is unavoidable. See the discussion of motivation in Snyder, Bruck, and Sapin, *op.cit.*, pp. 92–117; note that 25 of the 49 pages on "The Major Determinants of Action" are devoted to motives.

[13] A highly suggestive, but more abstract treatment of this teleological question is in Talcott Parsons, *The Structure of Social Action*, 2nd ed., Glencoe, Ill., 1949, especially in his analysis of Durkheim and Weber. It is interesting to note that for Parsons an act implies, *inter alia*, "a future state of affairs toward which the process of action is oriented," and he therefore comments that "in this sense and this sense only, the schema of action is inherently teleological" (p. 44).

ward outcomes of which they have little knowledge and over which they have less control, but that they nevertheless do prefer, and therefore select, particular outcomes and *attempt* to realize them by conscious formulation of strategies.

Also involved in the goal-seeking problem when we employ the nation-oriented model is the question of how and why certain nations pursue specific sorts of goals. While the question may be ignored in the system-oriented model or resolved by attributing identical goals to all national actors, the nation-as-actor approach demands that we investigate the processes by which national goals are selected, the internal and external factors that impinge on those processes, and the institutional framework from which they emerge. It is worthy of note that despite the strong predilection for the nation-oriented model in most of our texts, empirical or even deductive analyses of these processes are conspicuously few.[14] Again, one might attribute these lacunae to the methodological and conceptual inadequacies of the graduate training which international relations specialists traditionally receive.[15] But in any event, goals and motivations are both dependent and independent variables, and if we intend to explain a nation's foreign policy, we cannot settle for the mere postulation of these goals; we are compelled to go back a step and inquire into their genesis and the process by which they become the crucial variables that they seem to be in the behavior of nations.

There is still another dilemma involved in our selection of the nation-as-actor model, and that concerns the phenomenological issue: do we examine our actor's behavior in terms of the objective factors which allegedly influence that behavior, or do we do so in terms of the actor's *perception* of these "objective factors"? Though these two approaches are not completely exclusive of one another, they proceed from greatly different and often incompatible assumptions, and produce markedly divergent models of national behavior.[16]

---

[14] Among the exceptions are Haas and Whiting, *op. cit.*, chs. 2 and 3; and some of the chapters in Roy C. Macridis, ed., *Foreign Policy in World Politics*, Englewood Cliffs, N.J., 1958, especially that on West Germany by Karl Deutsch and Lewis Edinger.

[15] As early as 1934, Edith E. Ware noted that ". . . the study of international relations is no longer entirely a subject for political science or law, but that economics, history, sociology, geography—all the social sciences—are called upon to contribute towards the understanding . . . of the international system." See *The Study of International Relations in the United States*, New York, 1934, p. 172. For some contemporary suggestions, see Karl Deutsch, "The Place of Behavioral Sciences in Graduate Training in International Relations," *Behavioral Science*, III (July 1958), pp. 278–84; and J. David Singer, "The Relevance of the Behavioral Sciences to the Study of International Relations," *ibid.*, VI (October 1961), pp. 324–35.

[16] The father of phenomenological philosophy is generally acknowledged to be Edmund Husserl (1859–1938), author of *Ideas: General Introduction to Pure Phe-*

The first of these assumptions concerns the broad question of social causation. One view holds that individuals and groups respond in a quasi-deterministic fashion to the realities of physical environment, the acts or power of other individuals or groups, and similar "objective" and "real" forces or stimuli. An opposite view holds that individuals and groups are not influenced in their behavior by such objective forces, but by the fashion in which these forces are perceived and evaluated, however distorted or incomplete such perceptions may be. For adherents of this position, the only reality is the phenomenal—that which is discerned by the human senses; forces that are not discerned do not exist for that actor, and those that do exist do so only in the fashion in which they are perceived. Though it is difficult to accept the position that an individual, a group, or a nation is affected by such forces as climate, distance, or a neighbor's physical power only insofar as they are recognized and appraised, one must concede that perceptions will certainly affect the manner in which such forces are responded to. As has often been pointed out, an individual will fall to the ground when he steps out of a tenth-story window regardless of his perception of gravitational forces, but on the other hand such perception is a major factor in whether or not he steps out of the window in the first place.[17] The point here is that if we embrace a phenomenological view of causation, we will tend to utilize a phenomenological model for explanatory purposes.

The second assumption which bears on one's predilection for the phenomenological approach is more restricted, and is primarily a methodological one. Thus, it may be argued that any description of national behavior in a given international situation would be highly incomplete were it to ignore the link between the external forces at work upon the nation and its general foreign policy behavior. Furthermore, if our concern extends beyond the mere description of "what happens" to the realm of explanation, it could be contended that such omission of the cognitive and the perceptual linkage would be ontologically disastrous. How, it might be asked, can one speak of "causes" of a nation's policies when one has ignored the media by which external conditions and factors are translated into a policy decision? We may observe correlations be-

---

*nomenology*, New York, 1931, trans. by W. R. Boyce Gibson; the original was published in 1913 under the title *Iden zu einer reinen Phänomenologie und Phänomenologischen Philosophie*. Application of this approach to social psychology has come primarily through the work of Koffka and Lewin.
[17] This issue has been raised from time to time in all of the social sciences, but for an excellent discussion of it in terms of the present problem, see Harold and Margaret Sprout, *Man-Milieu Relationship Hypotheses in the Context of International Politics*, Princeton University, Center of International Studies, 1956, pp. 63–71.

tween all sorts of forces in the international system and the behavior of nations, but their causal relationship must remain strictly deductive and hypothetical in the absence of empirical investigation into the causal chain which allegedly links the two. Therefore, even if we are satisfied with the less-than-complete descriptive capabilities of a non-phenomenological model, we are still drawn to it if we are to make any progress in explanation.

The contrary view would hold that the above argument proceeds from an erroneous comprehension of the nature of explanation in social science. One is by no means required to trace every perception, transmission, and receipt between stimulus and response or input and output in order to explain the behavior of the nation or any other human group. Furthermore, who is to say that empirical observation—subject as it is to a host of errors—is any better a basis of explanation than informed deduction, inference, or analogy? Isn't an explanation which flows logically from a coherent theoretical model just as reliable as one based upon a misleading and elusive body of data, most of which is susceptible to analysis only by techniques and concepts foreign to political science and history?

This leads, in turn, to the third of the premises relevant to one's stand on the phenomenological issue: are the dimensions and characteristics of the policy-makers' phenomenal field empirically discernible? Or, more accurately, even if we are convinced that their perceptions and beliefs constitute a crucial variable in the explanation of a nation's foreign policy, can they be observed in an accurate and systematic fashion?[18] Furthermore, are we not required by the phenomenological model to go beyond a classification and description of such variables, and be drawn into the tangled web of relationships out of which they emerge? If we believe that these phenomenal variables are systematically observable, are explainable, and can be fitted into our explanation of a nation's behavior in the international system, then there is a further tendency to embrace the phenomenological approach. If not, or if we are convinced that the gathering of such data is inefficient or uneconomical, we will tend to shy clear of it.

The fourth issue in the phenomenological dispute concerns the very nature of the nation as an actor in international relations. Who or what is it that we study? Is it a distinct social entity with well-defined boundaries—a unity unto itself? Or is it an agglomeration of individuals,

---

[18] This is another of the criticisms leveled at the decision-making approach which, almost by definition, seems compelled to adopt some form of the phenomenological model. For a comprehensive treatment of the elements involved in human perception, see Karl Zener *et al.*, eds., "Inter-relationships Between Perception and Personality: A Symposium," *Journal of Personality*, XVIII (1949), pp. 1–266.

institutions, customs, and procedures? It should be quite evident that those who view the nation or the state as an integral social unit could not attach much utility to the phenomenological approach, particularly if they are prone to concretize or reify the abstraction. Such abstractions are incapable of perception, cognition, or anticipation (unless, of course, the reification goes so far as to anthropomorphize and assign to the abstraction such attributes as will, mind, or personality). On the other hand, if the nation or state is seen as a group of individuals operating within an institutional framework, then it makes perfect sense to focus on the phenomenal field of those individuals who participate in the policy-making process. In other words, *people* are capable of experiences, images, and expectations, while institutional abstractions are not, except in the metaphorical sense. Thus, if our actor cannot even have a phenomenal field, there is little point in employing a phenomenological approach.[19]

These, then, are some of the questions around which the phenomenological issue would seem to revolve. Those of us who think of social forces as operative regardless of the actor's awareness, who believe that explanation need not include all of the steps in a causal chain, who are dubious of the practicality of gathering phenomenal data, or who visualize the nation as a distinct entity apart from its individual members, will tend to reject the phenomenological approach.[20] Logically, only those who disagree with each of the above four assumptions would be *compelled* to adopt the approach. Disagreement with any one would be *sufficient* grounds for so doing.

The above represent some of the more significant implications and fascinating problems raised by the adoption of our second model. They seem to indicate that this sub-systemic orientation is likely to produce richer description and more satisfactory (from the empiricist's point of view) explanation of international relations, though its predictive power would appear no greater than the systemic orientation. But the descriptive and explanatory advantages are achieved only at the price of considerable methodological complexity.

IV. CONCLUSION

Having discussed some of the descriptive, explanatory, and predictive capabilities of these two possible levels of analysis, it might now be use-

---

[19] Many of these issues are raised in the ongoing debate over "methodological individualism," and are discussed cogently in Ernest Nagel, *The Structure of Science*, New York, 1961, pp. 535–46.

[20] Parenthetically, holders of these specific views should be less inclined to adopt the national or sub-systemic model in the first place.

ful to assess the relative utility of the two and attempt some general statement as to their prospective contributions to greater theoretical growth in the study of international relations.

In terms of description, we find that the systemic level produces a more comprehensive and total picture of international relations than does the national or sub-systemic level. On the other hand, the atomized and less coherent image produced by the lower level of analysis is somewhat balanced by its richer detail, greater depth, and more intensive portrayal.[21] As to explanation, there seems little doubt that the subsystemic or actor orientation is considerably more fruitful, permitting as it does a more thorough investigation of the processes by which foreign policies are made. Here we are enabled to go beyond the limitations imposed by the systemic level and to replace mere correlation with the more significant causation. And in terms of prediction, both orientations seem to offer a similar degree of promise. Here the issue is a function of what we seek to predict. Thus the policy-maker will tend to prefer predictions about the way in which nation $x$ or $y$ will react to a contemplated move on his own nation's part, while the scholar will probably prefer either generalized predictions regarding the behavior of a given class of nations or those regarding the system itself.

Does this summary add up to an overriding case for one or another of the two models? It would seem not. For a staggering variety of reasons the scholar may be more interested in one level than another at any given time and will undoubtedly shift his orientation according to his research needs. So the problem is really not one of deciding which level is most valuable to the discipline as a whole and then demanding that it be adhered to from now unto eternity.[22] Rather, it is one of realizing that there *is* this preliminary conceptual issue and that it must be temporarily resolved prior to any given research undertaking. And it must also be stressed that we have dealt here only with two of the more common orientations, and that many others are available and perhaps even more fruitful potentially than either of those selected here. Moreover, the

[21] In a review article dealing with two of the more recent and provocative efforts toward theory (Morton A. Kaplan, *System and Process in International Politics*, New York, 1957, and George Liska, *International Equilibrium*, Cambridge, Mass., 1957), Charles P. Kindleberger adds a further—if not altogether persuasive—argument in favor of the lower, sub-systemic level of analysis: "The total system is infinitely complex with everything interacting. One can discuss it intelligently, therefore, only bit by bit." "Scientific International Politics," *World Politics*, xi (October 1958), p. 86.
[22] It should also be kept in mind that one could conceivably develop a theoretical model which successfully embraces both of these levels of analysis without sacrificing conceptual clarity and internal consistency. In this writer's view, such has not been done to date, though Kaplan's *System and Process in International Politics* seems to come fairly close.

international system gives many indications of prospective change, and it may well be that existing institutional forms will take on new characteristics or that new ones will appear to take their place. As a matter of fact, if incapacity to perform its functions leads to the transformation or decay of an institution, we may expect a steady deterioration and even ultimate disappearance of the national state as a significant actor in the world political system.

However, even if the case for one or another of the possible levels of analysis cannot be made with any certainty, one must nevertheless maintain a continuing awareness as to their use. We may utilize one level here and another there, but we cannot afford to shift our orientation in the midst of a study. And when we do in fact make an original selection or replace one with another at appropriate times, we must do so with a full awareness of the descriptive, explanatory, and predictive implications of such choice.

A final point remains to be discussed. Despite this lengthy exegesis, one might still be prone to inquire whether this is not merely a sterile exercise in verbal gymnastics. What, it might be asked, is the difference between the two levels of analysis if the empirical referents remain essentially the same? Or, to put it another way, is there any difference between international relations and comparative foreign policy? Perhaps a few illustrations will illuminate the subtle but important differences which emerge when one's level of analysis shifts. One might, for example, postulate that when the international system is characterized by political conflict between two of its most powerful actors, there is a strong tendency for the system to bipolarize. This is a systemic-oriented proposition. A sub-systemic proposition, dealing with the same general empirical referents, would state that when a powerful actor finds itself in political conflict with another of approximate parity, it will tend to exert pressure on its weaker neighbors to join its coalition. Each proposition, assuming it is true, is theoretically useful by itself, but each is verified by a different intellectual operation. Moreover—and this is the crucial thing for theoretical development—one could not add these two kinds of statements to achieve a cumulative growth of empirical generalizations.

To illustrate further, one could, at the systemic level, postulate that when the distribution of power in the international system is highly diffused, it is more stable than when the discernible clustering of well-defined coalitions occurs. And at the sub-systemic or national level, the same empirical phenomena would produce this sort of proposition: when a nation's decision-makers find it difficult to categorize other nations readily as friend or foe, they tend to behave toward all in a more uniform and moderate fashion. Now, taking these two sets of propositions, how much cumulative usefulness would arise from attempting to merge and codify the systemic proposition from the first illustration with the sub-systemic proposition from the second, or vice versa? Representing different levels of analysis and couched in different frames of reference, they would defy theoretical integration; one may well be a corollary of the other, but they are not immediately combinable. A prior translation from one level to another must take place.

This, it is submitted, is quite crucial for the theoretical development of our discipline. With all of the current emphasis on the need for more empirical and data-gathering research as a prerequisite to theory-building, one finds little concern with the relationship among these separate and discrete data-gathering activities. Even if we were to declare a moratorium on deductive and speculative research for the next decade, and all of us were to labor diligently in the vineyards of historical and contemporary data, the state of international relations theory would probably be no more advanced at that time than it is now, unless such empirical activity becomes far more systematic. And "systematic" is used here to indicate the cumulative growth of inductive and deductive generalizations into an impressive array of statements conceptually related to one another and flowing from some common frame of reference. What that frame of reference should be, or will be, cannot be said with much certainty, but it does seem clear that it must exist. As long as we evade some of these crucial *a priori* decisions, our empiricism will amount to little more than an ever-growing potpourri of discrete, disparate, non-comparable, and isolated bits of information or extremely low-level generalizations. And, as such, they will make little contribution to the growth of a theory of international relations.

KENNETH W. THOMPSON

# *Normative Theory in International Relations*

International relations is a subject of growing importance because life and death issues hang in the balance. At one stage in history, it was no

SOURCE: Kenneth W. Thompson, "Normative Theory in International Relations," *Journal of International Affairs*, xxi (1967), 278–292. Copyright by the Board of Editors of the *Journal of International Affairs*. Permission to reprint is gratefully acknowledged to the Editors of the *Journal*.

more than intellectually stimulating to study the relations among nations, empires, and rulers. Today, a drama of awesome proportions is being played out on the world stage. The survival not only of men and nations but of mankind is at stake. The struggle for power is inseparably linked with the struggle for existence.

In measuring the consequences of national policies or objectives, the observer is bound sooner or later to invoke value questions. What is the value, for example, of a nation's independence as compared with the value of peace? What is the relative value of forestalling aggression or slowing down the arms race or building anti-missile defense systems or emphasizing butter rather than guns?

Every time the student raises a basic question of ends or means in the realm of war and peace, he very likely (whether implicitly or explicitly) is posing a value question. He is making normative assumptions, formulating positions regarding good or bad, better or worse, evil or more evil; and there are important benefits to be gained from bringing this fact to consciousness, both for him and for those who rally around. He should be willing to apply tests of reason, history, consistency, context, relevance, and priority to the position he espouses. More often than not, however, he excuses himself from this discipline and defends his position on the basis of authority, precedent, necessity, or law —leaving to his critics a broad area for debate. They take their stand on grounds he has long since passed over in his thinking. This explains why the ultimate norms on which current thinking is based are hidden or obscured. The current debate on Vietnam, the recurring discussion of emerging crises, and the historic controversy about internationalism and nationalism all reflect to some degree this absence of genuine dialogue.

### OBSTACLES AND POSSIBILITIES OF NORMATIVE THINKING

In part, the avoidance of normative debate stems from a prevailing emphasis on facts. Most foreign-policy issues—ratifying a treaty, approving a customs agreement, accepting a program of cultural exchange, issuing a visa, trading or not trading with friend or foe—involve painstaking judgments in a narrowly defined realm of fact. What are the "facts," for example, concerning the rights of a corporation to engage in business abroad? The original premise is generally lost sight of, left unexamined, or assumed because policy-makers operate, and indeed must operate, within an established framework. They assume, and from an operational standpoint are obliged to assume, that the facts to be determined are circumscribed and relatively simple in character. They are determined, as a rule, in terms of a specific checklist: What is national policy? What are the credentials of the firm? Has an invitation been issued? Does it have the capacity to operate abroad? What will its actions do for the national interest, etc., etc.? Rarely, if ever, are the underlying issues appraised, such as the relation of international business to the building of a more lasting peace, or the fostering of a healthier economy or a stronger polity abroad, or the priorities of such an endeavor in terms of a set of national and international priorities. There are certain stubborn obstacles in the makeup of international society that militate against using a scale of values as the basis for approving or rejecting concrete proposals concerning business, politics, or education abroad. When individuals and corporate bodies venture abroad, they do so not as the result of moral evaluations but from the standpoint of narrowly practical choices. Not ultimate right or wrong but questions of workability and practicality are normally controlling.

The environment in which international morality must be practiced is largely determined by the profound underlying forces such as individualism and nationalism. Moral action involves individual choice, and the narrowing areas of individualism limit the sphere of moral choice. The great choices seem to involve collective action. The solitary individual thus resigns himself to a state of powerlessness on the significant decisions of the day. The problems and issues are so complex and difficult that individuals are prone to conclude that they can contribute little to their solution. Men come to see themselves as objects rather than subjects of social and political action. In such a setting, the question of a just society loses its urgency. The individual who stands in danger of losing his identity also finds his moral concern weakened by a mass age.

Similarly, the force of nationalism tends to weaken the sense of solidarity men feel with the suffering and persecuted elsewhere in the world. Principles of right and wrong must be channeled through national agencies and interpreters. Here the domestic and international scene have certain analogies. With the former, programs of social welfare involving slum clearance and housing, help to the sick and aged, and widening opportunities for the poor and disadvantaged follow laws of rational organization. A vast machinery of social action has been instituted with the aim of serving the needy individual. If the "Good Samaritan" of our day wants to help someone, he must isolate himself more and more from those he wants to help behind a whole gamut of administrative machinery. It is obvious that those instruments are abstract and dehumanized; indeed, this is the condition of their effectiveness. Acts of love and compassion must be made part of an administrative case load. The great challenge in a collective era is discovering the human significance of anything that might otherwise become just another case. Organized social action hovers dangerously near the brink of the routine and procedural. The one antidote is remembering that the system's justification is the individual. This attitude and spirit must penetrate the organized structures of social action if deterioration and decay are to be avoided.

On the world scene, the need for a civilizing and informing moral attitude is equally urgent. In international affairs it is difficult to talk about ethics in general or to single out national policies that are wholly and unqualifiedly good. Nor is it always clear that on all questions in dispute the organized international community embraces justice. Those national leaders who declare that the United Nations, for example, embodies what is right and moral may, when confronting issues vital to the national interest, find their conception of justice at odds with the UN's. The real issue in debates over political ethics usually arises in the realm of means, not ends. This is why it is difficult and often pointless to talk about ethics in general, whether in terms of peace, justice, or international order. Decisions in foreign policy seldom involve simple and tidy choices. Actions stem from on-balance judgments. What is usually called for is an evaluation of the elements involved in a decision and the consequences likely to flow from each alternative course of action. In choices that are made, the best may be the enemy of the good. Not absolute truth but practical morality must be the guide.

In Jacques Maritain's words, "Means must be proportioned and appropriate to the end, since they are ways to the end, and, so to speak, the end itself is in its very process of 'coming into existence.'" Such a view of foreign policy must give heed to the call for restraint, to a sense of proportion and prudence. With John Dewey, we can say that "means and ends are two names for the same reality." Proximate morality may be the highest attainment in statecraft.

The focal point of moral purpose in international relations is the interests and goals of a nation. We start with the tacit assumption that responsible men will, broadly speaking, view national interest in similar terms. If this were not so, bipartisanship would be impossible. The present Secretary of State has observed that he has appeared before the committees of Congress in executive session more than two hundred times. He is able to recall only two occasions when the discussion of important issues was cast in partisan terms. On both sides of the aisle the controlling viewpoint was "what is right for the country." Congressmen off the hustings seek the best interests of their country. The Englishman T.H. Healy wrote to Lord Hugh Cecil, "Nationalism is what men will die for. Even the noble Lord would not die for the meridian of

Greenwich." If the national interest does not exhaust the possibility of ethical principles, it is always the necessary starting point.

This fact should never obscure the need for a decent respect for the opinions of mankind. If it is possible for political leaders to think responsibly about the national interest, they can also be expected to search for common interests with the spokesmen of other nations. If national interest is a fact, so is the mutality of national interests. There are common interests transcending narrow national interests. They form a network of shared relationships that draw together men of different national creeds and aspirations. For example, Germany today is sharply divided into opposing political systems. No one expects the differences between East and West Germany to dissolve overnight. If change can be expected it will come from a series of little steps or technical changes that may draw the country together or encourage a political settlement. Trade, cultural exchange, and limited tourism may, if practiced with patience and restraint, unlock the doors to greater unity. Even when existing political systems divide, common social, cultural, and economic interests may in time serve to reunite them.

No division is more profound and no cleavage greater than that separating the present rivals in the arms race. Looking out over the chasm that divides East and West, the late Secretary-General of the United Nations, Dag Hammarskjold, put forward a design for disarmament by "mutual example." He asked whether the Soviet Union and the United States did not have a common interest in limiting armaments and checking their spread to other powers. History will show that the great powers have inched ahead in the limitation of armaments. Bilateral disarmament in certain fields preceded the nuclear-test-ban treaty. There have been tacit agreements to limit at certain points the further accretion of various forms of military preparedness. There has been in recent years a corresponding respect by both sides for territorial boundaries in Western and Eastern Europe. Although there is still no overall peace settlement for World War II, the crises in Hungary and Cuba demonstrated a tacit acceptance of the other side's hegemony in its own sphere of influence.

Finally, international society is not bereft of certain broader principles of justice, freedom, and order. Their form may be embryonic in a half-organized world, but their existence is understood. In formulating their foreign policies, states seek points of correspondence between what they do and the broader principle. In foreign policy the concept of elemental right and wrong is never fully realized, but it can be approximated. Even the fact that states possess an awareness of injustice indicates the possibility of justice in foreign affairs, for a sense of injustice presupposes categories of justice to which leaders have recourse. Anti-colonialism is firmly rooted in certain general and inchoate notions of what is right. Often the right is but dimly perceived. Frequently, distributive justice is the highest attainment of states. The right may be as hazy and unclear as the shadows of Plato's cave. Yet these shadows are the beginnings of the necessary conditions for greater justice in the relations between states. As Reinhold Niebuhr has observed, "Our position is not an enviable one. Yet from an ultimate standpoint it need not be regretted. For a nation which cannot save itself without at the same time saving a whole world has the possibility of achieving a concurrence between its own interests and the general welfare; which must be regarded as the highest form of virtue in man's collective life." Order is the framework for the healthy growth of viable nation-states. A respect for national independence demands an international order to safeguard it. Freedom and justice presuppose order. If the world and its staunch supporters cannot preserve the international order, an early casualty is bound to be the survival of new and independent states.

Thus, there are layers of ethics in politics and international affairs. They deserve attention and study, especially since the strongest voices are those of crusaders and cynics. The ethical dimension comprises shades that are not black and white. Grays predominate; indeed, the distinguishing characteristics of political ethics are found in the recognition of the relativity of all ethical judgments. The centers of morality and religion in the land cannot stand aside from man's needs in this realm. For example, the church that teaches patience in all things should strive to inculcate this attitude toward world affairs. Foreign policy all too often is like a woman's work—it never ends. As every long-suffering housewife knows, even freezers and dishwashers have not changed this fact. In much the same way, the shining UN buildings, multilingual translation facilities, and instantaneous communications systems around the world have not prevented one challenge or conflict from following close on another.

The consequences of actions that were noble in themselves are seldom fully anticipated. For example, a well-deserved homeland for suffering and persecuted Jews has led to new tensions in the Middle East. The French Revolution brought in its wake Napoleon's armies on the move across Europe. Independence for the newer nations in our day is only the beginning of new trials and testing. "It is provided in the very essence of things," Walt Whitman declared, "that from any fruition of success, no matter what, shall come forth something to make a greater struggle necessary." Most of life is lived on the ground of successive crises. Peace and prosperity in an "America sailing on a summer sea" never provided the acid test of character. Rather, moral and spiritual resources are put to the test when peoples or nations teeter on the abyss of disaster, or when decisions have to be made for which there is neither present consensus nor future certainty. Ethical judgments, however painful and difficult, often reach a high point in clarity and resolve at the moment of moral crisis.

### THE EVOLUTION OF NORMATIVE THINKING

One approach to international relations that has enjoyed public and scholarly attention is that of the policy-oriented research. Respected institutions like the Brookings Institution have over the years contributed a steady stream of policy studies concerning various areas of the world.

One criticism of policy research has been that it is primarily value-free research. Scholars assume a degree of detachment denied the hard-pressed decision-maker. They enjoy a greater measure of freedom and a broader range of options than policy-makers. Choices that are conceivable for detached observers are often unthinkable for those whom the public holds accountable as guardians of the national interest. National values provide the framework for rational decision-making; standards for judging good and bad foreign policy are fixed by evolving conceptions of the national interest. A national statesman who justified policy by proclaiming that it served wider international goals at the expense of vital national interests would not long continue as his country's representative. The norms of a foreign office, however vaulting the values its spokesman affirms, must in the end be tested by their responsiveness to national security and national interest.

The normative emphasis in international studies in the aftermath of World War I derived from another source and reflected another perspective. In its early days as a separate discipline, international relations was reformist in outlook and dedicated to remedying international anarchy. The failure of the Senate to support the creation of the League of Nations was taken as an object lesson; it spurred American scholars to devote themselves to the task of laying the foundations for building an effective international organization. The purposes of the first chairs of international study were described in these terms. Occupants were to help create a climate of opinion favorable to new international institutions. The directives of scholars were therefore not primarily scientific. They had a mission: to assure that what had occurred with the repudiation of the League would not occur again. If scholarly writings often took on a moralistic and legalistic flavor, this was the underlying reason. International relations had a purpose and a norm, defined fairly simply and unequivocally as building "a commonwealth of nations." What contributed to this goal was viewed as positive and good, what detracted from it as negative and bad.

This version of a normative approach had certain undeniable strengths and virtues. It gave to the new discipline of international studies a definite and rather uncomplicated focus. It assisted university leaders in making clear-cut judgments on the requirements for filling new academic posts in an emerging field of study. Indeed, in the interwar period the overwhelming majority of professors in the field were authorities in one of two closely related "disciplines." Their major concern was either with international organization or with international law. Their chairs were so designated, and their writings and research reflected this emphasis. They undertook to prepare the way, successfully as it turned out, for a new system of international institutions.

While the normative view of international relations has continued into the present, interpreters and scholars have chosen to deal with more complex and less malleable realities. If the objective of the early stages of normative thinking was straightforward and simple, it grew more sophisticated and pragmatic in later phases. This can be made clear through stating the objectives of the two periods. The early objective was "peace through organization"; later it became "peace and justice through the convergence of interests, organization, and power."

Normative thinkers in recent times have felt constrained to look at international realities through bifocal lenses. On one hand, the development of an international community is, as earlier thinkers had proclaimed, indispensable to national survival in an interdependent world. On the other hand, nationalism is possibly the most stubbornly persistent reality of our time. It acts as the channel and, sometimes, as the transforming agent for worldwide ideological movements. It reshapes Communism to fit Russian, Chinese, and Yugoslav patterns. It may sometimes be disruptive, disorienting, and evil. It can also be constructive, integrating, and unifying. The once simple dichotomy of bad nationalism and good internationalism that prevailed in the early stage of normative writing is no longer sufficient. Communism is a world-wide internationalist movement seeking to remake the world in its image. How does the normative interpreter evaluate this form of internationalism alongside, say, the process of nation-building in newly independent states? Is it not too simple to cast the world in good and evil categories when most developments shade off into questions of relative good or evil for a particular moment in time?

Moreover, recent contributions to normative thought have set out to demonstrate that values and norms, like men and states, are plural and not single. Norms for groups and nations, like norms for individuals, are multiple and interrelated. Clarity and the beginnings of wisdom are not necessarily achieved through simplicity. This can be seen in any evaluation of the policies of a given state. The United States today is dedicated to "peace through international organization." It also es- pouses the goal of justice in the world. How are the goals of peace and justice to be maintained? What resolution is possible if they conflict? What if these norms, which are clear as general directives, point to con- flicting policies in practice? When is the norm of peace to be pursued at all costs and at the expense of justice, and when is justice to be the paramount goal in guiding the conduct of the United States? How are norms affected by technology and by the means of destruction? Is it true that the norms of international order and justice, which were su- preme in a pre-nuclear era, must be sacrificed to the pursuit of peace in the nuclear era?

There are other issues that arise for the normative thinker. What in- fluence does the stage of development of a nation-state have on the legitimate goals it holds and defends? Is isolationism or neutralism de- fensible for colonial America and newly independent India but in- defensible for Britain or the United States today? How do we distinguish between guiding principles for rich and poor nations? Can we draw a line between, say, the use of force that runs counter to the principles of the UN Charter and its employment in maintaining the unity of a threatened nation-state?

In short, students and observers who have written about norms in international society since World War II have placed far greater em- phasis on circumstances and the situation. They have tried to relate norms to context, and have put greater stress on the preconditions for viable rules and effective institutions than did their precursors following World War I. Their approach reflects, if you will, greater concern with the link between ethics and context; they are children of a trend of thought that some have described as "situational ethics."

International law as an expression of normative thinking reflects a similar emphasis. It looks at international obligations through spectacles that relate the conduct and behavior of states to forces and circum- stances. Today's international lawyers are more likely to ask questions like these: "What are the circumstances under which treaties and commit- ments are most likely to be observed?" "When will these obligations be set aside or bypassed, and when will they be transferred to larger in- ternational bodies?" Charles de Visscher, Wilfred Jenks, and Philip Jes- sup all have provided examples of this approach. So do the participants in projects sponsored by the Ford Foundation that are trying to establish links between the legal superstructure and the economic and political in- frastructure in various societies.

Thus, normative thinking is still an important feature  of international studies. It has lost none of its significance, nor is it any less central to the purpose and direction in which states and the world are moving. The temper and orientation have been altered, however: the spirit is more likely to be analytical and critical than crusading. Fortunately, able minds have been at work in each period of the developing study of international norms. Contributions in this area have helped to clarify the nature, structure, and framework of the working international system.

## VIETNAM AS A CASE STUDY IN POLITICAL AND NORMATIVE THINKING

The dialogue between those who support and those who oppose American policy in Vietnam flounders on conflicting moral assumptions. The acceptance of one or another premise leads inescapably to mutually irreconcilable moral and political conclusions. One trend of thought draws on historical and legal arguments that justify the defense of South Vietnam in the name of the commitments of four American Presidents. A nation's word is its bond, and our promise to come to the aid of a Southeast Asian country whose independence is threatened must be observed. Otherwise aggression unchecked at its source will spread and lead to a general conflagration, as in World War II. The other trend of thought puts the stress on the civil-war characteristics of the struggle. It condemns American policy-makers for intervening in an internal struggle, arguing that the major conflict was and is between local factions organized around the National Liberation Front and the government of South Vietnam. It points to the carnage and bloodshed that follow in the train of warfare once it breaks out and expands. The debate between these two viewpoints is unlikely to yield to arguments that are at odds with first premises.

Whether we like it or not, Americans are faced with what Dean Acheson was wont to call a factual situation. We are engaged in what has become a large-scale effort to resist a military and political invasion from North Vietnam. Whatever the elements of the struggle may have been at the outset, they now involve the movement of men and equipment from North Vietnam into South Vietnam. Our government and seemingly the majority of the American people are committed to turning back the troops led by four leading North Vietnamese generals in the South. On Christmas Day, 1966, two full-scale North Vietnamese divisions crossed the 17th parallel into South Vietnam. Eight hundred small craft moved down the coast the moment the air truce was announced to supply fighting men in the South.

What are the moral and political principles relevant to the "factual situation" this conflict has engendered? Two that come to mind—restraint and the use of diplomacy—are in the realm of means. They fall in the area Maritain described in declaring that means must be proportionate to ends. Critics who denounce and "view with alarm" run the risk of ignoring the partial "good" of policies in this area. This has been true for the Korean War, the British defense of Malaya, or American policy in Vietnam.

Restraint in politics or war can be a moral precept, and it is not an inconsiderable gain that the struggle in Vietnam remains a limited war. With the possible exception of some of the bombing in the North, American responses have been limited and measured. The Administration, all too conscious of the risks of a thermonuclear holocaust, has not expanded ground operations to the North. It has resisted calls of an often more belligerent Congress for all-out war and bombing in the North. It has held in check the spread of war fever and hysteria. Much as was done in nineteenth-century international politics, it has allowed the conflict to be circumscribed. In effect, a ring has been thrown around the belligerents and every effort has been made to resist the spread of the conflict. Indeed, the help of our major rival in the cold war, the Soviet Union, has been sought to limit the spread of the conflict.

Second, diplomacy has marched hand in hand with military activity. Strenuous and unremitting efforts have been made to explore ways for setting in motion peaceful processes that might bring the belligerents to the conference table. Every available diplomatic channel has been explored, sometimes admittedly with more compulsiveness than success. Meanwhile, endless discussions have gone on with the Soviet Union on other matters. Often unnoticed, significant advances have been made on such things as cultural exchange, trade, and the signing of the space treaty. Today the Soviet Union and the United States stand on the threshold of both a nuclear proliferation treaty and a consular treaty. Fifteen years ago, Winston Churchill hammered incessantly on the necessity of arming not to fight but to parley. The Administration has not lost sight of this advice, even though its achievements here must be measured more by deeds than by clear articulation.

A third moral and political principle that is relevant in a conflict-ridden world is the need to define the political objectives that inform and inspire a military conflict. Historically, the United States has fallen short of full clarity in formulating its goals. In World War I, the best Woodrow Wilson could do was to declare that our war aims were "to make the world safe for democracy." The diplomatic debacle at Versailles followed. In World War II, the goal was "unconditional surrender." The military conflict ran its course with the resulting division of Europe that carried the seeds of the struggle with the Soviet Union. Once more in Vietnam, little has been said that contributes to the cessation of conflict and the achievement of a peace. Many people doubt that the United States would expend the amount of blood and treasure pouring into South Vietnam if we did not plan to stay after the war. We have not been explicit about our political objectives and the kind of a political order in Southeast Asia that would be acceptable once the conflict came to an end. For example, what are our hopes for political cooperation among the states in the area? What is our goal for the status of the former Indochinese states? Would we accept a neutralization agreement internationally endorsed or guaranteed? What is our view about the withdrawal of air bases from the mainland of Asia? What kind of a defense perimeter do we have in mind? What do we see as our political objectives vis-à-vis China? Isolation? Containment? Or limited cooperation at some stage, say in curbing further nuclear proliferation?

There are limited steps of a moral and political character that are "imaginable" even in the depths of international rivalry and conflict. It is unfortunately the case that these partial "goods" are less appealing to moralists than are towering moral ends that comfort and reassure the conscience but leave the "factual situation" essentially as it was.

### NORMATIVE THEORY: ITS STATUS AND OPPORTUNITY

The complexities of the international scene and the urgency of current problems heighten the need for normative thinking. It would be reassuring to say that the literature abounds with serious writing on normative problems. The truth is that discussion of normative problems appears to lag both in status and prestige. It does not figure extensively in listings of research awards. Its spokesmen constitute no more than a handful of observers. Numerically superior by far are the so-called value-free social scientists. Behaviorist approaches to international-relations theory are currently in vogue. Nevertheless, the need for serious and exacting normative thinking is ever more clear. How can it be advanced? What is needed to spur first-rate minds to pursue such thinking? What qualities must an observer bring to the task?

First, the normative thinker must be prepared to take the long view of his subject. Normative thinking, like politics, is the slow boring of hard boards. It is less a matter of affirming the good than of probing for complex interrelationships between objective principles and hard facts. This effort may call for a marriage, or at least a sympathetic mutual awareness, of philosophy, history, and the social sciences. The philosopher and theologian are more likely to illuminate objective truths, and the historian or social scientist to explore empirical facts. To combine these skills, whether through one mind or many, is the first step in developing normative theory.

Second, every intellectual discipline has its tests that must be applied in studying problems. Normative thinking is no exception. The laws of philosophy and history apply. Normative thinking based on bad philosophy or bad history will not make a lasting contribution. At the same time, neither the traditional concerns of philosophy nor those of history will answer the need. A blending of interests and questions is called for, requiring traditionalists and students of contemporary issues to join hands.

In all this, the relevant guidelines include the tests of reason, history, and context. Attention must also be paid to relevance, continuity, and priority. Each guideline is surrounded by a body of experience that contributes to its usefulness in normative thinking. The task is to apply and translate rules and precepts more commonly associated with other fields. Rigorous study and analysis is the overall requirement.

The laws of reason bear on moral evaluation, especially when issues of international politics and diplomacy come into play. Writings on political reason make up a worthy chapter in the annals of political science. The guiding principle of reason assumes that ordering concepts can be chosen for relating otherwise independent events and data. Political reason historically has been associated with "reason of state." The observer proceeds with a rational map that sets out the course an independent state can be expected to follow in its national interest. The map assumes rationality on the part of policy-makers. It asserts not that all states at all times will adhere to the dictates of political reason but rather that a national imperative toward self-preservation will inform a nation's policies. In the long run, neither ideology nor visionary leaders are likely to override the hard demands of national interest. The moralist who sets out to plot the course a nation should follow cannot ignore the hard demands of political reason.

Likewise history and the traditional and geographic position of a nation must influence its moral and political outlook. Foreign policy is a product of the elements that determine a nation's position in the world. For example, the continuity of postwar American foreign policy is not the result of political uniformity or common membership in an elite or in *the* establishment. Presidents Roosevelt, Truman, Eisenhower, Kennedy, and Johnson came from different regions and social classes. They differed in temperament and outlook, and it would be difficult to equate their understanding of the world. Yet across all differences of experience, viewpoint, and party their foreign policies in the end were remarkably similar. The historic objectives and traditional interests of nations influence the shape of their external relations.

The context in which moral goals are pursued sets the framework for normative discussions. It is tempting to approach moral questions in general terms; their importance for normative theory is found in the concrete situation. For the statesman, his personal sense of right and wrong must accommodate to the demands of public responsibility. For President Lincoln as an individual, the practice of slavery was morally reprehensible. As the nation's chief executive, however, he was obliged to measure what he asked the nation to do by its effect on the union. Thus he declared that if he could preserve the union by freeing all the slaves he would do so; if the union could be preserved by freeing none of them, he would do that; or if he could save it by freeing some and leaving others as slaves he would do that. The test was the effect on the union. The President by his oath is pledged to defend and preserve the union, and in this context public morality overrides personal morality. That the two may conflict is well illustrated in certain Asian countries where continuing responsibility for meeting familial needs may clash with a leader's public trust.

Moral precepts must also be relevant. Law and justice more readily take form in an integrated society with effective machinery for lawmaking. Where institutions and community are lacking, legal prescriptions can be irrelevant. The problem in international society is the lack of widely accepted moral principles on which legal structures can be built. Philosophers have defined proximate morality as a body of mediating principles grounded in objective principles but more attuned to the given realities. Distributive justice is such a mediating concept that outlines working precepts of practical morality.

Finally, priorities must be drawn up both in general terms and for specific situations. It will not do to make an absolute out of a particular moral concept. The true situation with moral principles is that the actor in world affairs must choose not between good and evil but among competing moral principles. Justice may be a moral concern in one circumstance, while peace may take priority in another. Security is sometimes the controlling interest, while freedom may prevail at other times. Someone must formulate a scale of moral values relevant to given circumstances but subject to application under differing circumstances.

The point is that normative thought in international relations must pay heed to the guidelines of responsible analysis. The shape of international society—half organized and half anarchic—sets the framework. It would be as unreal for the moralist to ignore this as for the military analyst to overlook military realities. The opportunities for serious normative thinking rest on a full awareness of the elemental rules and guidelines for analysis.

Third, students of values must be prepared to deal with ambiguities and impalpables in much of their work. Thanks to logical positivism and modern analytical philosophy, some value questions can be dealt with precisely and in quantitative terms. For other facets of normative thought, the interplay of contingent, unpredictable factors and the tragic clash of conflicting values limit certainty and sharp definition. In this sphere, the most we can do is surround a problem, box it in, and point to the alternatives. The best writings on moral choice appear murky to the scientist or mathematician, but this results less from lack of clarity than from the intrinsic nature of the problem. The solitary individual, whether in personal or public life, is unlikely to face his dilemmas of moral choice through a mathematical equation. Rather, he will solve them existentially through trial and error, testing and probing, using his senses as well as his reason. A leading college president said recently, "I've seldom made the wrong decision when I trusted the feeling in my bones." This element of choice is not readily categorized; it resists simple generalization or transferability. Those who would recognize normative thinking in its full dimensions must take this into account.

These three aspects of the approach to revitalizing normative theory need further discussion. They are at most a part of the basic considerations germane to theorizing. Perhaps even this broad statement can help to suggest for others those aspects of intellectual activity unique to value study and those that bind it to other forms of humanistic and social-science study.

ROGER D. MASTERS

# *World Politics as a Primitive Political System*

## I. REASONS FOR COMPARING PRIMITIVE AND INTERNATIONAL POLITICS

Many primitive peoples have political systems which are very much like the international political system. If the characterization of world politics as mere "anarchy" is an exaggeration, surely anarchy moderated or inhibited by a balance of power is a fairly accurate description of the

SOURCE: Roger D. Masters, "World Politics As A Primitive Political System," *World Politics*, XVI (July 1964), 595–619. Reprinted by permission. [Note—The author's research has been undertaken with the assistance of a grant from the Stimson Fund, Yale University.]

rivalry between sovereign nation-states. The Nuer, a primitive African people, have been described as living in an "ordered anarchy" which depends on a "balanced opposition of political segments."[1] It is commonplace to describe the international system as lacking a government, so that "might makes right." "In Nuerland legislative, judicial and executive functions are not invested in any persons or councils"; hence, throughout the society, "the club and the spear are the sanctions of rights."[2]

To be sure, politics among the Nuer—or any other primitive people—is not identical to world politics, but however important the differences may be, a number of writers have suggested the possibility of comparing the two kinds of political systems.[3] Curiously enough, however, there has been virtually no effort to elaborate these similarities comprehensively from a theoretical point of view.[4]

It should be noted in passing that there are three more general reasons for comparing primitive and international political systems. An attempt to bridge the gap between political science and anthropology has merits because such cross-disciplinary endeavors may free one from unnecessarily narrow assumptions which often dominate research in a given field. This is particularly true with respect to political anthropology, since the political aspects of primitive society have often been only imperfectly analyzed.[5]

Secondly, it may not be amiss to point out that long before anthropology was established as a discipline, political philosophers analyzed the

[1] E. E. Evans-Pritchard, *The Nuer* (Oxford 1940), 181; *idem*, "The Nuer of the Southern Sudan," in M. Fortes and E. E. Evans-Pritchard, eds., *African Political Systems* (London 1940), 293.

[2] Evans-Pritchard, *The Nuer*, 162, 169. Cf. R. F. Barton, "Ifugao Law," *University of California Publications in American Archaeology and Ethnology*, xv (February 1915), 15.

[3] E.g., Hans Morgenthau, *Politics Among Nations* (1st edn., New York 1953), 221; George Modelski, "Agraria and Industria: Two Models of the International System," in Klaus Knorr and Sidney Verba, eds., *The International System* (Princeton 1961), 125–26; and David Easton, "Political Anthropology," in Bernard J. Siegel, ed., *Biennial Review of Anthropology 1959* (Stanford 1959), 235–36. At least one anthropologist was aware of the analogy: see R. F. Barton, *The Half-Way Sun* (New York 1930), 109–10; *idem*, *The Kalingas* (Chicago 1949), 101; and *idem*, "Ifugao Law," 100, 103. In his introduction to *The Kalingas*, E. A. Hoebel wrote: "International law is primitive law on a world scale" (p. 5). Cf. Hoebel's *The Law of Primitive Man* (Cambridge, Mass., 1954), 125–26, 318, 321, 330–33.

[4] Since this study was undertaken, an article has been published that marks a first step in this direction. See Chadwick F. Alger, "Comparison of Intranational and International Politics," *American Political Science Review*, LVII (June 1963), 414–19.

[5] In 1940, A. R. Radcliffe-Brown said: "The comparative study of political institutions, with special reference to the simpler societies, is an important branch of social anthropology which has not yet received the attention it deserves" (Preface, in Fortes and Evans-Pritchard, eds., *African Political Systems*, xi). More recently, David Easton has written: "Such a subfield [as political anthropology] does not yet exist" ("Political Anthropology," 210).

social and political antecedents of existing states and governments.[6] The idea of a "state of nature," in which men lived before the establishment of governments, plays an important role in the history of political philosophy. Although recent students of primitive society have argued that "the theories of political philosophers" are "of little scientific value,"[7] the existence of a tradition which considered the "state of nature" as relevant to any political theory may indicate that political scientists should consider primitive politics more fully than they now do.

This general point is of specific importance for the theory of international politics because it can be said that the modern theory of international relations took the notion of a "state of nature" as its model.[8] Since anthropologists have asserted that such a "state of nature" never existed, consideration of the empirical and theoretical relevance of the concept may well be in order; not the least of the advantages of a comparison between primitive and international politics would be a fuller understanding of the relevance of modern political philosophy to a theory of world politics.[9]

Finally, as Ragnar Numelin has shown, "international relations" (or its analog) exists among uncivilized peoples; the "discovery" of diplomacy cannot be attributed, as it customarily is, to the "historical" cultures of the Mediterranean or Orient.[10] Thus any exhaustive theory of world politics would have to comprehend the rivalry, warfare, and diplomacy of primitive peoples as genuine examples of "international politics."

## II. SIMILARITIES BETWEEN PRIMITIVE AND INTERNATIONAL POLITICS

At the outset, four elements common to politics within a number of primitive societies and international relations deserve mention: first, the absence of a formal government with power to judge and punish viola-

[6] E.g., Montaigne, *Essays,* I, xxiii ("Of Custom, and that We Should Not Easily Change a Law Received"), and I, xxxi ("Of Cannibals"); Rousseau, *Second Discourse,* esp. First Part and notes c-q; and Locke, *Second Treatise of Civil Government,* esp. chaps. 2 and 3.

[7] Fortes and Evans-Pritchard, *African Political Systems,* 4. See also Henry Sumner Maine's sharp criticism of Rousseau's conception of the "state of nature" in *Ancient Law* (New York 1874), 84–88, 299.

[8] On the relations between the concept of a "state of nature" and the prevailing theory of politics among sovereign states, see Kenneth N. Waltz, *Man, the State, and War* (New York 1959), esp. chaps. 6–8; and Richard H. Cox, *Locke on War and Peace* (Oxford 1960), esp. chap. 4.

[9] Cf. Kenneth N. Waltz, "Political Philosophy and the Study of International Relations," in William T. R. Fox, ed., *Theoretical Aspects of International Relations* (Notre Dame, Ind., 1959), 51–68; and Arnold Wolfers, "Political Theory and International Relations," in Arnold Wolfers and Laurence W. Martin, eds., *The Anglo-American Tradition in Foreign Affairs* (New Haven 1956), esp. xi-xiii.

[10] Ragnar Numelin, *The Beginnings of Diplomacy* (New York 1950), 125 *et passim.*

tions of law; second, the use of violence and "self-help" by the members of the system to achieve their objectives and enforce obligations; third, the derivation of law and moral obligations either from custom or from explicit, particular bargaining relationships (i.e., the absence of a formal legislative body operating on the basis of—and making—general rules); and fourth, a predominant organizational principle which establishes political units serving many functions in the overall social system.

The first three of these similarities between primitive and international politics are relatively self-evident when one considers those primitive societies which lack fully developed governments. The fourth, however, may not be as clear. In certain primitive societies, territorial political units are largely defined, especially in the eyes of their members, in terms of kinship groups which are reckoned either "unilaterally" (i.e., groups such as the "lineage," in which descent is in either the male or female line from a common ancestor), or "bilaterally" (i.e., the family group includes relatives of both mother and father, as in modern, "Western" society).[11] Different combinations or divisions of these groups, on a territorial basis, often provide the basic structure of the entire political system.

Although it is not normally noted, the international system of sovereign states is also organized largely on the basis of a single principle. In this case, the principle is that of "territorial sovereignty"—i.e., the conception that sovereignty "is always associated with the proprietorship of a limited portion of the earth's surface, and that 'sovereigns' *inter se* are to be deemed not *paramount*, but *absolute* owners of the state's territory."[12] This ultimate authority can, of course, be divided, as it is in federal states; but so, too, with the lineage principle in some primitive systems which are divided into different levels of units.[13]

In primitive societies like the Nuer, lineage or kinship groups perform a wide variety of functions, so that it is not possible to point to

[11] See Fortes and Evans-Pritchard, *African Political Systems,* 11; and Barton, "Ifugao Law," 92–94, 110. Carl Landé, in a stimulating unpublished paper entitled "Kinship and Politics in Pre-Modern and Non-Western Societies," has emphasized the different effects of these two types of kinship groups.

[12] Maine, *Ancient Law,* 99 (original italics).

[13] The foregoing comparison may appear to come strikingly close to the formulations of Maine (*ibid.,* 124–25) and Lewis H. Morgan (*Ancient Society* [New York 1877], 6–7)—formulations which have been criticized in recent years by anthropologists. See I. Schapera, *Government and Politics in Tribal Societies* (London 1956), 2–5. Despite the inadequacies of the conceptions of Maine and Morgan, especially with reference to their presumption of progress in human development, some distinction between primitive or traditional society, in which kinship and personal "status" play a predominant role, and modern territorial states, based on citizenship and contact, is today accepted by many social scientists. Indeed, it is paradoxical that while anthropologists have been attacking the Maine-Morgan dichotomy (by showing that

a specific action and define it as "political";[14] rather, there is a political element in many actions which simultaneously serve other purposes. This characteristic has been described in recent sociological literature as the "functional diffuseness" of traditional social structures.[15] The conception of "diffuseness" is thus opposed to "functional specificity" (i.e., the organization of a special group or institution to perform a given activity or function), which is supposed to prevail in all modern societies.

. . .

Up to this point we have tried to show two things: first, that there is a striking similarity between some primitive political systems and the modern international system; and second, that one element of this similarity is the "functional diffuseness" of political units in both types of system. If this is so, one cannot employ the polar opposites of "primitive" and "modern" or "functionally diffuse" and "functionally specific" as the basis of a comparative analysis of primitive political systems. Because primitive political systems vary enormously, one must explicitly distinguish the particular *kind* of primitive society which is supposed to present the greatest similarity to world politics.

In order to compare primitive and international politics, therefore, one needs a classification which distinguishes primitive societies in terms of their political structure. Although the typologies of primitive political systems hitherto developed by anthropologists have been imperfect, it will be useful to accept provisionally the distinction between primitive peoples which have developed some form of governmental institutions and those which have generally been called "stateless societies."[19]

---

all societies have a territorial element), sociologists and political scientists have been adopting the distinction from the works of Tönnies, Weber, Parsons, or Levy. E.g., see Fred W. Riggs, "Agraria and Industria—Toward a Typology of Comparative Administration," in William J. Siffin, ed., *Toward the Comparative Study of Public Administration* (Bloomington 1959), 28–30, III.

[14] E.g., according to Evans-Pritchard, "We do not therefore say that a man is acting politically or otherwise, but that between local groups there are relations of a structural order that can be called political" (*The Nuer*, 264–65).

[15] See Talcott Parsons, *The Social System* (Glencoe, Ill., 1951), 65–67.

[19] See Fortes and Evans-Pritchard, *African Political Systems*, 5–23; John Middleton and David Tait, eds., *Tribes Without Rulers* (London 1958), 1–3; Lucy Mair, *Primitive Government* (Baltimore 1962), Part 1; Schapera, *Government and Politics*, 63–64, 208–14; and Robert Lowie, *Social Organization* (New York 1948), chap. 14. For a critique of the categories used by anthropologists, see Easton, "Political Anthropology," 210–26.

The following comparison will focus on primitive societies that lack formal governments. Such systems may be described as having "diffuse leadership," since individuals or groups have influence without formally institutionalized coercive authority. There may be a "titular chief" in these societies, but such an individual, even together with other influential men, does not act as a ruler. Since the modern world, as a political system, shares this structural characteristic of "statelessness," a résumé of political life in primitive stateless societies will show the utility of comparing them to the international political system.

### III. "Self-Help" and Violence in Primitive Stateless Societies

In stateless systems, disputes cannot be referred to an impartial government backed by a police force. The characteristic pattern of responding to criminal or civil wrongs is "self-help": the individual or group which feels injured considers himself or itself legitimately responsible for punishing a crime or penalizing a tort. Self-help in these circumstances involves two stages which appear to be directly comparable to the functions of adjudication and enforcement in modern legal systems. In either system, first it is necessary to determine that a wrong has occurred and that a particular individual or group will be punished in a particular way; second, the punishment or penalty for that wrong must be enforced or implemented.

In the simplest primitive societies, both stages are accomplished by the individual or family that has been wronged. For example, when a kinship group discovers that one of its members has been murdered, the guilty individual and his kinship group will be identified and a retaliatory killing (or other punishment) will be inflicted by the wronged group. As Barton indicated in his study of Philippine headhunters, such self-enforcement of legal penalties[20] raises a crucial problem among stateless primitive peoples. The kinship group which enforces the *lex talionis* by killing a murderer or one of his kin sees this act as not only necessary, but also legitimate. Although unrelated bystanders may accept this interpretation, since retaliatory killing is customary, the kinship group which is penalized may not consider the retaliation to be a legitimate punishment.[21] When this occurs, there is often a tendency for crime and

[20] It must be emphasized that the retaliation is *legal*, being sanctioned by customary law (or, in Weber's terms, "traditional legitimacy"). Cf. Mair, *Primitive Government*, 16–19; and A. R. Radcliffe-Brown, *Structure and Function in Primitive Society* (Glencoe, Ill., 1952), chap. 12.

[21] See Barton, *The Kalingas*, 231. Note the parallel tendency in world politics: "One state's aggression is always another state's 'legitimate use of force to defend vital national interests'" (Inis L. Claude, Jr., "United Nations Use of Military Force," *Journal of Conflict Resolution*, vii [June 1963], 119).

punishment to "escalate" into a more or less permanent relation of "feud" between the kinship groups involved.[22]

In feuds, violence usually takes the form of sporadic surprise attacks by individuals or small groups. Hence a condition of feud should not be equated too completely with what we call "war";[23] rather, it is a condition of rivalry in which intermittent violence and aggression (e.g., seizure of property or person as well as retaliatory killing) appear legitimate to those who attack, and illegitimate to the victims. The similarity of this "state of feud" and a Hobbesian "state of nature" is obvious, with the important difference that kinship groups are often involved, instead of isolated individuals.

Although the notion of modern warfare cannot be accurately applied to all primitive intergroup fighting, primitive violence sometimes approximates a civilized war. The gradations of conflict arising out of self-help have been clarified by Tait and Middleton, who suggest that primitive feuds and wars be distinguished because only in the latter is there no obligation to attempt to settle the dispute.[24] They argue that within a restricted range (which varies from one primitive society to another) the more or less permanent condition of feud rivalry is rendered unlikely, if not impossible, by the existence of close kinship ties and relationships of "administrative organization."

At this level there may be a duel or the requirement that ritual acts of atonement be performed, but prolonged group rivalry is unlikely since the individuals concerned are all members of a single "nuclear group" (which is, normally, a local community, a kinship group, or both). Within such a local or family unit, disputes culminating in violence are not self-perpetuating; as in modern states, a punishment or penalty "atones" for a crime and thereby completes the legal case.[25]

• • •

This does not mean that such means of settling the feud are always

[22] Cf. Barton, *The Half-Way Sun*, chaps. 5 and 6. In some situations, however, a group may refrain from counterretaliation, either because the kinsman who was punished was offensive to his own kin or because the group lacks the power to react. As Carl Landé has pointed out to me, the principles of "an eye for an eye" and "might makes right" may, and often do, conflict in the operation of both primitive and international political systems.

[23] Numelin argues that organized, continuous warfare of the type known to civilized man is practically unknown among primitive peoples (*The Beginnings of Diplomacy*, chap. 2). Cf. Schapera, *Government and Politics*, 215, 219; and Melville J. Herskovits, *Cultural Anthropology* (New York 1955), 207–8.

[24] "Introduction," *Tribes Without Rulers*, 20–22. Cf. Radcliffe-Brown, *African Political Systems*, xx. . . .

[25] Tait and Middleton, *Tribes Without Rulers*, 19–20. See Barton, "Ifugao Law," 14–15, and the example, 120–21.

successful, nor that the settlement is in fact permanent. On the contrary, Evans-Pritchard concludes: "Though the chief admonishes the relatives of the dead man at the ceremonies of settlement that the feud is ended and must not be renewed, Nuer know that 'a feud never ends'. . . . There is no frequent fighting or continuous unabated hostility, but the sore rankles and the feud, though formally concluded, may at any time break out again."[28] Hence the settlement of a feud amounts to a truce—one might say a treaty, given the impermanence of similar settlements in international politics—between rival groups. Such a settlement may occur because feuding segments need to cooperate on other matters, but it cannot unite them into a harmonious unit without further steps, such as a marriage between the feuding families.[29]

Tait and Middleton use the term "jural community" to describe the unit within which disputes take the form of feuds to be settled by an established procedure.[30] Violence on this level tends to be limited in a way which presents very revealing similarities to procedures in international affairs: as with "limited war," there is a restriction on the means of violence used and the ends sought, and like some interstate treaties, each rival group is willing to end violence (if only temporarily) because of the need to cooperate with its rivals. Hence the settlement of a feud does not ordinarily preclude the recurrence of violence; as in international treaties, the parties are their own judges of the maintenance of the conditions of the peaceful settlement.[31]

• • •

Among stateless primitive peoples . . . social distance (which is highly correlated with geographical distance) decreases the likelihood that violence, should it occur, will be limited.[33] This spatial distinction

[28] *The Nuer*, 155. Cf. Barton, "Ifugao Law," 75: "Once started, a blood feud was well-nigh eternal (unless ended by a fusion of the families by means of marriage)."
[29] See the example in Barton, *The Half-Way Sun*, 115.
[30] "The jural community . . . is the widest grouping within which there are a moral obligation and a means ultimately to settle disputes peaceably" (*Tribes Without Rulers*, 9).
[31] Cf. the rarity of the emergence of what has been called a "security community" in international politics. Karl Deutsch, *et al.*, *Political Community and the North Atlantic Area* (Princeton 1957), chap. 1.
[33] The conquest of physical space by modern technology has altered the character of "social distance" without destroying it. Today differences in the kind of political regime tend to have effects similar to those of geographical distance between primitive tribes; because of their political principles, Communist regimes are those farthest from the United States even when they are close to us in miles. Cf. the concepts of "structural distance" (Evans-Pritchard, *The Nuer*, 113ff.) and "social distance" (Emory S. Bogardus, *Sociology* [4th edn., New York 1954], 535–36).

between those who are "far" and those who are "near" tends to produce a series of concentric zones around each group in many primitive worlds.[34] Where such zones have been found, the specific boundaries of each region are often unclear. Thus there is considerable evidence that, for a member of many primitive societies without a government, the group or "political community" to which allegiance is owed varies, depending on the dispute in question.[35]

This characteristic is related to one of the fundamental differences between many primitive political systems and world politics—namely, the fusion of various levels of social intercourse which we are accustomed to distinguish. In modern life, one can speak of a distinction between the level of a society (normally organized as a nation-state), that of a local community, and that of a family. For the primitive, the family or kinship group may include all residents of a locality; even if it does not, the kinship group or locality will tend to have many of the functions of a modern society without having either the political structure or the unique claim to allegiance of the modern state. As a consequence, parallels drawn between primitive political systems and international politics, however useful they may be in other respects, must take into consideration differences in the scope and powers of units in the two kinds of systems.[36]

Despite these differences, however, there are some striking similarities between primitive stateless societies and international political systems with respect to the role of violence in intergroup conflict. In both, there is a range of social relationships which is relatively exempt from self-perpetuating violence; within the "nuclear groups" composing both systems, the procedures for settling disputes or atoning for crimes are terminal, at least in principle. In both types of systems, intermittent, violent conflict between nuclear groups can be temporarily settled without removing the potentiality of further attacks. Violence is justified in the eyes of the aggressive group because the legal system permits self-help as a means of enforcing one's rights. Since the punished group de-

---

[34] See the similar diagrams in Barton, *The Half-Way Sun*, 114, and Evans-Pritchard, *The Nuer*, 114. Note that Barton distinguishes a "neutral zone" between the "home region" and the zone of feuding.

[35] See Mair, *Primitive Government*, 46–48, 104–6.

[36] The problem of units and levels of analysis has had surprisingly little attention in recent theorizing on international politics. For exceptions, see Karl Deutsch, *Political Community at the International Level* (Garden City, N.Y., 1954); Waltz, *Man, the State, and War;* and J. David Singer, "The Level-of-Analysis Problem in International Relations," in Knorr and Verba, eds., *The International System*, 77–92. Of particular importance is the relationship between a cultural community or "people" and organized "political communities." Cf. Gabriel A. Almond, "Comparative Political Systems," *Journal of Politics*, xviii (August 1956), 393–408.

nies this justification, there is a tendency for a conflict to erupt into an exchange of hostilities, a tendency which is restrained between those groups which consider themselves to be similar or "near" each other. These similarities indicate that the analogy between primitive political systems without governments and international politics is not merely fanciful; both appear to belong to a general class of political systems in which self-help or violence is an accepted and legitimate mode of procedure.

## IV. Order in Primitive Stateless Societies

In discussing the characteristics of violence in primitive societies which lack rulers, there has been an emphasis on the competitive relationship of opposed groups. When seen in this light, primitive society may seem to be a barely controlled anarchy in which security of life and limb is scarcely to be expected. Since this impression is inaccurate, it is of the greatest importance to emphasize the variety of political functions performed in primitive stateless societies.

•   •   •

The pacific functions of self-help can be clearly seen if one considers the circumstances in which violence does *not* arise out of conflict in a stateless primitive system. In the simplest of such societies, the necessities of cooperation tend to preclude violence within the family and locality, while the limitations of technology tend to restrict social intercourse to these relatively narrow groups; hence, among the technologically least developed primitives, feuding relations are rare and wars virtually unknown. In this kind of system, self-help and retaliation function effectively as the only forcible means for punishing crimes because social opprobrium is, in itself, a strong punishment.[38]

Among primitive peoples with a more complex stateless system, such as the Ifugao studied by Barton, there are many occasions for feuding or warfare, but actual violence does not arise out of every dispute. The limitation of violence between potentially feuding groups is related to the institutions which serve the function of settling feuds. The Ifugao "go-between" not only acts as a mediator in feuds which have caused deaths on either side, but also acts prior to the eruption of violence in an effort to prevent such killings. In negotiating disputes which have not yet led to killing, he emphasizes at every stage the dangers im-

[38] E.g., A. R. [Radcliffe-] Brown, *The Andaman Islanders* (Cambridge, Eng., 1922), 48–52, 84–87.

plicit in open feuding; by describing these dangers in detail, the "go-between" (with the backing of his own family and the local community at large) attempts to deter an attack by either of the opposed families.

. . .

Whether originating with a "go-between" or a member of a wronged group, advice that open feuding be avoided, or at least limited, is characteristic of a phenomenon which has recently received extensive attention in foreign affairs—namely, deterrence. Although it has sometimes been assumed that deterrence requires a rational calculation of the consequences of an attack, deterrence and self-help among primitive peoples do not presuppose a conscious strategic calculation of the type formalized by game theorists.[41] Thus the possibility of violent counterretaliation may, in itself and without further calculation, stabilize rivalries and limit conflicts when there is no governmental arbiter to enforce law and order.

. . .

The essential character of both self-help and deterrence in primitive society is . . . political in the broadest sense: when there is no government, retaliation and the threat of violence serve to unite social groups and maintain legal or moral criteria of right and wrong. This use of might to make right seems repugnant to civilized men, for it has been largely (though not completely) superseded within modern society; nonetheless, such a procedure is consonant with a particular kind of social order and cannot be dismissed as having been surpassed with the formation of the first political society. Primitive legal procedures may largely be confined to the international political system today, but on this level the uncivilized notions of self-help and retaliation continue to play a decisive role.[44]

. . .

V. INTERNATIONAL POLITICS AS A PRIMITIVE, STATELESS SYSTEM

The foregoing analysis has attempted to show how self-help, retaliation, and deterrence can be viewed as a characteristically primitive approach

[41] Sophisticated students of strategy have never assumed, of course, that rivals can deter each other only if their calculations are formulated in terms of game theory. Cf. Thomas Schelling's analogy of deterring a child, *The Strategy of Conflict* (Cambridge, Mass., 1960), 11. Nonetheless, popular analyses often assert that deterrence implies—and requires—rational calculation on both sides. E.g., Seymour Melman, *The Peace Race* (New York 1961), 22.

[44] Cf. Aristotle, *Nicomachean Ethics*, V.1130b30–1134a15.

to law and order. Through this focus on stateless primitive peoples, the reliance upon self-help and deterrence in international relations appears to be evidence that the world forms a political system that is in many respects similar to primitive systems. Although it is often argued that international law and politics are *sui generis*,[47] the utility of a comparison between international affairs and stateless primitive societies is shown by two characteristic similarities: first, the relation of law to violence as a means of organizing a coherent social system; and second, the relationship of custom to rivalry and bargaining as means of making and applying known rules.[48]

Although it is fashionable to describe international relations as a lawless anarchy,[49] and to admit that international law exists only on condition that it be called "weak" law,[50] these habitual opinions must be questioned. It is true that the international system permits and even sanctions a considerable amount of violence and bloodshed; but, as has been seen, there is a class of stateless political systems which have this characteristic because they depend upon self-help for the enforcement of law. In such systems law and violence are related in a way that is quite different from the internal political order under which civilized man is accustomed to live; if we speak of international "anarchy," it would be well to bear in mind that it is an "ordered anarchy."

To prove that international law is not necessarily "weak," one need only consider the functions of law in a political system. Hoffmann has suggested that any legal order has three functions: it should produce "security," "satisfaction," and "flexibility."[51] According to these criteria, a legal system dependent upon the self-enforcement of rights by autonomous groups (be they families or nation-states) is "strong" in all three respects.

Most obviously, "flexibility" is assured in a system which recog-

[47] E.g., Stanley Hoffman, "International Systems and International Law," in Knorr and Verba, eds., *The International System*, 205.

[48] The second of these characteristics is concerned, speaking crudely, with the relationship between what Almond has called the "political functions" of rule-making, rule application, and interest articulation, while the first corresponds roughly to his functions of interest aggregation and rule adjudication. The last of these functions, in a stateless system, should really be spoken of as rule enforcement, for obvious reasons. Cf. "Introduction," in Almond and Coleman, eds., *The Politics of the Developing Areas*, 17; and see note 82 below.

[49] Cf. Waltz, *Man, the State, and War*, chaps. 6 and 7. While the present essay is in complete agreement with Waltz's major theme (i.e., that war is a necessary consequence of the state system, since "in anarchy there is no automatic harmony"), his emphasis on the problem of war tends to understate the elements of legality and order in world politics.

[50] E.g., Hoffman, "International Systems and International Law," 206–7.

[51] *Ibid.*, 212.

nizes any change in power; to the extent that might makes right, changes in might produce changes in right. It may be somewhat less evident that international law produces a "satisfactory" solution for disputes, yet this is on the whole true because of the admitted impossibility of reversing the verdict of brute force.[52] And, finally, the stateless international system even produces a modicum of security, most especially through deterrence based upon a mutual recognition that rival nations will both be harmed (if not destroyed) by the use of their legitimate right to self-help. In this respect it is worth emphasizing that the nuclear age, with its awesome potentialities for destruction, has also seen a corresponding increase in the unwillingness of powerful nation-states to resort to overt war.[53]

•   •   •

The limitations as well as the importance of both violence and cooperation in world politics must therefore be equally emphasized in any total assessment of the international system. In so doing, the comparison with stateless primitive peoples serves the useful purpose of identifying the characteristic properties of a political system in which law is sanctioned by self-help. As among the primitives, retaliation is an acceptable means of righting a wrong, though it is true that civilized nations regard strict retaliation—"an eye for an eye"—as a more extreme recourse than do savage peoples.[58] As among stateless primitives, neutrality is possible, and non-involved groups often attempt to mediate conflict and induce rivals to cease fighting. As among stateless primitives, finally, the very possibility that conflict may escalate serves to deter violence on

---

[52] Although the "satisfaction" with defeat in war may be of short duration, this is not a necessary consequence of military defeat (as the pro-Western attitude of West Germany and Japan after World War II indicates). The limited durability of "satisfactory" settlements will be discussed below.

[53] Since World War II there have been numerous international incidents which, under prenuclear conditions, would probably have resulted in open warfare. Cf. Herman Kahn, "The Arms Race and Some of Its Hazards," in Donald G. Brennan, ed., *Arms Control, Disarmament, and National Security* (New York 1961), 93ff. On the security offered by the "impermeable" nation-state before the development of nuclear weapons, see John H. Herz, *International Politics in the Atomic Age* (New York 1959), Part 1.

[58] Henry S. Maine, *International Law* (New York 1888), 174–75. Primitive peoples do not always exact strict retaliation, however; the institution of a "weregild" or payment in lieu of retaliation is paralleled in international politics by reparations and other penalties exacted in the negotiation of peace treaties. Also, compare Morton A. Kaplan, "The Strategy of Limited Retaliation," Policy Memorandum No. 19 (Princeton, Center of International Studies, 1959), and, more generally, recent strategic discussions of "graduated deterrence"—e.g., Henry A. Kissinger, *The Necessity for Choice* (New York 1961), 65–70.

some occasions.[59] Hence the relation of law to force in the multistate system, like the "ordered anarchy" of primitive societies without governments, is derived from the lack of authoritative political institutions.

When we turn more directly to the decision-making process—the second characteristic mentioned above—it may be recalled that in many primitive political systems, especially those lacking governmental institutions, custom and bargaining are related in a crucial way, since they are the only methods for establishing enforceable rules. The same can be said of the international political system, for it too lacks an authoritative legislature or an all-powerful executive. International law can be said to be created in two major ways: a practice or rule either becomes a custom, having been followed for a considerable time, or it is adopted by mutual consent, as binding specific groups under particular circumstances. While the second of these legislative methods is relatively unambiguous to the extent that it produces formal treaties and agreements, the first produces customary law slowly and imperceptibly, so that in periods of rapid change one may wonder if any such law really exists. Over time, nonetheless, specific legal rules have been adopted and accepted as valid by the nation-states composing the modern international system.[60]

At any moment of time, international law seems to be chaotic and uncertain; "double standards" often appear to bind weak or lawabiding states, while permitting the ruthless or strong to satisfy their demands with impunity.[61] But when a longer-range view is taken and the world is considered as a stateless political system in which self-help is a legitimate means of legal procedure, disputes over the content of international law (like disputes over the legitimacy of each killing in a primitive

---

[59] Cf. Schelling, *The Strategy of Conflict*, chap. 8.

[60] On the character of international law and its sources, see James L. Brierly, *The Law of Nations* (4th edn., London 1949), 1–91, 229–36; Percy E. Corbett, *Law and Society in the Relations of States* (New York 1951), 3–52; and Morton A. Kaplan and Nicholas de B. Katzenbach, *The Political Foundations of International Law* (New York 1961), chap. 9. Some observers of international relations, following John Austin's legal theory, have doubted that a system without a single sovereign authority could have "true" law. For a criticism of this application of Austin's view, see Maine, *International Law*, 47–51.

[61] William Foltz has pointed out to me that there is also a parallel "reverse double standard" in both primitive and international systems; weak and unimportant groups are often permitted actions which major groups would not commit (or which would be strongly criticized if committed). Many primitive systems allow inferior lineages or castes wider latitude in many forms of conduct (dishonesty, petty thievery, public defamation, etc.) than is permitted major lineages or castes. As long as the stability of the system or the vital interests of a major group are not threatened, such behavior may be a useful safety valve. The behavior of so-called "nonaligned" states in the UN General Assembly offers an obvious parallel.

feud) become a predictable consequence of the system's structure. As the world is now organized, international law almost requires conflict concerning the substantive provisions relating to a given dispute, and warfare is a legal means of bargaining prior to the conclusion of more or less temporary settlements.[62]

One peculiar characteristic of laws in a stateless political system is thus the legitimization of dispute concerning the application of legal rights to particular circumstances. While it is usual in this context to emphasize the relationship of force to law (by pointing out that "might makes right" in anarchy), the frequency and necessity of disputes over the substance of rights have another consequence: the primacy of political rivalry. Within a society with a government, men whose interests conflict must channel their demands through a specific institutional structure, ultimately recognizing (in principle) the legitimacy of political attitudes which have been sanctioned by governmental decision.[63]

In international politics, this relatively terminal character of intrastate political decisions is often lacking; the policies of one's rivals need not be legitimized even by victory in warfare. In a sense, therefore, might does *not* make right in international politics (as, indeed, the French insisted after 1871 and the Germans after 1918). Like primitive feuds, international disputes are only temporarily settled; a settlement which precludes the possibility of further conflict is rare.[64] This means that political differences, and the interests upon which these differences are based, are often more visible in the world politics than in intrastate politics. Conflicting demands for the satisfaction of the desires of

[62] From the point of view of a systematic analysis, law need not be a "good." Indeed, law need not produce peaceful "order," though as civilized men we infer from our political experience that this *should* be so. Hence authorities on international law often feel compelled to go beyond mere restatements of accepted legal principles; the international law texts, long an important method of codifying customary international law, are frequently animated by a desire for reform. Cf. Maine, *International Law*, Lectures I, XII, *et passim*. Unlike the sphere of domestic politics, in which relativism sometimes seems tenable to scholars, international law and politics are difficult to treat in a wholly positivist fashion without thereby accepting as justifiable a condition of legal self-help and war which civilized men tend to reject as barbarous, if not unjust. Hence world politics is perhaps *the* area in which it is most evident that satisfactory political theory cannot divorce objectivity (and especially freedom from partisanship) from the quest for standards of justice.

[63] But note that, even in domestic politics, the legitimacy of governmental decisions may be challenged by those who are willing to be "bellicose." Cf. Bertrand de Jouvenel, *The Pure Theory of Politics* (New Haven 1963), 180ff.

[64] For the prerequisites for these rare cases, see the study cited in note 31. Note the function of "marriage" (between representatives of rival kinship groups in primitive societies and between ruling families in the earlier period of the modern state system) as a means of formalizing such a settlement.

one's own group—politics and rivalry—are therefore the prime factors in international relations.[65]

This primacy of political conflict in world affairs is especially important because of a further similarity between primitive and international politics. Just as some stateless primitive societies are differentiated into spatial "zones" of increasing opposition, so the world can be divided into areas which are politically "far" from each other.[66] Here again, a characteristic of world politics which often appears to be *sui generis* can be understood more broadly in the context of a comparison between primitive and international politics.

## VI. Some Differences Between Primitive and International Political Systems

In arguing that stateless primitive political systems resemble the international political system in many ways, the search for analogies should not obscure the massive differences which must have been only too easily noticed by the reader. By specifying some of these differences, however, it will be possible to distinguish those aspects in which world politics is unique from those that are due to the absence of a formally constituted world government. In particular, there are two general differences between primitive and international politics which will make it easier to see the limits of the structural similarity between the two. It will be necessary to consider, first, the role of political culture, and second, the impact of change.

Although it is usually assumed that the beliefs, manners, and customs of nonliterate peoples are homogeneous, many primitive societies are composed of heterogenous ethnic stocks; indeed, such heterogeneity is particularly important, for it appears to be related to the emergence of governmental institutions, at least among many African peoples.[67] Nonetheless, there is a marked tendency toward cultural homogeneity in primitive stateless societies, since most individuals accept without question the established way of life.[68] Although the application of traditional rules to specific cases may be and frequently is disputed, the rela-

---

[65] Cf. the "principle of political primacy" emphasized by Robert E. Osgood, *Limited War* (Chicago 1957), 13–15.

[66] "Blocs" and regional systems are, of course, ready examples. On the relationship between the global system and regional system in international politics, see George Liska, *Nations in Alliance* (Baltimore 1962), 19–20, 22–24, 259–62.

[67] See Schapera, *Government and Politics*, 124–25; and Mair, *Primitive Government*, chap. 5.

[68] Cf. Fortes and Evans-Pritchard, *African Political Systems*, 9–10.

tive stability of culture limits the kinds of change occurring in most primitive systems.[69]

In contrast, the international political system currently includes radically different political cultures. As Almond has shown, national political systems which face the task of integrating different political cultures are subject to strains that are absent in more homogeneous societies; *a fortiori*, this problem is even greater in a system which permits many antagonistic political cultures to organize themselves into autonomous nation-states.[70] In general, therefore, it could be argued that self-help and structural decentralization tend to produce a greater degree of instability in world politics than in most primitive stateless societies.[71]

An additional feature compounds this problem. The historical development of Western civilization, as it has increased man's control over nature and spread the effects of modern science throughout the world, has produced particularly sharp differences between political cultures, at the same time that it has brought these cultures into closer contact than was possible before the advent of modern technology. And, simultaneously with this intensification of the contact between different cultures, it has become apparent that technologically advanced societies are capable of what seems to be virtually infinite material progress, so that the most powerful nations can continuously increase their technological superiority over "backward" or "underdeveloped" states.

The main consequence of the interaction of modern, scientific technology upon cultural differences has been extraordinarily rapid change in world politics, of which the great increase in the number of nation-states is but the most superficial index.[72] The stateless structure of a primitive political system may be tolerably stable, despite the reliance upon self-help in legal enforcement; a similar structure, in the changing context of international politics, may well lead to chaos. Even in a primitive world, the contact of a more "advanced" people with a society with-

---

[69] Hence there may be disputes concerning the power and influence of opposed groups, but these conflicts are rarely ideological in character.

[70] See Almond, "Comparative Political Systems," 400–2. Cf. the importance of the nationality problem in the USSR.

[71] Note, however, that many primitive societies are not as stable and unchanging as is often believed. E.g., see Southall, *Alur Society*, 224–27, 236, *et passim*; and J. A. Barnes, *Politics in a Changing Society* (London 1954), chap. 2.

[72] On the distinction between "stable" and "revolutionary" international systems, see Hoffman, "International Systems and International Law," 208–11. Hoffmann suggests that three variables determine the stability or instability of an international system: (1) "the basic structure of the world," (2) "the technology of conflict," and (3) "the units' purposes" (*ibid.*, 207–8). In the present essay, emphasis is placed on the first of these variables—see below, section VII.

out governmental institutions has often produced a rapid domination of the latter by the former.[73] It is all the more to be expected, therefore, that the present structure of the international system is essentially transitional, and that quite considerable changes must be expected in the next century.

### VII. CONCLUSION: DIRECTIONS FOR RESEARCH

The reader may well wonder, at this point, whether the foregoing analysis has any theoretical significance: can the contrast between primitive stateless societies and the interstate system provide any substantive insights otherwise missed by students of world politics? The relative novelty of the comparison here proposed is not, in itself, sufficient justification of the endeavor. Almost eighty years ago, Henry Sumner Maine saw this parallel when he remarked: "Ancient jurisprudence, if perhaps a deceptive comparison may be employed, may be likened to international Law, filling nothing, as it were, except the interstices between the great groups which are the atoms of society."[74] While the parallels noted above may be nothing but a "deceptive comparison," Maine's formulation itself suggests the important element of similarity which promises to clarify our understanding of world politics.

Although both primitive and international politics can take place in "the interstices between the great groups which are the atoms of society," the "groups" which are "atoms" are not always the same. While this has obviously been true in international affairs at different times and places, it is no less so in primitive societies. As a result, there are an immense variety of types of primitive political systems, just as there have been widely different international political systems.

The question, then, is whether there are different patterns of groups —or different political structures—which can be identified as typical alternatives among primitive peoples; if this is the case, then perhaps the types of primitive political systems have similarities to the possible types of international political systems.

To date, there have been two major approaches to the construction of typologies of international systems: on the one hand, models of the international system have been defined in terms of behavioral rules,[75] and on the other, types of international systems have been distinguished on the basis of historical evidence.[76] Without entering into methodological

[73] Southall, *Alur Society*, 229–34.
[74] *Ancient Law*, 161.
[75] The most well-known example of this approach is, of course, Morton A. Kaplan's *System and Process in International Politics* (New York 1957), chap. 2.
[76] See Hoffman, "International Systems and International Law," 215–33; and Rosecrance, *Action and Reaction in World Politics*, esp. Part II.

discussion, it can be wondered whether both of these approaches have shortcomings: the former tends to be *ad hoc,* and the latter to be restricted to the periods one studies.[77] Given the orientation of recent theoretical efforts in political science, the construction of a structural typology of political systems would seem to be a useful supplement to other approaches.[78]

Because such a typology appears to derive from "structural-functional" theory, developed especially by some British anthropologists,[79] it would be well to specify more precisely what is meant by "structure," and why it is emphasized rather than "function." As Marion J. Levy, Jr., has suggested, the term "structure," in its most general sense, "means a pattern, i.e., an observable uniformity, of action or operation."[80] Levy adds: "Functions refer to what is done, and structure refers to how (including in the meaning of 'how' the concept 'by what') what is done is done. One refers to the results of actions (or empirical phenomena in general), and the other to the forms or patterns of action (or empirical phenomena in general). . . . The same empirical phenomenon may be an example of either a function or a structure, depending upon the point from which it is viewed. . . . An interest in the results of operation of a unit focuses attention on the concept of function. An interest in the patterns of operation focuses attention on structure. An interest in the results of operation of a unit and the implications of those results focuses attention on both function and structure since the implications that can be studied scientifically lie in their effects on observable uniformities."[81] As is evident, from the point of view of sociological theory it is impossible to develop a general theory which emphasizes solely either "structure" or "function." Nonetheless there are good reasons for suggesting that a structural typology precede refined "functional" analysis.

This advantage can best be shown by referring to Alger's analysis of the similarities between intranational and international politics. Although

---

[77] Cf. *ibid.,* chap. 1, and Stanley Hoffman, ed., *Contemporary Theory in International Relations* (Englewood Cliffs, N.J., 1960), 40–50, 174–84.

[78] It seems, for example, that the distinction between stateless systems and fully developed states is insufficient because it ignores an intermediary type which Southall called "pyramidal" or "segmentary states." In such systems, of which feudalism is but one example, there are a multiplicity of levels of authority, the most comprehensive of which is "paramount" without being "sovereign." See Southall, *Alur Society,* 241–60; and Barnes, *Politics in a Changing Society,* 47–53. Further development of the conception of such pyramidal systems and its application to world politics will be attempted in subsequent publications.

[79] E.g., see Radcliffe-Brown, *Structure and Function in Primitive Society,* esp. Introduction and chap. 10.

[80] Levy, *The Structure of Society,* 57.

[81] *Ibid.,* 60–62.

Alger suggests that Almond's list of political functions is useful for such a comparison,[82] when he turns to the parallel between primitive and international politics, he emphasizes three factors, derived from Easton's work, which are ultimately structural in character: namely, the differentiation of political roles and the contingency or continuity of their operation, the specialization of roles which control physical force, and the character of overlapping memberships.

The reason why Almond's political functions are not immediately useful in comparing primitive and international politics is not hard to see. As Alger remarked, "A headman of a primitive society may perform intermittently as interest articulator, aggregator, and rule-maker."[83] If Almond's functions are not performed by specialized individuals in many primitive societies, concentration on these functions may only emphasize the "diffuseness" of roles, without indicating the different patterns which emerge in different primitive systems. It is necessary to see in what kinds of situations different individuals act in different ways; functional categories derived from "modern" complex political systems may be simply inappropriate for the study of primitive societies.[84]

As Almond himself was at pains to point out, "The functional categories which one employs have to be adapted to the particular aspect of the political system with which one is concerned."[85] Since a comparison of primitive and international political systems must identify the "particular aspects" of each type of system which are analogous, the use of functional categories would seem to be unpromising at the outset. In contrast, the use of a structural typology of political systems, if it proves possible to define kinds of political structures which exist in *both* primitive and international politics, has a double advantage: this

[82] Alger emphasizes the similarities between international politics and the internal politics of both developing nations and primitive societies ("Comparison of Intranational and International Politics," 410–19). He suggests that the "input functions" ("political socialization and recruitment, interest articulation, interest aggregation, and political communication") are more relevant than the "output functions" ("rule-making, rule application, and rule adjudication"). Cf. Almond and Coleman, eds., *The Politics of the Developing Areas*, 16–17; and note 48 above.

[83] Alger, "Comparison of Intranational and International Politics," 412. Cf. Almond and Coleman, eds., 19.

[84] An additional critique which might be made is that the Almond functions imply a political teleology: since traditional, "diffuse" systems tend to be replaced by modern, "functionally specific" ones, analysis may be oriented toward finding those activities which favor the trend toward "modernity." Cf. Almond and Coleman, eds., 16–17. However minor the danger of this implication in the analysis of developing nations, it would certainly be erroneous in international politics, since we have no reason to believe that present tendencies will produce a world government in which Almond's political functions have been specialized.

[85] *Ibid.,* 16.

approach should permit one to see not only the similarities between systems, but also the sources of the differences between modern international politics and primitive political systems.[86]

Finally, it should be pointed out that research in this direction, while it appears to utilize recent theoretical approaches derived from anthropology, sociology, and behavioral political science, is not divorced from the problems posed by traditional political philosophy. By emphasizing the existence of a class of social systems in which no formally instituted governments are established, the relevance of the notion of a "state of nature" to international politics can be shown to be more than a mere by-product of "normative" theories developed by political philosophers.

At the same time, however, since the apparent "anarchy" of a "state of nature" is found in primitive societies, analysis of the various kinds of primitive political structures suggests that some of the implications of the "state of nature" doctrine in political philosophy are questionable. In particular, the phenomenon of stateless societies implies that even if one can speak of a "state of nature," such a condition cannot be used to prove that man is by nature an asocial being; as a result, the "state of nature" (whether in primitive or international politics) need not be considered the *natural* human condition, as opposed to the purely *conventional* political community or state. Hence the comparison of international and intranational politics—and, more specifically, the analysis of similarities between primitive and world politics—among other things leads us to a reassessment of the sufficiency of the theory of politics established by Hobbes and elaborated by Locke, Rousseau, and Kant.[87]

[86] In addition, an emphasis on structure should permit one to handle more explicitly the troublesome problem of defining the "actors" in the international system. Cf. Arnold Wolfers, "The Actors in International Politics," *Discord and Collaboration* (Baltimore 1962), 3–24. Alger seems to adopt the so-called "individuals-as-actors" approach, which raises some severe methodological problems; for example, he suggests (in applying Easton's work) that "international systems would tend to be distributed toward the contingent end of the continuum" which ranges from "contingent" to "continuous." This is a questionable conclusion if one considers that not only international organizations, but specific roles within national governments (e.g., "foreign minister"), function continuously in the modern state system. Cf. Alger, "Comparison of Intranational and International Politics," esp. 416, with the discussion above, p. 610. As Wolfers concluded: "While it would be dangerous for theorists to divert their primary attention from the nation-state and multistate systems which continue to occupy most of the stage of contemporary world politics, theory remains inadequate if it is unable to include such phenomena as overlapping authorities, split loyalties, and divided sovereignty, which were pre-eminent characteristics of medieval actors" ("Actors in International Politics," 24). The structural approach proposed here seems best suited to satisfy the theoretical requirements suggested by Wolfers.

[87] For a sophisticated attempt to show the continuing relevance of the philosophy of Rousseau as the basis of a theory of international politics, see Stanley Hoffman,

## STUDY QUESTIONS

1. What specific contributions to a better understanding of international relations are made by both classical-normative and the newer scientific-behavioral approaches? What are the limitations of each as discussed by Aron and Thompson?

2. Does Vital tend to agree or disagree with Aron's assertion that a "pure" theory of international relations is unattainable? Why? What explanatory functions should an adequate theory perform?

3. Why do international relations scholars regard the problem of analytical "levels" so important? Identify several of these levels and explain their analytical significance. Which of these do you regard as constituting the single most important dimension? Why?

4. Does the "balanced anarchy" of certain primitive societies offer any basic insights into the nature of the contemporary global, international system as claimed by Masters? If so, what variables would have to be explained by such a model of primitive society?

5. What is the unifying subject that Vital claims will render international relations an "integrated discipline"? Would Thompson and Singer agree? Why?

## SUGGESTIONS FOR FURTHER READING

ALGER, C. F. "International Relations: The Field," *International Encyclopedia of the Social Sciences*, Vol. VIII. New York: The Free Press, 1968, pp. 61–69.

BUTTERFIELD, HERBERT. "The Scientific vs. the Modernistic Approach," *International Affairs*, XXVII (October 1951), 411–422.

CORBETT, PERRY E. "Objectivity in the Study of International Affairs," *World Affairs*, IV (July 1950), 257–263.

DEUTSCH, KARL W. *Nationalism and Social Communication*. New York: John Wiley, 1953.

EASTON, DAVID. *The Political System*. New York: Alfred A. Knopf, 1953.

"Rousseau on War and Peace," *American Political Science Review*, LVII (June 1963), 317–33. Cf. Kenneth J. Waltz, "Kant, Liberalism, and War," *ibid.*, LVI (June 1962), 331–40.

FALK, R. A. *Law, Morality, and War in the Contemporary World*. New York: Frederick A. Praeger, 1963.

FISHER, R. (ed.). *International Conflict and Behavioral Science*. New York: Basic Books, 1964.

FOX, W. T. R. (ed.). *Theoretical Aspects of International Relations*. Notre Dame: Notre Dame Press, 1959.

HARRISON, H. V. *The Role of Theory in International Relations*. New York: Van Nostrand, 1964.

HERZ, JOHN J. *Political Realism and Political Idealism*. Chicago: University of Chicago Press, 1962.

HOFFMAN, STANLEY H. (ed.). *Contemporary Theory in International Relations*. Englewood Cliffs: Prentice-Hall, 1960.

HOFFMAN, STANLEY H. *The State of War: Essays in the Theory and Practice of International Politics*. New York: Frederick A. Praeger, 1965.

KAPLAN, MORTON M. and N. KATZENBACH. *Political Foundations of International Law*. New York: John Wiley, 1961.

KNORR, K. and S. VERBA (eds.). *The International System: Theoretical Essays*. Princeton: Princeton University Press, 1961.

MCCLELLAND, C. *Theory and the International System*. New York: The Macmillan Company, 1966.

MATHISEN, T. *Methodology in the Study of International Relations*. Oslo: Oslo University Press, 1959.

MORGENTHAU, H. J. *Politics Among Nations*. New York: Alfred A. Knopf, 1967.

PLATIG, E. R. *International Relations Research*. New York: Carnegie Endowment for International Peace, 1966.

RANSOM, H. H. "International Relations," *Journal of Politics*, XXX (May 1968), 345–371.

ROSECRANCE, R. N. *Action and Reaction in World Politics: International Systems in Perspective*. Boston: Little-Brown, 1963.

ROSENAU, J. N. *International Politics and Foreign Policy*. New York: The Free Press, 1961.

SCOTT, A. M. *The Functioning of the International System*. New York: The Macmillan Company, 1967.

SINGER, J. D. "The Relevance of the Behavioral Sciences to the Study of International Relations," *Behavioral Science*, VI (1961), 324–335.

SNYDER, R. C. "Some Recent Trends in International Relations Theory and Research," A. Ranney (ed.), *Essays on the Behavioral Study of Politics*. Urbana: University of Illinois Press, 1962.

TUCKER, R. W. "The Study of International Politics," *World Politics*, X (July 1958), 639–47.

WRIGHT, Q. *The Study of International Relations*. New York: Appleton-Century-Crofts, 1955.

# PART TWO □ DETERMINANTS
# OF POWER

P OWER PLAYS a crucial role in international politics. The importance of power becomes all the more clear in a world where each state pursues its national interests and where these interests (security, justice, peace, prosperity, pride, etc.) may be incompatible with those of other states. A state, therefore, must rely on power to protect its interests, maintain peace and order, and repel possible outside aggression. The task of measuring political power in world politics is a complex one. There are many determinants that contribute to and detract from it. As the selections in part two are read, bear in mind that it is difficult to measure a single power determinant since little in our revolutionary age remains fixed. For instance, a new weapon, a new raw material, a new technological breakthrough, an ideological appeal, a new leadership, and so on, may alter the entire set of international power relationship. Moreover, it is difficult to measure such intangible correlates of power as morale, ideology, political institutions and organizations, technology, and leadership.

In the following selections we shall examine such determinants of power as geography, military power and technology, the role of race, and finally, the contribution of domestic structures and leadership to national power and foreign policy.

Harold and Margaret Sprout, in the first selection, point out that man-made changes in the earth's surface have been significant. But more significant are the changes brought about by science, engineering, and technology. Revolutionary advances in science and technology have drastically altered the relative political-military values of location, space, distance, climate, terrain, and natural resources. The authors conclude that generally speaking the geographical layout of lands and seas no longer has the military-political values once attached to them. They support their arguments by citing the changing military-political values of Suez, Malta, Gibraltar, and other areas.

The rapid and continuing scientific and technological advances have affected not only the traditional military-political values of geo-graphical facts, but have also left their impact on the military power of states. In his selection, "Military Power and International Order," Michael Howard discusses the ominous development in weapon systems and changes in the patterns of war. Powers which possess the techno-logical know-how, wealth, and industrial capacity have developed weapon systems which can bring unacceptable destruction to the enemy and have also developed the capacity to deter any attack from a would-be aggressor. War, he writes, is an irrational instrument of foreign policy whose outcome is unpredictable. There is reluctance on the part of powers that possess nuclear weapons to use them. Howard discusses the impact of new weapons on the military and states rather strongly that politics must interpenetrate the military at all levels and that military commanders must refrain from shaping the international arena in their own image. On the other hand, he observes that statesmen must recognize the limitation of force. Military power can serve as an instrument of international affairs only if there is complete cooperation and mutual understanding between civilian and military leaders, and only if there is discipline and obedience in the ranks of the military and effective functioning of the process of command and control.

Going beyond Howard's discussion, Ciro Elliott Zoppo presents a detailed study of the impact of nuclear technology and multipolarity on international order. He points out that both the United States and the Soviet Union have refrained from using nuclear weapons in limited wars such as Korea. The capacity of nuclear weapons to inflict pain and destruction of great magnitude in a short time is what differen-tiates nuclear war from previous wars. Avoidance of nuclear confronta-tion appears to have become the "rule" of the international system. This rule, however, is dependent upon the willingness of the superpowers to run the risk of total war. Zoppo discusses the attitudes of both the United States and the Soviet Union with regard to the use of tactical nuclear weapons in local wars and the fear of escalation to a general nuclear war. This fear has had a tempering effect on the use of military force in local conflicts. Revolutionary powers, he states, who seek world hege-mony through the instrument of force, have been compelled to aban-don total war as a policy and to adopt a cautious use of military power. Zoppo adds that the technology of nuclear weapons is as important as their effects in influencing political expectations. He concludes that when a bipolar system of deterrence, which is the most stable international situation, "becomes transformed into a system of several major and/or minor independent nuclear powers, stability is likely to decrease."

In his analysis of race and color in international relations, Robert K. A. Gardiner writes that European control over Asia began to erode before the end of World War I. Japan, Russia, and the United States claimed positions for themselves in the East. National movements among the Afro-Asian peoples have been influenced by Woodrow Wilson's concept of self-determination. Japan demanded that racial equality be stated in the League of Nations' Covenant but failed. Non-white peoples were placed under the League's Mandate system and later on under the United Nations Trusteeship to assist them in achieving independence. Today, the Afro-Asian states constitute a clear majority in the United Nations, and they are asserting themselves on the international arena as well as within the United Nations. They are attempting to industrialize and modernize and it is unlikely they can remain under Western dominance. Gardiner observes that the role of race in international relations is ambiguous. He points to ANZUS and SEATO and states that it is difficult to draw a line between ideological, economic, political, and military motivations which bring Western and non-Western nations together. We live in an era of growing interdependence, he concludes.

In the final section, Henry A. Kissinger deals with the question of domestic structure and its impact on foreign policy. The domestic structure, he writes, determines the amount of social effort directed to foreign policy; affects the way the actions of other nations are interpreted; and finally, plays an important role in the elaboration of positive aims. He discusses the role of administrative structure and rigidity in the policies of the technologically advanced nations due in part to complexity in the decision-making process. Kissinger states that one of the purposes of bureaucracy is to make the decision-making process impersonal. For this reason, he believes, diplomacy tends to be rigid and turns into "an abstract bargaining process based on largely formal criteria such as "splitting the difference." This also tends to put technique before purpose and encourage inflexibility.

Kissinger also discusses three types of leadership groups: 1) the bureaucratic-pragmatic type; 2) the ideological type; and 3) the revolutionary-charismatic type. He concludes that these differences present both a challenge and an obstacle to the emergence of a stable international order.

HAROLD AND MARGARET SPROUT

*Geography and International Politics*
*in an Era of Revolutionary Change*

The earth is the stage upon which mankind enacts the drama of life.
From time immemorial men have speculated regarding the relations of
this earthly stage to human undertakings and accomplishments. Almost
every aspect of human affairs has been linked to the distribution and arrangement of things upon and close to the surface of the earth.

Students of that aspect of human affairs which we call "international politics" have long regarded the physical earth as a basic datum
of their subject. Every nation-state has a territorial base, a spatial section
of the earth's surface in the idiom of geographic science. Territory is one
of the absolute requisites of statehood. In nearly all international transactions involving some element of opposition, resistance, struggle, or
conflict, the factors of location, space, and distance between the interacting parties have been significant variables. This significance is embodied in the maxim, "Power is local." That is to say, political demands
are projected through space from one location to another upon the
earth's surface. Such operations involve expenditure of energy and consumption of other resources. A state's access to resources may decisively
affect its ability to impose its demands on other nations and, conversely,
to resist demands, pressures, and attacks made on it. In ways both obvious and obscure, the factors of climate—air temperature, relative hu-
midity, air circulation, barometric pressure, etc.—also appear to have

SOURCE: Harold and Margaret Sprout, "Geography and International Politics In An
Era of Revolutionary Change," *The Journal of Conflict Resolution,* IV (March 1960),
145–161. Reprinted by permission. [Note—This paper is one of the fruits of a program of study and research on the interrelations of geography and politics, supported
jointly by Princeton University and the Rockefeller Foundation, neither of which,
of course, bears any responsibility for judgments and conclusions expressed herein.]

directly and indirectly affected the distribution of political capabilities over the earth. Awareness of these various non-human factors, and notions as to their limiting effects, have commonly entered into the deliberations of national statesmen and appear on many occasions to have affected significantly the substance of policy decisions.

Today the relations between man and his non-human environment are decidedly in flux. As a result of revolutionary advances in technology and other social changes no less revolutionary, such relationships are probably more unstable than in any previous historical period. There are indications, moreover, that recent huge strides toward the conquest of nature may be altering in fundamental ways the patterns of human existence upon our planet. The function of this discussion is to examine certain aspects of this possibility. The discussion is limited to the phenomena commonly called "international relations" and, more precisely, "international politics." And we shall deal chiefly with the changing international significance of non-human factors of environment, with geographical configuration in particular, and to a lesser degree with distributions of economic resources and climate.

TERMS AND CONCEPTS

Throughout this discussion we shall be using certain terms and concepts which should be explicitly defined at the outset. *International politics* is one of these. By international politics we mean *only* those transactions and relations between or among nation-states in which some element of opposition, resistance, struggle, or conflict is involved.

Next, the terms *fact* and *factor*. Turning to the dictionary, one finds a fact defined as "something declared to have happened, or to have existed." A fact becomes a factor when it is identified as one of the components or elements of an aggregate which may contribute to an explanation or prediction of an event or state of affairs.

Third, the term *environment*. For the purposes of this discussion it will suffice to define "environment" simply as all phenomena in space and time which are external to the unit under consideration and to which that unit's activities or status may be significantly related. In the study of human affairs the ultimate environed unit is always an individual person. But, by a sort of analogical extension, the concept is loosely used with reference to human groups, including the nation-state. As defined above, the environment of an individual or group includes social, or human, as well as non-human factors. These non-human factors, it should be noted, represent only a fraction of the phenomena generally regarded by geographers as comprising the data of their science or discipline. For the more limited concept of non-human environment, geographers also use the terms *physical environment* and *natural environment*.

Finally, the terms *constants* and *variables*. Empirical phenomena may vary in space or through time, or both. Given the two dimensions —space and time—there are obviously four possible combinations: (1) phenomena constant both in space and through time; (2) phenomena constant in space but variable through time; (3) phenomena variable in space but constant through time; and (4) phenomena variable both in space and through time.

It may be doubted whether any phenomena are distributed absolutely evenly in space. Even such an apparent constant as the oxygen content of the air varies with altitude. With reference to the interactions and political relations of states, the variations of geographical phenomena in space are nearly always significant. This proposition is part of the basis of the geographer's well-recognized interest in this aspect of human affairs. It is likewise the basis of the political analyst's dependence upon geographic science for concepts, theories, and data regarding the distribution and arrangement of phenomena upon the earth.

It is probable that no empirical phenomena are absolutely constant through time. But there may be no significant variation through the time span involved in a particular transaction or sequence of events. Whether factors variable in space are also significantly variable through time depends both on the problem in hand and on the magnitude or the rate of change, or both, during the time span under consideration. Suppose, for example, the problem is to compare the relative abilities of the Soviet Union and the United States to supply agricultural tractors to India during the next six months. In this problem variations in space (factory capacities, raw materials on hand, etc.) are manifestly significant. On the other hand, variation of the spatial variables through time will probably turn out to be quite inconsequential. If, however, the time span is lengthened—say, to five years, in the problem stated— many factors treated as time constants in the short term may become significantly variable both in space and through time in the longer term.

The fourth category (factors variable in space and through time) is by far the most important in the context of international politics, especially for those who are concerned less with day-to-day statecraft than with larger patterns and longer-term trends. Most of the social factors of environment—population, technology, weapons systems, economic development, attitudes and values, institutions, and many others— are changing significantly through time and at different rates in different countries and regions. This fact of differential change is probably the most significant aspect of the social environment in which international statecraft is carried on in our time.

Geographical configurations—the layouts of lands and seas—always exhibit variations in space. But, with certain exceptions, these are among the more stable factors of environment through time spans generally of interest to the political analyst. However, as we shall explain more fully in a moment, even the most stable geographical configurations may be indirectly affected by changes in the social factors.

The distribution of useful materials—water, soil, minerals, etc.—highly variable in space, tends in our age to be differentially variable among countries and regions even through relatively short time spans. Climate, too, varies in space and through time. Both climate and natural resources are subject, like geographical configurations, to changes in significance as the result of changes in the social factors of environment.

### FACTORS AND RELATIONSHIPS

Environmental factors, whether constant or variable, can affect human affairs in only two ways. Such factors can be perceived, interpreted, and taken into account by the human actors under consideration. In this way, and in this way only, can environmental factors "influence" attitudes and decisions. The relation of environmental factors to performance and accomplishment (i.e., their relation to the operational consequences of decisions) is quite different. Such factors comprise a sort of matrix, figuratively speaking, which limits the execution of decisions. Limitations on performance and accomplishment are not necessarily dependent on the actor's perception. *Such limitations may be operative irrespective of whether or how the limiting factors are perceived in the process of reaching decisions.*

As we have emphasized on previous occasions, what matters in the explanation of decisions and policies is how the actor *imagined* his environment to be, not how it actually was, whereas what matters in the explanation of accomplishments is how the environment actually was, not how the actor imagined it to be. By suitable change of tense and substitution of assumptions (where necessary) regarding the future state of the environment, the same two propositions differentiate the prediction of policy decisions from the estimation of capabilities. Consistent observance of this simple distinction—between the relation of environmental factors to attitudes and decisions, on the one hand, and to accomplishments and capabilities, on the other—would help to avoid the confused and footless disputation which has characterized so much of the discussion of man-environment relationships.[1]

• • •

[1] Harold and Margaret Sprout, *Man-Milieu Relationship Hypotheses in the Context of International Politics* (Princeton, N.J.: Center of International Studies, 1956); and "Environmental Factors in the Study of International Politics," *Conflict Resolution,* I (1957), 309–28.

IMPLICATIONS OF ENVIRONMENTAL CHANGE

At any given time and place there is usually some range of fruitful choice with reference to a given sphere of human interest and activity. There may be choice among ends and choice among alternative means to desired ends. The range of fruitful choice is constantly changing. In some historical periods it changes slowly; in others, more rapidly, depending upon the nature and rate of changes among the non-human and social components of the environment. We are living through a period in which change is rapid and far-reaching and in which the political implications of change are probably more revolutionary than is generally appreciated.

With reference to the non-human environment, change presents two facets: changes in the non-human factors themselves, and changes in social factors which in turn alter the political properties or meaning of relatively stable non-human factors. Let us consider first the changes that take place in the non-human factors themselves.

Some of these changes, we may note in passing, arise from physical processes of nature: earth slipping, volcanoes erupting, rocks falling, water flowing and freezing, wind blowing, plants, animals, and micro-organisms reproducing, multiplying, or dying out, etc. Sometimes these "natural" processes produce human catastrophes such as earthquakes, floods, famines, and epidemics; occasionally, such catastrophes have affected in some degree the patterns of international politics.

Alongside these natural phenomena—and probably more important in the context of international politics—are changes in the earth wrought by the hand of man. Let us examine some of these briefly. With advancing technology—that is, with more effective tools and skills—men have increasingly changed the physical structure of the earth itself. They have dug canals and changed the course of rivers. They have built harbors and tunneled through mountains. They have cut down forests and planted new ones. They have depleted the soil and sometimes restored its fertility. They have made deserts bloom and have turned verdant landscapes into deserts. They have pumped irreplaceable oil and natural gas from underground reservoirs. They have consumed underground water faster than it could accumulate. They have smashed atoms and fused them. They have created new elements and transmuted matter into energy. In these and many other ways, men have altered at ever accelerating rate the structure of their earthly habitat.

Such structural changes have affected in greater or lesser degree the economic and military capabilities of nations and their political relations in peace and in war. A good historical example is the opening of the

Suez Canal in 1869. That engineering feat cleared a shipway across the desert which had separated the Mediterranean Sea from the Indian Ocean. The canal cut several thousand miles from voyages between European ports and the ports of southern and eastern Asia. It soon became one of the most heavily used trunk lines of *international* commerce. But the canal also became the strategic axis of the *internal* communications system of the British Empire. This led within a few years to British occupation of Egypt and British military domination of the canal. Thus it is probably no exaggeration to conclude that the opening of the Suez Canal altered the strategic geography of the British Empire and affected Britain's political relations with nearly every state and region.

As another example, consider the international implications of the heavy and progressive depletion of North American forests, soils, mineral fuels, ores, and other natural resources. This depletion has been going on for well over a century. The rate of depletion has turned sharply upward in recent decades. Consumption of natural resources reached record levels during World War II. It is climbing to still higher peaks in our time. These alterations of the physical geography of North America have various political implications. Not the least of these is the increasing dependence of the United States on imported iron ore and other basic raw materials in a period of continuing change in the international political relations of all states and regions.

The international consequences of man-made changes in the earth's surface and subsurface have been great in the past and seem likely to be even greater in the future. But, great as these changes have been, they are overshadowed and probably outweighed in their political effects by other changes—especially advances in science and engineering—which, while not actually altering the basic structure of the earth's surface substantially, have given new meanings and values to such geographic features as location, distance, terrain, climate, and natural resources.

Consider, for example, the changes which have taken place in the military properties of oceanic space during the last sixty or seventy years. Theories of sea power which appeared, in 1900, to be as permanent as the oceans themselves have become progressively obsolescent during the intervening years. Yet the oceans and connecting seas (one set of environmental factors) have remained approximately constant in terms of this particular development. Their size and shape have not changed significantly. But the activities which men can carry out upon the oceans and connecting seas have changed profoundly. Ships now have power plants designed to cruise greater distances without refueling. Methods for refueling at sea have been perfected for naval vessels. Submarines with automotive torpedoes have become formidable instrumentalities with which to challenge the passage of vessels upon the surface. Special ships have been designed for landing troops and heavy equipment on hostile open beaches. Aircraft have become powerful factors in the control of the sea and of lands beyond the seas. Submarines propelled by nuclear engines can remain beneath the surface for months at a time. Rockets with nuclear warheads can be launched from beneath the water's surface. These and many other technological advances have radically modified and continue to modify the military properties of oceanic space.

It would be difficult to exaggerate the importance of the giant and ever lengthening strides with which modern science and engineering are conquering space. Man has speeded up and enormously increased the capacity of transport and communications. He has created more and ever more deadly weapons systems with which to threaten, if not actually to destroy, his fellow men and all their works. He has made astounding advances in medicine, sanitation, weather forecasting, climatic adaptation, agriculture, metallurgy, and other branches of engineering and technology.

These achievements affect in many ways the range of fruitful choices open to the statesmen. Sometimes the effect has been narrowing; more often it has been broadening. In order to understand and appreciate the impact of these developments, the political properties and meanings of geographic facts have to be reconsidered in the light of technological and other social changes. If attention is directed to one set of environmental factors—oceanic space, in the example above—the change in the range of possible performance and accomplishment appears as an adaptation to a stable environment. But such adaptation appears, from a different perspective, to consist of alterations in another set of environmental factors—modes of transportation and design of weapons, in the example—alterations which change the social meaning, or properties, or implications of environmental factors which themselves may not have undergone significant structural change.

This interaction between human activities and the non-human environment has been going on ever since man emerged as a tool-inventing and tool-using creature. But, until a century or so ago, the rate of technological change was slow. Today the rate is rapid and seems to be still accelerating. The unsettling effects of new tools and new techniques on the political, military, and economic meaning of geographic layouts and configurations, climatic variations, and the distributions of useful earth materials have great and varied significance for the student of international politics.

It is out of the question, within the limited compass of this discussion, to undertake any comprehensive inventory of these effects. The most that we can do in the remaining pages is to raise a few issues and suggest some hypotheses both tentative and controversial.

*Changing significance of geographical configuration.*—At the close of the lecture to the Royal Geographical Society in 1904,[2] in which Mackinder outlined his geopolitical interpretation of history and advanced his hypothesis of the future predominance of the Eurasian "Heartland," one member of his audience rose to challenge the whole conception. This man was Leopold S. Amery, a name virtually unknown to most Americans despite his subsequent long career in the British public service.

Amery contended that a "great deal of this geographical distribution must lose its importance" with future advances in the means of transportation on land, upon the sea, and in the air. "The successful powers" of the future, he predicted, would be "those which have the greatest industrial basis." It would "not matter whether they are in the center of a continent or on an island; those people who have the industrial power and the power of invention and science will be able to defeat all others."[3]

Events of the past half-century have clearly gone some way toward confirming Amery's prediction. Naval forces can now refuel and carry out even major repairs at sea. This has reduced the military value of permanent oversea bases. Submarines, bombing planes, and ballistic missiles have eroded the former defensive strength of islands, peninsulas, promontories, and remote ports on coasts protected by mountains, deserts, or jungles. Airplanes have "shrunk" the widest oceans and continents and have surmounted refractory barriers of terrain and distance. Pipe lines, motor vehicles, and still expanding railway and highway grids have enormously increased the mobility of overland transport. These and other changes in weapons and transport have profoundly altered the relative political and military values of heartlands, marginal lands, and islands.

The physical layout of lands and seas, as emphasized above, has not changed substantially. The deserts, mountains, and prairies, the configuration of coast-lines, and other physical dimensions of our planet remain substantially unchanged. What has changed, and changed radically, is the political and military value of these geographic facts—changes resulting in large measure from the revolutionary advances of modern engineering and technology.

*Changing character of environmental limitations.*—Americans, Rus-

[2] H. J. MacKinder, "The Geographical Pivot of History," *Geographical Journal*, XXIII (1904), 421–44.
[3] Leopold S. Amery, Discussion of H. J. MacKinder, "The Geographical Pivot of History," *Geographical Journal, XXIII* (1904), 439–41.

sians, and others display understandable pride in the part which their respective nationalities have played, and are playing, in the massive twentieth-century assault on the non-human environment. From pride in achievement it is only a step to imagining that the world is "our oyster." Yet as the late Isaiah Bowman pungently observed, over twenty-five years ago, "For all his independence and ingenuity [man] can never wholly escape from his environment. He cannot move mountains without floating a bond issue. . . . Man conforms to many defective layouts because it would cost him too much to alter them."[4]

What Bowman seems to be suggesting—and it is even more true today than in the 1930's—is that the problem of overcoming the limitations of the non-human environment has become more economic than purely technological. In the technically advanced countries at least, sufficient engineering knowledge is available to accomplish a great deal more than is actually undertaken. More railroads and highways could be built and more airlines established. More ores could be mined and refined, and more synthetic substitutes for scarce natural resources could be produced. More people could be more adequately fed. More and better medical service could be provided. More buildings could be cooled in hot, damp climates. More swamps could be drained. Sea water could be desalted and more deserts irrigated. Explorations of outer space could be speeded up. Weapons could be further improved and military establishments generally strengthened. Industries could be relocated to make them less vulnerable to airborne nuclear attacks.

When such projects are contemplated, the issue is rarely one of technical capacity alone. The issues are rather: How much will it cost? What projects should have priority? Who is going to pay for it? Money spent on television sets, new motorcars, expensive vacations, and other ingredients of a high standard of living cannot be spent on fallout shelters, industrial relocation, or other projects designed to strengthen a country's defenses. Tolerance for austerity varies widely from one country to another. Sensitivity of politicians to public demands also varies from one political system to another. That is to say, limitations on public policy that are imposed by the social order have become in general more important—and in some countries very much more important—than limitations imposed by space, adverse climate, or any other set of non-human factors.

This is not to argue that technology has erased differentials in opportunities and limitations among nations. It is certainly true that many more units of energy are required to heat buildings in winter and to keep them tolerably cool in summer in the savage mid-continental

[4] Isaiah Bowman, *Geography in Relation to the Social Sciences* (New York: Charles Scribner's Sons, 1934), pp. 3–4.

climate of the American Middle West than in the milder climates of Britain and France. It is likewise true that greater expenditure of energy is required to haul ores and other heavy freights across the vast continental space of the Soviet Union than is required for similar tasks in a small compact country like Britain.

Every country has "natural" advantages and disadvantages in comparison with any other. Technological advances may narrow these differences, provided certain other conditions prevail. In any case, the consequence of achieving a higher level of productivity per capita is that this enables a people to pay a higher price for overcoming "natural" obstacles which, at a lower economic and technological level, were insurmountable. The more efficient a people's equipment, and the greater their skills, the greater becomes their potential capacity to master the limitations of the non-human environment—and do so at a price compatible with their conception of a tolerable standard of living.

From this perspective, one queries writings which attribute a certain absoluteness to the limitations set by the non-human environment. An example of this is a little book entitled *How Strong Is Russia?* by George Cressey of Syracuse University. In this book, published in 1954, Cressey seems to us to come very close to arguing that the non-human environment of the Soviet Union presents permanently disabling obstacles to successful Soviet competition with western Europe and the United States. Cressey writes:

> Geography has imposed permanent limitations on the development of the Soviet Union. Man can do much, but the restrictions of great distances, remoteness from the ocean, terrain, short growing seasons, inadequate and variable rainfall, and continentality will always remain. . . . The geographic potentials are very large, but the geographic limitations are formidable. . . . Premier Stalin gave his country the task "to overtake and surpass the capitalist world." From the standpoint of geography this does not appear possible. Limitations of location, climate, scattered resources, and continentality combine to create landscapes which no amount of planning can fully surmount. Whatever its government, Russia can never become a truly great world power.[5]

If these quotations accurately summarize Cressey's conclusions, it seems to us that he has seriously underestimated the implications of rapid technological advance and no differences in national political systems. No one could quarrel with the premise that every nation pays a price for its accomplishments and that the price tag may be higher or lower depending on the country's location, area, configuration, climate, mineral bodies, and other resources. But a deduction, from this premise, that a state with greater "natural" obstacles to overcome cannot al-

[5] G. B. Cressey, *How Strong Is Russia?* (Syracuse, N.Y.: Syracuse University Press, 1954), pp. 29, 98, 120.

locate more goods and services to the pursuit of political objectives, or play as influential a role as states more favorably endowed by "nature," would appear to be tenable only on one or both of the following assumptions: (1) that the period of rapid technological advance is drawing to a close and (2) that similar values and principles govern the allocation of goods and services in the Soviet Union as in other great states.

Neither of these assumptions is sound, in our judgment. All evidence known to us indicates that further technological breakthroughs are in prospect in such fields as nuclear fuels, climate control, plant breeding, etc. Such advances are likely in the future, as in the past, to diminish the handicaps of distance, area, location, or other non-human factors. Furthermore, governmental policies determining who gets what and how much vary widely from one political system to another. As already emphasized, values and demands vary, tolerance for austerity varies, sensitivity of politicians to public demands varies, ability of politicians to mold public opinion varies, and so do many other features of national political systems. This brings us back to our major conclusion in this section—that one of the consequences of rapid and continuing technological advance is to make limitations imposed by the social order relatively more significant politically than "natural" obstacles present in the non-human environment.

*Environmental limitations and social catastrophe.*—A rather different sort of environmental limitation on the modern state has been argued by Harrison Brown of the California Institute of Technology.[6] Brown emphasizes that the enormous and still rising consumption of mineral ores and fuels in recent years has depleted most of the more accessible and easily worked sources of non-renewable raw materials. From here on out, it will require deeper mines and oil wells, and more complicated industrial installations and processes, to reach and utilize the poorer-grade raw materials upon which industrial societies will have increasingly to depend.

Such dependence is all very well, Brown argues, so long as no nuclear war or other social catastrophe destroys the complicated installations and disrupts the increasingly complex and delicate industrial processes and interrelations. But he advances the profoundly disturbing thesis that, once destroyed, our fragile industrial civilization could never make a successful fresh start with the low-grade ores and more inaccessible fuels which would remain available.

This thesis is manifestly controversial. But it rests upon solid facts and should be carefully examined. Above all, its international political implications should be explored. If Brown's thesis is accepted, the con-

[6] Harrison Brown, *The Challenge of Man's Future* (New York: Viking Press, 1954), chapter vii.

clusion follows that our conquest of nature, of which twentieth-century man is so proud and boastful, is viable only in a universe from which total war fought with nuclear weapons is permanently excluded. A further implication latent in Brown's thesis is that nuclear war would probably disable countries in proportion roughly to their level of industrialization and to the geographical concentration of their industrial conurbations. In plain English, a reasonable inference from Brown's thesis is that a future general war would wipe out the densely inhabited industrial countries of western Europe, damage the United States and Soviet Union probably beyond recovery, and turn over the management of the earth to the Chinese Communists and other emerging nations of Asia and Africa.

*Modern arms and the territorial state.*—We come finally to the most controversial hypothesis of all. This hypothesis, put forward by John Herz of City College, New York,[7] holds that modern weapons systems are inexorably eroding the foundations of the territorial state itself. The point at issue is whether the territorial state, which for several centuries has been the basic unit of the international system, can much longer perform the supreme function for which it evolved—the function of providing a reasonable degree of safety for the person and property of its members.

Various hypotheses have been advanced to explain the integration of medieval towns and feudal communities into larger political-territorial units. At least one of the necessary conditions for this development seems to have been the "gunpowder revolution." The invention and improvement of firearms made castles and walled towns increasingly less defensible, that is to say, more easily penetrable by force. The same development, combined with some improvement in roads and haulage, made it possible to mobilize larger forces to defend larger geographical areas. More efficient weapons and communications likewise enlarged the geographical area which could be effectively policed and administered from a single capital. Thus the large-area state, in the words of Herz, "came finally to occupy the place that the castle or fortified town had previously held as a unit of impenetrability."

In the centuries that followed the formation of modern territorial nation-states, the prime function of statecraft was to make and to keep the country's geographical boundaries as impenetrable as possible. In pursuit of this objective—the direct antecedent of today's expanded concept of national security—much attention was given to achieving strong "natural boundaries." Among the coveted kinds of natural boundaries sea-

---

[7] J. H. Herz, "Rise and Demise of the Territorial State," *World Politics*, IX (1957), 473–93.

coasts ranked high, and a state that was wholly insular came to be regarded as fortunate indeed. Other forms of stong natural boundaries included rivers, mountains and other rough terrain, deserts, and jungles. Economic goods and services were poured into frontier fortifications, military roads, and other installations designed to strengthen "weak" and vulnerable boundaries.

Geographical space—between the state's boundaries and its vital centers of population and economic production—was likewise regarded as a strategic asset. Where space was deemed inadequate, a buffer zone of protected states—we would call them "satellites" today—might be created to absorb the shock of invasion. As late as 1918, Sir Halford MacKinder[8] outlined such a project to keep partially defeated Germany and Revolutionary Russia physically apart and to provide a security zone for western Europe. This project envisaged establishing a tier of small states in eastern Europe all the way from the Baltic to the Black Sea. The Peace Conference of 1919 did create such a buffer zone—with results that are well-known history.

By the end of World War I there was considerable evidence that developments in weapons were undermining the security of the territorial state. A long sequence of inventions had greatly increased the per capita firepower of military forces. Railroads, better roads, and motor vehicles had given greater overland mobility to this growing firepower. The development of mines, automotive torpedoes, and submarines provided more effective instruments with which to sink cargo shipping and to blockade marine frontiers. Aircraft, though still primitive, provided more than a hint of the possibility of overleaping even the most strongly fortified frontiers.

Subsequent development of air power transformed the hint into fearsome reality. For the first time in history it has become possible to project terrific firepower over great distances to attack the complex industrial conurbations upon which modern military power depends— and do so without blasting a path across fortified land frontiers or storming ashore on hostile open beaches. In the seesaw struggle between offensive and defensive weapons systems, the offense has decisively outrun the defense. There are rumors of antimissile missiles and other defensive innovations around the corner. Such a development might conceivably restore in some degree the shattered impenetrability of the territorial state. But it is noteworthy that many leading scientists and engineers are pessimistic of achieving any really effective defense against missileborne nuclear explosives.

[8] J. H. MacKinder, *Democratic Ideals and Reality*. Rev. ed. (New York: Henry Holt & Co., 1942).

In 1957 the British Government candidly recognized this state of affairs. Perhaps the most important sentence in its statement on defense that year was the frank admission that "there is at present no means of providing adequate protection for the people of this country against the consequences of an attack with nuclear weapons."[9]

Some reactions within the United States to this British candor were characteristic of the seeming inability of so many of us Americans to come to terms with the technological revolution in which we are caught. One comment, more or less typical of many others, was that the Western Allies ought to "work and plan hopefully toward an effective defense against hydrogen weapons rather than proclaiming and thus encouraging a sense of hopelessness among the people."[10] Certainly, such efforts will continue. But is it safe to ignore the opposite possibility—which may, indeed, be the more probable of the two—that no really effective defense can be perfected to protect nations against devastating airborne attacks with thermonuclear explosives?

If the latter turns out to be the case, future historians from the perspective of the twenty-first century (if somehow the ultimate catastrophe is avoided and if there are historians left to interpret the past) may well conclude that the combination of thermonuclear explosives, long-range bombing planes, and ballistic missiles made the territorial nation-state as unviable as the medieval castle became after the development of artillery.

These speculations all point to the conclusion that the technological revolution and other social changes taking place in our time are affecting the international political significance of location, distance, space, terrain, climate, and natural resources. Broadly speaking, the geographical layout of lands and seas and the configuration of the lands have lost much of the military-political value once attached to these factors. Insularity has less protective value. Commanding positions, athwart the trunk lines of international commerce—such as Gibraltar, Malta, Suez, and Singapore—no longer provide the leverage they formerly did. Outlying military installations become progressively less tenable, not only in a strictly military sense, but also because of the attitudes and policies of the new nations within whose territory many of them are located. Mountain passes, river valleys, and other "natural pathways" have likewise lost most of their political and military significance. The study of boundaries has changed in the main from analysis of military strength

[9] Harold Sprout, "Britain's Defense Program," in *Britain Today: Economics, Defense and Foreign Policy*, pp. 57–76. Princeton, N.J.: University Conference, May, 1959.
[10] James Reston, Article in the *New York Times*, April 5, 1957.

and weakness to analysis of transition zones where one culture merges into another. Attempts to achieve national "self-sufficiency" continue sporadically, but that struggle too is a lost cause, what with the progressive depletion of easily accessible resources and the extended list of materials required at the more advanced levels of economic development.

When all is said, countries and regions still differ, and these differences have political significance. They differ in stage of industrialization and urbanization and, consequently, in degrees of vulnerability to bombardment with nuclear weapons. Differences in economic development mean differences in ability to provide goods and services for military or other political purposes as well as to satisfy general consumer demands. Such differences still depend in some degree upon limitations implicit in the non-human environment; but, increasingly, they depend more on limitations imposed by the technological level and by the structure and operation of the national social order.

Nations still differ in attitudes, aspirations, and expectations as well as in their capacity to translate aspirations into solid accomplishments. Notions of what is desirable and what is possible, what should be supported and what should be resisted, are deeply rooted, as MacKinder emphasized, in each people's geographical and other preconceptions from the past. Time lag between environmental change and general awareness of such change and the consequences thereof is not a new phenomenon. But, because of the nature and rate of technological and other changes taking place today, the gap between image and reality seems to be both wider and more dangerous than in any period since the formation of the modern international system.

MICHAEL HOWARD

# Military Power and International Order

In his inaugural lecture, in January 1927, Sir Frederick Maurice chose as his subject 'The Uses of the Study of War'. These uses he saw as twofold.

The first, which most concerns the citizen, is to promote peace by promoting an understanding of the realities of war and of the problems which may lead to war. The second, which most concerns the professional, but also does or should concern the citizen, is to ensure that war, if it comes, is waged in the best possible way.

For, he pointed out,

A struggle between nations in which vital interests are involved is not merely the concern of professional soldiers, sailors and airmen, but affects directly every citizen and calls for the whole resources of the nation. We have learned that statecraft, economics, the supply of raw material, science and industry, are factors which are of prime importance to the issue, and we realise that the tendency is for the importance of the last two to increase . . .
Above all (he concluded) we have learned that war is a great evil.

The course of the Second World War was to bear out everything that he said. Its outcome was determined as much in the factories and shipyards and laboratories as on the battlefield itself. Its historians have to study the development of weapon-design and production, and problems of political, economic and industrial organisation, at least as deeply as the operations of the armed forces themselves. Yet it is quite clear that the development of weapons during the last 20 years has effected so

SOURCE: Michael Howard, "Military Power and International Order," *International Affairs*, XL (July, 1964), 397–408. Reprinted by permission of the author and publisher. [This is a slightly abridged version of Professor Howard's inaugural lecture delivered at King's College, London, on May 5, 1964.]

drastic a change in the nature of war that Sir Frederick's lecture can now properly be read only as a historical document from a previous era. Only by considering the context in which it was delivered and assessing the extent and significance of the changes which have since occurred can we take his words as a guide to our own studies and policies in the second half of the 20th century.

What was this context? It was that of the age of struggles between 'Nations in Arms' which had opened with the French Revolutionary Wars, developed through those great mid-century conflicts between nascent industrial communities, the American Civil War and the Franco-Prussian War, and reached its climax in the two World Wars which dominated the first half of this century. During this period, the development of the political authority and administrative expertise of the state made it possible to place at the disposal of the armed forces the entire resources of the nation in man-power, technical skill and industrial productivity. The development of science, engineering and industry made equally available to them, in great quantities, weapons of unprecedented destructive power. Equipped with these weapons, making full use of all developing means of transport by land, sea, and, ultimately, air, and drawing on national man-power to the point of exhaustion, the armed forces of the great nations of the Northern hemisphere were able to pursue on a gigantic scale the classical objectives of warfare: the defeat of the opposing forces, in order to disarm the enemy and confront him with the alternatives of annihilation or surrender; or at least a sufficient probability of defeat to make it sound policy for him to come to terms.

As the 20th century progressed the means of achieving this objective grew even more complex and sophisticated, but the object itself remained unaltered. The hopes expressed by inter-war theorists, that direct military confrontation might be avoided or mitigated by direct assaults on the morale of the enemy population, whether by propaganda, by blockade or by air attack, bore very little fruit. Command of the air could not be won without first destroying the enemy air force in a subtle and long-drawn-out battle of attrition; and without command of the air it was not possible to strike effectively either at the enemy population or at his sources of economic strength. Without command of the sea the economic base of maritime nations was hopelessly vulnerable; and command of the sea was the reward of a weary struggle, not simply between capital fleets as Mahan and his disciples had believed, but between submarines, escorts, aircraft and surface-raiders, equipped with the finest aids science could provide but ultimately dependent on the courage and skill of the men who manned them. Armies were still needed to seize or defend the bases on which command of the air or the sea depended and to exploit the opportunities which these advantages gave them; and even without these advantages skilful leadership, good weapons and stubborn troops could still inflict heavy losses and impose heartbreaking delays.

For all these reasons, and in spite of the growing complication of war in three elements, one can still trace in the Second World War the basic characteristics of the conflicts waged by Napoleon, by Ulysses S. Grant, by Moltke, and by Ludendorff and Haig. There was the mobilisation of the resources of the nation, involving a transformation of the peacetime pattern of the national economy. There was the conversion of those resources into effective military power; and there was the deployment of that power by military specialists, according to classical principles of strategy, for the defeat of the enemy armed forces.

It is of course an over-simplification to talk of the age of mass-warfare as 'beginning' in 1792. Eighteenth-century habits of military thought and organisation lingered long into the 19th and even the 20th centuries—perhaps longer in this sheltered country than anywhere else. Very few of Goethe's contemporaries could have understood what he meant by observing that a new age had opened when the French volunteers stood firm under the Prussian cannonade at Valmy on September 20, 1792. But there was no lack of would-be Goethes to proclaim the beginning of a new era on August 6, 1945, when the first atomic bomb was dropped on Hiroshima. In the short run they were wrong, just as Goethe was wrong. The atom bombs of 1945, for all their unprecedented power, were not immediately accepted by military planners as being, in themselves, decisive weapons of war. Their process of manufacture was so slow and expensive that it was several years before the United States had a stockpile sufficient to devastate a rival as large as the Soviet Union; while such bombs as were available could be transported to their targets only in sub-sonic, short-range manned bombers, vulnerable to fighter attack and anti-aircraft fire. When the world began to rearm again in 1950 the atom bomb was considered an ancillary and not a decisive weapon in a conflict which, in the view of responsible defence specialists on both sides, was likely to differ little in its basic requirements from the Second World War. The year 1945, like 1792, only provided a foretaste of what might come when the new technology got into its stride; that is, when thermonuclear replaced atomic explosives, and manned bombers were supplemented by ballistic missiles.

It is tempting to draw from this development sweeping and premature conclusions. There are still very few nuclear Powers in the world, and it seems unlikely that their number will increase very rapidly. A conflict today between, say, China and India, or between two African states, might well conform to the general pattern of European warfare over the past hundred years. But for the great industrial nations of the Northern hemisphere, that pattern is now radically altered. In order to confront one's adversary with the alternatives of annihilation or surrender it is no longer necessary to mobilise major forces and deploy them according to classical principles of strategy. It is unlikely that there will be either the need or the time to apply the techniques we learned in two world wars for the switching over of the national economy from a peacetime to a wartime footing. Those Powers which possess sufficient wealth, scientific expertise and industrial capacity have developed weapons-systems which poise the threat of inescapable and unaccountable destruction over the heads of their rivals even in time of deepest peace; and for nations so threatened military security can no longer be based on traditional principles of defence, mobilisation and counter-attack. It can be based only on the capacity to deter one's adversary by having available the capacity to inflict on him inescapable and unacceptable damage in return.

So much has been generally accepted for the past 10 years, and the dimensions of this new situation have been studied with encyclopaedic brilliance by a group of American scholars whose work must be the starting point for any student of military affairs today. They have patiently unravelled the problems of the technical and political requirements of deterrence. They have discussed the possible nature of a nuclear war, the alternative forms into which international conflict might be channelled, and the political measures needed to control the military forces we can now unleash. But many things remain unclear: not least of them the effect which this transformation in the nature of war is likely to have on that international order in which armed sovereign states peacefully coexist; always assuming that they remain armed and that they remain sovereign—two assumptions which at present it seems not unreasonable to make.

In offering some tentative remarks on this subject I shall consider briefly the nature both of war and of the international order within which it arises. I shall not, in dealing with the first, adopt the view that war is a disease of the body politic, a pathological condition which can be traced to abnormalities in the social or economic structure, or to the racial characteristics of particular peoples. One could list many such explanations of the causes of war, from 'aggressor nations' or the machinations of armament-manufacturers to particular kinds of ruling class—whether monarcho-feudal, as the Cobdenites believed 100 years ago, or bourgeois-capitalist, as the socialists believed 50 years later. All take as their starting point the assumption that peace is the natural condition of mankind, as health is of the human body. Such a view is understandable enough. It is a commendable reaction, not simply against the evils of war in themselves, but against the doctrines which were so widespread in Europe during the 19th and the earlier part of this century, that War is necessary to the health of the Race, that it is an intrinsic part of the dialectical mechanism of Progress or the biological mechanism of the Survival of the Fittest, a test of manhood to be strenuously prepared for and welcomed when it comes. The generation of Rupert Brooke had still to learn the lesson, on which Sir Frederick Maurice was to insist in 1927, that 'war is a great evil'.

But the historian and the political scientist cannot discuss war in terms of good or evil, normality or abnormality, health or disease. For them it is simply the use of violence by states for the enforcement, the protection or the extension of their political power. Some wars, under some circumstances, may be rational acts of policy; under others, they may not. Power, in itself, is something morally neutral, being no more than the capacity of individuals or groups to control and organise their environment to conform with their physical requirements or their code of moral values. The desire for, acquisition, and exercise of power is the raw material of politics, national and international, and violence may sometimes prove an effective means to secure or retain it. Within well-organised states groups can seldom achieve power by violence, save in a marginal or covert way; and power which is so achieved will be of a most transitory kind until it is transformed by prescriptive exercise or rational consent into effective authority. Yet in spite of the aspirations of internationalists since the 16th century, in spite of Hague Conferences, Kellogg Pacts, League Covenants and United Nations Charters, the use of violence remains among sovereign states as an accepted if rarely exercised instrument for the extension or protection of their power.

But the inhibitions on the use of violence between states are considerable. They are not grounded simply on humanitarian considerations, or on any formal respect for international law. Fundamentally they rest on the most naked kind of self-interest. The use of violence, between states as between individuals, is seldom the most effective way of settling disputes. It is expensive in its methods and unpredictable in its outcome; and these elements of expense and unpredictability have both grown enormously over the last 100 years. The advent of nuclear weapons has only intensified an aversion to the use of violence in international affairs, which has, with certain rather obvious exceptions, increasingly characterised the conduct of foreign policy by the major Powers since the latter part of the 19th century.

•   •   •

By 1914 governments and peoples were largely at cross-purposes. Since 1870 the size and expense of the war-machines, and the uncertainty of the consequences of war for society as a whole, made violence an increasingly unusable instrument for the conduct of international affairs. Defeat, even at the hands of a moderate and restrained adversary, might mean social revolution, as it nearly had for France in 1870 and Russia in 1905; while even a successful war involved a disturbance of the economic life of the nation whose consequences were quite unforeseeable. Clausewitz in his great work *On War* had suggested that 'policy', the adaptation of military means to political objectives, could convert the heavy battlesword of war into a light, handy rapier for use in limited conflicts; but the mass armies of 1870, of 1914 and of 1939 could not be wielded as rapiers in the cut and thrust of international politics. Indeed, so great was the expense of modern war, so heavy were the sacrifices that it entailed, that it was difficult to conceive of causes warranting having resort to it at all. Could the national resources really be mobilised and the youth of the nation really be sacrificed in hundreds of thousands for anything short of national survival, or some great ideological crusade?

So at least it appeared to the great Western democracies in the 1930s; and it was this sentiment that Hitler exploited with such superb and sinister skill. Mass war, as Britain and France had learned to fight it between 1914 and 1918, was not a rational instrument of foreign policy. French and British statesmen were naturally and properly unwilling to invoke it for such limited objectives as the preservation of the Rhineland from re-militarisation; or the prevention of the *Anschluss* of an acquiescent Austria with Germany; or to prevent the German population of the Sudetenland being accorded the privileges of self-determination which had been granted to other peoples in Central Europe; and there appeared to be no other instruments they could use instead. To suggest that Hitler could not have been planning for war because in 1939 the German economy was not fully mobilised nor the armed forces at full battle strength is to apply the standards of 1914 to a different situation. Hitler had not armed Germany, as Britain and France had systematically armed since 1935, for a full-scale, formal Armageddon. He had every hope that it might be avoided. But he had the means available to use violence as an instrument of policy in a limited but sufficient degree, and he had no more inhibitions about using it in foreign than he had in domestic affairs. The Western demoeracies, committed to a policy of total violence in international affairs or none at all, could only watch him paralysed; until they took up arms on a scale, and with a crusading purpose, which could result only in the destruction of Germany or of themselves, and quite conceivably of both.

We should not, therefore, overestimate the change brought about in international relations through the introduction of nuclear weapons. The reluctance to contemplate the use of such weapons, which is fortunately so characteristic of the Powers which at present possess them, is a continuation, although vastly intensified, of the reluctance to use the older techniques of mass war. Even as the statesmen of the 1930s found it difficult to conceive of a cause urgent enough to justify the use of the massive weapons of which they potentially disposed, so, *a fortiori*, is it still more difficult for us to foresee the political problem to which the destruction of a score of millions of civilians will provide the appropriate military solution. It is for this reason that political influence does not necessarily increase in direct proportion to the acquisition of nuclear power. Similarly, there is no cause to suppose that the capacity to use nuclear weapons will be any more effective as a deterrent to, or even as an agent of, disturbances of the international order than was, in the 1930s, the ability, given the will, to wage mass war. Those who wish to use violence as an instrument of policy—and since 1945 they have not been rare—can find, as did Hitler, more limited and effective forms; and those who hope to counter it need equally effective instruments for doing so.

Perhaps, indeed, it is necessary, in reassessing the place of military force in international affairs, to rid ourselves of the idea that if such force is employed it must necessarily be in a distinct 'war', formally declared, ending in a clear decision embodied in a peace treaty, taking place within a precise interval of time during which diplomatic relations between the belligerents are suspended and military operations proceed according to their own peculiar laws. We reveal the influence of this concept whenever we talk about 'the next war', or 'if war breaks out' or 'the need to deter war'. If an inescapable *casus belli* were to occur between nuclear Powers, there *might* follow a spasm of mutual destruction which the survivors, such as they were, would be justified in remembering as the Third World War; but such an outcome is by no means inevitable, and appears to be decreasingly likely. It seems more probable that a *casus belli* would provoke threats and, if necessary, execution of limited acts of violence, probably though not necessarily localised, probably though not necessarily non-nuclear; all accompanied by an intensification rather than a cessation of diplomatic intercourse. Instead of a formal state of war in which diplomacy was subordinated to the requirements of strategy, specific military operations might be carried out under the most rigorous political control. It will certainly no longer be enough for the statesman to give general guidance to a military machine which then proceeds according to its own laws. Politics must now interpenetrate military activity at every level as thoroughly as the nervous system penetrates the tissues of a human body, carrying to the smallest muscle the dictates of a controlling will. The demands on the military for discipline and self-sacrifice will be great beyond all precedent, and the opportunities for traditional honour and glory negligible. Regiments will bear as their battle honours the names, not of the battles they have fought, but those that they have averted.

The maintenance of armed forces for this role creates many problems. Such conflicts must be waged with forces in being, and the task for which they are recruited is a thankless one. The standard of technical expertise, already high, may become still more exacting; military commanders will need exceptional political wisdom as well as military skill; but they must refrain from attempting to shape the political world to their military image, as the French Army tried to do, so tragically, in Algeria. Indeed, the tendency which has been so general during the past 15 years of regarding all international relations as an extension of warfare, and the description of national policy in such terms as 'national strategy' or 'Cold War', betrays a dangerous confusion of categories and a fundamental misunderstanding of the nature of international affairs, even in an age of bitter ideological conflict.

On the other hand, statesmen now require a deeper understanding of military matters, of the needs and capabilities and limitations of armed forces, than they have ever needed in the past. Only if there is complete mutual understanding and co-operation between civil and military leaders, only if there is effective functioning of the mechanism of command and control, only if there is entire discipline and obedience in every rank of military hierarchy can military power serve as an instrument of international order at all, rather than one of international anarchy and world destruction.

The order which exists between sovereign states is very different in kind from that which they maintain within their borders, but it is in order none the less, though precarious in places and everywhere incomplete. There does exist a comity of nations, an international community transcending ideological and other rivalries. Its activities in many fields —those of commerce and communications, of health and diplomatic representation, of use of the high seas and of the air—are regulated by effective and precise provisions of international law, which are for the most part meticulously observed. But even in those aspects of international relations which international law does not regulate, order still obtains. It is preserved by certain conventions of behaviour established and adjusted by a continuing and subtle process of communication and negotiations, with which not even the most revolutionary of states— neither the United States in the 18th century nor the Soviet Union in the

20th—has ever found it possible to dispense for very long. This order is based on no system of positive law, nor of natural justice, nor of clearly defined rights, nor even of agreed values. It has never been very easy for sovereign states to agree about such things. Even if the differing pattern of their international development does not lead them to adopt divergent and conflicting ideologies, states are bound by their very nature to regard the maintenance of their own power as the main criterion of all their actions and to pursue that, whatever their noble professions to the contrary. International order is based rather on recognition of disagreement, and of the limitation on one's own capacity to secure agreement. It is based on the understanding by nations that their capacity to impose and extend their own favoured order is limited by the will and effective ability of other states to impose theirs. The conduct of international relations must therefore always be a delicate adjustment of power to power, a mutual exploration of intentions and capabilities, so as to find and preserve an order which, though fully satisfying to nobody, is just tolerable to all.

The power which states exercise in international affairs is compounded of many attributes, economic, diplomatic, cultural and ideological as well as military. But military power, the capacity to use violence for the protection, enforcement or extension of authority, remains an instrument with which no state has yet found it possible completely to dispense. Indeed, it is not easy to see how international relations could be conducted, and international order maintained, if it were totally absent. The capacity of states to defend themselves, and their evident willingness to do so, provides the basic framework within which the business of international negotiation is carried on. That this framework should be as wide and as flexible as possible hardly needs arguing; but if no such limits existed, if it were known that there were no extremes of surrender and humiliation beyond which a state could not be pressed, the maintenance of international order would surely be, not easier, but incalculably more difficult. It is significant that nearly every one of the new states which has emerged since the Second World War has considered it necessary to create at least a token military force, even when the strategic need has been as negligible as the financial capacity to support it. Such a force is not purely symbolic. The ultimate test of national independence remains in the nuclear what it was in the prenuclear age: whether people are prepared to risk their lives in order to secure and preserve it.

The thesis that military power is an intrinsic part of the structure of international order is not one which will meet with unanimous approval. Attitudes towards the place of armed forces in international relations fall somewhere between two extremes. On the one hand is the view that armed forces constitute a purely destabilising factor on the international scene, and that their abolition would lead to greater stability among nations. The arguments in favour of such a view are familiar and formidable, for it is true that the weapons which a nation considers necessary to its own defence will always be likely to appear to its neighbours as an actual or potential threat to themselves. The military preparations carried out by the Triple and Dual Alliances in pre-war Europe were inspired almost wholly by considerations of self-defence, but they appeared to offer reciprocally an intolerable threat, to be countered only by yet more intensive armament. It is no doubt as difficult today for the Soviet Union to believe in the purely defensive intentions of the bombers and missiles which ring her territory, and whose devastating powers our political and military leaders frequently extol, as it is for us to believe that the powerful units with which the Soviet Union could strike at Western Europe will never be used for aggressive purposes. In any case the 'Balance of Terror' is never wholly stable. It is maintained only by constant effort, heavy expense and the dedicated work of military specialists. Those specialists must constantly be thinking of the worst possible case, and it is not always easy under the circumstances to retain a sense of proportion and to realise that this may be the least probable case. It is simpler to judge the political intentions of a possible adversary according to his military capabilities; but the actions, writings and speeches stemming from such a judgment are likely to engender reciprocal alarm and bellicosity on the other side. The result is likely to be one of those arms races which inevitably, we are told, end in war.

Much of this is unfortunately and undeniably true. Yet there is all too little evidence to show that military impotence in itself leads to stability and order. The examples of China in 1931, of Abyssinia in 1935, of Czechoslovakia and her allies in 1938, and of Western empires in the Far East in 1941 are not encouraging. Violence can appear a perfectly rational instrument of policy to a state which stands to gain important strategic, economic or political advantages from the domination of helpless and disorganised neighbours; and the experience of the 1930s suggests that under such circumstances only the prospect of immediate and effective counter-violence can make it appear irrational.

At the other extreme we have the belief that military power is not merely one element of national power and international order, but the basic factor; and that no cheque in international politics can be honoured unless there is a full supply of military power in the bank to meet it. But such a view is really no more tenable than its opposite. There are many reasons which deter even the most powerful and ruthless states from attacking their neighbours; not least the inherent drawbacks of violence as an instrument of policy which we have already considered. In certain areas of the world—Scandinavia for nearly 200 years, and now at last perhaps Western Europe—social bonds have been forged between nations which make their military power increasingly irrelevant; while many states—our own not least—have exercised an influence in world politics out of all proportion to their military strength. . . .

●  ●  ●

CIRO   ELLIOTT   ZOPPO

## Nuclear Technology, Multipolarity, and International Stability

Traditional theory of international politics maintains that, other things being equal, a multipolar balance-of-power system is more stable than a bipolar system. Arms-control theory, on the other hand, generally contends that an increase in independent nuclear powers is a direct threat to the stability of the international system. A bipolar nuclear deterrent relationship is believed to be inherently more stable than one in which equilibrium is maintained among several nuclear powers in independent or alliance relationships. Though the relatively greater stability of a bipolar system may be preferred, its stability is, nevertheless, contingent. Maintaining the stability of mutual nuclear deterrence while restraining aggression is the primary goal of arms control.

The apparent contradiction between arms-control concepts and tra-

SOURCE: Ciro Elliott Zoppo, "Nuclear Technology, Multipolarity, and International Stability," *World Politics*, XVIII (July 1966), 579–606. Reprinted by permission. Some footnotes have been deleted. [Author's Note—This article was written while I was a Research Associate at the Harvard Center for International Affairs. The views expressed are mine. They should not be interpreted as reflecting the views of The RAND Corporation or the official opinion or policy of any of its governmental or private research sponsors.]

ditional balance-of-power theory arises, in part, from the different ordering of conditions believed to create stability, particularly with respect to the effects of military technology. Arms control focuses on the role of nuclear weapons, making deterrence the indispensable condition of international stability. It sees a unique correlation between the stability of deterrence at various levels of national armaments and the stability of the international system. International-relations theory, on the other hand, does not generally give preeminence to nuclear technology in the calculus of stability.[5] Most writers, while rating military *power* very high, include military *technology* as a factor of only relative importance. They note the possible far-reaching effects of nuclear weapons but do not directly relate stability in the international system to stability in nuclear deterrence.[6] The interrelation between the stability of deterrence and stability in the international system may, nevertheless, be fundamental. The invention of intercontinental missiles and nuclear warheads has brought into question traditional concepts about the nature of war, the uses of military force in the pursuit of national policy, and the role of military power in the maintenance of international stability.

The main reason for the decisive influence of nuclear weapons in the context of international stability is the awesome destructive potential of nuclear war and the unbelievably compressed time in which such destruction could take place. Moreover, no country wherever located and however strong militarily can, under current and foreseeable circumstances, realistically believe itself immune from the power and reach of nuclear weapons.

Nuclear weapons and their delivery mechanisms are manifestations of an unprecedented and spectacular intrusion of technology into politics. The interplay between the military applications of modern science and the foreign-policy goals of nations in an international system beset by intense ideological strife and power rivalry is a central problem of deterrence, the contemporary doctrine of international security, and its corollary, arms control. It is reflected in propaganda, the domestic politics of governments, and the diplomacy of the major powers.

[5] A notable exception is John H. Herz, *International Politics in the Nuclear Age* (New York, 1959).
[6] Stanley Hoffmann, "International Systems and International Law," in Klaus Knorr and Sidney Verba, eds., *The International System: Theoretical Essays* (Princeton 1961), 206–15; Kaplan, *System and Process,* 22–35. Kaplan has, however, suggested that the retaliatory power of ICBM's in large numbers is a stabilizing factor (p. 45), while postulating that increases in the destructive power of weapons may make it eventually possible for one of the major actors in the system to eliminate all other actors and establish a hierarchical system. He notes that such a system would be so nonintegrated and nonsolidary that dysfunctional tension would paramountly characterize it (p. 57).

Military nuclear technology has so far emerged only in the Communist camp and the Western Alliance, for nuclear technology is highly demanding of treasure and scientific talent. Relatively few powers seem presently capable of achieving major nuclear rank, though primitive nuclear capabilities are within reach of an increasing number of countries. Nuclear weapons have not only changed military power relationships between nuclear and nonnuclear states, but have also widened the gap between the superpowers and other major powers. The technical complexity and the cost of the delivery and command and control systems required to make nuclear warheads strategically effective against a superpower drastically reduce the chances that other nuclear powers in the system will achieve major rank. It is therefore likely that only the superpowers can fulfill the dynamic requirements of global deterrence. All declared aspirants to nuclear status have tested weapons. In addition to the United States and the Soviet Union, however, only Britain and France have so far produced as well as tested weapons, and have made public their strategic force goals. Chinese nuclear development is uncertain in scope if not in intention. Indeed, from the point of view of global politics, the actual or planned arsenals of these aspiring powers are debatable military and, to a degree, political assets.

Two important qualifications to these limitations should be mentioned. With the dissemination of information and knowledge about nuclear technology becoming increasingly unavoidable, it will become progressively easier and cheaper for middle-rank and even minor powers to develop and produce nuclear weapons. The costs for fabricating nuclear devices could be considerably less than those incurred by countries that pioneered in the development of nuclear conflict technology. About a dozen countries have or could have the option to go nuclear in the immediate future. Secondly, powers whose security requirements and political aspirations are regional, or powers faced with a local enemy not a superpower, would not need the sophisticated and costly delivery mechanisms required by the major powers to attain their goals. Many nations already possess jet bombers. Even missile technology is not completely excluded for some would-be nuclear powers. Nuclear military technology thus both spurs and limits national ambitions and in the process deeply influences international stability.

The inhibitions in the use of nuclear weapons fostered by their awesome destructiveness have magnified their importance as objects of political agitation and as instruments for political warfare. The surprises and the innovations of the technological arms race alone have created intense political issues in domestic and international politics. For example, the development of intercontinental ballistic missiles and the resulting loss of America's strategic invulnerability sparked a host of political problems in the Atlantic Alliance.[8] Heightened radioactive fallout from the testing of newly invented thermonuclear devices led to agitation, from 1954 on, against nuclear testing, and to dramatic national debate among scientists, politicians, and soldiers. It compelled international negotiations which led in 1963 to the banning of atmospheric nuclear tests. On the other hand, awareness of the singular properties of nuclear weapons has faced the leaders of expansionist and status quo powers alike with a dilemma over the means and scope of military power. These conditions tend to obscure customary distinctions between a stable and a revolutionary international system, and have qualified the use of military power at all levels of conflict for all states in the international system, but especially the major powers. Pertinent and important for stability has been the questioning of the concept of balancing the power of national units in the system through conflict or coalition diplomacy.

### THE DILEMMA OF EXPANIONIST GOALS, "ABSOLUTE" WEAPONS, AND NATIONAL SURVIVAL

Since the end of the Second World War, the methods used by revisionist nations have run the gamut from propaganda to warfare by regular armies in the field.[9] But except for local situations not directly involving the military presence of the contending superpowers, or their allies or satellites, the revolutionary dynamism in the international system has been generally curtailed, circumscribed, or smothered by tacit or explicit understanding between the two major antagonists of international politics. It is a paradox of the nuclear era that the original élan of revolutionary and revisionist powers is being replaced by concern lest violence surpass the bounds beyond which general war might occur in the system.

The use of military action by the principal actors—including the most outspoken revolutionary, Communist China—has been bridled.

---

[8] The ICBM has had a lasting political and military impact, but the strategic invulnerability of the United States had already been questioned before Sputnik. By 1955 the Soviet Union had created a small force of intercontinental bombers operational against the United States (Raymond L. Garthoff, *Soviet Strategy in the Nuclear Age,* rev. ed. [New York 1962], 173–79). The operational invulnerability of SAC had been questioned even earlier, though in different fashion. A study made for the Air Force found in 1954 that the overseas elements of American strategic air forces were vulnerable to surprise atomic attack (Albert Wohlstetter and others, *Selection and Use of Strategic Air Bases,* The RAND Corporation, R-266 [April 1954], released June 1962).

[9] Except when the context in which the term is used clearly indicates the contrary, a revisionist power may not be Communist.

Except for the bombardment of Hiroshima and Nagasaki at the end of World War II, the most powerful and decisive elements of the super-powers' military establishments, nuclear weapons, have not so far been used strategically or in local engagements. The national territories of the superpowers and their major allies, while becoming the main potential targets of nuclear war, have also become sanctuaries during peripheral conflicts. While the Soviet Union and China have deliberately fostered the local use of violence in Korea and Vietnam—conventional wars in-volving the military forces of one or more of the major powers—re-straint has been exercised and limits have been observed.

This has resulted neither from a lack of expansionist and revolution-ary aims on the part of the Soviet Union and China nor from the unwillingness of the United States and its allies to use force or the threat of force, including the threat to use nuclear weapons, to protect national interests. It has, rather, resulted increasingly from a dilemma engendered by the properties of nuclear weapons (and by the increase in American and Soviet nuclear carriers and their stockpiles) which have changed the destructiveness of military power from relative to near-absolute so that it can threaten—and possibly achieve within a matter of days or even hours—the destruction of national societies. Thus not-withstanding the intensity of the ideological commitment, the magnitude of possible destruction does not flow primarily from political in-tention[12] but from the characteristics of the weapons themselves and the operational imperatives they might dictate if nuclear war broke out *and became uncontrolled.* Not that nuclear war is inevitably all out war,[13] but even a limited strategic nuclear exchange between the super-powers, confined to strategic weapons and their supporting facilities, might result in collateral damage with high casualties and considerable destruction compressed into hours.[14]

[12] The example of Carthage notwithstanding, bidders for hegemony have generally sought to conquer or control, not destroy, other nations. The destruction of Carthage itself does not appreciably weaken this generalization. The Second Punic War, de-scribed by the historian Cary as "the World War of ancient times," ended, for all practical purposes, the rivalry between Rome and Carthage, establishing Roman hegemony in the Western Mediterranean and indirect but effective Roman control over Carthage. The third and final Punic War was unjustified on political and military grounds. Only the gallantry of the Carthaginians kept it from becoming a mere military execution. Anyway, the treatment meted out to them was not the usual Roman approach to conquest. See Max Cary, *A History of Rome* (London 1954), 156–94.

[13] Klaus Knorr and Thornton Read, *Limited Strategic War* (New York 1962), provides a rich discussion of hypothetical strategic but limited strikes.

[14] For example, it has been estimated that a Soviet counterforce strike limited to three hundred megatons could kill up to eleven percent of the American population. See Norman A. Hanumian, *The Relations of U.S. Fallout Casualties to U.S. and*

This capacity of nuclear weapons to compress drastically in time and to intensify greatly the magnitude of pain and destruction is one of the fundamental differences between nuclear war and previous wars. Even more salient is the fact that "you can punish your enemy before you have achieved victory, and if you design your force properly you can punish your enemy while going down to defeat."[15] As a result, competition and opposition among the major powers in the system have become strangely hobbled in the use of national military power to attain foreign-policy goals. And while threats of nuclear war have been made by both Soviet and American leaders in crisis or local-conflict situations, the avoidance of all-out nuclear war seems to have become an established "rule" of the international system.

That this rule has emerged in an era of ideological strife among major powers testifies to the impact on international politics of the nuclear technology of conflict. The validity of the rule is, however, contingent. Deterrence depends on the ability of both sides, particularly the politically defensive one, to keep credible, by demonstrating both military capacity and political resolve, the threat to go to war. The military capacity, built and maintained over time, must be capable of inflicting such pain and destruction on the enemy as to divest him of incentives for surprise or preemptive attack (either out of confidence or in desperation). Political resolve must be demonstrated in each crisis or conflict by a willingness to run the risk of general war.

Credibility is, therefore, a variable critically dependent on the contingencies of each crisis or conflict, as well as on previous performance. Each confrontation must test anew the validity of the rule. Yet under present circumstances, the magnitude of the costs that nuclear war is likely to visit (although not equally) upon attacker and defender alike tends to undermine the credibility of the threat to resort to general war. So while even expansionist and revolutionary powers have come to question whether general war serves the ends of policy, in crisis and conflict confrontation it becomes necessary to raise the threat of nuclear war by words and acts in order to maintain deterrence.

Under the impact of a dynamic nuclear military technology, expansionist goals are becoming increasingly qualified in fact if not in the rhetoric of the cold war. Until strategic superiority and inflexible de-

---

*Soviet Options*, The RAND Corporation, P-2412 (August 18, 1961), 9–14; or see Hanumian's statement to the Military Operations Subcommittee of the Committee on Government Operations, U.S. House of Representatives, 87th Cong., 1st Sess. (August 8, 1961), 207–33. Shelter programs would help considerably but would not eliminate casualties.

[15] Thomas C. Schelling, *The Nature of Deterrence*, Center for International Affairs, Harvard University (October 13, 1964).

termination were made jointly manifest by the United States in the 1962 Cuban missile crisis, the Soviet Union could attempt nuclear blackmail. Soviet miscalculations about raising the risk of general war prior to installing strategic missiles in Cuba and withdrawal in the face of over-whelming local United States superiority in conventional forces and the threat of potential escalation to a strategic nuclear exchange sug-gest that Communist powers, although more likely to probe for the limits of action, are nevertheless unwilling to risk central war. This has not generally been the case with the seekers of hegemony in the modern era. Two global wars in this century and the Napoleonic bid in the last attest to the contrary. Now, however, the ineludible need to accept the rule that there should be no resort to general war, except as *ultima ratio*, has led to doctrinal crisis—first within the Soviet leadership, then between the Communist governments of Russia and China—which is part of the broader conflict about prerogatives, ends, and the means of expanding communism.

The first, but abortive, effort to question war as an instrument of policy was made in 1954 by Malenkov, who declared that nuclear war would result in the destruction of world civilization—destruction, that is, of capitalist and Communist societies alike. Malenkov was made to recant. By 1956, however, his successor, Khrushchev, had publicly re-vised Communist dogma about the inevitability of all-out war between the Communist and capitalist camps. Further, by 1958, he had reversed this dogma, granting that a nuclear war "would cause immeasurable harm to all mankind." This questioning of general war as an instrument of policy by party leaders has continued and has been accompanied by a "gradual erosion of the dogma of inevitable communist victory," in the event of another war. Imperialistic drives, chained rather than excited by versatile strategic weaponry of global reach, lightning speed, a capability of near-total destruction, and an attendant operational doc-trine tending to favor surprise attack, would be a paradox indeed were it not for the severe inhibitions, alluded to earlier, in using nuclear war to achieve paramount national objectives.

If general war is not to decide whether the bid for hegemony by a superpower succeeds or is defeated, various tactical forms of conflict acquire more than customary importance in the contest to influence and control the international system. In some of these, such as the propa-ganda manipulation of the specter of nuclear holocaust by Communist leaders to inhibit the use of military force by Western nations, the action involved is mainly political. In others, violence is inextricably inter-woven with political acts. These situations have involved insurgencies, limited and local wars fought by regular military units, and terrorism by small, organized, subversive minorities.

Even at these lower levels of conflict, however, the nature of the nuclear deterrent relationship fetters the military actions of expansionist and defensive powers alike. Tactical nuclear weapons have not been used in combat. However, there are signs in recent military writings that the Soviet doctrine of the inevitability of escalation into general war might become qualified. And no firm doctrinal consensus against the use of nuclears in local conflicts exists among American writers on military strategy. Nevertheless, the Soviet Union has for some years officially asserted that local wars in which the nuclear powers use nuclear weapons will inevitably escalate to general war. The United States has equipped its forces with dual-capability weapons (i.e., with the option of using either nuclear or conventional warheads) and has declared its willingness to use nuclear weapons in local conflict if necessary. A deep psychological demarcation seems to exist in the minds of American policy-makers between conventional and nuclear weapons, however, and there are as yet no official indications that the distinction is fading. President Johnson's and Premier Kosygin's statements accompanying the escalation of the conflict in Vietnam are good illustrations. These attitudes on both sides have tended to limit the number of potential conflicts in which the superpowers participated and to localize or deflate the violence of those that occurred. Communist efforts to subvert the international system by exploiting, instigating, or militarily participating in local conflicts have been tempered by fear of escalation to nuclear war. This attenuation in the use of military instrumentalities has basically resulted from two conditions: first, Soviet strategic inferiority and the greater vulnerability of Soviet forces to preemption; and, second, the realization by the Soviet leadership that the political gains they might achieve by brandishing nuclear weapons would be dwarfed by the costs should miscalculation lead to war. At no time since nuclear weapons have become operational has the Soviet Union actually had superiority over the United States in strategic forces—though between 1957 and 1961 Premier Khrushchev attempted to exploit for political ends a fictitious Soviet superiority in missiles. This deception was finally exposed by the American government in 1961. Moreover, before measures reducing the vulnerability of strategic weapons to attack were implemented by the United States, and to a degree by the Soviet Union, reciprocal fears of surprise attack also aggravated the political tensions of the cold war.

In any case, if the polemics of the Sino-Soviet conflict are a valid guide, assessments of the risk of escalation from local conflict to nuclear war have become a vital consideration for the Soviet Union. The Chinese, like the Russians, have for some time also believed that general war between communism and capitalism is not inevitable. Both Russians and Chinese have favored indirect military assistance to "national liberation movements," but have been reluctant to participate overtly in insurgencies. The dispute has been about the limits of action permissible against the West without serious risk of precipitating nuclear war and about the degree of destruction such war might entail. In practice, the Chinese have been cautious. Nor do they seem unschooled in the implications of nuclear weapons. There is evidence for the view that the Chinese are strongly influenced by the possibility of American intervention with nuclear weapons in local conflict or in a war with China.

The United States, too, is confronted with a dilemma over means and ends. The expected effects of tactical nuclear weapons make it difficult, if not impossible, to discriminate between combatants and civilians in limited war and especially in insurgency. In such conflicts, where the political object is not to annihilate an enemy country but to defeat military or insurgent forces in order to reestablish political integrity, the use of nuclear weapons could subvert the rational use of military violence and negate the political object. For while force must be sufficient to attain the goals of policy it must not be so excessive as to cancel them.[28]

Thus it seems that the hiatus between expansionist goals and the use of military methods to achieve them has been crucially affected by the nuclear technology of conflict. But nuclear technology is also related to the character of Western, essentially American, military power and the political determination to use it. Whether the Soviets and the Chinese use the tactics of tension or those of détente depends significantly on the strength of the West and the resolve of its leaders to resist Communist probes, threats, and political maneuver. The Soviet leaders are

[28] The distinguished soldier and military historian J. F. C. Fuller in discussing the impact of nuclear weapons on war has cautioned against accepting them as simply another discovery like gunpowder by relating them to the political ends of warfare in the following words: ". . . Directly the political factor is introduced, in all wars, except those of the most primitive kind, the destructive means employed to achieve a profitable end must be limited. For example, when in feudal times the aim of a king was to bring his truculent barons to heel, the artillery of that period was found invaluable to deprive them of their power of resistance—their castles. But had its destructive effect been such that, not only their castles, but their retainers, serfs, orchards and cattle within a radius of several miles would be obliterated, nothing would have been left to bring to heel—the means would have swallowed the end (*The Conduct of War: 1789–1961* [New Brunswick 1961], 313).

Clausewitz has also made the point: "As war is no act of blind passion, but is dominated by the political object, the value of that object determines the measure of the sacrifices by which it is to be purchased. . . . As soon, therefore, as the expenditure of force becomes so great that the political object is no longer equal in value, this object must be given up . . ." (*On War*, trans. D. J. M. Jolles [New York 1943], 21).

aware that while the prospects of using war as a deliberate instrument of policy have greatly diminished, the political returns from exploiting the possession of military power may have increased. The salient strategic truth of our times may well be that "men's minds are the most profitable and perhaps the only suitable targets for the weapons of the nuclear age."[29]

This discussion does not address the highly problematic question of whether an international system of Communist states might be achieved through piecemeal subversion, insurrection, and coups d'etat. But it underscores *the essential role of states with nuclear capacity in defining the rules of interstate politics.* In the balance-of-power system, war was a legitimate, if not a preferred, means of reestablishing stability in the system. Neither the number of wars nor the participation of the great powers in them were crucial determinants of stability. Moreover, provided the existence of so-called essential actors was not threatened in defeat, minor states could be conquered, partitioned, or incorporated as a matter of political adjustment. An essential characteristic was that war was not to be fought for unlimited objectives by any of the great powers. We have been moving toward an international system in which political intentions are peculiarly shaped by "the state of the art" in military technology. Revolutionary powers, whose professed objective is the achievement of world hegemony through all the instrumentalities of state power, have been forced to forsake all-out war as an instrument of policy, and to show caution in the use of their military forces in the pursuit of national goals all along the spectrum of conflict.

The preoccupation with nuclear war arising from local conflict which shapes the dilemma of expansionist aims and qualifies use of military force in both large-scale and limited conflict reflects more than fear of miscalculation. It also stems from an awareness, by both the United States and the Soviet Union, of the contingent, perhaps transitory, nature of nuclear stability, which is the product of complex technical and political factors.

### STABILITY: INVULNERABILITY OF STRATEGIC FORCES AND THE SHARED RISK OF GENERAL WAR

Stability in the international system is the result of many factors in dynamic combination. Paramount is the interaction between political goals and military means. Nuclear technology critically shapes the modalities of the present system and directly affects the chances of maintaning international stability. Technology is centrally located in the

[29] Thomas W. Wolfe, *Some Factors Bearing on Soviet Attitudes Toward Disarmament,* The RAND Corportion, P-2766 (July 1963), 14.

process of deterrence. It is directly relevant to the probability of general war and to the possibilities of controlling nuclear war if it breaks out. The possible effects of nuclear warfare have increasingly narrowed the number of strategies that might permit the superpowers to exploit a temporary military advantage to achieve a more permanent and favorable distribution of power without risking unprecedented and prohibitive self-destruction. It is becoming increasingly true that strategic miscalculation might quickly and irreparably become a question of national survival for the most powerful as well as for minor powers. And on the stability of deterrence between the United States and the Soviet Union depends the stability of the international system itself.

In a word, because the new military technology has raised the issue of physical as much as political survival, technological factors have been elevated to a central concern with respect to maintaining stability in the system. Brodie stresses that prior to the Second World War changes in military technology, even when rapid, were confined to instruments having only tactical significance. The atomic bomb differed from "all previous military inventions in that its effects could not clearly be confined to the tactical." Since the introduction of nuclear weapons, "developments in the character, variety, and abundance of these weapons have affected . . . several distinct revolutions in military technology."[31] These have radically altered military strategy. Deterrence is informed not only by the state of political relations among antagonists, but also by their relationship within the context of military technology.

For example, it is hard to divorce technology from measures that make strategic weapons less vulnerable to surprise attack, technical intelligence more accurate, command and control more effective—all acts tending to forestall situations that might lead to inadvertent war, and thereby tending to enhance stability. Technology is also inseparable from acts that if taken beforehand might increase the chances of terminating war before the contestants expended all or most of their nuclear weapons. The impact of weapons and weapon systems on deterrence is not to be underestimated. The attainment of a steady-state peacetime operational deterrence is neither easy nor automatic.[32] . . . Maintaining deterrence during escalating conflict involving the superpowers may be-

---

[31] Bernard Brodie, "The Scientific Strategist," in Robert Gilpin and Christopher Wright, eds., *Scientists and National Policy-Making* (New York 1964), 242, 243, 250, 251.

[32] "Steady state" is used to describe a dynamic equilibrium that maintains stability by reacting adaptively to preserve the essential variables in the system. This has been called "the principle of ultrastability" and is stated formally as follows: "An ultrastable system acts selectively toward the fields of the main variables, rejecting those that lead the representative point to a critical state but retaining those that do not" (W. Ross Ashby, *Design for a Brain* [New York 1952], 91). In nuclear deterrence,

come very difficult, yet essential, during a limited nuclear conflict involving strategic strikes.

In 1962, the Kennedy administration amplified the concept of deterrence that underlay American national policy. Deterrence was now seen not only as a matter of comparative risks but also as a continuous, sometimes urgent, effort to undercut or neutralize the incentives for a surprise attack which nuclear forces might foster in the leaders of the Soviet Union—or as an effort to dampen preemptive urges on both sides. Deterrence was to be extended into general war itself. The administration revealed a strategic doctrine anchored to "flexible response." By this it meant a control of nuclear forces that discriminated between population and military targets in order to induce reciprocal restraints that might keep the fighting from spiraling into all-out war. Targeting enemy nuclear weapons instead of cities during the initial phase of the engagement could create the possibility of ending the war by negotiation—before the respective national societies became irreparably crippled by high fatalities, leaving only the urge for ultimate revenge.

The need to work constantly on the technological factors affecting the stability of mutual deterrence has been recognized by military doctrine. The influence of the nuclear technology of conflict in shaping international action is not amenable to precise measurement but cannot be denied. Even though this influence is not always obvious it can, under particular circumstances, become decisive. While the shift in emphasis from fighting general war to deterring it—a shift caused to a telling degree by this technology—has strongly influenced preconceptions about the use of military force held by the decision-makers in the system, the question of war-fighting remains, nevertheless, a significant consideration. The capacity to fight a nuclear war is basic to prewar and intrawar deterrence.

The dynamic nature of the technology of nuclear weapons is as important as their effects in shaping political expectations. Often unforeseen scientific and technological factors continually qualify the capabilities of existing weapons, suggest new ones, render others obsolete. In the course of a few years, these factors qualify and may radically change the international military environment, raising new political issues. The latter may involve attempts, such as the nuclear test ban, to control nuclear technology and, through such control, to curb the nuclear aspirations of additional countries.

---

"steady state" refers to the process of research and development, procurement, deployment, war-fighting capability, and declaratory policy which over time and taken together with environmental circumstances, including the capabilities and the intentions of potential enemies, would dynamically operate to maintain the deterrent balance.

Ironically, as the rapid advance of techniques for measuring the physical potential for waging war (the effects of nuclear weapons, for example) have made the assessment of the military capacity of nations more amenable to precise measurement and more systematic prediction, the rapid pace of technology has made military doctrine subject to rapid obsolescence, untested by war.[35] This rapid pace also complicates the problem of maintaining international stability, difficult to define and to operate even when the classical balance of power prevailed. Uncertainty about power calculations has persistently led nations to seek military superiority vis-à-vis their actual and potential enemies in order to gain a margin of safety that would allow them to maintain their independence. In contemporary terms this margin is defined by the means to limit damage to the nation, means resulting from a capability to disarm or intercept enemy weapons while terminating hostilities in such a way as to obtain national political goals through negotiation. The quest for military primacy may also create in nations that have gained an apparent edge over their antagonists strong urges to attempt to change the distribution of power in their own favor. On the other hand, nuclear weapons have greatly qualified these propositions as guides to policy.

Some kinds of strategic miscalculations may not only be irreversible

[35] A study on long-range forecasting in which eighty-two respondents participated—most of them professionally conversant with the characteristics and the problems of modern weapons—could suggest initially fifty-eight distinct weapon-systems developments. Even after dropping those which a consensus considered either unfeasible or of such limited feasibility as to make development in the foreseeable future very unlikely, there remained thirty-two possible systems of the future. While no implication is intended that these are forecasts of military instrumentalities in the offing, it might be interesting to list those weapon systems that the panel of experts predicted would become operational before 1980: tactical kiloton nuclear weapons used by ground troops; extensive use of devices that persuade without killing, such as water cannon and tear gas; miniature improved sensors and transmitters for reconnaissance and arms control; rapid mobility of men and light weapons to any point on earth for police action; incapacitating chemical agents; use of lasers for radar-type range-sensors, illuminators, and communications; incapacitating biological agents; cheap, lightweight rocket-type personnel armament (silent, plastic, match-lit projectiles, capable of single or gang firing); lethal biological agents; orbiting space reconnaissance stations; advanced techniques of propaganda, thought control, and opinion manipulation; effective antisubmarine capability; longer-endurance aircraft, perhaps nuclear-powered, for logistic supply or bombardment; biological agents destroying the will to resist; penetrating nuclear weapons for deep cratering; automated tactical capability (battlefield computers, robot sentries, television surveillance); ICBM's with other than nuclear warheads; and deep-diving submersibles made of materials that decrease detection probability (T. J. Gordon and O. Helmer, *Report on a Long-Range Forecasting Study*, The RAND Corporation, P-2982 [September 1964], 32–39 and Fig. II, i).

but become simply intolerable. Victory is likely to be pyrrhic. In our century, war has become total in the sense that it has been waged by total populations, with all available means, and for total political stakes. Nuclear weapons, while intensifying the devastation and pain of war and making the stakes greater than ever before, have changed at least one of these characteristics. Deterrence, by putting a premium on strategic forces in being, has created a situation in which the means for waging general war must be always at hand. Moreover, if the industrial-economic base exists and relevant skills are available, neither the production nor the use of strategic weapons involves most of a nation's manpower and skills. A sophisticated technology and a substantial industrial base are prerequisites for the production and the development of nuclear weaponry. But the effort required to develop and maintain strategic nuclear forces is not total in the sense that similar efforts were during the Second World War.

Finally, thermonuclear war (but not limited conflict involving the tactical use of nuclears) can be waged by armed forces relatively modest in size. And the decisions that might bring about the war itself ultimately rest more than ever on the judgment of a handful of decision-makers from the superpowers—perhaps only the Soviet Premier and the American President. The unprecedentedly compressed time available for critical decisions and the fact that strategic options must be built into force structures in advance have given a new meaning to miscalculation. One of the revolutionary characteristics of modern strategy is that "decisions are 'canned' in advance. . . . There is not much time for adaptation, new indoctrination, ironing out misunderstandings, and changing plans. The options that have been anticipated are programmed into weapon systems; those that have not been anticipated may be physically unavailable."[37]

This suggests a rather tenuous connection between the relative sizes of the opposing strategic forces and the likelihood of controlling events if miscalculation occurs. The characteristics or variety and the mode of employment of military forces—more than their total capacity for destruction—may become the decisive factor once the confrontation escalates from a local crisis or a conventional fight.

Nuclear weapons have also introduced novel ways of measuring military worth in the strategic realm. The number of weapons is important but is only one of the indices of power. Their reliability and accuracy, their yield, range, payload, speed, and vulnerability, as well as the variety and "mixes" of weapon systems, are at least as important. These indices, together with the number of potential targets, the warning

[37] Thomas C. Schelling, "Comment," in Knorr and Read, 257.

time available for the strategic forces to respond to attack, the resilience and flexibility of their control by the political authority, and so on, have become increasingly interrelated aspects of military potential.[38]

Superiority of forces, relative to an opponent, may, nevertheless, increase flexibility of response, and within certain limits reduce the number of fatalities.[39] The characteristics of weapon systems and their command and control, the capacity of the decision centers of both sides to survive the initial exchanges, capabilities for postattack reconnaissance, and the correspondence of war-fighting or targeting strategies chosen by the belligerents are also critical. But, as noted, once war starts, the capacity to exercise policy options by discriminating control of strategic forces might become as problematic as the timeliness in bringing hostilities to an end—though a rational, restrained conduct of war is nevertheless possible.

The problem of controlled central war is pervaded with uncertainties. Three kinds are major: technical, operational, and strategic. Technical uncertainty stems from potential inability to develop weapon systems with required features. Operational uncertainty results from the difficulty of predicting performance during actual combat. Strategic uncertainty is the most difficult to deal with because it involves such interactions between potential enemies as are hard to seize in advance. At the

---

[38] An example will be suggestive. If the effectiveness of a missile in destroying a military or demographic target is measured as the two-thirds power of the yield of its warhead, then an improvement by a factor of three in the yield-to-weight ratio would halve the number of missiles needed to kill a target. That is, two missiles with the improved characteristics would be the equivalent of four of the more primitive variety. Moreover, a given total yield does more damage in several small packages than in one large one. Finally, increases in the yield-to-weight ratio of warheads does more than merely increase their efficiency; it increases the flexibility of their uses (Kahn, 244, n. 13; and G. I. Pokrovsky, *Science and Technology in Contemporary War*, trans. R. L. Garthoff [New York, 1959], 74–76). Other illustrations of the kind of essential considerations that must be included in evaluating the military effectiveness of weapon systems and opposing strategic forces may be found in Glenn A. Kent, *On the Interaction of Opposing Forces Under Possible Arms Agreements*, Occasional Paper No. 5, Center for International Affairs, Harvard University (March 1963); and Jeremy J. Stone, "Bomber Disarmament," *World Politics*, XVII (October 1964), 13–39.

[39] Secretary McNamara has testified that for any given level of enemy offensive capability successive additions to each of various weapon systems have diminishing marginal value. That is, each increment added to existing strategic forces has progressively less and less effectiveness. See, "Statement of Secretary of Defense, March 2, 1965," Hearings before a Subcommittee of the Committee on Appropriations, U.S. House of Representatives, 89th Cong., 1st Sess. (1965), Part III, 35; and Statement of Secretary of Defense McNamara before the House Armed Services Committee on the Fiscal Year 1967–1971 Defense Program and 1967 Defense Budget (March 8, 1966), 47.

heart of this problem is the question of what the adversary power, or powers, will actually do—that is, the kind of force they build, the kind of attacks the power initiating the war will launch, and the effectiveness of the weapons used.

Currently, there seems to be little *declared* congruity between the deterrent and the general-war strategies the superpowers might choose in a conflict. The United States has been building a strategic force that, in addition to creating the option of separating military from urban targets, would also allow the staggering of a retaliatory strike into separate and successive waves. Lately, however, the emphasis has shifted toward a countervalue (population and industrial targets) doctrine. While it seems unlikely that the Soviet Union in an attack on the United States would fire all its weapons simultaneously in a salvo launch, Soviet strategic doctrine (seemingly rejecting the notion of the controlled use of strategic forces, that is, self-imposed and reciprocal restraints) stresses the all-out-nature of nuclear war. A Soviet strike that included major American cities would leave the United States little choice but to retaliate in kind. This may change as Soviet strategic weapons become increasingly secure against attack, because of measures reducing their vulnerability, and as they increase in numbers and variety. Moreover, currently enunciated doctrine need not exclude a more flexible and discriminating use of Soviet strategic forces if nuclear war occurs— a course not inimical to Soviet interests should strategic nuclear exchanges begin. Meanwhile, with inferior strategic forces the Soviet Union possibly believes that a doctrine of restraint might undermine the deterrent effect of its military posture. Marshal Krylov, commander-in-chief of Soviet Strategic Rocket Troops, has described the mission of his forces as "the destruction in the shortest possible time of the enemy's war-industry potential, the disruption of his government and military administration, the elimination of weapons of nuclear attack, and the annihilation of major troop concentrations, operations centers, arsenals and enterprises producing weapons of mass destruction."[44] Strategies remain seemingly incompatible. But with the publication of the second edition of Sokolovskii's *Soviet Military Strategy* in 1962, the strategic dialogue between the United States and the Soviet Union seems turned toward more genuinely reciprocal influence.

According to Secretary of Defense McNamara, the United States will have, during the 1960's, the capability of "completely destroying the Soviet Union as a civilized nation" with a retaliatory strike that would eliminate virtually all military targets in the Soviet Union while

---

[44] "Reliable Shield of Peace," *Pravda*, November 19, 1962, in *Current Digest of the Soviet Press* (December 16, 1964), 33.

retaining protected strategic forces in reserve for use against Soviet urban and industrial areas.[45] As time goes on and the Soviet Union continues to harden its missile sites and . . . to build missile-firing submarines, it will become increasingly difficult to destroy a substantial portion of [Soviet] residual forces." Even a "full first-strike capability . . . accompanied by vast programs of anti-missile, anti-bomber, and civil defense" could not preclude American casualties from running into the "tens of millions."[46] In a general war that occurred in the 1960's, American strategic forces could destroy the Soviet Union, Communist China, and their satellites as national societies under the "worst imaginable circumstances accompanying the outbreak of war."[47] But while this country could "win" a nuclear war, the cost would hardly allow the United States to consolidate a distribution of military and political power in its favor.[48]

Civil defense preparations are an important qualifier here. Extensive blast and, especially, fallout shelters, antimissile defense of cities and weapons, and related measures could significantly reduce the casualties of nuclear war. Such measures, however, do not presently exist and would take years to implement. Most important, a determined enemy could keep the potential number of fatalities high. Increases and innovations in offensive strategic systems might conceivably undercut the utility of defensive measures but not negate their relative usefulness. The deployment of additional weapon systems such as antiballistic missiles or bombardment satellites would have major psychological and political impact, creating additional opportunities for political and deterrent exploitation of nuclear weapons. But in the context of the arms race, such development might also lead to deployment of weapons with large explosive yields and might promote larger strategic forces. Whether this would lead to an increased capacity to inflict damage and fatalities should deterrence fail may depend on technological trade-offs between the offense and the defense and the circumstances of the war itself. Important qualifiers might result from the arms race. But without technological breakthroughs which no one has imagined, weapons develop-

[45] Cited in William W. Kaufmann, *The McNamara Strategy* (New York 1964), 5.

[46] U.S. Senate, Committee on Armed Services, Military Procurement Authorizations, Fiscal Year 1965, *Hearings*, 88th Cong., 2nd Sess. (1964), 30–32.

[47] Secretary McNamara, Address before the Platform Committee of the Democratic Party, *New York Times*, August 18, 1964.

[48] More than a few attack patterns and basic assumptions are tenable in projected general war exchanges and no definitive predictions can be made. Nevertheless, according to Secretary McNamara, "a full-scale nuclear exchange between the United States and the Soviet Union, lasting less than an hour, would kill almost 100 million Americans—the equivalent of 300 World War II's . . . and over 100 million Russians" (*ibid.*, quoted also in *U.S. News and World Report*, 55–56).

ment tends to reinforce the assumption that it is likely to become increasingly difficult to reduce the pain and damage of nuclear war.

Thus it seems that the number of strategies permitting the superpowers to turn a temporary military advantage into a long-range favorable distribution of power within the international system, without risking a degree of self-destruction of unprecedented and prohibitive magnitude, is shrinking.

We seem to be moving toward a situation in which miscalculation at the strategic level might become quickly and irretrievably a matter of political and—with some important qualifications—physical survival for the nations involved in the nuclear confrontation. What international decision-makers prematurely held as an image of nuclear war at the outset of the nuclear arms race is becoming a more accurate description of a range of possible postattack environments, in *uncontrolled* general war.

This suggests that while in the international system now prevailing a strategic edge in favor of the status quo superpower may be indispensable for maintaining the resolve of the superpowers to tolerate each other, in the long run, stability may also depend on whether the inferior superpower can feel that it possesses enough strategic capability to undercut with a relatively high degree of assurance its opponent's incentives for preemption. Conversely, and more crucial, an expansionist superpower would have to be made aware that it could not achieve its objectives through general war, or the threat of resort to nuclear war, without risking national suicide *even if it possessed strategic superiority*. The requirements for creating such a condition could be difficult to achieve and depend on predictions of the evolving technological and political environment which are contingent at best.

Stable mutual deterrence, when the defensive power is inferior or even equal to the offensive power, requires *at minimum strategic forces diversified at relatively large weapon inventories and capable of certain and utterly devastating retaliation*. The attacker must know that his survival as a viable nation-state would be put in jeopardy by his surprise or preemptive attack. With respect to the invulnerability of retaliatory capabilities, symmetry is mandatory. But the elusiveness of scientific breakthroughs and the rapid pace of technology may undermine this symmetry by threatening the obsolescence of strategic weapons and of the measures designed to frustrate a successful attack upon them. Thus the potential volatility of military technology promotes a qualitative arms race whose distinguishing feature may be ambiguity of signals between the superpowers about strategic force postures or about intentions to race for superiority or to stabilize at some kind of parity.

## Nuclear Multipolarity and International Stability

In addition to nuclear military technology and the "rules," conventions, and tacit understandings between the major powers, what distinguishes the present international system is the nature of the "signals," or the communication, between the superpowers in the context of the arms race and particularly in nuclear confrontations. For while the composition and the posture of opposing military forces suggest the limits and consequences of nuclear conflict, in a system based on deterrence the political value of nuclear weapons outstrips their military utility.

Deterrence, inherently a threat system, is concerned with the exploitation of potential force. As a strategy of conflict it is, therefore, essentially a universe of bargaining situations—a problem of communication between (or among) enemies in situations short of nuclear war (though bargaining may be even more crucial in intrawar deterrence). Deterrence, involving mutual interests as well as opposition, has for its object persuading an enemy that he should in his own interest avoid certain courses of action. At its purest, deterrence is the "skillful nonuse" of military forces.

Deterrence, while operating on a day-to-day basis, is tested during crises and limited conflicts. It would also operate in nuclear conflicts short of all-out war. Tacit and explicit bargaining by declaration and deed varies with each type of situation but is always present while deterrence prevails. The testing, the production, and the mode of deployment of weapon systems, the declarations of governments about their intended or possible purposes, increases or reductions in military appropriations, the stated willingness of governments to negotiate political conflicts, changes in weapon systems, the content of agreements with allies or neutrals, arms-control negotiations, tacit understandings about the limits of involvement and military action in peripheral clashes are samples of the communication process that serves to signal national intentions and constitutes the deterrent relationship between the superpowers.

Strategic nuclear confrontation in crisis or during limited conflict, on the other hand, is focused and tends toward an eclectic ordering of reciprocal signals. In such a situation, the technological dimension of weapons (for example, warning and control systems) acquires singular meaning from the possibility of accidents, false alarms, mechanical failures, unauthorized acts, *but primarily from the misapprehension of intentions these might occasion.* During the last few years the United States has implemented impressive organizational and technical safeguards, such as fail-safe procedures and permissive links, in the command and control of its nuclear weapons in order to prevent miscalculation. The Soviets too seem to have tight organizational control over their weapons. Nevertheless, acute problems of communication between enemies and allies are inherent in crises and limited conflicts. These problems have been aggravated by the advent of nuclear weapons since decisions might at some point become irreversible by greatly changing the physical and psychological environment in which competing decision-makers operate. It is difficult not to take decisions in the context of on-going situations. When these involve military actions, tactical considerations tend to obscure other equally or more important aspects of policy—such as political and long-range foreign policy objectives.

Reciprocal communication of intentions would be most demanding and fraught with uncertainties during an escalating conflict in which nuclear weapons were used—above all if escalation involved limited strikes against the territory of the superpowers or of a major ally. Communication in such circumstances becomes a form of bargaining indispensable for controlling events so that conflict retains the rationality needed to keep it from spiraling into general war. Deterrence must not, and need not, fail even during nuclear conflict short of all-out or "spasm" war. How demanding the diplomacy of nuclear confrontation it may be seen, however, from the fact that during the last crisis involving the danger of general war the United States did not consult with its allies until after the crisis had set its course.

The difficulties of maintaining the dynamic requirements for a stable deterrent system and the risks of miscalculation in crises and limited conflict would be severely multiplied by an increase in independent nuclear decision centers—which would in turn increase the fragmentation of coalitions and intensify local fears of aggression through regional arms races between traditional enemies or through the ideological involvement of the superpowers. When a bipolar system of deterrence, in which a potentially transitory nuclear standoff (resulting from the neutralization of opposing strategic forces) is the most stable international situation, becomes transformed into a system of several major and/or minor independent nuclear powers, stability is likely to decrease.

The very flexibility of alignment which brought stability to the balance-of-power system could become a serious threat to the maintenance of deterrence. All problems associated with maintaining nuclear stability would remain. Asymmetries in capabilities, military doctrines, and national goals might well become intolerable in a multipolar international system characterized by fluidity of political orientation or alignment and by latent breakthroughs in military technology. Initial experience with military nuclear development suggests that fledgling and adversary powers may not reach deterrent sufficiency at an even pace or with strategic symmetry. The complexity of deterrent calculations would be severely magnified for all powers in the system. Shifting deterrent relationships could confuse the signaling of intentions between the superpowers at tactical and strategic levels. Whatever modalities of nuclear power politics had been fostered between the United States and the Soviet Union by common experience in crisis confrontation might be called into question.

Clearly, whether or not international stability is drastically undermined depends on a host of factors, technological and political, but fundamentally on the pace, characteristics, and dimension of the increase in nuclear capabilities; the likelihood and degree of cooperation between the superpowers in thwarting proliferation; the nature of their involvement in regional conflict; and the recklessness with which additional nuclear capabilities are brandished. Much would depend upon concerted actions by established nuclear powers in preventing a diffusion of nuclear military technology—particularly if breakthroughs make the production of nuclear weapons a much less costly and complicated process.

Because the superpowers predominantly fashion the conventions of the international system, their use of military nuclear technology will crucially influence the behavior of nascent nuclear powers. It has been shown how the drastic and spectacular effects of this military technology and the image of general war it has created in the minds of international decision-makers have blunted the edge of the ideological rivalry between the superpowers and have led to a set of inhibitions reminiscent, in their effects, of the restraints in balance-of-power systems. Quite distinctive and of particular relevance to the subject at hand are the "rules," conventions, and tacit understandings between the superpowers on the *use* of nuclear weapons and related "signals," or the communication between the United States and the Soviet Union in the context of the arms race and during nuclear confrontations. The distinction made between nuclear and other weapons has been pivotal.

Although politically the image of strategic capability was aggressively exploited by Khrushchev, the *deterrent* use of nuclear weapons has been the distinguishing feature of superpower confrontation. While nuclear blackmail could increase an aggressor's political influence, political pressure so generated has not achieved important redistributions of power in the international system. Typically, the brandishing of nuclear threats has been most effective in thwarting attempts to expand political control rather than as a tool for attaining it. In this context, the political asymmetry between a defensive and democratic power and a dictatorial one should be noted. Soviet threats are more likely to be translated into political pressures when directed toward parliamentary democracies. In parliamentary countries, apprehensions and fears about nuclear war can more readily constrain governmental action. For whatever the likelihood of general war, its possibility directly affects domestic as well as international politics.

The actual employment of nuclear weapons in military conflict, even in limited and tactical fashion, would unavoidably restructure the attitudes of national decision-makers with regard to the role of nuclear weapons in international politics and would change the expectations about nuclear war held by leaders in emergent or would-be nuclear powers. These changes would manifest themselves primarily in a reassessment of the likelihood of escalation; and of the role of nuclear deterrence in conventional and limited conflict and in the parlance of crisis confrontation itself.

Whether the use of tactical nuclear weapons could increase their deterrent value with respect to conventional and nuclear aggression or could wash away those inhibitions about expansionist drives that seem to exist because of fears about inadvertent general war cannot be known in advance. But once the "firebreak" between conventional and nuclear weapons, now sanctified by practice, is erased by the use of nuclears, a central tenet of international communication will have been permanently altered.

"Conventions" about the use of nuclear weapons different from those now tacitly held will have to be worked out. Some other kind of obvious and controlling distinction to replace that between nuclear and conventional warfare might have to be discovered or invented and adopted by the nuclear powers to isolate the image of nuclear war from other more flexible and familiar applications of military force to political purpose. The shared risk of general war would remain as an inhibitor of rash political and military action. But at least during the transitional period leading to new, or renewed, expectations about escalation and the role of nuclear weapons, the ability to communicate strategic or policy intentions would be additionally burdened by the abolition of the nuclear conventional bench mark.

Other related understandings between the superpowers might be eliminated or questioned by the use of nuclears. The deterrent construction placed on nuclear weapons has spawned several other guidelines such as sanctuary notions, geographic limitations, a preference for the tactical over the strategic employment of military force, an inclination to choose military over population targets, and a strong reticence by a donor nation to share nuclear weapons without battlefield control. Selective, limited nuclear strikes—and probably also the battlefield use of nuclears—would tend to dissipate such distinctions in the policies of the superpowers and to influence deeply the expectations of other nuclear powers. Nuclear warfare, however limited and restrained, would

herald a basic change in the international competition. It would complicate communication among the nuclear powers in more immediate
ways than would the increase of nuclear powers in a system characterized by deterrent postures. The "noise" of a multilateral nuclear
crisis, and especially of a nuclear conflict, in which one country's tactical move could become another's strategic vulnerability, might swamp
deliberate and rational action.

A confrontation of several nuclear powers, with unequal capabilities
and with varying doctrines of employment, would increase the difficulty
of controlling events if for no other reason than because it might become difficult to ascribe responsibility for nuclear actions. Moreover,
a superpower's relative nuclear plenty, which allows various counterforce options, and an incipient or minor nuclear power's modesty of
means, which tends to dictate reliance on a countervalue strategy, may
lead to urges to preempt and tendencies toward hairtrigger action, especially on the part of the minor power. A superpower's ability to punish a minor but antagonistic nuclear power would depend, *inter alia*,
on the superpower's relationship with its major adversary and would
imply the latter's tacit tolerance of such action. Quite the opposite is likely, however, since a mutuality of interests between the
superpowers is least likely in a system in which their antagonism is the
most prominent feature of international politics and is muted primarily
by prudence dictated by the shared danger of general war.

Tolerance might be forthcoming if the inferior power in question
were an avowed and active enemy of both superpowers and without
ideological ties to either. Such political isolation is rare indeed. On the
contrary, even so-called neutral or nonaligned states may hope for a
measure of nuclear protection from one of the superpowers against a
common enemy. While a multilateral nuclear crisis or conflict in which
the ultimate sanction remained in the hands of the superpowers is both
more complicated and more delicate than those so far experienced in the
cold war, a crisis involving the superpowers and one of several minor
nuclear powers might be more destabilizing still. Each additional nuclear
decision-center increases the requirements for mutual adjustments in
relationships originally maintained solely by the superpowers and tested
anew with each change of leadership in Washington or Moscow.

The crucial variables of future encounters cannot be predicted with
much confidence. Much will depend on the circumstances of the particular crisis or conflict confrontation. The heightened requirements for
decision and the sobering knowledge of the inescapable political and
physical effects of nuclear alternatives might lead contending decision-
makers to examine their "acts of choice in crisis and during [the exami-
nation] to subdivide these possible acts in ways that make it feasible to

continue exercising choice."[57] Yet the use of nuclear weapons in a limited conflict involving several nuclear powers would tend to erode the deterrent relationship of the superpowers, already hedged by technological factors and sapped by ideological commitment.

An international system in which the political strategy of the major powers is acutely dependent on the state of a dynamic military technology is fragile. And it tends more toward national strategic autonomy, or ultimate strategic dependence on the nuclear umbrella of one or another superpower, then toward the aggregate balancing of national units for conquest, defense, or competition.

The peculiar properties of nuclear weapons may not have altered the basic control images of international politics more significantly than has the disruption caused by the rise of communism and its exploitation by expansionist powers in the system. It may be that traditional patterns —those that distinguished the European state system—will reassert themselves when nuclear technology ceases to be "an unsettling innovation" and having found "an equilibrium within its own compass . . . [becomes] absorbed in its larger environment." An international balance of this kind might have come into existence in the form of mutual nuclear deterrence between the Soviet Union and the United States. Beyond the attempt to work out some tacitly recognized rules for strategic confrontation, that is, deterrence doctrine and arms-control notions, however, the institutional response to the extraordinary challenges of the current international situation has been generally ineffective. In the area of political controls and organization, the challenge of nuclear weapons technology has hardly been met.

A regression to prenuclear rationales and methods because of inability to invent control techniques or organizational patterns of international politics appropriate to the new military technology would bode ill for the present system. The challenge to the nation-state system preceded intercontinental missiles and nuclear warheads, and the failure to meet it has been marked by two global, all-out wars. With the invention of nuclear weapons, the challenge has acquired greater urgency, for traditional patterns in the system favor war-fighting over deterrence, and the patterns developed in this century before nuclear weapons favor total over limited conflict.

Survival may not depend on acts taken in the technological sphere. It is decisions that initiate war. But decisions are shaped by the expectations generated by the environment in which leaders operate. And nu-

[57] Albert and Roberta Wohlstetter, *Controlling the Risks in Cuba*, Adelphi Papers 17, Institute for Strategic Studies (April 1965), 19, a stimulating analysis of the 1962 Cuban missile crisis in which the various reciprocal restraints and opportunities are discussed in the context of escalation.

clear technology is an intrinsic and important aspect of international politics.

An international system may be considered stable if it retains all of its essential characteristics; if no single nation becomes dominant; if most of its members survive; and if no all-out war occurs. It is clear that nuclear multipolarity might create conditions whose effects would tend to undermine, not enhance, international stability. How the super-powers adjust to the proliferation of nuclear capabilities among nations may become the real test of the deterrent system, for their behavior is normative. Stability does not depend only upon the number of major powers in the system. Power relationships, political alignments, national objectives, and the conduct of military operations also determine whether the acquisition of nuclear weapons by additional powers undermines stability. Arms competition and political antagonism are constant and normal features of international relations. The skill and timeliness with which the leaders of the major powers adjust to the winds of change may decide, nevertheless, whether the transition to the next international system will be evolutionary or violent.

R O B E R T  K .  A .  G A R D I N E R

## Race and Color in International Relations

I

• • •

War has proved to be the great catalyst of modern international relations. Even apparently inconclusive wars, such as the contemporary conflicts in Southeast Asia, do more to change the relations between na-

SOURCE: Robert K. A. Gardiner, "Race and Color in International Relations," *Daedalus*, XCVI (Spring 1967), 296–311. Reprinted with permission of *Daedalus*, Journal of the American Academy of Arts and Sciences, Boston, Mass. Summer 1967, "Color and Race."

tions—and not only those nations that are directly involved—than any other known phenomenon. This generalization is certainly true of World War I. Even though radical change in the configuration of international affairs had begun before World War I—and indeed helped to bring it about—nothing in international relations was ever the same after the war. Japan had already established itself as a force in world affairs, a fact explicitly recognized by Britain in 1902 when the two countries entered into an alliance, and underlined for all the world to see when Japan defeated Russia in 1905. Lancelot Lawton, writing in 1912, put the rise of Japan into sharp racial perspective when he said:

Japan leads the van in the march of Asia towards the attainment of her ideal, the recognition of equality with the nations of the West. The civilization of Japan may be superficial, but it is a militant civilization. The danger to the West lies in the existence of a state of indifference which may find unpreparedness when the time arrives for the inevitable conflict with the nations of the East. . . . Unless the West awakens to the imminence of danger, the predominance of the white over the yellow races will cease.[3]

Before World War I ended, it was clear that the "European Age" was coming to an end. Symbolic of the changed state of affairs was the United States' decision to enter the lists in 1917, after having pursued a policy of non-involvement in international conflicts during the nineteenth century. The concept of the "balance of power" had been rooted in the assumption of European dominance in world affairs; in 1917 President Woodrow Wilson served notice that the world had ceased to be an arena reserved for the elaborate acrobatics of European power politics. America's intervention—in the First, as in the Second World War—can be seen as a direct result of the recognition that its own security could be threatened by any grave disturbance of the *status quo* in Europe.[4]

Moreover, the United States was acutely aware that the Pacific was going to loom larger and larger in world affairs. "The empire that shifted from the Mediterranean," said Theodore Roosevelt in 1903, "will in the lifetime of those now children bid fair to shift once more westward to the Pacific." And again:

The Mediterranean era died with the discovery of America, the Atlantic era is now at the height of its development and must soon exhaust the resources at its command; the Pacific era, destined to be the greatest of all, is just at its dawn.[5]

[3] Lancelot Lawton, *Empires of the Far East* (London, 1912), cited by C. Northcote Parkinson, *East and West* (New York, 1965).
[4] Cf. Grayson Kirk, "World Perspectives, 1964," *Foreign Affairs* (October, 1964).
[5] Geoffrey Barraclough, *An Introduction to Contemporary History* (London, 1964), p. 70.

By the time that Roosevelt spoke, the United States had become a Pacific power. Its annexation of the Philippines and Guam at the end of the nineteenth century was perhaps a turning point. In 1899, when American Secretary of State John Hay issued his famous "open-door" declaration on Western dealings with China, he was announcing to the European powers—who had been proceeding on the assumption that they could carve up Asia among themselves as they had carved up Africa—that Asia was, indeed, a very different situation. American interests in China and in the Far East in general had now become a vital element in the world power equation. This left no room for the European technique of extending the balance-of-power game beyond Europe, as had been done by the partition of Africa.

Just as the emergence of the United States, Russia, and Japan as Pacific world powers ended the long period of Europe's unquestioned dominance in world affairs and transformed the character of international politics, so, too, the American entry into World War I and the Russian Revolution introduced the beginnings of a new pattern. The United States and Russia had been on the periphery of the international power struggle; they now appeared at the center, armed, moreover, with the beginnings of universal ideologies that were essentially revolutionary in character. With their ideology of "the self-determination of peoples," Wilson's Fourteen Points, says K. M. Pannikar, were "acclaimed as a doctrine of liberation" in Asia. On the other hand, "imperialism meant something totally different after Lenin's definition of it as the last phase of capitalism, and his insistence that the liberation of subject peoples from colonial domination was a part of the struggle against capitalism."[6]

While "the European civil war" of 1914-18 was destroying both Western solidarity and Europe's image outside the West, the peoples who had for so long been the victims of Western dominance were being offered new concepts of their own rights. In the year 1919 alone the "Fourth of May Movement" arose in China, the Destour party was born in Tunisia, and the first Pan-African Congress was held in Paris. By 1919 the nationalist movement in Indonesia had expanded to an organization of some two and a half million people calling for complete independence from the Dutch.

Up to this time, the race element in international conflicts had remained unexpressed. When, however, Japan, admitted as a full participant to the Peace Conference at Versailles in 1919, proposed that racial equality be written into the Covenant of the League of Nations, race came out into the open. The proposal was outvoted, but the point had been made.

[6] K. M. Pannikar, *Asia and Western Dominance* (London, 1953), pp. 199–200.

The Japanese move did not, of course, spring from a purely altruistic concern for the world's non-whites. Japan had its particular axe to grind: Japanese immigration to the West Coast of America had been drastically curtailed in the years preceding World War I. A direct presidential initiative had been needed in 1907, for example, to rescind a 1906 decree by the San Francisco School Board stipulating segregated schools for Japanese children.

The whole question of non-white immigration into white areas has very wide implications for relations between the white and the non-white worlds. Of the two major demands made by Japan at the Versailles Peace Conference, one was for title to its conquest of German-held territory in China's Shantung province, and the other for explicit recognition in the Covenant of the principle of racial equality. It was the property, not the principle, that Japan won.

After the sounding of this initial warning-bell, race was not destined to play an overt part in the working of the League of Nations, although it was impossible to be unaware of its brooding presence in the background of the Italo-Abyssinian conflict. The League itself was, with the exception of Liberia, Ethiopia, China, and Japan, an all-white and predominantly European affair.[7] That this should be so was never questioned even by the more far-sighted. As late as 1926, Sir Frederick (later to be Lord) Lugard could write of "the so-called awakening of the colored races."

What was significant in the evolution of this new attempt at organized and regulated confrontation among the nations of the world was the emergence of group alignments within the League—something that is usually described as the "bloc" system. Five such blocs have been identified in the assemblies of the League: the Latin American, the Commonwealth, the Scandinavian (with the occasional adherence of the Netherlands), and a group comprising Germany, Austria, Hungary, and, later, Italy; looser groupings of Balkan states also appeared from time to time.

The blocs operated as pressure groups or lobbying mechanisms for elections to the Council and to committees of the League. A Nominations Committee was finally established in an attempt to cut down on lobbying, and at the same time to meet the demands of the smaller nations, for whom bloc voting and lobbying had represented a certain "democratic" protection against the power and influence of their larger fellow-members. This committee functioned only during the last three years of the League's existence. The bloc system was to come into its

[7] Philip W. Quigg, *Africa: A Foreign Affairs Reader* (New York, 1964), p. 8.

own again when the United Nations Organization was created after
World War II.[8]

The League's Permanent Mandates Commission was to have tremendous importance for the political development of colored peoples.
The establishment of the mandate system—with its implicit guarantee
of eventual self-determination—and the explicit power of the League
of Nations to intervene in the exercise of the mandate by the mandatory
power introduced a new concept into relations between the dominant
white Westerners and the colored subject peoples. The decision of the
International Court of Justice on the case of South-West Africa is still
topical, as is the subsequent resolution of the U.N. General Assembly
revoking South Africa's mandate. With this exception, whenever a League
mandate was created, the path to eventual independence, passing through
the post-World War II freeway of the Trusteeship Council, has been
clear and unimpeded.

Thus, while the League was not precisely a major factor in the
evolution of international relations during the twenty-odd years that
separated the two World Wars, its influence in the area of dealings
with dependent—and mostly colored—peoples was real and lasting.


II

Churchill had perceived that within less than a year of the ending in
Europe of World War II, "from Stettin in the Baltic to Trieste in the Adri-
atic an iron curtain" had descended. Europe was no longer the center
of the world but, rather, a continent caught in the middle of a conflict
between two non-European super-powers—Russia and the United States.
The "dwarfing of Europe"[9] was progressing on another level as well,
the demographic—a process that had begun, according to some students, toward the end of the nineteenth century.

Demography is not all. Although Europe still maintains the inherent
advantages that its technological superiority conferred upon it (as is
witnessed in the rapid recovery of Western Germany in the postwar
years), this technology is no longer beyond the reach of non-European and non-Westernized countries. Russian, Japanese, and, to a lesser
extent, Communist Chinese examples demonstrate this. It is unlikely
that the two thirds of the world's population that inhabit Asia and Africa,
given the advantage of modern technology and their clearly growing
preoccupation with making that technology their own, will remain

[8] Cf. Thomas Hovet, Jr., *Bloc Politics in the United Nations* (Cambridge, 1960),
pp. 1–3.
[9] Cf. Barraclough, *An Introduction to Contemporary History*, pp. 69ff.

permanently in thrall to the less than 30 per cent known as "the West."

The ideological clash that divides the world into "East" and "West" may, of course, be pursued to the point of the final holocaust that nuclear warfare threatens. But, for the purposes of this discussion, one must assume that mankind will spare itself this suicidal denouement and, predicting survival, try to assess realistically the probable significance of these new facts of the contemporary world.

Demographers maintain, indeed, that for a considerable time to come the rate of growth of the colored two thirds of the world will be higher than that of the white minority. There will very likely be, therefore, increasing pressure from the world's population—and particularly the colored population—on available land space. Probable pressure points and trouble spots are not difficult to pick out. As long ago as the beginning of this century, the "white Australia" policy was introduced to protect what one writer called "a population less than the depleted population of Scotland" against "the congested millions of colored peoples just across the sea."[10] Only recently has legislation been introduced in the United States to mitigate some of the effects of previous laws, the unequivocal purpose of which had been to limit severely the immigration of those same "congested millions of colored peoples." About the same time that this legislation was being passed in the United States Congress, a Socialist government in Britain was preoccupied with measures to control the immigration of colored peoples.

The new states that have come into being since the end of World War II account for one quarter of the world's population; current estimates place the populations of the new Asian states alone at four times that of the European Economic Community. Granted the eventual acquisition of "Western" technology, a radical change has taken place in the world order. There are the beginnings, at least, of a shift of concern to what has been called the "Third World," whose populations are largely non-white. It is a long way from the days when the "Yellow Peril" was the white man's bugbear—when fear of Oriental competition was couched in purely racial terms. The emergence of the new states has provided a new kind of political education for the older members of the international community, and the new states themselves have been learning many of the sobering realities of statehood. Above all, the confrontations between the "Third World" and the old European world provide opportunities for bridging what may be described as the "cultural gap" between them. The very conventions and rituals of legal and diplomatic procedures serve to offer the scope needed for hammering out understanding and respect among nations.

[10] James Marchant, *Birth Rate and Empire* (London, 1917), quoted in Barraclough, *An Introduction to Contemporary History*, p. 76.

The new nations have in common their relative poverty, their underdevelopment; they all possess a technical and organizational capacity inadequate for exploiting their natural and human resources. One cannot strictly say that they have their color in common; yellow-skinned, black-skinned, or brown-skinned people, the bond they share is the fact that they are not white. This negative similarity has become a strong rallying point for them simply because of the experience of recent centuries when the white Westerner became increasingly conscious of himself as white and confidently assumed that his whiteness was a guarantee of his political, technical, and military pre-eminence.

The non-white, non-Western peoples, overwhelmed by the superior efficiency of European technology, accepted at first the white man's estimates—not only of himself, but of themselves also. Later, disillusionment, disgust, and a renewed self-respect set in, and the white man's standards were vehemently rejected. At Bandung in 1955, Jawaharlal Nehru spoke of this reaction when he said:

Has it come to this, that the leaders of thought who have given religion and all kinds of things to the world have to tag onto this kind of group or that, and be hangers-on of this party or the other. . . ? It is an intolerable thought to me that the great countries of Asia and Africa shall have come out of bondage into freedom only to degrade themselves in this way. . . . I will not tie myself to this degradation . . . and become a camp-follower of others.[11]

In Africa the same motives have given rise to the concept of "the African Personality," which is both a rejection of "Westernization" and a reassertion of the values and separate identity of Africa's own cultural heritage.

These movements of rejection and of self-assertion have had, as was to be expected, political repercussions as well. The most famous of these, the Bandung Conference of 1955, had its roots in the emergence of a fairly coherent Afro-Asian group at the United Nations during the Korean crisis of 1950. During the period immediately after World War II, the new nations gradually realized they had at least a number of negative reasons for making common cause in their international relations. President Sukarno said at Bandung: "This is the first intercontinental conference of colored peoples in the history of the world." While there may be several interpretations of the significance of this fact, that it was a fact cannot be disputed. The road from Bandung led to Belgrade, where many of the Bandung nations discovered they could make common cause with nations neither Asian nor African nor colored. It also led, in 1965, to the fruitless Algiers meeting, ruined by an ideological split in the Communist world, by a geographical argument

---

[11] Lawrence W. Martin, *Neutralism and Non-Alignment* (New York, 1962), p. 8.

about who is and who is not Asian, and by China's dilemma of whether to opt for the mantle of the true heir of Marx and Lenin or for that of leader of the "non-white" world.

### III

Though there is some community of interest among the non-white states, it is not a hermetic one. It cannot be hermetic because each of its single components is a country with its own history, culture, and, for the most part, language. The meetings of new partners usually must be conducted in languages not their own, languages borrowed from—or imposed by—former Western rulers; the radical African leader may feel closer to and find it easier to make contact with a Parisian than a Djakartan. One commentator suggests that "for many participants the [Bandung] conference seems to have been attractive as an emotional herding together for mutual reassurance in a puzzling world."[12] When even those nations best equipped in wealth and experience visibly flounder from crisis to crisis, it is not surprising that the new countries —uncertain of their direction, uncertain sometimes of the choices that may exist—should have tried to turn to one another for moral support and enlightenment.

But coherent co-operation between sovereign countries must be based on more than urgent impulses. Nothing less than self-interest will do—or, at least, what is imagined to be self-interest, under whatever guise it may appear, and ideology is perhaps one of its most popular contemporary guises. A variety of impulses has then combined to produce meaningful alignments among the newly emerged nations, just as in postwar Europe a mixture of national motives produced the Rome treaties of 1957.

These new alignments—the Arab League is the oldest, the Organization of African Unity, the youngest—came into being as a result of economic or political or politico-economic imperatives. That regional groupings would and should exist has been explicitly recognized in two twentieth-century attempts to regulate the world order by international organizations. The Covenant of the League of Nations did not affect "the validity of international engagements, such as treaties of arbitration or regional understandings . . . for securing the maintenance of peace"; Article 52 of the Charter of the United Nations makes very much the same provisions.

The workings of what have been called the "caucuses" within the United Nations constitute a separate study in themselves.[13] One school

[12] *Ibid.,* p. xiv.
[13] Cf. Hovet, *Bloc Politics in the United Nations.*

of thought condemns the "bloc" or "caucus" system on the ground that it involves a complicated and sometimes unprincipled process of vote-swapping which frequently leads to issues being neither debated nor voted upon according to their real merits. Another school contends that in a large organization such as the United Nations this kind of arrangement actually facilitates the process of negotiation and compromise which is an unavoidable element in international relations once the possibility of coercion is removed. It can also be argued, with some cogency, that the presence of many such groups in an international organization could obviate any tendency toward excessively rigid divisions on major issues. Flexibility and real regard for the different nuances in any given question would, thereby, be increased, resulting in greater possibilities of solution or compromise. This is a very significant thought which, logically extended, may be helpful in examining some of the directions international relations may take in the future.

In the context of the postwar world, one of the most striking multinational groupings is the Commonwealth of Nations. Starting life under the aegis of the Westminster Statute of 1931 as a loose association of Anglo-Saxon states, individually called dominions but collectively retaining the style of empire, this group now boasts an embryonic full-time Secretariat headed by an American from Canada and an African from Ghana.

The turning point for the "British" Commonwealth came in 1947, when the former imperial domain of India became the two independent states of India and Pakistan. Strains on the imperial concept, though of a significantly different sort, had, however, already begun to be felt in the first decades of this century. In the process of growing into their own sovereign personalities, Australia, New Zealand, and Canada, once the purest of imperial outposts, had learned that the essential problems of their independence could no longer be regulated from London; that the demographic pressures of the Far East and the geopolitical realities of life for an independent state in the Pacific were not European; that they must, on balance, be more sensitive to what was happening in the White House than to what was happening in Whitehall. Thus, the Commonwealth was one of the first political entities to reflect the weakening of European world hegemony.

When independence was granted to India and Pakistan, a new era decisively began. How new was even then not clearly visible; the lessons of Australia, New Zealand, and Canada had not been interpreted as pointing to an ultimate breakup of the Commonwealth. A Labour member of Parliament, Mr. Patrick Gordon-Walker, said in 1947 that while Mr. Churchill might "throw away" the Empire as George III had done with the American colonies, the Labour Government's aim was to "save it" by giving the colonies self-government. "If this plan comes off, the empire will be a very powerful idea indeed."[14] Mr. Gordon-Walker's idea was one of a multiracial community of free nations. In this sense, the British Commonwealth represents an experiment of capital importance for mankind, crowded together as it is on one planet.

The independence of Pakistan and India differed in quality from that which the "white dominions" had enjoyed up to that time. These countries were not tied to Britain by bonds of race; how was it, then, that despite the geopolitical pressures, despite the lack of racial affinity, these countries opted to remain in association with the former imperial power? The answer is complex, and possibly not fully known, though self-interest obviously played a role in this development.

The postwar Commonwealth has proved again that race is not the indispensable cement of international groupings. It has proved this positively, by the adherence of India and other republics—plus one independent federation, Malaysia. The 1965 war between India and Pakistan is negative proof of the fragility of racial bonds.

While the Commonwealth was fumbling along on its pragmatic path, theorists in continental Europe were at work. "Imagine," they said to themselves, "if 220,000,000 Africans and 200,000,000 Europeans could get together into an economic unit. With Europe's skills and techniques, and Africa's raw materials, one could create potentially the most powerful single bloc in the world."[15] The origins of the Eurafrica concept go back some forty years. Vernon McKay cites a book published in 1933 by a French writer, Eugene Guernier, entitled *L'Afrique —Champ d'expansion de l'Europe*. This work argues that a "longitudinal" view of geopolitics would make of Europe and Africa, after the immigration of fifteen to twenty million Europeans into Africa, one of these intercontinental units. Germany, too, got into the act; one German publicist cited by McKay called, in 1952, "for a strong Franco-German nucleus of a European community, without Britain, for the common exploitation of African resources." Europeanists in the United States seemed to subscribe to this idea on the assumption that Latin America was the special responsibility of the United States, and that Africa should be a special sphere of interest for Europe.

Several versions of this concept became current after World War II. They all had one thing in common: Europe came first; Africa, second. Africa was to be "Europe's dowry," a means of redressing Europe's losses "without the burdens of the colonial relationships."[16] Strategic considerations also came into play. "Africa is the natural complement

[14] Quoted in Vernon McKay, *Africa in World Politics* (New York, 1964), p. 27.
[15] Cf. *Ibid.*, pp. 124–37.
[16] *Ibid.*

of, and is vital to the defense, life, and subsistence of Europe," wrote a French commentator in 1957.

The French Community, inaugurated under President de Gaulle's Fifth Republic and buttressed by the association of former French dependencies with the European Common Market, provided a combination of the ideas of Eurafrica with the basic assumption of the British Commonwealth. First, Guinea chose independence outside the Community; not long after, the other eleven African members took the same road. Present trends are toward regional co-operation, with accompanying regional consciousness and regional pride, as expressed in the Organization of African Unity. But an association of Francophone countries is still an aspiration shared by France with her former dependencies. There is, therefore, the possibility of a world-wide French-speaking association based on historical and cultural links. African states that were former British or French dependencies must somehow reconcile their belonging to a British Commonwealth or a worldwide Franco-phone organization with their allegiance to the O.A.U. In a way, Britain and France face the same problem: how to be European states while belonging to non-European communities.

IV

Contemporary history throws a somewhat ambiguous light on the relationship between race and international affairs. At a given time, in a given situation, race will seem to have been a major consideration in the actions of nations. Yet in situations where the racial factor might be expected to dominate, nations are often guided by quite different considerations. Indeed, it is sometimes impossible to determine where to draw the line between race considerations and the ties of history and culture which can bring nations together.

This is illustrated by the case of white Australia. The European-settled subcontinent has recognized that its destiny is a Pacific destiny. In the past, Australia never thought of seeking an accommodation or understanding with its Pacific-Asian neighbors. Rather, Australia and New Zealand sought first the protection of the powerful British navy and then turned their eyes toward the United States. Were they appealing to their "kith and kin," or were they drawn by affinities of culture and history? What explains the near-panic at the turn of the century that led to the introduction of the "white Australia" policy? The sense of isolation in a "yellow sea" must have exacerbated the natural wish to have the protection and support of the "like" and to fend off what may have seemed the inevitable "swamping" of their country by "yellow hordes." Fifty years later, when the ANZUS security pact was signed by the United

States, Australia, and New Zealand, was it not possible to detect under-tones of white solidarity in the face of the "yellow masses" pressing on the Australasian subcontinent? It is hard to say; a similar treaty was signed with the brown-yellow Philippines. Also, the allies of the United States in the current Viet-Nam war consist of brown-yellow Southeast Asians as well as the white dominions.

Clearly it is difficult—sometimes impossible—to draw the line be-tween economic, political, and military motivations. The European Eco-nomic Community faces Comecon in an ideological as much as an economic confrontation. The Alliance for Progress was as much a political as an economic initiative. The growing disparity between the rich and the poor nations plays an important part in the ideological and power contest between the two megaliths of East and West. The economic contest has produced its own set of alignments. Aid has become a po-tent weapon in the struggle for allegiances, and the poor countries are gradually organizing themselves to ensure that they get from it the greatest benefit and the least harm, and avoid external economic, military, or ideological domination.

At the same time one cannot ignore a persistent feature of the age —the growing economic interdependence of communities. In the words of Thorsten Veblen, "As things stand now, no civilized country's in-dustrial system will work in isolation. . . . As an industrial unit, the nation is out of date." The case may be a little overstated, but it is true that industrial technology knows no borders and contains within itself the dynamic of internationalism. These developments, together with the growth of trade, are gradually but relentlessly forcing nations and races toward interdependence. Although the world is still very far from Gunnar Myrdal's dream of a "world economy," the volume and scope of contemporary international trade and its growth carry implica-tions of greater and greater international contacts and relations. Be-cause of this interdependence, it is permissible to look at the rules and regulations that govern international trade as a sort of universal "social contract."

There is also evidence of a trend toward an epoch of what can only be called universalism, some aspects of which are sometimes described as the "Americanization" of the world. Its overt forms are addiction to American ideas in dress, in the popular arts, in commercial design, and even in speech and mannerisms copied from film stars. This is effect. Two of the main causes would seem to be the tremendous material pre-ponderance of the United States in practically every area of life in this century, and the revolutionary developments that have taken place in international communications.

One cannot escape, however, the conviction that these are not more than the mechanics of the matter. Behind the mechanics there must be some quality in human nature that craves assimilation with its like. That the craving has so far found its satisfaction only in the more restricted groups of family or tribe or nation is an accident of geography and history. The economist's concept of the demonstration effect that applies equally within societies as among societies is a recognition of this tendency to imitate. In the past, the model, not the will, has been lacking, a lack which contemporary technologies have finally filled. Indeed, it is only partially accurate to speak of Americanization in this context. The victories of American soft drinks and blue jeans are easily matched by the conquests of the espresso machine, Zen Buddhism, the Calypso, and judo.

In the field of scholarship, institutions of higher education are now springing up in all parts of the world. The world of learning is, therefore, becoming truly universal. Guided by the principles of scientific objectivity, its members will appeal "neither to prejudice nor to authority," nor will they "confuse . . . the subjects [about] which they argue with race, politics, sex, or age."[17] These principles have been so conscientiously observed that Professor Jacob Bronowski is able to say: "A scientist who breaks this rule . . . is ignored. A scientist who finds that the rule has been broken in his laboratory . . . kills himself."[18] This is not only a comfort in a bewildering world but grounds for hope that the realization of world peace through the rule of law is not utopian.

The world is without doubt now approaching a stage where the rapid social and intellectual assimilation of all its inhabitants into a world community will be possible. Within this community there will be differences. One shall continue to observe a distinction but not a contradiction between the spirit of the community (*Volkgeist*) and the spirit of the age (*Zeitgeist*). It is also reasonable to accept that there will be a world outlook (*Weltanschauung*) all peoples can share.

There are some who hold the view that racism can ultimately be eliminated only through a process of wholesale miscegenation. This is, essentially, a sentimental analysis that both denies the countless crossings of the race barriers humane people have accomplished throughout history and ignores the occurrence of civil war, not to mention fratricide. The mixture of races is not a necessary precondition to international understanding. At the same time, the intermingling of all the strands of the human race would seem a natural outcome of the spreading of the media of mass communication and the speed of modern transportation.

[17] Jacob Bronowski, *Science and Human Values* (London, 1958), p. 64.
[18] *Ibid.*

The late President Kennedy drew attention to the common lot of man in the twentieth century when he said in his address to the General Assembly of the United Nations in 1961:

A nuclear disaster spread by wind and water and fear could well engulf the great and the small, the rich and the poor, the committed and the uncommitted alike. . . . We in this hall shall be remembered either as part of the generation that turned this planet into a flaring funeral pyre or the generation that met its vow to save succeeding generations from the scourge of war.[19]

Now that at least one non-white country has joined the ranks of nuclear powers—and others have the technology to do likewise—President Kennedy's words have an even more urgent ring. "Colored" and "white" both have their hands on the nuclear trigger. In the midst of these inexorable and irreversible processes, race or color scarcely qualifies as a decisive agent.

If I am optimistic about the long term, I am far less so about the short term. In what I call the short term—say, the next twenty-five years—the world will have to face the realities of the situations in Rhodesia and in South Africa. These will remain matrices of conflict between white and non-white nations. Battle lines will be drawn, roughly, along the emplacements of the now nearly ended colonial struggle. Added to this are the new tensions of race or tribe to be seen in some of the newly independent African countries and in certain parts of Southeast Asia. These are such bitter and dangerous conflicts that it is sometimes difficult to see them in the proper light and context.

The world is being obliged, through its increasing mastery over its resources and its increasing knowledge of itself, to regard itself as "one." Separate groupings of nations are more and more becoming just one aspect of a world society. This process of becoming "one" calls for action at various levels and in many spheres. It is of paramount importance that within states or communities discrimination be eliminated —especially in education, employment, housing, and the administration of justice. Between states, two steps have already been taken toward the building of a society of nations: the acceptance of the principle of self-determination of peoples and the respect for the sovereignty of states, however weak or poor. Efforts of communities to meet their daily needs in the economic field are both facilitating and making necessary the development of "one" world. The physical threat to the survival of the human race is terrifying. The greatest challenge to mankind is how to foster adjustments in conventional outlook and in minimum standards of be-

[19] Quoted in Arthur Schlesinger, Jr., *A Thousand Days: John F. Kennedy in the White House* (New York, 1965), p. 427.

havior in a fragmented world moving toward unity. Unity must not be confused with uniformity. It would be as absurd to expect a standard human type as to expect a uniform world culture. A world of free men must be a world of diversity.

HENRY A. KISSINGER

# Domestic Structure and Foreign Policy

## I. The Role of Domestic Structure

In the traditional conception, international relations are conducted by political units treated almost as personalities. The domestic structure is taken as given; foreign policy begins where domestic policy ends.

But this approach is appropriate only to stable periods because then the various components of the international system generally have similar conceptions of the "rules of the game." If the domestic structures are based on commensurable notions of what is just, a consensus about permissible aims and methods of foreign policy develops. If domestic structures are reasonably stable, temptations to use an adventurous foreign policy to achieve domestic cohesion are at a minimum. In these conditions, leaders will generally apply the same criteria and hold similar views about what constitutes a "reasonable" demand. This does not guarantee agreement, but it provides the condition for a meaningful dialogue, that is, it sets the stage for traditional diplomacy.

When the domestic structures are based on fundamentally different conceptions of what is just, the conduct of international affairs grows more complex. Then it becomes difficult even to define the nature of

SOURCE: Henry A. Kissinger, "Domestic Structure and Foreign Policy," *Daedalus*, XCV (Spring 1966), 503–529. Reprinted with permission of *Daedalus*, Journal of the American Academy of Arts and Sciences, Boston, Mass. Spring 1966, "Conditions of World Order."

disagreement because what seems most obvious to one side appears most problematic to the other. A policy dilemma arises because the pros and cons of a given course seem evenly balanced. The definition of what constitutes a problem and what criteria are relevant in "solving" it reflects to a considerable extent the domestic notions of what is just, the pressures produced by the decision-making process, and the experience which forms the leaders in their rise to eminence. When domestic structures—and the concept of legitimacy on which they are based—differ widely, statesmen can still meet, but their ability to persuade has been reduced for they no longer speak the same language.

This can occur even when no universal claims are made. Incompatible domestic structures can passively generate a gulf, simply because of the difficulty of achieving a consensus about the nature of "reasonable" aims and methods. But when one or more states claim universal applicability for their particular structure, schisms grow deep indeed. In that event, the domestic structure becomes not only an obstacle to understanding but one of the principal issues in international affairs. Its requirements condition the conception of alternatives; survival seems involved in every dispute. The symbolic aspect of foreign policy begins to overshadow the substantive component. It becomes difficult to consider a dispute "on its merits" because the disagreement seems finally to turn not on a specific issue but on a set of values as expressed in domestic arrangements. The consequences of such a state of affairs were explained by Edmund Burke during the French Revolution:

I never thought we could make peace with the system; because it was not for the sake of an object we pursued in rivalry with each other, but with the system itself that we were at war. As I understood the matter, we were at war not with its conduct but with its existence; convinced that its existence and its hostility were the same.[1]

Of course, the domestic structure is not irrelevant in any historical period. At a minimum, it determines the amount of the total social effort which can be devoted to foreign policy. The wars of the kings who governed by divine right were limited because feudal rulers, bound by customary law, could not levy income taxes or conscript their subjects. The French Revolution, which based its policy on a doctrine of popular will, mobilized resources on a truly national scale for the first time. This was one of the principal reasons for the startling successes of French arms against a hostile Europe which possessed greater over-all power. The ideological regimes of the twentieth century have utilized a still larger share of the national effort. This has enabled

[1] Edmund Burke, *Works* (London, 1826), Vol. VIII, pp. 214–215.

them to hold their own against an environment possessing far superior resources.

Aside from the allocation of resources, the domestic structure crucially affects the way the actions of other states are interpreted. To some extent, of course, every society finds itself in an environment not of its own making and has some of the main lines of its foreign policy imposed on it. Indeed, the pressure of the environment can grow so strong that it permits only one interpretation of its significance; Prussia in the eighteenth century and Israel in the contemporary period may have found themselves in this position.

But for the majority of states the margin of decision has been greater. The actual choice has been determined to a considerable degree by their interpretation of the environment and by their leaders' conception of alternatives. Napoleon rejected peace offers beyond the dreams of the kings who had ruled France by "divine right" because he was convinced that *any* settlement which demonstrated the limitations of his power was tantamount to his downfall. That Russia seeks to surround itself with a belt of friendly states in Eastern Europe is a product of geography and history. That it is attempting to do so by imposing a domestic structure based on a particular ideology is a result of conceptions supplied by its domestic structure.

The domestic structure is decisive finally in the elaboration of positive goals. The most difficult, indeed tragic, aspect of foreign policy is how to deal with the problem of conjecture. When the scope for action is greatest, knowledge on which to base such action is small or ambiguous. When knowledge becomes available, the ability to affect events is usually at a minimum. In 1936, no one could know whether Hitler was a misunderstood nationalist or a maniac. By the time certainty was achieved, it had to be paid for with millions of lives.

The conjectural element of foreign policy—the need to gear actions to an assessment that cannot be proved true when it is made—is never more crucial than in a revolutionary period. Then, the old order is obviously disintegrating while the shape of its replacement is highly uncertain. Everything depends, therefore, on some conception of the future. But varying domestic structures can easily produce different assessments of the significance of existing trends and, more importantly, clashing criteria for resolving these differences. This is the dilemma of our time.

Problems are novel; their scale is vast; their nature is often abstract and always psychological. In the past, international relations were confined to a limited geographic area. The various continents pursued their relations essentially in isolation from each other. Until the eighteenth century, other continents impinged on Europe only sporadically and for relatively brief periods. And when Europe extended its sway over much of the world, foreign policy became limited to the Western Powers with the single exception of Japan. The international system of the nineteenth century was to all practical purposes identical with the concert of Europe.

The period after World War II marks the first era of truly global foreign policy. Each major state is capable of producing consequences in every part of the globe by a direct application of its power or because ideas can be transmitted almost instantaneously or because ideological rivalry gives vast symbolic significance even to issues which are minor in geopolitical terms. The mere act of adjusting perspectives to so huge a scale would produce major dislocations. This problem is compounded by the emergence of so many new states. Since 1945, the number of participants in the international system has nearly doubled. In previous periods the addition of even one or two new states tended to lead to decades of instability until a new equilibrium was established and accepted. The emergence of scores of new states has magnified this difficulty many times over.

These upheavals would be challenge enough, but they are overshadowed by the risks posed by modern technology. Peace is maintained through the threat of mutual destruction based on weapons for which there has been no operational experience. Deterrence—the policy of preventing an action by confronting the opponent with risks he is unwilling to run—depends in the first instance on psychological criteria. What the potential aggressor believes is more crucial than what is objectively true. Deterrence occurs above all in the minds of men.

To achieve an international consensus on the significance of these developments would be a major task even if domestic structures were comparable. It becomes especially difficult when domestic structures differ widely and when universal claims are made on behalf of them. A systematic assessment of the impact of domestic structure on the conduct of international affairs would have to treat such factors as historical traditions, social values, and the economic system. But this would far transcend the scope of an article. For the purposes of this discussion we shall confine ourselves to sketching the impact of two factors only: administrative structure and the formative experience of leadership groups.

## II. The Impact of the Administrative Structure

In the contemporary period, the very nature of the governmental structure introduces an element of rigidity which operates more or less independently of the convictions of statesmen or the ideology which they represent. Issues are too complex and relevant facts too manifold to be dealt with on the basis of personal intuition. An institutionalization of decision-making is an inevitable by-product of the risks of international affairs in the nuclear age. Moreover, almost every modern state is dedicated to some theory of "planning"—the attempt to structure the future by understanding and, if necessary, manipulating the environment. Planning involves a quest for predictability and, above all, for "objectivity." There is a deliberate effort to reduce the relevant elements of a problem to a standard of average performance. The vast bureaucratic mechanisms that emerge develop a momentum and a vested interest of their own. As they grow more complex, their internal standards of operation are not necessarily commensurable with those of other countries or even with other bureaucratic structures in the same country. There is a trend toward autarky. A paradoxical consequence may be that increased control over the domestic environment is purchased at the price of loss of flexibility in international affairs.

• • •

The rigidity in the policies of the technologically advanced societies is in no small part due to the complexity of decision-making. Crucial problems may—and frequently do—go unrecognized for a long time. But once the decision-making apparatus has disgorged a policy, it becomes very difficult to change it. The alternative to the *status quo* is the prospect of repeating the whole anguishing process of arriving at decisions. This explains to some extent the curious phenomenon that decisions taken with enormous doubt and perhaps with a close division become practically sacrosanct once adopted. The whole administrative machinery swings behind their implementation as if activity could still all doubts.

Moreover, the reputation, indeed the political survival, of most leaders depends on their ability to realize their goals, however these may have been arrived at. Whether these goals are desirable is relatively less crucial. The time span by which administrative success is measured is considerably shorter than that by which historical achievement is determined. In heavily bureaucratized societies all pressures emphasize the first of these accomplishments.

Then, too, the staffs on which modern executives come to depend develop a momentum of their own. What starts out as an aid to decision-makers often turns into a practically autonomous organization whose internal problems structure and sometimes compound the issues which it was originally designed to solve. The decision-maker will always be aware of the morale of his staff. Though he has the authority, he cannot overrule it too frequently without impairing its efficiency;

and he may, in any event, lack the knowledge to do so. Placating the staff then becomes a major preoccupation of the executive. A form of administrative democracy results, in which a decision often reflects an attainable consensus rather than substantive conviction (or at least the two imperceptibly merge). The internal requirements of the bureaucracy may come to predominate over the purposes which it was intended to serve. This is probably even more true in highly institutionalized Communist states—such as the U.S.S.R.—than in the United States.

When the administrative machine grows very elaborate, the various levels of the decision-making process are separated by chasms which are obscured from the outside world by the complexity of the apparatus. Research often becomes a means to buy time and to assuage consciences. Studying a problem can turn into an escape from coming to grips with it. In the process, the gap between the technical competence of research staffs and what hard-pressed political leaders are capable of absorbing widens constantly. This heightens the insecurity of the executive and may thus compound either rigidity or arbitrariness or both. In many fields—strategy being a prime example—decision-makers may find it difficult to give as many hours to a problem as the expert has had years to study it. The ultimate decision often depends less on knowledge than on the ability to brief the top adminstrator—to present the facts in such a way that they can be absorbed rapidly. The effectiveness of briefing, however, puts a premium on theatrical qualities. Not everything that sounds plausible is correct, and many things which are correct may not sound plausible when they are first presented; and a second hearing is rare. The stage aspect of briefing may leave the decision-maker with a gnawing feeling of having been taken—even, and perhaps especially, when he does not know quite how.

Sophistication may thus encourage paralysis or a crude popularization which defeats its own purpose. The excessively theoretical approach of many research staffs overlooks the problem of the strain of decision-making in times of crisis. What is relevant for policy depends not only on academic truth but also on what can be implemented under stress. The technical staffs are frequently operating in a framework of theoretical standards while in fact their usefulness depends on essentially psychological criteria. To be politically meaningful, their proposals must involve answers to the following types of questions: Does the executive understand the proposal? Does he believe in it? Does he accept it as a guide to action or as an excuse for doing nothing? But if these kinds of concerns are given too much weight, the requirements of salesmanship will defeat substance.

The pragmatism of executives thus clashes with the theoretical bent of research or planning staffs. Executives as a rule take cognizance of a problem only when it emerges as an administrative issue. They thus unwittingly encourage bureaucratic contests as the only means of generating decisions. Or the various elements of the bureaucracy make a series of nonaggression pacts with each other and thus reduce the decision-maker to a benevolent constitutional monarch. As the special role of the executive increasingly becomes to choose between proposals generated administratively, decision-makers turn into arbiters rather than leaders. Whether they wait until a problem emerges as an administrative issue or until a crisis has demonstrated the irrelevance of the standard operating procedure, the modern decision-makers often find themselves the prisoners of their advisers.

Faced with an administrative machine which is both elaborate and fragmented, the executive is forced into essentially lateral means of control. Many of his public pronouncements, though ostensibly directed to outsiders, perform a perhaps more important role in laying down guidelines for the bureaucracy. The chief significance of a foreign policy speech by the President may thus be that it settles an internal debate in Washington (a public statement is more useful for this purpose than an administrative memorandum because it is harder to reverse). At the same time, the bureaucracy's awareness of this method of control tempts it to shortcut its debates by using pronouncements by the decision-makers as charters for special purposes. The executive thus finds himself confronted by proposals for public declarations which may be innocuous in themselves—and whose bureaucratic significance may be anything but obvious—but which can be used by some agency or department to launch a study or program which will restrict his freedom of decision later on.

All of this drives the executive in the direction of extra-bureaucratic means of decision. The practice of relying on special emissaries or personal envoys is an example; their status outside the bureaucracy frees them from some of its restraints. International agreements are sometimes possible only by ignoring safeguards against capricious action. It is a paradoxical aspect of modern bureaucracies that their quest for objectivity and calculability often leads to impasses which can be overcome only by essentially arbitrary decisions.

Such a mode of operation would involve a great risk of stagnation even in "normal" times. It becomes especially dangerous in a revolutionary period. For then, the problems which are most obtrusive may be least relevant. The issues which are most significant may not be suitable for administrative formulation and even when formulated may not lend themselves to bureaucratic consensus. When the issue is how to transform the existing framework, routine can become an additional obstacle to both comprehension and action.

This problem, serious enough *within* each society, is magnified in the conduct of international affairs. While the formal machinery of decision-making in developed countries shows many similarities, the criteria which influence decisions vary enormously. With each administrative machine increasingly absorbed in its own internal problems, diplomacy loses its flexibility. Leaders are extremely aware of the problems of placating their own bureaucracy; they cannot depart too far from its prescriptions without raising serious morale problems. Decisions are reached so painfully that the very anguish of decision-making acts as a brake on the give-and-take of traditional diplomacy.

This is true even *within* alliances. Meaningful consultation with other nations becomes very difficult when the internal process of decision-making already has some of the characteristics of compacts between quasi-sovereign entities. There is an increasing reluctance to hazard a hard-won domestic consensus in an international forum.

What is true within alliances—that is, among nations which have at least some common objectives—becomes even more acute in relations between antagonistic states or blocs. The gap created when two large bureaucracies generate goals largely in isolation from each other and on the basis of not necessarily commensurable criteria is magnified considerably by an ideological schism. The degree of ideological fervor is not decisive; the problem would exist even if the original ideological commitment had declined on either or both sides. The criteria for bureaucratic decision-making may continue to be influenced by ideology even after its élan has dissipated. Bureaucratic structures generate their own momentum which may more than counterbalance the loss of earlier fanaticism. In the early stages of a revolutionary movement, ideology is crucial and the accident of personalities can be decisive. The Reign of Terror in France was ended by the elimination of a single man, Robespierre. The Bolshevik revolution could hardly have taken place had Lenin not been on the famous train which crossed Germany into Russia. But once a revolution becomes institutionalized, the administrative structures which it has spawned develop their own vested interests. Ideology may grow less significant in creating commitment; it becomes pervasive in supplying criteria of administrative choice. Ideologies prevail by being taken for granted. Orthodoxy substitutes for conviction and produces its own form of rigidity.

In such circumstances, a meaningful dialogue across ideological dividing lines becomes extraordinarily difficult. The more elaborate the administrative structure, the less relevant an individual's view becomes —indeed one of the purposes of bureaucracy is to liberate decision-making from the accident of personalities. Thus while personal convictions may be modified, it requires a really monumental effort to alter bureaucratic commitments. And if change occurs, the bureaucracy prefers to move at its own pace and not be excessively influenced by statements or pressures of foreigners. For all these reasons, diplomacy tends to become rigid or to turn into an abstract bargaining process based on largely formal criteria such as "splitting the difference." Either course is self-defeating: the former because it negates the very purpose of diplomacy; the latter because it subordinates purpose to technique and because it may encourage intransigence. Indeed, the incentive for intransigence increases if it is known that the difference will generally be split.

Ideological differences are compounded because major parts of the world are only in the first stages of administrative evolution. Where the technologically advanced countries suffer from the inertia of over-administration, the developing areas often lack even the rudiments of effective bureaucracy. Where the advanced countries may drown in "facts," the emerging nations are frequently without the most elementary knowledge needed for forming a meaningful judgment or for implementing it once it has been taken. Where large bureaucracies operate in alternating spurts of rigidity and catastrophic (in relation to the bureaucracy) upheaval, the new states tend to take decisions on the basis of almost random pressures. The excessive institutionalization of one and the inadequate structure of the other inhibit international stability.

## III. The Nature of Leadership

Whatever one's view about the degree to which choices in international affairs are "objectively" determined, the decisions are made by individuals who will be above all conscious of the seeming multiplicity of options. Their understanding of the nature of their choice depends on many factors, including their experience during the rise to eminence.

The mediating, conciliatory style of British policy in the nineteenth century reflected, in part, the qualities encouraged during careers in Parliament and the values of a cohesive leadership group connected by ties of family and common education. The hysterical cast of the policy of Imperial Germany was given impetus by a domestic structure in which political parties were deprived of responsibility while ministers were obliged to balance a monarch by divine right against a Parliament composed of representatives without any prospect of ever holding office. Consensus could be achieved most easily through fits of national passion which in turn disquieted all of Germany's neighbors. Germany's foreign policy grew unstable because its domestic structure did little to discourage capricious improvisations; it may even have put a premium on them.

The collapse of the essentially aristocratic conception of foreign policy of the nineteenth century has made the career experiences of leaders even more crucial. An aristocracy—if it lives up to its values—will reject the arbitrariness of absolutist rule; and it will base itself on a notion of quality which discourages the temptations of demagoguery inherent in plebiscitarian democracy. Where position is felt to be a birthright, generosity is possible (though not guaranteed); flexibility is not inhibited by a commitment to perpetual success. Where a leader's estimate of himself is not completely dependent on his standing in an administrative structure, measures can be judged in terms of a conception of the future rather than of an almost compulsive desire to avoid even a temporary setback. When statesmen belonged to a community transcending national boundaries, there tended to be consensus on the criteria of what constituted a reasonable proposal. This did not prevent conflicts, but it did define their nature and encourage dialogue. The bane of aristocratic foreign policy was the risk of frivolousness, of a self-confidence unrelated to knowledge, and of too much emphasis on intuition.

In any event, ours is the age of the expert or the charismatic leader. The expert has his constituency—those who have a vested interest in commonly held opinions; elaborating and defining its consensus at a high level has, after all, made him an expert. Since the expert is often the product of the administrative dilemmas described earlier, he is usually in a poor position to transcend them. The charismatic leader, on the other hand, needs a perpetual revolution to maintain his position. Neither the expert nor the charismatic leader operates in an environment which puts a premium on long-range conceptions or on generosity or on subordinating the leader's ego to purposes which transcend his own career.

Leadership groups are formed by at least three factors: their experiences during their rise to eminence; the structure in which they must operate; the values of their society. Three contemporary types will be discussed here: (a) the bureaucratic-pragmatic type, (b) the ideological type, and (c) the revolutionary-charismatic type.

*Bureaucratic-pragmatic leadership.* The main example of this type of leadership is the American élite—though the leadership groups of other Western countries increasingly approximate the American pattern. Shaped by a society without fundamental social schisms (at least until the race problem became visible) and the product of an environment in which most recognized problems have proved soluble, its approach to policy is *ad hoc*, pragmatic, and somewhat mechanical.

Because pragmatism is based on the conviction that the context of events produces a solution, there is a tendency to await developments. The belief is prevalent that every problem will yield if attacked with sufficient energy. It is inconceivable, therefore, that delay might result in irretrievable disaster; at worst it is thought to require a redoubled effort later on. Problems are segmented into constituent elements, each of which is dealt with by experts in the special difficulty it involves. There is little emphasis or concern for their interrelationship. Technical issues enjoy more careful attention, and receive more sophisticated treatment, than political ones. Though the importance of intangibles is affirmed in theory, it is difficult to obtain a consensus on which factors are significant and even harder to find a meaningful mode for dealing with them. Things are done because one knows how to do them and not because one ought to do them. The criteria for dealing with trends which are conjectural are less well developed than those for immediate crises. Pragmatism, at least in its generally accepted form, is more concerned with method than with judgment; or rather it seeks to reduce judgment to methodology and value to knowledge.

This is reinforced by the special qualities of the professions—law and business—which furnish the core of the leadership groups in America. Lawyers—at least in the Anglo-Saxon tradition—prefer to deal with actual rather than hypothetical cases; they have little confidence in the possibility of stating a future issue abstractly. But planning by its very nature is hypothetical. Its success depends precisely on the ability to transcend the existing framework. Lawyers may be prepared to undertake this task; but they will do well in it only to the extent that they are able to overcome the special qualities encouraged by their profession. What comes naturally to lawyers in the Anglo-Saxon tradition is the sophisticated analysis of a series of *ad hoc* issues which emerge as problems through adversary proceedings. In so far as lawyers draw on the experience which forms them, they have a bias toward awaiting developments and toward operating within the definition of the problem as formulated by its chief spokesmen.

This has several consequences. It compounds the already powerful tendencies within American society to identify foreign policy with the solution of immediate issues. It produces great refinement of issues as they arise, but it also encourages the administrative dilemmas described earlier. Issues are dealt with only as the pressure of events imposes the need for resolving them. Then, each of the contending factions within the bureaucracy has a maximum incentive to state its case in its most extreme form because the ultimate outcome depends, to a considerable extent, on a bargaining process. The premium placed on advocacy turns decision-making into a series of adjustments among special interests— a process more suited to domestic than to foreign policy. This procedure neglects the long-range because the future has no administrative constituency and is, therefore, without representation in the adversary proceedings. Problems tend to be slighted until some agency or department is made responsible for them. When this occurs—usually when a difficulty has already grown acute—the relevant department becomes an all-out spokesman for its particular area of responsibility. The outcome usually depends more on the pressures of the persuasiveness of the contending advocates than on a concept of over-all purpose. While these tendencies exist to some extent in all bureaucracies they are particularly pronounced in the American system of government.

This explains in part the peculiar alternation of rigidity and spasms of flexibility in American diplomacy. On a given issue—be it the Berlin crisis or disarmament or the war in Viet-Nam—there generally exists a great reluctance to develop a negotiating position or a statement of objectives except in the most general terms. This stems from a desire not to prejudge the process of negotiations and above all to retain flexibility in the face of unforeseeable events. But when an approaching conference or some other pressures make the development of a position imperative and some office or individual is assigned the specific task, a sudden change occurs. Both personal and bureaucratic success are then identified with bringing the particular assignment to a conclusion. Where so much stock is placed in negotiating skill, a failure of a conference may be viewed as a reflection on the ability of the negotiator rather than on the objective difficulty of the subject. Confidence in the bargaining process causes American negotiators to be extremely sensitive to the tactical requirements of the conference table— sometimes at the expense of long-term considerations. In internal discussions, American negotiators—generally irrespective of their previous commitments—often become advocates for the maximum range of concessions; their legal background tempts them to act as mediators between Washington and the country with which they are negotiating.

The attitudes of the business élite reinforce the convictions of the legal profession. The American business executive rises through a process of selection which rewards the ability to manipulate the known—in itself a conciliatory procedure. The special skill of the executive is thought to consist in coordinating well-defined functions rather than in challenging them. The procedure is relatively effective in the business world, where the executive can often substitute decisiveness, long experience, and a wide range of personal acquaintance for reflectiveness. In international affairs, however—especially in a revolutionary situation—the strong will which is one of our business executives' notable traits may produce essentially arbitrary choices. Or unfamiliarity with the subject matter may have the opposite effect of turning the executive into a spokesman of his technical staffs. In either case, the business executive is even more dependent than the lawyer on the bureaucracy's formulation of the issue. The business élite is even less able or willing than the lawyer to recognize that the formulation of an issue, not the technical remedy, is usually the central problem.

All this gives American policy its particular cast. Problems are dealt with as they arise. Agreement on what constitutes a problem generally depends on an emerging crisis which settles the previously inconclusive disputes about priorities. When a problem is recognized, it is dealt with by a mobilization of all resources to overcome the immediate symptoms. This often involves the risk of slighting longer-term issues which may not yet have assumed crisis proportions and of overwhelming, perhaps even undermining, the structure of the area concerned by a flood of American technical experts proposing remedies on an American scale. Administrative decisions emerge from a compromise of conflicting pressures in which accidents of personality or persuasiveness play a crucial role. The compromise often reflects the maxim that "if two parties disagree the truth is usually somewhere in between." But the pedantic application of such truisms causes the various contenders to exaggerate their positions for bargaining purposes or to construct fictitious extremes to make their position appear moderate. In either case, internal bargaining predominates over substance.

The *ad hoc* tendency of our decision-makers and the reliance on adversary proceeding cause issues to be stated in black and white terms. This suppresses a feeling for nuance and makes it difficult to recognize the relationship between seemingly discrete events. Even with the perspective of a decade there is little consensus about the relationship between the actions culminating in the Suez fiasco and the French decision to enter the nuclear field; or about the inconsistency between the neutralization of Laos and the step-up of the military effort in Viet-Nam.

The same quality also produces a relatively low valuation of historical factors. Nations are treated as similar phenomena, and those states presenting similar immediate problems are treated similarly. Since many of our policy-makers first address themselves to an issue when it emerges as their area of responsibility, their approach to it is often highly anecdotal. Great weight is given to what people say and relatively little to the significance of these affirmations in terms of domestic structure or historical background. Agreement may be taken at face value and seen as reflecting more consensus than actually exists. Opposition tends to produce moral outrage which often assumes the form of personal animosity—the attitude of some American policy-makers toward President de Gaulle is a good example.

The legal background of our policy-makers produces a bias in favor of constitutional solutions. The issue of supra-nationalism or confederalism in Europe has been discussed largely in terms of the right of countries to make independent decisions. Much less weight has been given to the realities which would limit the application of a majority vote against a major country whatever the legal arrangements. (The fight over the application of Article 19 of the United Nations Charter was based on the same attitude.) Similarly, legal terms such as "integration" and "assignment" sometimes become ends in themselves and thus obscure the operational reality to which they refer. In short, the American leadership groups show high competence in dealing with technical issues, and much less virtuosity in mastering a historical process. And the policies of other Western countries exhibit variations of the American pattern. A lesser pragmatism in continental Europe is counter-balanced by a smaller ability to play a world-role.

*The ideological type of leadership.* As has been discussed above, the impact of ideology can persist long after its initial fervor has been spent. Whatever the ideological commitment of individual leaders, a lifetime spent in the Communist hierarchy must influence their basic categories of thought—especially since Communist ideology continues to perform important functions. It still furnishes the standard of truth and the guarantee of ultimate success. It provides a means for maintaining cohesion among the various Communist parties of the world. It supplies criteria for the settlement of disputes both within the bureaucracy of individual Communist countries and among the various Communist states.

However attenuated, Communist ideology is, in part, responsible for international tensions. This is less because of specific Marxist tactical prescriptions—with respect to which Communists have shown a high degree of flexibility—than because of the basic Marxist-Leninist categories for interpreting reality. Communist leaders never tire of affirming that Marxism-Leninism is the key element of their self-proclaimed superiority over the outside world; as Marxist-Leninists they are convinced that they understand the historical process better than the non-Communist world does.

The essence of Marxism-Leninism—and the reason that normal diplomacy with Communist states is so difficult—is the view that "objective" factors such as the social structure, the economic process, and, above all, the class struggle are more important than the personal convictions of statesmen. Belief in the predominance of objective factors explains the Soviet approach to the problem of security. If personal convictions are "subjective," Soviet security cannot be allowed to rest on the good will of other statesmen, especially those of a different social system. This produces a quest for what may be described as absolute security—the attempt to be so strong as to be independent of the decisions of other countries. But absolute security for one country means absolute security for all others; it can be achieved only by reducing other states to impotence. Thus an essentially defensive foreign policy can grow indistinguishable from traditional aggression.

The belief in the predominance of objective factors explains why, in the past, periods of détente have proved so precarious. When there is a choice between Western good will or a physical gain, the pressures to choose the latter have been overwhelming. The wartime friendship with the West was sacrificed to the possibility of establishing Communist-controlled governments in Eastern Europe. The spirit of Geneva did not survive the temptations offered by the prospect of undermining the Western position in the Middle East. The many overtures of the Kennedy administration were rebuffed until the Cuban missile crisis demonstrated that the balance of forces was not in fact favorable for a test of strength.

The reliance on objective factors has complicated negotiations between the West and the Communist countries. Communist negotiators find it difficult to admit that they could be swayed by the arguments of men who have, by definition, an inferior grasp of the laws of historical development. No matter what is said, they think that they understand their Western counterpart better than he understands himself. Concessions are possible, but they are made to "reality," not to individuals or to a bargaining process. Diplomacy becomes difficult when one of the parties considers the key element to negotiation—the give-and-take of the process of bargaining—as but a superstructure for factors not part of the negotiation itself.

Finally, whatever the decline in ideological fervor, orthodoxy requires the maintenance of a posture of ideological hostility to the non-Communist world even during a period of coexistence. Thus, in a reply to a Chinese challenge, the Communist Party of the U.S.S.R. declared: "We fully support the destruction of capitalism. We not only believe in the inevitable death of capitalism but we are doing everything possible for it to be accomplished through class struggle as quickly as possible."[2]

[2] "The Soviet Reply to the Chinese Letter," open letter of the Central Committee of the Communist Party of the Soviet Union as it appeared in *Pravda*, July 14, 1963, pp. 1–4; *The Current Digest of the Soviet Press*, Vol. XV, No. 28 (August 7, 1963), p. 23.

The wariness toward the outside world is reinforced by the personal experiences which Communist leaders have had on the road to eminence. In a system where there is no legitimate succession, a great deal of energy is absorbed in internal maneuvering. Leaders rise to the top by eliminating—sometimes physically, always bureaucratically—all possible opponents. Stalin had all individuals who helped him into power executed. Khrushchev disgraced Kaganovich, whose protegé he had been, and turned on Marshal Zhukov six months after being saved by him from a conspiracy of his other colleagues. Brezhnev and Kosygin owed their careers to Khrushchev; they nevertheless overthrew him and started a campaign of calumny against him within twenty-four hours of his dismissal.

Anyone succeeding in Communist leadership struggles must be single-minded, unemotional, dedicated, and, above all, motivated by an enormous desire for power. Nothing in the personal experience of Soviet leaders would lead them to accept protestations of good will at face value. Suspiciousness is inherent in their domestic position. It is unlikely that their attitude toward the outside world is more benign than toward their own colleagues or that they would expect more consideration from it.

The combination of personal qualities and ideological structure also affects relations *among* Communist states. Since national rivalries are thought to be the result of class conflict, they are expected to disappear wherever Socialism has triumphed. When disagreements occur they are dealt with by analogy to internal Communist disputes: by attempting to ostracize and then to destroy the opponent. The tendency to treat different opinions as manifestations of heresy causes disagreements to harden into bitter schisms. The debate between Communist China and the U.S.S.R. is in many respects more acrimonious than that between the U.S.S.R. and the non-Communist world.

Even though the basic conceptual categories of Communist leadership groups are similar, the impact of the domestic structure of the individual Communist states on international relations varies greatly. It makes a considerable difference whether an ideology has become institutionalized, as in the Soviet Union, or whether it is still impelled by its early revolutionary fervor, as in Communist China. Where ideology has become institutionalized a special form of pragmatism may develop. It may be just as empirical as that of the United States but it will operate in a different realm of "reality." A different philosophical basis leads to the emergence of another set of categories for the settlement of disputes, and these in turn generate another range of problems.

A Communist bureaucratic structure, however pragmatic, will have different priorities from ours; it will give greater weight to doctrinal considerations and conceptual problems. It is more than ritual when speeches of senior Soviet leaders begin with hour-long recitals of Communist ideology. Even if it were ritual, it must affect the definition of what is considered reasonable in internal arguments. Bureaucratization and pragmatism may lead to a loss of élan; they do not guarantee convergence of Western and Soviet thinking.

The more revolutionary manifestations of Communism, such as Communist China, still possess more ideological fervor, but, paradoxically, their structure may permit a wider latitude for new departures. Tactical intransigence and ideological vitality should not be confused with structural rigidity. Because the leadership bases its rule on a prestige which transcends bureaucratic authority, it has not yet given so many hostages to the administrative structure. If the leadership should change—or if its attitudes are modified—policy could probably be altered much more dramatically in Communist China than in the more institutionalized Communist countries.

*The charismatic-revolutionary type of leadership.* The contemporary international order is heavily influenced by yet another leadership type: the charismatic-revolutionary leader. For many of the leaders of the new nations the bureaucratic-pragmatic approach of the West is irrelevant because they are more interested in the future which they wish to construct than in the manipulation of the environment which dominates the thinking of the pragmatists. And ideology is not satisfactory because doctrine supplies rigid categories which overshadow the personal experiences which have provided the impetus for so many of the leaders of the new nations.

The type of individual who leads a struggle for independence has been sustained in the risks and suffering of such a course primarily by a commitment to a vision which enabled him to override conditions which had seemed overwhelmingly hostile. Revolutionaries are rarely motivated primarily by material considerations—though the illusion that they are persists in the West. Material incentives do not cause a man to risk his existence and to launch himself into the uncertainties of a revolutionary struggle. If Castro or Sukarno had been principally interested in economics, their talents would have guaranteed them a brilliant career in the societies they overthrew. What made their sacrifices worthwhile to them was a vision of the future—or a quest for political power. To revolutionaries the significant reality is the world which they are striving to bring about, not the world they are fighting to overcome.

This difference in perspective accounts for the inconclusiveness of much of the dialogue between the West and many of the leaders of the new countries. The West has a tendency to believe that the tensions in the emerging nations are caused by a low level of economic activity. To the apostles of economic development, raising the gross national product seems the key to political stability. They believe that it should receive the highest priority from the political leaders of new countries and supply their chief motivation.

But to the charismatic heads of many of the new nations, economic progress, while not unwelcome, offers too limited a scope for their ambitions. It can be achieved only by slow, painful, highly technical measures which contrast with the heroic exertions of the struggle for independence. Results are long-delayed; credit for them cannot be clearly established. If Castro were to act on the advice of theorists of economic development, the best he could hope for would be that after some decades he would lead a small progressive country—perhaps a Switzerland of the Caribbean. Compared to the prospect of leading a revolution throughout Latin America, this goal would appear trivial, boring, perhaps even unreal to him.

Moreover, to the extent that economic progress is achieved, it may magnify domestic political instability, at least in its early phases. Economic advance disrupts the traditional political structure. It thus places constant pressures on the incumbent leaders to re-establish the legitimacy of their rule. For this purpose a dramatic foreign policy is particularly apt. Many leaders of the new countries seem convinced that an adventurous foreign policy will not harm prospects for economic development and may even foster it. The competition of the superpowers makes it likely that economic assistance will be forthcoming regardless of the actions of the recipient. Indeed the more obstrusive their foreign policy the greater is their prospect of being wooed by the chief contenders.

The tendency toward a reckless policy is magnified by the uncertain sense of identity of many of the new nations. National boundaries often correspond to the administrative subdivisions established by the former colonial rulers. States thus have few of the attributes of nineteenth-century European nationalism: common language, common culture, or even common history. In many cases, the only common experience is a century or so of imperial rule. As a result, there is a great pressure toward authoritarian rule, and a high incentive to use foreign policy as a means of bringing about domestic cohesion.

Western-style democracy presupposes that society transcends the political realm; in that case opposition challenges a particular method of achieving common aims but not the existence of the state itself. In many of the new countries, by contrast, the state represents the primary, sometimes the sole, manifestation of social cohesion. Opposition can therefore easily appear as treason—apart from the fact that leaders who have spent several decades running the risks of revolutionary struggle or who have achieved power by a coup d'état are not likely to favor a system of government which makes them dispensable. Indeed the attraction of Communism for many of these leaders is not Marxist-Leninist economic theory but the legitimacy for authoritarian rule which it provides.

No matter what the system of government, many of the leaders of the new nations use foreign policy as a means to escape intractable internal difficulties and as a device to achieve domestic cohesion. The international arena provides an opportunity for the dramatic measures which are impossible at home. These are often cast in an anti-Western mold because this is the easiest way to recreate the struggle against imperial rule which is the principal unifying element for many new nations. The incentive is particularly strong because the rivalry of the nuclear powers eliminates many of the risks which previously were associated with an adventurous foreign policy—especially if that foreign policy is directed against the West which lacks any effective sanctions.

Traditional military pressure is largely precluded by the nuclear stalemate and respect for world opinion. But the West is neither prepared nor able to use the sanction which weighs most heavily on the new countries: the deliberate exploitation of their weak domestic structure. In many areas the ability to foment domestic unrest is a more potent weapon than traditional arms. Many of the leaders of the new countries will be prepared to ignore the classical panoply of power; but they will be very sensitive to the threat of domestic upheaval. States with a high capacity for exploiting domestic instability can use it as a tool of foreign policy. China, though lacking almost all forms of classical long-range military strength, is a growing factor in Africa. Weak states may be more concerned with a country's capacity to organize domestic unrest in their territory than with its capacity for physical destruction.

*Conclusion.* Contemporary domestic structures thus present an unprecedented challenge to the emergence of a stable international order. The bureaucratic-pragmatic societies concentrate on the manipulation of an empirical reality which they treat as given; the ideological societies are split between an essentially bureaucratic approach (though in a different realm of reality than the bureaucratic-pragmatic structures) and a group using ideology mainly for revolutionary ends. The new nations, in so far as they are active in international affairs, have a high incentive to seek in foreign policy the perpetuation of charismatic leadership.

These differences are a major obstacle to a consensus on what constitutes a "reasonable" proposal. A common diagnosis of the existing situation is hard to achieve, and it is even more difficult to concert measures for a solution. The situation is complicated by the one feature all types of leadership have in common: the premium put on short-term goals and the domestic need to succeed at all times. In the bureaucratic societies policy emerges from a compromise which often produces the least common denominator, and it is implemented by individuals whose reputation is made by administering the *status quo*. The leadership of the institutionalized ideological state may be even more the prisoner of essentially corporate bodies. Neither leadership can afford radical changes of course for they result in profound repercussions in its administrative structure. And the charismatic leaders of the new nations are like tightrope artists—one false step and they will plunge from their perch.

IV. DOMESTIC STRUCTURE AND FOREIGN POLICY:
THE PROSPECTS FOR WORLD ORDER

•   •   •

It must be admitted that if the domestic structures were considered in isolation, the prognosis would not be too hopeful. But domestic structures do not exist in a vacuum. They must respond to the requirements of the environment. And here all states find themselves face to face with the necessity of avoiding a nuclear holocaust. While this condition does not restrain all nations equally, it nevertheless defines a common task which technology will impose on even more countries as a direct responsibility.

Then, too, a certain similarity in the forms of administration may bring about common criteria of rationality. . . . Science and technology will spread. Improved communications may lead to the emergence of a common culture. The fissures between domestic structures and the different stages of evolution are important, but they may be outweighed by the increasing interdependence of humanity.

It would be tempting to end on this note and to base the hope for peace on the self-evidence of the need for it. But this would be too pat. The deepest problem of the contemporary international order may be that most of the debates which form the headlines of the day are peripheral to the basic division described in this article. The cleavage is not over particular political arrangements—except as symptoms—but between two styles of policy and two philosophical perspectives.

The two styles can be defined as the political as against the revo-lutionary approach to order or, reduced to personalities, as the distinc-tion between the statesman and the prophet.

The statesman manipulates reality; his first goal is survival; he feels responsible not only for the best but also for the worst conceivable outcome. His view of human nature is wary; he is conscious of many great hopes which have failed, of many good intentions that could not be realized, of selfishness and ambition and violence. He is, therefore, inclined to erect hedges against the possibility that even the most bril-liant idea might prove abortive and that the most eloquent formulation might hide ulterior motives. He will try to avoid certain experiments, not because he would object to the results if they succeeded, but be-cause he would feel himself responsibile for the consequences if they failed. He is suspicious of those who personalize foreign policy, for history teaches him the fragility of structures dependent on individuals. To the statesman, gradualism is the essence of stability; he represents an era of average performance, of gradual change and slow construction.

By contrast, the prophet is less concerned with manipulating than with creating reality. What is possible interests him less than what is "right." He offers his vision as the test and his good faith as a guarantee. He believes in total solutions; he is less absorbed in methodology than in purpose. He believes in the perfectibility of man. His approach is time-less and not dependent on circumstances. He objects to gradualism as an unnecessary concession to circumstance. He will risk everything be-cause his vision is the primary significant reality to him. Paradoxically, his more optimistic view of human nature makes him more intol-erant than the statesman. If truth is both knowable and attainable, only immortality or stupidity can keep man from realizing it. The prophet represents an era of exaltation, of great upheavals, of vast accomplish-ments, but also of enormous disasters.

The encounter between the political and the prophetic approach to policy is always somewhat inconclusive and frustrating. The test of the statesman is the permanence of the international structure under stress. The test of the prophet is inherent in his vision. The statesman will seek to reduce the prophet's intuition to precise measures; he judges ideas on their utility and not on their "truth." To the prophet this approach is almost sacrilegious because it represents the triumph of expediency over universal principles. To the statesman negotiation is the mechanism of stability because it presupposes that maintenance of the existing order is more important than any dispute within it. To the prophet negotiations can have only symbolic value—as a means of converting or demoralizing the opponent; truth, by definition, cannot be compromised.

Both approaches have prevailed at different periods in history. The political approach dominated European foreign policy between the end of the religious wars and the French Revolution and then again between the Congress of Vienna and the outbreak of World War I. The prophetic mode was in the ascendant during the great upheavals of the religious struggles and the period of the French Revolution, and in the contemporary uprisings in major parts of the world.

Both modes have produced considerable accomplishments, though the prophetic style is likely to involve the greater dislocations and more suffering. Each has its nemesis. The nemesis of the statesman is that equilibrium, though it may be the condition of stability, does not supply its own motivation; that of the prophet is the impossibility of sustaining a mood of exaltation without the risk of submerging man in the vastness of a vision and reducing him to a mere figure to be manipulated.

As for the difference in philosophical perspective, it may reflect the divergence of the two lines of thought which since the Renaissance have distinguished the West from the part of the world now called underdeveloped (with Russia occupying an intermediary position). The West is deeply committed to the notion that the real world is external to the observer, that knowledge consists of recording and classifying data—the more accurately the better. Cultures which escaped the early impact of Newtonian thinking have retained the essentially pre-Newtonian view that the real world is almost completely *internal* to the observer.

Although this attitude was a liability for centuries—because it prevented the development of the technology and consumer goods which the West enjoyed—it offers great flexibility with respect to the contemporary revolutionary turmoil. It enables the societies which do not share our cultural mode to alter reality by influencing the perspective of the observer—a process which we are largely unprepared to handle or even to perceive. And this can be accomplished under contemporary conditions without sacrificing technological progress. Technology comes as a gift; acquiring it in its advanced form does not presuppose the philosophical commitment that discovering it imposed on the West. Empirical reality has a much different significance for many of the new countries than for the West because in a certain sense they never went through the process of discovering it (with Russia again occupying an intermediary position). At the same time, the difference in philosophical perspective may cause us to seem cold, supercilious, lacking in compassion. The instability of the contemporary world order may thus have at its core a philosophical schism which makes the issues producing most political debates seem largely tangential.

Such differences in style and philosophical perspective are not unprecedented. What is novel is the global scale on which they occur and the risks which the failure to overcome them would entail. Historically, cleavages of lesser magnitude have been worked out dialectically, with one style of policy or one philosophical approach dominant in one era only to give way later to another conception of reality. And the transition was rarely free of violence. The challenge of our time is whether we can deal consciously and creatively with what in previous centuries was adjusted through a series of more or less violent and frequently catastrophic upheavals. We must construct an international order *before* a crisis imposes it as a necessity.

This is a question not of blueprints, but of attitudes. In fact the overconcern with technical blueprints is itself a symptom of our difficulties. Before the problem of order can be "dealt" with—even philosophically—we must be certain that the right questions are being asked.

We can point to some hopeful signs. The most sensitive thinkers of the West have recognized that excessive empiricism may lead to stagnation. In many of the new countries—and in some Communist ones as well—the second or third generation of leaders is in the process of freeing itself from the fervor and dogmatism of the early revolutionary period and of relating their actions to an environment which they helped to create. But these are as yet only the first tentative signs of progress on a course whose significance is not always understood. Indeed it is characteristic of an age of turmoil that it produces so many immediate issues that little time is left to penetrate their deeper meaning. The most serious problem therefore becomes the need to acquire a sufficiently wide perspective so that the present does not overwhelm the future.

## STUDY QUESTIONS

1. To what extent do differences in domestic structures help explain American versus Soviet viewpoints on war, arms control, and international order?

2. In what specific ways has the advent of nuclear weapons altered the conduct of nations and patterns of international affairs? In this connection, have

customary differences between military and civilian perspectives of the international arena been reduced or intensified? Why?

---

3. Describe the major typologies of leadership and their relevance for achieving political cohesion and progress in the newly emergent nations. Do you agree that some leaders of these nations utilize foreign policy as a deliberate technique for escaping internal difficulties?

---

4. Does race or geography appear to have a more profound impact on international relations? Why?

---

5. Describe the ways in which military power contributes to and detracts from a stable international system.

---

## SUGGESTIONS FOR FURTHER READING

BROGAN, D. W. *The American Character*. New York: Alfred A. Knopf, Inc., 1944; Vintage Books, 1956.

CARR, EDWARD HALLETT. *The Twenty-Years' Crisis 1919–1939*. London: Macmillan & Co., Ltd., 1951.

GARTHOFF, RAYMOND L. *Soviet Strategy in the Nuclear Age*. New York: Frederick A. Praeger, 1958.

HALPERIN, MORTON H. *Limited War in the Nuclear Age*. New York: John Wiley & Sons, Inc., 1963.

HILSMAN, ROGER. *Strategic Intelligence and National Decisions*. New York: The Free Press, 1956.

KNORR, KLAUS. *The War Potential of Nations*. Princeton: Princeton University Press, 1956.

LARUS, JOEL. *Nuclear Weapons Safety and the Common Defense*. Columbus: Ohio State University Press, 1967.

LONDON, KURT. *The Permanent Crisis*. Waltham, Massachusetts: Blaisdell Publishing Company, 1968.

MACKINDER, SIR HALFORD J. *Democratic Ideals and Reality*. New York: Henry Holt and Company, 1942.

ORGANSKY, KATHERINE and A. F. K. *Population and World Power*. New York: Alfred A. Knopf, Inc., 1961.

ROSENAU, JAMES N. *Domestic Sources of Foreign Policy*. New York: The Free Press, 1967.

SCHELLING, THOMAS C. *Arms and Influence*. New Haven: Yale University Press, 1966.

SKOLNIKOFF, EUGENE B. *Science, Technology, and American Foreign Policy*. Cambridge: The M.I.T. Press, 1967 .

SPROUT, HAROLD and MARGARET. *Foundations of International Politics*. Princeton: D. Van Nostrand Co., Inc., 1962.

WEIGERT, HANS W. *Generals and Geographers.* New York: Oxford University Press, 1942.

YOST, CHARLES. *The Insecurity of Nations: International Relations in the Twentieth Century.* New York: Frederick A. Praeger for the Council on Foreign Relations, 1968.

# PART THREE □ CONFLICT
# AND COEXISTENCE

P ERHAPS the most conspicuous characteristic of the international political scene is the existence of a hundred and twenty-five independent
states, with others on the road to independence. Europe is no longer the
center of international politics. European powers have been relegated to
the status of regional powers. The centers of power are found in the
United States and the Soviet Union, although China may become a
major power in the coming decades. Another center of power is emerging
in Asia and Africa, although these nations of the so-called "third world"
are still militarily and economically weak and depend upon the developed nations for technical and economic assistance.

The United States and the Soviet Union have emerged as nuclear
super-powers, and a relative balance of terror between the East and
West gives some assurance of peaceful coexistence. Fear of national destruction and possibly of humanity as a whole constitutes a strong incentive to avert the holocaust of nuclear war. States attempt to protect
and promote their interests while seeking at the same time to avoid war.
Ideological, economic, and political competition among differing political and social systems is the hallmark of contemporary international
relations.

The selections in part three present recent trends in the international arena. They examine the pattern of authority on the international scene, the emergence of polycentrism in the Soviet bloc, the
merits and disadvantages of bipolarity and multipolarity as systems of
power, and the alternatives that can be considered for the future. In the
last two sections, we find a contrasting discussion of the concept of
peaceful coexistence.

In his discussion of the pattern of authority on the international scene, Edward H. Buehrig points out that authority in the international arena is pluralistic. He analyzes the authority of the Catholic
Church and Islam, and discusses the Marxist view of authority. Buehrig
states that since World War II there has been a vast redistribution of

power due to the rise of many Afro-Asian states. He believes that it is difficult for a world that "just crossed the threshold of common existence" to establish a world government. The attempt first by the League of Nations and later by the United Nations to establish a world governed by law, peaceful change, and collective security, has had limited success. He points to the various difficulties in achieving such a world and states that the world pattern of authority "lack a capstone." Buehrig concludes that although the United Nations falls short of providing a dominant center of power and authority, it is active rather than passive.

George F. Kennan discusses the emergence of independent centers of political authority within the Communist bloc—the rise of polycentrism. He points to the conduct of Soviet-Yugoslov and Soviet-Chinese relations, especially in the post-Stalin period. Today there are two major ideological centers of communism: Moscow and Peking. Yugoslavia is independent. There are also a large number of influential Communist parties, not in power, which are bewildered by this division. Kennan is convinced that a complete restoration of unity is foreclosed, but a total break with all-out hostilities is improbable. He believes that Communist states are caught in a crisis of indecision with respect to the proper attitude that each state should adopt toward non-Communist countries. The former diplomat analyzes the impact of polycentrism on the internal and external affairs of East European regimes. He believes that the West, through its policy or behavior, can influence the choices of the East European states and he offers several courses of action.

In the next selection, R. N. Rosecrance presents the arguments of the proponents of bipolarity as an international system which, they claim, reduces conflicts in the international arena. Rosecrance offers a critique of their arguments and states that they seem to confuse bipolarity with détente. He also offers the argument of the proponents of multipolarity and a critique of this alternative as a desirable international system. Rosecrance presents an alternative system for the future which combines the desirable facets of bipolarity and multipolarity "without their attendant disabilities." He calls this alternative the intermediate international system. Rosecrance proceeds to discuss five basic characteristics of the system of bi-multipolarity. He concludes that although the bi-multipolar system does not eradicate conflict, it does limit the prospects of conflict to far smaller proportions than does either multipolarity or bipolarity: "If peace is the objective, a system combining bipolar and multipolar features may be a means of a reasonable approximation thereto."

In his analysis of the changes in alliance systems, Herbert S. Dinerstein discusses the changes in the concept of war as an instrument of foreign policy. Today, both the United States and the Soviet Union have a common interest in averting war. Both sides have acknowledged the status quo in Europe. Dinerstein analyzes the alliance systems in the pre-World War I and pre-World War II periods and the period since 1945. The present alliance system differs from previous ones in three respects: 1) the primacy of political goals; 2) the increase in the number of participants in the international system and the change in their relative power; and 3) the emergence of ideology as a determinant factor in international relations. Dinerstein discusses each of these characteristics and examines inter-alliance relations. He believes that at present the United States and the Soviet Union seem to accept roughly the existing balance of power. Also, he discusses the support of one superpower to a secondary power in rival alliances such as United States aid to Yugoslavia, Poland, and Rumania, and Soviet aid to Castro, then not yet communist. Moreover, he examines cross-alliance relationships between secondary alliance members. Finally, he surveys relationships between non-aligned powers and alliance members.

Moving from the discussion of recent transformation of the alliance systems to the concept of peaceful coexistence, Leon Lipson examines the concept as a principle or as a set of principles of international law. Lipson states that although the term "peaceful coexistence" has become a central slogan since 1956, it was used in Soviet literature in the early 1920s. It has been presented with vigor by Soviet representatives at international conferences. The principle of peaceful coexistence has been construed to include the five principles proclaimed in the Sino-Indian Pact of 1954 and their expanded version at the Bandung Conference of 1955. Soviet publicists have not been very much concerned about the purity of the list of principles as long as they serve their purposes. The Soviet doctrine of peaceful coexistence rejects pacifism, but when pacifist movements in the West tend to serve the objectives of Soviet foreign policy, pacifism is acclaimed. The Soviets also reject peaceful coexistence in the ideological sphere. Moreover, they view their wars as legal. Peaceful coexistence serves as a tactic in the conduct of Soviet foreign policy and its strategic uses vary from one audience to another. Lipson asserts that "the Soviet concept of PCX, in short, presupposes bipolarity and the cold war, rather than offering a way out of the cold war."

Concluding this part, Victor P. Karpov presents the Soviet concept of peaceful coexistence and its implications for international law. The concept of peaceful coexistence, he states, is a basic principle in Soviet foreign policy. The principle is not a tactical move on the part of the Soviet Union, it is "an indisputable fact" in a world of nations with different political, social, and economic systems. He asserts that the

Soviet Union seeks to achieve its objectives not by war but by peaceful competition. He defines coexistence as the struggle between two different social systems but by peaceful means. The principle of coexistence, he urges, must be universal. It has guided Soviet relations with other nations and is embodied in the United Nations Charter. He lists several basic principles of peaceful coexistence and states that the principle must be considered the basis of contemporary international law.

EDWARD H. BUEHRIG

## The International Pattern of Authority

The broad question posed here is how authority is distributed in the world and what shifts may be occurring in its pattern of distribution. Mainly, of course, authority is today allocated according to the Western State System, characterized in its legal mechanics by territorial rule among equals and in its political philosophy by consent of the governed. Conveniently dated from the Treaty of Westphalia and the French Revolution, the system is now more widespread than ever before.

Mingled with this dominant pattern, however, are remnants of the older religious systems. The Roman Catholic Church survives as a fascinating element in the contemporary structure of authority—nowhere more noteworthy than in Eastern Europe. Nor can Islam, though in serious disarray, be overlooked, when one considers the nuclear force with which in 1947 it erupted out of Indian society.

Communism and international organization are the newest claimants for possession of authority. Like the traditional religions, the former is a universal system, basing legitimacy on the truth of its doctrine. But, like them, it too has failed to provide a practical system for the gover-

SOURCE: Edward H. Buehrig, "The International Pattern of Authority," *World Politics*, XVII (April 1965), 369–385. Reprinted by permission.

nance of the world and has in its turn yielded to the workaday pattern of the Western State System. On the other hand, international organization is in the secular—which is to say, pragmatic—tradition of the Western State System, of which it is an outgrowth.

The contemporary pattern of authority is pluralistic in two respects. First of all, as between the Western State System and the ideologically based systems there is a radical difference of premise. Nationalism, the social cement of the territorial state, is neither universal in its claims nor, even within the confines of a single nation-state, is it (except in its pathological manifestations) exclusive of other loyalties. It is not constrained, as are the ideologies, to tie legitimate authority to a theology and to claim a monopoly on it. The nation-state could, however, without doing violence to its particularism, be part of a federal system. But in fact it is not. There is, then, a second respect in which the existing pattern is pluralistic: international law avowedly allocates authority to territorial sovereigns equal to each other. Thus, on top of competing though coexisting systems that seek to legitimize authority in essentially incompatible ways, the dominant system is itself, by virtue of its own internal principles, pluralistic.

The struggle for possession of authority is a constant theme of the drama of politics. What we have thus far witnessed in the twentieth century is the ability of the Catholic Church to hold its own; the shattering impact on Islam of its confrontation with the nation-state; the vain attempt of communism to supplant other systems; the spectacular multiplication of territorial sovereigns; and, despite many adversities, the development of international organization.

The broad survey here attempted shows that history has been more influential than logic in determining the contemporary pattern; and we may assume that circumstance will continue to mingle with intellectual endeavor to determine the pattern of the future. Certainly there is no prospect that the international pattern of authority will soon lend itself to an orderly diagrammatic presentation. Though it appears that international organization is the chief way in which the existing pattern is being modified, the concluding section of this article is not to be construed as arguing that the United Nations is a repository of authority in any but an equivocal sense. What has emerged is a certain autonomy of action, parallel, not superior, to the territorial state. Indeed, the latter is more than merely persistent. The argument is that it possesses its own utility and that international organization, despite its surprising vitality, cannot be pushed with profit beyond fairly narrow limits. Such as it is, however, international organization is the chief institutional response of the modern world to the extraordinary challenge of today's international politics.

I

Still part of the political landscape are two systems that were once rivals for universal allegiance, Christianity and Islam. Each ascribed legitimate authority to divine sanction; each arrogated to itself supreme authority, without equal; each, as is natural to authority based on religious faith, employed personal rather than territorial jurisdiction. For centuries these systems confronted each other, in theory mutually exclusive and in practice often hostile, each regarding the other as properly subject, on the one hand, to the Crusade and, on the other, to the Jihad.

Out of the Middle Ages there emerged in Europe a radically different pattern of authority, based on territorial jurisdiction and the assumption of equality between territorial sovereigns. It arose from many causes, one of which is here of particular interest. The new pattern at first assured the permanence of the split within Christendom; but ultimately it served to accommodate the schism, which could only have been exacerbated by continued belief in a supreme authority. Initially a rule of thumb was used. As between the Holy Roman Empire and the Lutherans of Northern Germany, the Treaty of Augsburg (1555) provided that the religion of the prince determined that of the people. The Treaty of Westphalia (1648) further emphasized territorial authority and expanded toleration of religious sects. Not until the American Constitution was the separation of church and state hit upon. Typically the European pattern today is a compromise between the formula of the Treaty of Augsburg and that of the American Constitution: an officially recognized and supported church, with allowance of non-conforming sects. Thus the dualism between religious and secular authority that has always characterized Western civilization continues today, but with the emphasis radically altered in favor of the latter.

The status of the Roman Catholic Church is the most notable feature of this continuing dualism. The Pope, more free than in the past from extraneous political pressure, continues to be exempt from mundane authority. The sovereignty of his person is augmented by the territorial independence of the Vatican City, by the immunities of members of the Curia, and by the diplomatic status of the representatives that the Holy See sends to and receives from other members of the international community: some, like the Netherlands, not predominantly Catholic and some, like Japan, not even predominantly Christian.

These are the formal attributes of authority of the Catholic Church today. No longer does it possess a territorial base capable of yielding taxes and soldiers. No longer does it exercise personal jurisdiction through its own law and its own courts (though the Uniat churches in

Lebanon, for example, still have exclusive control over the personal status of their members). No longer does it have a monopoly on education. Nor is the Church capable today of legitimizing the use of force or, as it so often attempted with varying success, of actually organizing collective military action. Still available are the sanctions based on faith: the interdict and excommunication.

Yet the surviving status of the Catholic Church, diminished though it is, might well be the envy of the United Nations. The Church has ancient and compelling symbols of authority. It has a strong economy, based variously or in combination on government subsidy, private contributions, and income from property—the latter sources often exempt from taxation by the territorial authority. Finally, it has a dedicated bureaucracy whose loyalty neither nationalism nor communism has seriously affected.

Despite an unequal struggle with the secular state, the Catholic Church, highly adaptable, actually emerged as a member of the new international community; and it remains so today, even as that community expands to include a majority of non-Christian states. As a sovereign corporation, the Church by the formal device of the concordat penetrates with its personal jurisdiction the territorial preserve of the nation-state—though its influence is not mainly dependent on, such formal means. Catholic political parties, for example, have been a significant postwar phenomenon in Europe.

Islam, meanwhile, has only in this century been forced into a showdown with the nation-state. Its confrontation has in two respects been less propitious than that of the Catholic Church. Lacking the organization and hierarchy of Catholicism, Islam cannot assert itself as a sovereign religious entity. The underlying difficulty, however, is still more profound. Islamic society has no tradition and little basis for distinguishing between secular and spiritual authority. Islamic law is all-inclusive; it is revealed; and it is applicable by religious courts on the basis of personal jurisdiction. Thus its claim to obedience is so extensive as to render the whole Islamic structure highly vulnerable to the nation-state, whose authority is territorially confined and can have only a mundane foundation. The expedient of dualism is not easily available to Islam.

## II

Communism has been rightly characterized as the would-be successor to the traditional religions as an ideological center of world authority. However, its challenge to the Western State System is not impressive. If, a century hence, there is a fundamental change in the existing pattern of territorial authority among equals, it seems unlikely that communism will prove to have been the precursor. Undeniably, however, there are universalistic presumptions in communism.

Communism's model of the future, considered as a purely theoretical construct, is not, as sometimes depicted by its opponents, a reincarnation of the Roman Empire. The fact is that Marxian thought, like much of the liberal thought of the time, was deeply affected by the optimism of the nineteenth century. But, whereas the liberal assumed that clashing interests would not harm but actually contribute to the general welfare, the Marxist, in ambivalent but sympathetic relation to anarchist thought, believed that the basic clash itself could be eliminated. Attributing the cause of friction in human relations to institutional arrangements (above all, private property) rather than to human nature as such, communism forecasts a world society in which—after a final convulsion—politics will have become anachronistic. The authority and power of the state will wither away, leaving only administration above, and below, voluntaristic and self-regulating economic and social groupings.

Thus the Communist model, highly Utopian, lacks any provision for authority, except the truth of its ideology. Actually, the egoism and prejudice of an often irrational human nature and the tribulations of a world threatening to overpopulate itself suggest that society is not soon to be emancipated from the play of political power and the restraint of authority. Man cannot escape the old dilemma, full of immense difficulty and moral hazard: How to use power and at the same time control it?

However, it must be emphasized that the disavowal of power in the ideal future has paradoxical consequences for communism's husbanding and use of power in the present. Since the future is so exceptionally attractive, the means to its attainment are not subject to restraint. Decisions of whatever character, whether touching on economics, education, art and literature, or on any other aspect of society, are typically made to turn on power considerations. Ideology renders the convinced believer undiscriminating as to the means of its furtherance. For the strength of his belief is not merely intellectual; it is psychologically tied to his innermost need for security.

This preoccupation with power, rationalized in terms of an imminent (and favorable) culmination of history, is the key to an understanding of the Communist outlook on the non-Communist world. Communist writings on international law, though increasingly conformist, suffer from a basic ambiguity. One perceives in them a division of the world that bears an unmistakable resemblance to what in Islamic law was made quite explicit. Islam was the "house of peace." Outside its borders—beyond the pale—was the "house of war." This classification placed the infidel at a juridical disadvantage; it clouded the legitimacy and justice of his authority and implied that his political existence was dependent on sufferance.

When communism speaks of the "peace zone" on the one hand and of the "imperialist camp" on the other, it is alleging a difference between itself and capitalism that cannot be resolved by policy, for it is represented as turning on structure and historical process—unaffected by subjective factors of intent. It is a difference in kind: something called communism is credited with progress and justice and with eventual triumph, and something called capitalism is identified with the decaying past, doomed by history itself to succumb to the new age.

It is notable that so sharp a qualitative distinction has failed to produce a systematic jurisprudence applicable to international politics. One inhibiting factor is the nonpolitical character of the model of the future that communism projects. But what about the strategy and tactics of the interim period, prior to the Utopian culmination?

Political power—advantage, that is, over opposition—is generated by an ideology that claims to explain the whole of history and that views events as ineluctably favoring its own preferences and predictions. Yet such a grand conception is bound to be wrong. Moreover, the "truth" is not immune to the perversity of its adherents, nor to the skepticism of nonbelievers. Actually the difficulties of implementing the universal pretensions of the Bolshevist revolution have been overwhelming. If in a simpler age Moslem jurisprudence had in fact to make substantial concessions to practicality, it is not surprising that in the modern world communism, despite a felt need, has failed to construct a juridical model rivaling that of the Western State System.

The Comintern possessed an interesting potential. Disdainful of the community of territorial states, its authority was based on ideology. Its hierarchy owed supreme loyalty to the corporate will, as did, in fact, all members of the Party. Authority was exercised through personal jurisdiction in disregard, often in violation, of the territorial jurisdiction of states. Here was an international organization that, despite profound differences of philosophy and objective, was in fact analogous to the Catholic Church—and in deadly combat with it.

Though communism continues as an international movement, the Comintern is now extinct. Long subjected to serving Russia's national interests, it was abolished by Stalin in his extremity in 1943. Its truncated successor, the Cominform, has also expired. There remain, however, without benefit of central organs of authority, periodic conferences of national Communist parties.

The failure of communism to sustain a dominant hierarchy is due not least to its own internal difficulties—to the irrepressible interests that cling to the particular, resisting absorption in the universal. Russia and China have not escaped the elemental frictions of politics: racial, territorial, economic, and, that most human of failings, rivalry for position. Moreover, the states of Eastern Europe have retained their national identities and have asserted themselves against the suffocating embrace of Moscow, essayed in the name of ideological fulfillment, yet hardly distinguishable from Russia's regard for her own security and welfare.

It is noteworthy that external resistance to the expansion of communism has failed to induce unity and central authority within the movement. Actually interaction between communism and the Western State System has eroded, not the prevailing system governing the allocation of authority, but the universal proclivities of communism itself. The innovations of the latter have atrophied and, despite its contempt for the justice of existing authority, communism has been obliged to conform to the pattern of diplomatic relations between equals, employing it even within its own sphere.

Innovation, meanwhile, has come from the West, in the form of international organization. To this, too, communism is adapting, but not without suspicion and often an ill-concealed disdain. Some forms of international organization communism has actually imported and applied to itself. Not only was the Cominform abortive. It was supplanted by the Warsaw Pact and Comecon, inspired respectively by the examples of NATO and the Common Market, though the importations lack the vitality of the originals.

## III

•  •  •

Since the Second World War, with a rush unprecedented in man's political history, filled though that history is with improbable happenings, a vast redistribution of authority has occurred. The pressures, a mingling typically of domestic and international politics, have been inexorable, producing catastrophic convulsions and grotesque political formations. It must be emphasized that the sudden proliferation of states has been a function not merely of receding European power but of new forces with which the new regimes, in their turn, must now contend. The location of authority within and among societies is what politics is about, but seldom has the attending controversy been so pervasive and so dangerous as today.

In times of great upheaval, existing patterns of authority are bound to undergo severe stress and strain. All the more striking, therefore, is the capacity of the Western State System not merely to survive but to expand; in the postwar period it has spread to virtually the whole land area of the earth. In its career of some three hundred years it has wrecked the universalistic systems of authority—the latter-day pretensions of communism no less than the traditional systems of Europe and Asia—and has supplanted as well the imperial extensions of Europe. What are we to say of territorial rule among equals in its time of final triumph?

It is remarkable that a system fashioned blindly by the crosscurrents of European history should transcend its parochial origin. The explanation cannot be simply that Europe imposed the system elsewhere, for Europe's own colonial rule has succumbed—beginning in North America in 1776. Rather the Renaissance produced a political outlook useful to an age, only just dawning, when all peoples were finally to interact with such intensity as to leave no alternative to the secularization of authority, at a level below the pretension of universal rule. That outlook was congenial to the notion that authority comes from below rather than from above; and in time the consent theory of political obligation eroded all other claims to legitimacy. From that point of view, it was inescapable that units of government should be territorial and juridically equal. An international law applicable to the whole world would seem bound to start with these assumptions—and only then to endeavor to mesh the general with the particular.

The contending forces in society have produced up to now about 125 units of authority, with prospect for still more. There is much cause for dismay in this outcome. Yet it would be invidious to dismiss the process as one of mere fragmentation. It is true, of course, that Islam (like Christianity before it) has been rent asunder. But its ideal had long since been corrupted and Ottoman rule had in its turn fallen into decay. Moreover, there was nothing in the imperial systems of Europe to suggest permanence. What has happened cannot, therefore, be represented as the breakdown of existing systems containing promise for the future.

There have always been difficulties with the nation-state both as an idea and as a practical device. The legitimization of authority in terms of the consent of the governed is a perplexing proposition: the will of the people is more metaphysical than it is tangible. There is also the question of how in actual fact authority can be allocated among the "peoples" of the world. Where does one "people" end and another begin? The West has struggled with these problems for a long time and, in consequence, they have begun to wear smooth. In the Americas and, more recently, in Europe (both east and west) there is substantial consensus as to the identity of nations and growing acquiescence (the German question apart) to existing boundaries. Outside of the West, however, these problems are many times intensified. Nor is it merely a matter in Africa and Asia of where lines should be drawn between units of authority. Still more fundamental is the question of their internal viability and capacity for meaningful self-direction.

The extreme decentralization of the Western State System has often been deplored, and the model of reform that most readily suggests itself is that of federation. Yet the degree of centralization envisioned by the advocates of world federation would not be without hazard. Actually the Western State System has the outstanding merit of keeping unlike things apart. At the system's inception the unity of Christendom was sacrificed to its pacification. If such an expedient could not then be avoided at the very heart of Western civilization, it seems fatuous to suppose that the world as a whole, having only just crossed the threshold of a common existence, could establish central organs of government without stultifying the attempt, or, worse, inducing mortal rivalry for control over them. Certainly the Communist and the non-Communist are not ready for the risks of so intimate an association.

The homeland of the Western State System, in a new burst of invention, has in this postwar period adopted ingenious ways of minimizing the economic consequences of boundaries and of promoting political solidarity. But what six European nations have done cannot be readily expanded in Europe itself. Nor is it an example that Russia and Eastern Europe, because of imbalance in political power and economic development, find easy to follow. It is, in fact, difficult to find situations that would warrant a similar attempt at extranational authority. Many combinations would be unprofitable, others sheer folly. For the United States and Canada to come closer together in common institutions would be a dubious thing. For the United States and Mexico to do so would set off an explosion.

Granting that territorial jurisdiction prevents a too intimate mixing of incompatible attitudes and of disparate interests, there is still the doctrine of equality, stultified, it is contended, by the vast differences of wealth and power among nations. Yet the doctrine, by its very assertion, achieves a certain reality. Nor is it wholly lacking in utility. It acts as a brake on the spread of control from the centers of economic and military power. That the postwar world has not in fact become polarized is not due to restraint in either Washington or Moscow but to the independent policy of nations resting often on little more than the juridical claim to equality. These nations have contrived to serve their material interests as well as satisfy their pride. They have extracted advantage by political means. Yet one cannot begrudge the freedom of action that enables them to chip away at the disproportionate wealth and power of the United States, Western Europe, and the Soviet Union.

## IV

A checkerboard pattern is admittedly a crude way of allocating authority, for the life of the world is not similarly compartmentalized. The rudimentary character of the Western State System has been an intellectual affront to the lawyer and the political scientist. Meanwhile, violence in international politics, always a moral issue, has become as well a problem of intense practical concern. At first in response to the impulse of reform and soon under the lash of two world wars, countless proposals have been made for improving the organization of the world. Governments have themselves entered the quest, relieving the oppressiveness of sheer speculation with the trial and error of schemes put into actual operation.

Responding to the needs of security, of welfare and convenience, and of human dignity, governments have created scores of international organizations (universal, regional, and bilateral), with new ones steadily being added. That these innovations are modifying the international pattern of authority is a fair assumption. However, precisely what is evolving it is not easy to say. Often the more significant results have been by-products of intentions which have themselves been frustrated. Certainly the experience of history is again being borne out. The variables are so numerous and often so obscure as to defy architectural presumptions about allocating authority.

The attempt of the League of Nations and the United Nations successively to order the world—through law, peaceful change, and collective security—has had indifferent success. Indeed, the Charter, as did the Covenant, draws back from subjecting legal disputes to compulsory jurisdiction and refrains, in the case of political disputes, from giving any organ of international organization the authority of binding settlement. For dealing with aggression, the United Nations Charter gives the Security Council corporate capacity to determine its existence and to commit the whole United Nations membership to the carrying out of sanctions against it. However, the attempt, in this one instance, to establish supreme authority over governments is palsied by the veto. More than a mere question of procedure, the veto reflects the underlying difficulty (indeed, improbability) of achieving in the Security Council a political fulcrum sufficiently stable to permit the imposition of an authoritative restraint on international politics.

The international pattern of authority lacks a capstone, and it is not likely in the forseeable future to acquire one. Instead of a vertical structuring of authority above the state, we have witnessed a lateral expansion of the international community to include numerous international organizations, which in a variety of ways have become a new independent variable in international relations.

Already acknowledged members of the international community, these institutions are still in process of legal evolution. Unlike the nation-state, they are not self-generating; nor are they, like the Church, a fixture of history. Yet, as international corporations created by treaty, they partake of the character of their sovereign creators and are subject to the jurisdiction of none. The headquarters of an international organization do not, like the Vatican City, enjoy a separate sovereignty. However, the authority of the host state is withdrawn, affording the organization a limited territorial control in its own precincts. The autonomy of international organization is further augmented through the immunities possessed, in varying degrees, from the highest through the lower ranks, by members of its secretariat. Permanent delegations from governments may be accredited to it. It also has the capacity to enter into formal agreements with others of its kind and with governments.

The legal autonomy enjoyed by international organization can provide the basis for legislative and administrative authority applicable to individuals. This potential has been most highly developed in the European Communities, especially the Coal and Steel Community, whose independent power of decision is notable not only for its scope but for its location in extraordinary degree in the High Authority, an organ composed of experts rather than representatives of governments. The Common Market, too, has wide authority, though in this instance the Council of Ministers is more heavily weighted in the making of decisions. Whether legislative or administrative, decisions are enforceable in the national courts and, ultimately, in the European Community Court of Justice, which is common to all three Communities, including the Atomic Energy Community. The genius of these arrangements is, through personal jurisdiction, the penetration laterally of the territorial jurisdiction of states. Moreover, the individual citizen may be party to litigation in the European Court, as may corporations, governments, and the Communities themselves. On a much wider basis than the six states comprising the Communities, Europe has adopted a treaty defining human rights, with a separate court of final appeal.

However, even without the potent aid of jurisdiction over individuals, international organization is capable of exploiting its legal autonomy in surprising ways. Thus the International Bank and the International Monetary Fund have money that they dispose of on their own conditions. In consequence, they are capable of imposing discipline on the economic and financial policies of governments. Such material inducements are not, however, plentifully available to international organization, lacking, as it does, possession of territory and all the perquisites that flow from control over territory.

The United Nations is a complex institution. As a forum in which national representatives confront each other in a parliamentary manner, it influences attitudes and behavior in many subtle ways. But in this role it is essentially passive. More interesting from the standpoint of the international pattern of authority is the performance by the United Nations of what Hammarskjöld called executive functions. How it manages to do this without legislative or jurisdictional authority, in the usual sense of these terms, and without material resources of its own is a matter of considerable interest.

In far greater degree than the League of Nations, the United Nations is more than the sum of its parts. To be sure, the Security Council, despite the encouragement of the Charter to admit political considerations into its decisions, has proved to be politically incapable of wielding the mandatory authority with which it is endowed. But the Charter, as well, increased the stature of the General Assembly and the Secretariat, the former by virtue of the two-thirds rule and the latter by virtue of the increased role of the Secretary-General; and in these instances the result has been not stultification but rather quite the opposite. The autonomy accorded these organs has under the stimulus of subsequent events developed in ways that were unexpected—not to say, unintended.

The Covenant of the League prescribed in substantive matters a voting formula of unanimity. The implications of the shift in the General Assembly of the United Nations to a rule of two-thirds of those present and voting are not at first glance apparent, for it is axiomatic that the Assembly does not have legislative power. The Assembly, in the words of Senator Vandenberg, was viewed as "the town hall of the world." Discussion might, of course, lead to the drafting of treaties on various subjects; but a treaty is not binding on a state until ratified by its government. Thus the particular voting formula employed by the General Assembly would seem to be of no tangible consequence. Yet, as regards the internal management of the Organization itself, the abandonment of unanimity has made a distinct difference. The use of the Secretariat for performing operational tasks in the field, some of which have been highly political in character, could hardly be undertaken except on the basis of a voting formula which permits dissent without precluding action. Thus, it may well be contended that the single most important difference between the Covenant and the Charter is in their voting provisions.

As the administrative arm of the United Nations, the Secretariat consists of civil servants subject, on the one hand, to the employer's normal means of control through the providing of a career and through the stimulation of loyalty to the leadership and purposes of the organization. However, beyond the normal kind of employment, the international civil servant is subject to a superior, the Secretary-General, whose personal status and autonomous role in the international community are unique, and whose subordinates are immune from territorial jurisdiction to the degree necessary for the performance of their official duties. The international civil servant may be denied admittance to a territory, but once on it he is not an alien in the ordinary sense. He is responsible for his official actions not to the territorial authority but to his principal. As regards its own hierarchy, therefore, the United Nations in a limited but nonetheless real sense exercises personal jurisdiction in the face of territorial sovereignty.

What, in combination, the General Assembly's power of resolution and the instrumentality of the Secretariat are capable of undertaking is illustrated by the United Nations Relief and Works Agency. Concerned with the Arab refugees, UNRWA operates within the territorial jurisdiction of four states, performing functions normally those of government itself: providing minimal food, clothing, and shelter; health services; and education. To accomplish these purposes it recruits and controls its own personnel, whose activities are related to the host states through diplomatic representation and negotiation. The legal basis for the enterprise is not a treaty but resolutions adopted by the General Assembly. These fall short, however, of being legislative in character, for they cannot impose the arrangement on the four Arab states concerned, whose consent is a *sine qua non.* Though they touch profoundly the welfare of the Arab refugees and the politics of the Middle East, the resolutions are internal to the United Nations itself, essentially directives of the General Assembly to its own civil servants.

The Congo is a further, more startling, illustration of the potency of resolutions addressed to the United Nations Secretariat. In this instance the Security Council (not the General Assembly) was the author. Responding to an appeal from the Congolese government, the resolutions instruct the Secretariat to undertake a wide range of activities, in pursuance of which the United Nations personnel, civil and military, is ancillary to the government of the Congo, yet subject to the control of the Secretary-General. Two authorities, one territorial in scope, the other limited in application to the personnel of the United Nations, are juxtaposed. Their relations, regulated on a diplomatic basis, are the subject of a special agreement between the Congo and the United Nations of November 1961 that strongly resembles a concordat. It is not surprising, however, that a line of demarcation between assistance to the Congolese government and intervention in its politics has proved difficult, if not impossible, to draw. As regards Katanga, the action of United Nations forces had an extraordinary result, profoundly affecting its relations with the central government.

When the history of this latter-day application of extraterritorial authority is written, it may be concluded that the nature of the task imposed on the United Nations required for its success nothing less than the assumption of full territorial responsibility. As a practical matter this is not an alternative easily available to the United Nations. It is not one, however, that is denied to it in principle. There is the interesting, if fleeting, precedent of West Irian. There, during the transition from Dutch to Indonesian rule, the United Nations, by General Assembly resolution (with Dutch concurrence), assumed the role of territorial ruler.

The exigencies of international politics, under the imperious restraint of the nuclear threat, are likely in the future to force further, even more varied, instances of action by the United Nations as an autonomous member of the international community. However, short of the Security Council's utilizing its full powers under Chapter VII of the Charter, the United Nations can proceed only on the basis of resolutions recommendatory in character and incapable, therefore, of imposing an action within the territory of a state without its consent.

There is as well a second, perhaps even more serious, stumbling block to the performance of executive tasks by the United Nations. Lacking resources of its own, it is dependent on its members for financial support. One alternative, illustrated by UNRWA, is to meet the cost on a voluntary basis. Some governments contribute, others don't. The other alternative is to assimilate the cost to the regular budget and to assess it against the whole membership—by two-thirds vote of the General Assembly. This course was adopted in the case of the Congo. It is a highly venturesome choice, for it probes the outer limits of what the authority of the United Nations is capable of attempting.

## V

Under the enormous pressure of politics—that great human paradox of abrasion and cooperation—the allocation of authority in the world has been subject to a fascinating variety of concepts and of institutional forms. Ideology, in search of its own security, typically claims universal authority—promising in return the pacification of mankind. Communism, reaching out for the mantle of exclusive legitimacy, is the most recent case in point. Yet politics so conceived is today an anachronism. The nuclear age requires maturity, and maturity demands that authority divorce itself from, not tie itself to, man's speculative concern about his destiny.

Admittedly the principles of territorial jurisdiction and equality between territorial sovereigns cannot be represented as seeking peace as a direct objective, placing it above national interest. It does not follow, however, that the Western State System is wholly mischievous. Lacking ideological pretension, it is not burdened with the invidious task of converting the nonbeliever. But this is not its only advantage. As we have suggested, the autonomy characterizing the units of the Western State System has positive utility. Nationalism is often an unlovely thing, and admittedly it is abetted by the parochialism of territorial rule. But the great political storms that we are witnessing in mid-twentieth century cannot be explained on the basis of nationalism alone. To see this, one need only compare the circumstances of the First World War with the great disparities of ideology and of welfare that separate many of the influential participants in today's international politics. Such societies, contrasting sharply in their very warp and woof, would surely be subject to greater rather than less tension were they to be thrown together in a hierarchical system.

It is wrong to suppose that order is essentially a problem involving the hierarchical structuring of authority. In some circumstances the appropriate linkage may not be the amalgamation of authority but the keeping-at-arm's-length that is precisely the virtue of the diplomatic pattern of intercourse. Disparities of the magnitude that exist today—not likely soon to abate—belie a mutuality of interest capable of supporting common institutions of government. Not uniform policy but a negotiating situation is called for in the differences between East and West, between haves and have-nots, and between the new and the older nations. Even within the Atlantic Community, consisting of similar societies with many common interests, we will have to concede that it is not merely the perversity of nationalism that prevents close economic and political integration and that frustrates a unified policy in relation to the rest of the world.

International organization, we have said, is the main institutional response of the twentieth century to the challenge of its international politics. Yet, if universal order is beyond the reach of ideology, and if the Western State System acquiesces in an admittedly difficult situation, the goal of international peace and security also escapes the embrace of international organization, which has not in fact been able to control events.

This is not surprising, considering how formidable the task. However, short of providing a dominant center of authority and power, international organization is not without purpose. The functional roles that it performs are, to be sure, piecemeal in their approach to international relations. But the agencies engaged in promoting social welfare and economic progress, over and above their specific accomplishments, achieve a more general result. Operating on the basis of the accumulated knowledge and developing skills of the social sciences, they serve to foster an empirical and rationalistic outlook on human relations, which for large parts of the world is still an innovation. What the economist, the sociologist, the political scientist, and the lawyer can do, given the maturity of their disciplines and the receptivity of society around them, is illustrated by the European Communities, which are a monument to social science.

In the political realm as such, international organization, though asserting itself in ways that were unforeseen, has converted autonomous membership in the international community into something more significant than mere juridical novelty. As a third party, international organization has been active rather than passive. Though failing to materialize as a framework of order and justice, it has functioned as a new variable, interacting independently with the numerous factors comprising today's international politics. The contemporary situation is significantly different from that prevailing at the comparable period after the First World War. Today international organization suffers not from desuetude but from problems generated by its own vitality.

GEORGE F. KENNAN

## *Polycentrism and Western Policy*

Much of the discussion in Western countries today of the problem of relations with world Communism centers around the recent disintegration of that extreme concentration of power in Moscow which characterized the Communist bloc in the immediate aftermath of the Second World War, and the emergence in its place of a plurality of independent or partially independent centers of political authority within the bloc: the growth, in other words, of what has come to be described as "polycentrism." There is widespread recognition that this process represents a fundamental change in the nature of world Communism as a political force on the world scene; and there is an instinctive awareness throughout Western opinion that no change of this order could fail to have important connotations for Western policy. But just what these connotations are is a question on which much uncertainty and confusion still prevail.

The historical development of the process of polycentrism, particularly as it has manifested itself in the growing differences between the Russian and Chinese Communists, is a subject to which a great deal of careful study has recently been devoted and on which there is already an excellent body of analytical literature. There is no need to attempt to recapitulate here the conclusions—remarkably unanimous, in the circumstances—at which leading scholars have arrived concerning the causes and course of this process. Suffice it to recall that it had its origins, generally speaking, in two great events of the year 1948: the forced defection of the Jugoslavs, and the Communist seizure of power in China. The unity of the bloc never fully recovered from the shock of

SOURCE: George F. Kennan, "Polycentrism and Western Policy," *Foreign Affairs,* XCII (January 1964), 171–183. Reprinted by special permission from *Foreign Affairs.* Copyright by the Council on Foreign Relations, Inc., New York.

the Jugoslav defection. Had the Jugoslavs undergone something like a counterrevolution—had they shaken off their own Communist dictatorship, adopted a form of government which permitted democratic freedoms, and relaxed the governmental hold on the economy to a point where the system would have been no longer classifiable as a Leninist-Marxist one—the effect on bloc unity would have been less; for then the defection could have been regarded simply as the loss of a position to the capitalist world: a regrettable setback but not unprecedented, and no fit cause of doubt or questioning for a movement which had always prided itself on its ability to pocket losses and to recover from them. But when the Jugoslavs failed to do any of these things—when the Jugoslav Communist Party remained in power, and Jugoslavia did not go over to the capitalist camp but carried on much as before, claiming to be a Communist state and talking like one but not recognizing the discipline of the bloc or accepting any political obligations toward it—this was really unsettling for those who had remained faithful; for it raised the appalling question whether monolithic unity and discipline were essential at all to the development of Marxian socialism: whether one could not be a perfectly good Communist without taking orders blindly from Moscow and without following slavishly the pattern of institutions and methods established by the Soviet Union.

And since the strains of Stalinist rule were greater in the more Westernized states of the satellite area of Eastern Europe than in Russia itself, this suggestion—that there might be more than one path to socialism—was particularly insidious in its effect on the satellite régimes. Many were the satellite Communists who, in the years following Tito's break with Stalin, groaned under the necessity of pursuing Stalinist policies obviously unfitted to the traditions and psychology of their country and stole envious looks at the Jugoslavs, who could now cut their cloth to suit their own figure and yet maintain the claim to be good Marxian socialists. It is instructive to reflect that precisely that feature of Jugoslav behavior which so many Americans today find it impossible to forgive, namely, that the Jugoslavs did not, so to speak, "go capitalist," but carried on as a Marxian-socialist state, was the factor which more than any other proved disrupting in its effect on bloc unity.

So long as Stalin remained alive, the effects of the Jugoslav defection could be reasonably well contained by the Moscow headquarters. But after his death, this proved no longer possible. The de-Stalinization campaign of the mid-fifties implied at least a partial justification of Tito's earlier defiance of Stalin's authority. It was awkward, in these circumstances, to leave the Jugoslavs wholly outside the camp; and Khrushchev felt it necessary to try to draw them back again—something which could be done only by conciliatory means. But this, implying

as it did at least a willingness to forgive the earlier Jugoslav defiance of
bloc discipline, proved unsettling in its effect on the other satellites, particularly the Poles and Hungarians, and had a good deal to do with the
events of 1956 in those two countries. For the Polish and Hungarian
Communists had to ask themselves: if Tito is to be forgiven and treated
with deference, where are the rewards of obedience? Why should
not we, too, select our own path?

As for China, rivalry between the Soviet and Chinese Communist
régimes was latent from the beginning, but it began to appear on the
surface only after Stalin's death; and it was not until 1957 that it began
to assume forms which threatened seriously to disturb bloc unity. It is
interesting to reflect that it was in part differing reactions to these same
events of 1956 that caused the Chinese-Soviet disagreements to become
acute. For what the Russians found necessary in absorbing the shock and
the lessons of Hungary proved intolerable to the Chinese, whose revolution was in a different stage and who had different political needs. Here
is seen how one thing leads to another, how the threads of causality lead
on from the original Jugoslav disaffection and the Chinese Communist
conquest of China in 1948—the one considered at the time a loss to
world Communism, the other a victory—to the polycentrism of today.
If there is any lesson in this, it is the demonstration of how poor we
all are, even the Communists, at knowing what is a victory and what is
a defeat.

We are now confronted with a situation in which what was once
a unified and disciplined bloc has disintegrated into something more like
an uneasy alliance between two ideologically similar commonwealths:
one grouped around the Soviet Union, the other around China. But even
that element of order and symmetry which this description would suggest is not complete, because one nominally Communist country, Jugoslavia, is not embraced in either of these alliances, and another, Albania,
is nominally and formally embraced in the one (it still belongs to the
Warsaw Pact) but is politically closer to the other. And beyond this
framework, there are a large number of Communist parties not in power
which are greatly torn and bewildered by this division; and some of
these parties have an important voice in bloc affairs, even though they
lack the prestige that comes of being in power in their respective countries.

Barring unforeseen disturbances in international affairs, I think this
state of affairs should be expected to endure, in its essential aspects, for a
long time. Efforts will be made, of course, at one point or another, to
patch up Soviet-Chinese differences and to restore something like the
previous unity. The Poles, who have always had a special hankering for
close relations with the Chinese Communists, are apt to be particularly

assiduous in trying to assuage the Chinese-Soviet differences. Perhaps at some point changes of personalities in Moscow and Peking will help. But such tendencies can scarcely go beyond a point. An attempt to establish either Moscow or Peking as the unchallenged center of the movement would today involve prohibitive strains. Communism has now come to embrace so wide a spectrum of requirements and compulsions on the part of the respective parties and régimes that any determined attempt to re-impose unity on the movement would merely cause it to break violently apart at one point or another. There can scarcely be any meeting ground today between, say, the Chinese Communist Party and the Communist Party of Italy that would not be disastrous to one or the other.

A complete restoration of unity seems therefore to be out. But a total break, to the point of all-out hostilities and the alliance of one or the other faction with parts of the non-Communist world, seems equally improbable. Excruciating as are the differences which have now developed within the world Communist camp, all of the disputants are aware that they have nothing to gain, and everything to lose, by tearing themselves to pieces. Chinese and Russians, furthermore, are both highly skilled at the delicate gradating of hostilities of every sort; and while it would not be surprising to see at some point the development of armed conflicts along the Soviet-Chinese frontier comparable in seriousness to those that developed between the Russians and the Japanese along the same frontier in 1938, it would be surprising to see them develop, any more than did those of 1938, into a full-fledged state of war between the disputants.

## II

While this state of affairs is, then, likely to last for some time in its major outlines, it allows of considerable variation and evolution in terms of the relations between various Communist countries and the non-Communist world. This is a point of great flux and uncertainty throughout the bloc. Not only do the Chinese-Soviet differences center around disagreements over this point, and not only are there further differences on this score between the Russians and individual satellite states of Eastern Europe, but almost every Communist party in the world is afflicted by sharp internal differences or gradations of opinion along these lines. It is not too much to say that the entire bloc is caught today in a great crisis of indecision over the basic question of the proper attitude of a Communist country toward non-Communist ones. The question is whether to think of the world in terms of an irreconcilable and deadly struggle between all that calls itself Communist and all that does not, a struggle bound to end in the relatively near future with the total destruction of one or both, or to recognize that the world socialist cause can be advanced by more complicated, more gradual, less dramatic and less immediate forms, not necessitating any effort to destroy all that is not Communist within our time, and even permitting, in the meanwhile, reasonably extensive and profitable and durable relations with individual non-Communist countries.

The lines of division of opinion over this issue are by no means clean; very often both viewpoints struggle against each other in the same troubled Communist breast. But this is in essence the question. It is this which is buried under the long ideological arguments as to whether socialism could conceivably, or could not conceivably, be achieved by means that did not involve violent revolution. It is this that underlies the arguments about the inevitability or non-inevitability of war. This is the explosive substance with which the controversial concept of "peaceful coexistence" is charged. And none of us, I am sure, can fail to note that this is only the mirror-replica of the similar question which divides Western public opinion and tortures the policy-makers of the Western countries.

It is important to recognize that the degree to which polycentrism has already advanced means that individual Communist countries now have a far wider area of choice than was the case some years ago in shaping not only their own relationship to the non-Communist world but also their internal institutions and policies. These two things are, in fact, closely connected; for the more internal institutions and policies come to resemble those that once prevailed in Stalin's Russia and/ or prevail today in China, the more one needs a state of apparent tension and danger in external relations, as a means of justifying them. And in both these fields, as I say, the smaller Communist countries, and particularly the Eastern European satellites, now enjoy a far wider range of independent decision than was once the case. At one time there was only one model; today there are a number of them: the Soviet, the Chinese, the Polish, the Jugoslav, etc. And the fact that Moscow and Peking both need the political support of the satellite parties, and are therefore obligated to compete for their favor, means that neither can afford to discipline them, beyond a point, if the paths they choose are not ones that meet with full approval on either side.

On the other hand, the area within which this freedom of choice exists is not unlimited; it has, in fact, certain very sharp limits, and it is important to bear these in mind.

The satellite régimes of Eastern Europe cannot, first of all, sever the bonds of military alliance which united them with the Russians. Jugoslavia, it is true, did this in effect; but one must remember that when this occurred, the Warsaw Pact did not yet exist—nor did the Atlantic Alliance. Further, the Jugoslavs had a very special geographic and political position.

Secondly, the satellite régimes cannot abandon the profession of fidelity to Marxist ideals or the monopoly of power which those ideals imply and purport to justify. To do anything like this would be to destroy the very theoretical basis on which their power rests, and to commit, in effect, political suicide.

What the satellite régimes *can* do, and are doing to some extent, is to shape their own internal economic and social institutions along more liberal lines, or at least individualistic lines. They can, furthermore, ease the restraints—as the Jugoslavs have done—on all forms of contact and dealings with non-Communist countries and their citizens. As a part of this process, they can resist—as the Rumanians are doing—efforts to pull them into a tight and exclusive trading association with other Communist countries; and they can insist on the right to expand their trade with non-Communist nations to a point where it constitutes an important element in their economic development.

Finally, while they cannot leave the Communist military alliance, the satellite régimes could, conceivably, if conditions were right, help to deëmphasize the military factor to a point where it would not stand in the way of at least a partial political rapprochement with some of their Western neighbors.

Altogether, then, the choices open to the satellite régimes cover a range which lies somewhere between the extremes of the full independence of the Jugoslavs on the one hand, and a slavish, timid clinging to Soviet patterns and authority on the other. This is a circumscribed range of choice; but what they do within it is by no means unimportant. It could, conceivably, make all the difference between a Communist orbit with which the West could coexist peacefully and without catastrophe over an indefinite time, and one with which it could not.

III

Now the West has it in its power, ideally speaking, to influence extensively, by its own policies and behavior, the choices that the satellite régimes make in this connection. It can reciprocate or fail to reciprocate moves to relax tensions and to facilitate collaboration in various fields. It can shape its policies in such a way as to create advantages and premiums for efforts on the part of the satellite governments to extend their relations with Western countries; or it can decline to create such advantages. It can exert itself to deëmphasize the military factor in the mutual relationship; or it can take the opposite course. Finally, and of overriding significance, it can show itself reconciled to the existence of these régimes, without accepting responsibility for them; and it can convey to them that they have nothing to fear from it if they will only refrain, themselves, from hostile and subversive policies; or it can hold to the thesis that its object is to overthrow them, and permit them to conclude that any concessions they may make will only be exploited, ultimately, to their disadvantage.

Obviously, in the totality of these choices, the West is confronted by a pervasive and fundamental problem of policy: whether to promote a trend toward further polycentrism, in the hope that there might prove to be a portion of the Communist world with which one could, in the long run, contrive to live, and that living with it and encouraging it to see advantages in a situation of coexistence might tend at least to narrow the area and power of that other portion with which one could not live, or could not *yet* live; or whether to discourage that trend, on the theory that a differentiation of outlook and authority among Communist powers does not materially affect their status as a threat to the security of the Western peoples, and that the impression of such a differentiation serves merely to disorient and demoralize Western resistance to the phenomenon of world Communism as a whole. This is the question facing Western policy-makers; and there can in my opinion be no doubt that the trend of political decision within the Communist world will be importantly influenced by the answers they find to it. It could well be argued, in fact, that if the major Western powers had full freedom of movement in devising their own policies, it would be within their power to determine whether the Chinese view, or the Soviet view, or perhaps a view more liberal than either, would ultimately prevail within the Communist camp.

Fortunately, or unfortunately, the major Western powers do not enjoy this full freedom of movement. In the case particularly of the United States and Western Germany, but also to some extent of the NATO powers in general, the area in which they could conceivably meet the problem of policy posed by the trend toward Communist polycentrism has been severely circumscribed in recent years either by engagements they have undertaken to one another or to parties outside of Europe or by policies to which they have so deeply committed themselves that any early renunciation of them would scarcely be feasible. A glance at their position with relation to the various points of flexibility in the position of the satellite régimes will suffice to demonstrate this.

If it is a question of alteration of the internal institutions and policies of the satellite régimes, it is evident, on the example of Jugoslavia, that neither the United States Congress nor the West German Government is inclined to attach importance to this factor. The Jugoslavs have abolished forced collectivization. They have adopted a system of management in industry fundamentally different from that prevailing in the Soviet Union. They have practically abandoned the active application of police terror. They have adopted policies on travel, contacts with foreigners and access to foreign informational media which seem closer to those of most Western countries than to those prevalent in the bloc. It is evident that none of this constitutes, in the eyes of our own Congress or of a great part of our public, any reason to treat Jugoslavia greatly differently from any other Communist country. A similar disposition seems to prevail in Bonn, if only as a reflection of the Hallstein doctrine, which bars diplomatic relations with any country recognizing the present East German régime. Since all of the satellites do recognize it, they are obliged to see in this doctrine at least a limitation to the possibilities of any future political rapproachement between themselves and the German Federal Republic.

When it comes to economic policy, a similar situation prevails. There are the NATO arrangements for economic controls. There are the various legislative restrictions prevailing in this country. There is, finally, the Common Market, established and being developed on principles that appear to leave no room for anything like the eventual economic reunification of the European Continent. It will be recalled that in the original Marshall Plan concept, American policy-makers were careful to leave open the possibility of the extension of the respective arrangements to the entire Continent, and to phrase the proposals in such a way that if the Eastern European régimes were to be excluded, they would have to exclude themselves, which, in effect, they then did. But the European Common Market has failed to include this feature either in letter or in spirit; and the impression is being given to the Eastern Europeans, including the Jugoslavs, that whatever may be the future of this novel and important entity, they are to have no place in it.

When it comes to the military factor and the question of its emphasis or deëmphasis, the bald fact is that the Western powers, over a period that now runs back for several years, have committed themselves more and more deeply against anything in the nature of a military disengagement in Europe. Not only do they reject the possibility of any extensive withdrawal of foreign troops from the Western part of the Continent, even if this were to be by way of reciprocation for a similar withdrawal of Soviet forces, but they appear to have set their face, in present circumstances, against anything in the nature of a European pact or a nonaggression pact between the NATO and Warsaw Pact members. They are also averse to any sort of arrangement for the de-nuclearization of the European area, even, again, if this were to be on a reciprocal basis. Finally, they have exhibited no very convincing evidence of any disposition to place effective limits on the rearmament of Western Germany, where one restriction after the other, established in earlier years, has quietly gone by the board, and where the Germans are now, in the view of everybody in Eastern Europe, well on the way to becoming in all essential respects a full-fledged nuclear power. Yet at the same time the Western powers, with the exception of the French, have been unwilling to recognize the finality of Germany's eastern frontiers; and the West German Government, with the blessing of the others, still pursues a policy of total irreconcilability toward the East German state.

These aspects of Western policy are not mentioned for the purpose of taking issue with them. Opinions can differ on the degree of their justification, individually or collectively. But even those who are enthusiastic about them should remember that there is a price to be paid for them in terms of their political effect on the Communist bloc. To the East European satellite leaders, faced with these attitudes, and noting the extreme rigidity with which they are adhered to by the Western governments, anything like a deëmphasis of the military factor in East-West relations can only appear today as discouragingly remote. In present circumstances, they can hope neither for the removal of Soviet forces from Eastern European positions which they now occupy, nor for any further East-West agreements that could take the heat off military tensions. Particularly discouraging and disturbing to them is the progressive rearmament of Western Germany against the background of a West German commitment to the liberation of Eastern Germany, even though that commitment professes to envisage only peaceful means. The effect which the combination of these two things has had on the feelings of people in Eastern Europe cannot be emphasized too strongly. Either one without the other might have been less unacceptable. A strong commitment to the reunification of Germany might have been tolerable if it had not been supported by a military policy designed to make Western Germany into one of the two strongest states in Western Europe. Or a rearmament of Western Germany, while never fully defensible in East European eyes, might have been more tolerable if it had been coupled with a greater readiness on the part of West German political leaders to *faire bonne mine à mauvais jeu*, to accept the existence of a Communist Germany at least as a regrettable necessity of the present epoch, and to regard the cause of German unification less as a programmatical commitment and more as an historical inevitability, to be left to the healing hand of time. But the spectre of the violent liberation of Eastern Germany, by means not resting on any agreement with the Russians, and coming either against the background of, or by means of, a revived German military ascendancy, unites both governments and peoples in Eastern Europe in a common reaction of horror and apprehension; for the Communist leaders there, however little they may like or respect Ulbricht, know that their own stability would not easily withstand the shock of the sudden and violent overthrow of his régime; and the peoples of Eastern Europe, including the Jugoslavs, see in this eventuality only the beginning of a reëstablishment of the German military ascendancy of unhappy memory throughout Eastern Europe, and 18 years have not been sufficient to allow the horror of this prospect to fade in their minds.

Behind all this, and connected with all of it, is the heavy extent of the Western commitment, and particularly the American and German commitment, to the eventual destruction of Communism generally. We have our Captive Nations Resolution; and the satellite régimes of Eastern Europe and Asia are specifically listed there as ones we have committed ourselves in effect to destroy. In the Far East, there is our similar commitment to the Nationalist Government on Taiwan, with all its far-reaching political ambitions. And Western opinion, not just in the NATO countries but in certain of the neutral European countries as well, is heavily affected by attitudes which are at least skeptical toward, and in some cases strongly averse to, any thought of an accommodation to the permanency of Communist power anywhere.

It is true that the West European NATO governments are in a somewhat better position to face this problem than is the United States. They are not committed to the Captive Nations Resolution. There is no formal reason why they should not, if they wished, shape the policies of the Common Market in such a way as to give to the Eastern European peoples a more reassuring impression of the prospects for their future relation to Western Europe in the economic field. In the case of export controls and other restrictive measures, the degree of their responsibility is obviously smaller than ours; and it would, presumably, be easier for them to take a more conciliatory line. Particularly is all this true of the Italians, whose understanding attitude has already helped to ease Jugoslavia's delicate relations with the West, and who, more than any other Western people, have possibilities for exerting a reassuring and helpful influence on the East European satellites. But further north, the German problem and the aversion to any discussion of disengagement still loom up on the horizon of the Eastern Europeans as impassable barriers to anything like such a lowering of tensions as would make it possible for them to create a basically new political relationship with the West; and for both of these situations, as they well know, Western Europeans are as responsible as ourselves.

It is clear, in these circumstances, that the West has, as of today, only limited possibilities for reciprocating any disposition the satellite countries might evince to reduce the dichotomy of the two worlds and to bridge the gap that divides present attitudes on both sides from the possibility of truly peaceful and mutually profitable coexistence. It is in a sense tragic that this should be the case just at a time when there is so great a longing for a better East-West relationship in the hearts of tens of millions of ordinary people in the East European area, and so important a willingness to move tentatively in this direction even on the part of certain of their Communist leaders. And the fact that things are this way is something which should give pause for thought not just to those who would. like to find ways of living peacefully with Communist neighbors but even to those who can contemplate no permanent reconciliation with world Communism; for to deny to the East even the possibility of the development of a better framework for coexistence is to affect the terms of the argument which goes on within the Communist camp and to forego the advantage which a division of opinion there provides. If there is really strength in unity, Communist leaders can only be grateful for a Western policy which slights the values of polycentrism and declines to encourage them; for a rigidly unreceptive Western attitude may eventually enforce upon a bloc a measure of unity which, by their own unaided effort, they could never have achieved.

To say that the West is in a poor position to encourage polycentrism is not, of course, to say that it will not continue to develop. There are instances in which, as in the case of Jugoslavia, the desire for national independence may be so strong that governments will wish for, and seek, relief from the disciplinary strictures of the bloc even if there is no apparent place for them, or even for good relations with them, in the Western scheme of things; and it is not to be assumed that they will find no means of achieving that relief. The West, after all, does not represent the entirety of the non-Communist world. There are other areas where the trauma of the conflict with world Communism has struck less deeply and where both the readiness to forget or ignore ideological differences and the willingness to look at international relations in terms other than those of military conflict will be greater; and people who feel the need of more independence of policy but see no place for themselves in the vision of Western statesmanship can look, as the Jugoslavs are already doing, in other directions for the alternative to isolation.

Polycentrism may thus continue to develop, in spite of, if not because of, the face which the West turns to the troubled and vacillating world of Communism. But there are risks involved here. There is a relatively short-term risk, from the standpoint of the danger of war and of the effect which an absence of polycentrism could have in increasing that danger. But even if military complications do not ensue, there is still the long-term question of the effect on the minds of those tens of millions of people in Communist countries who still look to the West with longing and with hope and who expect from it policies which take account of all the subtlety and contradiction of their position. If such a response on the Western side is not forthcoming, who can say how this will affect their attitudes in the more distant future? Will they be best influenced by a Western policy which, through its quixotic commitment to a highly unlikely violent liberation, appears to condemn them by implication either to the miseries of a new world war or to an indefinite further period of languishing under oppressive Communist régimes? Or will they be better influenced by a Western policy which accepts as its goal the less ambitious but more promising prospect of a relaxation of the severity of those régimes and, by the same token, of the barriers that separate their peoples from contact with the outside world? This is a question which Western policy-makers will do well to look at all over again, as the Chinese-Soviet conflict proceeds and as its effects continue to make themselves felt.

In the nineteenth century, the colonial mother-countries of the West alienated many millions of people in other parts of the world through lack of imagination and feeling toward those who were in effect within their power. There is, surely, a danger lest history record that Westerners of the twentieth century alienated just as many more through lack of imagination and feeling toward those who were in the power of their ideological adversaries.

R.  N.  ROSECRANCE

## *Bipolarity, Multipolarity, and the Future*

### 1. BIPOLARITY

The argument for bipolarity is dual: it is allegedly desirable, as opposed, say, to a multipolar international order; it is also a continuing
state of affairs. Four reasons are given to persuade us that a bipolar order
will reduce international violence. First, "with only two world powers
there are no peripheries" (Waltz, 1964, p. 882). This juxtaposition entails
a vital interest and involvement in all the outcomes of world politics.
Both the Soviets and the Americans must be concerned with happenings in widely separated areas of the globe—Korea, Cuba, Vietnam,
Eastern Europe, to name but a few. Far from leading to violence,
however, the commitment on opposite sides has led to a solid and de-
terminate balance. No expansion could be decisively successful; counterpressure is always applied. The very existence of serial confrontation
renders the balance more stable. Each counterposition of power discourages the next. There are no realms open to aggrandizement.

Second, not only is the competition extensive, but its intensity has
increased. The space race, economic growth, military preparedness, the
propaganda struggle, and domestic issues of all sorts have assumed significance in international relations. "Policy proceeds by imitation, with
occasional attempts to outflank" (Waltz, 1964, p. 883). Nothing escapes
calculation in terms of the international balance. By asserting the interests of the two great powers in even minor equilibrations of the balance, the bipolar international system keeps on an even keel; nice adjustments do not pass unnoticed. A third stabilizing factor is the "nearly

SOURCE: R. N. Rosecrance, "Bipolarity, Multipolarity, and the Future," *The Journal of Conflict Resolution*, X (September 1966), 314–327. Copyright 1966 by The University of Michigan. Reprinted by permission.

constant presence of pressure and the recurrence of crises" (Waltz, 1964, p. 883). Crises are natural and even desirable in a condition of conflict. If crises do not occur, it means that one side or the other is neglecting its own interests. Maintenance of the balance will then require small or large wars waged later on. As long as there are only two major protagonists, there can be no question of the impact caused by a favorable change in the position of one; there also, presumably, can be no uncertainty of an "equal and opposite reaction." "When possible enemies are several in number [however] unity of action among states is difficult to secure." Under bipolar conditions, moreover, "caution, moderation, and the management of crisis come to be of great . . . importance" (Waltz, 1964, p. 884). One pushes to the limit, but not beyond.

Fourth, and finally, the preponderant power of the two super-states means that minor shifts in the balance are not of decisive significance. The US "lost" China in 1949, the Soviet Union "lost" it in 1962, but neither change drastically altered the Russian-American equipoise. The two states were so strong they could accommodate change. While defection of a major Western European state would be significant, "a five percent growth rate sustained for three years would add to the American gross national product an amount greater than the entire gross national product of Britain or France or West Germany" (Waltz, 1964, p. 903). Rearmament, economic growth, scientific education— all these were means of internal compensation for international shifts in the balance. The US and the USSR confronted each other over each proximate issue, but few of the issues were of decisive importance.

Not only is bipolarity desirable—its proponents claim that it will continue indefinitely; it is a condition to which we must adjust. Patterns of economic growth indicate that the Soviet Union and the United States will have economic systems more than twice as large as any conceivable competitor until past the year 2000. Nor has the spread of nuclear weapons appreciably influenced the amount of power middle-ranking states can dispose. Britain's nuclear program, so it is argued, is dependent on the US, and while France may gain an independent capability, she is likely to find it vulnerable or useless in a crisis. If independent capabilities began to be significant militarily, the nuclear giants would merely increase their offensive or defensive postures (Waltz, 1964, pp. 894-95). As a result of modest exertions, the bipolar world would be restored.

## 2. BIPOLARITY: A CRITIQUE

There are, in rejoinder, three arguments against bipolarity as a desirable (or even as the best attainable) international system. The first is that bipolarity comprehends only one of the impulsions to expansion or aggression. While it may be true that international polarization helps to prevent successful expansion by either side, since it calls forth counterpressure by the opposing camp, it does not reduce motivations for expansion and may even increase them. Since the competition between poles is both intensive and extensive, each action by one will be viewed as a strategic gambit by the other. Even actions which may not be intended to have international reference will be seen in terms of the bipolar competition. This in turn must accentuate the political hostility between camps. The antagonism generated on one side by action of the other will be reciprocated, and the tempo of discord will increase. Since the competition is akin to that of a zero-sum game (see Waltz, 1964, p. 882), this is quite a natural outcome. Any advance in the position of one must take place at the expense of his adversary; hence the slightest improvement in the position of one must provoke the other to new exertions. The respective concern to advance or maintain one's position is realistic in the framework of a two-power competition. The psychological climate in which such a struggle takes place, moreover, is likely to be one of growing ill-will. At some point in this degenerative process one side may think not only of the risks consequent upon striking his opponent, but also of the risks he may suffer if he decides not to strike. Eventually reciprocal fears of surprise attack may grow to such a point that they cannot be endured. Preventive war may be seen to be preferable to war at the opponent's initiative.

A second disadvantage of the case for bipolarity is that two quite different notions of the term appear to be employed. According to one, the Soviet Union and the United States are engaged in a duel for world supremacy or, at minimum, in a struggle to maintain their relative positions. An action by one directly affects the position of the other; all international changes are of vital significance in that they affect the balance between the two. According to the other notion of bipolarity, however, substantial territorial and/or political changes can take place in international relations without impinging on the overarching stability. The US can "gain" or "lose" China without appreciable impact on the balance. If the latter is true, it is because international politics is not analogous to a two-person zero-sum game. The increment (or decrement) to the US is not a simultaneous loss (or gain) to the USSR. The "gain" is not at the expense of previously Soviet-held territory; the "loss" is not at the expense of previously American-held territory. China is an independent quantity in world politics, not merely a factor in Soviet or Western strength.[1] If this situation prevails, there can be

---

[1] It should be noted that it is not pertinent to argue that the magnitude of bipolar power *vis-à-vis* Chinese power is so great that a change in Chinese allegiance is in-

important shifts in the international balance which do not upset the basic relation between the US and the USSR. That relation, however, is no longer bipolar. All changes are either vital in that they directly affect the bipolar balance, or they are not vital in that they fail to do so.[2]

Thirdly, the prescription "peace by crisis" is a dubious palliative. It seems equivalent to saying that the world's most peaceful place is on the brink of war. Pacific features may be present in one sense, in that nations presumably try harder to avoid war when they are faced with it as an immediate prospect. But if the will to avoid war is greater, the proximity of war is also greater. Cuban and Vietnamese crises may be stabilizing in that they teach techniques of "crisis management," but they are destabilizing in that there is always the possibility that the lessons will not be learned. When one decides to fight fire with fire, he engages in a policy of calculated risks. At minimum, it is not unambiguously clear that serial crises are the best means to peace.

Bipolarity also seems to have been confused with *détente*. Under conditions of *détente* crises may be manageable, and peace may be preserved. But *détente* is directly contrary to one of the major formulations of bipolarity. *Détente* presumes that the interests of two parties can be advanced simultaneously. The zero-sum notion of bipolarity requires that the interests of one can be advanced only at the expense of those of the other. And if it is then maintained that the looser notion of bipolarity is to be accepted in consequence, one may rejoin that a loose bipolar system does not involve an absence of peripheries. The two poles may then remain partially indifferent and unaffected by even significant changes in the distribution of international power. Immediate countervailing pressures, then, are not called forth by each change in the status quo. Imbalance may emerge. In the result one must choose between two different international systems: a system in which change can be accommodated without drastic action by the two major camps and in which, as a result, disequilibrium can occur; or a system in which there is a taut balance maintained by vigilant employment of counterpressure and in which the antagonism between camps is likely to be very great. The first may permit *détente* but is not strictly bipolar; the second offers stringent bipolarity but rules out accommodation. The two notions are not compatible, and the argument for one undermines the contentions urged on behalf of the other.

---

significant. If Chinese power is very slight compared with both bipolar powers, the balance between poles is narrow enough to make a switch in alliance of great importance.

[2] Waltz recognizes but does not assign due weight to this contradiction (see Waltz, 1964, p. 903).

### 3. MULTIPOLARITY

If bipolarity does not pass muster as a "relevant utopia" for international relations, what of multipolarity? Does it have special advantages to offer? Again a dual argument may be given. Multipolarity, it is maintained, not only meets the requirements of a reasonable utopia, but it can be approximated in future international politics.[3] Aside from the feasibility of multipolarity, however, three basic reasons commend it to our attention as a desirable international system. First, multipolarity affords a greater number of interaction opportunities (Deutsch and Singer, 1964, pp. 392-96). The number of possible dyadic relationships in a multipolar system is very great, and it rises in increasing proportion to the number of states (poles). This plenitude of interacting partners means that there is a greatly reduced danger of mutually reinforcing antagonism between two states. Individual states will have associations with a great variety of others; their cross-cutting loyalties will tend to reduce hostility expressed toward one particular state or against one particular cause. Multipolarity, it is claimed, avoids the major disadvantage of a bipolar international order. Since world politics would not be a zero-sum game, action by one nation would not require an offsetting response by its single opponent. Instead of the mutual reinforcement of hostility expressed in terms of "positive feedback" there may be the dissipation of hostility through "negative feedback" (Deutsch and Singer, 1964, p. 393). Multipolarity, then, provides the basis for a stable social system; bipolarity cannot do so. In addition, not only does the need for the expression of augmented hostility fail to appear, but the availability of alternative partners makes possible a response other than direct challenge or military threat. If a state finds itself the object of hostility, it may respond indirectly by firming its connections with other states. This in turn preserves the peaceful atmosphere.

A second argument offered on behalf of multipolarity is that it diminishes the attention paid to other states (Deutsch and Singer, 1964, pp. 396-400); ". . . as the number of independent actors in the system increases, the share of its attention that any nation can devote to any other must of necessity decrease" (p. 396). Since a nation can only actively attend to a certain maximum number of other states at any given time, a large multipolar international system will mean that a number of national actions will not reach the threshold of international significance. Conflicts may be limited in this manner. "It is perhaps not

[3] Hedley Bull, for example, sees warrant for the view that in the next ten years "the system of polarization of power will cease to be recognizable; that other states will count for so much in world politics that the two present great powers will find it difficult, even when cooperating, to dominate them" (Bull, 1963, p. 21).

excessive to assume that the minimal attention ratio for an escalating conflict would have to be 1:9, since it does not seem likely that any country could be provoked very far into an escalating conflict with less than 10 percent of the foreign policy attention of its government devoted to the matter" (Deutsch and Singer, 1964, p. 399). An eleven-state world (assuming relative equality of power) would, then, avoid serious conflict (p. 398).

Thirdly, it is contended that a multipolar system, in contrast to bipolarity, has a dampening effect upon arms races. If a state, A, is allocating half of its military strength against B and half against C and D together, and B begins to rearm, A's countervailing increment is only half of what it would be if A and B were the only powers in the system. The typical bipolar model, involving an escalating arms race between two opposed powers, then fails to predict the outcome. Multipolarity is responsible for limiting the arms competition.

The proponents of multipolarity admit that there are circumstances under which an international system of many equivalent powers could become unstable. In present-day international politics there are powers more reckless than the Soviet Union and the United States. If these powers obtained a nuclear weapons capability they might use it in a disruptive fashion (Deutsch and Singer, 1964, p. 404). But ". . . *if the spread of nuclear weapons could be slowed down or controlled,* a transition from the bipolar international system of the early 1950s to an increasingly multipolar system in the 1960s might buy mankind some valuable time to seek some more dependable bases for world order" (p. 406; authors' emphasis). It is also acknowledged that, while multipolarity is most likely in the near future, in the long run there seems to be a tendency for multipolar systems to break down. "If the probability of states' perishing is small, but larger than zero, and the probability of substantial new powers' arising is zero . . . then the model will predict a diminishing number of effective contenders, leading eventually to a two-power world or to the survival of a single power. . ." (p. 405). Assuming restraint on the dispersion of nuclear weapons and imminent multipolarity in the immediate future, however, one can look forward to a more peaceful international environment.


### 4. MULTIPOLARITY: A CRITIQUE

The case of multipolarity offers remedies for certain of the disadvantages of bipolarity mentioned above. There should be no cause under multipolarity for total international concentration on the reciprocally reinforcing hostility between two states. Alternative interests, antagonisms, and connections should distract attention from a focused bilateral struggle. If two-power arms races develop, they should be of much less consequence than under bipolarity. At the same time, multipolarity has its unique deficiencies. At least three points may be raised against it.

First, it seems highly probable that a multipolar world order will increase the number of international conflicts, though it may possibly reduce their significance. A bipolar system can have but one antagonism; multipolarity, on the other hand, may have virtually numberless frictions. While the attentions of international actors will be dispersed throughout the system, the variety of national interests expressed will multiply. Inevitably, national interests are a complex amalgam of popular attitudes, tradition, geographic situation, economic and military strength, ideological orientation, and governmental structure. Since in a multipolar order a great number of states will be significant actors in the system, a bewildering range of claims and interests must ensue. As other writers have contended, conflict is partly a function of the degree of particularity in the international system (see Waltz, 1959). The greater the gamut of demands, the harder it must be to accommodate them. Thus multipolarity, by increasing diversity, must also increase conflicts of interest.

This assessment may be countered by the argument that the results of multipolar conflict will be much less catastrophic for the international system than the potential results of bipolar conflict; that:

$$P_{bc} \times R_{bc} > P_{mc} \times R_{mc}$$

where $P_{bc}$ and $R_{bc}$ are the probability and results of bipolar conflict and $P_{mc}$ and $R_{mc}$ are similar quantities for multipolar conflict. The expectation of bipolar conflict (probability times results) would be greater than the expectation of multipolar conflict. This reformulation, however, is open to two difficulties. First, it shows that the advantages of the multipolar system depend on the variable magnitudes assumed. If a multipolar order limits the consequences of conflict, it can scarcely diminish their number. If a bipolar system involves a serious conflict between the two poles, it at least reduces or eliminates conflict elsewhere in the system. The choice between systems, then, depends upon the size of the respective quantities in a given case. Second, if nuclear weapons are widely disseminated in a multipolar environment, bipolarity must be seen to be the better alternative. In such circumstances the greater frequency of multipolar conflict would be accompanied by devastating or disastrous results, and the probability-times-results formula above would suggest that a bipolar system is preferable.

The second major criticism of the case for multipolarity flows directly from these considerations. If a multipolar international order is as harmonious as its proponents claim, even widespread distribution of nuclear weapons should not destabilize the system. As new states enter, the ensuing diminution of national attention should reduce friction. If states really fail to pay attention to their fellows, what differences should diffusion of nuclear weapons make? That the dissemination of weapons is viewed as crucial, however, indicates that multipolar exponents recognize the latent conflict in a multistate system. States are reckless only if they are, or conceive themselves to be, embroiled in conflict. Those features of multipolarity with which we are familiar (in the nationalist, underdeveloped world) are not characterized by lack of interest or attention. They are marked by a highly political awareness of the postures and attitudes of other states. And if some states do not attend to one another, as might be assumed to be the case in the relations of—say— Thailand and Bolivia, this is by no means a general feature of underdeveloped politics. The occasional discontinuities in communication in one part of the system are more than compensated by the range and depth of contacts, both friendly and hostile, which occur in others. Since these contacts link states of very different national interests, they are bound to produce antagonism. And atomic weapons superimposed on antagonism are a recipe for instability.

Thirdly, a multipolar international system, while reducing the significance of any single change of alignment or military posture, inevitably compounds uncertainty. In a bipolar world, an adjustment in relative position of the two poles is important for the entire system. Changes, however, are relatively simple to predict. In a multipower world a single alteration in alliance combination or military prowess may not be decisive for the system as a whole, but its consequences are far more difficult to calculate (see Burns, 1957). The number of tentative combinations is astronomic; military dispositions may take myriad forms. Multipolarity, then, raises the difficulty of policy-making. Results may be altogether unforeseen; choice becomes very complex. Since multipolarity raises incalculability, the system finds it more difficult to achieve stable results. War may occur, not through a failure of will, but through a failure of comprehension.[4]

## 5. Toward an Alternative System

The respective disadvantages of bipolarity and multipolarity as monolithic images of future international systems should not blind us to their attractive features. Bipolarity provides for well-nigh automatic equilibration of the international balance; in addition, while reinforcing conflict between the two poles, it at least has the merit of preventing

[4] It is possible that the origins of World War I owe something to the inability to calculate policies of other states until it was too late to change them.

conflict elsewhere in the system. Multipolarity reduces the significance of major-power conflict by spreading antagonism uniformly through the system. What we should wish for a future relevant utopia is to combine the desirable facets of each without their attendant disabilities. In practice, even the adherents of one or the other find merit in a wider view. The devotees of bipolarity seem implicitly to include the *détente* (which was a response of the United States and the Soviet Union to their position in a larger international system); the proponents of multipolarity draw back when it is proposed that nuclear weapons be part of the multipolar diffusion of power.

The objective can be accurately described, though it is difficult to give it an appropriate name. The relations between two major powers would be strongly conditioned by the presence and activity of other states. This means that international politics would not be a zero-sum competition between two superpowers. The resources of the international system would not be entirely divided up between the two major states with future outcomes dependent upon a bilateral competition between them. Rather, resources would remain to be appropriated, and the rivalry between the two major protagonists would occur in the external international environment as well as in the national preserves of each. Because external avenues of possible expansion would exist, neither major state need presume that only a direct conflict with its antagonist could decide the issue. The bilateral conflict might be adjusted or equilibrated through actions in the external realm; gains by one power could be made up by countervailing gains by the other. Nor should serial appropriation decide the ultimate fate of the external international world. If the two great powers merely proceeded to apportion slices of the remaining international pie, they would in time be brought back to a strict bipolar confrontation, with all the horrendous consequences which this might involve. The multipolar features of the external sphere should prevent substantial transfers of real estate and political allegiance. Neither hegemony would be acceptable to burgeoning power centers of the external area; changes of alignment or international disposition would not barter the fundamental independence of external states. The bipolar powers would continue to seek advantages in the multipolar realm, but they would fail to eliminate multipolar orientations.

This failure, in turn, might lead to disenchantment with equilibration via the external realm. The bipolar powers might then seek direct advantages in an intensified struggle over the national position of each. If the multipolar challenge were sufficiently great, however, the bipolar states might reduce their own competition for the purpose of making occasional common cause in opposition to external claims.

Ultimately, the bipolar states might seek a *détente* based on mutual recognition of two rigidities: (1) the difficulty of achieving preponderance in direct internal competition; (2) the difficulty of making major gains in the external environment. Confronting external challenge, moreover, both might realize that the international status quo was preferable to possible foreshadowed deterioration. Since cooperation in international relations tends to be reinforced by conflict elsewhere in the system, resurgence of the multipolar region would produce a tendency toward bipolar agreement.

One of the uncertainties in such a situation would stem from reversals for either of the two major states in the multipolar realm. In order to recoup a lost position of strength, the bipolar states might be tempted to heighten the conflict between themselves to reinsure for a multipolar client the value of past association or alignment. And at present the United States has sought to reaffirm nuclear solidarity with its NATO allies by proposing a counterforce strategy directed against the Soviet Union. If the commitment to Europe is underscored in the one case, the *détente* with Russia is also affected. The multilateral nuclear force, designed to reassure several West European states, also generated Soviet opposition. On the other hand, Soviet attempts to reassure China and North Vietnam of the benefits of the Russian alliance are bound to impinge on US relations. Closer ties with China would inevitably weaken new-found bases of Western accord. In the short run, then, it seems likely that the US will have to accept some erosion of its past position in Europe, while the Soviets will have to adjust to a diminished role in both Eastern Europe and the Far East. If they fail to do so, it will be at the expense of cordiality at the bipolar level.

The maintenance of the *détente* is of fundamental international significance, both theoretical and practical. It is theoretically important because it avoids the antagonism of the zero-sum game in strict bipolar terms. It also obviates a general trend toward multipolarity, with the loss of control and increase in the frequency of conflict that this would involve. A modicum of bipolar cooperation dampens hostility in the external sphere; interventions may be at least partially designed for the purpose of preventing multipolar conflict that could threaten central bipolar stability. In practical terms the *détente* is the means by which the spread of nuclear weapons may be channelled, controlled, or halted. It should be observed that nuclear weapons do not affect the theoretical questions of conflict and cooperation. A measure of bipolar agreement has been achieved despite opposing nuclear weapons systems. The dispersion of weapons is important not because of the new conflicts which it creates, but because it sanctions radical options in the waging of old conflicts. In so doing it threatens the balance attained at the bipolar level. Nuclear weapons may also, over a considerable period of time, give the appearance of transforming a bipolar-multipolar order into a system of general multipolarity. This fundamental alteration would be unlikely to occur in fact, but it is one of a range of possible future outcomes.

If the *détente* is desirable, it is possible to have too much of a good thing. A total bipolar *rapprochement*, an end to the Cold War, would be likely to create a new bilateral tension between major power and multipower spheres. In practical terms it would represent a conflict of rich countries and poor countries, industrial states and agricultural states, European and colored races, northern and southern nations. This emergent bipolarity would demand a rapid spread of nuclear weapons in previously multipolar areas. It would require a hasty amalgamation of economic systems and pooling of industrial resources: the multipolar area would transform itself through a new political coordination. The zero-sum game might be played once again.

A bipolar-multipolar system, on the other hand, would seek to avoid the extremes of either parent form. Enough bipolar control of multipolar realms would take place to prevent extremes of conflict, or, if conflict could be averted, to dissociate bipolar interests from outcomes in the area. At the same time bipolar competition would continue in multipolar as well as bipolar regions. The two major states would act as regulators for conflict in the external areas; but multipolar states would act as mediators and buffers for conflicts between the bipolar powers. In neither case would conflict be eliminated, but it might be held in check. Indeed, if hostilities were suddenly eliminated in one realm but not the other, the result would be adverse to general stability. If conflict cannot be eradicated both generally and simultaneously, its abolition in one part is deleterious to the whole.

### 6. BI-MULTIPOLARITY

It is possible to list the characteristics of an immediate international system, a system of bi-multipolarity.

### A. *Relationship of Interests*

The significant feature of interests in such a system is that they would be partially opposed and partially harmonious. The relation between the bipolar nations would be cooperative in that it would reflect mutual interests in restraining conflict or challenge in the multipolar region. The relation between bipolar powers would be competitive in that each would seek to prevent the other from attaining predominance either militarily or in connections with the multipolar world. The multipolar states would have an equally ambivalent pattern of interests. In regard to one another there would be rivalries stemming from the variety of national perspectives and positions; there would also, however, be common interests in resisting the ambitions of the bipolar powers. In regard to the bipolar states there might be individual interests supporting military guarantees or economic assistance from one (or both) of the major powers. There would also be resistance to big-power encroachment. In no case, however, would the pattern of interests resemble that of a zero- or constant-sum game. Bipolar powers would not directly confront one another; multipolar powers would not develop irrevocable antagonisms among themselves; and the multipolar and bipolar worlds would not be completely opposed. Conflict within each sphere and between spheres would be restrained.

## B. *Equilibration*

Equilibration, or the redressing of the international balance, will be a more difficult task in a bipolar-multipolar structure than in a strictly bipolar world. Since in the latter system interests are so clearly opposed, any advantage accruing to one evidently must be made up by the other. In a bi-multipolar system where interests are cooperative as well as conflictual, the consequences of a change in the position of one state will be harder to estimate. Since relationships will be more harmonious, on the other hand, the need for equilibration will be significantly reduced.

## C. *Predictability*

Policy-making in a bi-multipolar system will be more difficult than in a system of bipolarity. A far greater range of separate national decisions must be considered. At the same time, since the bipolar states will exert an important influence on the trend of events in the multipolar fraction of the world, statesmen would not be confronted by the sheer indeterminacy of a strictly multipolar order. While shifts would be harder to predict than under general bipolarity, the momentousness of each shift would be appreciably less.

## D. *Probability of Overt Conflict*

The probability of war, whether local or general, would be much smaller than in a multipolar system. Conflict would be mitigated on two scores: a multipolar buffer might help prevent the two nuclear giants from coming to blows; and the restraining influence of the bipolar states might in turn prevent extreme conflict among multipolar powers. While simple bipolarity would not exist, the influence of two superpowers would be crucial in limiting the outcomes of the system.

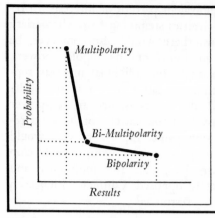 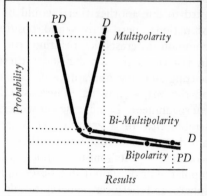

*Figure 1. Probability and results of overt conflict in the three different international systems.*

*Figure 2. Probability and results of overt conflict before (line PD) and after (line D) nuclear weapons have become available to a large number of states.*

## E. *Results of Overt Conflict*

The results of war, whether local or general, would be much more tolerable than in a bipolar system. Overt conflict would most generally take the form of wars among multipolar states, and while crises between bipolar states might not be ruled out, these would be tempered by recognition of significant mutual interests. As long as the *détente* continued, there would be few dangers of major nuclear war.

The probability and results of overt conflict in the three different international systems would be roughly as shown in Figure 1. The area of the dotted rectangle under the system-point in each instance indicates the amount of violence sustained by the international system. Bi-multipolarity does not eradicate violence, but it holds the prospect of limiting violence to far smaller proportions than does either bipolarity or multipolarity. If peace is the objective, a system combining bipolar and multipolar features may be a means of a reasonable approximation thereto.

### 7. DIFFUSION OF NUCLEAR WEAPONS

The situation depicted would change considerably if nuclear weapons began to be diffused among quite a number of states. The impact would be the greatest on a strictly multipolar system, for the incentives to acquisition would be substantial, and the disincentives involved in having to keep up with nuclear superpowers would be absent. Restraints on acquisition by the larger powers also would be lacking. In a bipolar

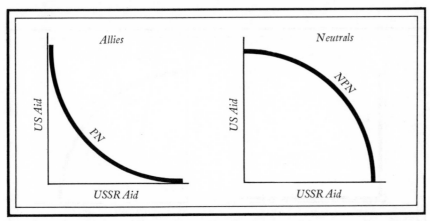

*Figure 3. Differential treatment received by allies and neutrals in terms of economic aid from the US and the USSR. PN is a "penalize neutralism" curve, while NPN is a "not penalize neutralism" curve.*

world nuclear weapons would add least to the dangers already confronted. A cataclysm between two halves of the world would be dangerous enough, even without nuclear bombs, though they would clearly enhance the war's destructive power. In an intermediate international environment, the process of nuclear diffusion would also raise levels of violence, but bipolar influence within the system would either reduce the scope of diffusion or limit its disruptive impact.

The results would be roughly as shown in Figure 2. If PD charts the results of international conflict in a prediffusion era, line D describes the outcomes after nuclear weapons have become available options for a large number of states. While bipolarity remains unattractive because of the dire consequences of conflict between the two protagonists, multipolarity has lost most of its previous advantages. Now the probability of conflict not only remains high, but the disastrous results of that conflict are clearly portrayed. Relative to the extremes of bipolarity on the one hand and multipolarity on the other, the intermediate system retains great appeal.

## 8. Bi-multipolarity and the Present International Scene

The system of bi-multipolarity should not be confused with the present international order. One of the major characteristics of the contemporary international scene resides in the difference in attitude and position of the allies of the great powers and neutral states. Two factors seem to account for this. On the one hand, nonaligned nations have received certain of the benefits of alliance protection and assistance without

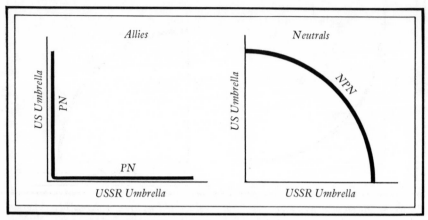

*Figure 4. Differential treatment received by allies and neutrals in the nuclear "umbrella" guarantees of the US and the USSR. As in Fig. 3, PN and NPN indicate policies of penalizing and not penalizing neutralism.*

pledging political allegiance to either bipolar camp. This continuing phenomenon has occasioned some disaffection among the formal allies of the two major powers. It has, in a measure, devalued the currency of alliance. On the other hand, the partial attempts at *détente* have made alliances seem less necessary. If a continuing Cold War were not the order of the day, former client powers would have less reason to guard, via great power alliances, against a sudden unfavorable change.

At the moment we seem to be in a phase in which the two major powers are placing enhanced emphasis on their formal alliances. The Soviet Union has come back into Far Eastern international relations, apparently striving to improve its ties with China and to reassert its influence in North Vietnam. Until recently, at least, the United States seemed engaged in an effort to reestablish a strong position within NATO. In both cases it remains unclear whether maintenance of a strong alliance position or an enduring atmosphere of *détente* and/or peaceful coexistence is most important. The issue is a complicated one in practice because any disengagement of interests, justified on grounds of relaxation of tension, may be interpreted by a bipolar opponent as a sign of weakness and a signal for adventure.

In the longer run, however, there are potentialities for the bipolar-multipolar world we have been discussing. It will probably involve treating nonaligned states somewhat less favorably and aligned nations somewhat more favorably than has been the case up to the present. It seems uncertain, however, that the two aligned camps will continue as presently organized into the indefinite future. The reasons for this

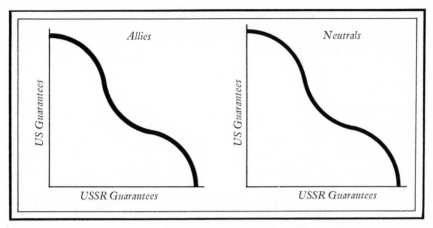

*Figure 5. A possible final equilibrium position for allies and neutrals with respect to economic and military guarantees from the US and the USSR.*

uncertainty can be seen in Figure 3.[5] The two diagrams show the differential treatment that allies and neutrals have received in the aid-giving behavior of the United States and the Soviet Union. Among neutrals, roughly speaking, the NPN (not penalize neutralism) curve has been followed, permitting a recipient country to receive sizable quantities of assistance from the opposing bipolar power. Among allies, on the other hand, the PN (penalize neutralism) curve has been followed, providing for substantial reductions of assistance as the ally in question gains additional aid from the opposing camp. If allies suffered in comparison to neutrals in terms of economic and other assistance, they had the compensation of participating in deterrence alliance systems, the protection of which was presumably denied to neutralist nations. As a result of the threatened spread of nuclear weapons today, however, it is no longer certain that allies alone may enjoy the benefits of deterrent protection. India, in particular, may be able to retain her nonalignment while participating in nuclear guarantees of the big powers. If this occurs generally in the neutralist world, an equivalent disproportion in the treatment of allies and neutrals might come to exist in the military sphere, as shown in Figure 4. Such outcomes would so disadvantage allies and reward neutrals that a considerable movement toward greater neutrality would have to be expected. A final equilibrium might be attained, covering both economic and military guarantees in roughly the form shown in Figure 5.

In such a case, of course, there would no longer be a difference between allies and neutrals. The growth of multipolar sentiment would

[5] I am indebted to Professor Albert O. Hirschman of Columbia University for the basic notions of the figures which follow (Hirschman, 1964).

presumably reinforce the *détente* between bipolar powers, and an important step in the direction of an intermediate international system would have been taken.

REFERENCES

BULL, HEDLEY. "Atlantic Military Problems: A Preliminary Essay," prepared for the Council on Foreign Relations meeting of November 20, 1963, p. 21.

BURNS, ARTHUR. "From Balance to Deterrence: A Theoretical Analysis," *World Politics*, 10, 4 (July 1957).

DEUTSCH, KARL, and J. DAVID SINGER. "Multipolar Power Systems and International Stability," *World Politics*, 16, 3 (April 1964), 390–406.

HIRSCHMAN, A. O. "The Stability of Neutralism: A Geometric Note," *American Economic Review*, 54 (1964), 94–100.

HOFFMANN, STANLEY. "International Relations—The Long Road to Theory," *World Politics*, 13, 3 (April 1961).

WALTZ, KENNETH N. "The Stability of a Bipolar World," *Daedalus* (Summer 1964).

———.*Man, the State, and War*. New York: 1959.

HERBERT S. DINERSTEIN

# The Transformation of Alliance Systems

## WAR AS AN INSTRUMENT OF POLICY

The investigation will begin with an examination of the change in the conception of war as an instrument of policy, treating separately the periods before the First and Second World Wars and the period since the Second World War.

SOURCE: Herbert S. Dinerstein, "The Transformation of Alliance Systems," *The American Political Science Review*, LIX (September 1965), 589–601. Reprinted by permission. [Author's Note—Any views expressed in this paper are those of the author. They should not be interpreted as reflecting the views of the RAND Corporation or the official opinion or policy of any of its governmental or private research sponsors.]

*Pre-World War I*

Before World War I statesmen believed, on the whole, that war could be profitable. Political leaders initiated wars, expecting gains commensurate with costs. The classic case comprised Bismarck's three wars against Denmark, Austria, and France, which achieved the unification of Germany at a cost probably no greater than expected.

The corollary to this assumption that some wars were worth the price was that some were not. Price was calculated not only in terms of prospective gain but also in terms of avoiding losses. Thus Great Britain reluctantly entered World War I pursuant to the guiding principle that no single nation—Germany in this case—should be permitted to dominate the European continent. Had any of the major powers before World War I foreseen its consequences, each would probably have been willing to accept greater shifts in the balance of power before engaging in war. The low tolerance for political loss in the European capitals of 1914 was a function of their underestimate of the cost of a general war.

*Pre-World War II*

For the victorious powers, the terrible, unexpected destructiveness of World War I produced a conception of war midway between that of 1914 and that of the present. Clausewitz's remark, made in a different context,[1] that "a conqueror is always a lover of peace," also applied to the Entente powers, since after 1918 a new war could bring them no great benefits. A profound anti-war spirit permeated all levels of British and French society. Consequently, in contrast with their position before World War I, Great Britain and France were willing to tolerate great and unfavorable changes in the balance of power before judging war to be necessary.

• • •

In the 1930s Germany viewed war as an instrument of policy, as "have-not" nations have traditionally done. Hitler's strong desire for German expansion was coupled with a belief that his enemies could be beaten one by one. Had he foreseen how many, how powerful, and how united his enemies would be, he might have been slower to provoke war. Between the two world wars Great Britain and France followed the traditional policy of victors: they upheld the *status quo* established by the last war, eschewed aggression for themselves and

[1] Karl von Clausewitz, *On War* (Modern Library, New York, 1943), p. 332.

deplored its practice by others. Their attitude toward war as an instrument to prevent losses had become more cautious since 1914, for they feared that air bombing would make the next war a cataclysm of destruction.[2] Consequently, they tolerated great defeats in Europe before resorting to war and exposed themselves to further defeats in the early years of the armed conflict.

## Post-World War II

Today, neither the Soviet Union nor the United States has any goals commensurate with the expected cost of a nuclear war. Hence, given the present balance of military power, the initiation of total war is unacceptable. With the development of nuclear weapons, *both* major powers have now all but ruled out large-scale nuclear war as an instrument of policy.

In the past the initiator of a war seldom thought it would be a total war; he always hoped to control the arena and intensity of war so as to maximize his chances of victory. Today it is commonly believed that a possible consequence of a direct military confrontation between the two super-powers would be a rapid transition to total war accompanied by unprecedented destruction. Both sides now say they will, and presumably intend to, retaliate with nuclear weapons if attacked with them on a large scale; but it is quite uncertain what lesser assaults, if any, would move them to nuclear war. Obviously both sides want to avoid such difficult decisions, and this is the basis of whatever mutual understanding exists. What differentiates the present situation from that preceding the outbreak of World War II is that *both* sides rather than *one* have rejected total war as an instrument of policy. Furthermore—in contrast to the situations preceding both world wars—the Soviet Union and the United States now have a very low tolerance for *any* changes in the balance of power in Europe. Since 1948 no changes comparable to those that took place in the periods 1904–1914 and 1933–1939 have occurred. The comparative rigidity of the present arrangements in Europe is to be explained, first, by the mutual awareness of the consequences of a nuclear war and, second, by the fear on both sides that any shift in the balance of power would cause the losing side to suffer further losses in rapid succession. Dominoes falling, has been the favored image. As early as December 1953, when the United States still enjoyed what was practically a monopoly in nuclear weapons, President Eisenhower stated the conviction that has dominated Amer-

---

[2] Chamberlain, particularly, and even Churchill, expected that aerial bombing would produce far more casualties than it actually did. However, 50,000 British civilians died in German air raids, a figure that would have seemed horrible enough to the statesmen of 1938.

ican attitudes ever since. By asserting that a nuclear war would mean the end of civilization, he implied that only the gravest threat to American interests could justify a decision to launch nuclear war. By maintaining American superiority in weapons, he reduced the likelihood that such threats would emanate from the Communist world.

• • •

## II. Is War Likely?

Before World War I, wars were more frequent than today. More than a dozen regular wars were fought between 1870 and 1914, almost all bilateral, and many of them could have expanded into larger wars. In addition, many international crises, almost all multilateral, threatened war. Since some of the wars of this period, including the two largest, the Franco-Prussian War and the Russo-Japanese War,[4] yielded benefits to the victor that were apparently commensurate with the sacrifices, the recurrence of similar wars was not "unthinkable."

At present the chances of a large-scale war with the most modern weapons seem small, certainly very much smaller than in say, 1913 or 1938. But the awful realization that the human race could be in jeopardy often dominates the imagination, obscures the reduced likelihood of war, and produces the emotionally based conviction in times of crisis, that war is likely, or inevitable in the long run unless radical changes are made in the international system. The truth, however, is that statesmen in the competing camps share a catastrophic view of the consequences of nuclear war, and this has made warfare *less* likely.

Not only general war, but apparently also wars on a smaller scale, with or without the employment of nuclear weapons, have become less likely. Only a few years ago it was generally expected that limited wars would become more likely when the Soviet Union had acquired nuclear parity. With both sides in possession of nuclear weaponry, the reasoning went, either side, trading on the common fear of a general nuclear war, might conduct war on a lower scale with relative impunity.

The validity of this prediction has not undergone a genuine test, since the United States has maintained nuclear preponderance. Although the Soviet Union has disposed of a substantial nuclear capability for some years now, the United States has enjoyed a mutually recognized superiority. In this situation both sides have been concerned about the

[4] It is not generally appreciated that the Japanese, despite their naval victories, were staggered by the extent of their losses and probably would have soon taken the initiative in suing for peace, had not Russia done so because of the revolutionary situation in the latter country. I am indebted to Paul Langer for this realization.

escalation of local conflicts and have sought to avoid them. Whether local wars would be more likely *if and when* the Soviet Union achieved
rough nuclear parity, or when China achieves a real nuclear capability,
can only be a matter for speculation.

### III. The Nature of the Alliance Systems

#### A. *Pre-World War I*

The great powers before World War I were organized in a balance
of power system first systematically described by Machiavelli. A power
shifted from one alliance to another, either to "balance" another power
or a coalition which had become too strong, or to place itself in a position
to gain territory at the expense of a former ally. In the nineteenth and
early twentieth centuries, nations sought territorial alterations within Europe, competed for empire in Asia and Africa, jockeyed for positions
of advantage in the expected demise of the Ottoman Empire. Some, but
not all, of their goals were interchangeable. Thus Italy, by alliance with
the Central Powers, increased its chances of getting the territories it
claimed on the French Riviera, but thereby relinquished claims to *irredenta* in the Austro-Hungarian Empire. And Bismarck tried, but
failed, to compensate France for the loss of Alsace-Lorraine by holding
out opportunities in Africa. But it was not only the prospect of gains
that caused nations to shift from one alliance to another. Fear of loss
could be equally, or more impelling. Thus, the German naval program of the turn of the century played a major role in persuading
France and Great Britain that they had more to fear from Germany
than from each other.

In contrast to the present, ideology was not an inhibition to diplomatic realignments (*renversements des alliances*). The ideological differences between Imperial Russia and Republican France and Liberal England were residual; for neither the Russians on the one hand, nor the
French on the other, were intent on a political revolution within
the other country (unlike the period from 1791–1815). These nations
formed an *entente* which survived the crisis preceding the war, three
years of war, and the democratic revolution of February 1917, only to
collapse after the victory of the Communists in October 1917.

Great powers shifted their alignments rapidly and radically. For
example, in 1898 in the Fashoda crisis, Great Britain and France were
on the brink of war over competing ambitions in Africa. The crisis that
erupted brought the two countries closer to war than they had been
for many years. The French, for a combination of domestic and
foreign policy reasons, yielded and war was avoided. The name ap-

plied to this easement was *détente*. Several years later, largely because of a changed perception of the danger from Germany, the two powers formed an *entente*—practically an alliance—first settling territorial disputes between themselves on a basis of give and take. Thus, they proceeded from the brink of war immediately to a *détente* and eventually to an *entente*. A *détente* sometimes developed into an *entente*; enemies sometimes became friends. How much, or how little, this has changed we shall examine shortly.

Remaining outside the alliance system was only possible for countries without territorial ambitions and against whom others did not have territorial claims. Even so, in time of war or imminent war, another power might invade for strategic reasons. Of course, distant and powerful nations separated by oceans, like the United States, could remain outside the system of alliances.

## B. *Pre-World War II*

By World War II the character of the system had begun to change in that the *status quo* and the revisionist groups were more firmly fixed in their positions. France, Great Britain, and the new states of Eastern Europe, created in part at the expense of Germany and of Russia, supported the *status quo*. Germany, especially after Hitler's rise to power, was revisionist, and the Soviet Union shunted between the two positions, although it was basically revisionist.[5] Neither the Soviet Union nor any other major power was able to remain neutral. Small powers like Austria, the Baltic States, and Finland, outside the major alliance systems, or secured only by bilateral nonaggression pacts, lost their independence to the revisionist powers. Even within the *status quo* alliance system, weaker powers did not enjoy genuine security. Although the great powers never formally renounced their obligations to Czechoslovakia, in essence they abandoned her to Germany. Before the First World War neutrality would not necessarily survive the outbreak of war; before the second, even membership in an alliance did not protect weaker powers from absorption before the inception of general war. How different the position of the weak and unaligned has become!

[5] The Soviet Union was revisionist when Germany was weak, a defender of the *status quo* after Hitler came to power, and revisionist again in 1939 when it seized the opportunity to gain territory and remain neutral in a war between its foes. The *status quo* position of the Soviet Union at various times must be distinguished from that of Great Britain and France, for unlike them it had great expectations of radical favorable chances in the future. The Soviet Union favored the *status quo* when its relative weakness permitted no other course, but was prepared to shift when opportunities for aggrandizement offered themselves. Professor Vernon V. Aspaturian suggested this and other formulations.

In the interwar period, the threat of internal revolution inhibited the formation of alliances. For example, the Franco-Russian treaty of mutual assistance signed in 1935 was never implemented by joint military arrangements as in the case of the Franco-Russian alliance whose negotiation was completed in 1894. Although the alliance proved abortive for more reasons than the ideological tension between Republican France and the Communist Soviet Union, ideology did play a major role.

## The Present

1. GENERAL CHARACTER   Alliances now differ in three large respects: (1) political goals have superseded military; (2) the relative power and the number of participant states have altered significantly; and (3) ideology has become a major factor.

   *a. The primacy of political goals.* The determination of the major powers to avoid war, noted above, has caused a qualitative change in international relations. The expectation that war can be avoided makes the primary purpose of alliances deterrence of war rather than preparation for its conduct. Although success in the former purpose is dependent on the latter, the primacy of deterrence is of great consequence. The great questions of war and peace are the almost exclusive concern of the Soviet Union and the United States; the secondary powers in both alliances benefit, or suffer, from the military balance produced by the rivalry of the two greatest powers. But the influence of secondary powers on the balance of power in comparison with their influence in earlier alliances is modest. The relations between the two greatest powers are increasingly conducted on the assumption that outstanding issues will be resolved only by political means. The secondary members of both alliance systems pursue their particular goals in the confidence that there will be no world war. Thus conflicts with the hegemonic power within each alliance involve only political and economic costs. The question of isolation and abandonment in a world war need hardly be considered. The Chinese Communists would hardly have permitted relations with the Soviet Union to deteriorate to the point of withdrawal of Soviet military aid if they had expected war with the United States; de Gaulle would not have presumed to challenge the American position in Western Europe if he expected a world war. Hence secondary powers, while less influential in alliance military arrangements, enjoy more freedom of action within the alliance. The consequences of this increased freedom of action are quite different for each system. They will be examined at the point where intra-alliance arrangements are discussed.

   *b. The increase in the number of participants in the international system and the change in their relative power.* Since the Second World War the distribution of power within the international system has changed significantly. Earlier there were greater powers (more than two); secondary participants in alliances who, at the lower end of the power spectrum, merged with client states protected by a major power and without a genuinely independent foreign policy; and finally a great fraction of the world's population, largely non-European, lived in colonies or semi-independent political entities.

At present there are two super-powers, the Soviet Union and the United States. In time, probably, Communist China and, possibly, a united Western Europe will join the ranks of the super-powers. But now the gulf in power between the largest power in each alliance and the next largest is greater than ever before. Consequently, the very magnitude of the power of the two greatest states creates, despite their rivalry, some common concerns and common interests not shared by their allies.

By now almost all the former colonies and semi-independent states have become independent and have largely remained unaligned. The reduced likelihood of world war makes it possible for them to contemplate continued existence without becoming minor members of a diplomatic system. They no longer worry that their independence would constitute the victor's spoils in a new world war. From being the objects of international politics they have become active participants, adjusting and readjusting their relationships with each other and with the major powers. And client states, especially in Eastern Europe, as we shall see, are increasingly asserting some control over their own foreign policy.

*c. Ideology.* Soon after the conclusion of the Second World War it became a truism that ideology was the major determinant in international relations. But like many truisms it turned out to be a half-truth. As early as 1948 Yugoslavia, after ejection from the Communist camp, was able to survive as an "unaligned" nation. The Soviet Union failed to gobble up weak nations on its periphery and communize them on the model of the Eastern European nations largely because, both before and after it acquired nuclear weapons, the Soviet Union feared a large war that might result from aggression against a small country protected within the American alliance system. The American system of guarantees and alliances of the 1950s has been much criticized of late on the ground that the Soviet Union was really unaggressive and that the system extended American commitments beyond American strength and willingness to play a world role. But the success of the policy of the containment of Soviet expansion by superior military strength does not prove that containment was unnecessary. It was just because some countries joined in the effort to contain the Soviet Union that other countries could afford non-alignment and enjoy the freedom of a position between the two main antagonists. But whatever the origin of the present security of the smaller powers, the present reality is that both diplomatic and ideological non-alignment are realistic policies for the weaker nations in the international system.

After 1947 it was widely believed, on both sides, that the passage of a particular country from one camp to the other, regardless of its size, would precipitate a series of such changes. In the West this fear rested on the over-facile assumption that Western European nations, which had not been occupied by Soviet troops, were as much in danger of communization as the Eastern European countries had been. In the Soviet Union, on the other hand, it was feared that the successful departure of Yugoslavia from the Soviet satellite system would be emulated. This fear lay at the basis of the brutal imposition of strict police controls in all the satellite states after 1948. Since then in Europe both sides have felt that any alteration of the *status quo* would produce a chain reaction.

But the very stability, caused in part by the mutually shared apprehension of the consequences of change, has produced a measure of relaxation. The conversion of some of the satellite states of Eastern Europe into client states with incipient independent foreign policies has been an embarrassment, and may presage serious losses; but it has not been a disaster for the Soviet Union. Castro's personal conversion to Communism, which (given his position) meant the communization of Cuba, caused great agitation in the United States. But it is now tolerated largely because of Castro's failure to spread the revolution, the relatively minor importance of Cuba, and the frustration of the Soviet attempt to make a major strategic change on the basis of a political victory in a small country.

In the overall balance of power, new Communist states, ideologically much diluted and little controlled by the largest Communist state or states, may become important. If, again, modernizing dictators adopt Communism and impose the new faith on their people like the pagan princes converted to Christianity, will it be an extension of the international power of Communism or a dilution of its strength? It all depends on what happens to such states. If some stumble and founder, then the pattern maintained since 1920 when Hungary ceased being a Communist state will have been broken—communization will no longer be irreversible, and each case can be separately assessed on its own terms. If on the other hand, each new regime consolidates itself (and no established regimes abandon Communism), then forceful measures to prevent what will seem to be permanent losses can be expected. Thus, ideology will play a greater role in international relations or a reduced role; the present situation seems to be transitional.

Very likely the importance of ideology in foreign policy calculations will persist longest in areas vital to the interests of the greatest powers. For example, it is difficult for the near and proximate future to imagine political changes in Europe in which ideology would not figure largely. Reckoning on the basis of power politics alone, the Soviet Union would have much to gain from the abandonment of the Communist regime in Eastern Germany. A serious proposal to Western Germany for reunification on the basis of demilitarized neutrality would have good chances of acceptance and at the very least would precipitate a major political crisis in Western Germany. Such a settlement, presumably including the settlement of the Polish (and Czech) western borders, would constitute a political settlement in Europe which would probably bring in its train major modifications of NATO and the Warsaw Pact. The enormous saving in money would greatly ease the dilemma of resource allocation within the Soviet Union. This projection of future events seems unrealistic only because the ideological value of Eastern Germany cannot be exchanged for other values. But the reconversion of Castro, or the collapse of his regime would probably not be viewed as fraught with disaster by the Soviet Union.

2. INTER-ALLIANCE RELATIONS *a. As between the United States and the Soviet Union.* Earlier the familiar point was made that the Soviet Union and the United States have a common interest in avoiding nuclear war. But beyond that common interest, rivalry is the keynote of the relationship. In that rivalry, relative military strength is crucial. At present both sides accept United States superiority in nuclear weapons, but Soviet acceptance followed upon efforts to create a balance more favorable to the Soviet Union. The Soviet Union failed to convert its priority in ballistic missiles into a superiority in intercontinental forces, largely, probably, because of its industrial and economic inferiority. It also failed in its effort to alter the military balance by the expedient of putting medium and intermediate-range missiles into Cuba in the fall of 1962. For the Soviet Union, a test-ban treaty promised to, and has tended to, stabilize the weapons balance at roughly the present level, namely an inferior Soviet position in intercontinental nuclear weaponry. The Soviet Union probably accepted such a state of affairs for the interim, at least, because the alternatives might be worse. A continuation of the arms race at a faster pace might well produce no relative advantage. The economic cost, which the Soviet Union can ill afford, might well be paid without military and political improvements relative to the United States, perhaps even with a decline in the Soviet Union's

relative position. The United States, on the other hand, enjoying a military superiority which it believes has contributed to the frustration of Soviet aims in Cuba, West Berlin, and elsewhere, is willing to continue the present situation. It is uncertain, of course, whether opportunities, especially in the technological sphere, to alter the weapons balance will emerge and be exploited by the Soviet Union. But at present the United States and the Soviet Union seem to accept roughly the present balance because the former finds it satisfactory and the latter can see no way to alter it significantly for the better.

An unusual feature of the treaty, and significant for the altered nature of international relations, was that both the Soviet Union and the United States knew that a major ally of each would refuse to sign it. The leading powers of the rival alliances thus agreed on a major issue concerning which, one differed with France and the other with Communist China—both disagreements being between allies. Furthermore, the conclusion of the treaty legally bound the signatories to resist their allies' demands for assistance in developing nuclear weapons. Whatever political costs were involved in opposing the wishes of their alliance partners the United States and the Soviet Union were ready to bear. Both major powers opposed the further proliferation of nuclear weapons, and the treaty represented a common resolve not to assist in such proliferation. It was generally recognized, however, that even without help France and Communist China could acquire nuclear weapons by their own efforts.

The corollary of the Soviet and American determination to reduce the danger of war by controlling nuclear weapons as much and as long as possible by themselves is the determination to avoid small-scale conflicts which could grow into larger ones, eventually threatening war. Most often this has meant the frustration of a secondary ally's desire to use force to his own advantage. The two super-powers, in a sense, have a tacit pact to keep the peace even if it frustrates an ally's ambitions. Thus the United States vetoed the Anglo-French-Israeli adventure in Suez, with the Soviet Union adding menace from the sidelines. Whatever the extent of Chinese desires in India in the fall of 1962, the joint—though not concerted—United States and Soviet support of India set limits on Chinese objectives. In both cases it was a nonaligned nation that was protected against an ally. As a consequence, the United States and Soviet partnership in keeping the peace reduces the policy alternatives traditionally enjoyed by secondary members of an alliance. Thus, not only the nuclear powers, but their weaker allies, also must pursue their foreign policy objectives with much less reliance on military force as an instrument to attain desired goals.

The recognition of an area of common Soviet-American interest, symbolized by the test-ban treaty, has been referred to as a *détente*. But unlike the traditional *détente*, the present arrangements cannot be converted into an *entente, i.e.,* the alliances cannot be reshuffled because several essential features are lacking.

First, the present situation is essentially bipolar, since as has already been remarked, the difference between the power of the strongest member of each alliance and the next strongest is unprecedentedly great. Traditionally, great powers shifted from one alliance to another because another power of the same size was perceived as threatening. Thus the British *Entente cordiale* with France in 1904 required the existence of a Germany. At present the Soviet Union and the United States have no peers in power.

Second, in most reversals of alliances at least one partner was revisionist, that is, considered territory held by another power as rightfully belonging to itself. Thus the Anglo-French *entente cordiale* of 1904 eventually brought Alsace-Lorraine back to France; the Italian shift from the Triple Alliance to the Triple Entente brought them Fiume, etc. Now *both* the Soviet Union and the United States, having been victorious in the last war, are essentially *status quo* powers. This generalization requires serious modification only when the present arrangements for Germany are challenged, but hardly at any other time.

Concerted action to keep the peace between two powers is not equivalent to common action to ward off a common threat from a third power, or to gain something at the expense of third powers. Unless and until the Soviet Union and the United States perceive a threat from a third power of equal rank, or both develop aggrandizing goals which can be achieved only at the expense of third powers of equal rank, the necessary basis for the conversion of *détente* to *entente*, for the reversal of alliances, does not exist.

Thus even if the ideological tension between the Soviet Union and the United States diminishes rather than intensifies, they can only become more friendly; they cannot become friends.

But from the point of view of secondary allies, this partial accommodation between the two super-powers has some of the features of a reversal of alliances, especially if the accommodation is in an area of vital interest to the secondary power. Thus, in the Chinese view, the Soviet accommodation with the United States on the peace issue has deprived the Chinese of practically every advantage which the alliance had afforded. But unlike the classic reversal of alliances, the Chinese do not find themselves in another diplomatic constellation. The improvement in the relations between the two super-powers does not lead to the reshuffling of alliances but to alterations within each alliance which will be considered subsequently.

*b. As between a super-power and a secondary power in a rival alliance.* On several occasions the United States and the Soviet Union have given limited support to a secondary power in the rival system in order to increase the leverage of that power in relation to the hegemonic power, with the object of reducing the cohesion of the rival system. American aid to Yugoslavia was an example of such a tactic—after the fact to be sure, but relevant nonetheless. After the increase in Poland's independence in 1956, United States aid to Poland was offered in the hope of consolidating that independence rather than out of any farther reaching community of Polish and American foreign policy interests. Recently, Rumania has taken first steps toward similar arrangements. Other East European Communist states may well follow suit. Thus far these measures have not caused departures from the Warsaw Pact, but have rather contributed to the process of desatellitization in Eastern Europe.

Similarly in Cuba, the Soviet Union offered Castro, then not yet a Communist, limited political and economic assistance with the purpose of reducing the cohesion of the American diplomatic system in the Caribbean. Castro, a modernizing *caudillo*, deemed it necessary to provoke sharp conflict with the United States in order to demonstrate that he was not merely another dictator, who after eloquent promises of reform would relapse into corruption. In order to guarantee continued Soviet support and also to control his own Communist Party, Castro declared himself and Cuba to be Communist. If Paris was worth a mass to Henry IV, Cuba was worth a party card to Castro. In contrast to the Russian and Chinese revolutions, which derived largely from internal impulses with subsequent effects on foreign policy alignments, the basic impulse in Cuba was in the realm of foreign policy with subsequent effects on domestic policy.

Attempts by both the United States and the Soviet Union to weaken the rival coalition by approaches to some of its members seem to be a permanent rather than a transitory phenomenon.

*c. As between secondary members of rival alliance systems.* The main purpose of cross-alliance relationships between secondary alliance members is to gain leverage as against the alliance hegemon, often on issues which are of secondary importance to the hegemonic power but of primary importance to the weaker power. For the United States, relations with Pakistan are important, but no more important than relations with a dozen other powers. For Pakistan nothing is more important than the Indian problem. Hence Pakistan's arrangements with China have as their main motive the improvement of her position *vis-à-vis* India.

The Franco-Chinese exchange of courtesies (*rapprochement* would describe more than has occurred), was motivated by considerations of lesser urgency than the Pakistani-Chinese gestures of friendship. The French desire a larger voice in allied policy in general, and in Southeast Asian policy in particular, but their national interest in that area can only be residual and sentimental. It is more a case of, "I will be heard." For the Chinese it represents a symbolic escape from the diplomatic isolation caused by the Sino-Soviet breach.

Recently, both the French and the Germans have sought to improve their relations with some of the Eastern European countries. In part the motive resembles that of the United States in seeking to stimulate the growth of the independence of these states from the Soviet Union, but in part it expresses the rivalry of France and Germany for dominance in Europe.

In these cases, to greater or lesser extent, the approaches of second-rank members of one alliance to second-rank members of another alliance have been un-ideological and represent an effort to satisfy desires thwarted by the hegemonic power. Thus Pakistan wants a settlement of the Kashmir dispute which the United States will not support; France wants to be the first power in Western Europe; the countries of Eastern Europe want to improve their bargaining power with the Soviet Union by establishing better relations with France and especially West Germany.

Since only the hegemonic power can satisfy the demands represented by these cross-alliance overtures between secondary powers, these overtures do not lead to switching alliances. After all, it is the United States, not China, to whom Pakistan must look for effective pressure for its solution of the Kashmir question. France wants American acceptance of its claim to primacy in Europe; Soviet or Chinese assent is meaningless. Poland and Rumania require Soviet acceptance of their desire for greater freedom in foreign policy. West Germany or France cannot satisfy that wish, they can only serve as instruments for its accomplishment. Therefore, these approaches to members of the rival alliance are really methods of improving negotiatory power against the hegemonic power. The basic impulse is from within the alliance, not from without.

*d. As between non-aligned powers and alliance members.* (*1*) *Competition between members of rival alliances for influence with the non-aligned.* In the immediate postwar period, only the Western alliance system drew non-aligned states to itself. These states fell into several categories: first, states against whom the Soviet Union or China had territorial claims or was presumed to have territorial ambitions (Turkey and Iran in the Near East). In the Far East, South Korea and South Vietnam were under threat when not under attack.

A second category of states entering the American mid-eastern and far eastern alliance systems comprised those who wanted American economic or political aid but were under no immediate threat from either the Soviet Union or China. Iraq, Pakistan, and the Philippines are the obvious cases. Most new states, however, perceiving no threat from the main Communist states, and hoping for economic support from both systems, have remained unaligned.

When it was realized that the Soviet Union had abandoned the policy of the absorption of contiguous states out of fear of the consequences, states in the tier beyond those immediately bordering on the Soviet Union and China dropped whatever ideas they had had of joining a Western defense system, thus putting a term to the Western process of alliance building.

Furthermore, beginning in 1955, the Soviet Union began to furnish military, and sometimes economic, support, especially to former colonies who were at odds with their former imperial masters. Indonesia and Egypt are the two most important in this category.

For the great majority of the non-aligned countries, national interest is best served by joining neither alliance system and being wooed by both. Above it was argued that the international tension produced by the communization of new states (the unaligned or underdeveloped, or both, being the most likely candidates) would not remain at its present level. It would either increase or decrease. If concern increases, efforts to draw unaligned countries into alliance systems would resume, with the leaders of the unaligned countries seeking to exploit the advantages of the middle position. In a period of intense rivalry for their allegiance, the leaders of non-aligned countries could combine appeals to magnanimity with the threat or promise to move from one camp into another. But this is a threat of limited utility, because all concerned know that the first choice for the unaligned is the medial position.

If fears for the definitive passage of presently unaligned (or loosely aligned) powers to one of the systems decline, the bargaining power of the unaligned will be sharply reduced. They will be reduced to a position commensurate with their power. They can appeal to the magnanimity of the great powers, but they cannot negotiate effectively because they have little to give or withhold.

The super-powers in their rivalry and mutual fear of war have permitted the birth of a host of new nations and have protected their independence. These now act on the international stage, but the political importance of any single one of these nations becomes a multiple of its true power only when it becomes an object of rivalry between the two super-powers.

(2) *Competition between members of the same alliance system for*

*influence among uncommitted states.* The first area of Sino-Soviet rivalry for influence in underdeveloped countries has been Southeast Asia. By the time of the Bandung Conference at the latest, it was clear that Sino-Soviet rivalry for the adherence of the unaligned was at least as important as Communist-capitalist rivalry.

Since the Soviet signature of the test-ban treaty, the Chinese have challenged Soviet influence wherever they could: in Africa, in the Near East, in Latin America, and even in Europe. This competition is really a function of intra-alliance dissension, to the examination of which we shall now proceed.

Competition within the non-Communist alliance for influence among the unaligned, by contrast, is of slight significance, because no conflict comparable to the Sino-Soviet conflict exists. Greek-Turkish rivalry in Cyprus, however sharp, is consequently localized; and French oil interests in North Africa, as against other European powers, are not the occasion of NATO's troubles.

*a. The non-Communist alliance system.* The purpose of the non-Communist alliance system or, more correctly, systems, is the containment of the Communist states. This is a familiar goal in international diplomacy, namely, not allowing an opponent to grow too strong. Two novelties characterized this effort: its geographical scope and its duration. The French Revolution, in its time, also presented a threat to the established political order, but it was essentially confined to Europe, and conclusively contained in 1815, only a quarter century after its beginning. The Communist Revolution is almost half a century old and still presents challenges in many parts of the world.

The ideological character of the Communist system has impelled a search in the non-Communist alliance for a suitable ideological label for its system, but none has been found, for the internal regimes of the member nations are based on different principles. Outside of Western Europe, only in countries populated by settlers from Northwestern Europe, and in Japan, are societies based on a broad consensus. In most of Latin America, the Near and Middle and Far East, ruling strata are too narrow and middle classes too small to make representative democracy a genuine possibility at present. Although frequently deplored, this political diversity in the non-Communist alliance is a source of strength rather than weakness, as we shall presently see.

The non-Communist alliance system truly deserves the appellation of polycentric because it is a congeries of alliances with different purposes suited to the different threats posed by Communism in various parts of the world. In each of these alliances, the hegemonic power, the United States, plays a different role.

In the NATO alliance, after setting into motion the economic and

political restoration of Western Europe, the United States by the maintenance of nuclear military superiority has limited the options open to
Communist expansion. Since 1948 when Czechoslovakia became a
Communist country, the Communist state system has made no progress
in Europe. Hence the anti-Communist purpose of the NATO alliance
has receded into the background, and NATO's main task is to maintain a credible deterrent against the Soviet Union. Since this task has
been successfully accomplished, its importance tends to be forgotten,
except when the Soviet Union offers a challenge such as the Berlin
crisis, or even more dramatic, the Cuban missile crisis.

With security against both internal and external threats seemingly
assured, the nations of Western Europe can and do devote much of
their energies to jockeying for favored positions, as against each other,
and as against the hegemonic power of the United States. France has
put herself forward as the claimant for leadership in Europe. Western
Germany cannot compete for this position despite her greater economic
resources, because the unresolved problem of unification makes her
politically dependent on the United States. The issues on which the
NATO allies differ are well publicized: the sharing of nuclear control
in NATO, the terms of economic integration, support for Western Germany's position on the Berlin issue and what lies behind it—the political future of all Germany. Yet despite these very genuine differences,
the system is not disintegrating, but is rather rearranging the relationship of its parts. After all, the economic integration of part of Western
Europe goes forward; economically Western Europe and the United
States are growing closer rather than apart. The basic stability of the
NATO alliance can be explained on two grounds. First, no claimant
for second place presents a genuine challenge to United States power.
China may someday be a greater power than the Soviet Union, but
neither France nor Germany can challenge the preeminence of the
United States. Thus de Gaulle is claiming the position of the first
among the secondary powers in the alliance, rather than the position
of first in the alliance. Since goals are limited, the conflict does not
pass beyond a certain point. Second, the modesty of NATO's goals
makes it an alliance which can withstand a great deal of turbulence.
Since its main purpose is to prevent the spread of Communism and
Soviet power in Europe, differences which do not threaten the
accomplishment of that objective are not really subversive. If the purpose
of NATO encompassed a common political direction of all Western
Europe, or a common economic policy directed from the center, then
NATO would be even more disrupted than the Soviet system in
Eastern Europe. It is because the true purpose of NATO is *merely*

anti-Communist that the alliance is capable of accommodating so much change.

A striking feature of the NATO alliance system is the limited power of hegemonic partner. The Cyprus issue illustrates the increased independence of the weaker power within the alliance. In a traditional alliance system, both Greece and Turkey would have had to consider the consequences of defying the wishes of the hegemonic partner for peace in Cyprus. The Turks would have had to calculate that bad relations with the United States might encourage the Soviet Union to press its claims once again for *irredenta* in Eastern Anatolia. The Greeks, for their part, would have had to worry that bad relations with the United States would encourage Yugoslavia or Bulgaria, or both, to renew claims for Greek Macedonia. But neither Greece nor Turkey need concern themselves overmuch about such contingencies, because in a common desire to avoid territorial conflicts which might cause even greater conflicts, the Soviet Union and the United States have consistently avoided territorial conflicts in Europe in which both alliances were involved. The consequence has been to make territorial conflict within alliances easier.

The problems of the hegemonic power in the CENTO and SEATO alliances are very different from those in NATO. In the band of territory stretching from the Bosporus to the China Sea, the economic base for political institutions of the Western European type does not exist. Unresolved internal, political, and economic problems of varying intensity characterize every member of the CENTO and SEATO alliances. And in Vietnam, a situation exists which the Communists expected would be common to the majority of the former colonies.

The speed and relative ease of decolonization since World War II has come as a surprise to all. Communist theorists expected that the imperial powers and the colonies would have been involved in long armed conflict, during which the national liberationist movement would have been captured by Communist parties. However, only in Indo-China is the Communist Party engaged in active combat to become the successor to a colonial regime.

In Vietnam, therefore, the United States is trying in the midst of a civil war to create the political conditions in which democracy might be able to grow, and it is not an easy task. Had the British been as reluctant to face the necessity of liquidating empire as the French, Burma today might be in the position of Vietnam, rather than an independent and unified country.

In the CENTO and SEATO alliances the hegemonic power has two tasks: first to create the conditions for economic growth, which it is hoped will permit the establishment of broadly based governments of the West European type in which the internal threat is practically nonexistent; and second, as in Vietnam, to aid a regime actually engaged in a civil war with Communists.

The role of the United States as the hegemonic power in Latin America is again very different. Opposition to the extension of the Communist state system is a very different task in Latin America than in Europe or Asia. The geographical proximity of part of Latin America enables it to play a role in the military relationship between the two super-powers. The United States' successful opposition to the emplacement of missiles in Cuba was in pursuit of the goal of maintaining strategic superiority over the Soviet Union. As pointed out earlier, Soviet acceptance of this relationship is the condition of the existing *détente* between the super powers.

A second United States purpose in Latin America is to prevent the establishment of Communist regimes in these countries. The hegemonic position of the United States in this alliance is complicated, first, by the circumstance that the danger from Communism is internal rather than external. The United States and Latin America are in a very uneasy relationship because of their different assumptions about the nature of their relationship. Although Latin American countries display a very wide variety of stages of development, they share the belief that the United States plays a dominant role in the affairs of each country. For each country of Latin America the United States is the most important foreign power; for the United States, each Latin American country is only one of many. The natural consequence is resentment at neglect.

Second, the belief is almost universal in Latin America that United States policy toward Latin America is largely determined by American private investors in Latin America.

Third, any United States involvement in the internal affairs of Latin American countries awakens the suspicion that North American imperialism is again active.

Yet the very formulation of the problem necessitated active North American involvement in Latin American internal affairs. The operative theory in the United States is that the unresolved developmental problems of Latin America may create good opportunities for Communism, and that therefore it is in the interests of the United States to help Latin American countries develop their economies.

In Latin America, however, the danger of Communism from within is not perceived as so great, and the dominant feeling is that the United States *owes* Latin America assistance because of the profits that American business has made in the last century. Moreover, the United States, it is believed, owes such a debt even if the businesses of its citizens are confiscated.

The situation is further complicated by vacillations in the United States judgment as to the danger of Communism in Latin America. The Cuban conversion to Communism, at first seen as a pattern for the future, is now increasingly perceived both by the Soviet Union and the United States as unique. As the danger of Communism is perceived to diminish, quite naturally United States interest in Latin America declines.

The Rio Pact is not, then, a traditional alliance against a foreign threat but an agreement about United States economic and military assistance against internal threats, variously perceived by the signatories of the pacts. Is this a transitional or a permanent feature of the international scene? The answer seems to depend very much on the future prospects of Communism discussed above. If Communism loses as well as gains, then new variants of syncretic Communism in Latin America, if they emerge, will probably be viewed as reversible phenomena which might do world Communism more harm than good in the long run. If on the other hand, Communism continues to gain, the pressure for intervention before and after the fact of conversion will be high.[6]

*b. The Communist alliance system.* The members of the Communist alliance system share with the members of the non-Communist alliance system the security from war which results from the common interests of the two super-powers in keeping the likelihood of war low. But beyond this the resemblance ceases. The major distinguishing features of the Communist alliance are the following: (1) It is a fragmented system meant to be universal. (2) It is divided into revisionist and *status quo* powers. (3) Its members have territorial and economic claims against each other.

The greatest difficulty in the Communist alliance system is to establish a common agreement on its goals. As we have seen in the non-Communist alliance system where the purpose is essentially to contain Communism, the alliance system is divided into different parts in accordance with the nature of the task, with the United States being the hegemonial power in each of the sub-alliances. No such satisfactory solution is possible in the Communist alliance because its goals go far beyond containing the opponent; they encompass, eventually, overwhelming him. It has not been possible to reach agreement on how to do so safely in a world full of nuclear weapons.

For a long time the Communist camp could preserve the fiction of

[6] These lines, like the rest of the paper, were written in March 1965. No changes have been made in the text to accommodate subsequent events like the Dominican crisis.

the existence of a correct political and military strategy to be discovered by divination from the entrails of Marxism. While the *pontifex maximus* was established in Moscow, the question of variant interpretations never arose. But just as the United States and the Soviet Union finally succeeded in establishing the security of their respective allies from attack, the primacy of Moscow was challenged from within the Communist alliance system by China, and the leadership of the United States within the Atlantic Alliance was sharply disputed by de Gaulle. The protected secondary powers challenged the hegemon, but the consequences were much more serious for the Communist system.

For one, the main challenger, Communist China, was potentially a greater power than the Soviet Union, which lent a special bitterness to the conflict. Second, the problem of mutual economic aid is much more severe in the Communist camp than in the other. In the non-Communist system, in each of the sub-alliances, economic demands have been made only on the hegemon, that is, the United States. In Western Europe economic assistance is no longer necessary; in other areas the extent of economic assistance is under continuous assessment. But in the Communist camp the direction of demands has been reversed. The Soviet Union at one time exploited Eastern Europe, but since 1956 it has responded to demands upon itself from Eastern Europe. The Soviet Union also exploited China by reasserting Tsarist rights in the Treaty Ports and on the Manchurian railroad. Moreover, as has been revealed since, the Chinese Communists had to pay for Soviet military aid during the Korean War. After Stalin's death the flow of demands was reversed until 1960, when the Soviet program of military and economic assistance came to an end.

These reversals in the flow of economic wealth are profoundly disturbing to the Communist camp because a critical goal for all its members, including the hegemonic power, is the attainment of the standard of living of the advanced Western capitalist countries. Since the United States has already attained this goal, offering assistance to its allies does not mean postponing the achievement of the aim of an adequately fed and clothed population.

A further cause for division in the Communist alliance is the existence of *status quo* and revisionist powers. These claims are not only against members of the non-Communist alliance, but against each other.

The Soviet Union, being a victor in the last war, is essentially a satisfied power territorially. Communist China is not, having active claims to Taiwan and inactive but not abandoned claims in Southeast Asia. A common policy of pressing these claims would produce gains for China, not the Soviet Union, and what is more, the costs to the Soviet Union are higher. Soviet support of Chinese territorial claims could cause conflict with the United States, but even if that were avoided it would most probably produce a new phase of the arms race with the attendant economic embarrassment of the Soviet Union. Since China is too far behind the United States in weapons to be in competition, this cost does not enter into her calculations.

Thus in the Communist alliance, agreement cannot be reached on a common policy of promoting the expansion of Communism, nor on some scheme for sharing economic resources to build Communism in each country. The frustration produced by these differences is so high that Communist China has raised her territorial claims against the Soviet Union and Outer Mongolia and has encouraged Rumania to raise the question of Bessarabia obliquely. Poland, Czechoslovakia, and East Germany have not claimed the territory they lost to the Soviet Union, but these demands are just beneath the surface.

Originally, in the Communist system the tendency was for each country's internal institutions to be pressed into conformity with those of the Soviet Union; but since Stalin's death diversification rather than *Gleichschaltung* has been the trend. This aggravates internal political problems in the Soviet Union. For example, the freedom of action of Soviet leaders in domestic agricultural policy is limited by the existence of a Poland without collective farms.

Within the Western system the necessity to maintain uniformity in the political regimes of all its members has never been felt, and centrifugal tendencies do not create pressures for domestic reforms. As the originally looser system becomes more so, there is a little feedback in internal politics. As the rigid system loosens, however, the feedback is significant and, what must be deeply disturbing, of dimensions difficult to foresee and assess.

Thus it is hard to imagine Eastern Europe as anything but much altered ten years from now and Western Europe as remaining essentially the same. Paradoxically, it seems that the cohesion of the Communist alliance system, once pressed into a rigid mold, will suffer much greater disintegration than the always loose non-Communist system. And the multiplication of ideological variants of Communism probably will eventually attenuate the ideological force of Communism.

Perhaps the second half of the twentieth century will indeed be the time of the end of ideology and a time of peace.

LEON LIPSON

## Peaceful Coexistence

### INTRODUCTION

"Peaceful coexistence" deserves provisionally to be examined as a principle or a set of principles of international law: not simply as a description of contemporary international relations, not as an index to a
mood or as an expression for something desired, but as something proclaimed to be the basis for contemporary international law and indeed
the most important principle within it. . . .

A Polish Ambassador to India has written (in 1961) that coexistence is the norm applicable to present-day international relations, that
coexistence besides being a concept of international relations becomes
also a concept of the law of nations, that the principles of international
law applied to contemporary relations are the principles of the conduct
of coexistence, and that international law is the law of coexistence. The
man who is perhaps the most eminent currently active Soviet scholar
of international law, Professor Gregory Tunkin, said in 1959, "A new
page in the development of international law constitutes the principle
of peaceful coexistence," and, in 1963, "There is every ground to call
present-day international law the law of peaceful coexistence."

The Committee on Peaceful Coexistence of the Soviet Association of
International Law declared in 1962, "The principle of peaceful coexistence is a universally recognized principle of modern international
law; . . . whereas international law of the past was a law of war and

SOURCE: Leon Lipson, "Peaceful Coexistence," *Law And Contemporary Problems*,
XXIX (Autumn 1964), 871–881. Reprinted by permission from a symposium, "The
Soviet Impact on International Law," appearing in *Law and Contemporary Problems*,
published by the Duke University School of Law, Durham, North Carolina. Copyright 1964, by Duke University. [Note—The substance of this article was delivered
as an address at the School of Law of Duke University in February, 1964. Recent
events have not materially altered the situation.]

peace, it has today become a law of peace and peaceful coexistence."
The draft declaration of principles of peaceful coexistence submitted
by the Association proposed that the United Nations proclaim that the
principle of peaceful coexistence is a fundamental principle of modern
international law.

• • •

### The Fight for the Slogan

The term "peaceful coexistence" as such has been found in Soviet
literature, bearing as early a date as 1920. Contemporary Soviet writing
ascribes the idea to Lenin; he does not seem to have used the term.
The Soviet scholars who inveigh against the sin of quotationism have
not been able to commit it in this instance. Western scholars have recalled that it was Chicherin, the People's Commissar for Foreign Affairs, who referred to the peace treaty with Estonia in 1920 as the first
experiment in peaceful coexistence with bourgeois states. Twenty years
later, the bourgeois state of Estonia having been rescued by Soviet
forces, it became unnecessary to coexist with her except in the sense
that the robin in Don Marquis' poem coexisted with the worm it had
swallowed. The first experiment in peaceful coexistence had been unilaterally successful.

It is true the slogan has become central only since about 1956. At
that time it took off from the Pancha Shila, the five principles which
had been proclaimed in the Sino-Indian Pact of 1954 and expanded in
the Bandung Declaration of 1955. As a proclaimed principle of international law, peaceful coexistence has been treated in numerous Soviet
monographs and articles since 1956 and has been pressed with vigor
by Soviet representatives at national meetings of governmental
and non-governmental organizations. The thrust of the massive effort
now being exerted in many forums is to place that which is called
principles of peaceful coexistence in the center of contemporary international law.

To this end, the purity of the slogan as such is defended against
objection from without or within. Thus, in the summer of 1962 when an
attempt was made in the International Law Association to change the title
of the relevant committee by dropping the term "coexistence" so as to
bring the title in line with that which was used in the United Nations,
the Soviet delegation quit work in the committee until the change of
name was blocked. In 1963 at a meeting of the Soviet Association of International Law one Soviet jurist made the error of depreciating the slogan in
a similar way. He is reported as having contended that the principles
of cooperation and friendly relations between states (a term used in
the United Nations) were identical with the principles of peaceful co-

existence. On this he was opposed, according to published report, by eight speakers who were named and others who were not; no one is reported to have risen to his defense. . . . Here it suffices to note that the phrase "principles of peaceful coexistence" is sacred. . . .

## II. THE CONTENT OF PCX

When PCX is offered as a legal principle and an envelope for subordinate legal principles, it is natural to seek a list, representative or exhaustive, and a principle of organization that gives unity to the list. It will not do to say that PCX in international law means that men ought to live in peace. That would be little more than to describe the commonplaces in international relations, as Professor Jennings of Cambridge has said. Nor is it enough to say that PCX means that men should live in peace and collaboration. That would be a desirable outcome, and it may be a good thing to express the aspiration, but we should not have gone far along the road to proving that something new had arrived in international law.

It is not hard to find a list; the hard thing is to find which list to use. In view of the friendly Soviet references to the Pancha Shila, we might begin there. We find that the five principles are mutual respect for territorial integrity and sovereignty, mutual non-aggression, non-interference in each other's internal affairs, equality and mutual benefit, and peaceful coexistence itself. These are noble if not quite clear; if they were more clear they might not sound quite so noble. Some aid to interpretation may be found in the course taken by Sino-Indian relations since the signing of the agreement in 1954.

We note that PCX is number five on the list. Does it embrace all or any of the others? Does any of the others embrace No. 5 as well as others on the list? In the mid-1950s several Soviet authors took up the five principles and gave to all of them the term "The Principles of Peaceful Coexistence." That was the period in which the Leninist origin of the idea was discovered.

In the Bandung Conference of 1955 the list had swollen to ten. The first four principles of the Sino-Indian Pact survive in altered or lengthened form. Several new ones included (among others) respect for fundamental human rights and for the purposes and principles of the Charter of the United Nations, respect for the right of each nation to defend itself singly or collectively in conformity with the Charter of the United Nations, abstention from the use of arrangements of collective defense to serve the particular interests of any of the big powers, abstention by any country from exerting pressure on other countries, and respect for justice and international obligations. Coexistence was lifted from the list of enumerated principles to the caption of the list.

By 1961 a politically authoritative list had appeared in Part One of the Program of the Communist Party of the Soviet Union. There PCX was defined as implying

renunciation of war as a means of settling international disputes and their solution by negotiation; equality, mutual understanding and trust between countries; consideration for each other's interests; non-interference in internal affairs; recognition of the right of every people to solve all the problems of their country by themselves; strict respect for the sovereignty and territorial integrity of all countries; promotion of economic and cultural cooperation on the basis of equality and mutual benefit.

One may note certain features of these and other lists besides the fluidity of their contents. Most of the items stressed and most of the reasons advanced in their support have been conspicuous for failure to specify a concrete secondary content; that is, a content that is sufficiently arguable to have meaning. Where the content is arguable, it is tendentious. For example, the proclamation of the inalienable right of peoples to their natural resources is silent upon the form or extent of compensation or other redress in the event of expropriation. For another example, in the Soviet draft declaration submitted to the International Law Association in 1962 the proclamation of the equality of states was accompanied by the sentence, "States shall be represented in international organizations with consideration for the fact of the existence at present of three large political groupings." It is easy to see that that rider was mounted on a *troika*.

On the whole, Soviet publicists have not shown themselves jealous of the purity of the list. The slogan is one thing; the content of the principles is something else. Soviet jurists have included some principles designed to have general appeal and some that were designed for particular advantage. They have been hospitable to lists advanced by others if only the others were willing to go along with the idea that an agreed list of PCX should be worked out. Even their opposition to certain principles in competing lists, principles that likewise were designed for particular advantage, has been relatively mild. We shall presently consider an explanation for the generality and fluidity of these enumerations.

One of the ways of testing the content of PCX is to ask whether the suggested extension of the term points to all of the particulars that normally would be considered. For instance, arbitral or judicial determination of legal issues between states is not a principle of peaceful coexistence in Soviet formulation. Now, one of the Bandung principles of 1955 was settlement of all international disputes by peaceful means such as negotiation, conciliation, arbitration, or judicial settlement, as well as other peaceful means of the parties' own choice in conformity with the Charter of the United Nations. It is true that the residual phrase, "other peaceful means of the parties' own choice," can be read so as to require consent of the parties in each case before resort to arbitration or judicial settlement, or indeed any of the other specified peaceful means. Still, the reference to arbitration and judicial settlement is there.

In the Soviet lists arbitration and judicial settlement are smothered. Some time ago Professor Jennings asked whether this refusal to submit legal disputes to legal determination was a part of the concept of peaceful coexistence. If it was, he said, Professor Tunkin might be thought not progressive but somewhat reactionary. Chairman Khrushchev, in his New Year's message in 1964 to heads of state of other governments on the settlement of territorial disputes, proposed four points for an international agreement on the settlement of territorial disputes. The fourth point was an undertaking to settle all territorial disputes exclusively by peaceful means such as negotiation, mediation, conciliatory procedure, and also other peaceful means at the choice of the parties concerned in conformity with the Charter of the United Nations. The accordance with the Bandung Declaration is almost exact. The only exceptions are the limitation of the subject matter to territorial disputes, which after all was the general subject of the New Year's message; the insertion of a reference to mediation; and the consistent absence of a reference to arbitration or judicial settlement.

Also conspicuously absent from Soviet lists of principles of PCX is condemnation of war as such. Wars that serve the ends of Soviet foreign policy have never been termed illegal. They are given the label of wars of national liberation or revolutionary civil war or wars against the counterrevolution and are accepted as just. Sometimes the implicit *eirenicon* is that the wars being outlawed are wars between states. The abjuration of war as a means of settlement of disputes between states ought to be read with the emphasis on "between states"; disputes that are not between states may well be subject to settlement by war. Soviet doctrine has consistently preserved the negative pregnant.

So PCX is not the same as pacifism. Soviet doctrine has never accepted pacifism; but at times when the movements of pacifist interest groups or pressure groups or groups of principle in the Open World have happened to serve the ends of Soviet foreign policy, pacifism has been acclaimed exoterically. Soviet international lawyers tell us that the *jus ad bellum* is now obsolete, but they still distinguish between rightful wars and wrongful wars. A book entitled *Peace, Freedom and You,* published in Prague in 1963, is quoted in a recent

Western study as containing the statement: "Peaceful coexistence creates the most favorable conditions for the fight of the oppressed nations against their imperialist oppressors. Peaceful coexistence means the maximum support to the oppressed nations, including arms."

A third absent item is a principle that would uphold free international interchange of ideas. Peaceful coexistence in the sphere of ideology has been repudiated by Soviet leaders and writers in many statements directed principally at the Soviet population but used also in the context of the Sino-Soviet dispute. As recently as 1961 Chairman Khrushchev referred to the policy of peaceful coexistence as representing in its social content a "form of intensive, economic, political, and ideological struggle of the proletariat against the aggressive forces of imperialism in the international arena"; the current Program of the Communist Party uses similar language. When it was suggested in a Soviet forum that an enumeration of principles of friendly relations between states, suggested by a Czechoslovak delegation, was transferable to PCX, the orthodox critics pointed out that such an identification ignored the character of the relationship between socialist and capitalist states as a form of the class struggle.

• • •

Another way of testing the context of PCX in international law is to reduce the general ideas to manageable proportions by imagining cases. Here the imagination ought not to be confined to illustration from Soviet practice, for the idea that it is worth working out PCX in international law has won support in other quarters. If, for example, the United States' support of the Bay of Pigs invasion of Cuba is to be justified under international law, then we have a better idea of what the justifying speaker means by the principle of non-intervention. If the Indian embrace of Goa or the Israeli advance in Sinai is praised as the righting of historic wrongs or as preventive counteraction, then we have a better idea of what the speaker means by the principle of settlement of territorial disputes by peaceful means. If the Soviet suppression of the Hungarian revolution of 1956 is supported as justifiable in international law, we have a clearer notion of the supposed content of the principle of non-interference in the internal affairs of other states. If the events that have taken place in the last three or four years along the Sino-Indian border are an explication of the inner meaning of Pancha Shila, then some of the mystery of the mysterious Orient is dispelled. If the annexation of the Baltic states during the period of the Soviet-Nazi pact is defended on the ground of the plebiscites carefully arranged there, then we can understand better the meaning being attached by the speaker to the principle of self-determination.

III. The Strategy of the Campaign

Is the idea of PCX taken seriously by its Soviet proponents as a guide for Soviet foreign policy, or is it put forward to advance that policy, or both? A full answer would lead us into a general discussion of international relations in the cold war, of the Soviet system, of the détente and the Sino-Soviet split, of the multiple audiences for Soviet statement on peaceful coexistence and their reciprocal eavesdropping. Here a few pertinent episodes must suffice.

When the leaders of the Soviet regime were somewhat more candid than they have since become, it was reasonably clear that the idea of PCX was to serve as a tactic in the conduct of foreign policy. In 1922 Lenin wrote to Chicherin when Chicherin represented Russia at the Genoa Conference:

We Communists have our own Communist program, the Third International. Nevertheless, we consider it our duty as merchants to support (even if there is only one chance in ten thousand) the pacifists in the other [bourgeois] camp. It will be both biting and amicable and will help to demoralize the enemy. With such tactics we will win even if Genoa fails.

Though expressed in universal terms, in practice the principles of PCX have seemed to be used to indicate duties of states outside the Soviet bloc but rights of states inside the Soviet bloc. One small example is worth our attention because the evidence, noticed by some close readers of the Soviet press, was so striking. Early in 1962, Mr. Suslov, a chief Soviet Marxist theoretician, made a speech at a conference of Soviet university teachers in the social sciences. His speech was published in *Pravda* on February 4th. The *Pravda* report had him saying: "Peaceful coexistence means . . . the rejection of war, the settlement of disputes between states through negotiations. It means the refusal to export revolution and to export counterrevolution." The symmetry of the last sentence is the thing to notice. Thirteen days later the same speech was published again in the chief Soviet magazine of general political theory, *Kommunist*. In that version, peaceful coexistence means ". . . the refusal to violate the territorial integrity of states, the inadmissibility of the export of counterrevolution." The reference to the refusal to export what the Soviet leaders call revolution was omitted; and the action seems not merely an omission but a deletion, made at a late stage of the printing in *Kommunist*, perhaps from galley proof or page proof, for the key sentence in *Kommunist* is now very widely spaced.

The strategic uses of "principles of PCX" vary with the audience. Afro-Asian audiences are assured that the Soviet Union sides with them in their campaigns for the Pancha Shila and, more fundamentally, that the Soviet Union as an important European power takes seriously a form of words that the Afro-Asians take seriously. With certain other audiences the aim is to influence non-Soviet disarmament, to attract East-West trade, to enlist support for various other current objectives of Soviet foreign policy. With Communist audiences the declaration of adherence to PCX is a taking of sides on one of the main issues between the Chinese and Soviet Communist leaders, which may be defined as the question whether the expansion of the Communist system can be rapidly achieved without actions that increase the risk of world-wide nuclear war.

Recently, before a Soviet audience, some Soviet international lawyers took pains to distinguish the concept of peaceful coexistence "as the fundamental principle of international law which is also the basis of the foreign policy of peace-loving states" from "the concept of coexistence of the two systems as an indication of the stage of history referred to by V. I. Lenin, a stage which is inevitable by virtue of the fact that the socialist revolution does not triumph simultaneously in all countries." All of the audiences eavesdrop on one another with differing success. That complicates the task of Soviet publicists, but they are assisted by the durable propensity of us all to hear what we wish to hear and to close our ears to what we would rather not hear.

PCX obtains only between states of different social systems, to use Soviet language. In the last analysis that comes down to states with diverse attitudes toward the Soviet Union. Relationships between states in the open world are not characterized in Soviet terminology as PCX; neither are relationships between states in what Soviet writers call the socialist camp. Between socialist countries the governing principles are those of proletarian internationalism, a term now being replaced (since the proclamation of the end of the period of dictatorship of the proletariat) by the term socialist internationalism. Principles of PCX are no part of the law of socialist internationalism, because there can be no class struggle between comradely, freely collaborating, brotherly states, and principles of PCX are meant to guide the class struggle.

In the higher phase of interstate relations that has been attained within the socialist camp, as we are told, genuine equality prevails. The principle of nonaggression becomes superfluous between socialist countries, for under those conditions aggression is too unthinkable to be worth warding off. The rights of national minorities are so well protected in socialist countries that there is no point in recognizing the principle of the protection of national minorities as being a principle of international law for those states. The provisions of the declaration on the rights of man with regard to the protection of democratic rights and freedoms of the representatives of various nations are likewise read out of the field of play for this part of the world. So are the provisions of the Convention on Genocide, and so it goes with slightly varying language for the principle of the equality of states, for the principle of non-intervention in the internal affairs of other states, and others.

What ought we to make of the idea that emerges: that legal principles are not applicable to him who propounds them if he states that he never violates them? The Soviet writers at this point would appear to be distinguishing their polity from lesser breeds within the Law. From the standpoint of international relations, what underlies this limitation of the principles of PCX to relationships between the Soviet bloc and the open world is the implication that that is the only important confrontation in the world today. The Soviet concept of PCX, in short, presupposes bipolarity and the cold war, rather than offering a way out of the cold war. Indeed, when combined with the repudiation of peaceful coexistence in the realm of ideology, it furnishes a Soviet equivalent of the cold war. The emphasis upon confrontation between socialism so-called and imperialism so-called lines up states on two sides of the Iron Curtain, ignores *pro tem* other bases of division and alliance, purports to set out rules for the conduct of states across the Curtain, and scores points in the Sino-Soviet debate.

## IV  PCX and Customary International Law

We can now arrive at some conjectures as to the utility of PCX in Soviet plans for the development of international law, after rehearsing briefly the position of the Soviet Union in the international legal community and recalling some of the other techniques the Soviet Union has applied in order to improve that position. The Soviet Union began its statehood under conditions of Soviet theory that implicitly denied the validity of traditional international law as the regulating idea of the system of nation-states. Upon coming into the international community the Soviet Union was very much in a minority. Even today, though it is stronger with satellites and friends in power and out of power throughout the world, the Soviet Union finds it useful for morale and ideology to emphasize at times that it is beleaguered by a hostile majority. Not only were many of the doctrines of international law disagreeable or hampering to Soviet leaders but the process by which international law was made and applied seemed under Soviet analysis to be necessarily exclusive and anti-Soviet. The facts indeed lent some support to this opinion despite the elements of humbug and hypocrisy that disfigured its expression.

In such a situation Soviet theory in international law, whatever it twists in regard to the course of Soviet foreign relations, made use of a variety of techniques to depreciate existing processes of the development of international law and to enlarge the role to be reserved for the Soviet Union in those processes. There was the time when international law was generally repudiated. Later, international law was to be accepted during a period of transition, admitted to be necessary before the time when international law could be discarded along with the general system of separate nation-states. There was the assertion that a state whose polity was based upon a new and just social theory had the right and duty to repudiate those particular doctrines of international law that offended that theory. There was the continued insistence upon the primacy of treaties as sources of international law, the belittling of the role of custom, the stress upon the necessity of the consent of a state before that state could be bound by a rule. When the United Nations Charter was adopted, with institutional arrangements allowing a very important role to the Soviet Union and its text corresponding in many ways to demands upon which Soviet representatives had insisted, Soviet publicists extolled what was called the international law of the Charter over what was called traditional or, indeed, obsolete international law. . . .

• • •

### Conclusion

If we now find PCX as principles of international law to be either truisms or religious dogmas (like the reference, in the Soviet draft declaration of principles of PCX, to "mankind's advance toward the most just social system which is Communism") or tactics in particular Soviet moves in foreign policy, or an effort to secure the veto in the formation and application of customary international law, does it follow that we ought to oppose any further effort to codify and declare the principles of PCX?

There is respectable argument to the negative. We are urged that we ought to consider the difficulties that even the best modern Soviet international lawyers must face in coping with the heritage of the past, in the policy of the Chinese Communists, in the views of some of their own Soviet colleagues, in their personal inner debate. We are urged to allow for the technical underdevelopment of Soviet international law: underdevelopment due not to any lack of intellectual quality but to years of isolation and difficulties of training, political interference, the constrictions of Soviet dogma. We are urged to be grateful for the relatively mild expression, the relatively friendly approach. We are urged not to set our faces against the de-Stalinization of the cold war. The *détente,* we are told, is genuine but it is fragile, it requires concessions. If Soviet international lawyers find one form of words so agreeable to them or so binding upon them by virtue of politically authoritative pronouncement, then the concession here is in an area that will not do much harm.

• • •

VICTOR P. KARPOV

## *The Soviet Concept of Peaceful Coexistence and Its Implications for International Law*

### I PEACEFUL COEXISTENCE AND SOVIET FOREIGN POLICY

The concept of peaceful coexistence has always been the general line of Soviet foreign policy. Of course, this concept has been liable to some development and improvement but its very emergence was a result of the Great October Revolution which gave birth to the socialist system.

From its very inception the Soviet state proclaimed peaceful coexistence as the basic principle of its foreign policy. The fact that the very first political act of the Soviet Russia was the Decree on Peace, the decree on stopping the bloody war, is not to be considered an accident.

The peaceful coexistence policy is not a tactical move on the part of the Soviet Union. Our desire for peace and peaceful coexistence springs from the very nature of our socialist society in which there are no social groups interested in profiting by means of war or by the arms race.

SOURCE: Victor P. Karpov, "The Soviet Concept of Peaceful Coexistence And Its Implications For International Law," *Law And Contemporary Problems,* XXIX (Autumn 1964), 858–864. Reprinted by permission from a symposium, "The Soviet Impact on International Law," appearing in *Law and Contemporary Problems,* published by the Duke University School of Law, Durham, North Carolina. Copyright, 1964, by Duke University.

Moreover, the principle of peaceful coexistence is the only realistic policy to pursue nowadays when the world consists of nations belonging to different social systems—capitalism and socialism. In view of the present alignment of forces in the world and of the progress of military technique, it is impossible to find any other sound basis for relations between countries except that of peaceful coexistence. We cannot even discuss this principle in terms whether we should "accept" or "reject" it. The point is that today peaceful coexistence is *an indisputable fact* of international life and not someone's request or suggestion. Peaceful coexistence is an objective necessity stemming from the contemporary stage of the development of human society.

If we face facts squarely, we should admit that the essence of world politics now is the character of relations between the two main socioeconomic systems—capitalism and socialism. And capitalist and socialist countries exist side by side on our planet. The rise of socialism was an inevitable objective historical development. However, the capitalist world refused to recognize this fact and has repeatedly resorted to war to destroy its unwelcome neighbor. It is common knowledge that all these attempts have turned out to be futile.

The attempts to solve differences between the two systems by means of war have always been costly for the common people. They resulted in millions of killed and wounded, in thousands of destroyed towns and villages, and in senseless losses of human energy and ingenuity.

And now the very character of modern nuclear warfare makes planning for war as a means of settling differences between the two systems obvious insanity. None of these systems can rely upon war to secure its victory over the other. The Soviet Union does not need any war to secure victory over capitalism, although the Soviet people believe in such a victory.

It is not war that should settle the controversy between the two systems. In the final analysis, it will not be the system which produces the greatest quantity of means of destruction that will triumph, but the system which produces the most of material and spiritual values, which provides man with a better life. We are absolutely sure that one cannot drive people to paradise with a club, or drive them to communism by means of war.

Communists do not conceal from anyone their desire to attract all people of the world to the side of socialism. This is regarded by them as their prime international task. But the question is: by what means is that cause to be advanced? We are not going to attain it by unleashing wars, nor by forcing our way of life on other nations. It is through creative labor, through the great constructive force of the liberated peoples, through the revolutionary energy of the working people, that we are going to raise the prestige of socialism and to win it more and more support on the part of various nations.

Some people say that communism promotes the cause of peaceful coexistence because this favors communism and brings it certain advantage. These people are right. Peaceful coexistence, we feel, really favors our cause, the cause of socialism. And we do not conceal our belief that, in the long run, peaceful competition between socialism and capitalism will result in an overall victory for socialism.

But that would be a fair competition—a competition in the best possible satisfaction of all man's needs. Why should nations be afraid of that kind of competition? If they are sure that their cause is right, they should wholeheartedly accept this competition and do their best to win it. And if there are countries reluctant to be engaged in peaceful economic competition with the socialist countries one can but suggest that they rely more on their arms and armies in competition with socialism than on their productive capacities.

Coexistence is a continuation of the struggle between the two social systems, but struggle by peaceful means, without resort to war, without interference by one state in the internal affairs of another. It is a competition in peaceful endeavors. It implies reciprocal concessions and compromises—I would say mutual adaptation—in the sphere of interstate relations as regards the settlement of urgent practical issues in order to preserve and strengthen peace.

The point at issue now is not whether or not there should be peaceful coexistence. In fact, since socialism and capitalism are not at war they are in practice coexisting. And if we want to avoid the lunacy of world nuclear war we should coexist. The only alternative we have nowadays is between peaceful coexistence and nuclear holocaust. There are no other choices.

But the point is that we should coexist on a reasonable basis.

There are some people in the West who willy-nilly accept the necessity to coexist with the Soviet Union because, although it belongs to another social system, it is a powerful nation and possesses mighty weapons. But as soon as a question arises of peaceful coexistence between a big Western power and a smaller country, these people prefer methods of coercion—economic, political and even military threats. That, of course, is a wrong attitude; and it can bring about very grave consequences.

The principle of peaceful coexistence should be universal. It should be based on the assumption that every country, big or small, chooses for itself or borrows from its neighbors what it thinks fit, without any outside imposition. This is a precondition, the only one that can make coexistence genuinely peaceful and good-neighborly.

In short, coexistence on a reasonable basis presupposes the recognition of the existence of different social systems, the recognition of the right of every people to deal independently with all political and social problems of its own country, respect for the sovereignty of other nations, adherence to the principle of noninterference in internal affairs of other countries, and the settlement of all international issues by negotiation.

Thus, the Soviet view of peaceful coexistence of countries with different social and political systems does not simply imply an absence of war or a state of temporary and unstable armistice. It provides for the maintenance of friendly economic and political relations and envisages the establishment and development of a variety of forms of peaceful international cooperation.

And we believe that the realization of the Soviet proposals for general and complete disarmament under strict international control, the immediate and final abolition of the disgraceful colonial system, the conclusion of a German peace treaty, and the normalization on its basis of the situation in West Berlin would remove the chief causes of existing international tensions, destroy the very machinery of war, and enable all peoples to go calmly about their peaceful and creative labor.

## II  Peaceful Coexistence and International Law

The principle of peaceful coexistence is more and more widely adhered to by states in their international relations. It has won not only the widest moral support on the part of the peoples, but also international legal recognition. The countries of the socialist camp are guided precisely by this principle in their relations with other countries.

The principle of peaceful coexistence is reflected in the decisions of the Bandung Conference of Asian and African countries. Many countries of Europe, Asia, and Africa have solemnly proclaimed it as the basis of their foreign policy. And this idea was more than once unanimously supported in the resolutions of the United Nations General Assembly (for instance, decisions of 12th, 13th and subsequent sessions). It is very significant that the 17th session of the General Assembly unanimously resolved on December 18, 1962, to undertake further studies to promote and codify international legal principles of friendly relations and cooperation between states.

If we have a look at the United Nations Charter itself we can find out that it is based on the principle of peaceful coexistence although it does not use this very word. In its Preamble, the United Nations Charter, for example, states that the member countries undertake "to practice tolerance and live together in peace with one another as good neighbors," and to unite their "strength to maintain international peace and security." By that, the U.N. Charter in fact provides for the practice of what we call peaceful coexistence. Some other articles of the U.N. Charter are also based on a tacit recognition of this principle, and also on the recognition of such principles as the sovereign equality of states (Article 2 (1)), non-intervention (Article 2(7)), the equality and self-determination of peoples (Article 1(2)), territorial integrity (Article 2(4)), and so on.

The well-known clause providing for unanimity of the permanent members of the Security Council when major decisions are to be taken is also a reflection of the principle of coexistence. In fact, if this clause had not been included into the U.N. Charter, we might have witnessed situations when a group of nations representing one social system would have tried to impose its will on another nation or other nations representing a different social system. Such a hypothetical situation would have led inevitably to complete disregard of principle of peaceful coexistence of states with different social systems and cannot but lead to the violation of the goals of the United Nations and to a dangerous aggravation of international tension.

The majority rule cannot be applied to the relations between different social systems. Such relations are inevitably to be based on mutual respect for the sovereign equality of nations, peaceful negotiation, and reasonable compromise.

That is why we consider very dangerous all attempts to change the U.N. Charter so that the unanimity rule in the Security Council is abolished. This could lead only to the collapse of the United Nations. In this connection I would like to mention the case of so-called Soviet "failure" to pay for the U.N. operations in the Middle East and in the Congo: to mention it because some governments try to resolve the financial crisis of the United Nations at the expense of the Soviet Union by using methods which run absolutely counter to the principles of international law if this law is understood properly.

This is the essence of the case: Attempts are being made to apply Article 19 of the U.N. Charter to the question of reimbursement of the expenditures incurred by U.N. operations in the Middle East and the Congo. But Article 19 has nothing to do with these cases; it can be applied only to the arrears in members' payments to the regular budget. Decisions on reimbursement for the expenditures for the Middle East and Congo operations were adopted by the General Assembly, bypassing the Security Council and usurping the rights of the Security Council against the clear provisions of the Charter. (According to the Charter, the General Assembly makes *recommendations* that are not obligatory for those countries which did not vote for them.)

The same goes for the decisions of the International Court of Justice which is being used to prove the alleged legality of this illegal attempt. Incidentally, the United States does not recognize that decisions of the International Court of Justice are obligatory in all cases, and has made a reservation to this effect while ratifying the Statute of the Court.

The Soviet Union's position in this case is clear. We feel that the responsibility for the consequences of aggression, including financial implications, should be borne by those who have committed the acts of aggression. Any other approach would only encourage aggressors. It is primarily and precisely for this reason that the Soviet Union is not sharing, and will not share, the expenditures for the U.N. operations in the Middle East and the Congo.

We are not going to change our position under any pressure. Our position is just, and we are not inclined to compromise it. On March 21 of this year, the Soviet government issued a warning that in case of any attempt to act along the mentioned unlawful lines, the Soviet Union may be obliged to reconsider its attitude toward the U.N. activities in general.

A theoretical basis, so to say, of the attempts to make the U.S.S.R. pay for those U.N. emergency operations can be easily found in the concepts which claim that international law should prevail over the national or municipal law. This attitude is completely alien to the principle of peaceful coexistence, as it entails an encroachment upon the sovereign rights of nations and opens avenues for interference into their domestic affairs.

The same goes for the proposal to grant obligatory jurisdiction to the International Court of Justice, which some American lawyers view as one of the ways to improve the "rule of law" in international relations. This is not only contrary to the spirit of peaceful coexistence but at the same time is not adequate in present circumstances. The most burning international issues, such as the liquidation of colonial system or the solution of the West Berlin question, are *political* problems first of all, and cannot be solved by a court or an arbitration alone.

These are, broadly speaking, the main prerequisites that should ensure the application of the principle of peaceful coexistence to international law.

III   THE BASIC PRINCIPLES OF PEACEFUL COEXISTENCE

Speaking more specifically, we can trace the following, more detailed provisions which constitute the essence of the peaceful coexistence and which, in our understanding, should be reflected in the international law.

1. *Renunciation of war as means of settling international disputes, and their solution by negotiation.*

Compliance with this principle should lead to adoption of specific measures that would exclude war from the life of human society both by way of solemn obligations of states and by measures of physical disarmament that would liquidate all means of waging war. To achieve this goal, the Soviet government proposes the general and complete disarmament program, various measures of partial disarmament, and a non-aggression pact between the NATO and Warsaw Pact countries. Recently the Soviet government advanced a new program to this effect, which provides for an international agreement to renounce the use or threat of force in territorial and border disputes between nations. This agreement should include the following provisions:

(a) a solemn undertaking not to resort to force to alter existing borders;

(b) the acknowledgment that the territories of states should not, even temporarily, be the object of any invasion, attack, military occupation, or any other forcible measure directly or indirectly undertaken by other states for whatever political, economic, strategic, border or any other considerations;

(c) a firm statement that neither differences in social and state systems, nor refusal to grant recognition or absence of diplomatic relations, nor any other pretext may serve as a basis for the violation by one state of the territorial integrity of another;

(d) a commitment to solve all territorial disputes by peaceful means in conformity with the United Nations Charter.

2. *Equality, mutual understanding and trust between countries.*

3. *Consideration for each other's interests.*

4. *Non-interference in internal affairs of other countries.*

5. *Recognition of the right of all peoples to solve all the problems of their countries by themselves.* This should provide for all countries to refrain from "exporting" revolution or counter-revolution. Communists do believe that the idea of communism will ultimately triumph throughout the world, just as it triumphed already in the Soviet Union and in some other countries. But when we say that in competition with capitalism the socialist system will win, this does not signify by any means that we shall achieve that victory by interfering in the internal affairs of non-socialist countries. Our confidence in the victory of communism is based on a knowledge of the laws governing the development of human society. Just as in its time capitalism, as the more progressive system, took the place of feudalism, so will capitalism be inevitably replaced by the more progressive and just social system—communism.

6. *Strict respect for the sovereignty and territorial integrity of all countries.* This principle should be strictly observed; and its observance is, of course, incompatible with some resolutions that have from time to time been adopted by the American Congress, as those calling for "liberation" of some integral parts of Soviet Union—of the Ukraine, Byelorussia, Lithuania, Latvia, Estonia, Armenia, Azerbaijan, Georgia, Kazakhstan, Turkmenistan and even some "Ural Area." I would say that this is roughly the same as if the parliament of Mexico, for example, would have passed a resolution demanding that Texas, Arizona, and California be "liberated from American slavery." Such an attitude, of course, is incompatible with the principle of peaceful coexistence and with international law in general.

7. *Promotion of economic and cultural cooperation on the basis of complete equality and mutual benefit.* This should lead to abolition of all forms of economic blockade, of economic sanctions, or trade discrimination.

### Conclusion

The Soviet Union has consistently pursued, and will pursue, the policy of peaceful coexistence of states with different social systems.

We are convinced that the principle of peaceful coexistence should be the basis of the whole structure of contemporary international law. Only if it is based on the principle of peaceful coexistence can the international law best promote the cause of peace and mutual understanding between nations.

## STUDY QUESTIONS

1. Attempts on the part of the League of Nations and the United Nations to achieve such goals as world law, peaceful change, and collective security, have met with limited success. Discuss the reasons why greater success has not been achieved, with particular reference to the Marxist view of power, and the role of United Nations executive agencies in facilitating the emergence of international patterns of authority.

2. Discuss the meaning and origins of polycentrism in the Communist bloc. How has it affected the internal and external affairs of various East European regimes, and in what sense does it create risks and opportunities for American foreign policy?

3. Bipolarity, multipolarity, and bi-multipolarity are each advanced as desirable models for international order. Discuss the meaning, strengths, and weaknesses of each.

4. Identify and describe the major alliance systems in the world today. Evaluate the role of the United States in various alliance arrangements.

5. Various nations and international bodies have addressed themselves to the general doctrine of peaceful coexistence. What are the major principles of that doctrine? Over what issues do the coexistence views of Lipson and Karpov diverge? Why?

## SUGGESTIONS FOR FURTHER READING

BRZEZINSKI, ZBIGNIEW. *The Soviet Bloc: Unity and Conflict.* Rev. ed. Cambridge: Harvard University Press, 1961.

CLEVELAND, HAROLD VAN B. *The Atlantic Idea and Its European Rivals.* New York: McGraw Hill, 1966.

DALLIN, ALEXANDER (ed.). *Diversity in International Communism: A Documentary Record, 1961–1963.* New York: Columbia University Press, 1963.

GOLDMAN, MARSHALL I. *Soviet Foreign Aid.* New York: Frederick A. Praeger, 1967.

GRIFFITH, WILLIAM E. (ed.). *Communism in Europe,* 2 vols. Cambridge: The M.I.T. Press, 1965, 1966.

HALLE, LOUIS J. *The Cold War as History.* New York: Harper & Row, 1967.

HOVELICK, ARNOLD L., and MYRON RUSH. *Strategic Power and Soviet Foreign Policy.* Chicago: University of Chicago Press, 1966.

KAPLAN, JACOB J. *The Challenge of Foreign Aid.* New York: Frederick A. Praeger, 1967.

KISSINGER, HENRY A. *The Troubled Partnership: A Reappraisal of the Atlantic Alliance.* New York: McGraw Hill, 1965.

LAQUEUR, WALTER and LEOPOLD LABEDZ (eds.). *Polycentrism: The New Factor in International Communism.* New York: Frederick A. Praeger, 1962.

MONTGOMERY, JOHN D. *Foreign Aid and International Politics.* Englewood Cliffs: Prentice-Hall, 1967.

OSGOOD, ROBERT ENDICOTT. *NATO, the Entangling Alliance.* Chicago: University of Chicago Press, 1962.

SCHUMAN, FREDERICK L. *The Cold War: Retrospect and Prospect.* 2nd edition, Baton Rouge: Louisiana State University Press, 1967.

SHULMAN, MARSHALL D. *Beyond the Cold War.* New Haven: Yale University Press, 1966.

ULAM, ADAM B. *Expansion and Coexistence.* New York: Frederick A. Praeger, 1968.

ZAGORIA, DONALD S. *The Sino-Soviet Conflict,* 1956–1961. Princeton: Princeton University Press, 1962.

# PART FOUR □ SOCIAL-
# PSYCHOLOGICAL ASPECTS
# OF INTERNATIONAL BEHAVIOR

$A$NY EXAMINATION of the behavior of states in the international arena must take into account the thinking, feeling, orientation, and background of the decision-makers. Individuals who have been invested with legal authority, and not states, make public policies. The decision-makers are influenced by internal pressures and cross pressures. Likewise they are influenced directly or indirectly by actions of other states. The behavior of decision-makers and their advisers is governed by considerations that include economics, ideology, culture, religion, patriotism, and national interest. In this part we examine the influence of such factors as social ideology, world public opinion, cultural exchange, and psychological patterns on the behavior of nation-states.

Philip Worchel, in his article "Social Ideology and Reactions to International Events," presents an empirical study which tests certain hypotheses derived from a theory of social ideology concerning international conflict. He describes in detail the procedure of his investigation, the subjects (students in given public and private institutions of higher learning), the methods, and the results of the study. He concludes that aggression is associated with negative orientation toward others; that is, the higher the tendency to view others as "bad," "weak," or mere "objects," the greater the tendency to recommend aggression as a response to attack from others. The reverse is true for negotiation and self-blame; that is, the more positive the conception toward others, the greater the willingness to negotiate. Also, he concludes that the more positive the orientation toward others, the less the tendency toward authoritarianism and ethnocentrism.

In the second article, Hans J. Morgenthau discusses world public opinion and states that it is a presumed force which governments seem to curry. Major powers, such as the United States and the Soviet Union, compete with each other in supporting anti-colonial movements because world public opinion supports such movements. He maintains that the United States has been particularly solicitous of world public opinion. But Morgenthau believes that world public opinion is a myth. He alludes to existing world political realities such as the attitudes of different nations to the Korean conflict and discusses three lessons for the foreign policy of the United States.

Cultural exchange plays an important role in the relations among nations. Charles Frankel, who served as Assistant Secretary of State for Educational and Cultural Affairs, examines the role of intellectuals in international affairs. He points out the ways in which intellectuals can influence international affairs and discusses the differences in outlook between American intellectuals and most intellectuals in foreign countries. He emphasizes that these differences are in degree. National pride plays an important role in the process of cultural communications between the United States and other developed countries, and he gives Japan and Western Europe as examples. In the emergent nations, he states, there is fear of "cultural imperialism." There is anger at the destruction of certain traditional habits and values. The United States is the most conspicuous country that has plunged into modernization and industrialization. Other countries have also followed this course and Frankel believes their changing way of life reflects the changed aspirations and opportunities of their people rather than American propaganda and pressure.

According to Frankel, a sense of community can be developed by the discovery of shared problems in the industrial countries and all other countries moving toward industrialization. In this way a responsive dialogue between the intellectuals of different states can exert influence in finding rational resolutions for international conflicts. Frankel is convinced that although contacts between intellectuals may not lead to agreement among them, they help "to undermine organized fantasies." "Cultural exchange," he points out, "encourages the qualifying of rigid generalizations and the tempering of stereotypes about people in other nations, and it exercises a countervailing pressure against both intellectual and political inertia."

In the concluding article, Anthony F. C. Wallace states that few societies have not experienced war at least once. War is viewed by some as a natural phenomena and by others as the result of social or psychopathology. Wallace focuses his attention on the psychological preparation of a society for war and discusses the process of mobilization as the central theme in psychological preparation for war. He also discusses the impersonality of war and states that war is "conducted by persons whose private motives . . . are highly diversified." Wallace concludes that unpopular wars occur "as a result of a perversion of administrative process rather than as a result of popular folly."

PHILIP WORCHEL

# Social Ideology and Reactions to International Events

## Introduction

The present study stems from an assumption that reactions to international events are derivatives of interpersonal orientations which, in turn, are determined in part by one's ideology concerning the nature of his fellow-man. As a product of his socialization, man develops a set of beliefs in which others are conceptualized as (1) either good or bad, (2) "weak" or "strong," (3) "object" or "human." Each pattern of beliefs leads to certain implications regarding the kind of formal and informal controls—political, economic, and social—that a group must establish if it is to maintain itself as a viable organization.

The conception of man as innately good is central to a philosophy that endorses a positive approach designed to elicit socially beneficial responses, whereas the conception that man is bad leads to a punitive system deemed necessary for suppressing his natural inclination to make socially detrimental choices.

The power structure required in the decision-making process is influenced by the conception of man as "weak" or "strong." If the mass is generally perceived as "weak" then it is necessary for the few

SOURCE: Philip Worchel, "Social Ideology and Reactions to International Events," *Journal of Conflict Resolution*, XI (December 1967), 414–430. Reprinted by permission. [Note—The investigation was supported by a grant from the Office of Naval Research under contract NONR–375 (19).]

"strong" to dictate the choices for all (authoritarian approach). In a democratic organization, each person is assumed to be capable of sharing in the decision process.

The "object" orientation views others as instruments for self-gain with little regard for their welfare, whereas in the humanistic orientation a concern for the welfare and feelings of others is basic. The "object–human" conception is particularly influential in determining the economic aspect of an organization.

The present project does not attempt to assess the interrelationship of these conceptual dimensions nor to study each separately, but rather to investigate the effects of the two extreme conceptual patterns.

The investigation to be described represents an attempt to extend the theoretical formulation concerning the significance of social ideology in international behavior. Gladstone and Taylor (1959) state the basic assumption of such a theory, namely, that each individual has an ideology in terms of which he interprets the communications he receives and makes decisions for action. Sufficient evidence has been accumulated to demonstrate the relationship of personal characteristics to the perception of international events. Christiansen (1959) presents an excellent review and additional data to support a "generalization" hypothesis, i.e., that there is a connection between people's attitudes towards foreign affairs and their ways of reacting in interpersonal relationships. Levinson (1957) has shown that unfavorable attitudes towards international cooperation measures are associated with the basic personality syndrome of authoritarianism. The ideological conception of man as bad, weak, and "object" is an integral part of the authoritarian syndrome.

Fensterwald (1958), in his study of American isolationism and expansionism, states that logic alone would never lead one to conclude that there was any close connection between attitudes toward childraising or the punishment of sex offenders and attitudes toward the conduct of foreign relations. The correlations between the International Scale and the Domestic Scale, however, suggest such a conclusion. Smith and Rosen (1958) present evidence for a negative correlation of the F Scale with "world-mindedness." In interviews with extreme respondents they also found that the more world-minded individuals were more equalitarian in outlook, less stereotyped, and more likely to view personal problems as internal rather than external. MacKinnon and Centers (1956) report that "equalitarians" and "authoritarians" not only differed in expected ways in their attitudes toward trade with the USSR, but were also likely to give quite dissimilar types of reasons in support of their positions. Punitive considerations were mentioned more often by authoritarians as a reason against trade, whereas economic benefit was an argument distinctive of authoritarians who favored trade. Thus the high value placed on punishment and the motivating influence of self-gain seem to be important characteristics of the authoritarian person. Faris (1960) also found that the less authoritarian a person is, the more likely he is to be low on jingoism (exaggerated patriotism) and on expectations of war; the more authoritarian, the more likely he is to be high on jingoism. Bay, Gullväg, Ofstad, and Tønnessen report that power-oriented nationalism is related to the authoritarian syndrome, whereas a people-oriented nationalism is not. An "object" conception of man probably undelies the power-oriented nationalism, while a humanistic conception is essential to a people-oriented nationalism.

It is the purpose of the present investigation to test the following major hypothesis derived from our theory of social ideology and international behavior: that the more positive the conception of man as basically good, strong, and humanistic, the greater the tendency to advocate negotiation in international conflicts, to accept international controls, and to recommend economic aid to other nations. In addition, it is predicted that the more positive the orientation, the less the ethnocentrism and authoritarianism.

PROCEDURE

*Instruments*

The final battery of tests used in the present project consisted of three major scales: the International Scale, the Traditional Family Ideology Scale (Levinson and Huffman, 1955), and the Social Orientation Scale. The International Scale also included items to assess (a) ethnocentrism, (b) group identification, and (c) internationalism. These instruments are reproduced in appendices to this article.

*International Scale.* The International Scale was similar in format to the one used by Christiansen (1959) to measure reactions of Norwegians to hypothetical international conflicts involving Norway. Each respondent indicated his first and second choice from six alternative ways of resolving the conflict. In our scale, the 18 items consisted of hypothetical and actual incidents involving the United states *vis-à-vis* a West-bloc (nine items) or East-bloc nation (nine items) followed by four alternative suggestions for dealing with the conflict: (1) negotiation, (2) aggression, (3) self-initiated remedial action implying self-blame, and (4) avoidance of any action. Each of the nine West-bloc and nine East-bloc incidents included three items involving direct physical aggression (violent) against a symbol representing the United States (e.g., flag, embassy), three items of indirect (nonviolent) action against the United States (e.g., economic), and three items of direct aggressive action against a citizen of the United States (e.g., arrest, attack). Every East-bloc incident was matched with a West-bloc item so that the nature of conflict (violent, nonviolent, and individual) and the four choices for resolving conflict were very similar, thus permitting direct comparisons of reactions to the two kinds of items. For example, the two following items represent direct physical attack (violent) against a symbol of the US by a West-bloc and an East-bloc nation respectively (the word in parentheses following each choice indicates the scoring category):

During a student riot in Turkey, our flag was torn down without the police attempting to prevent the action.
29. Demand that the Turkish government apologize for this action *(aggression)*
30. Meet with the Turkish officials to find out the causes of such action. *(negotiation)*
31. Increase our efforts to improve our relations with Turkey. *(self-blame)*
32. Do nothing; the feeling will die down in time. *(avoidance)*

The US flag on our Legation was torn down by a group of Bulgarian students while the police looked on.
73. Demand an apology from the Bulgarian government. *(aggression)*
74. Arrange a meeting with the Bulgarian officials to reduce causes of antagonism. *(negotiation)*
75. Increase our efforts to improve our relations with Bulgaria. *(self-blame)*
76. Do nothing; one has to expect such things in a tense world situation. *(avoidance)*

All the items in the scale were presented in a planned order so that no two successive incidents contained the same source of attack (East or West) or the same nature of attack (violent, nonviolent, or individual). The respondent indicated his degree of agreement with each of the four alternative modes of reactions on a six-point scale varying from $-3$ (very strong disagreement) to $+3$ (very strong agreement). The zero-point was omitted in order to force the respondent to make a positive or negative choice. In scoring the responses, three points were added to each rating, converting the scale so that it ran from 0 to $+6$.

In addition to the 18 incidents in the scale, there were three incidents, nonconflictual in nature, which served as "fillers" and as measures of ethnocentrism, internationalism, and willingness to aid another nation. The first two were selected from the Nationalism Scale of Terhune (1964) and consist of items 41-44 and items 57-60 in Appendix A. The sum of the four ratings from $-3$ (very strong disagreement) to $+3$ (very strong agreement) in each of the two incidents provided the measures for internationalism and ethnocentrism respectively (12 points were added to the total scores to convert them to all positive numbers).

The other nonconflictual incident involves items 13-16 in Appendix A. Only the last item, 16 ("Refuse to send any aid whatsoever"), was scored as a measure of the willingness of the subject to aid a potential enemy (Cuba); three points were added to the six-point scale.

All of the items in the scale were subjected to a preliminary analysis following administration to a class of 76 students in an introductory history class at the University of Texas. Items which discriminated poorly were eliminated from the scale. To determine item reliability, the final scale was then administered to an introductory sociology class consisting of 65 students (31 males and 34 females) planning to major in engineering, sociology, psychology, or business. The correlations for the subtotal aggression scores with the total retaliation score varied from .45 to .60; for the negotiation items, from .36 to .60; for the self-blame items, from .32 to .61; and for the avoidance items, from .31 to .56. All these correlations were significant at the .01 level. Test-retest reliability was determined by administering the scale to a class of 35 students in political science at Southwest Texas State College in San Marcos, Texas, and then retesting them five months later.[2] Test-retest correlations for the total retaliation, negotiation, self-blame, and avoidance scores were .77, .60, .77, and .51 respectively.

*Traditional Family Ideology Scale* (TFI). In order to obtain some measure of the validity of our Social Orientation Scale and, at the same time, to determine the relationship between authoritarianism within the family organization and reactions to international events, eight items were selected from the abbreviated 12-item scale of Traditional Family Ideology constructed by Levinson and Huffman (1955). They reported a correlation of .65 between their scale and the Ethnocentrism Scale, and a correlation of .73 with the Authoritarian Scale. In another study (Gilbert and Levinson, 1956), the TFI was shown to correlate .70 with a Custodialism Scale designed to assess authoritarian policies in mental hospital personnel and policies. Subjects rated each item on the six-point scale of agreement. Unfortunately, all items are negatively worded so that response set is not eliminated. The score (+24) was used as an index of authoritarianism in the family relationships; high scores represent high authoritarianism.

*Social Orientation Scale.* The theoretical formulation of social ideology guided the construction of items for the Social Orientation Scale. The final scale, after a number of preliminary explorations, consisted of 20 items designed to assess the "good-bad," the "weak-strong," and the "object-human" orientations (see Appendix C). As with the International Scale, respondents were to indicate their degree of agreement on a six-point scale varying from —3 (very strong disagreement) to +3 (very

[2] The assistance of Dr. E. de Shazo, Southwest Texas State College, San Marcos, Texas, in administering the tests is gratefully acknowledged.

strong agreement). In scoring the test, positive items were reversed so that high scores represent the "bad-weak-object" end of the continuum and low scores represent the "good-strong-humanistic" end (60 points were added to the total scores to eliminate negative scores).

For item analysis and to obtain evidence on validity, the Social Orientation Scale and the F Scale were administered to a class of 38 students registered for a course in finance at the University of Texas. The correlations of each item with the total scores on the Social Orientation Scale varied from .16 to .67. Thirteen of the 20 items correlated from .43 to .67 (significant at the .01 level), five items ranged from .33 to .42 (significant at the .05 level), and the other two were .16 and .21. The mean score of the entire class was 13.08 with a standard deviation of 14.67. The product-moment correlation between the Social Orientation Scale and the F Scale was .51, indicating a significant degree of relationship. A factor analysis was performed on the Social Orientation Scale, yielding six factors. The detailed results of the factor analysis will not be reported here (65.74 percent total variation extracted).

*Subjects*

To obtain a wide range of college subjects, attending both public and private institutions in the US, in addition to the University of Texas (South Central), staff members of psychology departments in seven other universities located in the Northeast (Brown), Southeast (Florida), North Central (Chicago and Knox), Southwest (Arizona), Far West (Los Angeles), and Northwest (Montana) were contacted for assistance in administering the battery of tests. The purpose of the study was explained to each staff member, specific instructions for administration were provided, and a time schedule was set for the testing so that all subjects could be tested at about the same time (first weeks of November 1965). Two of the universities (Los Angeles and Chicago) could not comply with the time schedule and had to be excluded from the study. At each of the other six universities, four public and two private, the tests were administered by the staff member to students enrolled in the introductory psychology class.[3] A total of 1,219 subjects, 691 males and 528 females, completed the questionnaire.

Table 1 shows the number of subjects in each university according to sex, major area, and socioeconomic class. The last was determined from information as to father's occupation and education. Initially five classes were established: (1) professional and salaried officials, (2) self-

[3] Appreciation is expressed to Dr. Anthony Davids, Brown University; Dr. V. Tempone, University of Arizona; Dr. M. E. Shaw, University of Florida; Dr. R. C. Ammons, Montana State University; and Dr. G. R. Francis, Knox College, for their assistance in administering the scales.

employed, owner or manager, (3) technical and salaried employees, (4) craftsmen, (5) white- and blue-collar workers. In the final coding, however, the five categories were reduced to three: upper class (1 and 2), middle class (3), and lower class (4 and 5). As can be seen from Table 1, the universities were not matched in any of our three variables of sex, major area, and socioeconomic class. It is not suggested that our sample, even as a total group, is representative of the college population of the United States. This would have been most difficult to obtain and of little value in testing our theoretical formulation.

## Method

The battery of tests was administered whenever possible during the regular class hour. In one university, however, this was not feasible, and the students were permitted to take the questionnaires home. They were all informed that the purpose of the study was to assess student attitudes on international events and on some common social problems. They were asked to fill in the information on sex, age, date, class, major

TABLE 1. *Number of Subjects in Each University According to Sex, Major Area, and Socioeconomic Class*

| | Ari-zona | Brown | Florida | Knox | Montana | Texas | Private | Public | Total* |
|---|---|---|---|---|---|---|---|---|---|
| *Sex:* | | | | | | | | | |
| Male | 74 | 123 | 59 | 57 | 159 | 219 | 180 | 511 | 691 |
| Female | 73 | 64 | 99 | 65 | 82 | 145 | 129 | 399 | 528 |
| *Major Area:* | | | | | | | | | |
| Soc. science | 30 | 83 | 47 | 36 | 33 | 58 | 119 | 168 | 287 |
| Nat. science | 27 | 30 | 42 | 23 | 57 | 119 | 53 | 245 | 298 |
| Humanities | 19 | 36 | 15 | 32 | 37 | 46 | 68 | 117 | 185 |
| Education | 33 | 0 | 41 | 8 | 39 | 42 | 8 | 155 | 163 |
| Other | 38 | 38 | 13 | 23 | 76 | 97 | 61 | 224 | 285 |
| *Socioeconomic Class:* | | | | | | | | | |
| Upper | 35 | 90 | 57 | 45 | 73 | 165 | 135 | 330 | 465 |
| Middle | 64 | 83 | 73 | 40 | 89 | 149 | 123 | 375 | 498 |
| Lower | 44 | 12 | 28 | 37 | 80 | 49 | 49 | 201 | 250 |

* The number of subjects in each category does not total the same as in some cases sex, major area, or socioeconomic class was not indicated on the questionnaire.

area of study, place of birth, place of longest residence, and father's and mother's education and occupation. Names were optional, that is, if the subject felt reluctant to give his name he could omit the item (in only 15 cases, however, were names omitted). They were informed that the results of the questionnaire would be made available to them after the tests were scored and analyzed.

The instructions for the International Scale were as follows:

This scale describes a series of hypothetical international situations. You are to state what ought to be done in these situations. Following each situation, there will be listed four reactions. You are to state how strongly you would follow *each* and *every* reaction. Your answers are not to be written in this booklet, but on a separate answer sheet. Write the number which best describes how strongly you would follow that particular reaction according to the following scale:

+3 feel *very strongly* that I would recommend this reaction
+2 feel *strongly* that I would recommend this reaction
+1 feel *somewhat strongly* that I would recommend this reaction
−1 feel *somewhat strongly* that I would not recommend this reaction
−2 feel *strongly* that I would not recommend this reaction
−3 feel *very strongly* that I would not recommend this reaction

## RESULTS

*Response to international conflict.* The mean total reactions for aggression, negotiation, self-blame, and avoidance are presented in Table 2. The mean score of 83.35 for negotiation indicates an average absolute rating of "strong agreement" and is the most preferred response of the four reactions. The second most popular response is some US-initiated action to reduce tension, suggesting an awareness of some blame for the crisis. The mean score of 70.33 indicates an average rating of "somewhat strong agreement." The least recommended actions are aggression

TABLE 2 *Mean Reactions to Anti-US Acts According to the Source and Nature of Attack*

| Reaction | Total | West | East | F-ratio | Violent | Non-violent | Individual | F-ratio |
|---|---|---|---|---|---|---|---|---|
| Aggression | 50.09 | 23.64 | 26.45 | 238.77*** | 20.70 | 12.37 | 17.02 | 645.18*** |
| Negotiation | 83.35 | 42.33 | 41.02 | 100.99*** | 29.30 | 25.81 | 28.24 | 353.49*** |
| Self-blame | 70.33 | 35.99 | 34.34 | 91.75*** | 26.83 | 16.56 | 26.94 | 3,272.56*** |
| Avoidance | 26.38 | 11.41 | 14.97 | 583.49*** | 7.40 | 10.38 | 8.60 | 173.97*** |

*** Significant at the .001 level.

and avoidance in that order. The mean of 50.09 for aggression lies near the hypothetical "neither agree nor disagree" point on the scale, while that for avoidance (26.38) lies on the "somewhat strong disagreement" point. The F-ratio for reaction type is significant far beyond the .001 level.

*Source of attack.* In regard to the source of attack, agreement is significantly higher for an aggressive reaction when the attack originates from East-bloc than from West-bloc nations (see Table 2). The F-ratio of 238.77 is significant far beyond the .001 level. The situation is reversed for the negotiation and self-blame reactions, that is, there is significantly higher agreement for negotiation and self-blame when the conflict involves a West-bloc than an East-bloc nation (F-ratios of 100.99 and 91.75 respectively). The avoidance response is greater for an East-bloc crisis than one involving a West-bloc nation. The difference between the means yields and F-ratio of 583.49, which is significant far beyond the .001 level.

*Nature of attack.* A violent or direct physical attack upon a symbol of the US elicits the greatest agreement to retaliate with an aggressive response. The attack on a citizen produced a stronger recommendation for an aggressive reaction than one involving a nonviolent act against the US (F-ratio of 645.18). There is, however, less willingness to negotiate a conflict involving a nonviolent action than one involving a violent action against the US or one against a citizen of the US (F-ratio of 353.49). A similar pattern of responses is found with self-blame reaction, that is, least willingness to accept blame for a nonviolent action and much greater readiness to admit responsibility in actions involving

TABLE 3  *Means and F-Ratios for Each University on All Scales*

| Scale | Arizona | Brown | Florida | Knox | Montana | Texas | F-ratio |
|---|---|---|---|---|---|---|---|
| *International Scale:* | | | | | | | |
| Aggression | 53.65 | 48.47 | 50.25 | 46.82 | 50.49 | 50.10 | 2.33* |
| Negotiation | 84.04 | 82.21 | 85.38 | 84.36 | 82.96 | 81.63 | 2.50* |
| Self-blame | 70.62 | 68.53 | 73.13 | 71.83 | 73.02 | 68.27 | 5.06*** |
| Avoidance | 25.07 | 28.53 | 25.48 | 28.26 | 27.90 | 24.85 | 3.27** |
| *Item 16* | | | | | | | |
| (No aid to Cuba) | 1.00 | .93 | 1.21 | .61 | 1.26 | 1.15 | 3.47** |
| *Items 41–44* | | | | | | | |
| (Internationalism) | 15.64 | 17.22 | 16.87 | 17.01 | 15.54 | 15.70 | 8.25*** |
| *Items 57–60* | | | | | | | |
| (Ethnocentrism) | 15.71 | 12.78 | 14.65 | 13.89 | 14.71 | 15.23 | 8.62*** |
| *Traditional Family Ideology Scale* | 19.93 | 16.50 | 16.22 | 15.70 | 21.06 | 20.48 | 16.27*** |
| *Social Orientation Scale* | 65.10 | 60.71 | 60.60 | 61.12 | 66.48 | 67.30 | 12.33*** |

* Significant at the .05 level.
** Significant at the .01 level.
*** Significant at the .001 level.

a violent attack against the US or against a citizen. The F-ratio of 3272.56 is significant far beyond the .001 level. Avoidance is more highly recommended for a crisis involving a nonviolent action than one involving a "violent-US" or action directed against a citizen (F-ratio of 173.97).

*University*. Table 3 shows the means scores on all scales for each university and the F-ratios. On all but three scales the differences in the means for the universities yielded F-ratios which were significant beyond the .001 level. For avoidance reaction and "No aid to Cuba" the differences were significant beyond the .01 level, but for aggression and negotiation the F-ratios of 2.33 and 2.50 were significant only at the .05 level. It is interesting to note that the two private universities (Brown and Knox) had the lowest aggression and avoidance scores. They also disagreed most strongly with the item "No aid to Cuba," and they had the highest scores on internationalism and the lowest on ethnocentrism. Together with Florida, they also showed the least authoritarianism on the Traditional Family Ideology Scale and the most positive conception of others.

*Major Area*. Table 4 shows the results on all scales according to the major area of study. All the F-ratios but two (self-blame and avoidance) were significant beyond the .01 level. On the reactions to the international incidents, the education majors were lowest in aggression and highest in negotiation and self-blame; the natural science majors were among the highest in aggressive reactions and lowest in negotiation and self-blame. On the item "No aid to Cuba," the social science majors and humanities students disagreed most strongly. The social science majors also received the highest scores on internationalism, the lowest scores on ethnocentrism, the highest on the TFI, and the lowest on the Social Orientation Scale.

*Sex*. The mean scores on all the scales and the F-ratios for sex are shown in Table 5. All the means but three (avoidance, internationalism, ethnocentrism) were significant beyond the .001 level. On the International Scale, the females were less aggressive in their reactions, were more self-blaming, and preferred negotiation more than the males. On "No aid to Cuba," the females were more strongly disagreeing than the males. As would be expected, the females were also less authoritarian in family relationships (TFI) and more positively oriented toward people in general.

*Class*. Socioeconomic class did not seem to be a significant variable in any of our scales. The only score that approached significance (less than the .05 level) was that for self-blame on the International Scale. The lower class seemed to feel more strongly than the other two classes about the responsibility of the US to initiate action for reducing tension.

*Correlations of reactions to international crises*. Table 6 presents the product-moment correlations of the subscales with the four types of reactions to international conflicts. Our hypotheses were concerned primarily with the Social Orientation Scale. This scale was significantly

TABLE 4   *Means and F-ratios for All Major Areas on All Scales*

| | Mean | | | | | |
| --- | --- | --- | --- | --- | --- | --- |
| | Soc. science | Nat. science | Humani- ties | Educ. | Other | F-ratio |
| *International Scale* | | | | | | |
| Aggression | 48.66 | 52.30 | 48.21 | 46.99 | 52.03 | 4.20** |
| Negotiation | 83.66 | 80.64 | 82.85 | 86.58 | 82.96 | 5.90*** |
| Self-blame | 70.95 | 68.68 | 70.43 | 72.11 | 70.85 | 2.72* |
| Avoidance | 26.72 | 26.93 | 26.57 | 25.31 | 26.37 | .40 |
| *Item 16* | | | | | | |
| (No aid to Cuba) | .87 | 1.18 | .85 | .99 | 1.34 | 4.49** |
| *Items 41–44* | | | | | | |
| (Internationalism) | 16.90 | 15.95 | 16.45 | 15.67 | 15.80 | 4.46** |
| *Items 57–60* | | | | | | |
| (Ethnocentrism) | 13.76 | 14.93 | 14.16 | 14.91 | 15.19 | 4.00** |
| *Traditional Family* | | | | | | |
| *Ideology Scale* | 17.08 | 20.51 | 18.37 | 18.12 | 19.78 | 7.21*** |
| *Social Orientation* | | | | | | |
| *Scale* | 61.34 | 66.70 | 61.40 | 63.52 | 67.44 | 12.91*** |

\* Significant at the .05 level.
\*\* Significant at the .01 level.
\*\*\* Significant at the .001 level.

correlated with all four reactions. Aggression is associated with negative orientation towards others, that is, the higher the tendency to view others as bad, weak, and "object," the greater the tendency to recommend aggression as a response to attack from other nations. The reverse is true for negotiation and self-blame, that is, those with more positive feelings toward others tended to prefer more strongly the reactions of negotiation and self-initiated US action to reduce tension. The TFI presents a somewhat similar picture. Subjects who preferred the authoritarian orientation also preferred aggression. Ethnocentrism yielded the highest correlation with aggression, that is, the greater the ethnocentrism the greater the preference for the aggressive reaction. The more internationalistic the person is, the less he prefers aggression and the more he prefers negotiation and self-initiated reactions (self-blame). Results are very similar for the item on refusal to give aid to Cuba (item 16 in Appendix A). Those who tend to agree with the statement are more likely to recommend aggression and less likely to recommend negotiation or self-initiated action. All the results on our scales therefore seem to be consistent both with our hypotheses and with each other.

*Intercorrelations of scales.* Table 7 presents the intercorrelations of the four reactions to the international incidents. As would be expected,

TABLE 5  *Means and F-ratios for Sex and Socioeconomic Class on All Scales*

| Scale | Mean | | | Mean | | | |
|---|---|---|---|---|---|---|---|
| | Male | Female | F-ratio | Upper class | Middle class | Lower class | F-ratio |
| International Scale | | | | | | | |
| Aggression | 54.48 | 44.26 | 105.86*** | 49.68 | 49.75 | 51.32 | .80 |
| Negotiation | 81.50 | 85.00 | 22.50*** | 83.00 | 82.40 | 84.53 | 2.30 |
| Self-blame | 68.82 | 72.71 | 21.24*** | 70.81 | 69.40 | 72.14 | 3.10* |
| Avoidance | 26.76 | 26.11 | .67 | 26.63 | 26.57 | 25.94 | .23 |
| Item 16 | | | | | | | |
| (No aid to Cuba) | 1.33 | .74 | 42.07*** | 1.16 | 1.01 | 1.04 | 1.14 |
| Items 41-55 | | | | | | | |
| (Internationalism) | 15.97 | 16.44 | 4.53* | 16.27 | 16.15 | 16.00 | .42 |
| Items 57-60 | | | | | | | |
| (Ethnocentrism) | 14.71 | 14.47 | .72 | 14.34 | 14.72 | 14.80 | 1.01 |
| Traditional Family | | | | | | | |
| Ideology Scale | 20.65 | 16.60 | 70.27*** | 18.54 | 18.77 | 19.72 | 1.60 |
| Social Orientation | | | | | | | |
| Scale | 66.76 | 61.26 | 53.96*** | 63.78 | 64.16 | 65.77 | 1.93 |

\* Significant at the .05 level.
\*\* Significant at the .01 level.
\*\*\* Significant at the .001 level.

aggression is negatively related to self-blame and avoidance, while negotiation is positively related to self-blame but negatively related to avoidance. Those who prefer to negotiate international conflicts are much more likely to admit self-blame and deny an avoidance response. Table 8 presents the intercorrelations of all the remaining scales. Almost all of the intercorrelations are significant beyond the .01 level. Of particular interest is the Social Orientation Scale. Those who tend to perceive others positively tend to disagree with the statement of "No aid to Cuba," to be more internationalistic and less ethnocentric, and to prefer a more democratic family relationship. The internationalists tend to disagree with "No aid to Cuba" and recommend a more democratic family life.

## Discussion

The present study was an attempt to test certain hypotheses derived from a theory of social ideology concerning reactions to international conflicts. Two general ideological patterns were specified: the good-strong-"human" and the bad-weak-"object" conceptions of others. The results confirm the predictions, namely, that the positive conception of the "other person" would be associated with a greater willingness to support negotiation and to admit the responsibility of one's own nation in an international crisis; and conversely, that the more negative the conception, the greater the tendency to advocate aggression and to deny

TABLE 6 *Product-Moment Correlations of Scale Items with Reactions to Anti-US Acts (N = 1,219)*

| Scale | Aggression | Negotiation | Self-blame | Avoidance |
|---|---|---|---|---|
| *Item 16* | | | | |
| (No aid to Cuba) | .22** | −.19** | −.20** | .02 |
| *Items 41–44* | | | | |
| (Internationalism) | −.15** | .27** | .32** | .03 |
| *Items 57–60* | | | | |
| (Ethnocentrism) | .36** | −.01 | −.07* | −.09** |
| *Traditional Family* | | | | |
| *Ideology Scale* | .22** | −.08** | −.01 | .07* |
| *Social Orientation Scale* | .27** | −.17** | −.15** | .07* |

\* Significant at the .05 level.
\*\* Significant at the .01 level.

that one's own nation might be at fault. In addition, the interrelationships of the scales show that subjects with a negative person-orientation, as predicted, tend to accept a more authoritarian relationship within the family, are more ethnocentric, and are more likely to refuse aid to a potential enemy even when that nation has suffered a catastrophe.

These results not only confirm our theoretical formulation but demonstrate the validity of the Social Orientation Scale. The data are also consistent with the findings about the influences of authoritarianism, ethnocentrism, and dogmatism on international perception (Christiansen, 1959; Levinson, 1957; Smith and Rosen, 1958; Stagner, 1946). Our findings are also similar to those of Stagner *et al.* (1942).

Though the correlational evidence of the present study does not permit any conclusions as to causal relationships, descriptions of authoritarian, ethnocentric, and dogmatic personalities and studies of child-rearing practices yield indirect evidence of the central nature of social ideology (Frenkel-Brunswick, 1950; Guetzkow, 1955; Rokeach, 1960). Experimental studies of games also indicate the significance of ideology in the strategy of the player (Deutsch, 1960; Lutzker, 1960). Using the

Social Orientation Scale as a measure of social ideology, Mueller and Worchel (1966) found that those with a positive orientation toward others were more likely to trust the other player and cooperate with him for mutual and long-term gain than were those with a negative orientation, who were apparently motivated by immediate self-gain. The low but significant correlations with the International Scale in our study, however, indicate that only a small portion of the variance in reactions to international conflicts can be accounted for by the variation in Social Orientation scores. Other factors have to be considered in any comprehensive theory of international behavior. Kelman (1955) states that there are at least two other factors besides attitudinal variables that affect the final level of interaction between nations, namely, societal factors and

TABLE 7  *Intercorrelations of Reactions to Anti-US Acts (N = 1,219)*

|  | *Negotiation* | *Self-blame* | *Avoidance* |
|---|---|---|---|
| Aggression | −.03 | −.20** | −.15** |
| Negotiation |  | .53** | −.33** |
| Self-blame |  |  | −.06* |

\* Significant at the .05 level.
\*\* Significant at the .01 level.

TABLE 8  *Intercorrelations Between Scale Items (N = 1,219)*

|  | *41–44* | *57–60* | *TFI* | *Social orientation* |
|---|---|---|---|---|
| *Item 16* (No aid to Cuba) | −.27** | .16** | .09 | .21** |
| *Items 41–44* (Internationalism) |  | −.21** | −.10** | −.22** |
| *Items 57–60* (Ethnocentrism) |  |  | .22** | .26** |
| *Traditional Family Ideology Scale* |  |  |  | .45** |

\* Significant at the .05 level.
\*\* Significant at the .01 level.

structural factors. Scott (1958–59) adds to these the factor of the nature of the international event. In our study, both the source and the nature of the anti-US act were significant factors in influencing the degree of support for each of the four responses. For example, aggression was more strongly endorsed when the conflict originated in an East-bloc nation or when it involved a violent attack on a symbol of the US.

Cultural variables have frequently been mentioned as important determinants of international behavior (Gladstone, 1955; Katz, 1965; Kelman, 1955; Sawyer, 1965; Scott, 1958-59). Scott points out that "from a sociopsychological point of view, a person's attitudes towards events in his life are conditioned by the norms of his associates and of his positive reference groups" (1958-59, p. 470). The differences between the sexes in our study are probably due to the different emphasis on the expression of aggression. It is difficult to offer any interpretation of the differences in reactions to international conflicts among the universities or between public and private universities because there are many confounding variables. The preponderance of social science majors in the private universities and the much larger proportion of males in the public universities could well account for the observed differences in reactions. The uneven distribution of the sexes in major areas of study might also explain the greater preference for negotiation and the greater disagreement with aggression among social science and education majors. More females than males tend to major in these areas as compared to the natural sciences. It is interesting to note, however, that the social science majors received the lowest Social Orientation scores; that is, expressed the most positive orientation toward others.

The lack of any really significant differences in our scales among the three socioeconomic classes seems quite surprising in view of the differences reported in other studies. In an analysis of the data from United Nations studies, Scott (1958-59) points out that persons of lower socioeconomic status are less likely to support cooperative measures in international conflicts and are more likely to advocate either violence or withdrawal than persons of the middle class. Miller and Swanson (1953) have proposed that the socialization procedures within the various social classes result in different opportunities for learning favored defense mechanisms in reacting to frustrations. It is very probable that our college subjects in the lower socioeconomic class would be classified as middle-class on any absolute scale of income, education, and occupation of parents. The differences in socioeconomic class among our subjects are, in all probability, much less than would be found in the general population.

The overwhelming support of negotiation by our college subjects, regardless of the source or nature of attack on the US, seems to substantiate the conclusion by Katz (1965) that there is a popular basis in advanced technological nations for political cooperation and for the peaceful settlements of international disputes. He reasons that there is some tendency in these nations toward divorcing the cultural identity of the people from doctrines of statism, and therefore that "Americans can derive major satisfactions from being American without loving their government." As a consequence, a "reported insult to the American flag is not as widely perceived with a sense of personal outrage as was once the case."

Looked at in another way, the more secure the nation—economically, militarily, and politically—the less sensitive are the people to insults to national honor. They are also more likely to "look within" to find fault than to blame the other nation. This may account for the large support given to self-blame, that is, blaming one's own nation for the international crisis. Dollard, Doob, Miller, Mowrer, and Sears (1939) have suggested that Americans pride themselves on being "masters of their fate"; they therefore tend to blame only themselves for their frustrations and incline toward self-aggression when they fail. If this mechanism can be generalized to international frustration, one might expect Americans to blame their own nation in international crises. Unfortunately, our data, demonstrating considerable support for negotiation and self-blame, seem to have little impact on politicians, who feel that unless they react aggressively to foreign affronts they will be swept out of office.

REFERENCES

ADORNO, W. E., E. FRENKEL-BRUNSWICK, D. J. LEVINSON, AND R. N. SANFORD. *The Authoritarian Personality.* New York: Harper, 1950.

BAY, C., I. GULLVÅG, H. OFSTAD, AND H. TONNESSEN. *Nationalism: A Study of Identification with People and Power.* Oslo: Institute of Social Research, 1950 (mimeographed).

CHRISTIANSEN, B. *Attitudes towards Foreign Affairs as a Function of Personality.* Oslo: Oslo University Press, 1959.

DEUTSCH, M. "The Effect of Motivational Orientation upon Trust and Suspicion," *Human Relations,* 13 (1960), 123–40.

DOLLARD, J., L. W. DOOB, N. E. MILLER, O. H. MOWRER, AND R. R. SEARS. *Frustration and Aggression.* New Haven: Yale University Press, 1939.

FARIS, C. D. "Selected Attitudes on Foreign Affairs as Correlates of Authoritarianism and Political Anomie," *Journal of Politics,* 22 (1960), 50–67.

FENSTERWALD, B., JR. "American Isolationism and Expansionism," *Journal of Conflict Resolution,* 2, 4 (Dec. 1958), 280–307.

GILBERT, D. C., AND D. J. LEVINSON. "Ideology, Personality, and Institutional Policy in the Mental Hospital," *Journal of Abnormal and Social Psychology,* 53 (1956), 263–71.

GLADSTONE, A. I. "The Possibility of Predicting Reactions to International Events," *Journal of Social Issues,* 11 (1955) 21–28.

GLADSTONE, A. I., AND M. A. TAYLOR. "Threat-Related Attitudes and Reactions to Communications about International Events," *Journal of Conflict Resolution,* 2, 1 (March 1958), 17–28.

GUETZKOW, H. *Multiple Loyalties: Theoretical Approach to a Problem in International Organization.* Princeton University, Center for Research on World Political Institutions, Publication No. 4 (1955), 1–62.

KATZ, D. "Nationalism and Strategies of International Conflict Resolution." In

H. Kelman (ed.), *International Behavior*. New York: Holt, Rinehart, Winston, 1965, 356–90.

KELMAN, H. C. "Societal, Attitudinal, and Structural Factors in International Relations," *Journal of Social Issues*, 11 (1955), 42–56.

LEVINSON, D. J. "Authoritarian Personality and Foreign Policy," *Journal of Conflict Resolution*, 1, 1 (March 1957), 37–47.

LEVINSON, D. J., AND P. E. HUFFMAN. "Traditional Family Ideology and Its Relation to Personality," *Journal of Personality*, 23 (1955), 251–73.

LUTZKER, D. R. "Internationalism as a Predictor of Cooperative Behavior," *Journal of Conflict Resolution*, 4, 4 (Dec. 1960), 426–30.

MACKINNON, W. J., AND R. CENTERS. "Authoritarianism and Internationalism," *Public Opinion Quarterly*, 20 (1956), 621–30.

MUELLER, L., AND P. WORCHEL. "Social Ideology and Game Behavior," unpublished manuscript, 1967.

SAWYER, J., AND H. GUETZKOW. "Bargaining and Negotiation in International Relations." In H. C. Kelman (ed.), *International Behavior*. New York: Holt, Rinehart, Winston, 1965, 464–520.

SCOTT, W. A. "Correlates of International Attitudes," *Public Opinion Quarterly* 22 (1958–59), 464–72.

SMITH, H. P., AND E. W. ROSEN. "Some Psychological Correlates of World Mindedness and Authoritarianism," *Journal of Personality*, 26 (1958), 170–83.

STAGNER, R. "Nationalism." In L. P. Harriman (ed.), *Encyclopedia of Psychology*. New York: Philosophical Library, 1946, 404–407.

———, J. F. BROWN, R. H. GUNDLACH, AND R. K. WHITE. "A Survey of Public Opinion on the Prevention of War," *Journal of Social Psychology*, 16 (1942), 109–30.

TERHUNE, K. W. "Nationalism among Foreign and American Students: an Exploratory Study," *Journal of Conflict Resolution*, 8, 3 (Sept. 1964), 256–70.

APPENDICES

## A. International Scale

Our Embassy in Brazil was burned during student riots while the police looked on and did nothing to prevent the action.

1. Threaten to break off diplomatic relations unless proper compensation is made and those responsible punished.
2. Request a meeting with the Brazilian government to smooth out causes of friction.
3. Try to find out what we did to antagonize the Brazilian officials.
4. Build a new Embassy building; in time the tension will die down.

Yugloslavia has decided that US diplomats are to be restricted in their travel about the country.

5. Arrange a conference with the Yugoslav officials to modify their position.
6. Do nothing; the Yugoslav government has the right to decide this issue.
7. Blame ourselves for not being more friendly to Yugoslavia.
8. Institute the same restrictions on Yugoslav diplomats in US.

A US citizen has been arrested and imprisoned in Argentina without the officials giving any reason.
9. Do nothing; he will probably be released soon anyway.
10. Demand immediate release or threaten to undertake reprisals.
11. Suggest a meeting of representatives of both countries to investigate the case.
12. Review our actions to determine the causes of this apparently unprovoked action.

Cuba experiences a severe tornado wiping out much property and human life.
13. We should send all aid possible immediately.
14. We should send aid only under certain conditions.
15. Send only emergency supplies of medicine.
16. Refuse to send any aid whatsoever.

Our US Ambassador to Greece was attacked by a mob of anti-American Greeks as he called upon the Prime Minister.
17. Demand punishment for those responsible and better protection of our officials.
18. Request a meeting with the Greek officials to reduce anti-American feeling.
19. Modify our foreign policy towards Greece to improve our relations.
20. Do nothing; one has to expect such things during tense periods.

China has begun an extensive propaganda campaign against the US over several shortwave radio stations.
21. Get the United Nations to take the matter up for discussion.
22. Do nothing; people will pay little attention to it anyway.
23. Modify our position to remove any basis to their propaganda.
24. Start jamming or do the same thing.

A US citizen has been attacked in Chile by a student mob.
25. Forget it; it is just one of those momentary incidents.
26. Demand proper compensation and a promise to prevent such future actions.
27. Suggest a meeting with Chilean officials to reduce any causes for antagonism.
28. Review our policy towards Chile to eliminate cause of such behavior.

During a student riot in Turkey, our flag was torn down without the police attempting to prevent the action.
29. Demand that the Turkish government apologize for this action.
30. Meet with the Turkish officials to find out the causes of such anti-American feeling.
31. Increase our efforts to improve our relations with Turkey.

32. Do nothing; the feeling will die down in time.

USSR has instituted strict trade restrictions against the US.
33. Set up trade conferences with USSR in order to remove the restrictions.
34. There is nothing we can do since each country has a right to set up its own economic policy.
35. Examine our own economic policies to determine what precipitated this action.
36. Retaliate by instituting the same trade restrictions against the USSR.

US tourists in Peru are met with signs saying "Yankee go home."
37. Nothing to do; it will die down in time.
38. Demand more efficient protection or threaten economic reprisals.
39. Arrange a conference with Peruvian officials to prevent such actions.
40. Find out what we are doing to arouse such feelings.

As a means of maintaining peace throughout the world, it has been suggested that:
41. International barriers, such as tariffs and immigration restrictions, should be removed.
42. My country should participate more actively to help achieve peaceful solutions to conflicts among nations.
43. My country should actively strive to improve the United Nations.
44. It is in the best interests of one's own country to be concerned with the welfare of other nations as well.

A US Legation in Poland has been blown up during government-inspired student riots.
45. Threaten to break off diplomatic relations unless proper compensation is made and those responsible punished.
46. Request a meeting with the Polish government to eliminate causes of friction.
47. Try to find out what we did to cause such action.
48. Build a new Legation; such things are bound to happen during tense periods.

Spain has decided to limit the movements of US diplomats.
49. Request a meeting with the Spanish officials to remove this restriction.
50. Do nothing; the Spanish government has the right to do this.
51. Blame ourselves for not being more friendly to the Spanish government.
52. Do the same to the Spanish diplomats in our country.

US tourists have complained that they have been met by anti-American slogans and insults by East German persons during their visit in the area.
53. There is nothing we can do; such incidents will happen from time to time.
54. Demand better protection for our citizens in the area or threaten retaliatory action.
55. Call a meeting with East German officials to find ways of stopping such behavior.
56. Find ways of improving our relations.

For the welfare of our own country it has been suggested that:

57. It is only natural that our country should put its own interests first.
58. To the degree possible, our country should be both economically and politically independent of all other nations.
59. Our country should strive for power in the world.
60. The best way for our people to progress is to maintain themselves as a distinct and independent nation.

As he left the Embassy building our US Ambassador to Hungary was booed and spat upon by a mob of Hungarians.

61. Demand punishment for those responsible and better protection.
62. Discuss the situation with the Hungarian government to eliminate further actions of this nature.
63. Review our policy towards Hungary to minimize any cause of friction.
64. Do nothing; such things do happen from time to time.

France has initiated anti-American propaganda over her short wave radio stations.

65. Take the matter up in the United Nations.
66. Ignore it; few will pay attention to it anyway.
67. Analyze their propaganda to see if there is any truth to it.
68. Start jamming or do the same thing to France.

A US citizen has been attacked by a student mob in Rumania.

69. Do nothing; it is just an isolated action.
70. Demand compensation and proper police protection in the future.
71. Suggest a joint meeting of US and Rumanian officials to eliminate causes of friction.
72. Determine what we did to arouse such action.

The US flag on our Legation was torn down by a group of Bulgarian students while the police just looked on.

73. Demand an apology from the Bulgarian government.
74. Arrange a meeting with the Bulgarian government officials to reduce causes of antagonism.
75. Increase our efforts to improve our relations with Bulgaria.
76. Do nothing; one has to expect such things in a tense world situation.

The British Prime Minister issued a decree reducing US imports to Britain.

77. Arrange a conference with Britain to modify its decree.
78. Do nothing; Britain has a right to establish its own trade policy.
79. Modify our own policy so as to remove any reason for their action.
80. Institute the same restrictions against Britain.

A US citizen has been arrested in Czechoslovakia for no apparent reason.

81. Take it calmly; police can make a mistake.
82. Demand to have him returned or undertake reprisals.
83. Suggest that the case be investigated by representatives of both countries.
84. Examine our own actions to see what we did to cause this action.

## B. Traditional Family Ideology Scale

1. A child should not be allowed to talk back to his parents, or else he would lose respect for them.
2. Women who want to remove the word *obey* from the marriage service don't understand what it means to be a wife.
3. The facts on crime and sexual immorality show that we will have to crack down harder on young people if we are going to save our moral standards.
4. A well-raised child is one who doesn't have to be told twice to do something.
5. Some equality in marriage is a good thing, but by and large the husband ought to have the main say-so in family matters.
6. It helps the child in the long run if he is made to conform to his parents' ideas.
7. A wife does better to vote the way her husband does, because he probably knows more about such things.
8. It goes against nature to place women in positions of authority over men.

## C. Social Orientation Scale

1. Once a criminal, always a criminal. Therefore, criminals should be sentenced to long prison terms in order to protect society.
2. Many people vote without knowing the issues or the candidates. The right to vote should be restricted to those who demonstrate a knowledge of American history and government.
3. Man being what he is, there will always be wars. Therefore it is best that we maintain the strongest military force to deter others from attacking us.
4. The alcoholic is basically a weak person who is escaping from his problems and responsibilities. He should never be given a position of authority and responsibility.
5. The insane person can be successfully treated and returned to society as good as he ever was. We should provide more and better hospitals.
6. There are people who get into one accident after another. They should not be given a license to drive a car.
7. People enjoy reading 'trash,' going to sexy movies, and seeing one Western after another on TV. There is no use trying to provide them with better programs and intelligent newspapers.
8. Familiarity breeds contempt. Those who hold positions of authority and responsibility should always maintain a certain distance from those working under them.
9. Too many people convicted of murder and sentenced to be executed escape punishment. Laws should be "tightened up" to prevent unnecessary delays in carrying out the sentence.
10. It is a waste of time and money to try to reduce the number of "dropouts" from school. Many of them are better off going to work anyway.
11. We can eliminate much poverty by providing skilled training, better employment opportunities, and counseling.

12. Immigrants only add to our unemployment problem. We should restrict admission to our country to those possessing skills needed by industry.

13. Delinquents come from bad homes and poor neighborhoods. We can reduce the number of delinquents by eradicating slums, providing more recreational facilities and better schools.

14. In general, the mentally retarded or "feeble-minded" will always be a burden to society. At best, we should care for them in state institutions.

15. It is only the fear of punishment that deters many from becoming criminals. Police forces should be increased and punishment for violations of the law should be more severe.

16. It has been estimated that about one-third of marriages end in divorce. Regardless of what we do there are people who will never be happily married.

17. Labor unions have grown much too powerful. Legislation should be passed that would provide more government control over unions.

18. The people cannot be trusted to vote for the most capable man to be a judge. Judges should be appointed by the governor.

19. Leaders are born, not made. We should spend more time locating these leaders than training the people to become leaders.

20. Automatic pay increases for any job should be abolished as they tend to promote inefficiency.

H A N S   J .   M O R G E N T H A U

# Is World Public Opinion a Myth?

Since the beginning of history, governments in their relations with one another have had to yield from time to time to military threats and diplomatic pressure. Government A would try to induce Government B to embark upon a certain course of action through the promise of benefits or the threat of disadvantages.

SOURCE: Hans J. Morgenthau, "Is World Public Opinion a Myth?" *New York Times Magazine* (March 25, 1962), 23, 126–127. © 1962 by the New York Times Company. Reprinted by permission.

In our period of history, a third force has arisen—invisible, intangible, imponderable—before which governments seem to stand in awe and whose favor they appear to curry: world public opinion. The United States and the Soviet Union compete with each other in supporting anti-colonial movements because world public opinion supports them, too. The United States and the Soviet Union have been spending much time and effort on elaborating and debating disarmament proposals, not in the expectation that the other side would accept them but out of deference to world public opinion.

The United States has been, throughout its history, particularly solicitous of public opinion, at home and abroad. Tocqueville called public opinion "the predominant authority" in America and faith in it "a species of religion." The Declaration of Independence itself owes its existence to the conviction of the Founding Fathers that "a decent respect to the opinions of mankind requires that they should declare the causes which impel them to the separation." Woodrow Wilson invoked the same force in his address to the Paris Peace Conference of Jan. 25, 1919:

\* \* \* We are assembled under very peculiar conditions of world opinion. I may say without straining the point that we are not representatives of governments, but representatives of peoples. It will not suffice to satisfy governmental circles anywhere. It is necessary that we should satisfy the opinion of mankind.

Less than five months before the outbreak of the Second World War, Cordell Hull, then American Secretary of State, maintained that "a public opinion, the most potent of all forces for peace, is more strongly developing throughout the world." The New York Times stated on Nov. 15, 1947, that the General Assembly of the United Nations was capable "of mobilizing world opinion, which, in the last analysis, determines the international balance of power."

When last year the Government of the United States refused to commit American troops to the invasion of Cuba—an action it would have taken, say, fifty years ago almost as a matter of course—it was in good measure motivated by the fear of world public opinion. And its hesitation to resume atmospheric testing has been similarly motivated.

What is this thing called "world public opinion," which nobody has ever seen or heard or touched, which has no ambassadors nor armies but has a way of sometimes prevailing over both? Is world public opinion but a myth, a figment of the imagination of unduly apprehensive governments, or is it a fact of experience, something of real power which governments do well to take into account?

Those who believe in the reality of world public opinion imagine it as a kind of national public opinion writ large, a public opinion which performs the same functions for humanity as the several national public opinions do for their respective national societies. World public opinion is supposed to transcend national boundaries and to unite members of different nations in a consensus with regard to certain international issues.

Whenever the government of a nation takes a certain action on the international scene which contravenes the opinion of mankind, humanity is supposed to rise, regardless of national affiliations, and take its stand against that government. That government would then find itself in about the same position as an individual who has acted against the public opinion of his nation. World public opinion will either compel it to conform with its standards or punish it for its deviation from them.

If such is the meaning generally attributed to world public opinion, then it is safe to say that world public opinion does not exist. For there can be no public opinion without an integrated society whose members can act and react in concert with regard to common interests and on behalf of common values.

It is true that there is at the bottom of all political contentions and conflicts an irreducible minimum of psychological traits and aspirations which are the common possession of all mankind. All human beings want to live and, hence, want the things necessary for life. All human beings want to be free and, hence, want to have those opportunities for self-expression and self-development which their particular culture considers to be desirable. All human beings seek power and, hence, seek social distinctions, again varying with the particular pattern of their culture, that put them ahead of and above their fellow men.

Upon this psychological foundation, the same for all men, rises an edifice of philosophical convictions, ethical postulates and political aspirations. These, too, might be shared by all men under certain conditions, but actually they are not. They might be shared by all if the conditions under which men can satisfy their desire to live, to be free, and to have power were similar all over the world, and if the conditions under which such satisfaction is withheld and must be striven for were also similar everywhere.

If this were so, the experience, common to all men, of what men seek, of what they are able to obtain, of what they are denied, and of what they must struggle for would indeed create a community of convictions, postulates and aspirations which would provide the common standards of evaluation for world public opinion. Any violation of the standards of this world public opinion, against and by whomever committed, would call forth spontaneous reactions on the part of humanity; for, in view of the hypothetical similarity of all conditions, all men would fear that what happens to one group might happen to any group.

But reality does not correspond to this hypothetical assumption of similarity of conditions throughout the world. The variations of the standard of living range from mass starvation to abundance; the variations in freedom from tyranny to democracy from economic slavery to equality; the variations in power from extreme inequalities and unbridled one-man rule to wide distribution of power subject to constitutional limitations.

One nation enjoys freedom, yet starves; another nation is well fed, but longs for freedom; still another enjoys security of life and individual freedom, but smarts under the rule of an autocratic government. In consequence, while philosophically the similarities of standards are considerable throughout the world—most political philosophies agree in their evaluation of the common good, of law, peace and order, of life, liberty and the pursuit of happiness—moral judgments and political evaluations show wide divergencies.

The same moral and political concepts take on different meanings in different environments. Justice and democracy mean one thing here, something quite different there. A move on the international scene decried by one group as immoral and unjust is praised by another as the opposite.

Thus the contrast between the community of psychological traits and elemental aspirations, on the one hand, and the absence of shared experiences, universal moral convictions and common political aspirations, on the other, far from providing evidence for the existence of a world public opinion, rather demonstrates its impossibility, as humanity is constituted in our age.

Humanity is constituted not as one great society pursuing common aims, but as a multitude of national societies reflecting the most diverse conditions, interests and aspirations. What all men have in common is filtered through, colored and hence transformed by, the particular national societies to which they belong. This interposition of nationalism between the aspirations of mankind and world public opinion, so called, is most strikingly revealed in mankind's attitude toward war.

No opinion is more widely held anywhere in the world than the abhorrence of war. When they think and speak of war in this context, the men on the streets of Washington, Moscow, Peiping, New Delhi, London, Paris and Madrid have pretty much the same thing in mind: that is, war waged with the modern means of mass destruction. There appears to exist a genuine world public opinion with respect to war. But here again the appearances are deceptive.

Humanity is united in its opposition to war in so far as that opposition manifests itself in philosophic terms, moral postulates and abstract political aspirations—that is, with regard to war as such, war in the abstract. But humanity thus united reveals its impotence, and the apparent world public opinion splits into its national components, when the issue is no longer war as such, in the abstract, but a particular war, this particular war; not any war, but war here and now.

In such circumstances, the universal condemnation of war undergoes a significant change in focus. The opposition to war as such is transformed into opposition to the nation that threatens to start, or actually has started, a particular war, and it so happens that this nation is always identical with the national enemy whose belligerent attitude threatens the national interest and, therefore, must be opposed as a threat to peace.

In other words, out of the common soil of the universal condemnation of war grow specific acts of condemnation directed against whoever threatens through war the interests of particular nations.

The attitude of the different nations to the Korean War bears out this analysis. The Korean War was universally condemned by "world public opinion." Yet, while the Soviet Union and its supporters blamed the United States and its allies for it, the latter regarded North Korea and China as the aggressors, supported by the Soviet Union, and the "neutrals," such as India, divided the blame between the two camps.

The actual participation of the different nations in this war was similarly determined by their conceptions of the national interest. Nations such as China and the United States, whose interests were directly affected by the war and who had the power to protect them, bore the war's main burden. Others, such as France, with only limited interests and resources, took a correspondingly limited part in the war. Still others, such as Denmark, without interest or resources, and India, with a positive interest in abstention, took no active part at all.

When we speak then of world public opinion, we cannot mean what we say. What we can refer to is only a number of national public opinions, favorable or unfavorable to a particular policy. From the recognition of this fact, three lessons for the foreign policy of the United States follow.

*First,* public opinion in foreign countries is one factor among many that the foreign policy of the United States must take into account. The equation which goes into the making of a foreign policy contains many factors—political, military, economic, psychological—brought to bear upon one's own nation, one's allies, one's enemies and the uncommitted nations. The effect a certain policy is likely to have upon public opinion in a foreign country may be given by the policy makers an important or even decisive weight, as compared with all the other factors to be considered in the formulation of a foreign policy.

However, it ought not to be assumed a priori that the reaction of public opinion in a foreign country must necessarily outweigh all the other factors involved. Each situation must be considered on its merits, and in consequence the weight to be given to foreign public opinion will change with circumstances.

*Second,* on the basis of recent historical experience, a good case can be made for the proposition that we have tended to overestimate greatly the importance of public opinion both at home and abroad. Successive Administrations have refrained from taking an initiative in foreign policy, which they would have otherwise taken, because they were afraid of the reaction of public opinion both in this country and among our allies or the uncommitted nations.

Yet public opinion is not a fixed entity which restricts foreign policy within insurmountable barriers. Quite to the contrary, it responds to leadership; it is the product of somebody's leadership, and if it isn't yours it is likely to be your enemy's. It has been said that God is on the side of the strongest battalions. Whatever one may think of this statement, there is no doubt that public opinion has a way of accommodating itself to successful political action.

Public opinion in many countries was opposed to the Russian reconquest of Hungary and the Chinese conquest of Tibet. But, since the interventions have been successful, public opinion has reconciled itself to that success, while at best continuing to deplore it.

*Third,* a certain foreign policy is likely to evoke both a positive and a negative response from public opinion abroad. This is almost inevitable in view of the different interests at stake and of the different values being brought to bear. While the policy maker may be concerned about the negative response, especially since it is likely to be particularly vociferous, he ought to be encouraged by the positive one. There are all kinds of opinions abroad, and the policy maker ought not to give all of them equal weight.

In the reference of the Declaration of Independence to "a decent respect to the opinions of mankind," the accent is on "decent." Not every opinion is worthy of the same respect as any other, because not every opinion is as good as any other in terms of our interests and values.

Instead of catering to a "world public opinion," which as such has no reality, it might be the beginning of wisdom in dealing with the several national public opinions, which are a factor to be reckoned with, if we were to form a clear opinion of ourselves and what we are about in our relations with other nations. Only if we have standards of evaluation which have their roots in the soil of our interests and values can we deal justly and successfully with the opinions of other nations, reflecting their interests and values.

CHARLES   FRANKEL

## *The Scribblers and International Relations*

The large-scale entrance of the United States Government into the field of international cultural relations is a relatively recent phenomenon, dating only from World War II. Much has been said in this brief period about the importance of cultural relations for the resolution of international conflicts and the achievement of American foreign-policy objectives. However, there has been relatively little discussion of cultural relations that has attempted to cut beneath the widely accepted conventions that it is good for people in different countries to know one another personally, and good for the United States if other nations realize that we do indeed have a culture. In particular, one special purpose of cultural relations, and one peculiar and troublesome set of problems which they present, have been given less attention than they merit. These have to do with the role of intellectuals in international affairs, and with some of the special characteristics of the relation between American intellectuals and intellectuals elsewhere.

It would hopelessly simplify the harsh complexity of most international conflicts, and it would ascribe more influence to intellectuals than they have, to say that international conflict has its source in the quarrels of intellectuals. Nevertheless, there is a kind of devious truth in this statement. The influence over international affairs of "the scribbling set," as the Duke of Wellington once called the intellectuals with less than complete affection, is greater than is commonly thought—greater, certainly, than one would suppose from the frequent complaints of intellectuals themselves that people in power are suspicious of them and averse to listening to them.

SOURCE: Charles Frankel, "The Scribblers And International Relations," *Foreign Affairs*, XL (October 1965), 1–14. Reprinted by special permission from *Foreign Affairs*. Copyright by the Council on Foreign Relations, Inc., New York.

There are a number of ways in which this influence is exercized. One of the most obvious is the relation of intellectuals to the language of international conflict and accommodation. International affairs are peculiarly susceptible to galloping abstractions—"Communism," "Africa," "Imperialism," "the Free World." Nowhere else do massive stereotypes and personified ideas play a larger role; nowhere do they do more to rigidify disagreement, to give it a quality of necessity and higher nobility, and to turn otherwise manageable conflicts into unmanageable ones. And intellectuals, more than most other groups, have the power to create, dignify, inflate, criticize, moderate or puncture these abstractions. The character of international life is influenced by the language that comes to be used in public to explain what is going on, to justify the positions that are taken, or to negotiate disputes. The quality of this language is something which intellectuals do much to affect.

There are some other even more apparent ways in which intellectuals exercise influence over international affairs. The pivotal audiences abroad to whom United States educational and cultural programs are addressed, for example, are composed of intellectuals.[1] The effect which these programs have on our relations with other countries depends decisively on the reactions of intellectuals to them. This is true even when educational and cultural programs have other audiences in mind. The target for an educational project of the Agency for

---

[1] It would take us far afield to define the phrase "the intellectuals" with the thoroughness it deserves. Briefly, however, it refers to a social category. As I am using it here, it says nothing about the inner capacities (or incapacities) of mind of the people who belong to this category. First of all, an intellectual is simply a man whose principal occupation involves dealing with words or symbols at a fairly high level of complexity. He is, in this broad sense, a "scribbler." (Of course, the idea of what is "complex" is a relative matter. It depends on the surrounding educational and cultural context. In countries where educational levels are low, the notions of "complexity" are naturally more relaxed. Merely being a university student, or even a high-school graduate, can be enough to qualify an individual as an intellectual—a significant factor that affects the political influence of students in countries marked by low literacy.) Secondly, an intellectual is a man who, in addition to his specialized knowledge or with the help of such knowledge, concerns himself with issues of general public importance, and addresses himself to people outside his own professional field. Specialized knowledge in itself is not enough to make a man an intellectual. The late Norbert Wiener, for example, was an intellectual, in this meaning of the term, not because he made technical contributions to cybernetics but because he also discussed "the human use of human beings." Finally, it should be noted that to be an intellectual is not entirely a matter of self-election. In every society, there are associations, clubs, cliques, cafés and periodicals that are identified as "intellectual." Admission to them may be a wholly informal affair, but the fact that an individual has been admitted to them is part of what is meant by calling him an "intellectual." In this sense, intellectuals compose a reasonably definite social category, even though, just as in the case of businessmen, doctors or criminals, there are a fairly large number of borderline cases that cannot be classified one way or the other.

International Development may be primary- or secondary-school students, but without the understanding and coöperation of local teachers, school administrators and officials of education ministries, it is not likely to succeed. Some of the State Department's cultural presentations—for example, a jazz band or a touring movie star—may be aimed at a mass audience, but their reception depends to a considerable extent on the amount and kind of attention they receive from editors, critics and broadcasters. Of all United States agencies conducting large educational programs abroad, probably only the Peace Corps can achieve its purposes without major reliance on the good will of foreign intellectuals; and even its programs can be compromised by these groups if they wish to do so.

These aspects of the influence of intellectuals are reflections of a deeper role that intellectuals play in contemporary societies. As a consequence of the growing practical importance of such fields as law, medicine, science, economics, education and journalism, and, to a larger extent, as a consequence of the secularization of society, an outstanding feature of modern history has been the rise of intellectuals to positions of pivotal importance in society. Indeed, as the role played by intellectuals in most of the emerging nations illustrates, this trend is an essential part of what we mean by the "modernization" of a society. And the role of intellectuals has not been simply that of giving practical counsel or supplying technical know-how. It has been that of serving as a "censorclass" for the community. Located in the universities, the press, the theatre and the arts, the intellectuals in almost all societies are a major group from whom members of the educated and semi-educated publics draw their opinions about the character and moral quality of their society.

The attitudes which the individual members of a society hold toward its reigning institutions do not depend simply on their judgment of the efficiency of these institutions. Such attitudes depend also on whether individuals find these institutions congruent with their general *Weltanschauung*, and can justify them in a language which they regard as appropriate for discussing such matters. Thus, relatively few Americans or foreigners find fault with American institutions on the ground of their inefficiency. The more usual denunciation is that America is "materialistic." In other words, the stability and strength of social and political institutions depend not only on their practical performance but on their symbolic *legitimacy*. And to a considerable extent, the secular intellectuals of modern nations have supplanted the clergy as the principal suppliers and endorsers of the symbols of legitimacy. "Capitalism," "socialism," "freedom," "justice," "exploitation," "alienation," etc., with the special reverberations they now carry, are intellectuals' terms.

The significance of this for foreign policy is as great as it is for domestic affairs. Over the long run, a major nation's foreign policy is unlikely to succeed, or will, at any rate, become more costly and more completely dependent on violence and the threat of violence, if it loses the understanding and sympathy of intellectuals in other countries and at home. It is against this background that we may turn to consider certain curious features of the relation between American and foreign intellectuals. For the attitudes of intellectual groups abroad are peculiarly relevant to an understanding of the nature and difficulties of the tasks that are somewhat loosely and happily lumped together under the heading of "cultural relations."

## II

It is tempting, and only too common, when describing the attitudes of foreign intellectuals, to label them with the generic term, "anti-American." But this is almost certainly misleading. The attitudes to which this label is applied are not infrequently accompanied by great courtesy and friendship toward individual Americans, by avid interest in American intellectual, literary and artistic achievements, and even by basic sympathy with the long-range objectives of American foreign policy. "Anti-Americanism," so-called, is in fact a complex and elusive phenomenon composed of many separate strands, a good number of which have little to do intrinsically with American culture as such. Instead of concentrating on anti-Americanism, which begs many questions, it is preferable to try to unravel these strands and to see what they imply with regard to the problem of communication between articulate representatives of American and foreign cultures.

Obviously, there are grave dangers of oversimplification in any attempt to characterize the intellectuals of the United States or of other countries in a few broad strokes. The ethnic, social and political differences between the intellectuals of different countries are frequently very great, and, within individual countries, intellectual groups are commonly divided into sub-groups and factions that are in sharp disagreement with one another. So far as the remarks that are about to be made are concerned, it should be borne in mind that they describe, on the whole, the attitudes of the most vocal and visible members of intellectual groups, and that they apply with least force to the English-speaking and Scandinavian countries, and probably with greatest force to the intellectuals of the emerging countries. It should also be stressed that we are discussing differences between American intellectuals and others that are differences in degree, and not absolute, categorical contrasts. Within the framework of such reservations, however, a number of generalizations may be hazarded.

To begin with, the basic intellectual perspective of the dominant groups in the intellectual circles of most foreign countries tends to be different from that which prevails among most leading representatives of American scholarship and intellectual life. Setting specialists in the physical sciences aside, the education and mental formation of most foreign intellectuals is literary in character, and their approach to social issues is marked by a high degree of reliance on broad and abstract theories and ideals. In contrast, American scholars, particularly those in the social sciences, tend to be more empirical, more concerned with refined problems of methodology, and more anti-ideological. Where foreign intellectuals enjoy using comprehensive intellectual schemes, often carrying heavy philosophical and metaphysical overtones, to explain and interpret specific trends, American scholars and social observers tend to be skeptical, perhaps overly skeptical, of broad generalizations and value-judgments.

This difference in basic intellectual outlook leads to other differences, sometimes more apparent than real, but important none the less because they are felt to be real. Thus, to a considerable extent, intellectuals abroad are likely to be leftist in their political sentiments. In contrast, American scholars and intellectuals, although in fact they may be anything but conservative, are nevertheless frequently perceived by their foreign colleagues as adherents of the status quo. The reason has less to do with their explicit political sentiments than with their intellectual style. By and large, they tend to be "problem-oriented." That is to say, they generally shun sweeping verdicts on the state of society, and prefer, by training and inclination, to break down large issues into their smaller parts, formulating these as limited problems which manageable programs of inquiry or reform may reasonably be expected to solve. Accordingly, to others with different traditions, American scholars are likely to seem at best mildly reformist or meliorist. Their concern to deal with limited problems one by one suggests that they are merely tinkering with a social system with whose fundamental aspects they are in sympathy.

Moreover, this impression which foreign intellectuals have of American intellectual culture is complemented and complicated by another impression which they are also likely to have. Leftist though they may be in their political sentiments, many foreign intellectuals also tend to be aristocratic in their educational, esthetic and cultural ideals. Although American intellectuals may often share the foreigner's disdain for "leveling-downwards" and "mass culture," they are less often as stringent and uncompromising in their declarations of principle. They are likely to be more tolerant of the theory and practice of American mass education. They are less prone to see inherent conflicts between "democracy" and "excellence," or "industrial society" and "individual freedom." And while they may recognize a conflict between "the sciences" and "the humanities," they do not so often draw the absolute line between these two spheres that intellectuals in other parts of the world do. In sum, although an antagonism between "the two cultures" exists in the United States, it is probably less pronounced in this country than in any other. In consequence, if American intellectuals strike others as too conservative from one point of view, they often seem too modernist, too supinely afloat on the wave of the future, from another point of view.[2]

The issue is practical, indeed economic and political, as well as moral and theoretical. In the United States itself, the introduction of new intellectual materials that require new intellectual skills if they are to be mastered, and particularly the introduction of methods of social inquiry marked by indifference to traditional ideological positions, have encountered resistance on many occasions and in many places. This resistance is likely to be all the greater when, in a given country, such materials and methods appear to be an import from abroad. A revision of secondary-school curricula, the return of students trained in the United States in American methods of empirical social inquiry, the introduction by visiting American scholars of the American style in sociology and political science, can all imply or seem to imply the upsetting of established learning in a host country. Without intending to do so, American programs of educational and cultural exchange can thus threaten the estab-

[2] Although we are not discussing established facts about American intellectuals, but only the views which intellectuals elsewhere tend to hold of them, some apparently important exceptions to these generalizations may nevertheless come to mind. Men like Robert Oppenheimer or Linus Pauling are obviously not perceived either as conservatives or as apologists for technocracy by intellectuals abroad. Again, the activities of many American professors with regard to civil rights or Viet Nam would seem to fall into the pattern of political activity characteristic of the most visible and vocal intellectual circles abroad. And there are, of course, well-known intellectual journals of opinion in the United States, usually literary in their focus, whose tone of alienation from contemporary American culture resembles the tone of similar journals abroad.

Nevertheless, while these examples indicate that the contrast we are drawing must be carefully shaded, they also underscore its basic truth. Dr. Pauling, for example, has been a radical critic of American military policy, and Dr. Oppenheimer has gained fame not only as a physicist but as a social philosopher concerned about the relation of science to humanistic civilization. Yet neither can be identified as the spokesman of a general political position that can be given systematic formulation. Again, there is no evidence that the great majority of professors who have taken part in Viet Nam demonstrations are critics of the American political or social system in general, or even that they are opposed to the major aspects of American foreign policy such as NATO or foreign aid. And when we turn to literary journals of opinion, we find in them not only ideology, but also a high content of anti-ideology. To many foreign intellectuals, all this is likely to suggest that American intellectuals are strangely indifferent, or perhaps even hostile, to questions of first principles.

lished system of status and prestige in academic and intellectual circles abroad.

To this must be added other sources of potential misunderstanding. The labels that American and foreign intellectuals use to discuss social systems are different. Discussions by most foreign intellectuals still turn on words like "socialism" and "capitalism," the former being almost invariably a eulogistic term, the latter almost invariably pejorative. It is difficult for foreign intellectuals to join issue with intellectuals like those from the United States, who seem so often to be indifferent to the distinction intended by these words, and who tend to suggest, indeed, that the words are misleading.

There are allied difficulties in connection with attitudes toward religion. In many countries, the intellectuals, particularly the younger ones, are predominantly not religious or are militantly anti-religious. At the very least, they are not usually Protestant Christians, and are therefore likely to be puzzled or put off by the special religious rhetoric that characterizes many American political statements. And even if American scholars and intellectuals do not echo this rhetoric, they may still puzzle their foreign counterparts. For there is little in the experience of the latter to prepare them to understand attitudes toward religion—ranging from ingenious reconstructions of traditional religious thought through cheerful tolerance of all religion to indifference to the question—which are likely to characterize intellectuals who have grown up in a society where religious pluralism is well established.

Such differences in outlook are sharpened by differences in the history and in the social position and function of intellectual groups in the United States and other countries. Students, scholars, writers and artists abroad tend to be discriminable and visible groups in their society. Often they have relatively little active contact with other social groups. Indeed, they often perceive themselves, and are perceived, as a separate social *class*, with a distinct outlook and a special social mission. They are the vanguard of the forces of enlightenment, the spokesmen for modernization or freedom or the emerging national culture, the keepers of the national conscience. American intellectuals, in comparison, have less ambitious conceptions of their role, and less consciousness of themselves as a class, just as American businessmen, workers and government functionaries also tend to have less class-consciousness.

This difference between American intellectuals and intellectuals abroad runs parallel to one another. By and large, foreign intellectuals think of themselves as performing their special functions precisely when they keep their distance from the centers of power governing their society. They are prepared to identify themselves with the powers-that-be only when, in turn, they can identify these powers-that-be with themselves—

only when they believe, that is to say, that government, the economy and the social structure are being systematically rebuilt in accordance with the principles which they hold. From such a point of view, it is one thing to take and use power for "revolutionary" purposes; it is quite another thing to serve those who have power, and who use it merely to keep things going or to patch things up. Accordingly, for many foreign intellectuals, to advise government, to counsel industry, to bring technical expertise to bear on specific social problems, seems to be equivalent to the renunciation of one's status as an intellectual. American scholars, in contrast, are less inclined to regard a close identification with power as inherently contaminating. They find it easier to think of practical service to government, industry or the community in neutral, non-political terms.

It is worth saying again that we are speaking here only of differences in degree. There are a number of American scholars and intellectuals who regard any form of close association with government or industry as an abandonment of their intellectual independence. And there are many scholars and intellectuals not only in Western Europe, but in Asia, Africa and Latin America, who have undertaken practical tasks of leadership and counseling, and have moved back and forth between the universities, the professions and government service. But to some extent this reflects the tempo of development and the shortage of manpower in the emerging countries; and to some extent it reflects the congruence of the official revolutionary ideologies of these countries with the principles of the scholars and intellectuals concerned. Broadly speaking, even though the difference between American and foreign intellectuals may be a matter of degree, it remains a significant difference. Fewer American scholars and students think of themselves as generalized intellectuals; they think of their social role simply as that of men possessing special knowledge, like doctors or engineers. More foreign scholars and students are self-consciously intellectuals, and think of their social role as that of secular priests—general guides, critics and judges of their society.

Behind these different attitudes toward identification with power there are often, of course, objective differences in the social situation and political realities of different countries. In some countries in Latin America, for example, the people who hold power in government or the economy are deeply hostile both to intellectuals and to social reform. It is not a mistake or a dogmatic ideological illusion for an intellectual in such circumstances to view an alliance with power as a defection from principle. But behind such attitudes toward identification with power there are also certain pervasive attitudes toward power itself. The notion that political practice inescapably involves moral compromise goes back to Plato, pervades Western philosophy and Western common sense, and has become part of the heritage of intellectuals in most countries in the world. In the West, it is reinforced by traditional suspicions of worldly pomp and power inherited from Prophetic and Christian teachings. In many other civilizations, it is reinforced by religious and philosophical ideas that condemn the material world as the scene of illusion and temptation. And just as in the West, people may hold these views and yet proclaim themselves philosophical materialists. The obvious fact should perhaps also be mentioned that the objective experience of most human beings in relation to the wielders of political power has been a bitter one. This is easily forgotten by many Americans, including intellectuals, but it separates American history from the history of most other nations in the world.

In any case, whatever the sources of such views, they are widespread, and they have considerable influence in many parts of the world on intellectual attitudes toward power, and, indeed, toward the very nature of politics, government and social authority. And given such inherited attitudes toward power and identification with it, it should not be surprising that intellectual groups abroad—or, at any rate, some of the most articulate and influential elements among them—should be negatively predisposed toward American society and American policy. To be critical of power almost automatically entails that one be critical of the country that, above all others, possesses and epitomizes worldly success, wealth and influence. Needless to say, actual American deeds and pronouncements also have much to do with the attitudes toward the United States of intellectuals abroad. But it is naïve to imagine, so long as the United States occupies the position in the world that it does, and so long as the intellectuals of most other societies retain their traditional cast of mind with regard to their social mission and their relation to power, that American policy will not have to contend with an undertow of suspicion against it on the part of intellectuals in other countries.

Finally, major historical trends affect and complicate the relationship of American culture to other cultures. In the emerging societies, intellectuals are usually deeply committed to the modernization of their society, and resent any implication that they are less "progressive" in their thinking than their fellow intellectuals in the West. In practical terms, this means that they are eager to show themselves to be, in significant respects, westernized. At the same time, they cannot help but associate Western culture with a memory of injustice and of the subordination of their own native culture. In consequence, they very often have equivocal feelings toward Western culture, including its American version. This is one reason for the appeal of Marxism, a philosophy which, at one and the same time, offers both a convenient synthesis of

Western tradition and a radical critique of that tradition. Marxism allows the intellectual of non-Western societies to feel that he is taking advantage of Western thought without being taken in by it. In contrast, any United States program of educational or cultural exchange with a developing country, much as it may be to the interest of both sides, almost inevitably raises the spectre of "cultural imperialism."

In the emerging nations, Americans may hear their country accused of playing a devious and self-interested game. In the more developed nations, they may hear American policy condemned for its innocence and optimism. Nevertheless, while the difficulties that appear in relations with the intellectuals of the developed countries are not quite the same as those that affect relations with the underdeveloped countries, they are in certain respects analogous. Feelings of national pride, American and foreign, play a role in the process of cultural communication between the United States and other economically advanced societies, and the events of the last quarter-century have exacerbated these feelings. In Japan it cannot help but be difficult for intellectuals to separate their response to American culture from their memory of defeat, occupation and tutelage by the Americans. In Western Europe the American presence is a standing reminder of a war in which everybody in the West but the Americans suffered a major loss of status. Under the circumstances, an emphasis on America's unfitness for leadership—on the incongruence between America's economic and military power and her cultural immaturity—is perhaps to be expected.

Moreover, underneath these feelings there is a deeper one, akin to the feelings of those in the emerging countries who fear "cultural imperialism." It is anger at the destruction of hereditary standards and amenities by the advance of technology and the mass market. The jukebox, the snack bar, the traffic jam, the supermarket, and the patterns of aspiration and emulation they symbolize, have become universal phenomena in developed nations. They suggest the coming of an homogenized international civilization which people who like their own native idiosyncrasies are bound to resent and resist. When they do so, there is a natural tendency for them to resent and resist American culture. For these phenomena have been carried to their most extreme form in the United States, and are associated with a process known around the world as "Americanization."

The association is in fact largely adventitious. The United States is undoubtedly the most conspicuous example of a country that has plunged heavily into the process variously known as "modernization" or "industrialization." But other countries have now also plunged into this process, and their changing style of life reflects the changed opportunities and aspirations of their own populations rather than American pressure or propaganda. As has often been observed, there are no laws forcing people elsewhere to queue up to see Hollywood movies, to leave domestic service for work in factories, to import American slang into their language, or to strive to obtain the products of mass-production, American style. They seem to have made such choices of their own free will. Nevertheless, even though the United States may simply be a convenient scapegoat on whom these revolutionary changes can be blamed, the fact remains that there are special overtones in the relationship of foreign intellectuals to American culture. For American culture, or what is thought to be American culture, is a lively and painful domestic issue in their own societies—not a piece of exotica, or simply another country's way of life, but a living example and option for their own country in which they must acquiesce or against which they must struggle.

## III

Is the moral of this tale that there are insurmountable obstacles in the path of good cultural relations between the United States and other nations? Under any circumstances, communication between members of different cultures is a difficult and delicate affair. This question can be answered only if we are clear about what we mean by "good cultural relations" and what the functions of such relations are. If we think that it is a function of such relations to effect a grand international ideological merger, the problems that have been mentioned are very probably insuperable. And if we think that it is an object of cultural relations to "sell" a point of view, we are probably asking for what is equally impossible, and for what destroys the power of exchange programs to do what they are peculiarly capable of doing. On the other hand, the problems that have been mentioned help us to focus more precisely on some of the central and proper functions of such programs. And when these functions are fixed clearly in mind, these problems are not necessarily barriers to communication. On the contrary, they are potential ties, if approached with realistic objectives in mind, between articulate Americans and the articulate citizens of other countries.

The overhanging problem of using technological progress to enhance rather than destroy humane values and the aesthetic quality of life is only one among many examples that might be given. With regard to this problem, Americans are certainly in no position to give instruction to others; but neither are others in a position to point the finger of scorn at us. It is a problem for all industrial civilizations, and for all societies moving toward industrialization, and it invites not the exchange of invidious comparisons but joint concern and inquiry. A sense of community can be developed not only by the announcement of common values but by the discovery of problems that are shared. And it is against this background that we can understand why the emergence of habits of disciplined and responsive discourse between the intellectuals of different nations can have much to do with the chances for the rational resolution of international conflicts.

What, then, are the functions of programs for improving and intensifying the process of communication between intellectuals of different countries? There are many, but among them is the tempering and subverting of stereotypes, and the creation of opportunities for discourse that will encourage intellectuals in different countries to speak to each other rather than past each other. For stereotypes, and the habit of talking about different things at different levels of discourse, block the process of locating and defining the problems around which a sense of intellectual community might be developed.

Needless to say, personal and continuing contact between intellectuals from different nations may not lead to agreement among them or even to sympathy. But the evidence is considerable that such contact tends to undermine the organized fantasies that grow up, and that intellectuals themselves often nurture, when close and personal contacts are missing. Cultural exchange encourages the qualifying of rigid generalizations and the tempering of stereotypes about people in other nations, and it exercises a countervailing pressure against both intellectual and political inertia. As the relations between the United States and the Soviet Union over the last decade illustrate, there is a notable tendency in international affairs to persist in analyses and policies that do not fit new facts or fit them only inexactly. Vested interests, intellectual and practical, which have piled up around the old analyses, conspire to produce this result. A vigorous program to facilitate communication, particularly personal communication, between the intellectuals of different countries is a way of preventing the hardening of the arteries of international communication in general. It can discipline international discourse in the simple sense that it can help bring it closer to the complex and changing facts.

More than this, cultural exchange, if it is conducted with such a purpose in mind, can help at once to limit and enlarge the process of international intellectual communication. On one side, it can lead to the discovery and localization of questions that provide promising themes for joint discussion and study outside a context of political negotiation or competing national interests. City planning, the relation of the mass media to education or to inherited cultural traditions, the advantages and the limits of new methods of social inquiry, are only a few examples. This localization of issues by intellectuals can help in the gradual development of a vocabulary for international communication that avoids the great conflicts of ideologies, and that paves the way for more effective forms of international communication.

But the process of international communication among intellectuals also needs to be enlarged. The character and moral significance of the radical changes taking place in twentieth-century civilizations are any civilized man's concern. Given a reasonable effort on the part of intellectuals to listen to each other and to try to make sense to each other, direct intellectual confrontations may contribute to a kind of international discourse that exists now only fitfully and precariously. If there is a point in avoiding angry forms of high ideological recrimination, there is no point in avoiding the discussion of high intellectual themes. It is particularly important for American intellectuals, with their sophisticated methodologies, their love of concrete problems and their suspicion of broad abstractions, to remember this. What the much used and much abused word "democracy" means, what the relation is between individual freedom and the emergence of massive forms of social organization, what the function of intellect itself is in a technical and specialized society—these are questions with roots that go far back in the history of intellectual discussion. It is clear that even men of thorough reasonableness and good will will not come to the same conclusions about them. But it is equally clear that if men do not talk to each other about such questions at all, they are not likely to understand each other very well. And this causes trouble when they turn to the more practical matters on which international accommodation depends.

ANTHONY F. C. WALLACE

## Psychological Preparations for War

War is the sanctioned use of lethal weapons by members of one society against members of another. It is carried out by trained persons working

SOURCE: Anthony F. C. Wallace, "Psychological Preparations for War" in Morton Fried, Marvin Harris, and Robert Murphy, eds., *War: The Anthropology of Armed Conflict and Aggression* (Garden City, 1968), pp. 173–180. Copyright © 1968 by Doubleday & Company, Inc.; copyright 1967 by The Museum of Natural History. Reprinted by permission of Doubleday & Company, Inc.

in teams that are directed by a separate policy-making group and supported in various ways by the non-combatant population. Generally, but not necessarily, war is reciprocal. There are few, if any, societies that have not engaged in at least one war in the course of their known history, and some have been known to wage wars continuously for generations at a stretch.

Because war is apparently perverse, being both painful and sought after, people frequently give psychological explanations for it. Those who think about it with resignation, or with favor, conclude that making war is part of human nature, like making love; others are equally convinced that nothing so evil can be explained except as the result of social- or psychopathology. In this discussion, however, we shall not be concerned to answer the ultimate question, but a more limited one: What, if any, psychological preparation is required for a society to enter *a* war?

## THE STATE OF MOBILIZATION

The principal psychological preparation for war is the training of all members of the society to participate efficiently in a social process that I shall call mobilization. I do not refer here simply to military mobilization in the modern sense of calling up reservists and drafting hitherto uncommitted men and resources to a war, although that is one instance of the larger phenomenon. Rather, I refer to the fact that all human societies, and the societies of many of the higher primates below man, are observed to exist alternately in two states. In one of these, lone individuals and a variety of subgroups occupy themselves in resting and in diversified and complexly co-ordinated economic, sexual, educational, and other activities. In the other state, the population arranges itself precisely into three well-defined groups—the policy-makers, the young males, and the females and children—and the entire society co-ordinates its activities under the leadership of recognized authority toward the achievement of a single task. The former state I shall call the relaxed state; the latter, the mobilized state; and mobilization is the process of transformation from the relaxed to the mobilized state.

•  •  •

## THE PROCESS OF MOBILIZATION

In order for a society to shift from the relaxed to the mobilized state, the population must receive a releasing stimulus, in response to which everyone promptly disposes himself according to a plan. Obviously the stimulus must be broadcast in order that all members of the population receive it quickly, correctly, and simultaneously. For a small band, most of whose members are always within earshot of one another, this is relatively easy. But the larger the group, the more difficult it is to prevent the communication from being distorted in transmission, from reaching individuals at different times, and from being seriously delayed in reaching some. Hence, as a society increases in size and as its territorial boundaries enlarge, cultural innovations are required that will ensure speed and reliability in communication of the releasing stimulus and any associated instructions. This requirement has probably prompted many tribal and early urban societies to invent special language codes, systems of graphic symbols, broadcast devices, and roads and other transportation methods, and to train men in the arts of precise memorization of messages and of rapid and careful travel.

It is also obviously desirable, although not necessary, that the releasing stimulus not merely elicit a disciplined response but evoke a motivational system appropriate to the action to be taken. Here the society enters into a kind of conspiracy with itself to combine the alerting signal with symbolic content that, given a certain distribution of modal personality variables, will arouse maximum desirable emotion. The releasing stimulus is therefore apt to be—particularly in the case of mobilization for war—a report that a certain kind of event has occurred to which people with that character type will respond with anger, determination, fear, or whatever affective state is desired by the communicating group. For Iroquois Indians, this symbolically arousing stimulus was always a report that a kinsman had been killed and that a survivor demanded revenge. For twentieth-century Americans, the symbolically arousing stimulus is apt to be the report that helpless Americans or their allies are being held prisoner or are under attack, and must be rescued.

It is important to note, however, that this embellishment of the releasing stimulus is not, and cannot be, necessary to ensure mobilization. A population is composed of persons with a variety of character structures and personal motives, many with limited intelligence and others suffering from greater or lesser degrees of psychopathology, and mobilization must proceed independent of private motive. Hence, atrocity stories, scare reports, and the like are never adequate to ensure mobilization; indeed, in some situations, such as medical emergencies, they appear to interfere with it. Thus the intensity of the emotion aroused must not be so high as to preoccupy the person being mobilized; the symbol must function more as a rationalization for personal sacrifice than as a stimulus toward unrestrained violence or flight.

TRAINING FOR MOBILIZATION

It is apparent that the shift from the relaxed to the mobilized state must be taken by people who have already learned what to do in response to the releasing stimulus. In all societies this learning probably occurs very early in life, and very largely without didactic instruction, in the course of the child's living through the alternating states of relaxation and mobilization. He learns, while acquiring the language, and by constant observation and participation, the difference between the two states and the nature of the three main status groups characteristic of the mobilized state. And as he grows older, he is trained more and more explicitly to recognize the releasing stimulus, to take orders, and to play specific roles in one of the groups.

One critically necessary feature of this learning is the development of a readiness to move from a situation characterized by considerable personal freedom and democratic, consensual decision making to a hierarchical and authoritarian structural pose. In many band and tribal cultures there is little in the way of coercive authority exercised in the making of decisions during the relaxed state but a very high degree of it in states of mobilization. Thus, among the Iroquois daily life in the village was largely managed by tradition, supplemented by consensual decision when alternative policies had to be chosen, and children were generally given a great deal of freedom. The Iroquois were famous, at least among European observers, for their intolerance of personal constraint. But when a war party mobilized, the participants suddenly assumed a posture of rigorous discipline under the command of a captain who had unquestioned and absolute authority during the military mission. At the end of the expedition, however, this authority terminated, and the captain's influence after that depended entirely on the willingness of other citizens to take his advice in council.

How the early Iroquois trained their children to be able to switch structural pose is not clear from the records available to us now. But a great deal of information is at hand to reveal how our own children are trained to switch poses. A classic example is the school fire drill, which, in addition to improving the chances of evacuating a school quickly in case of fire, provides a general model of how to mobilize in an emergency. At the sound of the alarm, the physical disposition and social relationships of the children abruptly change from the relaxed order characteristic of class or play group to the exact discipline of the fire drill line of march. Similar training in mobilization is given in athletic activities and in popular literature and film, where the training takes the form of play and spectator sport. The principle that is communicated in such exercises, apart from their specific utility, is that when the mobilization signal is heard, automatic obedience to recognized authority is required and assumes priority over other motives.

## THE IMPERSONALITY OF WAR

So far, we have discussed the phenomenon of mobilization as the central theme in psychological preparation for war. But what of the fear, suspicion, and hatred of "the enemy," traditionally believed to be prerequisites for war, that are often invoked by the releasing signal? It is my contention that far from being necessary, these attitudes are almost irrelevant to war except as rationalizations. Human beings generally reserve their settled fears, suspicions, and hatreds for those closest to them: kinsmen, neighbors, and colleagues. Today's enemy in war is yesterday's stranger and tomorrow's ally. The psychological target of lethal weapons in war is an abstraction rather than a person (as the saying goes, "I have nothing against you personally"); hence any member of a society that at the moment happens to be classified as an enemy is apt, in one way or another, to be fair game (with "no hard feelings," of course). Few soldiers ever personally kill anybody; those who kill often do not actually see what they hit; and most never push a button, pull a trigger, or throw a grenade in combat.

War is never really total; its aim is never the absolute annihilation of the enemy and all his works; death and destruction are limited by more or less arbitrary restraints concerning the weapons to be used, the treatment of prisoners, civilians, and non-military targets, and the goals of military action. Thus, being removed from hate, war is also relatively free of guilt. This is not to say that some persons may not displace domestic hate upon foreign enemies by psychiatrically familiar mechanisms of defense, nor that bereaved persons, or those who have suffered personal threat or injury, do not experience, at least for a time, a very personal hatred. But such feelings are not a reliable indicator of efficiency in combat, where an ability to maintain cognitive orientation and a commitment to task-completion in noisy, fatiguing, and dangerous surroundings may be much more important than a high level of primitive urges to fight-or-flight.

Nor can war usefully be regarded as essentially an outgrowth of mass hysteria or mass movements, although some wars, and some events in most wars, are affected by such contagious enthusiasms. A religiously dedicated population, for instance, is likely to be easy to mobilize and difficult to defeat. But the action of a mob in sacking a building or in lynching a neighbor is almost the opposite of war, for it is directed toward the matériel and persons of one's own community, and by definition is carried out without communication of the releasing signal by authority.

Thus, in our own technologically sophisticated society, it is readily apparent that it is possible for half of the national budget and a substantial proportion of our young men to be mobilized to fight an enemy seen by few and rarely recognized even when seen. Lethal weapons are employed by technicians who never set eyes on their human targets. Nor can the other side claim a much more personal focus of their military activities. War is an extremely impersonal business conducted by persons whose private motives—apart from the motive of efficient participation in the state of mobilization—are highly diversified.

## The Interests Served by War

We have, so far, discussed the psychological preparations required for a people as a whole to conduct war effectively and have argued that little more is required than a population trained to respond affirmatively to the mobilization signal and to carry out orders from recognized authority. But what determines the communication of this signal?

The signal must be given by a person or group recognized as having the responsibility to do so when the situation requires it. This, in contemporary industrial societies, is apt to include at least some of the persons who will make policy during the mobilization state, but in general it is not necessary that the body that gives the signal for war be the body that directs the conduct and arranges the termination of the war. It is obvious enough that this signal will be given when an authorized person perceives that a threat exists to the continued functioning of the system that cannot be met by the society without shifting to the mobilized state and using lethal weapons against members of another society. When the society is under physical attack itself, the danger is obvious, and war may be the only alternative to abandoning hope of maintaining, or returning to, the traditional form of relaxed state; it may even be the only alternative to destruction. But sometimes even when no serious attack is threatened, the authorized body communicates the releasing signal, the society mobilizes, begins to use lethal weapons, and initiates an extremely costly and, sometimes, fatal conflict.

I have already suggested that war is often perverse. It is well known to pacifist and soldier alike that many wars are unnecessary, disastrous, even catastrophic mistakes. They do not serve the purpose, whatever it may be, for which the society has mobilized, and they cause immense suffering and damage. The sense of moral outrage that such events arouse does not carry us far, however, in trying to understand how these disasters happen. Political witch-hunting and accusations of psycho-pathology and criminal conspiracy may simply obscure the facts. In one minor war whose inception is very well documented—the Black Hawk War between the United States and the Sac and Fox Indians in 1832— the record clearly shows that—the responsible policy-making bodies on both sides were *not* in favor of war. An irresponsible insistence by an Indian faction on crossing the Mississippi River to join forces with a religious prophet, and lack of discipline in an Illinois militia detachment, precipitated the first firing of guns, and a sequence of events followed mechanically that resulted in the death, from disease, starvation, and bullets, of several hundred Indians and whites. The critical event was a misunderstanding. The Indians, disillusioned with their prophet, attempted to surrender to the militia before a shot was fired in order to gain free passage back across the Mississippi to their tribal territory. The militia were drunk, had no interpreter, and were unaccustomed to discipline, and fired on the peace party. In the ensuing melee the militia were de-feated by the Indian warriors, who then fled with their women and children in an effort to escape across the river by a different route. But the use of lethal weapons on a militia detachment automatically set in motion a sequence of communications that resulted in the mobilization signal being given by the President of the United States. The Sac and Fox council, however, refused to broadcast *their* signal, and the fighting was restricted to the east bank of the Mississippi; the Indian territory across the river was not attacked.

Such examples could, of course, be multiplied *ad nauseam*. The point they illustrate is that unwanted wars—and most wars are now unwanted— occur as a result of a perversion of administrative process rather than as a result of popular folly. The types and sources of such perversions are complex. In some cases, the psychopathology of administrative per-sonnel is evidently responsible (the case of Nazi Germany is the best example of this type). In other cases, responsible and intelligent admin-istrators attempting to act in the best long-term interests of their society are precipitated by misinformation, communication failures, and a rigid, poorly designed system of decision making into unnecessarily mobilizing the society for war.

From this point of view, it would appear that the administrative structure of any society—and every society has an administrative struc-ture at least latent during the relaxation phase and active during its mobi-lization phases—is extraordinarily vulnerable to perversion in regard to war decisions.

•   •   •

## STUDY QUESTIONS

1. What are some of the basic relationships between social ideology and personal responses to international events? Do these relationships hold as validly for members of political elites as for those of the masses? Explain.

2. Describe the strengths, weaknesses, and uses of the idea of "world public opinion." Does that idea play a major role in the formulation and execution of American foreign policy?

3. How do intellectuals respond to and influence the course of world politics? Can you think of any reasons why, in the present era, intellectuals are widely regarded with skepticism and even hostility?

4. In what sense does mobilization for war consist in a series of "psychological preparations" of the citizenry and social institutions? What social functions, apart from war, do such preparations play?

## SUGGESTIONS FOR FURTHER READING

BARGHOORN, FREDERICK CHARLES. *The Soviet Cultural Offensive*. Princeton: Princeton University Press, 1960.

————. *Soviet Foreign Propaganda*. Princeton: Princeton University Press, 1964.

CANTRIL, HADLEY (ed.). *Tensions that Cause War*. Urbana: University of Illinois Press, 1951.

COOMBS, PHILIP H. *The Fourth Dimension of Foreign Policy: Educational and Cultural Affairs*. New York: Harper & Row, 1964.

DURBIN, E. F. M., AND JOHN BOWLBY. *Personal Aggressiveness and War*. New York: Columbia University Press, 1939.

FRANKEL, CHARLES. *The Neglected Aspect of Foreign Affairs*. Washington: Brookings Institute, 1966.

FROMM, ERICH. *Escape from Freedom*. New York: Rinehart, 1941.

KELMAN, HERBERT C. (ed.). *International Behavior, A Social-Psychological Analysis*. New York: Holt, Rinehart and Winston, 1965.

KLINEBERG, OTTO. *The Human Dimension in International Relations*. New York: Holt, Rinehart and Winston, 1964.

LASSWELL, HAROLD D. *Power and Personality*. New York: W. W. Norton, 1948.

PEAR, T. H. (ed.). *Psychological Factors of Peace and War*. New York: Philosophical Library, 1950.

RESTON, JAMES. *The Artillery of the Press: Its Influence on American Foreign Policy.* New York: Harper & Row, 1967.

SINGER, J. DAVID (ed.). *Human Behavior and International Politics, Contributions from the Social-Psychological Sciences.* Chicago: Rand McNally, 1965.

WHITAKER, URBAN G., JR. *Propaganda and International Relations.* San Francisco: Chandler, 1960.

# PART FIVE □ THE UNITED STATES
# IN THE WORLD ARENA

Since 1945 the United States has become the major actor in Western
Europe, the Middle East, Southeast Asia, and the Far East. Until recently many of the countries in these regions were considered primarily
within the British and/or French spheres of influence. However, because
of enfeebled British and French economies and their decline in power
and prestige, the onus of solving many of the intricate problems facing
these regions devolved primarily on the United States. The American
effort to solve some of the problems of Asia, Europe, and the Middle
East, has been manifested in the Truman Doctrine, the Marshall Plan,
NATO, the Point Four Program, SEATO, CENTO, and the Eisenhower
Doctrine, to mention only a few. Moreover, the United States has shown
determination to defend or support friendly nations threatened by Communist aggression or subversion.

American policy in many regions of the world has encountered
a series of dilemmas. Among them are the conflicting interests of the
Western powers, the rise of national movements, internal subversion, regional conflicts, civil wars, and overt or covert Communist threats. The
selections in this part point out some of the problems that face the United
States as a major power in a changed and changing world.

Professor Martin C. Needler describes the foreign policy of the
United States during the nineteenth century with regard to the Western
Hemisphere and the outside world. He analyzes major divisions among
Americans as they approach questions of foreign policy and changes in
the international arena. He examines the erosion of the cold war, the
break-up of bipolarity and especially the weakening of the East-West
alliance system, and the role of the new states on the international scene.
Needler believes that an evolution is taking place in the structure of the
international community based on different premises from those of the
past. Finally, he discusses what United States policy should be in a
transformed world community.

In his address "Toward a Strategy of Peace" President John F. Kennedy spoke of the necessity for peace and of the need for reexamination of our attitudes toward peace and disarmament. Peace, he stated, is a process that can be had only by the actions of many nations. It means mutual tolerance and resolution of conflicts by just and peaceful means. No political or social system is so evil that its people must be looked upon as lacking in virtue. The Soviet Union and the United States both abhor war. The United States seeks relaxation of tensions, supports the United Nations, and stands ready to carry out its commitments in Europe. The Communist drive to impose their economic and political system on other nations, however, is a major cause of world tension. Peace requires an understanding as well as an increased contact and communication with the Soviets. The late President addressed his final remarks to peace and freedom at home.

John Paton Davies, Jr. states that many American leaders, in the past as well as the present, view the United States as a country with a mission to inspire other peoples and nations with American ideas and ideals, achievements, and way of life. This proselytization is carried out by both private and public sectors of society. Davies discusses missionary activities in China and Japan and points out some of the other lessons that may be learned from the past. He also discusses some of the reasons for lack of sympathy for the United States and the background of anti-Americanism in many countries. Furthermore, Davies discusses the struggle with the Communists for men's minds, and points out the relevance of the American and Russian Revolutions to the developing nations. He asserts the need to understand that we are moving out of the stage of political philosophy and entering the stage of know-how, where we are in the vanguard. Americans, finally, he concludes, must learn to be more relaxed and more modest.

Extending Davies' discussion, J. William Fulbright states that America is at a critical juncture where it may lose its perspective with regard to what lies within its power and what lies beyond it. "Power," he writes, "confuses itself with virtue and tends also to take itself for omnipotence." Senator Fulbright fears that the United States may over-extend itself beyond its capacities. He discusses in detail the power drive of nations and states urging that the sources of that drive lie not in economic, balance of power, and historical forces, but in the fears and hopes in men's minds. Great nations tend to equate their power with virtue and their responsibilities with a universal mission. He expresses the hope that the United States will exercise power with wisdom. He sees arrogance of power in American behavior in foreign countries.

Fulbright also questions the ability of the United States to establish democracy in a country with an alien political culture in which the essential conditions of democracy are lacking, especially in Vietnam. He points out the disfunctional impact of America's richness and strength on the poverty-stricken and weak Vietnamese. He believes that our difficulty in Southeast Asia stems from the use of "the wrong kind of power." Also, we face difficulty from our presumed failure to understand the alarm of other nations in adjusting to the very existence of such a great power, and from our own lack of self-confidence. Fulbright concludes that we must be friends of social revolution and social justice.

In the final article Zbigniew Brzezinski, who served as a member of the Policy Planning Council of the Department of State, analyzes five major changes in international politics and discusses their implications for United States foreign policy.

# MARTIN C. NEEDLER

## Understanding Foreign Policy

### THE CHANGING AMERICAN ATTITUDE

If one takes a broad historical perspective, it can be seen that the American approach to foreign policy has undergone a drastic shift from its original assumptions. The foreign policies of the United States during the nineteenth century are summed up in the Monroe Doctrine; although usually treated as establishing a line of policy for the United States in the Western Hemisphere, the Monroe Doctrine actually did not establish a policy towards a single problem so much as delineate the scope of the whole range of national foreign affairs activities. In effect the doctrine marked out the Western Hemisphere as the field of action for the United States; and as the European powers were not expected to intervene in

SOURCE: Martin C. Needler, *Understanding Foreign Policy*, (New York: Holt, Rinehart and Winston, Inc., 1966), pp. 255–272. Copyright © 1966 by Holt, Rinehart and Winston, Inc. Reprinted by permission of Holt, Rinehart and Winston, Inc.

the Americas, the United States, for its part, would not intervene in Europe.[1]

The area circumscribed by the Monroe Doctrine was held to for a hundred years; the republic followed a policy of intermittent and limited imperialism with respect to the continent of North America and the adjacent waters, and one of noninvolvement with respect to the politics of the rest of the world.[2] In these respects it resembled the policies of the newly independent states of today.

But the effective arena of action of national arms and statesmanship—the northern part of the Western Hemisphere—had its own peculiar characteristics, and these set their impress on American thinking about foreign policy. Foremost among these characteristics was the fact that around most of its perimeter the United States encountered only power vacuums. The exception was to the north. An attempt had been made to conquer Canada in the War of 1812, without success; thereafter the frontier was stabilized on an amicable basis, with the United States to entertain neither hopes of annexing the British dominions to the north, nor fears of invasion from that direction. And the Monroe Doctrine explicitly recognized the possession by the European powers of the colonies then still in their hands.

To the west, to the southeast and southwest, however, no countervailing power presented itself. To the west only handfuls of primitive aborigines stood in the path of expansion to the Rocky Mountains; to the southwest a Mexico in continual political turmoil, corrupt and divided against itself, could not defend its distant outlying provinces; to the southeast, in the Caribbean, the small tropical and sub-tropical republics were not even able to govern themselves, much less to offer resistance to the incursions of North American power—or so it seemed— while the decaying remnant of the Spanish colonial empire seemed about to collapse of its own accord.

Given this absence of countervailing power in areas in which expansion could be contemplated, foreign policy designs could mature without needing to take the opposition of other states into account. The foreign and Indian wars in which the United States was engaged in the century between the War of 1812 and World War I invariably ended in victory for the United States, and no effective external check to American expansion presented itself. As the political controversy between the supporters of imperialism and the anti-imperialists developed, the argument was couched exclusively in terms of American wishes,

[1] "In the wars of the European powers in matters relating to themselves we have never taken any part, nor does it comport with our policy to do so."
[2] Thus even the United States occupation of Guam and the Philippines was the unanticipated consequence of a war originating in the Caribbean over Cuba.

not in terms of any realities in the outside world that might present obstacles to the gratification of those wishes. Thus the anti-imperialists, such as William Graham Sumner, argued that the United States should refrain from following the imperialist path not because of the external difficulties involved in the construction of an empire, but because such a policy would mean that the republic would not be true to itself, that the possession of colonies would impair the democratic political system and the American political personality.

The bond between the views of the simple republican opponents of imperialism, who judged foreign policy by reference to the norms of domestic political behavior, and the vulgar self-assertiveness of the super-patriots of imperialism, like Senator Beveridge, is that both were concerned exclusively with the national self and not at all with any limits placed on American policies by the world outside the national borders. With justification, therefore, the century of simple imperialism and simple anti-imperialism that preceded American involvement in World War I can be regarded as a sort of infantile stage of the development of national policy, in that the United States, like the very young infant, had not yet had to adjust its behavior to take account of the realities of a cold, indifferent, and often hostile world; the country had not yet made the transition from the pleasure principle to the reality principle, as it were.

Of course many differences exist among Americans as they approach questions of foreign policy. Perhaps the major division that exists today, however, is between those who have accepted the realities implied in the American assumption of a great power role in international politics, on the one hand—although they differ among themselves over policies to be followed in specific situations—and, on the other, those who would set foreign policies while ignoring the existence of a world outside the United States. The latter may resemble the imperialists of the turn of the century in believing in American omnipotence, in believing that the simple use of force will produce the desired results without cost—those who meet every problem of foreign policy with the recommendation to send in the Marines or to drop nuclear bombs. But there are also among us successors to the anti-imperialists of seventy-five years ago, who attempt likewise to ignore the realities of the world outside our borders, and who counsel that foreign policy should be set by reference only to the ideals of domestic political life. United States policy to the outside world, in this conception, should be an extension of domestic social policy, and should become a colossal welfare program, supervised by an international legislature. However, it is hardly less naïve to believe that peace and justice can be achieved by treating everyone nicely, campaigning against poverty, and "educating for the world citizenship"—

desirable though these activities may be in themselves—than to think that policy problems can be resolved by conquering or bombing those who seem to be causing difficulties. There is naïveté on both Right and Left.

A great many commentators on foreign policy have identified their own positions with that of either Right or Left described above, which they have then termed "realistic." The neo-imperialist view passes as realistic because it takes the apparently sophisticated line that issues can be resolved only by force; the welfare-oriented approach to foreign policy passes itself off as more realistic because it is directed at removing the "real" causes of unrest and war: poverty, ignorance, and disease. Actually, however, realism inheres in neither position. The crucial principle of realism as it applies in present American foreign policy is that the field of American international concerns is no longer a power vacuum in which the only determinant of action need be American desires. One is surely entitled to believe that the United States should pursue its "interests" rather than its "ideals," or some interests more than others, or some interests more than some ideals; inevitably, individuals vary widely over the importance that each attaches to a given social or political system, to money, or indeed to the value of human life itself. The criterion of realism, however, is that it values actions not in themselves, but in reference to their consequences, and to be able to estimate the consequences of acts requires some understanding of the realities of the world in which action takes place. Acting with foreknowledge of the consequences of actions is at the same time the definition of responsibility. Whatever the ultimate goals it is designed to serve, a responsible and "realistic" foreign policy is distinguished by its consideration of consequences. It is a policy of forethought, not of emotional reaction; dominated by design, not by slogan; aware of necessary costs, as much as of imagined benefits.

## THE CHANGING WORLD SITUATION

The external reality within whose framework policy must be executed is constantly changing. All too often a foreign policy thought to be realistic is addressed not to the reality of the moment but to a reality that has already become obsolete. This danger must especially be guarded against in American foreign policy, since the United States emerged onto the world scene in the midst of a configuration of circumstances that impressed a certain mould on policy, but that is today no longer the dominant pattern of world politics.

The United States participated actively in the whole range of international affairs for the first time with World War I, and indeed the events of that war were what drew the Americans into participation.

The style of behavior that the situation imposed on the United States was that of straightforward combat against a clearly defined enemy. After a period of withdrawal, the United States reentered the arena of international politics under a similar set of circumstances; in 1941 the requirement was again for all-out combat against a well-defined enemy. World War II had hardly ended before the familiar pattern imposed itself yet another time, with the Soviet Union assuming the role that had been played twice before by Germany.

The problem for United States policy today is to break out of a conception of world politics limited to that of a straightforward conflict between two camps, and to adjust to a world more complex, more difficult to understand, yet probably more typical of the normal characteristics of international politics in the long run. Adjustment to this newly emerging world situation will mark the final attainment by the United States of maturity as a world power.

### The Eroding of the Cold War

Let us first consider the recent changes in the theme that has dominated American thinking about international relations for nearly twenty years, the confrontation with the Soviet Union. As the world became set in the pattern that it had assumed by 1949, it became commonplace to describe the peculiar characteristics of the era as the bipolarity of power and the rigidity of alliances. American thinking became dominated by the fact of the military threat posed by the Soviet Union, and troubles that developed elsewhere in the world were typically ascribed to the activities of Soviet agents, which was generally plausible, and sometimes true, but which never gave a complete description of international reality.

Today the Cold War continues, but its bitterness has softened and it is becoming merely one among several dominant themes of international relations; it can no longer be regarded as the only one that matters. Various causes can be adduced for this change. It was certainly facilitated by the death of Stalin, and the rise of a Communist China; but the present softening of the Cold War is also the eventual result of the policy of containment that the United States adopted in President Truman's day as its response to Soviet expansionism. If it is true that a powerful state tends to expand into neighboring "power vacuums," it appears equally true that the expansionist urge steadily atrophies when opportunities for its gratification are denied it.

The history of the Cold War can thus be told in terms of its increasing moderation as steadily narrowing limits were placed on the scope of the conflict between the two superpowers. One might say that the code of Cold-War behavior followed today by the United States and the Soviet Union represents a sort of "case law" that has grown out of a series of significant limiting cases that have served to define the boundaries of the scope of conflict between the two states. The major "cases" in this regard are the Berlin blockade and the subsequent airlift; the Korean war; the Soviet repression of the Hungarian uprising of 1956; President Eisenhower's discontinuation of U-2 flights over the Soviet Union; and the Cuban missile crisis of 1962.

By its action in the Berlin blockade in airlifting supplies to the besieged city, the United States made clear that it would defend the positions it occupied but that it would employ no more force than necessary to this end; the Soviet Union, in refraining from taking action against the planes that were participating in the airlift, demonstrated that its expansionist moves were likewise limited by considerations of rationality and economy of force. In the case of Korea, the United States showed itself willing to enter actual combat if necessary to hold back Communist expansionism, while both sides showed an appreciation of the importance of limiting the arena of conflict to avoid its escalation into a full-scale world war. By not intervening in the Hungarian uprising of 1956, the United States conceded that it would respect the immediate Soviet security zone of the Eastern European satellites, despite the talk of "liberation" that had been general during the 1952 election campaign. In calling off the flights over the Soviet Union by U-2 planes after the failure of the Paris summit conference of 1960, the United States implicitly acknowledged that the dangers of world conflict inherent in the balance of terror imposed a respect for the territorial integrity of the major antagonist, and an obligation to refrain from humiliating acts. The Cuban missile crisis of fall 1962—when Khrushchev withdrew Soviet missiles already emplaced on the island of Cuba and destroyed their launching sites—parallels in some respects the action of the United States in relation to the Hungarian uprising. That is, the Soviet dictator acknowledged that his attempt to intervene directly in the zone of immediate security of the United States was a bluff that could be called, that is, was an initiative that fell outside the scope of legitimate conflict in the Cold War. It is noteworthy that many commentators understood that there was somehow a connection, however paradoxical it might seem, between the fact that the Soviet Union was forced to back down in the Cuban missile crisis and the improvement of the international atmosphere that made possible the subsequent negotiation of the nuclear test ban treaty. The connection between the two events is simply that in backing down in the Cuban missile crisis the Soviet Union was forced to acknowledge that the Cold War could only be carried on given a set of basic agreements between the two principal protagonists; the fact that each had now accepted the inviolability of the immediate security zone of the other meant that, with respect to a considerable portion of the world's surface, each had, in his own mind, accepted the existence of a *status quo* that he did not favor for its own sake.

One way of looking at the series of events that forms the history of the Cold War is as a learning process for the Soviet Union. Just as the United States, as it became involved in world politics, had to adjust its behavior from the norms consonant with a position of hegemony in North America to those of a participant in world balance-of-power maneuvers, the Soviet Union, similarly, had to make the transition from angry young rebel, bent on self-gratification in defiance of the norms of international society, to responsible middle-aged statesman, conscious of the obligations to world peace and order that rest on his shoulders.

If the Cold War ground rules include: respect for the territory of the opponent and for his immediate security zone; the prohibition of invasions across international boundaries aimed at total conquest; and the limitation to the minimum level of the scope of any overt conflict; then the main dimension in which the Cold War continues today is in the form of "cat's paw" war and *coup d'état*, conflict between the two power blocs disguised as civil war or civil disturbance. Thus the United States tries not to involve its own troops in Cold War fighting; if they should be directly committed, as in South Vietnam, it is only with great reluctance and as a last resort, while every attempt is made to cut short the conflict. Similarly, the Soviet Union has always held back from a direct confrontation of arms. It remains to be seen what norms will guide Chinese conduct as China succeeds an increasingly passive Soviet Union as the principal American antagonist. The author would assume, however, that a similar process of adjustment to a new *status quo* will set in—after it has been possible to stabilize the boundaries to China's expansion.

## THE BREAK-UP OF BIPOLARITY

The evolution in the ground rules of the Cold War has been complemented by an evolution in the structure of the Soviet bloc. This has generally been characterized as "polycentrism," that is, the emergence of several centers of initiative and direction within the Communist camp, supplanting the single center of authority allowed during Stalin's reign. Tito's break from the Cominform was followed eventually by a loosening of ties that allowed Poland to pursue independent policies; China and Albania diverged enough from the Soviet line to bring about a series of direct public attacks between their leaders and those of the Soviet Union; the accession of Cuba to the Soviet bloc introduced into the Soviet commonwealth an erratic and idiosyncratic partner; and with the divergence of Romania from the Soviet line on bloc economic policy, it became clear that despite the ideological sympathies that bind the "people's republics" to the Soviet state, divergent national interests continue to exist, and to impose themselves on national policy.

At the same time the ideological bond becomes less significant as the ideology itself becomes less relevant to the needs of domestic policy. Thus, faced with low standards of living and with the desire to improve them, and having learned from the doctrinaire mistakes of the past, the "Leninist" flexibility of the Communist leaderships leads them increasingly to set economic policy in terms of the maximization of production by the introduction of norms of economic rationality. The outcome of this process, however, differs less and less from the mixed-economy pragmatism that characterizes government economic policy outside the Soviet sphere. This resemblance became even plainer under the influence of Khrushchev's dictum that Soviet planners and administrators must build a better economy by learning from advances made in the West, a principle carried even further by Khrushchev's successors.

It is noteworthy that at the same time as the organization of the Soviet economy and the policies of Soviet planners tend to come closer to those found in the West, a parallel development is beginning in the political sphere. The theoretical basis for the political changes that are taking place in the Soviet Union is that of a reinterpretation of the manner in which Soviet society will approach the era of pure communism, the final stage of history in Marxist thought. Under Stalin the attainment of communism tended to be pushed further and further into the indefinite future, or even to be used to justify the extreme political repression of Stalin's day; Stalin even went so far as to announce the thesis that the era of communism would arrive "dialectically," that is, the state would "wither away" only after it had attained its maximum development—in other words, after the apparatus of police oppression had reached its maximum. This doctrine has now been repudiated by the Soviet leadership, which has taken the line that communism is achieved progressively—that is, repression and central direction of Soviet life are steadily to be deemphasized or eliminated in the progressive achievement of pure communism. In practice this means that control of the economy is being decentralized, and the role of the secret police has been limited.

Clearly, if ideology plays a smaller role in the governing of the Soviet Union, and is in any case interpreted so that it counsels policies not very dissimilar from those followed in the West, the whole thesis of ideological conflict with the West is steadily eroded.

A modification in the Soviet concept of conflict with the West has indeed taken place. As the West's policy of containment has taken hold, and as it has become clear that the expansion of Soviet power by military means is no longer possible, the emphasis in Soviet thinking on foreign policy has changed until the coming dominance of communism everywhere in the world is perceived more as a historical development that will evolve of its own accord than as the first imperative of Soviet foreign policy. It appears likely to the writer that this belief in the eventual victory of communism in the world will steadily weaken over time until it comes to resemble the average nominal Christian's faith in the Second Coming—it may be believed in vaguely at some level of consciousness, without in any way affecting day-to-day behavior.

Pressure to abandon an aggressively expansionist foreign policy derives also from the increasing desire among Soviet citizens and the Soviet leadership to limit expenditures on defense, foreign aid, and probes of outer space, in the interest of diverting resources into the production of consumer goods to raise the low Soviet standard of living. The level of national security and space expenditures clearly constitutes a substantial strain for the less than affluent Soviet economy, and with increasing technological sophistication costs in these areas of expenditure tend to rise steeply unless a deliberate decision is made to deemphasize the policies that call for such expenditures.

The tendency is, therefore, for the Soviet Union to become increasingly contented with the territorial *status quo*, in practice if not in principle. This does not mean that the basic prestige-and-power conflict with the United States will disappear, but only that it will subside in significance to become one among the principal conflicts that will dominate international politics, losing its place as the single, most urgent, overriding conflict; and because of the relatively increasing importance of problem areas outside the clash between Soviet and American power, relations between the two states will take on some components of common interest, so that Soviet-American relations will not need to be relations of pure antagonism.

The major dichotomy in international relations will then tend to become not that between the Soviet bloc and states loyal to the American alliance, but between states generally satisfied with the *status quo* and prepared to contemplate changes in it only by peaceful means, on the one hand, and, on the other, revisionist, expansionist, and aggressive states. The states comprised in this latter category will vary, as new personalities or political movements assume leadership; but if it continues to include the Soviet Union in some respects, it will extend at least equally well to embrace Communist China, Indonesia, and perhaps the United Arab Republic or Ghana.

Just as the emergence of polycentrism among Communist states acted to unfreeze the balance-of-power situation of 1949, comparable developments have begun to take place among the states of the Western alliance. The Western alliance was never a "bloc," as the Soviet Union and her allies were, despite the vigorous efforts of Secretary of State Dulles to include all non-Communist states in military alliances with the United States and to regard neutrals outside them virtually as enemies. Dulles' image of the world was never altogether realistic, however, since the United States has always had predominantly defensive policy aims, and has thus shared interests in common with all states that wished to maintain their independence and the formally friendly relations among states normal to diplomatic practice. This was clearly revealed when the United States came to the aid of India after the Chinese attack of 1962, despite the fact that India was not an American ally.

New tendencies have emerged, however, that have weakened the cohesion the Western alliance used to possess. The most salient of these is the development of an independent foreign policy line by France under the leadership of President de Gaulle, which has often taken curious directions, in some cases inimical to the interests of the United States and of the Western alliance. At the same time the coming to independence of most of the former European colonies has meant in many cases that territories once included in the Western alliance are now neutralist; a comparable development has been taking place in Latin America, where such a traditionally staunch ally of the United States as Brazil began under President Quadros to refer to itself as nonaligned.

A NEW BALANCE OF POWER?

In the 1950s it became fashionable to descry in the trends immanent in world politics the emergence of a new balance-of-power system in which the United States and the Soviet Union would be joined, depending on the tastes of the observer, by two or three other new great powers. Communist China was invariably accorded a place in this putative new world system, usually along with a united Europe, sometimes a strengthened British Commonwealth, perhaps a growing India, or some configuration of nonaligned African and Asian states. What was actually occurring, however, was not the revival of a classic European balance of power in which several states of roughly equal power checked the aggressive intentions of others by forming temporary countervailing alliances, but a quite different set of relations.

The more fluid situation that has in fact emerged might more appropriately be described as a "field of power" in which all kinds of influences are exerted in every direction by a variety of states differing widely in size and wealth. It should be noted that in this new "field of power" a state's influence on events is determined not merely by the military and economic power it can muster, but by its symbolic position, its sympathetic ties with other states, the fanaticism of its devotion to a given policy aim, or its strategic position in relation to the world's major alliances—that is, a state's influence is partly determined by its capacity to serve as a symbol, rather than its capacity for marshalling military and economic resources. For example, the role that Yugoslavia has been able to play in the world, as a Communist state that broke with the Soviet bloc, accepted aid from the West, and maintained its political independence from both blocs, has nothing to do with the size of the country. Israel's ability to enlist the support of the United States and other powers against hostile moves of the Arab states is constant and reliable, but is based on sympathy for Israel's people and their ideals, not on tangible power factors. Cuba has been able to defy the United States and create difficulties for American policies in Latin America; Romania has forced the Soviet Union to modify her plans for the economic integration of Eastern Europe; Pakistan has succeeded in securing a favorable settlement of a territorial dispute with Communist China.

Why has it been possible for smaller states to exercise this freedom of maneuver and thus obtain some of their foreign policy goals? Why do not the major powers of the world simply arrange affairs to their own liking, coercing the smaller states to fall in line with their wishes willy-nilly? One has to answer, in the first place, that very often the devotion with which an aim is pursued can be a substitute for more tangible factors of power. In other words, a state that is prepared to do more to secure a desired end may be in a stronger relative position than a state nominally more powerful that is not prepared to make similar exertions. An example of the application of this principle is provided by the situation of a large power conducting a military occupation of another country. Normally—at least after its initial enthusiasm has worn off—the people of the occupying state are less than eager about the whole business, which makes it necessary for large numbers of young men to spend tours of duty away from their homes. Normally, one must add to this picture friction with that of the population of the occupied state. If the local population in addition harasses the occupying army, and certainly if it conducts a terrorist or guerilla campaign, the political pressures on the home government for the withdrawal of troops will be substantial. In a situation of this kind the cards are stacked in favor of the native population of the territory, even if the occupying power is prepared to go to great lengths to maintain its control. A striking illustration of this type of situation was provided by the case of the French in Algeria, who over a period of seven years brought the manpower and economic resources of a large and developed state to bear in the attempt to end the resistance of the Moslem population to French rule, only eventually to yield the point and withdraw.

United States experience is equally instructive. Although the military occupations of Japan and Germany constituted very easy duty for the American soldiers involved, and although no serious difficulties were presented by the attitudes of local populations, the United States never felt comfortable in the role of an occupying power. During the Marine occupations of Haiti, the Dominican Republic, and Nicaragua early in the century, there was indeed resistance from the local populations that became guerrilla war, with the result of extreme alienation from the local population, the unpopularity of the occupations back home, and the eventual withdrawal of American forces. That a similar situation might ensue should be borne in mind by those who advocate American invasion of Cuba to overthrow the government of Fidel Castro; in that case one would have to add to the picture the suitability of the Sierra Maestra for guerrilla operations.

The possibilities of the coercion of small states by the major world powers are also limited by several other factors. The desire of each of the superpowers to avoid an armed conflict with the other may create an area of maneuver for a smaller power—as it did in the case of Yugoslavia. The major Cold War protagonists also make some effort to create a favorable impression of their policies in the "battle for men's minds" (which the present writer believes a vastly overrated component of the Cold War struggle) and for this reason shrink from more obvious acts of coercion, unless they bear directly on national security interests, as in the Hungarian case. In addition to these attitudinal limits presented by the world outside, the larger states tend to be limited in their willingness to coerce smaller states by unfavorable attitudes among their own populations, and indeed among policy makers themselves, who, with the easing of the Cold War, are tending to lose that sense of mission that might otherwise prompt them to support greater costs for the sake of the domination of other states.

## THE EMERGING SHAPE OF THE FUTURE WORLD

As one gains perspective on the changes that have occurred, and are occurring, in the structure of international relations in recent times, it becomes clear that an evolution is taking place in the direction of a world community based on different premises from those of the past. Without any assurance as to exactly how far the process will go, although it clearly will not extend in any foreseeable future to the extreme of actual world government in the standard sense, there is a sense in which it can be said that many institutions of a world government are emerging. This semigovernment has its focus in the UN, but its chief characteristic is that it is not limited to any one organization but consists of an inter-locking grid of specialized and regional groupings—the OAS,[3] the Brit-ish Commonwealth, OECD,[4] NATO, GATT,[5] the World Bank, and a host of others. The resulting network of obligations to consult, and of resolutions that can be taken by qualified majorities in international organ-izations, seems to be creating norms of international behavior; the lynch-pin of the system is of course the United States as the richest and most powerful nation.

Anyone who has followed the trend of opinion expressed in the standards to which statesmen appeal in public speeches, or in the dominant themes of discussion in the UN General Assembly, can even dimly perceive that a sort of common world ideology is emerging. The prin-ciples of this ideology, which constitutes a sort of incipient world con-science, are: the peaceful settlement of disputes, the independence of nation-states, the protection of individual human rights, and the promo-tion of economic development.

It may still be too fanciful to refer to this web of organizations as a "world government"; but the system at least attempts to perform the major functions that a government has. That is, it tries to maintain order, and when fighting breaks out in an area where the local jurisdiction does not seem able to handle it, some international method of restoring order is attempted. It may well be that U Thant's major achievement as Secretary General will be to achieve the regular use of UN peace-keeping forces in those chronic trouble spots where the major Cold War protag-onists do not confront each other.

The system has also been able to make adjustments in the *status quo*, where revisionist claims were felt to be just; it undoubtedly acts to protect and promote trade, and to foster educational, scientific, and cultural activ-ities. Finally, through the various aid and development assistance pro-grams, the emerging world system has begun to perform that charac-teristic function of modern government: to redistribute income by means of welfare programs from the more well-to-do to the poorer sections of the community.

Clearly, this emerging system of consensus, of interlocking organiza-tions identified by their initials, of fitful and irregular attempts at remedy-ing the world's ills, falls considerably short of government in the normal sense. In response to those who believe in the necessity and possibility of world government in order to meet the world's problems, however, one has to point out that it is perhaps unnecessary to be mechanical or

[3] The Organization of American States.
[4] The Organization for Economic Cooperation and Development.
[5] The General Agreement on Tariffs and Trade.

dogmatic, or overly symmetrical, in one's conception of what a "world government" is.

## THE UNITED STATES AND WORLD TRENDS

Although specific situations may often have results disadvantageous to the United States, viewed in a long-term perspective the emerging constants of international affairs should on the whole give Americans cause for satisfaction and not alarm. The world of today is, after all, based increasingly on distinctively American premises, and is guided by characteristically American principles. The very existence of a world organization that tends, albeit slowly, to become the focus of international relations is due eminently to American efforts, is faithful to the tradition of Woodrow Wilson, and conforms to typical American predilections. The norm of national independence on which the dominant anticolonial sentiment in the UN is based is an idea introduced into the practice of the modern world by the American Revolution. The concern for human rights that is increasingly becoming an international norm is in perfect consonance with American attitudes, our own Declaration of Independence and Bill of Rights being among the most important examples of the translation of the concern for individual human freedom from an aspiration to the nominal reality of official documents. The limits that the international community attempts to place upon the outbreak of violence are to be welcomed by all men of good will, and not least by the nation that attempted to make World War I the "war to end all wars." The obsession with economic development that currently dominates all the countries of the globe, and that is embodied in a host of international agencies, is one of the most characteristically American features of today's world, Americans having been long distinguished by their concern with economic and material progress. Even the institutional devices increasingly adopted as the world seeks to organize itself derive from ideas of unmistakably American origin. Federalism, which is emerging among many former colonial states and perhaps in Europe itself, is an American invention; while the intra-American system, which was given impulse from both North America and South America, is the model for the regional organizations that are beginning to take shape in other parts of the globe.

Americans may, therefore, be forgiven if they feel satisfaction as they contemplate the theses and organizational forms prevailing in the world; it is a world largely created on American principles, and in the American image.

## POLICY FOR THE FUTURE

What line of policy should the United States take in the changed and changing world that today confronts us? The first of the general considerations that should inform policy is the unequivocal acceptance of the change in the American sphere of action from the quarter of the globe to which it was confined during the nineteenth century to the world scene on which the United States acts today. Acceptance of this change entails in turn acknowledgment that in the sphere in which it must act today the United States is not omnipotent. Paradoxically, the vast increase of the power of the United States has resulted in an appreciation of the limits of national power itself. Even that most creative and ingenious statesman who did more than anyone else to shape the reality of his time, Bismarck, wrote that human beings cannot consciously create the forces that move the world; they can only recognize the tendencies of the time, and, by climbing aboard, may hope to steer them a little this way or that. In George F. Kennan's striking phrase, the maker of foreign policy is not so much a mechanic as a gardener.

Within the range of the limited hopes and expectations defined by recognition of this fact, the United States in its foreign policies should, of course, be concerned to pursue its national interests; but in determining what constitutes American interests in stressing some elements of the whole complex of national interests rather than others, and in the choice of means that are to be employed, equally knowledgeable and public-spirited people may legitimately differ. While the views that follow are the writer's own, he believes that they will secure a wide measure of agreement.

Preeminent among the national interests of the United States is the interest in the existence of a stable, secure, and ordered world. In the isolationist years it was believed that America was best off in ignoring the rest of the world. Although old-style isolationism is no longer possible, it remains true that the United States will be the better off the less disturbance in the outside world upsets the normal activities of Americans. As the most affluent of the world's states, with the most ramified overseas economic and cultural interests, the United States stands to lose the most by outbreaks of violence and irrational behavior. At the same time, because of American affluence and power, the private individuals who are the bearers of American trade and ideas can in a stable world expect to have their efforts attended by more than average success.

Because of this power and economic strength of the United States, the priority of various national goals is rather different for American policy makers than it is for those of other states. That is, the interest in the preservation of a stable and secure world order is logically accorded higher priority and the interest in defending any specific economic investment is less than for other states, since it is less easy to damage the American economy by damaging any one of its elements.

Because of the American interest in a stable and secure world, the general concern of diplomats to interpret national interests so that they are complementary and not antagonistic to the interests of other states must have special weight with American policy makers. At the same time it is clear that the whole range of national interests can never be absolutely compatible with the interests of all other states, and disagreements are regularly to be expected, even between the United States and her closest allies. The existence of such disagreements over secondary points, however, should not be allowed to interfere with otherwise good relations between them.

A point arrives on the continuum of friendly relations with another state, nevertheless, at which disagreements in objectives between the two become great enough that general amity with occasional minor differences becomes transformed into a policy of settled opposition and antagonism. At what point does this occur? What is it that determines whether the relations between the United States and another country will in general be friendly—despite existing disagreements—or will in general be hostile despite existing common interests? The present writer would suggest that the demarcation of lines between the relations of amity and those of enmity lies at the point where another state opposes *on principle* any policy of the United States, no matter what it is, and refuses even to attempt to negotiate differences in good faith. During most of the administration of Fidel Castro, the government of Cuba has placed itself in this position, as has the government of Communist China. It is an attitude that the government of the Soviet Union used normally to take, but assumes less frequently as time goes on. What this amounts to saying is that the United States can coexist with any state that is prepared to coexist with the United States.

The continuing attempt to coexist peacefully with other states does not, and cannot, mean that the United States is indifferent to what occurs elsewhere in the world, even when what occurs lies clearly within the domestic jurisdiction of other states. Even if one takes the position that it is not the function of United States policy to attempt to impose certain principles of constitutional behavior or economic or social policy on the governments of other states, the United States must necessarily become involved in the internal politics of other countries. Despite all of the principles of international law relative to sovereignty and to the sanctity of a state's domestic jurisdiction, the policies of the world's most powerful state necessarily have repercussions in the domestic affairs of other countries. A change in American tariff or import quota regulations can cause either boom or collapse in the economies of other states; signs of excessive United States friendliness or unfriendliness to an incumbent government can cause its domestic opposition to give up in despair, or to attempt a *coup d'état*; a change in some of the technical requirements for United States foreign aid can cause a drastic shift in the direction of another country's economic growth. Taking into account the magnitude of the effect of United States actions on the domestic situation in other states, therefore, the question becomes not "Should the United States influence developments within other states?" but rather "Should the influence that the United States has be exercised consciously and in keeping with the goals of national policy, or inadvertently and at random?" If one takes the view that responsible action on the part of the United States decision makers entails a consciousness of the effect of their acts, then it seems to the present writer that the only question to be decided is that of the direction in which the United States would like to see the domestic political, economic, and social structures of other states develop.

This question has been squarely and explicitly faced in relation to the Alliance for Progress, which constitutes in part a United States aid program, and in part an agreement among the American states as to the directions in which they wish the structures of their domestic lives to evolve.

In the writer's view there has been an overeagerness among commentators to "write off" the Alliance for Progress before its effects have made themselves felt, and before the initial procedural problems have been overcome. It should surely be acknowledged that the conception of the Alliance has taken a giant step towards meeting the justified charge that, ". . . America's foreign policy headaches around the globe today stem less from information or organization deficiencies than from lack of clearly articulated foreign policy objectives beyond anti-communism."[6]

In a democratic society there are, of course, divergent points of view; and even where general agreement can be secured in principle, formidable difficulties present themselves in the application of principles to specific cases. The author believes nevertheless that recent history suggests that there are certain general ideas with which most Americans agree that provide the framework within which policy can be made. These can be summarized as follows:

States should be encouraged to maintain their autonomy and should be prepared to defend themselves against outside aggression. Their readiness to do so will reduce the possibility of aggressive war. At the same time states should actually take up arms only as a last resort, and should strive to hold to a minimum any fighting that does break out; they should be willing to compromise their differences with other states; and they should be prepared to make financial and other sacrifices to maintain an international organization that can facilitate the process of mutual ac-

[6] Harry Howe Ransom, "Secret Mission in an Open Society," New York *Times* Magazine, May 21, 1961.

commodation. Domestically, a government should be organized on democratic principles where feasible; it should govern in an environment of freedom and respect for individual rights; and, while the presumption should always be in favor of private property and individual initiative, the aim of its economic policies should be to help assure the material well-being of the greatest number of people under its jurisdiction.

In the period since the first days of America's involvement in world affairs as a major power, a tradition of national policy has been building up, reflecting the learning processes that have gone on. The general willingness of Americans to accept this tradition was what Senator Goldwater found himself up against, when he urged departures from the standing assumptions of foreign policy during his 1964 presidential campaign.

As time goes on the American foreign policy tradition will be refined and elaborated to meet new situations. If United States policy makers and the American people themselves do not allow the frustrations inherent in the inevitable minor setbacks of policy to weaken their commitment to abiding national principles, then it seems to the present writer that it will become increasingly apparent to the newer nations, whose experience in world affairs is still limited, that the principled yet nonaggressive and compromising spirit that has most often characterized American policy provides the soundest basis for the conduct of world affairs in an era of change, challenge, and hope.

JOHN F. KENNEDY

*Toward a Strategy of Peace*

"There are few earthly things more beautiful than a University," wrote John Masefield, in his tribute to the English universities—and

SOURCE: President John F. Kennedy, "Toward a Strategy of Peace," *The Department of State Bulletin*, XLIX (July 1, 1963), 2–6. [Note—this address was made at commencement exercises at The American University, Washington, D.C., on June 10. This is the White House press release, as-delivered text.]

his words are equally true here. He did not refer to spires and towers, to campus greens and ivied walls. He admired the splendid beauty of the university, he said, because it was "a place where those who hate ignorance may strive to know, where those who perceive truth may strive to make others see."

I have, therefore, chosen this time and this place to discuss a topic on which ignorance too often abounds and the truth is too rarely perceived—yet it is the most important topic on earth: world peace.

What kind of peace do I mean? What kind of peace do we seek? Not a *Pax Americana* enforced on the world by American weapons of war. Not the peace of the grave or the security of the slave. I am talking about genuine peace, the kind of peace that makes life on earth worth living, the kind that enables men and nations to grow and to hope and to build a better life for their children—not merely peace for Americans but peace for all men and women, not merely peace in our time but peace for all time.

I speak of peace because of the new face of war. Total war makes no sense in an age when great powers can maintain large and relatively invulnerable nuclear forces and refuse to surrender without resort to those forces. It makes no sense in an age when a single nuclear weapon contains almost 10 times the explosive force delivered by all of the Allied air forces in the Second World War. It makes no sense in an age when the deadly poisons produced by a nuclear exchange would be carried by the wind and water and soil and seed to the far corners of the globe and to generations yet unborn.

Today the expenditure of billions of dollars every year on weapons acquired for the purpose of making sure we never need to use them is essential to keeping the peace. But surely the acquisition of such idle stockpiles—which can only destroy and never create—is not the only, much less the most efficient, means of assuring peace.

I speak of peace, therefore, as the necessary rational end of rational men. I realize that the pursuit of peace is not as dramatic as the pursuit of war, and frequently the words of the pursuer fall on deaf ears. But we have no more urgent task.

Some say that it is useless to speak of world peace or world law or world disarmament—and that it will be useless until the leaders of the Soviet Union adopt a more enlightened attitude. I hope they do. I believe we can help them do it. But I also believe that we must reexamine our own attitude, as individuals and as a nation, for our attitude is as essential as theirs. And every graduate of this school, every thoughtful citizen who despairs of war and wishes to bring peace, should begin by looking inward—by examining his own attitude toward the possibilities of peace, toward the Soviet Union, toward the course of the cold war, and toward freedom and peace here at home.

## THE POSSIBILITIES OF PEACE

First: Let us examine our attitude toward peace itself. Too many of us think it is impossible. Too many think it unreal. But that is a dangerous, defeatist belief. It leads to the conclusion that war is inevitable, that mankind is doomed, that we are gripped by forces we cannot control.

We need not accept that view. Our problems are manmade; therefore they can be solved by man. And man can be as big as he wants. No problem of human destiny is beyond human beings. Man's reason and spirit have often solved the seemingly unsolvable, and we believe they can do it again.

I am not referring to the absolute, infinite concept of universal peace and good will of which some fantasies and fanatics dream. I do not deny the values of hopes and dreams, but we merely invite discouragement and incredulity by making that our only and immediate goal.

Let us focus instead on a more practical, more attainable peace, based not on a sudden revolution in human nature but on a gradual evolution in human institutions—on a series of concrete actions and effective agreements which are in the interest of all concerned. There is no single, simple key to this peace, no grand or magic formula to be adopted by one or two powers. Genuine peace must be the product of many nations, the sum of many acts. It must be dynamic, not static, changing to meet the challenge of each new generation. For peace is a process, a way of solving problems.

With such a peace there will still be quarrels and conflicting interests, as there are within families and nations. World peace, like community peace, does not require that each man love his neighbor; it requires only that they live together in mutual tolerance, submitting their disputes to a just and peaceful settlement. And history teaches us that enmities between nations, as between individuals, do not last forever. However fixed our likes and dislikes may seem, the tide of time and events will often bring surprising changes in the relations between nations and neighbors.

So let us persevere. Peace need not be impracticable, and war need not be inevitable. By defining our goal more clearly, by making it seem more manageable and less remote, we can help all peoples to see it, to draw hope from it, and to move irresistibly toward it.

## COMMON INTERESTS OF U.S. AND SOVIET UNION

Second: Let us reexamine our attitude toward the Soviet Union. It is discouraging to think that their leaders may actually believe what their propagandists write. It is discouraging to read a recent authoritative Soviet text on military strategy and find, on page after page, wholly baseless and incredible claims—such as the allegation that "American imperialist circles are preparing to unleash different types of wars . . . that there is a very real threat of a preventive war being unleashed by American imperialists against the Soviet Union . . . [and that] the political aims of the American imperialists are to enslave economically and politically the European and other capitalist countries . . . [and] to achieve world domination . . . by means of aggressive wars."

Truly as it was written long ago: "The wicked flee when no man pursueth." Yet it is sad to read these Soviet statements—to realize the extent of the gulf between us. But it is also a warning—a warning to the American people not to fall into the same trap as the Soviets, not to see only a distorted and desperate view of the other side, not to see conflict as inevitable, accommodation as impossible, and communication as nothing more than an exchange of threats.

No government or social system is so evil that its people must be considered as lacking in virtue. As Americans we find communism profoundly repugnant as a negation of personal freedom and dignity. But we can still hail the Russian people for their many achievements—in science and space, in economic and industrial growth, in culture and in acts of courage.

Among the many traits the peoples of our two countries have in common, none is stronger than our mutual abhorrence of war. Almost unique among the major world powers, we have never been at war with each other. And no nation in the history of battle ever suffered more than the Soviet Union suffered in the course of the Second World War. At least 20 million lost their lives. Countless millions of homes and farms were burned or sacked. A third of the nation's territory, including nearly two-thirds of its industrial base, was turned into a wasteland—a loss equivalent to the devastation of this country east of Chicago.

Today, should total war ever break out again—no matter how—our two countries would become the primary targets. It is an ironical but accurate fact that the two strongest powers are the two in the most danger of devastation. All we have built, all we have worked for, would be destroyed in the first 24 hours. And even in the cold war, which brings burdens and dangers to so many countries—including this nation's closest allies—our two countries bear the heaviest burdens. For we are both devoting massive sums of money to weapons that could be better devoted to combating ignorance, poverty, and disease. We are both caught up in a vicious and dangerous cycle in which suspicion on one side breeds suspicion on the other and new weapons beget counterweapons.

In short, both the United States and its allies, and the Soviet Union and its allies, have a mutually deep interest in a just and genuine peace and in halting the arms race. Agreements to this end are in the interests of the Soviet Union as well as ours, and even the most hostile nations can be relied upon to accept and keep those treaty obligations, and only those treaty obligations, which are in their own interest.

So let us not be blind to our differences, but let us also direct attention to our common interests and to the means by which those differences can be resolved. And if we cannot end now our differences, at least we can help make the world safe for diversity. For in the final analysis our most basic common link is that we all inhabit this planet. We all breathe the same air. We all cherish our children's future. And we are all mortal.

### THE PURSUIT OF PEACE

Third: Let us reexamine our attitude toward the cold war, remembering that we are not engaged in a debate, seeking to pile up debating points. We are not here distributing blame or pointing the finger of judgment. We must deal with the world as it is and not as it might have been had the history of the last 18 years been different.

We must, therefore, persevere in the search for peace in the hope that constructive changes within the Communist bloc might bring within reach solutions which now seem beyond us. We must conduct our affairs in such a way that it becomes in the Communists' interest to agree on a genuine peace. Above all, while defending our own vital interests, nuclear powers must avert those confrontations which bring an adversary to a choice of either a humiliating retreat or a nuclear war. To adopt that kind of course in the nuclear age would be evidence only of the bankruptcy of our policy—or of a collective death wish for the world.

To secure these ends, America's weapons are nonprovocative, carefully controlled, designed to deter, and capable of selective use. Our military forces are committed to peace and disciplined in self-restraint. Our diplomats are instructed to avoid unnecessary irritants and purely rhetorical hostility.

For we can seek a relaxation of tensions without relaxing our guard. And, for our part, we do not need to use threats to prove that we are resolute. We do not need to jam foreign broadcasts out of fear our faith will be eroded. We are unwilling to impose our system on any unwilling people, but we are willing and able to engage in peaceful competition with any people on earth.

Meanwhile we seek to strengthen the United Nations, to help solve its financial problems, to make it a more effective instrument of peace, to develop it into a genuine world security system—a system capable of resolving disputes on the basis of law, of insuring the security of the large and the small, and of creating conditions under which arms can finally be abolished.

At the same time we seek to keep peace inside the non-Communist world, where many nations, all of them our friends, are divided over issues which weaken Western unity, which invite Communist intervention, or which threaten to erupt into war. Our efforts in West New Guinea, in the Congo, in the Middle East, and in the Indian subcontinent have been persistent and patient despite criticism from both sides. We have also tried to set an example for others—by seeking to adjust small but significant differences with our own closest neighbors in Mexico and in Canada.

Speaking of other nations, I wish to make one point clear. We are bound to many nations by alliances. Those alliances exist because our concern and theirs substantially overlap. Our commitment to defend Western Europe and West Berlin, for example, stands undiminished because of the identity of our vital interests. The United States will make no deal with the Soviet Union at the expense of other nations and other peoples, not merely because they are our partners but also because their interests and ours converge.

Our interests converge, however, not only in defending the frontiers of freedom but in pursuing the paths of peace. It is our hope—and the purpose of Allied policies—to convince the Soviet Union that she, too, should let each nation choose its own future, so long as that choice does not interfere with the choices of others. The Communist drive to impose their political and economic system on others is the primary cause of world tension today. For there can be no doubt that, if all nations could refrain from interfering in the self-determination of others, the peace would be much more assured.

This will require a new effort to achieve world law, a new context for world discussions. It will require increased understanding between the Soviets and ourselves. And increased understanding will require increased contact and communication. One step in this direction is the proposed arrangement for a direct line between Moscow and Washington, to avoid on each side the dangerous delays, misunderstandings, and misreadings of the other's actions which might occur at a time of crisis.

We have also been talking in Geneva about other first-step measures of arms control, designed to limit the intensity of the arms race and to reduce the risks of accidental war. Our primary long-range interest in Geneva, however, is general and complete disarmament, designed to take place by stages, permitting parallel political developments to build the new institutions of peace which would take the place of arms. The pursuit of disarmament has been an effort of this Government since the 1920's. It has been urgently sought by the past three administrations. And however dim the prospects may be today, we intend to continue this effort—to continue it in order that all countries, including our own, can better grasp what the problems and possibilities of disarmament are.

The one major area of these negotiations where the end is in sight, yet where a fresh start is badly needed, is in a treaty to outlaw nuclear tests. The conclusion of such a treaty—so near and yet so far—would check the spiraling arms race in one of its most dangerous areas. It would place the nuclear powers in a position to deal more effectively with one of the greatest hazards which man faces in 1963, the further spread of nuclear arms. It would increase our security; it would decrease the prospects of war. Surely this goal is sufficiently important to require our steady pursuit, yielding neither to the temptation to give up the whole effort nor the temptation to give up our insistence on vital and responsible safeguards.

I am taking this opportunity, therefore, to announce two important decisions in this regard.

First: Chairman Khrushchev, Prime Minister Macmillan, and I have agreed that high-level discussions will shortly begin in Moscow looking toward early agreement on a comprehensive test ban treaty. Our hopes must be tempered with the caution of history, but with our hopes go the hopes of all mankind.

Second: To make clear our good faith and solemn convictions on the matter, I now declare that the United States does not propose to conduct nuclear tests in the atmosphere so long as other states do not do so. We will not be the first to resume. Such a declaration is no substitute for a formal binding treaty, but I hope it will help us achieve one. Nor would such a treaty be a substitute for disarmament, but I hope it will help us achieve it.


PEACE AND HUMAN RIGHTS

Finally, my fellow Americans, let us examine our attitude toward peace and freedom here at home. The quality and spirit of our own society must justify and support our efforts abroad. We must show it in the dedication of our own lives, as many of you who are graduating today will have a unique opportunity to do, by serving without pay in the Peace Corps abroad or in the proposed National Service Corps here at home.

But wherever we are, we must all, in our daily lives, live up to the age-old faith that peace and freedom walk together. In too many of our cities today the peace is not secure because freedom is incomplete.

It is the responsibility of the executive branch at all levels of government—local, State, and national—to provide and protect that freedom for all of our citizens by all means within their authority. It is the responsibility of the legislative branch at all levels, wherever that authority is not now adequate, to make it adequate. And it is the responsibility of all citizens in all sections of this country to respect the rights of all others and to respect the law of the land.

All this is not unrelated to world peace. "When a man's ways please the Lord," the Scriptures tell us, "he maketh even his enemies to be at peace with him." And is not peace, in the last analysis, basically a matter of human rights—the right to live out our lives without fear of devastation, the right to breathe air as nature provided it, the right of future generations to a healthy existence?

While we proceed to safeguard our national interests, let us also safeguard human interests. And the elimination of war and arms is clearly in the interests of both. No treaty, however much it may be to the advantage of all, however tightly it may be worded, can provide absolute security against the risks of deception and evasion. But it can, if it is sufficiently effective in its enforcement and if it is sufficiently in the interests of its signers, offer far more security and far fewer risks than an unabated, uncontrolled, unpredictable arms race.

The United States, as the world knows, will never start a war. We do not want a war. We do not now expect a war. This generation of Americans has already had enough—more than enough—of war and hate and oppression. We shall be prepared if others wish it. We shall be alert to try to stop it. But we shall also do our part to build a world of peace where the weak are safe and the strong are just. We are not helpless before that task or hopeless of its success. Confident and unafraid, we labor on—not toward a strategy of annihilation but toward a strategy of peace.

JOHN   PATON   DAVIES,   JR.

## In Search of Monsters

From Greenland's icy mountains to India's coral strand, for a century and a half, thousands of Americans have struggled to propagate the faith and convert the heathen. It was, and still is, a selfless, dedicated commitment to change the beliefs and lives of other men.

This labor of persuasion was from the beginning regarded as belonging within what is now fashionably called the private sector, for the American government had no role in the proselytization of foreigners.

Only a generation ago, the general inclination was that, as a nation, we should mind our own business. In the public sector, the United States "has abstained from interference in the concerns of others," said John Quincy Adams, "even when the conflict has been for principles to which she clings, as to the last vital drop that visits the heart."

Recognizing that this was a Fourth of July oration but not taking it, in our manner, as mere bombast because of that, we would do well by our sense of perspective to listen to some of the other things Mr. Adams had to say.

Wherever the standard of freedom and independence has been and shall be unfurled, there will her heart, her benedictions, and her prayers be. But she goes not abroad in search of monsters to destroy. She is the well-wisher to the freedom and independence of all. She is the champion and vindicator only of her own. She will recommend the general cause by the countenance of her voice, and the benignant sympathy of her example. She well knows that by once enlisting under other banners than her own, were they even the banners of foreign independence, she would involve herself beyond the power of extrication, in all the wars of interest and intrigue, of individual avarice, envy and

SOURCE: John Paton Davies, Jr., *Foreign and Other Affairs* (New York: W.W. Norton Co., Inc., 1964), pp. 201–219. Reprinted by permission of W.W. Norton & Company, Inc. Copyright © 1966, 1964 by W.W. Norton & Company, Inc.

ambition, which assume the colors and usurp the standard of freedom. . . .
She might become the dictatress of the world. She would be no longer the
ruler of her own spirit.

Mr. Adams and some of the other gentlemen who got us going as
a nation were shrewd judges of human nature, including our own. They
were far too perceptive to become infatuated by the surface phenomena
they saw abroad. And they modestly understood the limitations of what
we could do beyond our own jurisdiction and the dangers of overreach-
ing ourselves.

Another Bostonian, 141 years later, in his 1962 State of the Union
Message, proclaimed: "People everywhere, in spite of occasional disap-
pointments, look to us—not to our wealth or power, but to the splendor
of our ideals. For our nation is commissioned by history to be either an
observer of freedom's failure or the cause of its success."

History had here acquired alien godlike attributes. Proselytization
had swelled from spiritual to secular concern, from private consecration
to public function. The Federal Government was ordained by history
to busy itself with saving the political heathen in foreign lands, converting them by example and by good works from the sin of unrepresentative government.

We were told that foreigners looked to us for leadership. It was
our mission to inspire people in distant lands with the revolutionary
impact of American life, achievement, and dreams so that they would
cherish freedom and embrace the idea of a world community of harmonious, independent states, as envisaged in the United Nations Charter.

This is a large and diffuse undertaking for a government. And proselytization by bureaucracy is new to us. The general proposition of trying to inspire foreigners with a revolutionary idea is, however, as old
as the Christian missionary movement. Many of the government's opinion-
forming techniques, which may seem to be innovations, are well established in the history of the church's activities in foreign fields. The experiences of the past in inspiration and persuasion illuminate the groping
efforts of the present.

In the sixteenth century the first Jesuits arrived in China. They
were tolerated and finally accepted by the suspicious, archaic court at
Peking, more because of their representation of the life and achievements of the West than for their religion. Matteo Ricci, the leader of
the group, was a scholar and by all accounts a man of exceptional stature.
He and his successors tactfully avoided contesting Confucian rites for
somewhat the same reasons that our policy now is to avoid condemning
neutralism as immoral. Imputations of immorality usually leave the
listener unmoved, unless to the disadvantage of the moralist.

Anticipating the activities of our cultural attachés and information officers, these Jesuits brought and later published books and expounded on Western accomplishments and dreams. Like our aid missions, they introduced Western scientific knowledge and techniques and told of Occidental methods of education. And in the manner of a Military Assistance Advisory Group, they taught the Chinese how to cast brass cannon.

For three and a half centuries Catholic and then Protestant missionaries in China propagated not only the Christian faith but also the Western point of view: individualism, human rights, and, from the nineteenth century onward, freedom. They also taught the Western way of doing things: the scientific method, mechanization, and technology.

Dwarfing our present worldwide governmental programs in effort, if not cash, expended, this private-sector proselytization had in China during the third decade of this century more than ten thousand American and European missionaries in person-to-person programs, over a hundred Christian colleges and universities, some seven hundred high schools, more than four thousand primary schools, and in excess of five hundred hospitals and clinics.

In mass media, the output was prodigious. Catholic production alone in secular matters included thirteen scientific periodicals and forty-nine dealing with social, cultural, and educational subjects. In addition to their own publications, the Protestants opened in 1936 a radio station.

Our student-exchange programs have their precedents in the thousands of Chinese students who for at least two generations went to the United States and Western Europe for higher education. Many of them became the leaders in the "modernization" of China.

All of this was done not without sacrifice. Most readily there comes to mind the 221 missionary men, women, and children slaughtered in the Boxer Rebellion. More recently, in the five years 1929–1934, bandits or Communists kidnapped or killed fifty-four missionaries.

What came of this prolonged outpouring of love, labor, and blood?

Less than 1 per cent of the population of China was converted to Christianity. China was but superficially modernized and was torn by dissension. The massive bulk of Chinese existed in a Malthusian cycle, illiterate, impoverished, and fatalistic.

Then came the culmination. Three hundred and fifty years of enlightenment from the West was extinguished by an ideological movement that had existed in China for less than thirty years. Communism then undertook the modernization of China by force.

But this is only part of the object lesson for us. There was also Japan. There the impact of the West had a revolutionary effect. Shortly after Commodore Perry "opened" Japan, the Japanese themselves began, in 1868, the Meiji Reformation. In a little more than thirty years, they had made themselves enough of a power to challenge the Russian Empire and then defeat it on land and sea.

In this underdeveloped country the example of Western life and achievements, the instruction of missionaries, and the education of young Japanese in the West created a revolution, as it had not in China. In one generation, Japan was well on the way to modernization and status as a world power.

The Japanese continued on this course, selecting from the West what they calculated would add to their power, commercially, industrially, politically, and militarily. That from the West for which they felt no need, they slighted or ignored. Less than half of 1 per cent of the Japanese adopted Christianity.

The culmination of Japan's eager acceptance of Western life and achievements was Pearl Harbor. After defeating the Japanese, we imposed on them, through military occupation and rule, democracy and a recognition of the values of freedom and of a world community of harmonious and independent states, as laid down in the UN Charter.

There should be some lessons for the present out of this past. One lesson is that opinion-forming will probably fail if what we have to say is not, in the mind of our audience, relevant to its own situation. That was one of the great problems with the Chinese. As Confucianists, the idea of salvation was implausible; as Buddhists, it seemed unnecessary. Individualism was meaningless, when not shameful, in a civilization rooted in the family system. Human rights and freedom had long ago been appropriately delineated by Confucius; any fault lay with the misdeeds of the magistrate, and it would be unseemly for a barbarian, however well-intentioned, to speak out boldly in such matters.

As for the mechanical contrivances of the West, entertaining, useful, and desirable—but how to create large mechanized enterprises, how to industrialize in the absence of mutual confidence, governmental competence, skilled workers, capital accumulation, and a social stigma on short fingernails. These continue to be relevant questions to irrelevant exhortations to sluggish, corrupt, undisciplined, and impoverished societies that they get their countries moving and revolutionize themselves after the example of our life, achievement, and dreams.

Another lesson is that people even of the same race can vary tremendously in national personality, as did the Chinese and the Japanese. Programming and projecting the U.S.A. may, because of differing character, outlook, and energy in the recipients, influence Country X in one direction, Country Y in another, and Country Z scarcely at all. The number of differing reactions will correspond to the number of "target" countries.

To inspire a nation by our life, achievements, and dreams to the degree that it modernizes itself does not guarantee that it will thereby be converted to a live-and-let-live policy in its international relations. It may elect a contrary course and turn on us. Or it may go its own self-assertive way without respect to us or the UN Charter.

Turning more particularly to our present battle for men's minds, the conditions of the conflict are not entirely favorable to us. Much is made of reservoirs of goodwill for the United States. This is true, for such reservoirs do exist. But it is also true that a characteristic of many reservoirs is that they are dammed up. A pervasive unsympathy for us holds back the natural flow of such goodwill as may exist.

The unsympathy varies from petty irritations to unreasoning hostility. Even the people nearest to us, our next-door neighbor, speaking the same language and sharing pretty much the same origins and culture—the Canadians—are somewhat less than uncritical of us. There is so much of us, we intrude upon them, and we have long taken them for granted.

The quality of the wet sheepdog in the parlor, demonstrative, well disposed, sniffing everyone, into everything, likewise irritates our European friends. They are grateful to us, of course, as a watchdog. But when we tug at their sleeves to go out and hunt Castros with us, the familiar human reaction is: "Don't be a nuisance, go chase your own Cubans."

More serious is the anti-Americanism in the underdeveloped countries this side of the Curtain. For the underdeveloped peoples, the primitive force of race—racial suspicions, resentments, and hatreds—may prove to be stronger than ideology. It is generations deep in the passions of Asia and Africa. It is not absent among the nonwhites of Latin America. That we are predominantly white is sufficient to aggravate the fester of nationalism, to find indignant self-virtue in every publicized act of segregation or violence against the American Negro, and to inflate and nurture insults, as visitors to our shores, in encounters with sorely beset New York policemen, hotel receptionists, gentlemen's clubs, and Howard Johnson hostesses.

Race is also the fuel of ideology. Anti-imperialism is felt with fervor long after its weight has been lifted, not simply because of distant political or economic relationships but more likely because of past or present personal humiliations by white men.

The same holds true of communism. Its appeal among underdeveloped peoples is stimulated by racial grudges. This is because Marxism-Leninism is not only militantly anti-imperialist but is also loud in its protestations for racial equality. Largely overlooked is Russian light pigmentation, extensive racial prejudices in the U.S.S.R., and Soviet imperialism from Mongolia through Central Asia to East Germany.

That the Russians are white is not, however, entirely disregarded. Primitive color prejudice exists between the Russians and the Chinese, a common ideology notwithstanding. The Chinese have sought to exploit this elemental antipathy among other nonwhite Communists, to the Kremlin's intense indignation, trying to turn them against Moscow and into alignment with Peking, which pretends to be the capital of colored communism.

The white man's whiteness is not his sole burden nowadays in treating with underdeveloped nations. In our case we also encounter the natural envy of the poor. We are the richest of the rich nations, and in our bounty we have bestowed benefits upon the poor countries with unprecedented liberality. This is the cause of an embarrassed beholdingness, inverted into resentment, in the proud. In those of a practical bent, the embarrassment is soon quelled by rising expectations of continuing benefits as an accustomed due. A lessening of the benefits naturally produces a sense of being unjustly deprived of what has become a right.

American intervention, before we became the Good Neighbor, left in Latin-American memories that have not died out, an apprehension of United States power cracking down on them. That we have been for over thirty years bland as mother's milk, and more freely flowing, matters little. Yanqui imperialism remains a specter in the Latin mind.

Being white, rich, and reformed imperialists makes for something of a propaganda handicap. What do we do about foreign antipathy?

Possibly the first thing to do is to stop being so agitated about it.

We might with profit consider a predecessor in preeminent power, the British. No one liked the British much. For their part, they recognized foreign dislike for its worth, including the valid criticism therein. But they did not become obsessed by unpopularity. Nor did they waste energy in vainly combating those international neuroses that were curable only by (if even by that) Britain's disappearance from the face of the earth.

What was usually taken for British arrogance was merely British boredom. Generations of Britons had learned the futility of explaining to alien minds the rationale of worldwide power and its attendant responsibilities.

But ours is another temperament. However composed we may become, whatever aplomb we may muster, we feel the necessity of reacting to the ideological offensive of the Communists. We cannot simply ignore pervasive and persistent thought-aggression throughout the world, damaging to our interests.

So, as a government, we react. The fact that in a generally unsympathetic world situation our government does react is in contrast to the missionary movement. Christian proselytization was spontaneous; it was on the offensive. Our agitated opinion-forming is not spontaneous. It is a defensive reflex, a response to Soviet ideological aggression. Were it not for the communist menace, we would scarcely have embarked on this, unnatural for us, proselytization of foreigners by the Federal bureaucracy and circulating celebrities.

With the Communists on the offensive and with us on the defensive, the battle for men's minds is snarled in a double paradox. To the bewildered foreigner serious enough to make a try at sorting out the issues, our identifiable outlook is in apparent conflict: (*a*) the Christian ethic of political principles enunciated by the founders of the Republic and (*b*) the materialistic, hedonistic philosophy produced by our industrial and merchandising genius.

The second paradox derives from the ideological confrontation between us and the Communists. Our case is publicly stated on alternative (*a*): we represent the spiritual, idealistic, humanistic values. We consider them, "the splendor of our ideals," to be revolutionary in their impact on the unconverted. The communist dogma is aggressively materialistic. Yet our attraction for foreigners is our superlatively successful materialism, "our wealth or power," the level of which it is the communist ideal to equal and overtake. Perversely, the communist magnetism for the underdeveloped peoples is ideas, theory, and, save the mark, idealism—else there would be no communist fanaticism, which is a perversion of idealism.

Our mosaic of traditional beliefs, the totality of which we call democracy, has relevance and deeply treasured significance for us. But for others, American democracy is particularly American, remote, and inapplicable to themselves. As for the lessons of the American Revolution, they seem academic to the Asian, African, or Latin American, having little bearing on the extremity in which he finds himself.

The American Revolution is in time, magnitude, and intensity far distant from what goes on in modern revolutionary situations—from the October Revolution in Russia, to the long-drawn-out upheaval in China, to the feverish frustrations of Arab socialism in North Africa and the Near East, and to the machete Marxist performance in Brazil. It is the difference between an uprising commanded by disaffected gentry and a desperate, groping, ignorant compulsion among those who feel their only hope is to overturn and smash not only the old regime but the whole social order and to replace it with almost any blatant denial of what they live under, almost any sort of plebeian dispensation.

The American Revolution was essentially conservative. The revolutions of the underdeveloped countries are metamorphic, boundless in impulse to wreck and make over. As such they present an exciting opportunity to power-hungry schemers, those who, as Hamilton observed, begin "their career by paying an obsequious court to the people, commencing demagogues and ending tyrants."

What Jefferson and Patrick Henry had to say about liberty and the pursuit of happiness was regarded as worthily revolutionary by the educated minority in underdeveloped countries when they, too, were colonials, but now that they are sovereign, the revolutionary oligarchies view such sentiments as counterrevolutionary.

In contrast, the combination of American materialism and American pop culture is one of the most potent influences ever loosed on the world. The appeal is nearly universal because merchandising creativity, research, and development meant it to be so. The infinite permutations of plastics, luminescence, frigidity, moving metal parts, heat, extrusions, electrical impulses, petrochemical fibers, swoosh of air in and swish of air out, artificial flavors, sonic effects, and liquid concentrates diluted outdo the total philosophical and moral output of our Founding Fathers. "This," simple people everywhere sigh and say, "ah, this is America."

And if for lack of cash the foreigner cannot buy such tangible bliss on earth, we offer to rich and poor alike everyman's effortless Nirvana: on film, tape, radio, and TV and in McCallism-Playboyism. This is our immaterial thrust, our un-ideology, the power of which we fail to appreciate.

Some Americans are ashamed of the success abroad of this neopubescent way of life. It is not putting our best foot forward. That is true. But there it is. And it must be admitted that the message is comprehensible to all and appallingly popular with most.

The utilitarian, the vapid and the vulgar of our life, achievements and dreams homogenize into a successful revolutionary export. A measure of the revolutionary success is that the communist rulers regard the blend as a distracting and subversive influence which, if allowed free entry, would undermine Marxism-Leninism. This is one of the main reasons for the Iron Curtain.

Being an open society, Western Europe is succumbing to this revolution of flatulence. The appeal is relevant, and with Europe's growing affluence the revolutionary goals are attainable by almost everyone. Quality and taste are fighting a counterrevolutionary rearguard action. But the odds are against them.

With the underdeveloped countries it is yet another story. The materialistic appeal of the Miami Beach blend is there, but it is usually not relevant because it is, for most, unattainable. It excites revolutionary impulses that need money to be satisfied. Poverty thwarts fulfillment. The pop culture stimulates the rising expectations with dreams of possessing that which, upon confrontation with reality, is priced beyond possession.

The result of this revolutionary force on the emergent poor is resentful frustration, heightening the basic discontent of poverty. From there it is but a step to a will to revolt and receptivity to any plausible scheme of violent revolution. This is where communism, in theory and insurrectionary technique, appears to be relevant to backward peoples, not because they like Russians or Chinese or want to be ruled by them. Quite the contrary. It is because many of them are drawn to authority, purpose, mass solidarity, violent revolt, a shared formula for self-realization, the government's taking problems off their shoulders and promises of security in a utopian collective society. The less enured to choice and decision a people, the more attractive this simplifying formula.

The practical aspirant to power in the underdeveloped countries tends toward the totalitarian choice because—quite aside from the agreeable coincidence that he, the government, and the "people" might merge into one, with him as the father of the trinity—he recognizes that his people are not equal to what we understand by democracy. And the people themselves, after colonial rule, submission to native tyrants, or "governing themselves" through scalawags and weaklings, are receptive to totalitarianism in which the simple man finds spurious realization as an individual in local party meetings, "popular" demonstrations, and possession of a militiaman's gun, while actually losing his individuality in the socially secured people.

This is what happened in Cuba. And in Cuba, as elsewhere under Communist tyranny, the people soon found themselves betrayed by what was purported to be their revolution.

And yet, since mid-century, the spread of communism as a projection of Soviet power in the world has not been extensive.

One of the three facets of communism, its technique of insurrection, has been less than wholly successful since the Chinese revolution. The technique was effective in Cuba and partially so in Indochina. In Greece, Iran, the Philippines, and Malaya the uprisings failed. In the future, communist insurrections may succeed in some Latin-American countries.

There is a second facet of communism—ideology in its fundamentalist Marxist-Leninist expression—but it has not gained significant ground. Communism as an infallible unitary doctrine has been fragmented by the Russo-Chinese quarrel and the growth of polycentrism. Communist ideology has been borrowed from in dilutions and unlikely admixtures by some of the new states in Asia and Africa. The Marxist-Islamic brew in some sub-Saharan nations of Africa is an example. And nationalist variants of communism may come to power through democratic elections in a few Latin American countries.

Another facet, the communist system of domination and rule, has been more extensively drawn upon, but also in diffused form. This is so, not necessarily because the revolutionary oligarchies were tender of heart, but because of a pervasive temperamental disarray. The one-party Afrosocialist dictatorship of the immortal Osagyefo Kwame Nkrumah is a case in point. Nevertheless, species of authoritarianism derived from Leninism will probably be the most enduring legacy of communism in the underdeveloped states, with eventually little or no allegiance to its originators.

Rampant nationalism in the underdeveloped nations, particularly the new ones, has been the strongest antibody to the extension of Soviet authority and power. Backward governments have accepted from the Communists, Russian and Chinese, insurrectionary techniques, ideology, and totalitarian systems, but always with reservations and modifications. It is, of course, a dangerous game. If the emergent nation becomes dependent upon Moscow or Peking, as Cuba in its selfmade chaos did, the risk is great of penetration of control mechanisms and take-over. If this happens, the country becomes an adjunct of Soviet or Chinese power. Otherwise the power advantages to Moscow or Peking are conditional, most obviously with respect to the economic cost of trying to maintain control.

While ideology is a mishmash in the backward countries, in the rest of the world it is obsolescent. This is most evident in Western Europe, its breeding ground, from whence emerged Marxism, nazism, and fascism, for Western Europe was to ideologies what the Near and Middle East were to religions. Notwithstanding the popularity of socialism, ideology is passé in Western Europe because it has been made largely irrelevant by the orderly adoption of many moderate socialist principles, the success of the Marshall Plan, and a consequent social equilibrium. The only possible revival of rampant ideology would seem to be in the event that Western Europe suffers a prolonged depression.

As for the communist countries, ideology is kept nominally alive by the system of domination, including isolation, and by rote. People have lived before on what had ceased to have fresh and vital meaning to them, so long as the familiar outward forms and structures remained. With time, the rub of internal and external contradictions will erode even the system encasing the people.

The truth is that our battle for men's minds in the past decade has gone much better than we have anxiously imagined. The principal reason is that communism has done poorly for Moscow and Peking, largely as a result of their own economic botches and of the vigor of nationalism in the new countries, the old countries, and in the communist camp itself.

The industrialized countries of the West have, in contrast, flourished beyond expectation and become a symbol of success. This does not of course provide an answer in the minds of the underdeveloped peoples to their own problems. They want to get where we are without going through a slow growth process. But the contrast between the Communists and the West has raised doubts about blind adherence to Marxism.

Obviously some of what we are trying to do in opinion-forming is futile. Some of it is silly. And some is even damaging. Foreigners, like us, are stubborn folk, not much moved by alien exhortation unless it suits their book. What we have to say about ourselves is rarely assimilable by others, even when understood. What we offer is, in part, taken; what is learned may be used against us—as what is taken from our enemy may be used against him. What we deem ordinary and even shoddy is admired and pathetically emulated. What we cherish is spurned.

We are preoccupied with ideology. We fail to distinguish between hostile ideology associated with power, which is a real threat, and hostile ideology without significant power, which is impotent enmity.

More significantly, we are insufficiently aware that civilization is moving out of the epoch of political philosophies and entering the era of know-how, with us in the vanguard.

Should the lagging countries move forward and not sink into a bog of squalor and chaos, it will be mainly because administrative and technical know-how is applied. It will not be because of ideology—or even the adoption of universal suffrage and a bicameral legislature. And if the Communists are to sober from their doctrinal hallucinations, it will be because the pragmatic possessors of know-how—the only element capable of bringing the communist countries up from their material inferiority—wear down the fanatics.

Our approach to the so-called battle for men's minds should be more relaxed and modest. It should be more modest in claims of what our life, achievements, and dreams can do for others in an uncertain world. It should be more modest in the scope of "programs" undertaken, the size of staffs engaged therein, and the number of gallivanting political celebrities roaming the face of the earth creating what Dr. Daniel J. Boorstin calls pseudo-events. And rather than expostulating—in effect to ourselves without meaning to our auditors—we would more often better be silent.

Most important of all, it is not what we say abroad that is vital. Our first obligation is to ourselves, that at home we fulfill in integrity our native heritage and promise, that we be the ruler of our own spirit.

J .   W I L L I A M   F U L B R I G H T

## *The Arrogance of Power*

America is the most fortunate of nations—fortunate in her rich territory, fortunate in having had a century of relative peace in which to develop that territory, fortunate in her diverse and talented population, fortunate in the institutions devised by the founding fathers and in the wisdom of those who have adapted those institutions to a changing world.

For the most part America has made good use of her blessings, especially in her internal life but also in her foreign relations. Having done so much and succeeded so well, America is now at that historical point at which a great nation is in danger of losing its perspective on what exactly is within the realm of its power and what is beyond it. Other great nations, reaching this critical juncture, have aspired to too much, and by overextension of effort have declined and then fallen.

The causes of the malady are not entirely clear but its recurrence is one of the uniformities of history: power tends to confuse itself with virtue and a great nation is peculiarly susceptible to the idea that its power is a sign of God's favor, conferring upon it a special responsibility for other nations—to make them richer and happier and wiser, to remake them, that is, in its own shining image. Power confuses itself with virtue and tends also to take itself for omnipotence. Once imbued with the idea of a mission, a great nation easily assumes that it has the means as well as the duty to do God's work. The Lord, after all, surely would not choose you as His agent and then deny you the sword with which to work His will. German soldiers in the First World War wore belt

SOURCE: J. William Fulbright, from *The Arrogance of Power* (New York: Vintage Books, 1966), pp. 3–22, 255–258. © Copyright 1966 by J. William Fulbright. Reprinted by permission of Random House, Inc.

buckles imprinted with the words "*Gott mit uns.*" It was approximately under this kind of infatuation—an exaggerated sense of power and an imaginary sense of mission—that the Athenians attacked Syracuse and Napoleon and then Hitler invaded Russia. In plain words, they over-extended their commitments and they came to grief.

I do not think for a moment that America, with her deeply rooted democratic traditions, is likely to embark upon a campaign to dominate the world in the manner of a Hitler or Napoleon. What I do fear is that she may be drifting into commitments which, though generous and benevolent in intent, are so far-reaching as to exceed even America's great capacities. At the same time, it is my hope—and I emphasize it because it underlies all of the criticisms and proposals to be made in these pages—that America will escape those fatal temptations of power which have ruined other great nations and will instead confine herself to doing only that good in the world which she *can* do, both by direct effort and by the force of her own example.

The stakes are high indeed: they include not only America's con-tinued greatness but nothing less than the survival of the human race in an era when, for the first time in human history, a living generation has the power of veto over the survival of the next.

## THE POWER DRIVE OF NATIONS

When the abstractions and subtleties of political science have been exhausted, there remain the most basic unanswered questions about war and peace and why nations contest the issues they contest and why they even care about them. As Aldous Huxley has written:

There may be arguments about the best way of raising wheat in a cold climate or of re-afforesting a denuded mountain. But such arguments never lead to organized slaughter. Organized slaughter is the result of arguments about such questions as the following: Which is the best nation? The best religion? The best political theory? The best form of government? Why are other people so stupid and wicked? Why can't they see how good and intelligent *we* are? Why do they resist our beneficent efforts to bring them under our control and make them like ourselves?[1]

Many of the wars fought by man—I am tempted to say most— have been fought over such abstractions. The more I puzzle over the great wars of history, the more I am inclined to the view that the causes attributed to them—territory, markets, resources, the defense or per-petuation of great principles—were not the root causes at all but rather

[1] Aldous Huxley, "The Politics of Ecology" (Santa Barbara: Center for the Study of Democratic Institutions, 1963), p. 6.

explanations or excuses for certain unfathomable drives of human nature. For lack of a clear and precise understanding of exactly what these motives are, I refer to them as the "arrogance of power"—as a psychological need that nations seem to have in order to prove that they are bigger, better, or stronger than other nations. Implicit in this drive is the assumption, even on the part of normally peaceful nations, that force is the ultimate proof of superiority—that when a nation shows that it has the stronger army, it is also proving that it has better people, better institutions, better principles, and, in general, a better civilization.

Evidence for my proposition is found in the remarkable discrepancy between the apparent and hidden causes of some modern wars and the discrepancy between their causes and ultimate consequences.

The precipitating cause of the Franco-Prussian War of 1870, for example, was a dispute over the succession to the Spanish throne, and the ostensible "underlying" cause was French resistance to the unification of Germany. The war was followed by the completion of German unification—which probably could have been achieved without war—but it was also followed by the loss of Alsace-Lorraine, the humiliation of France, and the emergence of Germany as the greatest power in Europe, which could not have been achieved without war. The peace treaty, incidentally, said nothing about the Spanish throne, which everyone apparently had forgotten. One wonders to what extent the Germans were motivated simply by the desire to cut those haughty Frenchmen down to size and have a good excuse to build another monument in Berlin.

The United States went to war in 1898 for the stated purpose of liberating Cuba from Spanish tyranny, but after winning the war—a war which Spain had been willing to pay a high price to avoid—the United States brought the liberated Cubans under an American protectorate and incidentally annexed the Philippines, because, according to President McKinley, the Lord told him it was America's duty "to educate the Filipinos, and uplift and civilize and Christianize them, and by God's grace do the very best we could by them, as our fellowmen for whom Christ also died."[2]

Isn't it interesting that the voice was the voice of the Lord but the words were those of Theodore Roosevelt, Henry Cabot Lodge, and Admiral Mahan, those "imperialists of 1898" who wanted America to have an empire just because a big, powerful country like the United States *ought* to have an empire? The spirit of the times was expressed by Albert Beveridge, soon thereafter to be elected to the United States Senate, who proclaimed Americans to be "a conquering race": "We

[2] Quoted in Samuel Flagg Bemis, *A Diplomatic History of the United States* (New York: Henry Holt, 1955), p. 472.

must obey our blood and occupy new markets and if necessary new lands," he said, because "In the Almighty's infinite plan . . . debased civilizations and decaying races" must disappear "before the higher civilization of the nobler and more virile types of man."[3]

In 1914 all Europe went to war, ostensibly because the heir to the Austrian throne had been assassinated at Sarajevo, but really because that murder became the symbolic focus of the incredibly delicate sensibilities of the great nations of Europe. The events of the summer of 1914 were a melodrama of abnormal psychology: Austria had to humiliate Serbia in order not to be humiliated herself but Austria's effort at recovering self-esteem was profoundly humiliating to Russia; Russia was allied to France, who had been feeling generally humiliated since 1871, and Austria in turn was allied to Germany, whose pride required that she support Austria no matter how insanely Austria behaved and who may in any case have felt that it would be fun to give the German Army another swing down the Champs-Élysées. For these ennobling reasons the world was plunged into a war which took tens of millions of lives, precipitated the Russian Revolution, and set in motion the events that led to another world war, a war which took tens of millions more lives and precipitated the worldwide revolutions of our time, revolutions whose consequences are beyond the foresight of any of us now alive.

The causes and consequences of war may have more to do with pathology than with politics, more to do with irrational pressures of pride and pain than with rational calculations of advantage and profit. There is a Washington story, perhaps apocryphal, that the military intellectuals in the Pentagon conducted an experiment in which they fed data derived from the events of the summer of 1914 into a computer and that, after weighing and digesting the evidence, the machine assured its users that there was no danger of war. What this "proves," if anything, is that computers are more rational than men; it also suggests that if there is a root cause of human conflict and of the power drive of nations, it lies not in economic aspirations, historical forces, or the workings of the balance of power, but in the ordinary hopes and fears of the human mind.

It has been said that buried in every woman's secret soul is a drum majorette; it might also be said that in all of our souls there is a bit of the missionary. We all like telling people what to do, which is perfectly all right except that most people do not like being told what to do. I have given my wife some splendid suggestions on household management but she has been so consistently ungrateful for my advice that I

[3] Quoted in Barbara Tuchman, *The Proud Tower* (New York: Macmillan, 1966), p. 153.

have stopped offering it. The phenomenon is explained by the Canadian psychiatrist and former Director-General of the World Health Organization, Brock Chisholm, who writes:

. . . Man's method of dealing with difficulties in the past has always been to tell everyone else how they should behave. We've all been doing that for centuries.

It should be clear by now that this no longer does any good. Everybody has by now been told by everybody else how he should behave. . . . The criticism is not effective; it never has been, and it never is going to be. . . .[4]

Ineffective though it has been, the giving—and enforcement—of all this unsolicited advice has at least until recently been compatible with the survival of the human race. Man is now, however, for the first time, in a situation in which the survival of his species is in jeopardy. Other forms of life have been endangered and many destroyed by changes in their natural environment; man is menaced by a change of environment which he himself has wrought by the invention of nuclear weapons and ballistic missiles. Our power to kill has become universal, creating a radically new situation which, if we are to survive, requires us to adopt some radically new attitudes about the giving and enforcement of advice and in general about human and international relations.

The enormity of the danger of extinction of our species is dulled by the frequency with which it is stated, as if a familiar threat of catastrophe were no threat at all. We seem to feel somehow that because the hydrogen bomb has not killed us yet, it is never going to kill us. This is a dangerous assumption because it encourages the retention of traditional attitudes about world politics when our responsibility, in Dr. Chisholm's words, is nothing less than "to re-examine all of the attitudes of our ancestors and to select from those attitudes things which we, on our own authority in these present circumstances, with our knowledge, recognize as still valid in this new kind of world. . . ."[5]

The attitude above all others which I feel sure is no longer valid is the arrogance of power, the tendency of great nations to equate power with virtue and major responsibilities with a universal mission. The dilemmas involved are pre-eminently American dilemmas, not because America has weaknesses that others do not have but because America is powerful as no nation has ever been before, and the discrepancy between her power and the power of others appears to be increasing. One may hope that America, with her vast resources and democratic traditions, with her diverse and creative population, will find the wisdom

[4] Brock Chisholm, *Prescription for Survival* (New York: Columbia University Press, 1957), p. 54.
[5] *Ibid.*, p. 9.

to match her power; but one can hardly be confident because the wisdom required is greater wisdom than any great nation has ever shown before. It must be rooted, as Dr. Chisholm says, in the re-examination of "all of the attitudes of our ancestors."

It is a tall order. Perhaps one can begin to fill it by an attempt to assess the attitudes of Americans toward other peoples and some of the effects of America's power on small countries whom she has tried to help.

INNOCENTS ABROAD

There are signs of the arrogance of power in the way Americans act when they go to foreign countries. Foreigners frequently comment on the contrast between the behavior of Americans at home and abroad: in our own country, they say, we are hospitable and considerate, but as soon as we get outside our own borders something seems to get into us and wherever we are we become noisy and demanding and we strut around as if we owned the place. The British used to say during the war that the trouble with the Yanks was that they were "overpaid, over-sexed, and over here." During a recent vacation in Mexico, I noticed in a small-town airport two groups of students on holiday, one group Japanese, the other American. The Japanese were neatly dressed and were talking and laughing in a manner that neither annoyed anybody nor particularly called attention to themselves. The Americans, on the other hand, were disporting themselves in a conspicious and offensive manner, stamping around the waiting room in sloppy clothes, drinking beer, and shouting to each other as if no one else were there.

This kind of scene, unfortunately, has become familiar in many parts of the world. I do not wish to exaggerate its significance, but I have the feeling that just as there was once something special about being a Roman or a Spaniard or an Englishman, there is now something about the consciousness of being an American abroad, something about the consciousness of belonging to the biggest, richest country in the world, that encourages people who are perfectly well behaved at home to become boorish when they are in somebody else's country and to treat the local citizens as if they were not really there.

One reason Americans abroad may act as though they "own the place" is that in many places they very nearly do: American companies may dominate large segments of a country's economy; American products are advertised on billboards and displayed in shop windows; American hotels and snack bars are available to protect American tourists from foreign influence; American soldiers may be stationed in the country, and even if they are not, the population are probably well aware that their very survival depends on the wisdom with which America uses her immense military power.

I think that when any American goes abroad, he carries an unconscious knowledge of all this power with him and it affects his behavior, just as it once affected the behavior of Greeks and Romans, of Spaniards, Germans, and Englishmen, in the brief high noons of their respective ascendancies. It was the arrogance of their power that led nineteenth-century Englishmen to suppose that if they shouted at a foreigner loud enough in English he was bound to understand, or that now leads Americans to behave like Mark Twain's "innocents abroad," who reported on their travels in Europe that

> The people of those foreign countries are very, very ignorant. They looked curiously at the costumes we had brought from the wilds of America. They observed that we talked loudly at table sometimes. . . . In Paris they just simply opened their eyes and stared when we spoke to them in French! We never did succeed in making these idiots understand their own language.[6]

## THE FATAL IMPACT

Reflecting on his voyages to Polynesia in the late eighteenth century, Captain Cook later wrote that "It would have been better for these people never to have known us." In a book on European explorations of the South Pacific, Alan Moorehead relates how the Tahitians and the Australian aborigines were corrupted by the white man's diseases, alcohol, firearms, laws, and concepts of morality, by what Moorehead calls "the long down-slide into Western civilization." The first missionaries to Tahiti, says Moorehead, were "determined to recreate the island in the image of lower-middle-class Protestant England. . . . They kept hammering away at the Tahitian way of life until it crumbled before them, and within two decades they had achieved precisely what they set out to do."[7] It is said that the first missionaries to Hawaii went for the purpose of explaining to the Polynesians that it was sinful to work on Sunday, only to discover that in those bountiful islands nobody worked on any day.

Even when acting with the best of intentions, Americans, like other Western peoples who have carried their civilizations abroad, have had something of the same "fatal impact" on smaller nations that European explorers had on the Tahitians and the native Australians. We have not harmed people because we wished to; on the contrary, more often than

[6] Mark Twain, *The Innocents Abroad* (New York: The Thistle Press, 1962), p. 494.
[7] Alan Moorehead, *The Fatal Impact* (New York: Harper & Row, 1966), pp. 61, 80–81.

not we have wanted to help people and, in some very important respects, we have helped them. Americans have brought medicine and education, manufactures and modern techniques to many places in the world; but they have also brought themselves and the condescending attitudes of a people whose very success breeds disdain for other cultures. Bringing power without understanding, Americans as well as Europeans have had a devastating effect in less advanced areas of the world; without knowing they were doing it, they have shattered traditional societies, disrupted fragile economies and undermined peoples' self-confidence by the invidious example of their own power and efficiency. They have done this in many instances simply by being big and strong, by giving good advice, by intruding on people who have not wanted them but could not resist them.

The missionary instinct seems to run deep in human nature, and the bigger and stronger and richer we are, the more we feel suited to the missionary task, the more indeed we consider it our duty. Dr. Chisholm relates the story of an eminent cleric who had been proselyting the Eskimos and said: "You know, for years we couldn't do anything with those Eskimos at all; they didn't have any sin. We had to teach them sin for years before we could do anything with them."[8] I am reminded of the three Boy Scouts who reported to their scoutmaster that as their good deed for the day they had helped an old lady to cross the street.

"That's fine," said the scoutmaster, "but why did it take three of you?"

"Well," they explained, "she didn't want to go."

The good deed above all the others that Americans feel qualified to perform is the teaching of democracy. Let us consider the results of some American good deeds in various parts of the world.

Over the years since President Monroe proclaimed his doctrine, Latin Americans have had the advantages of United States tutelage in fiscal responsibility, in collective security, and in the techniques of democracy. If they have fallen short in any of these fields, the thought presents itself that the fault may lie as much with the teacher as with the pupils.

When President Theodore Roosevelt announced his "corollary" to the Monroe Doctrine in 1905, he solemnly declared that he regarded the future interventions thus sanctified as a "burden" and a "responsibility" and an obligation to "international equity." Not once, so far as I know, has the United States regarded itself as intervening in a Latin American country for selfish or unworthy motives—a view not necessarily shared, however, by the beneficiaries. Whatever reassurance the purity of our motives may give must be shaken a little by the thought

[8] Chisholm, *op. cit.*, pp. 55–56.

that probably no country in human history has ever intervened in another except for motives it regarded as excellent.

For all our noble intentions, the countries which have had most of the tutelage in democracy by United States Marines have not been particularly democratic. These include Haiti, which is under a brutal and superstitious dictatorship; the Dominican Republic, which languished under the brutal Trujillo dictatorship for thirty years and whose second elected government since the overthrow of Trujillo is threatened, like the first, by the power of a military oligarchy; and of course Cuba, which, as no one needs to be reminded, has replaced its traditional right-wing dictatorships with a communist dictatorship.

Maybe, in the light of this extraordinary record of accomplishment, it is time for us to reconsider our teaching methods. Maybe we are not really cut out for the job of spreading the gospel of democracy. Maybe it would profit us to concentrate on our own democracy instead of trying to inflict our particular version of it on all those ungrateful Latin Americans who stubbornly oppose their North American benefactors instead of the "real" enemies whom we have so graciously chosen for them. And maybe—just maybe—if we left our neighbors to make their own judgments and their own mistakes, and confined our assistance to matters of economics and technology instead of philosophy, maybe then they would begin to find the democracy and the dignity that have largely eluded them, and we in turn might begin to find the love and gratitude that we seem to crave.

Korea is another example. We went to war in 1950 to defend South Korea against the Russian-inspired aggression of North Korea. I think that American intervention was justified and necessary: we were defending a country that clearly wanted to be defended, whose army was willing to fight and fought well, and whose government, though dictatorial, was patriotic and commanded the support of the people. Throughout the war, however, the United States emphasized as one of its war aims the survival of the Republic of Korea as a "free society," something which it was not then and is not now. We lost 33,629 American lives in that war and have since spent $5.61 billion on direct military and economic aid and a great deal more on indirect aid to South Korea. The country, nonetheless, remained until recently in a condition of virtual economic stagnation and political instability. Only now is economic progress being made, but the truly surprising fact is that having fought a war for three years to defend the freedom of South Korea, most Americans quickly lost interest in the state of the ward for whom they had sacrificed so much. It is doubtful that more than a handful of Americans now know or care whether South Korea is a "free society."

We are now engaged in a war to "defend freedom" in South Vietnam. Unlike the Republic of Korea, South Vietnam has an army which fights without notable success and a weak, dictatorial government which does not command the loyalty of the South Vietnamese people. The official war aims of the United States government, as I understand them, are to defeat what is regarded as North Vietnamese aggression, to demonstrate the futility of what the communists call "wars of national liberation," and to create conditions under which the South Vietnamese people will be able freely to determine their own future.

I have not the slightest doubt of the sincerity of the President and the Vice-President and the Secretaries of State and Defense in propounding these aims. What I do doubt, and doubt very much, is the ability of the United States to achieve these aims by the means being used. I do not question the power of our weapons and the efficiency of our logistics; I cannot say these things delight me as they seem to delight some of our officials, but they are certainly impressive. What I do question is the ability of the United States or any other Western nation to go into a small, alien, undeveloped Asian nation and create stability where there is chaos, the will to fight where there is defeatism, democracy where there is no tradition of it, and honest government where corruption is almost a way of life.

In the spring of 1966 demonstrators in Saigon burned American jeeps, tried to assault American soldiers, and marched through the streets shouting "Down with American imperialists," while a Buddhist leader made a speech equating the United States with the communists as a threat to South Vietnamese independence. Most Americans are understandably shocked and angered to encounter expressions of hostility from people who would long since have been under the rule of the Viet Cong but for the sacrifice of American lives and money. Why, we may ask, are they so shockingly ungrateful? Surely they must know that their very right to parade and protest and demonstrate depends on the Americans who are defending them.

The answer, I think, is that "fatal impact" of the rich and strong on the poor and weak. Dependent on it though the Vietnamese are, American strength is a reproach to their weakness, American wealth a mockery of their poverty, American success a reminder of their failures. What they resent is the disruptive effect of our strong culture upon their fragile one, an effect which we can no more avoid having than a man can help being bigger than a child. What they fear, I think rightly, is that traditional Vietnamese society cannot survive the American economic and cultural impact.

The evidence of that "fatal impact" is seen in the daily life of Saigon. A *New York Times* correspondent reported—and his information matches that of other observers on the scene—that many Vietnamese find it necessary to put their wives or daughters to work as bar girls or to peddle them to American soldiers as mistresses; that it is not unusual to hear a report that a Vietnamese soldier has committed suicide out of shame because his wife has been working as a bar girl; that Vietnamese have trouble getting taxicabs because drivers will not stop for them, preferring to pick up American soldiers who will pay outrageous fares without complaint; that as a result of the American influx bar girls, prostitutes, pimps, bar owners, and taxi drivers have risen to the higher levels of the economic pyramid; that middle-class Vietnamese families have difficulty renting homes because Americans have driven the rents beyond their reach, and some Vietnamese families have actually been evicted from houses and apartments by landlords who prefer to rent to the affluent Americans; that Vietnamese civil servants, junior army officers, and enlisted men are unable to support their families because of the inflation generated by American spending and the purchasing power of the G.I.s. One Vietnamese explained to the *New York Times* reporter that "Any time legions of prosperous white men descend on a rudimentary Asian society, you are bound to have trouble." Another said: "We Vietnamese are somewhat xenophobe. We don't like foreigners, any kind of foreigners, so that you shouldn't be surprised that we don't like you."[9]

Sincere though it is, the American effort to build the foundations of freedom in South Vietnam is thus having an effect quite different from the one intended. "All this struggling and striving to make the world better is a great mistake," said George Bernard Shaw, "not because it isn't a good thing to improve the world if you know how to do it, but because striving and struggling is the worst way you could set about doing anything."[10]

One wonders how much the American commitment to Vietnamese freedom is also a commitment to American pride—the two seem to have become part of the same package. When we talk about the freedom of South Vietnam, we may be thinking about how disagreeable it would be to accept a solution short of victory; we may be thinking about how our pride would be injured if we settled for less than we set out to achieve; we may be thinking about our reputation as a great power, fearing that a compromise settlement would shame us before the world, marking us as a second-rate people with flagging courage and determination.

Such fears are as nonsensical as their opposite, the presumption of a universal mission. They are simply unworthy of the richest, most powerful, most productive, and best educated people in the world. One

[9] Neil Sheehan, "Anti-Americanism Grows in Vietnam," *The New York Times*, April 24, 1966, p. 3.
[10] George Bernard Shaw, *Cashel Byron's Profession* (1886), Chapter 5.

can understand an uncompromising attitude on the part of such countries as China or France: both have been struck low in this century and a certain amount of arrogance may be helpful to them in recovering their pride. It is much less comprehensible on the part of the United States—a nation whose modern history has been an almost uninterrupted chronicle of success, a nation which by now should be so sure of its own power as to be capable of magnanimity, a nation which by now should be able to act on the proposition that, as George Kennan said, "there is more respect to be won in the opinion of the world by a resolute and courageous liquidation of unsound positions than in the most stubborn pursuit of extravagant or unpromising objectives."[11]

The cause of our difficulties in Southeast Asia is not a deficiency of power but an excess of the wrong kind of power, which results in a feeling of impotence when it fails to achieve its desired ends. We are still acting like Boy Scouts dragging reluctant old ladies across streets they do not want to cross. We are trying to remake Vietnamese society, a task which certainly cannot be accomplished by force and which probably cannot be accomplished by any means available to outsiders. The objective may be desirable, but it is not feasible. As Shaw said: "Religion is a great force—the only real motive force in the world; but what you fellows don't understand is that you must get at a man through his own religion and not through yours."[12]

With the best intentions in the world the United States has involved itself deeply in the affairs of developing nations in Asia and Latin America, practicing what has been called a kind of "welfare imperialism." Our honest purpose is the advancement of development and democracy, to which end it has been thought necessary to destroy ancient and unproductive modes of life. In this latter function we have been successful, perhaps more successful than we know. Bringing skills and knowledge, money and resources in amounts hitherto unknown in traditional societies, the Americans have overcome indigenous groups and interests and become the dominant force in a number of countries. Far from being bumbling, wasteful, and incompetent, as critics have charged, American government officials, technicians, and economists have been strikingly successful in breaking down the barriers to change in ancient but fragile cultures.

Here, however, our success ends. Traditional rulers, institutions, and

[11] George F. Kennan, "Supplemental Foreign Assistance Fiscal Year 1966—Vietnam," *Hearings Before the Committee on Foreign Relations,* United States Senate, 89th Congress, 2nd Session on S. 2793, Part I (Washington: U.S. Government Printing Office, 1966), p. 335.
[12] George Bernard Shaw, *Getting Married* (1911).

ways of life have crumbled under the fatal impact of American wealth and power but they have not been replaced by new institutions and new ways of life, nor has their breakdown ushered in an era of democracy and development. It has rather ushered in an era of disorder and demoralization because in the course of destroying old ways of doing things, we have also destroyed the self-confidence and self-reliance without which no society can build indigenous institutions. Inspiring as we have such great awe of our efficiency and wealth, we have reduced some of the intended beneficiaries of our generosity to a condition of dependency and self-denigration. We have done this for the most part inadvertently: with every good intention we have intruded on fragile societies, and our intrusion, though successful in uprooting traditional ways of life, has been strikingly unsuccessful in implanting the democracy and advancing the development which are the honest aims of our "welfare imperialism."

## AMERICAN EMPIRE OR AMERICAN EXAMPLE?

Despite its dangerous and unproductive consequences, the idea of being responsible for the whole world seems to be flattering to Americans and I am afraid it is turning our heads, just as the sense of universal responsibility turned the heads of ancient Romans and nineteenth-century British.

In 1965 Henry Fairlie, a British political writer for *The Spectator* and *The Daily Telegraph*, wrote what he called "A Cheer for American Imperialism."[13] An empire, he said, "has no justification except its own existence." It must never contract; it "wastes treasure and life"; its commitments "are without rhyme or reason." Nonetheless, according to Fairlie, the "American empire" is uniquely benevolent, devoted as it is to individual liberty and the rule of law, and having performed such services as getting the author released from a Yugoslav jail simply by his threatening to involve the American Consul, a service which he describes as "sublime."

What romantic nonsense this is. And what dangerous nonsense in the age of nuclear weapons. The idea of an "American empire" might be dismissed as the arrant imagining of a British Gunga Din except that it surely strikes a responsive chord in at least a corner of the usually sensible and humane American mind. It calls to mind the slogans of the past about the shot fired at Concord being heard 'round the world, about "manifest destiny" and "making the world safe for democracy," and the demand for "unconditional surrender" in World War II. It calls to

[13] *The New York Times Magazine*, July 11, 1965.

mind President McKinley taking counsel with the Supreme Being about his duty to the benighted Filipinos.

The "Blessings-of-Civilization Trust," as Mark Twain called it, may have been a "Daisy" in its day, uplifting for the soul and good for business besides, but its day is past. It is past because the great majority of the human race is demanding dignity and independence, not the honor of a supine role in an American empire. It is past because whatever claim America may make for the universal domain of her ideas and values is balanced by the communist counter-claim, armed like our own with nuclear weapons. And, most of all, it is past because it never should have begun, because we are not God's chosen saviour of mankind but only one of mankind's more successful and fortunate branches, endowed by our Creator with about the same capacity for good and evil, no more or less, than the rest of humanity.

An excessive preoccupation with foreign relations over a long period of time is more than a manifestation of arrogance; it is a drain on the power that gave rise to it, because it diverts a nation from the sources of its strength, which are in its domestic life. A nation immersed in foreign affairs is expending its capital, human as well as material; sooner or later that capital must be renewed by some diversion of creative energies from foreign to domestic pursuits. I would doubt that any nation has achieved a durable greatness by conducting a "strong" foreign policy, but many have been ruined by expending their energies in foreign adventures while allowing their domestic bases to deteriorate. The United States emerged as a world power in the twentieth century, not because of what it had done in foreign relations but because it had spent the nineteenth century developing the North American continent; by contrast, the Austrian and Turkish empires collapsed in the twentieth century in large part because they had so long neglected their internal development and organization.

If America has a service to perform in the world—and I believe she has—it is in large part the service of her own example. In our excessive involvement in the affairs of other countries we are not only living off our assets and denying our own people the proper enjoyment of their resources, we are also denying the world the example of a free society enjoying its freedom to the fullest. This is regrettable indeed for a nation that aspires to teach democracy to other nations, because, as Edmund Burke said, "Example is the school of mankind, and they will learn at no other."[14]

The missionary instinct in foreign affairs may, in a curious way, reflect a deficiency rather than an excess of national self-confidence. In

[14] Edmund Burke, "On a Regicide Peace" (1796).

America's case the evidence of a lack of self-confidence is our apparent need for constant proof and reassurance, our nagging desire for popularity, our bitterness and confusion when foreigners fail to appreciate our generosity and good intentions. Lacking an appreciation of the dimensions of our own power, we fail to understand our enormous and disruptive impact on the world; we fail to understand that no matter how good our intentions—and they are, in most cases, decent enough—other nations are alarmed by the very existence of such great power, which, whatever its benevolence, cannot help but remind them of their own helplessness before it.

Those who lack self-assurance are also likely to lack magnanimity, because the one is the condition of the other. Only a nation at peace with itself, with its transgressions as well as its achievements, is capable of a generous understanding of others. Only when we Americans can acknowledge our own past aggressive behavior—in such instances, for example, as the Indian wars and the wars against Mexico and Spain— will we acquire some perspective on the aggressive behavior of others; only when we can understand the human implications of the chasm between American affluence and the poverty of most of the rest of mankind will we be able to understand why the American "way of life" which is so dear to us has few lessons and limited appeal to the poverty-stricken majority of the human race.

It is a curiosity of human nature that lack of self-assurance seems to breed an exaggerated sense of power and mission. When a nation is very powerful but lacking in self-confidence, it is likely to behave in a manner dangerous to itself and to others. Feeling the need to prove what is obvious to everyone else, it begins to confuse great power with unlimited power and great responsibility with total responsibility: it can admit of no error; it must win every argument, no matter how trivial. For lack of an appreciation of how truly powerful it is, the nation begins to lose wisdom and perspective and, with them, the strength and understanding that it takes to be magnanimous to smaller and weaker nations.

Gradually but unmistakably America is showing signs of that arrogance of power which has afflicted, weakened, and in some cases destroyed great nations in the past. In so doing we are not living up to our capacity and promise as a civilized example for the world. The measure of our falling short is the measure of the patriot's duty of dissent.

•   •   •

AN IDEA MANKIND CAN HOLD TO

Favored as it is, by history, by wealth, and by the vitality and basic decency of its diverse population, it is conceivable, though hardly likely, that America will do something that no other great nation has ever tried to do—to effect a fundamental change in the nature of international relations. It has been my purpose . . . to suggest some ways in which we might proceed with this great work. All that I have proposed in these pages—that we make ourselves the friend of social revolution, that we make our own society an example of human happiness, that we go beyond simple reciprocity in the effort to reconcile hostile worlds—has been based on two major premises: first, that, at this moment in history at which the human race has become capable of destroying itself, it is not merely desirable but essential that the competitive instinct of nations be brought under control; and second, that America, as the most powerful nation, is the only nation equipped to lead the world in an effort to change the nature of its politics.

If we accept this leadership, we will have contributed to the world "an idea mankind can hold to." Perhaps that idea can be defined as the proposition that the nation performs its essential function not in its capacity as a *power*, but in its capacity as a *society*, or, to put it simply, that the primary business of the nation is not itself but its people.

Obviously, to bring about fundamental changes in the world we would have to take certain chances: we would have to take the chance that other countries could not so misinterpret a generous initiative on our part as to bring about a calamity; we would have to take a chance that later if not sooner, nations which have been hostile to us would respond to reason and decency with reason and decency. The risks involved are great but they are far less than the risks of traditional methods of international relations in the nuclear age.

If we are interested in bringing about fundamental changes in the world, we must start by resolving some critical questions of our foreign relations: Are we to be the friend or the enemy of the social revolutions of Asia, Africa, and Latin America? Are we to regard the communist countries as more or less normal states with whom we can have more or less normal relations, or are we to regard them indiscriminately as purveyors of an evil ideology with whom we can never reconcile? And finally, are we to regard ourselves as a friend, counselor, and example for those around the world who seek freedom and who also want our help, or are we to play the role of God's avenging angel, the appointed missionary of freedom in a benighted world?

The answers to these questions depend on which of the two Americas is speaking. There are no inevitable or predetermined answers because our past has prepared us to be either tolerant or puritanical, generous or selfish, sensible or romantic, humanly concerned or morally obsessed, in our relations with the outside world.

For my own part, I prefer the America of Lincoln and Adlai Stevenson. I prefer to have my country the friend rather than the enemy of demands for social justice; I prefer to have the communists treated as human beings, with all the human capacity for good and bad, for wisdom and folly, rather than as embodiments of an evil abstraction; and I prefer to see my country in the role of sympathetic friend to humanity rather than its stern and prideful schoolmaster.

There are many respects in which America, if she can bring herself to act with the magnanimity and the empathy which are appropriate to her size and power, can be an intelligent example to the world. We have the opportunity to set an example of generous understanding in our relations with China, of practical cooperation for peace in our relations with Russia, of reliable and respectful partnership in our relations with Western Europe, of material helpfulness without moral presumption in our relations with developing nations, of abstention from the temptations of hegemony in our relations with Latin America, and of the all-around advantages of minding one's own business in our relations with everybody. Most of all, we have the opportunity to serve as an example of democracy to the world by the way in which we run our own society. America, in the words of John Quincy Adams, should be "the well-wisher to the freedom and independence of all" but "the champion and vindicator only of her own."[15]

If we can bring ourselves so to act, we will have overcome the dangers of the arrogance of power. It would involve, no doubt, the loss of certain glories, but that seems a price worth paying for the probable rewards, which are the happiness of America and the peace of the world.

[15] John Quincy Adams, July 4, 1821, Washington, D.C. Reported in *The National Intelligencer*, July 11, 1821.

ZBIGNIEW   BRZEZINSKI

*The Implications of Change*
*for United States Foreign Policy*

International politics is dominated by crises. The result is that we often mistake these crises for the reality of international politics. Going from crisis to crisis, we simply lose sight of the more basic and often more important changes that imperceptibly reshape the world in which we live.

It is useful, therefore, sometimes to pause and ask in a detached way: What is the nature of our era? What is really changing in international politics? By posing these questions we become better equipped to discuss the implications of historical trends for U.S. foreign policy. Definition of a broad framework of that kind in turn enables us to see in sharper relief our true interests and goals in specific regions of the world, such as Europe or Asia. Accordingly, in these remarks I would like to first turn to the problem of change in international politics and then discuss the implications of these changes for the U.S. posture in world affairs.

As I look at international politics, I see five major changes taking place, together fundamentally altering the nature of international relations in our day. The changes are not obvious, because they are slow; but their cumulative impact is most important.

SOURCE: Zbigniew Brzezinski, "The Implications of Change for United States Foreign Policy," *The Department of State Bulletin*, LVII (July 3, 1967), 19–23.

## WANING OF IDEOLOGICAL CONFLICTS

1. *The first involves the waning of ideological conflicts among the more developed nations of the world.*

Since the time of the French Revolution, conflicts between states have been profoundly emotionalized by mass struggles induced by a mixture of ideology and nationalism. Where that mixture was particularly intense, as in the case of nazism, the conflicts which resulted were particularly bloody and destructive. By and large, during the last 150 years or so relations among the more advanced states, particularly in Europe, have been poisoned by the emotionalizing impact of absolute doctrinal answers concerning most of the basic issues of humanity.

This condition is waning due to a variety of factors.

First of all, nuclear weapons have necessitated greater and greater restraint in relations among states. The realization of the enormous destructiveness of nuclear conflict has had a most sobering effect on statesmen. Hitherto one could calculate the cost and the potential advantages of war; today, this simply is no longer possible, and thus even the most bitter ideological hatreds have to be restrained by common sense.

Secondly, just as important, we are realizing more fully that social change is such an enormously complex and interrelated process, with so many variables, that it cannot be reduced to a few simple ideological formulas, as was the case in the early stages of industrialization. Ideological attitudes are thus giving way to a problem-solving, engineering approach to social change.

Thirdly, communism, the principal, and until recently the most militant, revolutionary ideology of our day, is dead—communism is dead as an ideology in the sense that it is no longer capable of mobilizing unified global support. On the contrary, it is increasingly fragmented by conflicts among constituent units and parties. This has contributed to ideological disillusionment among its members. Communist states, Communist movements, and Communist subversion are still very important on the international scene, but Communist ideology as a vital force is no longer with us.

Revolutionary movements in different parts of the world instead relate themselves more specifically to local radical traditions and try to exploit local opportunities. Thus, the common doctrine and its alleged universal validity are being diluted by specific adaptations. The process is destroying the universal appeal and global effectiveness of ideology.

All of that, cumulatively, prompts the waning of the ideological age in relations, particularly among the developed nations. The role of ideology is still quite important in relations among the less developed states, where problems are simpler, where issues can be translated into black-and-white propositions, and where absolute doctrinal categories still appear superficially relevant.

## SHIFT IN FOCUS OF VIOLENCE

2. *Closely connected with the waning ideological conflicts among the more developed nations of the world is the decline of violence among these states.* During approximately the last 150 years, the international scene has been dominated by conflicts fought principally among the more advanced and largely European nations of the world. The focus of violence today is shifting to the third world. Increasingly, conflicts are either between some of the developed nations and the less developed nations; or increasingly, instability in the underdeveloped world is itself the source of global tensions. It is thus a basic reversal of the dominant pattern of the recent past.

The new restraint on violence displayed by the more advanced states in relations among one another is also largely due to the nuclear age. It should be acknowledged that without the presence of nuclear weapons a major war probably would have erupted in the course of the last 20 years. Given the range of conflicts, the frequent tensions, and the occasional clashes between the United States and the Soviet Union, in almost any other era in history a war between them probably would have ensued. The presence of nuclear weapons has introduced an overriding factor of restraint into relations among the more advanced states and has helped to preserve world peace.

This restraint is still largely absent insofar as relations among the less developed states are concerned. Moreover, the ideological passions and the nationalist tensions have not yet run their full course; and consequently the propensity toward total reactions, total commitment, and total violence is still quite high.

Without discussing the pros and cons of the Vietnamese war, it offers a good example of the generalization made above. It reflects the shift of focus in global affairs from conflicts between the developed states to a conflict that involves a wealthy and highly advanced country in an effort to create regional stability. The unwillingness of the Soviet Union to become totally involved in the conflict stems from the greater realization of its own interest in preserving peace in the nuclear age and also from the gradual waning of its ideology, which weakens its sense of total identification with every revolutionary movement in the world.

## TREND TOWARD POSTNATIONALISM

3. *The third generalization is the proposition that we are witnessing the end of the supremacy of the nation-state on the international scene.*

This process is far from consummated, but nonetheless the trend seems to me to be irreversible. It is not only a matter of security inter-dependence among allied states. It is also a matter of psychological change. People through history have expanded their sense of identification. At first, men identified themselves with their families, then with their villages, then with their towns, then with their regions and provinces, then with their nations. Now increasingly people are beginning to identify with their continents and regions. This change has been induced by the necessities of economic development and of the technological revolution, by changes in the means of communication—all of which cause people to identify themselves more and more with wider, more global human interests.

### GLOBAL POWER OF THE UNITED STATES

4. *The fourth major change which has taken place in our times is the emergence of the United States as the preponderant world power.* The conventional view is that since 1945 we have seen three basic stages of international development: First of all, U.S. nuclear monopoly; secondly, bipolarity, based on two homogeneous alliances rigidly confronting each other; and now increasingly polycentrism, with many states playing the international game.

I submit that this is a wrong perspective; in fact, the sequence has been the opposite. The first postwar era—1945-50—was essentially a polycentric era. The United States was largely disarmed. It had a nuclear monopoly, to be sure, but its nuclear power was essentially apocalyptic; it was not applicable—it was only usable in circumstances which everyone wished to avoid—hence it was not politically relevant. The United States was disarmed, it was only beginning to be involved in Europe, hardly involved in Asia—and there were still two major empires on the scene, the French and the British. The Russians were asserting their regional control over Central Europe, but they were not yet involved in Asia. Asia itself was in turmoil. This truly was the polycentric era.

It gave way to the era of bipolarity, of dichotomic confrontation, if you will, between two alliances—one led by the Soviet Union, one led by the United States. The Soviet Union during this time acquired nuclear capacity, and under Khrushchev it misjudged its nuclear power and attempted to pursue between 1958 and 1962 a policy designed to assert Soviet global supremacy. These years were dominated by the Soviet effort to throw the West out of Berlin, to put missiles in Cuba and to force a showdown. However, Khrushchev discovered in 1962 that the Soviet Union still had only apocalyptic power. Its nuclear power was not relevant when faced with U.S. power, which by then had become much more complex and much more usable in a far greater diversity of situations.

Thus in the last few years the United States successfully stared Khrushchev down in Cuba, it protected its interests in the Dominican Republic and in the Congo—and today it is doing it in Viet-Nam. Yet the Soviet Union did not dare to react even in the area of its regional domination: Berlin. Today, the Soviet Union is in effect a regional power, concentrating primarily on Europe and on the growing danger from China. Our power during this ensuing period has become applicable power, with a long-range delivery system, with the means of asserting itself on the basis of a global reach.

Moreover, recent years—and this is much more important—have witnessed continued economic growth in this country; they have seen the expansion and appearance on the world scene of U.S. technological know-how. Increasingly, the U.S. way of life, our styles, our patterns of living, are setting the example. Today, if there is a creative society in the world, it is the United States—in the sense that everyone, very frequently without knowing it, is imitating it. However, paradoxically because the United States is the only global power, it finds it increasingly difficult to concentrate its resources or its policy on any specific region of the world. This often creates sharp dilemmas and difficulties, difficulties with which we will have to live because our involvement is also a major factor of stability in the world.

### THE GROWING FRAGMENTATION OF THE WORLD

5. *The fifth major change involves the growing fragmentation of the world, not only between the developed states and the underdeveloped—which is, of course, much talked about—but the increasing fragmentation of the developed world.* I have particularly in mind the growing difference between the United States and the rest of the advanced world. The United States is becoming a new society, a society no longer shaped by the impact of the industrial process on social, economic, and political life. That impact still shapes European life; if you look at the changes in the nature of the European political elite, if you look at problems of employment or unemployment or welfare, if you look at efforts to create greater access to education in Europe—all of these are manifestations of the impact of the industrial process on a formerly rural and traditional society.

The United States is no longer in this kind of historical era. Increasingly, our social dilemmas are of leisure, well-being, automation, psychic well-being, alienation of the youth (usually from well-to-do middle-class families). All of that is connected with a standard of living which has become relatively stable and high, connected with a society which is well-to-do but in many respects has new dilemmas of purpose and meaning. We are becoming, in effect, a post-industrial society, in which computers and communications are shaping more and more our way of life. Our education and our image of the world are shaped more by television and less and less by sequential, logical media such as books and newspapers. If the Europeans are today experiencing the automobile revolution—which extends physical mobility—Americans are undergoing an electronic revolution, which extends our senses and nervous systems.

All of this induces new perspectives and new attitudes and sharpens the difference between us and the rest of the developed world. It also creates underlying tension, in addition to the obvious problems of foreign policy, such as the Kennedy Round, the problem of NATO, the problem of East-West relations, and so forth.

## U.S. FOREIGN POLICY IN A TIME OF CHANGE

If there is any merit in this highly generalized analysis of the nature of change in our time, what are its implications for U.S. foreign policy?

First of all, we should not become ideological latecomers. We have traditionally been the pragmatic society, free of ideological shackles. It would be unfortunate if now we succumbed to internal and external ideologization, either because of belated anti-Communist rigidity at a time when the Communist world is becoming fragmented or because of radical reactions to internal dilemmas, the new dilemmas of our society that I spoke about. It would be unfortunate if these new dilemmas, inherent in the United States' becoming a new type of society, were responded to on the basis of essentially irrelevant, outmoded, 19th-century ideological formulations. Yes, this is the great danger, particularly with the New Left, which is looking for ideological guidance and only too often turns to outmoded anarchistic, Trotskyite, or nihilistic doctrines, doctrines completely irrelevant to the new dilemmas of our society.

Secondly, in our foreign policy we ought to avoid the prescriptions of the extreme right or the extreme left. The right only too often says, erroneously, that to protect a better America we ought to stay out of the world. The New Left says that to build a better America we have to stay out of the world. Both are wrong, because today our global involvement and our preponderance of power is such that our disinvolvement would create international chaos of enormous proportions. Our involvement is an historical fact—there is no way of ending it. One can debate about the forms it ought to take, about its scope and the way it is applied, but one cannot any longer debate in absolutist terms should we or should we not be involved.

Thirdly, we should not underestimate, because of our own historical formation, the role of revolutionary nationalism in the world. While we have to pursue the task of building a world of cooperative communities, we have to realize that revolutionary nationalism is a stage of development which in many cases cannot be avoided. We should therefore be very careful not to get overinvolved in conflicts, with the result that we are pitched against revolutionary nationalisms, making us appear as impediments to social change.

This raises the extremely complicated issue of intervention. Under what conditions should we or should we not intervene? It is extraordinarily difficult to define clear-cut criteria; but as a broad generalization, it might be said that intervention is justified whenever its absence will create regional instability of expanding proportions. It has to be judged largely on its international merits and not in terms of specific domestic consequences within individual states. It is that distinction which justifies intervention—it is that distinction which warrants our involvement today in the effort to create regional stability in Southeast Asia.

Fourthly, in seeking ties with the developed nations of the world, particularly with Western Europe, we have to emphasize in addition to specific political and security arrangements, increasingly efforts addressed to the fundamental social dilemmas which are inherent in the widening gap between the United States and Western Europe. We ought to try to share and distribute our new knowledge and technological skills, because this is the unique asset of the postindustrial society. At the same time we should try to make the industrial societies more aware of the novel character of our problems. By learning from us they can perhaps avoid some of our difficulties. We have to forge new social bonds, especially between our younger generation and the younger Europeans—and urgently so, for we are at a time in history when the two continents find themselves in different historical eras.

Finally, to apply these remarks cumulatively and briefly to Europe: Since the ideological age is waning, since the developed world is increasingly becoming the zone of tranquillity, since the United States is playing a predominant role in the world, and since we are in a new historical era which gives us special assets, it is our task to develop a broader approach for Europe, the purpose of which . . . is to end gradually through reconciliation the cold war, a remnant of the civil war that has divided the most advanced parts of the world for the last 150 years.

Thus we need to adapt the Atlantic concept to the post-cold-war era. We should strive increasingly to shape a community of the developed nations which will contain four basic components: The United States;

a more homogeneous and integrated Western Europe in close ties with the United States but also in increasingly close linkage with Eastern Europe; an Eastern Europe which will gradually begin to stand on its own feet and engage in subregional integration more independently of the Soviet Union while in turn retaining its ties with the Soviet Union; a Soviet Union which would also be drawn into constructive relationships with Western Europe and the United States.

Only by developing such a community of the developed nations, of which Japan should naturally be a member, can we try to assure a measure of order to a world which otherwise will be increasingly dominated by chaos.

If we look 20 years ahead, we can see clearly a challenge to the survival of organized society in several parts of the world. When we look 20 years ahead in the developed parts of the world and particularly in the United States, where the scientific, technological, medical, and chemical revolutions are progressing most rapidly, we can increasingly see a challenge to the individual as a mysterious, autonomous human being.

We cannot effectively respond to these twin challenges if we are at the same time pre-occupied with ideological and doctrinal conflicts which no longer have much relevance to the fundamental concerns of our day. Given the traditional American quest for human freedom and today's U.S. global power, we have the opportunity and the responsibility to take the lead in responding to these twin challenges.


## STUDY QUESTIONS


1. What foreign policy direction should the United States pursue in a changing world? Consider conflicting viewpoints among the American people discussed by Needler, and the major changes in patterns of international politics traced by Brzezinski.

2. Discuss the meaning of the policy of "containment" and evaluate its success, through specific examples, for American foreign policy.

3. What is the substance of the argument that peaceful relations with the Soviet Union have become increasingly possible because of the latter's growing contentment with the status quo and the existence of common interests between the United States and the Soviet Union? Is this viewpoint corroborated by President Kennedy's address?

4. Does Fulbright's concept of the "arrogance of power" provide a convincing explanation of anti-Americanism in various parts of the world? What courses of action might be followed in alleviating anti-Americanism?

5. Do the American and Russian revolutions offer any "lesson" to the leaders of developing societies in Asia, Africa, and Latin America? Is American policy in Vietnam and the developing areas consistent with your understanding of the American revolutionary heritage?

## SUGGESTIONS FOR FURTHER READING

ALMOND, GABRIEL A. *The American People and Foreign Policy.* New York: Harcourt, Brace & World, 1956.

BURDETTE, FRANKLIN L., (ed.). *Conduct of American Diplomacy.* Princeton: D. Van Nostrand, 1967.

CARLETON, WILLIAM G. *The Revolution in American Foreign Policy.* New York: Random House, 1963.

CARROLL, HOLBERT N. *The House of Representatives and Foreign Affairs.* Rev. ed. Boston: Little, Brown and Company, 1966.

CRABB, CECIL V., Jr. *American Foreign Policy in the Nuclear Age.* 2nd ed., New York: Harper & Row, 1965.

DAHL, ROBERT A. *Congress and Foreign Policy.* New York: Harcourt, Brace & World, 1950.

FULBRIGHT, J. WILLIAM. *The Arrogance of Power.* New York: Random House, 1966.

———. *Old Myths and New Realities.* New York: Random House, 1964.

HILSMAN, ROGER, and ROBERT GOOD (eds.). *Foreign Policy in the Sixties: The Issues and the Instruments.* Baltimore: Johns Hopkins Press, 1965.

KISSINGER, HENRY A. *The Necessity for Choice: Prospects of American Foreign Policy.* New York: Harper & Row, 1961.

LERCHE, CHARLES O., Jr. *Foreign Policy of the American People.* 2nd ed. Englewood Cliffs: Prentice-Hall, 1961.

PERKINS, DEXTER. *The American Approach to Foreign Policy.* London: Oxford University Press, 1962.

PERKINS, DEXTER. *America's Quest for Peace.* Bloomington: Indiana University Press, 1962.

ROBINSON, JAMES A. *Congress and Foreign Policy-Making.* 2nd ed. Homewood, Illinois: Dorsey Press, 1967.

WESTERFIELD, BRADFORD. *The Instruments of America's Foreign Policy.* New York: Thomas Y. Crowell, 1963.

# PART SIX □ WORLD ORDER: PROBLEMS AND PROSPECTS OF TRANSFORMATION

$R$ELATIONS among states are characterized by competition, cooperation, conflict, and accommodation. On the international scene where states of varying political, economic, social, and ideological systems must co-exist, some kind of international law and/or organization is simply inevitable. International law and international politics are intertwined because civilized nations in their relations with one another are presumed to operate within a certain accepted body of rules or principles.

The framers of the United Nations Organization pledged themselves to establish peace where all nations can live safely and "in freedom from fear and want." They also stated in the Atlantic Charter their aim to establish a permanent and wider system of general security. The task of the United Nations is to maintain international peace and security and remove threats to international peace and order by peaceful means. The organization is designed to develop friendly relations and encourage cooperation among nations in solving problems of an economic, social, cultural, and humanitarian nature. The United Nations is to serve as the center for harmonizing the actions of nations as they seek to attain these goals.

The task of the United Nations was hampered from the start by big power conflicts and ideological struggle. Its efforts to promote and solve economic, social, and humanitarian problems also have been hampered by civil wars, internal discord, strife, and hatred. The fact that the United Nations has been able to survive in a divided political world and exercise moral influence in averting major war is significant. What the United Nations can accomplish will depend on cooperation among nations. The late President John F. Kennedy remarked in 1961 that:

Never have the nations of the world had so much to lose—or so much to gain. Together we shall save our planet, or together we shall perish in its flames.

*383*

Save it we can—and save it we must—and then shall we earn the eternal thanks of mankind and, as peacemakers, the eternal blessing of God.

The selections in this part deal with various views of the United Nations, United Nations diplomacy, the role of regionalism and the United Nations, the old international law and the new, the concept of community, and the future of the United Nations.

In his annual report to the General Assembly shortly before his death, Secretary-General Dag Hammarskjöld, expressed his perception of how members of the United Nations view the role of the organization and its place in the international arena. He stated that there are those who view the organization as static conference machinery for discussing conflicts in the hope of achieving peaceful coexistence. On the other hand, there are those who view the United Nations as a dynamic instrument entrusted by its members with the responsibility for solving conflicts of interests by peaceful means "in a spirit of objectivity and in implementation of the principles and purposes of the Charter." Hammarskjöld believed that the former view "can refer to history and to the traditions of national policies of the past" while the latter view "can point to the needs of the present and of the future" in an interdependent world where nation-states possess instruments of destruction hitherto unknown in the past. The late Secretary-General believed that the second view of the organization is more in consonance with the purposes and principles of the United Nations. He presented an analysis of the principles of the organization, and the character of its decisions and its structure. He concluded that the United Nations is a crucial instrument for peace and world order in a divided political world.

Diplomacy has been defined as the "business of communicating between governments." Diplomacy is the most important instrument used by nation-states in the management of their international relations. Prior to World War I diplomacy was mainly secret. Negotiations and sometimes the substance of specific proposals remained undisclosed. After World War I reformers like Woodrow Wilson called for open covenants and condemned private understandings of any kind. Wilson asserted the right of the people to know what commitments, obligations, and promises their governments had made, insisting that governments in Western democracies are responsible to the people and their representatives.

In the article, "United Nations Diplomacy," Thomas Hovet, Jr., states that a blending of public and quiet diplomacy is displayed at the United Nations. This mixture of public and quiet diplomacy, giving uniqueness to United Nations diplomacy, has been influenced by three factors: 1) the growth of the role of the Secretary-General; 2) the establishment of permanent missions; and 3) the development of blocs and groups. In addition, Hovet discusses diplomatic functions as manifested by the experience, skill, and orientation of individual delegates.

Francis O. Wilcox, in his article, "Regionalism and the United Nations," discusses the role that regional organizations might play in conjunction with the United Nations in maintaining peace and security. He alludes to three fundamental concessions made by the framers of the United Nations in the direction of regionalism. The intent of the framers of the organization, he notes, was to establish a flexible framework whereby the United Nations and regional organizations can function harmoniously. In his analysis of relationships between the United Nations and the regional organizations, he states that both the North Atlantic Treaty Organization (NATO), and the Southeast Asian Treaty Organization (SEATO) "neglected to establish any regional relationship or commitments of this kind." Nations deemphasize the need for coordinating regional actions with the United Nations and emphasize the importance of independent action. Wilcox notes that with the exception of the Organization of American States (OAS) and the Organization of African Unity (OAU), regional organizations have been far less active in the peaceful solution of disputes than the framers of the United Nations had hoped. The author discusses the reasons why most regional organizations have played a limited role in the peaceful settlement of disputes.

Wilcox states that in the view of some members, there have been "highly disturbing changes" in the relationship between the United Nations and regional organizations with regard to enforcement actions. He concludes, however, that neither regional organizations nor the United Nations have functioned effectively particularly with regard to peaceful settlement of disputes. Yet, despite many unresolved disputes in the international arena, nuclear war has been averted. "To that extent," he adds, "the deterring power of some of our regional agencies coupled with the moral force and the peacekeeping activities of the United Nations have been successful."

The next selection moves from a general discussion of the United Nations and regionalism to an examination of international law and order. In his article, "International Law: The Old and The New," Charles G. Fenwick notes that the old international law failed and that rules such as neutrality proved to be inconsistent and irrational. An inconclusive line was drawn between the old international law and the new when Woodrow Wilson called for a system of collective security for the maintenance of peace. However, the first step toward the new international law was taken on January 1, 1942, when the United Nations Declaration was signed. Later, the Atlantic Charter laid the foundation for a general system of collective security. The United Nations Charter speaks not only of collective security but also of the peaceful settlement of international disputes. Fenwick points out that although on the issue of collective security the new international law is ineffective, both the Security Council and the General Assembly exercise a strong moral influence upon the preservation and maintenance of peace and order. Fenwick concludes that despite the tendency to develop international law and encourage cooperation among nations, the future of world order and law is dim due to the "invention of the new instruments of destruction."

In the final article Richard W. Van Wagenen states that the United Nations "is a community-building institution." On the whole, he adds, the United Nations is not a security-community, although it is moving toward the eventual building of such a community. He believes that the integrative works of the United Nations system should be strengthened by taking on tasks which can be successfully handled and which appear to add to the authority and legitimacy of the United Nations system.

DAG HAMMARSKJÖLD

# Two Differing Concepts
# of United Nations Assayed

## I

Debates and events during the year since the publication of the last report to the General Assembly have brought to the fore different concepts of the United Nations, the character of the Organization, its authority and its structure.

On the one side, it has in various ways become clear that certain members conceive of the Organization as a static conference machinery for resolving conflicts of interest and ideologies with a view to peaceful coexistence, within the Charter, to be served by a Secretariat which is

SOURCE: Dag Hammarskjöld, "Two Differing Concepts of United Nations Assayed," *United Nations Review*, VIII (September 1961), 12–17, 34–35.

to be regarded not as fully internationalized but as representing within its ranks those very interests and ideologies.

Other members have made it clear that they conceive of the Organization primarily as a dynamic instrument of governments through which they, jointly and for the same purpose, should seek such reconciliation but through which they should also try to develop forms of executive action, undertaken on behalf of all members, and aiming at forestalling conflicts and resolving them, once they have arisen, by appropriate diplomatic or political means, in a spirit of objectivity and in implementation of the principles and purposes of the Charter.

Naturally, the latter concept takes as its starting point the conference concept, but it regards it only as a starting point, envisaging the possibility of continued growth to increasingly effective forms of active international cooperation, adapted to experience, and served by a Secretariat of which it is required that, whatever the background and the views of its individual members, their actions be guided solely by the principles of the Charter, the decisions of the main organs and the interests of the Organization itself.

The first concept can refer to history and to the traditions of national policies of the past. The second can point to the needs of the present and of the future in a world of ever-closer international interdependence where nations have at their disposal armaments of hitherto unknown destructive strength. The first one is firmly anchored in the time-honored philosophy of sovereign national states in armed competition of which the most that may be expected in the international field is that they achieve a peaceful coexistence. The second one envisages possibilities of intergovernmental action overriding such a philosophy, and opens the road toward more developed and increasingly effective forms of constructive international cooperation.

It is clearly for the governments, members of the Organization, and for these governments only, to make their choice and decide on the direction in which they wish the Organization to develop. However, it may be appropriate to study these two concepts in terms of the purposes of the Organization as laid down in the Charter and, in this context, also to consider the character and the significance of the decisions of the Organization as well as its structure.

## II

The purposes and principles of the Charter are set out in its preamble and further developed in a series of articles, including some which may seem to be primarily of a procedural or administrative nature. Together, these parts of the Charter lay down some basic rules of international ethics by which all member states have committed themselves to be guided. To a large extent, the rules reflect standards accepted as binding for life within states. Thus, they appear, in the main, as a projection into the international arena and the international community of purposes and principles already accepted as being of national validity. In this sense, the Charter takes a first step in the direction of an organized international community, and this independently of the organs set up for international cooperation. Due to different traditions, the state of social development and the character of national institutions, wide variations naturally exist as to the application in national life of the principles reflected in the Charter, but it is not too difficult to recognize the common elements behind those differences. It is therefore not surprising that such principles of national application could be transposed into an agreed basis also for international behavior and cooperation.

In the preamble to the Charter, member nations have reaffirmed their faith "in the equal rights of men and women and of nations large and small," a principle which also has found many other expressions in the Charter.

Thus, it restates the basic democratic principle of equal political rights, independently of the position of the individual or of the member country in respect of its strength, as determined by territory, population or wealth. The words just quoted must, however, be considered as going further and imply an endorsement as well of a right to equal economic opportunities.

It is in the light of the first principle that the Charter has established a system of equal votes, expressing "the sovereign equality of all its members," and has committed the Organization to the furtherance of self-determination, self-government and independence. On the same basis, the Charter requires universal respect for an observance of human rights and fundamental freedoms for all "without distinction as to race, sex, language or religion."

It is in the light of the latter principle—or, perhaps, the latter aspect of the same basic principle—that the Charter, in Article 55, has committed the members to the promotion of higher standards of living, full employment and conditions of economic and social progress and development as well as to solutions of international economic and related problems. The pledge of all members to take joint and separate action, in cooperation with the Organization, for the achievement of these purposes has been the basis for the far-reaching economic and technical assistance channelled through or administered by the Organization, and may rightly be considered as the basic obligation reflected also in such economic and technical assistance as member governments have been giving, on a bilateral basis, outside the framework of the Organization.

It would seem that those who regard the Organization as a conference machinery, "neutral" in relation to the direction of policies on a national or international basis and serving solely as an instrument for the solution of conflicts by reconciliation, do not pay adequate attention to those essential principles of the Charter to which reference has just been made. The terms of the Charter are explicit as regards the equal political rights of nations as well as of individuals and, although this second principle may be considered only as implicit in the terms of the Charter, they are clear also as regards the demand for equal economic opportunities for all individuals and nations. So as to avoid any misunderstanding, the Charter directly states that the basic democratic principles are applicable to nations "large and small" and to individuals without distinction "as to race, sex, language and religion," qualifications that obviously could be extended to cover also other criteria such as, for example, those of an ideological character which have been used or may be used as a basis for political or economic discrimination.

In the practical work of the Organization these basic principles have been of special significance in relation to countries under colonial rule or in other ways under foreign domination. The General Assembly has translated the principles into action intended to establish through self-determination a free and independent life as sovereign states for peoples who have expressed in democratic forms their wish for such a status. Decisive action has in many cases been taken by member governments, and then the United Nations has had only to lend its support to their efforts. In other cases, the main responsibility has fallen on the Organization itself. The resolution on colonialism, adopted by the General Assembly at its fifteenth session, may be regarded as a comprehensive restatement in elaborated form of the principle laid down in the Charter. Results of developments so far have been reflected in the birth of a great number of new national states and a revolutionary widening of the membership of the Organization.

The demand for equal economic opportunities has, likewise, been—and remains—of special significance in relation to those very countries which have more recently entered the international arena as new states. This is natural in view of the fact that, mostly, they have been in an unfavorable economic position, which is reflected in a much lower per capita income, rate of capital supply and degree of technical development, while their political independence and sovereignty require a fair measure of economic stability and economic possibilities in order to gain substance and full viability.

In working for the translation into practical realities in international life of the democratic principles which are basic to the Charter, the Organization has thus assumed a most active role and it has done so with success, demonstrating both the need and the possibilities for such action.

Further, in the preamble to the Charter it is stated to be a principle and purpose of the Organization "to establish conditions under which justice and respect for the obligations arising from treaties and other sources of international law can be maintained." In these words—to which, naturally, counterparts may be found in other parts of the Charter—it gives expression to another basic democratic principle, that of the rule of law. In order to promote this principle, the Charter established the International Court of Justice, but the principle permeates the approach of the Charter to international problems far beyond the sphere of competence of the Court. As in national life, the principle of justice—which obviously implies also the principle of objectivity and equity in the consideration of all matters before the General Assembly or the Security Council—must be considered as applicable without distinction or discrimination, with one measure and one standard valid for the strong as well as for the weak. Thus, the demand of the Charter for a rule of law aims at the substitution of right for might and makes of the Organization the natural protector of rights which countries, without it, might find it more difficult to assert and to get respected.

The principle of justice can be regarded as flowing naturally from the principles of equal political rights and equal economic opportunities, but it has an independent life and carries, of itself, the world community as far in the direction of an organized international system as the two first-mentioned principles. It has deep roots in the history of the efforts of man to eliminate from international life the anarchy which he had already much earlier overcome on the national level, deeper indeed than the political and economic principles which, as is well known, were much later to get full acceptance also in national life. Long before the United Nations and long before even the League of Nations, governments were working toward a rule of justice in international life through which they hoped to establish an international community based on law, without parliamentary or executive organs, but with a judicial procedure through which law and justice could be made to apply.

The Charter states and develops the three principles mentioned here as a means to an end: "to save succeeding generations from the scourge of war." This adds emphasis to the concept, clearly implied in the Charter, of an international community for which the Organization is an instrument and an expression and in which anarchic tendencies in international life are to be curbed by the introduction of a system of equal political rights, equal economic opportunities and the rule of law. However, the

Charter goes one step further, drawing a logical conclusion both from the ultimate aim of the Organization and from the three principles. Thus, it outlaws the use of armed force "save in the common interest." Obviously, the Charter cannot, on the one side, establish a rule of law and the principle of equal rights for "nations large and small" and, on the other hand, permit the use of armed force for national ends, contrary to those principles and, therefore, not "in the common interest." Were nations, under the Charter, to be allowed, by the use of their military strength, to achieve ends contrary to the principle of the equality of members and the principle of justice, it would obviously deprive those very principles of all substance and significance. One practical expression of this approach, which may be mentioned here, is that the organs of the United Nations have consistently maintained that the use of force, contrary to the Charter as interpreted by those organs, cannot be permitted to yield results which can be accepted as valid by the Organization and as establishing new rights.

In the Charter, the right to the use of force is somewhat more extensive than may seem to be the case from a superficial reading of the phrase "save in the common interest." Thus, apart from military action undertaken pursuant to a decision of the Security Council for repression of aggression—that is, for upholding the basic Charter principles—the Charter opens the door to the use of armed force by a nation in exercise of its inherent right to resist armed attack. This is a point on which, both in theory and in practice, the development of international law is still at a very early stage. As is well known, no agreement has been reached on a definition of aggression, beyond that found in Article 2, paragraph 4, of the Charter, and the Organization has several times had to face situations in which, therefore, the rights and wrongs in a specific case of conflict have not been clarified. It would be a vitally important step forward if wider agreement could be reached regarding the criteria to be applied in order to distinguish between legitimate and illegitimate use of force. History is only too rich in examples of armed aggression claimed as action in self-defence. How could it be otherwise, when most cases of armed conflict are so deeply rooted in a history of clashes of interests and rights, even if, up to the fatal moment of the first shot, those clashes have not involved recourse to the use of armed force?

In recognition of this situation and in the light of historical experience, the Charter makes yet another projection into international life of solutions to conflicts tested in national life, and establishes the final principle that the Organization shall "bring about by peaceful means and in conformity with the principles of justice and international law, adjustment or settlement of international disputes or situations which might lead to a breach of the peace." This principle, as quoted here from Article 1 of the Charter, is further developed specifically in Article 33, which requires parties to any dispute, the consequence of which is likely to endanger the maintenance of international peace and security, to "seek a solution by negotiation, inquiry, mediation, conciliation, arbitration, judicial settlement, resort to regional agencies or arrangements, or other peaceful means of their own choice." It is in this sphere that the Security Council has had, and is likely to continue to have, its main significance, both directly as a forum before which any dispute threatening peace and security can be brought up for debate and as an organ which directly, or through appropriate agents, may assist the parties in finding a way out and, by preventive diplomacy, may forestall the outbreak of an armed conflict. It seems appropriate here to draw attention especially to the right of the Security Council under Article 40 to "call upon the parties concerned to comply with such provisional measures as it deems necessary or desirable" for the prevention of any aggravation of a situation threatening peace and security, and to the obligation of members to comply with a decision on such measures.

It is in the light of the approach to international coexistence in our world today, which is thus to be found in the Charter, that judgment has to be passed on the validity of the different conceptions of the Organization which in recent times have become increasingly apparent. As already pointed out, the basic principles regarding the political equality of nations and their right to equal economic opportunities are difficult to reconcile with the view that the Organization is to be regarded only as a conference machinery for the solution, by debate and joint decisions, of conflicts of interest or ideology. It seems even more difficult to reconcile these principles with a view according to which equality among members should be reflected in the establishment of a balance between power blocs or other groupings of nations. The same difficulty is apparent as regards the principle of justice and the principle of prohibiting the use of armed force. It is easier to apply the conference concept to the principle of prevention of conflict through negotiation, but also on this point the difficulties become considerable if it is recognized that such solutions as may be sought by the Organization should be solutions based on the rules of equality and justice.

## III

The General Assembly, the Security Council and other collective organs of the United Nations have features in common with a standing international diplomatic conference, but their procedures go beyond the forms of such a conference and show aspects of a parliamentary or quasi-parliamentary character.

While decisions of a conference, in order to commit its participants, must be based on their subsequent acceptance of the decisions, the organs of the United Nations act on the basis of voting, with the decisions being adopted if supported by a majority. However, the decisions of the Assembly have, as regards member states, only the character of recommendations (except for financial assessments and certain other types of organizational action) so that obligations like those arising out of an agreement, coming into force after a conference, do not normally flow from them. But although the decisions, legally, are only recommendations, they introduce an important element by expressing a majority consensus on the issue under consideration.

Naturally, such a formula leaves scope for a gradual development in practice of the weight of the decisions. To the extent that more respect, in fact, is shown to General Assembly recommendations by the member states, they may come more and more close to being recognized as decisions having a binding effect on those concerned, particularly when they involve the application of the binding principles of the Charter and of international law.

Both those who regard a gradual increase in the weight of decisions of the General Assembly as necessary, if progress is to be registered in the direction of organized peaceful coexistence within the Charter, and those who oppose such a development, have to recognize that, with certain variations in individual cases, the practice still is very close to the restrictive Charter formula. Experience shows that even countries which have voted for a certain decision may, later on, basing themselves on its character of merely being a recommendation, refuse to follow it or fail to support its implementation, financially or in other respects.

What has been said applies generally to the collective organs of the Organization, but, as is well known, the Charter has gone one step further beyond the conference concept, in the direction of the parliamentary concept, in the case of the Security Council. In Article 25 member states of the United Nations have agreed to "accept and carry out the decisions of the Security Council in accordance with the present Charter," thus, by agreement, making the decisions of the Council mandatory, except, of course, when such decisions take the form of "recommendations" within the terms of Chapter VI or certain other Articles of the Charter. They have further, in Article 49, undertaken to "join in affording mutual assistance in carrying out the measures decided upon by the Security Council."

This agreed mandatory nature of certain Security Council decisions might have led to a demand for unanimity in the Council, a unanimity which was the rule for the Council of the League of Nations. Even so, however, the arrangement would have gone beyond the conference principle with its requirement that no decision reached in an international organ should be binding on an individual member short of his agreement. With the present arrangements, requiring a majority of [nine] and the concurring votes of the permanent members, a bridge between the traditional conference approach and a parliamentary approach is provided by the commitment in Article 25 to agree to the carrying out of the decisions in the Council which should be considered as giving the Council its authority by general delegation as indeed stated in Article 24, paragraph 1.

What clearly remains within the Council of the traditional conference and agreement pattern is the condition that its decisions of a nonprocedural character must be supported by the unanimous vote of the five permanent members, thus avoiding for those members the risk of being bound by a decision of the Council which has not met with their agreement. It may be observed that this special position for the permanent members, apart from other reasons, has the justification that, without such a rule, the other members of the organization, in complying with a Security Council decision, might find themselves unwillingly drawn into a big power conflict.

In spite of the delegated authority which the Council may be considered as exercising, and the condition that decisions must be agreed to by the permanent members, the experience of the Organization, as regards the implementation of Council decisions, is uneven and does not indicate full acceptance in practice of Article 25. In this case also, examples can be given of a tendency to regard decisions, even when taken under Chapter VII, as recommendations binding only to the extent that the party concerned has freely committed itself to carry them out; there is here a clear dichotomy between the aims of the Charter and the general political practice at its present stage of development. Such cases refer not only to members outside the Council, or, perhaps, members inside the Council, who have not supported a specific decision, but also to members within the Council who have cast their votes in favor of a decision but who later on are found to reserve for themselves at least a right to interpret the decision in ways which seem to be at variance with the intentions of the Council. The ambiguity of this situation emerges with special force in cases where such attitudes have been taken by permanent members of the Council, who are considered to shoulder the responsibility for the maintenance of peace and security which is reflected in the special position they hold within the Council. Obviously, the problem whether the intended legal weight is given to decisions of the Security Council arises in practice not only in cases of noncompliance but also in cases of a refusal to shoulder the financial consequences of a decision of the Council.

These observations—which have been limited to a reminder of the Charter rules and a factual reminder also of the experiences in practice—point to a situation which in any evaluation of the United Nations must be given the most serious consideration by members. For the judgment on the various concepts of the United Nations which are put forward, it is one thing to note what the Charter stipulates; it is an entirely different but ultimately more important question as to what the situation is in practice and what, in fact, is the weight given to decisions of the Organization when they go beyond the conference pattern of agreement.

For those who maintain the conference concept of the Organization, it is natural to side-step the mandatory nature of decisions by the Security Council. For those who take a different view, it is equally natural and essential to work for a full and general acceptance of the Charter rules. Were those to be right who hold that the Charter, on the points discussed here and, maybe, also as regards the five basic principles discussed in the first part of this introduction, is ahead of our time and the political possibilities which it offers, such a view still would not seem to justify the conclusion that the clear approach of the Charter should be abandoned. Rather, it would indicate that member nations jointly should increase their efforts to make political realities gradually come closer to the pattern established by the Charter.

In the light of such considerations, the significance of the outcome of every single conflict on which the Organization has to take a stand and the weight given to its decisions in such a conflict stand out very clearly. A failure to gain respect for decisions or actions of the Organization within the terms of the Charter is often called a failure for the Organization. It would seem more correct to regard it as a failure of the world community, through its member nations and in particular those most directly concerned, to cooperate in order, step by step, to make the Charter a living reality in practical political action as it is already in law.

Were such cooperation, for which the responsibility naturally rests with each single member as well as with all members collectively, not to come about, and were the respect for the obligations flowing from Article 25 of the Charter to be allowed to diminish, this would spell the end of the possibilities of the Organization to grow into what the Charter indicates as the clear intention of the founders, as also of all hopes to see the Organization grow into an increasingly effective instrument, with increasing respect for recommendations of the General Assembly as well.

What this would mean for the value of the Organization as protector of the aims, principles and rights it was set up to further and safeguard is obvious. The effort through the Organization to find a way by which the world community might, step by step, grow into organized international cooperation within the Charter must either progress or recede. Those whose reactions to the work of the Organization hamper its development or reduce its possibilities of effective action may have to shoulder the responsibility for a return to a state of affairs which governments had already found too dangerous after the First World War.

## IV

The growth of the United Nations out of the historic conference pattern—which, as observed earlier in this introduction, at all events naturally remains the starting point in all efforts of the Organization— is clearly reflected in what, in the light of experience, may seem to be a lack of balance in the Charter. While great attention is given to the principles and purposes, and considerable space is devoted to an elaboration of what may be called the parliamentary aspects of the Organization, little is said about executive arrangements. This does not mean that the Charter in any way closes the door to such arrangements or to executive action, but only that, at the stage of international thinking crystallized in the Charter, the conference approach still was predominant, and that the needs for executive action, if the new Organization was to live up to expectations and to its obligations under the Charter, had not yet attracted the attention they were to receive in response to later developments.

The key clause on the executive side may be considered to be Article 24, in which it is said that "in order to assure prompt and effective action by the United Nations, its members confer on the Security Council primary responsibility for the maintenance of international peace and security."

On that basis the Security Council is given the right, under Article 29, to establish such subsidiary organs as it deems necessary for the performance of its functions, the right under Article 40 to decide on so-called provisional measures, the right to use, for the purposes of the Charter, under certain conditions, armed forces made available to the Council, the right under Article 48 to request from governments action on the Council's behalf, as well as the right to request of the Secretary-General to "perform . . . such functions as are entrusted to him" by the Council.

The various clauses here briefly enumerated open a wide range of possibilities for executive action undertaken by, and under the aegis of, the Security Council. However, no specific machinery is set up for such action by the Council, apart from the Military Staff Committee, with planning responsibilities in the field of the possible use of armed force by the Security Council under Chapter VII of the Charter. In fact, therefore, the executive functions and their form have been left largely to practice, and it is in the field of the practices of the Organization that cases may be found in the light of which it is now possible to evaluate the ways in which the Organization may develop its possibilities for diplomatic, political or military intervention of an executive nature in the field.

The forms used for executive action by the Security Council—or when the Council has not been able to reach decisions, in some cases, by the General Assembly—are varied and are to be explained by an effort to adjust the measures to the needs of each single situation. However, some main types are recurrent. Subcommittees have been set up for fact-finding or negotiation on the spot. Missions have been placed in areas of conflict for the purpose of observation and local negotiation. Observer groups of a temporary nature have been sent out. And, finally, police forces under the aegis of the United Nations have been organized for the assistance of the governments concerned with a view to upholding the principles of the Charter. As these, or many of these, arrangements require centralized administrative measures, which cannot be performed by the Council or the General Assembly, members have to a large extent used the possibility to request the Secretary-General to perform special functions by instructing him to take the necessary executive steps for implementation of the action decided upon. This has been done under Article 98, as quoted above, and has represented a development in practice of the duties of the Secretary-General under Article 97.

The character of the mandates has, in many cases, been such that in carrying out his functions the Secretary-General has found himself forced also to interpret the decisions in the light of the Charter, United Nations precedents and the aims and intentions expressed by the members. When that has been the case, the Secretary-General has been under the obligation to seek guidance, to all possible extent, from the main organs; but when such guidance has not been forthcoming, developments have sometimes led to situations in which he has had to shoulder responsibility for certain limited political functions, which may be considered to be in line with the spirit of Article 99 but which legally have been based on decisions of the main organs themselves, under Article 98, and thus the exclusive responsibility of member states acting through these organs. Naturally, in carrying out such functions the Secretariat has remained fully subject to the decisions of the political bodies.

This whole development has lately become a matter of controversy, natural and, indeed, unavoidable in the light of differences of approach to the role of the Organization to which attention has been drawn earlier in this introduction. While the development is welcomed by member nations which feel a need of growth as regards the possibilities of the Organization to engage in executive action in protection of the Charter principles, it is rejected by those who maintain the conference concept of the Organization. The different opinions expressed on the development are only superficially related to this or that specific action and the way in which it is considered to have been carried through. They are also only superficially related to the choice of means used for translating decisions into action. The discussion regarding the development of executive functions is basically one confronting the same fundamentally different concepts of the Organization and its place in international politics, which could be seen also in the different attitudes toward the legal weight of decisions of the Organization.

It is in this context that the principle embodied in Article 100 of the Charter is of decisive significance. This principle, which has a long history, establishes the international and independent character of the Secretariat. Thus, it is said that the Secretary-General and the staff of the Secretariat "shall not seek or receive instructions from any Government or from any other authority external to the Organization," and that they "shall refrain from any action which might reflect on their position as international officials responsible only to the Organization." In the same Article, the members of the United Nations undertake to respect "the exclusively international character of the responsibilities of the Secretary-General and the staff and not to seek to influence them in the discharge of their responsibilities."

The significance of the principle stated in Article 100 is a dual one. It envisages a Secretariat so organized and developed as to be able to serve as a neutral instrument for the Organization, were its main organs to wish to use the Secretariat in the way which has been mentioned above and for which Article 98 has opened possibilities. But in doing so, the principle also indicates an intention to use the Secretariat for such functions as would require that it have an exclusively international character.

In the traditional conference pattern, participants in a meeting are mostly serviced by a secretariat drawn from the same countries as the participants themselves, and constituting a mixed group regarding which there is no need to demand or maintain an exclusively international character. It is therefore natural that those who favor the conference approach to the United Nations tend to give to Article 100 another interpretation than the one which the text calls for, especially in the light of its historical background and its background also in other clauses of the Charter.

There is no reason to go more deeply into this special problem here. Suffice it to say that, while the Organization, if regarded as a standing diplomatic conference, might well be serviced by a fully international Secretariat but does not need it, the other approach to the Organization and its role cannot be satisfied with anything less than a secretariat of an exclusively international character, and thus cannot be reconciled with a secretariat composed on party lines and on the assumption that the interests represented in the main organs in this manner should be represented and advocated also within the Secretariat. Thus, again, the choice between conflicting views on the United Nations Secretariat is basically a choice between conflicting views on the Organization, its functions and its future.

In order to avoid possible misunderstandings, it should be pointed out here that there is no contradiction at all between a demand for a truly international Secretariat and a demand, found in the Charter itself, for as wide a "geographical" distribution of posts within the Secretariat as possible. It is, indeed, necessary precisely in order to maintain the exclusively international character of the Secretariat that it be so composed as to achieve a balanced distribution of posts on all levels among all regions. This, however, is clearly something entirely different from a balanced representation of trends or ideologies. In fact, if a realistic representation of such trends is considered desirable, it can and should be achieved without any assumption of political representation within the ranks of the Secretariat, by a satisfactory distribution of posts based on geographical criteria.

The exclusively international character of the Secretariat is not tied to its composition but to the spirit in which it works and to its insulation from outside influences, as stated in Article 100. While it may be said that no man is neutral in the sense that he is without opinions or ideals, it is just as true that, in spite of this, a neutral Secretariat is possible. Anyone of integrity, not subjected to undue pressures, can, regardless of his own views, readily act in an "exclusively international" spirit and can be guided in his actions·on behalf of the Organization solely by its interests and principles and by the instructions of its organs.

## V

After this brief review of the principles of the Organization, of the character of its decisions and of its structure, especially as regards arrangements for executive action, presented only as a background for the consideration of what basic concepts and approaches should guide the development of the Organization, it may be appropriate, in conclusion, to give attention to the activities of the Organization and their relevance to the current international situation.

For years the Organization has been a focal point for efforts to achieve disarmament. This may still be considered as the main standing item on the agenda of the General Assembly. However, in recent years these efforts of the Organization have been running parallel to other efforts which are either outside of it or only loosely tied to the work of the United Nations. This may be justified on the basis that a very limited number of countries hold key positions in the field of armaments, so that any effort on a universal basis and by voting, to reach a decision having practical force, would be ineffective, unless founded on a basic agreement between those few parties mostly concerned. Therefore, direct negotiations between those countries are an essential first step to the solution, through the United Nations, of the disarmament problem, and do not in any way derogate from the responsibilities or rights of the Organization.

The situation may serve as an example of a problem which has become increasingly important in the life of the Organization: the right way in which to balance the weight of the big powers and their security interests against the rights of the majority of member nations. Such a majority naturally cannot expect the big powers, in questions of vital concern to them, with their superior military and economic strength, automatically to accept a majority verdict. On the other hand, the big powers cannot, as members of the world community, and with their dependence on all other nations, set themselves above, or disregard the views of, the majority of nations. An effort to balance the big power element and the majority element is found in the Charter rules regarding the respective competence of the General Assembly and the Security Council and regarding the special position of the big powers within the Council. Other efforts to solve the same problem are reflected in the way in which the disarmament problem has been attacked in recent years. No fully satisfactory or definitive formula has been found, but it must be sought, and it is to be hoped that when the time comes for a Charter revision, agreement may be reached on a satisfactory solution.

What is true of the disarmament problem is, of course, true also of those more specific questions in which security interests of big powers are or may be directly involved, as for example the Berlin problem. The community of nations, represented in the United Nations, has a vital interest in a peaceful solution, based on justice, of any question which—like this one—unless brought to a satisfactory solution, might come to represent a threat to peace and security. However, the problem of the balance to be struck between the rights and obligations of the big powers and the rights and obligations of all other nations applies, in a very direct way, also to this problem which is now so seriously preoccupying the minds of all peoples and their leaders. The United Nations with its wide membership is not, and can, perhaps, not aspire to be, a focal point in the debate on an issue such as the Berlin question, or in the efforts to solve it, but the Organization cannot, for that reason, be considered as an outside party which has no right to make its voice heard should a situation develop which would threaten those very interests which the United Nations is to safeguard and for the defence of which it was intended to provide all member nations with an instrument and a forum.

Reference has already been made in this introduction to the work of the Organization devoted to furthering self-determination, self-government and independence for all peoples. In that context it was recalled that the General Assembly, at its last session, adopted a resolution regarding the colonial problem which elaborates the basic principles of the Charter in their application to this problem.

This is, likewise, a question which for years has been before the General Assembly and it is likely to remain a major item until a final result is achieved which reflects full implementation of the basic principles in the direction indicated by last year's resolution. Experience has shown that peaceful progress in that direction cannot be guaranteed solely by decisions of the General Assembly or the Security Council, within the framework of a conference pattern. Executive action is necessary, and neither the General Assembly nor the Security Council—which has had to deal with situations in which the liquidation of the colonial system has led to acute conflict—has abstained from such action in support of the lines upheld. As in the past, executive action by the Organization in the future will undoubtedly also be found necessary if it is to render the service expected from it under the terms of the Charter.

It is in conflicts relating to the development toward full self-government and independence that the Organization has faced its most complicated tasks in the executive field. It is also in the case of executive action in this context that different concepts of the Organization and of its decisions and structure have their most pointed expressions. As regards this specific aspect of the work of the United Nations, the front line has not been the usual one between different bloc interests, but more one between a great number of nations with aims natural especially for those which recently have been under colonial rule or under other forms of foreign domination, and a limited number of powers with other aims and predominant interests. This seems understandable if one takes into account that a majority of nations wishes to stand aside from the big power conflicts, while power blocs or big powers tend to safeguard their positions and security by efforts to maintain or extend an influence over newly emerging areas. The United Nations easily becomes a focal point for such conflicting interests as the majority looks to the Organization for support in their policy of independence also in relation to such efforts, while power blocs or countries with other aims may see in the United Nations an obstacle in the way of their policies to the extent that the Organization provides the desired support. How this is reflected in the attitude toward the development of the executive functions of the United Nations can be illustrated by numerous examples. It may be appropriate in this context to say in passing a word about the problem of the Congo and the activities of the United Nations in that country.

Different interests and powers outside Africa have seen in the Congo situation a possibility of developments with strong impact on their international position. They have therefore, naturally, held strong views on the direction in which they would like to see developments in the Congo turn and—with the lack of political traditions in the country and without the stability which political institutions can get only by being tested through experience—the doors have been opened for efforts to influence developments by supporting this or that faction or this or that personality.

True to its principles, the United Nations has had to be guided in its operation solely by the interest of the Congolese people and by their right to decide freely for themselves, without any outside influences and with full knowledge of facts. Therefore, the Organization, throughout the first year of its work in the Congo, up to the point when Parliament reassembled and invested a new national Government, has refused—what many may have wished—to permit the weight of its resources to be used in support of any faction so as thereby to prejudge in any way the outcome of a choice which belonged solely to the Congolese people. It has also had to pursue a line which, by safeguarding the free choice of the people, implied resistance against all efforts from outside to influence the outcome. In doing so, the Organization has been put in a position in which those within the country who felt disappointed in not getting the support of the Organization were led to suspect that others were in a more favored position and, therefore, accused the Organization of partiality, and in which, further, such outside elements as tried to get or protect a foothold within the country, when meeting an obstacle in the United Nations, made similar accusations.

If, as it is sincerely to be hoped, the recent national reconciliation, achieved by Parliament and its elected representatives of the people, provides a stable basis for a peaceful future in a fully independent and unified Congo, this would definitely confirm the correctness of the line pursued by the United Nations in the Congo. In fact, what was achieved by Parliament early in August may be said to have been done with sufficient clarity. It is a thankless and easily misunderstood role for the Organization to remain neutral in relation to a situation of domestic conflict and to provide active assistance only by protecting the rights and possibilities of the people to find their own way, but it remains the only manner in which the Organization can serve its proclaimed purpose of futhering the full independence of the people in the true and unqualified sense of the word.

The United Nations may be called upon again to assist in similar ways. Whatever mistakes in detail and on specific points critics may ascribe to the Organization in the highly complicated situation in the Congo, it is to be hoped that they do not lead members to revise the basic rules which guide the United Nations activities in such situations, as laid down in the first report of the Secretary-General to the Security Council on the Congo question, which the Council, a year ago, found reason unanimously to commend.

Closely related to a policy aiming at self-government and independence for all is the question of economic and technical assistance, especially during the first years of independence of a new member state. The United Nations and its agencies and affiliated organs have at their disposal only very modest means for the purpose, but a rich experience has been gathered and the personnel resources are not inconsiderable.

Last year the Economic and Social Council and the General Assembly had to consider proposals designed to open up new possibilities for the Organization to respond to the demands of member governments facing all the problems of newly achieved independence. Naturally, the problems which are of special importance for such countries are basically the same as those which face all countries which have been left behind in economic development. Therefore, the urgent attention required by newly independent countries in this respect can in no way justify a discrimination in their favor against other countries with similar difficulties.

This year the General Assembly will have before it proposals initiated by the Scientific Advisory Committee and endorsed by the Economic and Social Council for a conference, under United Nations aegis, intended to provide possibilities for a break-through in the application of the technical achievements of present times to the problems of the economically less developed countries. It is sincerely to be hoped that, in the interest of international cooperation and the acceleration of the economic progress of those countries, this proposal will meet with the approval of the General Assembly.

So far, the economic and technical activities of the United Nations have been less influenced by the conflict between different concepts of the role of the Organization than its activities in other fields. However, it is impossible to isolate the economic and technical problems from the general question discussed in this introduction. While receiving countries should have full freedom to take assistance from whatever source they find appropriate, they should not be barred, if they so wish, from getting all the assistance they need through United Nations channels or under United Nations aegis. The Organization is far from being able to meet all such demands, as donor nations continue to show a strong preference for bilateral approaches on a national or a group basis. Again, the problem arises of the basic concept of the United Nations. With the conference approach to the work of the Organization a choice is made also in favor of bilateral assistance, while the alternative approach opens the door to a development under which international assistance, in implementation of the principle of equal economic opportunities for all, would be channelled through the Organization or its related agencies to all the extent that this is desired by the recipient countries and is within the capacity of the Organization.

Basic to the United Nations approach to economic and technical assistance is the principle, under all circumstances, that, although the Organization has to follow its own rules and maintain its own independence, its services are exclusively designed to meet the wishes of the recipient government, without the possibility of any ulterior motives and free from the risk of any possible influence on the national or international policies of that government. Whatever development the executive activities of the Organization may show in the field, there should never be any suspicion that the world community would wish or, indeed, could ever wish to maintain for itself, through the United Nations, a position of power or control in a member country. Were political groups in a country really to believe in such a risk, the explanation would seem to be that, as has indeed happened in the case of governments of member countries with long-established independence, they may find it difficult to accept the judgment of the majority of the nations of the world as to what in a specific situation is necessary in order to safeguard international peace and security, when such a judgment appears to be in conflict with the immediate aims of the group. With growing respect for the decisions of the Organization and growing understanding of its principles, the risks for such misinterpretations should be eliminated.

•    •    •

THOMAS HOVET, JR.

# United Nations Diplomacy

Diplomacy in the United Nations has been characterized in many ways. Traditionally it has been called multilateral diplomacy, public diplomacy, conference diplomacy, or parliamentary diplomacy. On occasion it has been termed bloc diplomacy, diplomacy by groups, and even diplomacy by majorities. When the diplomatic processes in the United Nations have been more comparable to the classical methods of diplomacy, the methods there have been referred to as private or quiet diplomacy. When the features of public and quiet diplomatic methods were combined, the diplomatic process in the United Nations has been characterized as preventive diplomacy or the diplomacy of reconciliation.

The key to any understanding of United Nations diplomacy is a recognition of the role the organization plays as an instrument of diplomacy. As a diplomatic instrument the United Nations is, in some senses, a permanent international conference. Representatives . . . are in almost continual attendance at the headquarters in Manhattan of the Organization, and their very presence provides a ready atmosphere for constant diplomatic negotiations. As a center for harmonizing the actions of states the United Nations provides a formal framework for diplomatic operations. In the thirteenth Annual Report of the Secretary-General, the late Dag Hammarskjöld wrote that ". . . as an instrument for reconciliation and for worldwide co-operation the United Nations represents a necessary addition to the traditional methods of diplomacy as exercised on a bilateral or regional basis." Within the framework of its formal

SOURCE: Thomas Hovet, Jr., "United Nations Diplomacy," *Journal of International Affairs*, XVII (1963), 29–41. Copyright by the Board of Editors of the *Journal of International Affairs*. Permission to reprint is gratefully acknowledged to the Editors of the *Journal*.

organization and agreed procedures the United Nations provides a diplomatic instrument that can be used at a moment's notice. While the preliminary negotiations for an *ad hoc* multilateral international conference may require months or even years to agree upon the procedures for the conference, the United Nations provides a framework already established to which states can bring their problems without delay. Because most states have established permanent missions at the United Nations headquarters, a state that does not want to avail itself of the formal procedures of the United Nations can have easy contact with the diplomats of other states and carry on negotiations in the traditions of the more classical forms of diplomacy. To the newer and smaller states which may not be able to afford diplomatic representation in a wide variety of countries, this center of diplomatic activity at the United Nations may provide their primary area of contact with other states. Thus the United Nations is not only a diplomatic instrument itself, but it is also a center of diplomatic activity constantly available to states in their negotiations with other states.

Surveying the evolution of the diplomatic method in the United Nations, it appears that the process has evolved from one which stressed public or conference diplomacy to one which stresses private or quiet diplomacy. The use of "evolution" may be an oversimplification because diplomacy in the United Nations has not really been of one type or the other. The development of the diplomatic method in the United Nations has seen an increasing recognition of the possibilities of supplementing conference diplomacy with quiet diplomacy. Secretary-General Hammarskjöld constantly argued for a greater awareness of the variety of diplomatic techniques that could be realized within the setting of the United Nations. In his tenth Annual Report, the Secretary-General explained that

Within the framework of the Charter there are many possibilities, as yet largely unexplored, for variation of practices. The United Nations is at a very early stage in that development. . . . It is my hope that solid progress can be made in the coming years in developing new forms of contact, new methods of deliberation and new techniques of reconciliation. . . .

The problem of diplomacy in the United Nations has been a question of evolving an adjustment between the processes of conference and quiet diplomacy. Diplomatic methods are in a constant state of evolution. A process applied in one situation may or may not be used in other situations. The problem for the diplomat in the United Nations is to recognize the strengths and weaknesses of particular diplomatic techniques, and to adjust to new diplomatic methods that may or may not require the particular type of skills generally associated with diplomacy in its classical sense. Diplomatic techniques in the United Nations can be called successful if they provide an atmosphere which allows negotiations to continue, and unsuccessful if the method or combination of methods inhibits the process of negotiation.

### PUBLIC DIPLOMACY

The emphasis on conference or public diplomacy in the United Nations is not only related to the adjustment of the diplomatic method to the growth of representative government, the impact of scientific developments, especially in the area of communications, and the experiences of the League of Nations; it also reflects concepts inherent in the minds of the drafters of the United Nations Charter. Basic to this type of diplomacy is a belief in the importance of public discussion and in the importance of world public opinion. By focusing the spotlight of public opinion on a situation, it is felt that this public exposure can freeze a situation and prevent a chain of events that might lead to conflict. At the same time there is a feeling that public discussion of an issue provides an opportunity for states not directly involved in the situation to make their influence felt in resolving the issue. The focus of publicity on the actions of a particular state threatening the peace may place that state not in an offensive but rather in a defensive position in which it must justify and explain its actions. In many instances the use of this type of public diplomacy in the United Nations has had a bearing on the adjustment of a problem. The public discussions in the Security Council and the General Assembly in 1960 undoubtedly had an influence in minimizing the actions of the United States and the Soviet Union in the Congo. The Security Council considerations of the situation in Iran in 1946 had an influence on the withdrawal of Soviet troops from that country. The actions in 1956 of Great Britain and France in the Suez were curtailed by exposure to the spotlight of public discussion in the United Nations. The public consideration in the General Assembly in 1953 and 1954 of the Burmese complaint over the presence of Chinese Nationalist troops within its borders was a determining factor in the withdrawal of those forces. The public discussion in the Security Council in 1962 was a factor in the easing of tensions between the United States and the Soviet Union over the presence of Soviet missiles in Cuba. The states administering Trust Territories and Non-Self-Governing Territories have continually been forced to justify their policies publicly in the Trusteeship Council and the General Assembly, and there can be little doubt that their policies in these territories have been modified as a result. The continual discussions in conference of economic and social questions have served to isolate fundamental problems and to make all states aware of the variety of attitudes on these crucial issues.

While it is apparent that conference or public diplomacy in the United Nations has been a factor in preventing many particular situations from getting out of hand, it is just as clear that adjustment of a situation often cannot be resolved by public discussion. Public diplomacy may expose the issue, but its resolution is generally the result of quiet diplomacy. Too often, policy positions taken in the public eye of conference diplomacy prevent states from adjusting their attitudes on an issue. Public diplomacy places stress not on negotiation but on "success" or "failure." Having once taken a strong public policy position a state cannot easily adjust its position without having it interpreted as a concession; a public shift of policy is often interpreted as a diplomatic defeat. With its emphasis on formal voting and other procedures, public diplomacy in the United Nations often results in competition between states. The spotlight of publicity places undue pressure on a state not on its ability to adjust to a situation, but on its ability to preserve its position. Delegates are tempted to play to the public arena instead of concentrating on negotiations that will resolve the problem; they may ridicule the representatives of other states because it is pleasing to their fellow countrymen, but it does not help the process of negotiation. They are constantly motivated to prove to the public in their own countries that they are defending national policy. In a sense they are placed in a position of acting as if they were representatives in a parliament, their constituents being the people in their own country. But they are not parliamentary representatives, because the United Nations is not a parliament.

The fact that resolutions are adopted in the United Nations by majority vote means that the diplomats are often tempted to negotiate for votes, not to negotiate for the adjustment of problems. The public spotlight emphasizes votes, not the resolution of international problems. The public spotlight de-emphasizes the fact that resolutions are not laws, but merely recommendations. The public spotlight inclines the representatives of states to take stands on issues which may not be of vital interest to their countries. In the resumed Thirteenth Session, for example, the Indian ambassador took a public stand on a question of the nature of elections in the Trust Territory of the Camerouns under French Administration. By his public stand he found himself in a position of being at odds with the representatives from all the African states. His motive may have been to seek what he thought was a proper action, but the result of taking this position in public meant that he openly antagonized a number of states on an issue that was of vital concern to them but of little concern to his country. Had his suggestions been made in private the ensuing animosity would have been negligible, because he could have reversed his position without any loss of prestige for India. Having taken the position in public, he could not reverse himself. Thus on an issue of no major importance to India he found himself creating not only conflict between India and the African states, but an atmosphere of animosity that would transfer to other issues at other times.

The ability to win votes and to pass resolutions, however, may not resolve issues. Between 1946 and 1962, fifty-six resolutions have been passed by the General Assembly, for example, on the question of South West Africa, more resolutions than have been passed on any other issue before the United Nations. Yet none of these resolutions has had any major impact upon the policies of South Africa towards the territory of South West Africa. Even if South Africa might want to adjust its policies towards South West Africa, it would be difficult to do so because it would appear to the South African public as if the Government were not defending its national interest. Any adjustment of its policy in the face of these resolutions would be intepreted as a defeat for the South African Government. Thus, in the face of these resolutions, the South African Government has become more adamant. Rather than reducing the conflict between South Africa and the other states, the tension has increased.

## QUIET DIPLOMACY

While public diplomacy has an important role, especially in certain types of situations, it is apparent that the success of diplomacy in the United Nations depends upon the use of public diplomatic methods in conjunction with more quiet forms of diplomacy. If there has been the development of a distinctive diplomatic method in the United Nations, it has been the development of a wide variety of techniques that provide an opportunity to intermingle and balance public and private procedures of diplomacy.

This blending of public and quiet diplomacy gives a uniqueness to the diplomatic method of the United Nations that has been influenced by at least three factors: the growth of the role of the Secretary-General, the establishment of permanent missions, and the development of caucusing groups and blocs. Each of these three elements is, in a sense, an outgrowth of the nature of public diplomacy in the United Nations, but the significance of these elements has really been felt in the environment they have created for the development of quiet diplomacy.

As the United Nations developed and the agenda of each organ expanded, the Headquarters became the location for a continual round of meetings. The General Assembly hardly finishes its sessions before the Trusteeship Council and the Economic and Social Council together with their commissions and committees, are in session. Moreover, the Security Council is organized so as to be able to meet at any moment. Even if a state is not a member of one or another of these organs, its ability to keep abreast of the issues demands that it have some sort of permanent representation at United Nations Headquarters. By 1962 almost all of the members of the United Nations had permanent missions located at the seat of the Organization. It is natural that the existence of these permanent missions provides a basis for continual contact between nations. States are thus provided with another area of diplomatic contact in addition to the normal exchange of ambassadors. In some respects, contact between states at the United Nations has the advantage of being more informal than contact between ambassadors at a national capital. The existence of these permanent missions, therefore, provides a convenient framework for quiet diplomacy.

With the impact of the Cold War frustrating the anticipated development of the Security Council, the role of the General Assembly has increased and so, too, has the role of the Secretary-General. While the concept of the role of the Secretary-General has evolved in many ways . . . the most significant aspect of this development has been the tendency of delegates to thrust heavy responsibilities upon the Secretary-General. While the General Assembly in 1956 agreed upon the creation of a United Nations Emergency Force in the Middle East, it gave the Secretary-General the responsibility of attending to the details involved in establishing such a force. His success in carrying out these tasks, and many similar ones, has influenced the General Assembly and the other organs to entrust even more responsibilities to him. In part, the willingness to give these responsibilities to the Secretary-General have been an expression of confidence in him as a person. During the tenure of Dag Hammarskjöld, the tendency to "let Dag do it" was a tribute to his ability to facilitate, through the devices of quiet diplomacy, a resolution of issues that could not be brought to fruition by public diplomacy. Gradually the Office of the Secretary-General has developed as a third factor in diplomatic negotiations.

The Secretary-General serves as a catalyst in facilitating quiet diplomacy. An issue may be brought to public attention, as was the Cuban situation in the fall of 1962, but once the issue has been exposed, the negotiations between the United States and the Soviet Union were not only conducted quietly between their permanent missions, but also through the good offices of the Secretary-General which served as a medium for the exchange of views and as a source of suggestions of means for negotiation and reconciliation. Having the maintenance of peace as his only interest in an issue, the Secretary-General can use his initiative in facilitating negotiations. His success in encouraging negotiations depends upon the degree to which states have confidence in his role as a catalyst in the negotiations; consequently, his role is limited if states feel that he is concerned with a particular solution of a problem. In order to maintain this role as a catalytic force the Secretary-General has resorted to a number of techniques, one of the most important being the creation of informal advisory committees. The United Nations Emergency Force Advisory Committee and the Advisory Committee on the Congo were created by the Secretary-General to provide a diplomatic sounding board in which he could weigh with the delegations concerned the moves he intended to take in implementing resolutions of the General Assembly and the Security Council. The efforts of the Secretary-General have not been the efforts of secret diplomacy. His concern has been with the preliminary phase of behind-the-scenes negotiations in preparation for reaching open covenants with public diplomacy. From the very beginnings of the United Nations, the Office of the Secretary-General has served as a go-between for states in preliminary negotiations. Traditionally, the Office of the Secretary-General has not entered negotiations unless it has been requested by one of the parties to an issue. However, the Secretary-General has not always waited for states to call upon his assistance in facilitating negotiations, but at times has taken the initiative; an example was the Beck-Friis mission to Cambodia and Thailand. Nevertheless, the extent to which the Secretary-General may of his own initiative enter into this quiet phase of United Nations negotiations depends heavily upon his personal rapport with the delegations. Therefore, the role of the Secretary-General is two-fold: it may be a role in the preliminary stages before the public discussion of an issue; or it may enter in the phases that follow a public discussion. Both roles are concerned with making it possible for negotiations to proceed.

The third element that has facilitated the development of quiet diplomacy in conjunction with public diplomacy at the United Nations has been the gradual evolution of caucusing groups and blocs within the membership of the Organization. While groups of states with similar interests were initially drawn together primarily to agree upon candidates for election to the non-permanent seats on the Security Council and the other organs, these groups have gradually emerged as an informal diplomatic apparatus.

*   *   *

Caucusing groups are concerned with attempts to mobilize strength to influence formal decisions of the various organs of the United Nations.

But they also perform a significant role in preliminary stages of negotiation before the public debates, votes, and resolutions. The very informal Commonwealth Group, for example, is not concerned with agreeing on common policies, its members belong to a number of other groups, and the meetings of the Commonwealth Group therefore provide informal means of expressing various points of view. These caucusing groups constitute a channel of communications between countries with similar interests. They can, within their meetings, work for an accommodation of viewpoints to prevent clashes within the arena of the public debates that would lead to a hardening of relations. In the Sixteenth Session of the General Assembly, for example, Nigeria and Guinea were in disagreement in the plenary debate over a procedural point on the consideration of items on the agenda. Before the discussion became too involved, Ghana proposed that the Assembly adjourn to allow the African Group time to see if it could work out the difficulty. At the next session of the Assembly the Delegate of Madagascar, as chairman of the African Group, announced that the issue had been resolved and he proposed a compromise procedure which had the support of both Guinea and Nigeria.

Concerned as they are with achieving support for formal proposals, the group-majority recognizes that unless concessions are made to gain that support, it may only create friction and bitterness. Negotiations between groups, then, often tend to blunt an otherwise sharply worded resolution. Where public consideration tends to separate issues, negotiation within and between groups can relate concessions on one issue to concessions on other issues. New delegations and delegates can test their skills with other states in an informal caucus atmosphere of frank exchange that is not possible within a more formal public discussion. A state can thus test a proposal without fear that it is publicly taking a viewpoint that cannot be adjusted.

One of the fundamental difficulties in dealing with any international issue is the problem of determining precisely what is actually at dispute. The groups in their discussions provide a place in which delegations can share information informally, and thus assist in determining what is the point at issue. Questions can be asked without embarrassment in this group process, and delegations can become better informed on the problems that will be considered at a later time in the public debates.

In addition to the permanent missions, the role of the Secretary-General, the function of the group process, and the very nature of the composition of the General Assembly also provide a bridge between public and quiet diplomacy that is unique. The fact that in session after session more and more foreign ministers, prime ministers, and chiefs of state attend General Assembly meetings means that there is an opportunity for contact between states that is unparallelled. While foreign ministers participate in the public debates, especially in the initial stages of the Assembly, they also use the opportunity to meet informally with their counterparts from other countries. Even their participation in the General Assembly is significant. The foreign ministers usually participate in the so-called general debate at the beginning of each General Assembly session. The general debate provides these foreign policy leaders with an opportunity to assess the current nature of international problems from a new perspective. It also provides all members with an awareness of the general philosophical approach of each state to significant problems. The Charter provides for the Security Council to serve on occasion as a meeting ground of heads of state. While this development has been encouraged by the Secretary-General, it has not come into operation.

As the United Nations evolves, these various developments create a bridge between techniques of public and quiet diplomacy. It is not easy, however, to develop the proper balance between the areas in which quiet diplomacy is most useful and those areas in which public diplomacy is most useful. One problem lies in the nature of the diplomatic skills that are required. It is an unusual delegate who is skilled in the techniques of both public and quiet diplomacy. A diplomat used to more traditional forms of diplomacy may be shocked at his first experience in the General Assembly where the procedure is more similar to that of a parliament or a state legislature. Skills may be needed in coping with the rules of procedure. In this situation the member of a delegation who may have come up through the ranks of a political party will find himself more at home. He is familiar with parliamentary give and take. Such an individual, however, may become so concerned with manipulating the procedure that he will lose sight of the fact that the United Nations is not a parliament, that success is measured not in passing resolutions but in providing means through which negotiations can continue. There is a temptation to insult other delegates, a temptation to consider resolutions passed as victories, and a temptation to demonstrate proficiency in the use of procedural rules. Such temptations, if not curbed, can create more disharmony than advance the cause of peace.

The delegate accustomed to more traditional forms of diplomacy may be inclined to overlook elements in United Nations diplomatic method that are necessary for the achievement of his tasks. For example, he may confine his contacts with delegations to the ambassadorial level. But within the United Nations, the interplay is as much between delegations as between leaders of delegations. Within each delegation individuals are assigned particular tasks, and to some extent they develop areas of speciality upon which their delegation leaders place considerable reliance. Depending upon the category of issue that is being considered, there are, sometimes, informal leaders within a delegation whose influence is substantial in determining the policy attitudes of a delegation. Successful negotiation may depend, therefore, upon discerning the identity of these leaders. The delegation that confines its contacts to the ambassadorial level may, as a result, find its negotiations fruitless. Successful negotiation between delegations should involve contact at every level so as to provide useful intelligence on the latitude of instructions given to delegations, and therefore the areas within which an accommodation of viewpoints can be negotiated.

Most of the major powers have a problem in this process of the interplay of public and private diplomacy precisely because they are major powers, with wide interests in virtually all issues before the United Nations. Their latitude for give and take may be limited because of this universality of interests. Conversely, smaller states must be constantly aware that, though they may build voting majorities, no resolutions in the United Nations can be realistic unless concessions are made to the power relationships among the larger states.

The United Nations has only begun to explore the variety of techniques of diplomacy that are at its disposal to facilitate negotiations between states. While all of its attempts have not been successful, it has nonetheless achieved success in a variety of cases. One of its most notable developments has been in the area of what Mr. Hammarskjöld called preventive diplomacy—that which combines both elements of public and quiet diplomacy. In the Introduction to the fifteenth Annual Report, the late Secretary-General explained that

. . . preventive diplomacy . . . is of special significance in cases where the original conflict may be said either to be the result of, or to imply risks for, the creation of a power vacuum between the main blocs. Preventive action in such cases must, in the first place, aim at filling the vacuum so that it will not provoke action from any of the major parties, the initiative for which might be taken for preventive purposes but might in turn lead to a counter action from the other sides. The ways in which a vacuum can be filled by the United Nations so as to forestall such initiatives differ from case to case, but they have this in common: temporarily, and pending the filling of the vacuum by normal means, the United Nations enters the picture on the basis of its non-commitment to any power bloc, so as to provide to the extent possible a guarantee in relation to all parties against initiatives from others. . . .

This type of preventive diplomacy has been exercised by the United Nations in different circumstances and with different techniques. In Greece, the Special Committee on the Balkans focused attention upon foreign sources of subversion. The United Nations Observation Group in Lebanon checked reports of foreign intervention. In Laos, a Security Council sub-committee verified whether a crisis existed. In the Congo, the United

Nations prevented intervention by outside powers by providing assistance in the maintenance of law and order when the established government there collapsed. These cases illustrate the fact that although the diplomatic method evolving in the United Nations has the ability to achieve concrete results, its full potential has not been reached. Progress is nevertheless being made, for the ability to produce conditions in which negotiations can proceed is a mark of good diplomacy.

At the same time that a distinctive diplomatic method is gradually evolving, the expansion in United Nations membership is creating problems for diplomacy. The procedures and the structure of the General Assembly are being strained by the size of its membership. There are more issues on the agenda, more delegates desiring to speak, more draft resolutions submitted, more amendments introduced, more votes requested, more meetings to attend, and more delegates to be consulted. As the sessions become longer, it is more difficult for foreign ministers and heads of states to participate, except for brief periods. Delegations, especially small ones, are severely taxed in providing representatives to attend the increased number of meetings. States cannot afford to allow key individuals in their foreign offices to spend one-third or one-half of their time at the United Nations. They must either rotate personnel attending sessions there or else send less qualified officials. On the other hand, to be effective, public diplomacy needs persons experienced in its procedures and qualified to deal with the issues being considered.

Up to the present the evolution of diplomatic method in the United Nations has been concerned with an expansion of opportunities for quiet diplomacy. In the future the adjustment of procedures of public diplomacy to the enlarged membership will probably be the more serious problem faced by the world body. The ability of the United Nations to balance techniques of public and quiet diplomacy will depend upon the successful development of workable procedures integrating the two diplomatic methods.

FRANCIS O. WILCOX

## Regionalism and the United Nations

Old soldiers may "just fade away" as General Douglas MacArthur reminded us, but the controversy over the relative merits of regionalism and globalism in international organization will ever be with us. That question generated as much heat as any other issue at San Francisco in 1945 with the possible exception of the veto. In more recent years the inadequacies of the United Nations, the changing nature of the Cold War, the growth and expansion of regional organizations, the proliferation of nuclear weapons, and the continued shrinking of the universe have kept the heat of this controversy at a relatively high level.

At one extreme are those staunch supporters of regionalism who contend that regional arrangements are a natural outgrowth of international cooperation and desirable stepping-stones toward world organization. Those who defend this view argue that regional agencies are not only compatible with the United Nations but, in reality, constitute an indispensable element in its successful growth and functioning. At the other end of the spectrum are those who insist that some regional agencies are little more than old-fashioned military alliances that foment great-power rivalries, weaken the effectiveness of the United Nations, and undermine the principle of collective security.

The issue, of course, has its practical aspects. Many people in this country, convinced that state sovereignty must yield further ground if the world is to survive in a nuclear age, have supported the creation of an Atlantic Union or a Free World Federation. Still others, perhaps disillusioned by the relative weakness of the United Nations, have urged the development of a stronger Atlantic Community or a concert of the free nations. Although the problem does not necessarily involve making

SOURCE: Francis O. Wilcox, "Regionalism and the United Nations," *International Organization*, XIX (Summer 1965), 789–811. Reprinted by permission.

a choice between organizing the world on a regional or a global basis, it is by no means clear how such organizations would fit into the present world order and what their relations with the United Nations would be.

After twenty years of experience in the peace and security field, it seems pertinent to inquire again whether the goals of regional agencies like the North Atlantic Treaty Organization (NATO), the Arab League, and the Organization of African Unity (OAU) are in harmony with the objectives of the United Nations. Have the efforts of the regional agencies conflicted with the United Nations or have they effectively supplemented its work? To what extent has the balance between the two concepts, so carefully worked out at San Francisco, been changed? Is there any real inconsistency in our efforts to deal with peace and security problems through both regional and global organizations?

## THE SAN FRANCISCO CONFERENCE

In 1943, during the early stages of planning for the postwar world, some of the leaders of the democratic countries placed a rather surprising amount of emphasis on the concept of regionalism. Winston Churchill, who apparently had misgivings about the establishment of a worldwide organization, urged the creation of a number of regional councils through which the great nations might exercise their leadership in the world. By the time the Dumbarton Oaks Conversations convened, however, the Great Powers agreed that the new world organization should be given clear and unchallenged authority to deal with the basic issues of war and peace. They also recognized, with less enthusiasm, the valuable collateral role that regional organizations might play. As a result, the Dumbarton Oaks Proposals rather grudgingly provided that nothing in the UN Charter should preclude the existence of regional agencies provided they were "consistent with the purposes and principles of the Organization." Such organizations might play a constructive role, the conferees conceded, in the settlement of local disputes "either on the initiative of the states concerned or by reference from the Security Council." Moreover, it was agreed that in certain circumstances, the Security Council might utilize regional agencies for enforcement action with the understanding that this could be done only when authorized by the Council.[1]

At the United Nations Conference on International Organization at San Francisco the constant emphasis on the veto brought the regional issue to a white heat. The Latin countries, not willing to give up what they already had for something not yet within their grasp, insisted that

[1] "Proposals for the Establishment of a General International Organization," Department of State *Bulletin*, October 8, 1944 (Vol. 11, 276), p. 372.

the veto must not be permitted to block regional action in the Americas. On the other hand, members of the United States delegation, although responsive to the entreaties of the other American republics, remained fearful that the United Nations would be fatally weakened if regional groupings of states were authorized to take action without going through the Security Council. As Senator Arthur Vandenberg put it, "The Monroe Doctrine is protected only if we kick the daylights out of the world organization."[2]

In the end, hope was tempered with reality as three fundamental concessions were made in the direction of regionalism. The first amendments to the Dumbarton Oaks Proposals were designed to encourage states involved in local disputes to utilize regional agencies in their attempts to work out an amicable adjustment before turning to the Security Council for help. The result of several language changes was to reaffirm the compatibility of the regional and global approaches to the peaceful settlement of disputes and to provide a viable formula under which the two systems might function in mutual harmony. Regional agencies, to be sure, were not given exclusive jurisdiction over regional disputes; but they were given elbowroom to deal with local disputes in the first instance, and the Security Council was even urged to encourage and facilitate such attempts. On the other hand, the Charter reserved the basic right of the Council to deal with *any* dispute, whether regional, interregional, or global in character, whenever it needed to do so to discharge its primary responsibility for the maintenance of peace.

A second set of amendments dealt with the problem created by the existence of mutual assistance pacts, like the Anglo-Soviet Treaty of 1942,[3] and their integration into the United Nations system. The Conference met this issue head on by inserting Article 53 into the Charter providing for the utilization, where appropriate, of regional arrangements by the Security Council for enforcement action. "But," declares Article 53,

no enforcement action shall be taken under regional arrangements . . . without the authorization of the Security Council, with the exception of measures against any enemy state . . . or in regional arrangements directed against renewal of aggressive policy on the part of any such state. . . .

---

[2] Arthur H. Vandenberg, Jr., *The Private Papers of Senator Vandenberg* (Boston: Houghton Mifflin, 1952), p. 188.
[3] Treaty of Alliance in the War against Hitlerite Germany and Her Associates in Europe and of Collaboration and Mutual Assistance Thereafter Concluded between the Union of Soviet Socialist Republics and the United Kingdom of Great Britain and Northern Ireland, signed at London, May 26, 1942.

The intent here is clear; while prior authorization of the Council is normally required for regional enforcement action, that requirement is waived with respect to measures taken against the resurgence of aggression by former enemy states.

Finally, the most important amendment recognized the right of individual and collective self-defense against armed attack. This amendment (Article 51) admitted the right of Member States to defend themselves "until the Security Council has taken the measures necessary to maintain international peace and security." In such an event, however, the defensive steps taken by Members were to be "immediately" reported to the Council and

shall not in any way affect the authority and responsibility of the Security Council . . . to take at any time such action as it deems necessary . . . to maintain or restore international peace and security.

Although these language changes may be criticized by some as a bundle of ambiguous compromises, what the framers of the Charter intended to do is reasonably clear. They intended to establish a flexible framework within which existing and future regional agencies and the United Nations might function together harmoniously, the one lending support and encouragement to the other in their mutually complementary tasks. They intended to underline the primary role of the regional agencies in the settlement of local disputes, and they obviously wished to recognize the inherent right of states to defend themselves against armed attack, veto or no veto. They did not intend, however, to "kick the daylights out of the world organization" or to detract from its primary responsibility for the maintenance of world peace.

## THE BALANCE BEGINS TO SHIFT

One interesting shift in the delicate balance established at San Francisco—which is often overlooked—is reflected in the provisions of the treaties that have been negotiated setting up the various regional arrangements.[4] At the outset many supporters of the UN had grave doubts about the wisdom of developing regional instrumentalities like the Inter-American Treaty of Reciprocal Assistance (Rio Treaty) and the North Atlantic Treaty for fear of detracting from the influence and prestige of the UN and impairing its effectiveness. To reassure the skeptics, the regional and other security arrangements concluded since 1947 have traditionally contained repeated references to the United Nations. The Rio Treaty, in addition to the preamble, carries such references in eight of

[4] See Norman J. Padelford, "Regional Organizations and the United Nations," *International Organization*, May 1954 (Vol. 8, No. 2), pp. 211 ff.

its substantive articles. Five of the fourteen articles of the North Atlantic Treaty, again apart from the preamble, pay homage to the UN and its Charter.

The depth of this feeling of loyalty for the United Nations was clearly demonstrated in this country in 1948 at the time of the passage of the Vandenberg Resolution by the United States Senate. In retrospect it is worth noting that the Resolution was sold to the Senate and to the American people primarily as a constructive program for strengthening the United Nations. Very little was said at the time about the much more important fact that its provisions, in effect, gave the President a green light to negotiate the North Atlantic Treaty.

A year later, when the NATO pact came before the Senate for debate, the Committee on Foreign Relations reiterated its strong support for the United Nations. "The treaty is expressly subordinated to the purposes, principles, and provisions of the UN Charter," declared the Committee, "and is designed to foster those conditions of peace and stability in the world which are essential if the United Nations is to function successfully."[5] This protective interest in the United Nations continued in evidence at nearly every hearing conducted by the Committee on important foreign policy matters. Thus, in 1954, during the hearings on the Southeast Asia Collective Defense Treaty, Secretary of State John Foster Dulles made clear that the Treaty did not disturb in the slightest United States obligations under the United Nations. "I can say categorically," declared Mr. Dulles, "that in my opinion this neither adds one jot or tittle nor subtracts one jot or tittle, from our objective as expressed in the Charter of the United Nations."[6]

Despite these repeated acknowledgments of the responsibility of the UN with respect to world peace, the language of the regional agreements entered into by the United States and other countries has tended to become less specific in its reference to the United Nations. The Rio Treaty, concluded shortly after the San Francisco Conference, was closely geared to the peaceful settlement and enforcement machinery of the United Nations. It is true that the Treaty was based on Article 51 of the Charter which reiterates "the inherent right of individual or collective self-defense" against armed attack. But it is also tied specifically to Article 54 under which the Security Council must be kept informed of activities either planned or undertaken by regional agencies with respect to the maintenance of peace. In this fashion, the Rio Treaty recognizes Chapter VIII of the Charter which clearly subordinates regional enforce-

[5] U.S. Congress, Senate, *Senate Executive Report* 8, 81st Congress, 1st Session, 1949.
[6] U.S. Congress, Senate, *Senate Executive Report* 1, 84th Congress, 1st Session, 1955, p. 10.

ment activities to the overriding jurisdiction of the United Nations.[7]

Both the NATO pact and the Southeast Asia Treaty Organization (SEATO) pact conveniently neglect to establish any regional relationship or commitments of this kind. The North Atlantic Treaty refers only to Article 51 and requires only that any measures taken against an armed attack "shall immediately be reported to the Security Council." Such measures, according to the Treaty, are to be terminated when the Council has taken the steps necessary "to restore and maintain international peace and security." Since no mention is made of Articles 52-54 of the Charter, the presumption is to be drawn that its signatories did not consider NATO a regional arrangement in the strict sense of that term. The SEATO pact, concluded in 1954, reiterates the principle that collective defense arrangements do not alter the rights and obligations of the parties under the Charter or the responsibility of the UN for the maintenance of peace. Unlike its predecessors, the Rio Treaty and the NATO pact, it does not refer to any particular article of the Charter. Like both the Rio Treaty and the North Atlantic Treaty, it does require that measures taken against a common danger should be immediately reported to the Security Council, but it does not require that such action cease in the event the Security Council is able to restore peace and security.[8]

The significance of these changes is obvious. As the Cold War intensified, the parties to the newer arrangements considered it desirable to avoid the burdensome limitations and restrictions found in the regional articles of the Charter. It can be argued, of course, that the significance is more symbolic than real. Yet from both a legal and a practical point of view the net effect is to reduce the reliance of the parties on the UN and to deemphasize the need for coordinating regional action with the United Nations. Rightly or wrongly, the emphasis is less on teamwork and more on independent action. The signatories are thus free to act in an emergency without the possible delays and handicaps imposed by the restrictive language of Chapter VIII.

In any event there is no doubt that these trends created considerable concern in UN circles. In the *Annual Report of the Secretary-General* issued in 1954, Dag Hammarskjöld called attention to important developments outside the United Nations—but inside its sphere of interest—which required serious consideration.

[7] U.S. Congress, Senate, *Review of the United Nations Charter*, 83rd Congress, 2nd Session, 1954, Document 164, p. 204.
[8] The Charter of the OAU, the newest of the regional agencies, places even less emphasis on the United Nations. For the text of the Charter, see Boutros-Ghali, Boutros, "The Addis Ababa Charter," *International Conciliation*, January 1964 (No. 546), pp. 53–62.

To fail to use the United Nations machinery on those matters for which Governments have given to the Organization a special or primary responsibility under the Charter, or to improvise other arrangements without overriding practical and political reasons—to act thus may tend to weaken the position of the Organization and to reduce its influence and effectiveness, even when the ultimate purpose which it is intended to serve is a United Nations purpose.[9]

Mr. Hammarskjöld pointed out that appropriate use of regional arrangements in the maintenance of peace was recognized and encouraged by the Charter. Nevertheless, where states choose to resort to such arrangements in the first instance, he said, "that choice should not be permitted to cast any doubt on the ultimate responsibility of the United Nations."

This was only one of many appeals to reason issued by Mr. Hammarskjöld during his career, and it struck a responsive chord in the hearts of many people. He was enough of a realist to know that he could not—even if he so desired—stem the tide of collective defense pacts. But he also recognized the imperative need to strike a proper balance between the regional and world organizations. For unless Member States kept in mind their long-range interests in building a strong and effective United Nations, they might be tempted, for short-run advantages, to turn to other organizations in particular situations, thus weakening the UN and damaging the cause of world peace. He did not tell the Member States that they should have no other gods before them; he merely reminded them in his inimitable Swedish-English where their primary loyalties must lie if they were ever to arrive at the promised land.

PEACEFUL SETTLEMENT OF DISPUTES

A second shift in the balance between the regional organizations and the United Nations stems from the fact that the regional agencies have been far less active in the peaceful settlement of disputes than the framers of the Charter anticipated. With the exception of the Organization of American States (OAS), and more recently the Organization of African Unity (OAU), these agencies apparently have not recognized activity in this field to be among their prime objectives. As a result it cannot be said that any clear-cut pattern of working relationships or any satisfactory division of labor between the regional organizations and the United Nations has been developed. Moreover, the regional agencies have not eased the burden of the United Nations very much by

[9] *Annual Report of the Secretary General on the Work of the Organization, 1 July 1953 30 June 1954* (General Assembly *Official Records* [9th session], Supplement No. 1), p. xi.

serving either as a shock absorber or as a court of first resort for the settlement of local disputes.

There would appear to be at least three basic reasons why most regional agencies have played only a limited role in the peaceful settlement process. The first obviously flows from the inability of the United Nations to create the kind of enforcement machinery contemplated in the Charter. Peaceful settlement has a very intimate relationship with collective measures to keep the peace. The certainty of punitive action against those who disturb the peace increases considerably the probability that states will resolve their differences by peaceful means. On the other hand, without the deterring impact of an effective sanctions system some states may be far more inclined to take the law into their own hands, ignoring or bypassing the peaceful settlement machinery that is available to them. One can only hazard a guess, but in all likelihood if the Security Council had been able to discharge effectively its responsibility for the maintenance of peace, many more disputes of a local character would have been settled at the regional level.

In the second place, we sometimes forget that regional defense organizations were not created for the purpose of resolving differences between their own members. In NATO, as in other organizations of the alliance type, the basis of consensus among its members does not normally extend to the peaceful resolution of disputes that are unrelated to its *external* function. As Secretary of State John Foster Dulles pointed out in 1956: "NATO has not been organized as a regional association, nor has it any policy or jurisdiction to deal with disputes as between the members."[10] One of NATO's strengths lies in the fact that it has a fairly limited and precise mission to perform—the collective defense of the NATO area against aggression. In the early years of the Organization it was believed that if this commitment were broadened so as to include the extra burden of settling regional disputes, the unity of purpose of NATO might suffer and the alliance subjected to undesirable stresses and strains.

Yet the link between friendly relations and cooperative action in the defense field is an obvious one and regional alliance members have been increasingly willing to admit a degree of joint responsibility in this regard. In 1956 the report of the "NATO Committee of Three Wise Men," the Foreign Ministers of Canada, Italy, and Norway, acknowledged that it was "of crucial importance" in the development of political cooperation in NATO to avoid serious intermember disputes and to settle them quickly whenever they occurred. As a result of their recommendations, NATO members not only reaffirmed their obligations to settle

[10] Department of State *Bulletin*, June 4, 1956 (Vol. 34, No. 884), pp. 925–926.

such disputes by peaceful means, but they also agreed to submit them to good office procedures *within* NATO "before resorting to any other international agency."[11] Since that time NATO members have increased both the breadth and the depth of their consultations in their attempt to settle disputes before they arise and to work out common policies on problems of mutual interest.

The third and perhaps the most important reason most regional organizations do not play a significant role in the peaceful settlement of disputes stems from the serious limitations on their membership. How could the Central Treaty Organization (CENTO) or SEATO possibly serve as a helpful factor in resolving the sharp differences between Pakistan and Afghanistan or the Kashmir dispute between India and Pakistan as long as India and Afghanistan are nonmembers? How could the Arab League be expected to settle the Palestine refugee problem or deal satisfactorily with the border clashes between Israel and its neighbors as long as Israel is not a member? How could NATO assure jurisdiction over the dispute between Italy and Austria over South Tyrol in view of the Austrian policy of nonalignment? How could SEATO make a useful contribution to the peaceful settlement of the serious differences between Malaysia and Indonesia when neither country is a member?

The conclusions are obvious. It is no doubt true that the friendly relations that normally exist among the members of an alliance have had a certain prenatal effect in preventing potential disputes within the alliance from coming to the fore. But the fact remains that most of the difficult issues of the postwar era—Algeria, Cyprus, West Irian, the Congo (Leopoldville), Cuba, Angola, Suez, and many more—have not been settled at the regional level but have found their way into the broader forum of the United Nations. Whether this situation is due primarily to the fact that some regional organizations are ill-equipped to perform the peaceful settlement function, whether it is due to the desire of some states to gain political and propaganda advantages by taking their cases to a world forum, or whether it is due to the obvious fact that the Cold War has tended to convert many local differences into worldwide issues, it does suggest that every effort should be made to strengthen the peace-keeping machinery of the United Nations.

As far as the settlement of African disputes is concerned, the OAU could perform a valuable service for the United Nations. This function may be of special importance in Africa, which is a hodgepodge of nations with many poorly drawn frontiers and built-in boundary disputes. During its short life the OAU has already offered constructive help in bringing several difficult disputes within manageable bounds. The first of these

---

[11] "Non-Military Co-operation in NATO: Text of the Report of the Committee of Three," *NATO Letter*, January 1, 1957 (Vol. 5, Special Supplement to No. 1), p. 8.

was the frontier controversy between Algeria and Morocco, which smoldered under an uneasy truce for a year and then threatened to develop into open warfare. Following the creation of a seven-member arbitration commission by the OAU Council of Ministers in November 1963, a cease-fire was negotiated with the help of Emperor Haile Selassie of Ethiopia and President Modibo Keita of Mali. The "spirit of Addis" was also instrumental in stimulating Mali and Mauritania to sign a frontier delimitation treaty in July 1963. Finally, the long-standing and bitter dispute between Ethiopia and Somalia was eased considerably in February 1964, following a special appeal by the OAU Council of Ministers.

From a legal point of view the relationship between the regional organizations and the United Nations in the peacemaking field remains basically unchanged. For the most part there has been little competition for jurisdiction although sharp controversies have arisen between the OAS and the United Nations in connection with several important disputes. The first occurred in 1954 when the government of Guatemala simultaneously requested the OAS and the Security Council to take the necessary steps to bring to an end the attacks launched against it by Nicaragua and Honduras. In submitting its case to the Security Council the Guatemalan government in effect bypassed the OAS, contending that it had a right under the UN Charter to appeal directly to the Council for help. The United States, supported by certain Latin American states, insisted that OAS members were obliged to submit such disputes initially to the OAS which functioned as a court of first appeal in the western hemisphere. After a long procedural wrangle the Security Council failed to adopt the agenda by a vote of 4 in favor, 5 opposed, with 2 abstentions, in effect turning the dispute over to the OAS for futher consideration.

Although the arguments were heavily weighted on the legal side, the motives in the transfer were largely political. The United States, together with Honduras and Nicaragua, hoped to unseat the Guatemalan government and thus supported regional jurisdiction in order to keep the Security Council out of the controversy. In the end the United States got what it wanted because it had the votes. What is important to note, however, is that the Security Council did not admit the exclusive jurisdiction of the OAS, nor did it admit any lack of authority to deal with the matter. The United Kingdom representative stated the views of the majority of the Council's members when he said: "For the Security Council to divest itself of its ultimate responsibility would be gravely to prejudice the moral authority of the United Nations. . . ."[12]

---

[12] On these issues, see Inis L. Claude, Jr., "The OAS, the UN, and the United States," *International Conciliation*, March 1964 (No. 547), p. 27.

The controversy between Cuba and the United States tested the central issue in much the same way with much the same result. Does a state involved in a dispute have a right to exercise its preference and take the issue to the United Nations even though a regional organization may be dealing with the matter at the time? Cuba, in calling for a meeting of the Security Council in July 1960 to consider its complaint against the United States, insisted that it had such a right. The United States contended that Cuba was legally obligated by the Rio Treaty to take the matter *first* to the OAS; however, in any event, the Security Council ought not to take any action until the problem had been dealt with by the appropriate organ of the OAS.

In the end the Security Council, without denying its own competence, turned the problem over to the OAS. This was done for pragmatic reasons. The Latin American members of the Council, Argentina and Ecuador, argued that disputes of this kind should normally be resolved within the framework of regional organizations, but in no case should a Member be denied access to the United Nations. Subsequent debate in the Security Council and the General Assembly during later stages of the Cuban crisis tended to underline these general principles.

Two other cases are of interest in this connection. The first had to do with a dispute between the Dominican Republic and Haiti which was brought before the Security Council at Haiti's request in May 1963. The second had to do with a complaint filed by Panama against the United States in January 1964. In both these cases the complaining parties agreed that the Security Council should step aside and permit the OAS to work out a solution to the problems involved. Meanwhile, in accordance with the desires of the parties, the Council retained the cases on its agenda, thus maintaining a posture of watchful waiting as the OAS proceeded with its task. In no way did these cooperative ventures impair the right of OAS members to have access to the aggressor. Since these measures fell short of the use of armed force, the OAS *reported* the action to the Security Council but apparently did not consider it necessary to seek the approval of the Council for their application.[13]

But the Soviet Union, with one eye on the developing Cuban crisis, had other ideas. The Soviet representative requested a meeting of the Security Council and urged the Council to give its formal approval to the sanctions voted by the OAS against the Dominican Republic. In this fashion he sought to establish, for future reference, the authority of the United Nations to coordinate and control OAS enforcement measures. Said the Soviet representative:

[13] See Manuel Canyes, *The Organization of American States and the United Nations* (Washington, D.C.: Pan American Union, 1963), pp. 52 ff.

Without authorization from the Security Council, the taking of enforcement action by regional agencies would be contrary to the Charter of the United Nations.[14]

This is at least a debatable point. The United States' argument that Security Council approval should be limited to enforcement action that involves the use of military power and should not be required for the limited kind of political and economic sanctions the OAS invoked against the Dominican Republic certainly has some merit. Clearly it is within the power of *any* sovereign state—without violating the Charter—to sever diplomatic or economic relations or to interrupt its communications with another state. Why, then, should UN approval be necessary for the same kind of action undertaken by a few states individually or by a *group* of states acting together?

Admittedly this argument would have carried more weight in the Council if its historical roots had been more impressive. The fact is, however, that from 1943 on, considerable evidence had piled up to support the Soviet contention that economic and financial sanctions should be treated as enforcement measures under Article 53 and therefore subject to UN control.[15] In any event, the Council members rallied to the support of the United States and by a vote of 9 in favor, none opposed, with 2 abstentions, approved a resolution by which the Council merely "takes note" of the regional measures against the Dominican Republic. Whether support for the United States was based on pragmatic or legal grounds is not entirely clear. What is clear is that the Security Council by its action in this case gave considerable impetus to regional autonomy.

Still further impetus resulted from the Cuban crisis. When the OAS in 1962 voted to exclude Cuba from participation in the inter-American system and to apply certain economic sanctions, Cuba took its case to the Security Council, contending that without the Council's approval such measures were illegal. As might be expected, the United States based its position in part on the precedent established in the Dominican case. But this time the central issue revolved not so much around the right of the OAS to apply enforcement measures under the Charter as it did around the general relationship between the UN and the regional agencies. Thus, the Soviet representative solemnly warned against the desirability of freeing regional organizations from the overall control of the Security Council and underlined the risks that were involved in arbitrary action in Africa, Asia, and Latin America if the regional agen-

[14] Security Council *Official Records* (15th year), 893rd meeting, September 8, 1960, p. 4.
[15] See Claude, *International Conciliation*, No. 547, pp. 48 ff.

cies usurped the authority of the Council. For its part the United States just as solemnly warned against the deadening impact of the Soviet veto and the dilution of regional efforts on behalf of peace if they were subject to the direction and control of the Security Council. "The principal issue," said United States Ambassador Adlai E. Stevenson,

is whether a regional organization . . . has the right to manage its own affairs and to defend itself against a foreign-dominated Government, or whether the Soviet Union is to be allowed to paralyze that organization's activities through the exercise of the veto power in this Council.[16]

Although the final votes were inconclusive, they seemed to substantiate the proposition that the United Nations, veto or no veto, should not be permitted to block regional enforcement activity of this kind.

One further step was taken in October 1962 at the height of the Cuban missile crisis. At that time the OAS Council approved a resolution calling upon its members to take certain measures, "including the use of armed force," in support of the course of action embarked upon earlier by the United States. This was a historic event; among other things it was the first time the OAS had approved the application of *military* sanctions. Under more normal circumstances this might have stirred up a jurisdictional battle of considerable proportions. On this occasion, however, the United States took its case to *both* the OAS and the UN, calling upon *both* organizations to help avert a possible nuclear conflict. It is important to note that the United States apparently did not assume that it was necessary to seek the approval of the Council under Article 53 for the action taken by the OAS. Rather, it based its case on the principle of regional autonomy and the right of the OAS to take effective action without interference from the United Nations. And although the Soviet representative once more raised his voice in protest, the compelling need for great-power cooperation became apparent. As a result, the jurisdictional quarrel faded into the background as the two organizations joined hands to help find a way out of the dilemma.

Significantly enough, in these cases before the OAS, the Soviet Union departed from its traditional conservative position with respect to the authority of international organization and assumed a new role as the great defender of a strong and effective United Nations. The United States, on the other hand, in arguing for the jurisdiction of the OAS, has often found itself in the embarrassing position of opposing a vigorous and expansive role for the United Nations. This change in policy is obviously due to a determination on the part of the United States to avoid the desultory effect of the Soviet veto. It does not mean that

[16] Security Council *Official Records* (17th year), 993rd meeting, March 15, 1962, p. 14.

the United States government has rejected the principle that the primary responsibility for world order should rest with the United Nations. It does mean that the precise relationships between regional and world organizations must be worked out in each case in the light of the policy considerations that are involved and the need for effective action.

Unlike the OAS, the OAU has not been involved in any jurisdictional squabbles with the UN in connection with collective measures. To the contrary, the African states have taken the lead in the United Nations in promoting and encouraging the use of collective action against the Republic of South Africa and Portugal in a whole series of resolutions going back to 1961. Meanwhile, in its efforts to rid the continent of colonialism, the OAU has itself approved many nonpeaceful measures against both South Africa and Portugal. At Addis Ababa in May 1963, the Summit Conference of Independent African States urged the severance of diplomatic and consular relations, a total economic boycott of the two countries, the creation of liberation armies in various African states, as well as the establishment of a special coordinating committee to help in the liberation of dependent African territories.[17] Also, at its Cairo meeting in July 1964, the OAU went beyond the United Nations resolutions regarding air and sea transport by calling for the denial of rights to *any* aircraft or ship en route to or coming from South Africa or Portugal.

It may be argued that these resolutions are couched in the form of recommendations and carry with them no binding obligations for the members of the OAU. Nevertheless, they have set in train a series of developments both within and outside Africa that could be of great importance. Persistent efforts have been made either to boycott Portugal's and South Africa's participation in or to expel them from various United Nations organs and agencies. Some of the more militant African countries are heavily engaged in training freedom fighters and saboteurs. The OAU's African Liberation Committee (Committee of Nine) has raised a sizable sum—against a budget of some $4,000,000 a year—much of which is being used for propaganda purposes in colonial areas. And a subcommittee made up of Algeria, Egypt, and Guinea has drafted proposals for military aid for the liberation movement.

Governments may differ, as they obviously do, over the precise meaning of "enforcement action" and whether the joint measures taken by the OAS and the OAU legally require the approval of the Security Council. The fact is, Security Council at any time; in no way did they challenge the jurisdiction or the competence of the United Nations.

[17] See Norman J. Padelford, "The Organization of African Unity," *International Organization, Summer* 1964 (Vol. 18, No. 3), pp. 521, 536–540.

Despite all this pulling and tugging, from a legal point of view the basic relationship between the United Nations and the regional organizations remains relatively unchanged. Practically, however, it is apparent that the United Nations has yielded some jurisdictional ground to the OAS. It is particularly interesting to note that in all these cases, even though they joined the United States in supporting regional action, a good many Latin American countries carefully safeguarded the right of OAS members to take their problems to the United Nations at any time.

### COLLECTIVE ACTION

As far as enforcement action is concerned, the relationships between the United Nations and the regional organizations have undergone far-reaching and, in the eyes of some people, highly disturbing changes. By their words and their deeds the OAS, the OAU, the Arab League, and, to a lesser extent, collective defense organizations like NATO, CENTO, and SEATO have either disregarded the authority of the United Nations or have taken positive steps to avoid the controls over regional action contemplated by the Charter. In some cases political, economic, and even military sanctions have been applied without the approval of the Security Council; in other cases the necessity for reporting enforcement measures to the United Nations appears to have been overlooked or ignored. The result has been that the authority of the Council to coordinate or control the enforcement activities of regional agencies has been sadly diluted.

The economic boycott of Israel, which was instituted by the Arab League in line with its policy of strangling Israel economically, is a case in point. As is well-known, the boycott was designed to achieve its purpose in two ways: by preventing trade between Israel and the Arab world, and by black-listing foreign companies and ships doing business with Israel. Regardless of the merits of the case—and the historical justification advanced by the Arab countries—the boycott certainly was not in keeping with the persistent efforts of the United Nations to improve relations between Israel and its neighbors nor was it ever submitted to the Security Council for formal approval.

It is in connection with the activities of the OAS, however, that the authority of the United Nations received its first formal challenge and its first formal setback. The matter initially came to a head at a meeting of the ministers of foreign affairs of the OAS in San José in 1960. At that meeting the foreign ministers condemned the Dominican Republic for intervention and aggression against Venezuela and voted to set in train a series of diplomatic and economic sanctions, including suspension of trade in arms, against the Dominican Republic. . . . The

United Nations has been jockeyed into a position of relative inferiority so that the ties between the regional agencies and the world Organization exist "at the practical pleasure" of the regional agencies.[18] As Ambassador Francis Plimpton of the United States stated the case on March 23, 1962, after the Security Council vote on the Cuban proposal: "By its action today, the Security Council has forthrightly, resolutely and decisively upheld the integrity and independence of regional organizations."[19]

## UNITED STATES POLICY

During the 1950's, the United States was often accused of worrying too much about security and of suffering from what some critics called an acute case of "regional pactitis." From other quarters the United States was accused of being softheaded and sentimental and putting too much emphasis on a relatively weak and ineffective United Nations in a world where national power remains the determining factor. Despite these criticisms the United States has continued to put its eggs in both these baskets. There seems little likelihood that this policy will undergo any substantial change in the near future. United States leaders continue to believe that the country has an important role to play in an international community in which many states both large and small, together with regional groupings of various kinds and appropriate global international organization, can make constructive contributions to peace and world order. The long-range goal of the United States remains a worldwide community of free nations.

It is not difficult to compile an impressive list of limitations on regional action in the peace and security field. There are the built-in handicaps inherent in most regional organizations because of their limited mission and their restricted geographic and functional jurisdiction. They are simply not geared to deal with many important problems that demand solution in a complex world. Moreover, some regional agencies, the OAU and the Arab League among them, are torn by internal stresses and strains and lack that unity of purpose that is so essential for effective action. Some like SEATO and CENTO, as we have pointed out above, suffer from understandable but significant gaps in membership. And some are incapable of vigorous and effective action precisely because they lack vigorous and effective leadership. Even more important, for most of the agencies, is the preemptive influence of the Cold War, for it has transformed many regional problems into world problems by re-

---

[18] E. S. Furniss, Jr., "A Re-examination of Regional Arrangements," *Journal of International Affairs* (New York), May 1955 (Vol. 9, No. 2), p. 84.
[19] Security Council *Official Records* (17th year), 998th meeting, March 23, 1962, p. 30.

quiring that they be dealt with in a broader forum where both the United States and the Soviet Union are represented.

Despite these limitations, from the point of view of the United States, regional defense arrangements have served a number of extremely useful purposes. In the first place, they served notice to the entire world that the United States and its allies openly recognized the serious nature of the Communist threat and stood ready to take common action to meet it. In the second place, they stimulated the efforts of the treaty states to help themselves and each other, thus encouraging a higher degree of unity and teamwork than would have been possible through simple bilateral arrangements. Moreover, from a political point of view they provided an acceptable method and organizational framework for the introduction of United States power and influence into various regions of the world where weakness and instability invited Communist aggression.

It is, of course, impossible to prove that the existence of arrangements like NATO, SEATO, and CENTO actually stemmed Communist aggressive designs against the non-Communist countries of Western Europe and of Asia. One can only speculate about what *might* have happened if such organizations had not been created. This much, however, is perfectly clear: The *threat* of Soviet aggression had so permeated Western European thinking by 1949 and had stimulated such a feeling of fear and insecurity that real progress toward political stability and economic growth became impossible. NATO dissipated this fear and, together with the Marshall Plan, ushered Europe into a period of development and prosperity unparalleled in modern times. The case for SEATO and CENTO may be somewhat less obvious. The fact that Mao Tse-tung and other Communist leaders have repeatedly denounced them, however, would suggest that they have served not only as an irritant but also as a brake upon the expansionist ambitions of the Communist powers.

Prior to the assassination of President John F. Kennedy, Administration leaders placed a good deal of emphasis upon the so-called "grand design" in which a developed and integrated Atlantic Community would serve as the central core of strength of a worldwide community of free nations. Although these terms were never very clearly defined, it was apparent that President Kennedy's hopes for a strengthened Atlantic Community were conditioned by a realization that the United States is a global power with heavy commitments in Asia, Africa, Latin America, the Middle East, and Europe. He realized, too, that any move on the part of the United States to confine its interests to Europe or to Latin America would gravely weaken United States foreign policy and undermine its role as a world power. Administration leaders therefore frequently referred to the important work of the OAS, SEATO, CENTO, and other evolving organizations of the new nations and considered them—together with the Atlantic Community—as the "potential components" of a worldwide community of free nations. This development, they believed, would also contribute to a "stronger and more effective United Nations" and thus to the building of a broader world order.[20]

Since President Lyndon B. Johnson took over the White House, more attention has been given to domestic matters and relatively little has been said about the grand design. Administration leaders appear to take a somewhat more pragmatic approach to a pluralistic world—a "world of great diversity with many centers of power and influence . . . coming into better focus."[21] They recognize, on the one hand, that a genuine world community is not within our grasp either now or in the foreseeable future. They also realize that regional organizations are unequipped to cope with many important problems which are global in character and which are only made more difficult by attempts to distort them or squeeze them into regional molds. Speaking in Washington on March 11, 1965, Ambassador Adlai E. Stevenson put it this way:

For the foreseeable future we will have to pursue world peace and world order in a combination of ways: bilaterally, multilaterally, regionally, and through the U.N. There must be continuous flexibility about this. Each of these methods has its limitations, as well as advantages.[22]

From the United States point of view the Cuban missile crisis illustrates very well the constructive results that can flow from cooperative action between a regional organization and the United Nations. Certainly the timely support of the United States position by the OAS coupled with direct bilateral negotiations between the Soviet Union and the United States were instrumental in preventing the outbreak of hostilities that might have escalated into nuclear war. But equally helpful was the indispensable role of the United Nations. It afforded an essential world forum for the presentation of the United States' case, it made possible extremely valuable diplomatic contacts, and, last but by no means least, it made available the unique assistance of a highly qualified third party, Secretary-General U Thant. In this instance surely, regional action combined with global diplomacy and direct negotiations all helped materially in bringing about the desired results.

In this connection some supporters of the United Nations have vigorously criticized the United States for "bypassing" the Organization and urging the solution of disputes in other forums. This treatment, it

[20] See Francis O. Wilcox and H. Field Haviland, Jr. (ed.), *The Atlantic Community: Progress and Prospects* (New York: Frederick A. Praeger, 1963), pp. 186 ff.
[21] Speech of United States Secretary of State Dean Rusk, New York City, January 10, 1964.
[22] Speech before the Overseas Writers Club.

is argued, tends to expose the weaknesses of the United Nations and downgrade its influence in the world community. Would it not be better to encourage its development and strengthen its capacity to cope with difficult situations by turning to it more often? How can we expect it to discharge its responsibilities if we deliberately ignore it and avoid its jurisdiction?

While these arguments have some merit, it seems to me they overlook two fundamental considerations. In the first place, the Charter does not urge Member States to dump all their problems on the UN doorstep; to the contrary, it enjoins them to make every effort to settle their disputes elsewhere, resorting to the United Nations only if other methods of peaceful settlement prove unsatisfactory. Secondly, it neither helps the cause of world peace nor strengthens the United Nations when we ask it to perform impossible tasks. In the field of diplomacy, practice does not necessarily make for perfection; clearly the Member States can do the United Nations more harm than good by overburdening it with difficult problems.

In facing this dilemma the United States has used a pragmatic approach in which each case is examined on its merits. In the light of available facts, where can a particular problem be dealt with most effectively—in the United Nations, in a regional context, or through the channels of bilateral diplomacy? Will debate in the United Nations tend to exacerbate the dispute or is there a reasonable chance that it will help facilitate settlement? Will such action further the objectives of United States policy—which include the strengthening of the United Nations—or will it hamper their achievement? Responding to questions like these, the United States strongly supported UN action in Iran, Greece, Suez, and the Congo (Leopoldville) and in the later stages of the crisis over Cyprus. The United States favored regional jurisdiction in the Guatemalan and Cuban cases and it opposed, for what appeared to be sound reasons, UN intervention during the early stages of the Algerian and Cyprus disputes. The Administration has been unwilling, at least until April 1965, to invoke UN assistance in Berlin and South Vietnam because it did not feel, in view of the unique nature of the controversies and the parties involved, that the United Nations could make any useful contribution to these differences.

It is a mistake to assume, as some people apparently do, that the United Nations is an end in itself. It is only a means, and only one of the means, through which the United States and other countries can work toward a more orderly world. True, we can do a real disservice to the cause of international organization by arbitrarily preventing it from dealing with serious matters that urgently cry for peaceful adjustment. At the same time we must recognize the practical limitations on its use. In a world where goodwill and sincerity of purpose are scarce commodities and where states may bring their problems to international organizations in order to gain political advantage rather than to seek a just settlement, it would be a mistake to impose too heavy a burden upon the United Nations unless we are sure the Great Powers stand ready to support it.

### Toward the Future

The experience of the last twenty years suggests that it is easy to overemphasize the effectiveness of regional organizations in the peace-making process. Physical proximity often breeds controversy and in many instances the people of a particular region are less well equipped than outsiders to settle their own differences. Indeed, where disputes are deep-seated and bitter, the objective approach, the neutral facilities, and the constructive encouragement of countries or organizations outside the region are sometimes more acceptable to the conflicting parties than the assistance proffered by neighboring states.

In making these observations, one can not deny the obvious advantages of regionalism. Clearly a smaller organization, such as the OAS or the OAU, which is restricted geographically to nations in relatively close proximity to each other, can create the kind of machinery its members need to cope with their common problems more effectively than a world organization. States located several thousand miles away from each other, separated by vast differences in historical background, culture, language, and political and economic interests, may find it difficult to appreciate as fully as they should the mutual problems that afford them a common basis for cooperative action. Even more important, most states have not accepted the idea that world peace is indivisible. Insofar as collective action to repel aggression is concerned, they are inclined to respond with far greater speed and vigor to a security threat in their own area than to a distant danger whose focal point is far from their own frontiers.

The advantages of a global approach toward peace and security are equally obvious and equally persuasive. It is extremely difficult, for example, to determine with any degree of precision the geographic confines of a region or to decide which states should logically belong to a regional organization. NATO, SEATO, CENTO, and even the OAS, with their curious mélange of members, offer ample proof for this observation. Moreover, even within a well-defined regional area, states sharing the same linguistic and cultural backgrounds may differ sharply with respect to ideology and political institutions. In a world torn by Cold War cleavages such differences place serious limitations upon the effectiveness of regional action.

But still more convincing in practice is the striking fact that world problems simply do not recognize regional boundary lines. Even problems that are local at the outset often spill over into other regions of the world and assume a significance all out of proportion to their original importance. This was certainly true of the controversy between Italy and Austria over the problem of South Tyrol which eventually found its way into the General Assembly. It was also true of the dispute over Cyprus which was localized for many months until it erupted and became a threat to world peace. It is particularly true of many problems that take on Cold War overtones and by that fact cut across regional frontiers.

The obvious fact is that neither the United Nations nor the regional agencies have functioned as effectively as we would like, particularly with respect to peaceful settlement. Indeed, as one writer reminds us, the list of armed conflicts that have taken place since World War II "is probably as large as during any comparable period in history."[23] Literally dozens of controversies simmer on in varying degrees of intensity, without being submitted to any of the regional agencies for consideration or settlement. And many dangerously explosive disputes—including Laos, Berlin, and South Vietnam—go on indefinitely without finding a place on the agenda of the United Nations. This reluctance of states to turn to established organs for help is undoubtedly due to a variety of factors, but it stems primarily from the realization by the states involved that in submitting their problems to a multilateral forum they lose a certain element of control over their solution.

Yet despite the plethora of unresolved disputes that plague the international community, we have managed to muddle through twenty years of UN history without plunging the world into nuclear war. To that extent the deterring power of some of our regional agencies coupled with the moral force and the peacekeeping activities of the United Nations have been successful. A good many serious crises, including more recent situations in Algeria, West Irian, Lebanon, the Suez, and Cuba, have been met and are fading into history. Moreover, most of the open conflicts that have arisen have been limited both in terms of the weapons used and in terms of their geographic scope. In no case have nuclear weapons been called upon; and in nearly every instance the conflicts have been kept within the borders of a single state. Most important is the fact that the two superpowers have at all times avoided becoming involved in direct hostilities against each other.

Whether primary credit for these successes should be accorded to the United Nations or the regional agencies may be debatable. What is not debatable is the obvious fact that few if any burning issues have been resolved at the regional level. It is equally clear that the United Nations has served as a court of last resort handling many of the tough problems that have proved too hot to handle elsewhere. At the same

[23] Evan Luard, *Peace and Opinion* (London: Oxford University Press, 1962), pp. 35–38.

time, inasmuch as the United Nations has not had at its disposal the armed forces needed to keep the peace, most reasonable men would probably agree that regional organizations and alliances have made an invaluable contribution to world order.

Clearly such general organizations as the OAS, the Arab League, and probably the OAU will continue to have an important role to play on the world stage. The future of regional defense organizations like NATO, SEATO, and the Warsaw Treaty Organization will depend, to a large extent, upon the intensity of the Cold War and the nature of the security threat to which member states are subjected in a changing world. . . .

●   ●   ●

. . . If anything like a reasonable balance is to be maintained between the regional and the universal, the United Nations must be reshaped to meet the realities of a new era. What we have had, during the past nineteen years, is basically a free world peacekeeping mechanism with the United Nations providing the moral and legal support. This is no longer feasible. What we should do now is to strengthen the Organization, first, by building a greater sense of responsibility in UN decision making and, second, by developing a more universal basis of support for UN peacekeeping operations. Unless these things can be done, more and more states may feel compelled to pursue their national interests increasingly outside the United Nations system either by a greater use of regional machinery or through bilateral action of an objectionable kind.

CHARLES G. FENWICK

# International Law: The Old and the New

The Hague Conference of 1907 is over and the delegates return to their respective countries. Aspirations for the pacific settlement of

SOURCE: Charles G. Fenwick, "International Law: The Old And The New," *American Journal of International Law*, LX (July 1966), 475–483. Reprinted by permission,

international disputes have been voiced and a list of possible arbitrators has been drawn up described by the formal name of the Permanent Court of Arbitration. Well and good! No obligation was accepted to have recourse to the Court, but at least the Conference went so far as to declare its acceptance of "the principle of compulsory arbitration" and its applicability to international agreements. At the same time the Conference declared that the divergencies of opinion in respect to compulsory arbitration "have not exceeded the bounds of judicial controversy," and that the delegates, in the course of their long collaboration, had succeeded "in evolving a very lofty conception of the common welfare of humanity."

What "lofty conception" could it have been? Hypocrisy, no! Just an expression of the limited outlook of the governments of 1907, and the limited area of international law at the beginning of the century. Dr. Scott, my professor, just back from the Conference, held out to us the hope that a first step had been taken towards the establishment of a permanent Judicial Arbitration Court, possessed, as it was said, of a sense of judicial responsibility. A draft convention had been proposed which would bring the Court into effect when an agreement could be reached upon a method of selecting the judges. The matter did not seem to be urgent, however, except indeed to Dr. Scott.

But the failure of the Hague Conference to provide more adequate procedures for the pacific settlement of international disputes is pardonable in relation to its more grievous failure to make provision for some system of co-operative defense to replace the balance of power in Europe. Here were the delegates of the nations, assembled in conference, and no constructive idea was so much as suggested. That the balance of power was inherently unstable, and would almost inevitably break down in time, seemed to trouble no one. The hard fact was that war was accepted as part of the normal condition of things. Nationalism had reached the point where war was not only a procedure of self-defense, it was to a degree a test of the virility of a nation, and the ability to make war gave it a right to speak with a measure of authority in determining the policies of the nations.

The result was that out of thirteen conventions adopted at the Hague Conference eleven related to the conduct of the next war. Could practical statesmen actually have believed that the rules so meticulously laid down would be observed in the stress of the major conflict that was to be anticipated? They knew the weapons already in use and could have imagined those that might be invented. Could they not have foreseen that possible new weapons would render rules prescribed for old weapons no longer practicable? At this distance of time the word "naïve" seems best to describe their attitude. So conflicting were the views of the leading maritime Powers at the London Naval Conference a year later that the Declaration adopted there remained unratified. What would not have been contraband ten years before might now be.

Few will contest today the statement that of all major wars the war of 1914 had least justification. There were no moral issues at stake, there was no real threat to the security of Austria-Hungary, merely the issue whether a stronger state might punish a weaker state for an act for which the weaker state could not reasonably be held responsible. What an act of folly, to risk a major war for so little! How unstable a balance of power that could have been upset for so little! Why was a third Hague Conference not called to meet the situation? The answer is that no provision had been made in 1907 for a meeting to prevent war; the only thought was how the war was to be fought. The exchanges of telegrams from members of the Triple Alliance to members of the Dual Alliance read at this date as a confused crossing of purposes. No one really wanted war, but all were prepared for it; and it just came. Britain did not seem to be seriously aware that she might become involved. The Triple Entente was a looser bond than the Triple Alliance. The United States, far off across the wide Atlantic, could see no national interest of its own that might have led it to make an offer of mediation or conciliation. Europe was politically a world of its own.

With war itself in 1914 came the test whether the conditions of war had now changed so much as to justify new instruments and new methods. Was the submarine a justifiable instrument of warfare when it could not meet the traditional conditions under which merchant ships of the enemy might be destroyed? Was it justifiable to "ration" neutral countries lest their excess of production of food and supplies might find its way to a neighboring enemy? Was it permissible to use guns of such long range that it was impossible to direct the fire against military installations and not hit churches and monuments?

In like manner the traditional rules of neutrality were put to their severest test, and their inconsistencies and irrationalities were soon manifest: a country could make loans and sell munitions in vast quantities to one of the belligerents and still remain neutral; it could allow itself to become economically involved in the war and yet remain politically apart from the conflict. If, in view of changed conditions, it made a concession to one side, it was immediately accused by the other of lack of neutrality. At long last, as controversy followed controversy, President Wilson came to declare that " the business of neutrality is over," and that no nation must henceforth be permitted to declare war and set in motion forces so destructive to the normal commerce of peaceful nations. Something must be done to put an end to war itself, since by its very nature it put the neutral state in a position where it must either abandon its neutral rights or fight to maintain them.

The proposal by President Wilson in the Treaty of Versailles of a collective responsibility for the maintenance of peace was a far-reaching one, and it may be said to have marked a line, however inconclusively, between the old international law and the new. There was not, indeed, much hope that without the stabilizing influence of the United States the League of Nations could succeed in making the guarantees of Article 10 of the Covenant effective. But for all that, the principle had been proclaimed that the members of the League were henceforth responsible for the protection of the territorial integrity and political independence of the other members of the League, and that any war or threat of war, whether immediately affecting a particular member of the League or not, was a matter of concern to the whole League, which should take any action considered effectual to safeguard the peace. The proposal was, in point of law, a constructive one of the first order, but in such sharp contrast to the law of 1914 that a majority of the American people were unable to recognize it in the presence of the political confusion of postwar Europe. More serious than that, the proposal to guarantee the independence and territorial integrity of the members of the League did not seem to take into account the fact that many of the territorial arrangements of the Treaty were clearly not so far final as to justify guaranteeing their permanence.

But if the United States would not join the League of Nations, what could it do for peace? Something had to be done to distract the advocates of the League from their idealistic objective and at the same time forestall what appeared to be a new race in armaments. The Washington Conference met in 1922 and agreed upon an over-all ratio of 5-5-3-1.7-1.7 for the United States, Great Britain, France, Japan and Italy. But the ratio was confined to capital ships only, leaving other smaller craft, cruisers, destroyers and submarines, untouched. The agreement was sensational, but little attention was paid to the fact that there was no provision for collective security, the cornerstone of any effective system of peace. International law remained as it was: each state was responsible for its own security, except insofar as a member of the League of Nations might rely upon the provisions of the Covenant. It was almost unpatriotic, at the moment, to suggest that the fundamental weakness of international law, the right of each state to take the law into its own hands, had been overlooked for something that appeared tangible and practicable. The illusion was of short duration.

The additional substitute offered for the refusal of the United States to accept the obligations of the Covenant, known as the Kellogg-Briand Pact, reads at this date as a combination of dramatic idealism and political naïveté. Recourse to war was solemnly condemned and renounced as an instrument of national policy; and a pledge was given that the settlement of all disputes of whatever nature should never be sought except by pacific means. But as if the abstract character of the declaration might have gone too far, an exchange of identic notes made exception of the right of self-defense as interpreted by each state for itself, the only issue on which a nation might be expected to go to war. As in the case of the Washington Conference, the illusion that something constructive had been done for peace was short-lived.

The breakdown of international law came with the defiance by Japan of its pledge made at the time of the Disarmament Conference to respect the Open Door in China, and with the open and unashamed seizure of Manchuria in clear violation of the Covenant, the Nine-Power Treaty, and the Kellogg Pact. But who was to take action to defend the agreements? The League of Nations could do no more than appoint a commission to study the crisis; the United States limited itself to a note to the aggressor that it would not recognize any situation brought about contrary to the obligations of the Kellogg Pact, a reprimand so ineffective as to encourage, or at least not discourage, other aggressors to take the law into their own hands. The rape of Ethiopia followed, with nothing more than economic sanctions by the League against the aggressor, stopping short of the sanction against shipments of oil which might have brought the dictator to a stop. The repudiation of the Treaty of Versailles by the Nazi leader followed. The worst could now be expected, if Chamberlain had been able to read the signs of the times.

As the war clouds gathered, the United States might have thrown its weight against the aggressors and warned them of its determination not to see principles of international law defied with impunity. But we seemed to have no national interest of our own in the maintenance of international law and order. Instead we took the course of modifying the application of the international law of neutrality, so as to prevent any possibility that conditions might arise again such as had brought the United States into the war in 1917. Legislation was adopted prohibiting the making of loans to belligerents or the sale of munitions, both legal under the law of 1914. The result was to give the green light to Hitler and enable him to plan his policies of aggression in the knowledge that Great Britain would not be ready for a war and could not obtain munitions from the United States if war came.

As in 1914, only in a far more drastic form, the violations of international law literally stunned the American people. Neutrality offered no protection against the aggressor. Now at last it was clear that the United States did have a vital national interest of its own in the maintenance of international law and order. The triumph of ruthless aggression in Europe might well mean a danger to the security of the United States, even across the barrier of the Atlantic Ocean. An inter-American conference met at Havana in 1940 and adopted the principle of collective security for the Western Hemisphere—an attack upon one is an attack upon all. Shortly after, the President of the United States, abandoning its technical position of neutrality, met with the British Prime Minister on the high seas and adopted the Atlantic Charter, a definite pledge of co-operation for a better international law "after the final destruction of Nazi tyranny." Neutrality was now at an end, even before Pearl Harbor brought the United States into the war.

The Declaration of United Nations of January 1, 1942, succeeding to the Atlantic Charter, marked the first step towards a new international law. For the time it was an alliance of the 26 states at war with the Axis Powers; but it laid the foundation of the collective security system drafted at Dumbarton Oaks and finally adopted at San Francisco on June 26, 1945. The terms of the Charter were clear and definite, clarifying the obligations of Article 10 of the Covenant of the League of Nations and creating procedures for enforcement. A concession had to be made in giving a veto to the five permanent members constituting, with [ten] elected members, the Security Council, although the veto did not extend to procedural matters. Regional security groups were recognized, and provision was made that in the event of an armed attack they might retain their "inherent right of individual or collective self-defense" until such time as the Security Council should take the means necessary to maintain the peace. A second foundation stone was laid in the provisions for the peaceful settlement of international disputes, which are all comprehensive, although reference to the International Court of Justice is qualified by the consent of the parties, manifested in advance for a limited group of cases by states signing the Optional Clause.

Some twenty or more years have gone by since the principles of a new international law were adopted, since the Charter was signed and the substance of the law was extended into the fields of economic, social and cultural relations. What has been the experience of those years? How far have the ideals of the Charter been put into practice, been made a living reality, been reduced from the abstract to the concrete? Unhappily, on the crucial issue of collective security the new law has simply proved ineffective. The first principle of all law, national as well as international, is the collective responsibility of the whole community for the protection of its individual members. When that goes, the cornerstone of the edifice is shaken. Doubtless the veto power of the permanent members of the Security Council has on occasion prevented decisions that might have resulted in more decisive action to prevent aggression. But far more serious has been an element not taken into account in the formulation of the Charter, the discovery of nuclear energy and the invention of the atomic bomb. Here, within a year of the adoption of the Charter, was a weapon of such a formidable character as to change the underlying assumptions of collective security. For it put the individual state in the position of facing complete annihilation if called upon to take action against a Power in possession of the atomic bomb. The result was that a new balance of power arose, described popularly as a "balance of terror," in which the national security of the United States, itself possessing the bomb, was dependent upon its ability to survive an initial devastating attack and be able to strike back and inflict equal devastation upon the aggressor.

The years succeeding 1946 were thus years of tense competition in the development of nuclear weapons and in the means by which they might be made effective against a potential enemy. The strongest deterrent against the use of the bomb, apart from the inherent immorality of a weapon that could not by its very nature be brought within the traditional laws of war, was the fact that neither side could anticipate victory; both would lose more than they could gain. Limitation of nuclear weapons was attempted; but the Soviet Union was unwilling to permit local inspection of the observance of an agreement. The Test Ban Treaty of 1963 was restricted to new inventions and improvements and did not extend to the limitation of existing stocks of atomic warheads or methods of long-range bombardment. Thus, while the principle of collective security still holds, the application of the principle is for the time ineffective, as are the pledges of pacific settlement listed in the Charter. A number of states soon made it clear that they could not recognize the obligations of the Charter when the conditions under which they had signed the treaty had been so completely changed. The term "neutralism" came into use, not in the sense of neutral states in relation to belligerents under the old law, but in the sense of an unwillingness to take sides in issues bearing upon the "cold war" between the two leading atomic Powers.

However, in spite of the ineffectiveness of the procedures established in the Charter for the enforcement of the principle of collective security, there is no question that both the Security Council and the General Assembly exercise a strong moral influence upon the maintenance of law and order in the international community. The existence of a general forum where problems can be discussed and resolutions adopted makes it possible to meet critical situations before they reach the point of a dangerous crisis. The General Assembly thus acts as a sort of permanent mediatory body before which grievances can be brought and tensions kept under control. In this process the declarations and resolutions of the General Assembly are slowly acquiring an authority beyond the legal obligation of the document. It is a question, however, whether, in view of the large number of former colonial dependencies admitted to membership of the United Nations, the principle of equal voting should be continued in the General Assembly. Does the "sovereign equality" proclaimed by the Charter extend beyond the fundamental area of national self-government and include also the equal right of a state, whatever its size and resources, to determine the financial obligations of the Members. That would be in a sense a denial of the principle itself, and it would defeat rather than promote co-operation. In administrative problems the solution is often to be found in the composition of committees of the Assembly.

Substantial progress has been made in meeting legal problems arising in the normal intercourse of states. Here the International Law Commission established by the General Assembly has been an effective agency for the progressive development of the law, both in its studies of specific problems and in the draft projects it has prepared for conferences, such as that on the Law of the Sea at Geneva in 1958 and those on Diplomatic Intercourse and Immunities of 1961, and on Consular Relations of 1963.

Of significance in recent years has been the tendency to develop rules of international law governing problems of private international law, including the conflict of laws, judicial assistance, and uniformity of legislation. The importance of obtaining a more definite regulation of these topics has obviously grown with the very great increase of commercial relations between states and the attendant increase in communication and travel. A new law of outer space is in the process of development, which falls within a special category of its own.

The law of 1906 was the law of the Western World; so also the law of 1945 in respect to principles and rules not included in the Charter of the United Nations. Did the admission of half a hundred new Asian and African states into the United Nations imply their acceptance of the existing law of the Western World? Doubtless some modification of traditional rules was to be expected, especially where the traditional rule affected adversely the new state by reason of its former colonial status, as in respect to principles of succession and the legal status of natural resources. Perhaps it may even be said to be a matter of surprise that so much respect has been shown for the traditions of Western Europe, apart from occasional psychopathic reactions that relate rather to matter of policy than of general international law.

But the story of the new international law is as yet but half told. Equally important—more important it may prove to be—has been the extension of international law into the new areas of economic and social cooperation. Contrast the law of 1906 with that of 1966 and we are in a sense worlds apart. On the eve of the first World War the struggle of the manufacturing countries for foreign markets went on without restraint, accompanied by a corresponding struggle for supplies of the raw materials of industry that were essential to manufacture. In both cases the control of a colony gave the colonial Power a practical monopoly of both supplies and markets. To protect its commercial interests a state had to have a powerful army and a powerful navy, and these in turn made necessary more economic resources, so that political and economic imperialism proceeded hand in hand. The Constitution of the International Labor Organization, incorporated in the Treaty of Versailles, recognized the need of establishing standards of social justice as a basis of peace, and the long list of draft conventions submitted to the members covered all of the important problems of labor policy. But these were practically lost in the political conflicts that followed the close of the war. The rivalry between the leading Powers appeared to increase rather than diminish, and the financial depression that followed led to an even closer national control of policies of trade and commerce, which in turn increased the political tension.

It was only with the adoption of the Atlantic Charter and the wider Declaration of United Nations that it came to be realized that the hope of a new political order was dependent upon removing the economic causes of war and setting up an ideal of social reconstruction. The barriers to the trade and raw materials of the world must be removed; labor standards must be improved, and social security assured to the people of all countries. The pledges of the Declaration took definite shape in the Charter of the United Nations. The Economic and Social Council is the central co-ordinating body of a group of "specialized agencies" which, although associated with the United Nations, have a separate institutional character which enables them to develop their own law and functions without being dependent upon the political elements of the Security Council and the General Assembly. In addition there are innumerable non-governmental organizations devoted to practically every aspect of human interest cutting across state lines.

A new world has now been opened up in which the old international law of rights and duties is being supplemented by an international law of cooperation, which is slowly building up a body of international common interests which may, in the course of the years, accomplish what the more strictly political elements of the rule of law have thus far been unable to accomplish. Nationalism is for the moment dominant, perhaps, because statehood has taken on a larger meaning with the newly emancipated colonial dependencies, and, in two outstanding cases, from the recourse to political power to further ideological conceptions of economic welfare. But it is the faith and hope of the Western World that the wide range of economic and social activities of the new governmental and non-governmental organizations cannot fail in time to strengthen the bonds of international unity and the realization that the rule of law conceived in a larger sense of justice, is the hope of progress.

Supplementing the economic and social program of the United Nations, and equally far-reaching in its ultimate effects, is the declaration in the preamble of the Charter "to reaffirm faith in fundamental human rights, in the dignity and worth of the human person, in the equal rights of men and women and of nations large and small." The objective is repeated in Article I of the Charter, which enumerates among the Purposes of the United Nations "to achieve international cooperation in solving international problems of an economic, social, cultural, or humanitarian character, and in promoting and encouraging respect for human rights and fundamental freedoms for all without distinction as to race, sex, language, or religion." This was followed by the Universal Declaration of Human Rights enumerating in detail the rights contemplated in the Charter.

Here, for the first time in the history of international law, was an act of the whole community of states, looking behind the formal organization of their governments to the individual human beings who constitute the legal body of the state. It creates, in a sense, a bond of unity cutting across state lines and restricting the sovereignty of the state in a vital area of its domestic life. The individual has thus been accepted as a subject as well as an object of international law, and it is to be expected that, as emphasis upon his human needs increases, the existing over-emphasis upon nationalism may lose something of its present appeal. In a separate field, the Educational, Scientific and Cultural Organization (UNESCO) is seeking to break down the intellectual and moral barriers between states and to promote the "moral disarmament" of the nations, which is declared to be an essential condition of peaceful relations. The task is a vast one, but already enough progress has been made to justify belief in its ultimate success.

*International law, the old and the new.* Looking only at the principles of international law that have come into being, at the widening range of its precepts, at the proclamation of high ideals of co-operation and at the concrete agencies actually functioning, great advances in the law have been made; so great, indeed, that even the idealists of sixty years ago would scarcely believe in the reality of what has taken place. Unhappily the prospect of a world of law and order remains dim, not so much because of the conflict of ideologies between the leading states, which time might moderate by degrees, but because of the invention of the new instruments of destruction, which, in the chance hands of a fanatic, might start a succession of crises beyond the control of the governments that realize their deadly character. The need of controlling so dangerous an instrument of destruction is clear, if only action can be taken in time. The danger is too great to postpone the issue.

RICHARD  W.  VAN  WAGENEN

# The Concept of Community and the Future of the United Nations

It may be unthinkable, even unimaginable, that the United Nations could itself become a true "community" in the near future. It is *not* unthinkable that the UN may be pushing the present disarray a little closer to that goal. The popular press abounds with loose references to the "world community," but men who have thought deeply and hard-headedly about this prospect have also hinted in that direction, using various terms for the same thing. To quote only two, Lincoln P. Bloomfield calmly mentions "the universal society of which the United Nations is the forerunner"[1] and Richard N. Gardner believes that a "genuine world community is waiting to be born. . . ."[2]

• • •

[1] *The United Nations and U.S. Foreign Policy: A New Look at the National Interest* (Boston: Little, Brown and Company, 1960), p. 233. He wisely warned that there is no evidence that purely "functional" interrelationships will lead by any natural or automatic process to political integration, or even that integration as such will eventually be the dominant trend. (*Ibid.*, p. 230).

[2] Richard N. Gardner, *In Pursuit of World Order* (New York: Frederick A. Praeger, 1964), p. 262.

SOURCE: Richard W. Van Wagenen, "The Concept of Community and the Future of the United Nations," *International Organization*, XIX (Summer 1965), 812–827. Reprinted by permission.

Looking at the record of the United Nations over the first twenty years and applying political judgment and common sense, we are likely to conclude that, on balance, the UN is a community-building institution. The line of reasoning is familiar. As the technology of transportation and other forms of communication squeeze the globe into a sphere that is a fraction of its former size, global institutions have been invented or have grown from regional functional institutions. They do not grow as fast as the need for them, but there is a new realization that many things which have to be done *cannot* be done on a less-than-global basis, among them the regulation of transport and communication, the control of outer space, the control of disease, and above all the control of massive armed conflict.

If the doctrine of functionalism is taken at face value, the next step is to reason that the performance of these tasks, especially the economic and social ones in which the UN is so deeply engaged, will strengthen the sense of community over wide areas. This will help to build institutions which in turn strengthen the consensus needed for political community. A benign spiral then carries that sense of community to a point where the institutions gradually grow strong enough to support enforceable law. Such authority, in turn, may be able to check war, the greatest of dangers to man at the present time. The UN is the nearest thing we have to a global political institution. Therefore, to strengthen the UN in structure and function is to provide community-building authority.

There is probably a sound basis for this line of reasoning, but it still represents only a belief. We find it persuasive in the light of the many activities, most of them successful, which have been carried on by the UN in its first two decades. The situation is suggested by Adlai Stevenson, who gives the UN a large share of the credit:

The central trend of our times is the emergence of what, for lack of a better label, might be called a policy of cease-fire and peaceful change. I would suggest . . . that we may be approaching something close to a world consensus on such a policy. . . . Cease-fire and peaceful change may strike some as a curious way to describe a period so jammed by violence, by disorder, by quarrels among the nations—an era so lacking in law and order. But I do not speak wistfully; I speak from the record. It is precisely the fact that so much violence and so many quarrels *have not led to war* that puts a special mark on our times.[4]

---

[4] Address at Princeton University, March 23, 1964, published in Andrew W. Cordier and Wilder Foote (ed.), *The Quest for Peace: The Dag Hammarskjöld Memorial Lectures* (New York: Columbia University Press, 1965), p. 57. For a differing estimate by another respected statesman, see Herbert Hoover in Raymond A. Moore, Jr. (ed.), *The United Nations Reconsidered* (Columbia: University of South Carolina Press, 1963), pp. 80–82. For a strong proposal for action on clearly functionalist

Convinced as we may be, for reasons of good judgment and desperation in unequal parts, that the UN is most assuredly worth supporting, we are left with a question: Did the UN really have much to do with the development of "cease-fire and peaceful change" or would this progress have come anyhow, swept forward by the facts of life? Indeed, does this alleged progress really exist? As analysts, we are uneasy until we have explored the intellectual basis—at least the underlying definitions and concepts—of the favorable assumption through social science research.

## PREMISES AND CONSIDERATIONS OF THEORY

In exploring the second approach, the first thing to note is that the concept of community is elusive and slippery. Any number of scholars, especially sociologists and political scientists, have tried to grip it. The variables involved are almost infinite. The concept is crucial at various levels from the village to the globe; understanding seems to vary inversely with the height of the level so that the international is the most opaque of all. We are not concerned with other levels except as theory developed for studying them is useful at the international level. We do not need to start, therefore, with a comprehensive framework.[5] Rather, we seek a theory which is limited in two respects: It speaks to the international level and it points to the minimal kind of community needed to maintain peace.

We are interested at this point in trying to learn how the existence and operation of the UN may contribute to its strength as an international peacekeeping agency. Is there any sign of UN "community building" as a basis for institutional strength? Is there any secular trend slanting upward or downward through the pointed peaks and rounded valleys of UN crises, from the Iranian case of 1946 to the constitutional crisis of 1965? Does the UN itself have anything positive to do with that trend?

As to the "minimal or maximal" issue, it is a reasonable question whether those parts of the preamble calling for relief from the "scourge of war" and for the establishment of "conditions under which justice and respect for the obligations arising from treaties and other sources of international law can be maintained" are more basic than those parts

---

lines but outside the UN, see the thoughtful speech, "Approaches to International Community," to have been delivered on March 6, 1965, at Pennsylvania State University by Senator J. W. Fulbright.

[5] Such as that of Philip Jacob and Henry Teune in the opening chapter of Philip E. Jacob and James V. Toscano (ed.), *The Integration of Political Communities* (Philadelphia, Penna.: J. B. Lippincott Company, 1964).

reaffirming "faith in fundamental human rights" and encouraging "social progress and better standards of life in larger freedom." It is almost a cliché to say that peace is not merely the absence of war. But the absence of war is itself a valid overriding objective. What is specifically prohibited in the Charter is the unilateral use of force except in self-defense; if this is achieved, at least the "security" aim of the term "international peace and security" is realized.

To state a value premise, we believe that the war-prevention objective is the more fundamental because progress in the other elements of human welfare is impossible without this prerequisite. Yet the old question remains unanswered: Is a high level of welfare—economic and social and political—itself a prerequisite to a community cohesive enough to support institutions for keeping the peace? We take the minimal position: that where the object is peaceful change, the whole list of prerequisite or companion values is not necessary.

This drives us to the concept of security-community and integration as defined and elaborated some years ago in exploring "expanding community" as a focus for research.[6]

A *security-community* is considered to be a group which has become integrated, where *integration* is defined as the attainment of a sense of community, accompanied by formal or informal institutions and practices, sufficiently strong and widespread to assure peaceful change among members of a group with "reasonable" certainty over a "long" period of time.[7]

To avoid circularity, "sense of community" and "peaceful change" were further defined, leading to the necessity of handling also the classic legal and psychological problem of "authority."[8]

When applied to the UN, this set of definitions does not reveal the basis of authority for what the Organization does and the lack of authority for what it does not do. How can it push toward a security-community over as wide an area as possible? How can it promote the process of integration?[9] We are referring to what has been called the "ultimate task":

to convert the world into a pluralistic society marked by a high adjustment potential—by the existence of component parts which are susceptible of regulation in their relationships with each other and with the whole, through the processes of political accommodation.[10]

[6] Richard W. Van Wagenen, *Research in the International Organization Field: Some Notes on a Possible Focus* (Princeton, N.J.: Center for Research on World Political Institutions, 1952).

[7] *Ibid.*, pp. 10–11.

[8] *Ibid.*

[9] The word is used to mean both the process and the condition.

[10] Inis L. Claude, Jr., *Power and International Relations* (New York: Random House, 1962), p. 284.

We are thinking sociologically of

the possibility that the level of organization in the world may be raised, so to speak, so that a more inclusive social system comes to incorporate the national States.[11]

This would be incorporation to the minimum extent needed for a security-community, that is, for integration.

It is quite true, as a thoughtful scholar has put it, that

the competition of states can be pursued by means short of violence but still far in excess of those used by even sharply opposed political parties which accept the basic constitutional order of a state.[12]

Yet it is the habit of this very pursuit short of violence that is the proximate and perhaps the ultimate goal we seek. Even though Stanley Hoffmann is correct in separating for purposes of analysis two different phenomena, the relations between individuals or groups across national boundaries ("transnational society") and competition and cooperation of states having no common authority above them,[13] the study of the integrative process seems to underlie both.

In the most thorough and sophisticated analysis of the doctrine of functionalism so far in print, Ernst Haas defines integration in a way not inconsistent with the definition we have just cited, provided both are used in the sense of process and not of condition:

If the present international scene is conceived of as a series of interacting and mingling national environments, and in terms of their participation in international organizations, then integration would describe the process of *increasing* the interaction and the mingling so as to obscure the boundaries between the system of international organizations and the environment provided by their nation-state members.[14]

This is a more limited use of the word, but consistent especially when we note that Mr. Haas considers

modern nation-states as communities whose basic consensus is restricted to agreement on the *procedure* for maintaining order and settling disputes among groups, for carrying out well-understood functions.[15]

[11] Robert C. Angell, in *The Nature of Conflict* (Paris: United Nations Educational, Scientific and Cultural Organization, 1957), p. 205.
[12] Stanley Hoffmann, "Discord in Community: The North Atlantic Area as a Partial International System," *International Organization*, Summer 1963 (Vol. 17, No. 3), pp. 526–527.
[13] *Ibid.*, p. 525. There is room for disagreement that as a tool of analysis "the word *community* does more harm than good. . . ."
[14] Ernst B. Haas, *Beyond the Nation-State: Functionalism and International Organization* (Stanford, Calif.: Stanford University Press, 1964), p. 29.
[15] *Ibid.*, p. 39.

We are dealing with the United Nations as an organization. Concerning the outcomes of organizations, Mr. Haas identifies three types of decision-making processes or, as he calls them, recurrent patterns of outcomes. The least demanding is accommodation on the basis of the minimum common denominator, pleasing only the least cooperative bargaining partner. The other two are more demanding and carry the participants farther along the path toward integration: accommodation by splitting the difference and accommodation "on the basis of deliberately or inadvertently upgrading the common interests of the parties." Mr. Haas believes that

the proof of an organizational impact lies in the appearance of a new set of general interests that command respect among the members—in short, a new world task.

There are three specific indicators: institutional autonomy, authority ("grudging implementation bestowed on organizational acts"), and legitimacy. He believes that the position of the UN system could be summed up convincingly if the degree of its legitimacy could be specified. [16]

His pioneering studies exploring integration in the European setting are well-known.[17] It is quite a jump from a set of nuclear European politico-economic organizations to a single-purpose functional worldwide international organization (the International Labor Organization [ILO]) and from there to a general-purpose political organization (the UN). Ernst Haas' work lends encouragement to those who would like to make this second leap.

The other lead toward assessing the integrative possibilities of the UN comes from the indicators devised by Karl Deutsch[18] in order to apply the Princeton concept of integration and security-community[19] and to develop it for exploring the integration of the North Atlantic area.[20] Again there is a conceptual leap from the historical cases of integration to the North Atlantic area and from there to the UN.

In the Princeton study *dis*integrative conditions were not handled systematically except in the case of amalgamated security-communities

[16] *Ibid.*, pp. 111, 131–133.
[17] Especially *The Uniting of Europe* (Stanford, Calif.: Stanford University Press, 1958) and *Consensus Formation in the Council of Europe* (Berkeley: University of California Press, 1960).
[18] *Political Community at the International Level: Problems of Definition and Measurement* (Garden City, N.Y.: Doubleday, 1954).
[19] See p. 815 above.
[20] Karl W. Deutsch and others, *Political Community and the North Atlantic Area: International Organization in the Light of Historical Experience* (Princeton, N.J.: Princeton University Press, 1957).

in history[21] so that we are unable to explore by this means whether the UN may be promoting some unknown disintegrative conditions at the same time it may be promoting integrative ones. . . .

•     •     •

Obviously the UN system as a whole is not a security-community and perhaps it never will be. Some groups of its Members already constitute such communities. The United States and Canada provide the clearest example and there are many others. Some are at the other end of the scale, for example, Israel and Jordan. Most are in between. Does the UN system promote or deter the process of international integration among large groupings of at least its non-Communist membership?

Do the findings of the Princeton historical studies have any application here?

One of the three conditions that were found to be *essential but not sufficient* for attainment of a security-community was

a compatibility of the main values held by the relevant strata of all the political units involved; and with this condition there sometimes had to be also a tacit agreement to deprive any remaining incompatible values of their political significance.[24]

What can be construed as main values and relevant strata is wide open as far as the UN system is concerned. Values such as democracy and constitutionalism do not have equivalent meanings among many of the Members or among the revelant strata of society within Member States although they do have equivalent meanings among a majority of the Members having at least a bare majority of the population represented in the UN. Such broad values as social rights and economic welfare have a wide acceptance although the meaning of the terms is not identical everywhere. Prestige and independence are certainly among the main values of a nation-state, but they need referents: prestige in the eyes of whom, and independence from whom?

Our question is narrower, however, in two ways: 1) Integration does not ask congruence, only compatibility; peaceful coexistence, if it is genuine and permanent, is sufficient to uphold a security-community. 2) The present situation is not so much our concern as whether the UN promotes for the future any closer compatibility of values or the defusing of incompatible ones.

[21] Since the amalgamated security-community is beyond even the most visionary notions about the future of the UN, only those parts of the study found relevant to pluralistic security-communities will be applied here.

[24] Deutsch and others, p. 123.

It is a temptation to decide that one value, an overwhelming desire to settle conflicts by peaceful (nonphysical) means, is more basic than any other in assessing progress toward a security-community. But this has not been proven, either as to its validity or as to its embodiment in national policies. Only two of the larger Members of the UN in 1964 or 1965 were on record with a policy of first-strike military force against another Member—the United Arab Republic (and its allies) and Indonesia—and by the end of the year one had resigned its membership. Two other Members came close to outright war in 1964 and it is not certain that they will avoid battle over Cyprus in the future. The availability of a UN alternative on the ground, which was not the case when three major Members of the UN undertook in 1956 to settle another problem by physical means, may have made some difference. The most that can be said about this indicator at present is close to simple assertion: Most students and observers of the UN system would probably judge that major national values are rendered slightly more compatible by constant exposure to each other in the UN system.

The second condition found to be essential was mutual responsiveness: mutual sympathy or loyalties, trust and consideration, at least some identification in terms of self-images and interests, and ability to predict behavior—a process of social learning.[25] Is there really much doubt that this kind of learning goes on in the UN? Clearly the Organization serves as more than a magnifier of existing images, merely enhancing congruences and incongruities alike. It also helps to predict behavior. The perpetual attention to, communication of, and perception of needs are there, as is at least some identification in terms of self-images and interests. Constant communication is one of the advantages of parliamentary diplomacy most frequently celebrated.[26]

•  •  •

The third condition found to be essential was

a multiplicity of ranges of communication and transactions between the units involved, and also a fairly wide range of different functions and services, together with the organizations to carry them out.[31]

The same judgment applies to this criterion as to the one calling for

---

[25] *Ibid.*, p. 129.

[26] Outside the formal agenda the General Assembly has become the world's greatest switchboard for bilateral diplomacy. . . . In New York last fall, in a period of 11 days, I conferred with the foreign ministers or heads of government of 54 nations. (United States Secretary of State Dean Rusk, in Cordier and Foote, p. 74, referring to the fall of 1963.)

[31] Deutsch and others, p. 144.

mutual responsiveness. There seems little doubt that the operation of the far-flung UN system meets this condition even though these operations are spread very thinly among the myriad contacts already flourishing outside that system—messages, face-to-face contacts, and especially trade. The operations are certainly pervasive.[32] But the question remains whether these are keeping up with the increasing number of participating people and units in the world. If not, the effect may be integrative but fail to be net integrative.

•  •  •

Moving from indicators arising from the study of historical cases in limited geographical areas, we can ask what can be done with indicators arising from the study of a contemporary international organiation performing a definite but limited function on an almost worldwide basis.

Those developed by Ernst Haas are of two kinds: 1) As to procedures, there should be a greater integrative effect as they move from minimum common denominator into accommodation by splitting the difference and still farther into upgrading the common interests of the parties. 2) If the result of the operations is increased autonomy, authority, or legitimacy for the organization, and especially legitimacy, there is an integrative effect.

Most decisions in the UN are doubtless of the "minimum common denominator" sort, with little compromise involved. These are found in many fields—gestures of condemnation against South Africa, the Kashmir dispute, a declaration of human rights in place of conventions, and the like. Most of these decisions are the ones that do not move from the corridors into the conference rooms because feelers have shown that an alternative has too little chance to survive. Compromise then takes the form of agreed inaction, sometimes quiet and sometimes noisy. Some of the noisy instances might be called the senatorial courtesy cases, where a matter that obviously concerns the UN is brought forward but laid aside after it is made clear that one Member would "take a walk" if pressed—the instances concerning Hyderabad, Goa, and Algeria, for example. Probably the greatest of these is the current constitutional crisis, where the will and wisdom to avoid confrontation on Article 19 have halted the General Assembly in its tracks. Even ILO, by far the most carefully studied agency in the UN system, usually operates on this

---

[32] "We must recognize that there is a United Nations angle, presently or prospectively, to every major subject of foreign policy." (United States Assistant Secretary of State Harlan Cleveland, in Francis O. Wilcox and H. Field Haviland, Jr. [ed.], *The United States and the United Nations* [Baltimore, Md.: The Johns Hopkins Press, 1961], p. 147.)

basis of the minimum common denominator, according to Ernst Haas.[39]

There is ample evidence that the two more advanced procedures specified by Mr. Haas are also found frequently in the conduct of UN business. Compromising the final bargaining positions of Members is done each year when the budget tries to squeeze between the cutters and the spenders. It is also done in revising the scale of assessments and recently when the Committee of Experts on the Review of the Activities and Organization of the Secretariat revised the formula for geographical distribution of Secretariat members among the competing interests. The Secretary-General's mediation work, for example, the ground-breaking Beck-Friis mission to Cambodia and Thailand in 1959 and the mission to Laos later that year, might be considered in the third category, but to be conservative we can consider it here. The fact that these missions did not permanently solve the problems facing them (just as the mediation job in Cyprus has not yet succeeded) does not surprise those familiar with international politics or subtract much from the efficacy of such operations at the time. The "opting out" technique is an odd example of this procedure. By this we mean that the failure of certain members to buy UN bonds does not stop the sale of bonds to other Members, nor does the failure of some Members to pledge toward voluntarily supported programs such as the Expanded Program of Technical Assistance (EPTA) and the UN Children's Fund (UNICEF) veto those operations.

The third and most advanced procedure is naturally harder to identify in the UN context, but two or three kinds of operations seem to involve upgrading the common interests of the parties. One is international military force authorized by a worldwide body, a "new world task" of recent times. Despite their distinctly different purposes, the UN Emergency Force (UNEF), the UN Operation in the Congo (ONUC), and the UN Peacekeeping Force in Cyprus (UNFICYP) are good examples. These are not simply the implementation of an existing will to peace, but a little bit more. Another kind of operation in this category is economic planning and execution on a multi-national scale, a task of large dimensions and poor coordination. Within the UN system the main agencies are the International Monetary Fund (IMF), the International Bank for Reconstruction and Development (IBRD) and its two affiliates, the other specialized agencies in the economic field, the Special Fund, EPTA, and the four regional economic commissions. Some of these operations mesh with each other, but that does not bring them very close to such regional non-UN organizations as the Inter-American Development Bank (IDB) of the Organization of American States (OAS)

[39] Haas, *Beyond the Nation-State,* p. 445.

or the Development Assistance Committee (DAC) of the Organization for Economic Cooperation and Development (OECD). It is debatable whether the more successful these organizations become the more strongly they will give economic support to an existing political nationalism and hence have a disintegrative effect from the standpoint of the community as a whole. Yet they tend more and more to coordinate their efforts and at least some of them realize that not every country needs a steel mill.[40] It is the national foreign aid programs that cater more to the desire for unwarranted self-sufficiency.

•     •     •

Turning to the factor of institutional autonomy mentioned by Mr. Haas, it may be noted first that the Secretary-General's authority has gone up and down.[44] Trygve Lie asserted more leadership than he is generally given credit for and achieved a considerable image of authority and autonomy before being turned upon by one of the major powers. Dag Hammarskjöld exhibited surefooted leadership, reaching a point where he was given political jobs to perform without specific instructions. This began with the United States flyers in Communist China (late 1954) and moved to the observation task in Lebanon (1958) and to the Congo operation in 1960. He went still further philosophically in his Oxford address shortly before his death.[45] It is doubtful that he would have been able to push that quite revolutionary stretching exercise, but his work may foreshadow a long-range trend in the direction of autonomy and authority if the Organization survives the present downdraft.

There is little doubt about the favorable effect of IBRD representatives and field missions in creating respect for the Bank, but the reluctance of staff members to advertise their connection with the UN

[40] Two recent publications of the UN illustrate this emphasis upon transnational approaches: *Possibilities of Integrated Industrial Development in Central America* (UN Document E/CN.12/683/Rev.1); and *The Economic Development of Latin America in the Post-War Period* (UN Document E/CN.12/659/Rev.1). On the grand scale, the Mekong River program involves 25 countries within and outside the Economic Commission for Asia and the Far East (ECAFE) region plus twelve UN organs or units.

[44] See Charles Winchmore, "The Secretariat: Retrospect and Prospect," earlier in this volume.

[45] He stated his belief that the Secretary-General could "resolve controversial questions on a truly international basis without obtaining the formal decision of the organs . . . ," since the

principles of the Charter are . . . supplemented by the body of legal doctrine and precepts that have been accepted by States generally, and particularly as manifested in the resolutions of UN organs.

(*The International Civil Servant in Law and in Fact* [Oxford: Clarendon Press, 1961], pp. 24–25.)

makes it likely that no more than the outer rim of the Bank's halo touches the UN system as a whole. The halo seems to be stretching, however, as the Bank's new President brings the Bank closer to the UN and the other specialized agencies. Evidence of the influence of UN Resident Representatives is not scarce but has never been fully analyzed. As of 1964, their increasing utility has been noted, save in the task of country programming.[46] The impact of these 83 offices headed by either a Resident Representative or a Deputy, all engaged in economic and social activities of interest to the local population, varies from country to country and from situation to situation, but it is unknown in terms of their authority-building function. The same is true for Directors of UN Information Centers and indeed for the effect of the entire UN information program. . . .

•   •   •

The distinction Ernst Haas makes between authority and legitimacy is an important one from the standpoint of creating a real security-community,[48] yet one of these includes the other. It would be hard to imagine legitimacy without authority, but authority without legitimacy is commonplace.[49] If research could follow the suggestion Mr. Haas makes, we could learn something significant about integrative progress. He proposes that

a rough measure of legitimacy can be provided by distilling from the historical material the situations in which member states invoke the purposes and principles of the UN to justify some item of national policy, such invocation being at the same time accompanied by an expansion of the global task.[50]

This index would be rough indeed, but if it sidestepped the trap of false cause-and-effect, it would be worth making. Citing UN principles might be more of a justification than a true motive for something which a Member government wanted to do, seeking legitimation from the UN in the same way that battling troops seek the legitimation of God for

[46] Gerard J. Mangone, *The United Nations Resident Representative: A Case of Administrative Institution-Building* (unpublished paper, 1964), pp. 27, 79.

[48] Legitimacy provides a presumption of "repetition or expansion of peaceful change procedures . . . ," whereas mere authority does not. (Haas, *Beyond the Nation-State*, p. 133.)

[49] For example, one would suppose that the UN Truce Supervision Organization (UNTSO) is a good case of at least some authority without legitimacy at present, asking again an old question: "What is the consensus-forming effect, not simply the immediate agreement-reaching effect, of the United Nations' mixed commissions in Palestine?" (Van Wagenen, p. 44.)

[50] Haas, *Beyond the Nation-State*, p. 133.

their cause. Yet the mere fact that the blessing is sought would tend to build up the legitimacy of the blesser.

• • •

## THE ESCALATION OF COMMUNITY

The conclusions are more suggestive than conclusive in response to our opening questions: Is there any sign of "community building"? Is there any secular trend slanting upward or downward? Does the UN itself have anything positive to do with that trend? While the UN undoubtedly does some disintegrative and many nonintegrative things, it also does many apparently integrative things in integrative ways. It is not too exuberant to say that the net direction seems to be integrative, tending toward the eventual building of a security-community broader than we have today.

There is no way to be sure of a security-community before time has delivered the pragmatic test. Yet it is likely that the work of the UN system and the personal contact which that work entails will help to grow more of what we have been calling pluralistic security-communities where they do not yet exist.[52] This conclusion, however, evades a crucial question: Is it more dangerous to have fewer and tighter communities on a less-than-global level than to leave things as they are? Also, we cannot forget that if evidence of a trend toward integration appears on the international political scene it is impossible to estimate how much credit is due to the UN system.

How can the integrative work of the UN be stregthened? Activities should be undertaken which build muscle without the danger of hernia. These are activities that lead to the expansion of tasks that are successfully handled and that appear to increase the authority and later the legitimacy of the UN system.

In practical terms, this means that within the margins of maneuver open to Members the UN should be given jobs to do which 1) are conspicuously related to the UN, 2) have a good chance of success in a technical or administrative sense, 3) involve the lives of many influential people in several significant Member States, and 4) bring tangible rewards to Members, if possible including the prevention of expensive wars.

This simple formulation may seem self-evident enough in logic and unattainable enough in practice to invite concrete illustration. The

[52] Perhaps in Central America, parts of the Indian subcontinent and Southeast Asia, or some of the Arab states, for example.

most convincing examples are the normal activities of the specialized agencies, which are at present by no means conspicuous enough.[53] Greater use of the International Court of Justice would be helpful in cases where advisory opinions are certain to be accepted and where decisions are most likely to be executed. The field of human rights also offers an opportunity that may have been underrated.[54] Further practice is recommended in forming UN peacekeeping operations where they have a fair chance of being conspicuously successful in the eyes of many Members of the UN. Proposals for designating national contigents and for drafting logistical head starts and other plans are in this realm and have already begun. A greater use of UN observers is also indicated. Arms control and outer space lie before us. The bed of the sea in some parts of the world is pregnant with resources and awaits community action to prevent fighting over their ownership. Indeed, the subtle "side effects" coming out of *any* operation bear close watching.

• • •

## STUDY QUESTIONS

1. Explain the "static" and "dynamic" concepts of the United Nations. Which of these concepts more nearly embraces the idea of the U.N. as a "community building" institution? Is the Secretariat as presently constituted adequate to the promotion of an international security-community?

2. In what sense does the practice of requiring the unanimous vote of the five permanent members of the Security Council facilitate the promotion of the underlying principles of the U.N.? Cite examples of discrepancies between these principles and the general practice of member nations.

3. In what legal and other ways, and with degree of success, have regional organizations attempted to supplement the role of the U.N. in the peaceful settlement of disputes? What is the American view of the relationship between regional organizations and the U.N.?

4. What is the theoretical and practical role of international law in achieving collective security within the framework of the U.N.? In this connection,

[53] As with the reporting of public affairs at any level, the monotony of the unexciting brings about the monopoly of the exciting.
[54] See especially, Percy E. Corbett, *The Individual and World Society* (Princeton, N.J.: Center for Research on World Political Institutions, 1953), pp. 47–59; and Gardner, Chapter 10.

what is meant by the "new" international law, and how successful has it been in increasing collective security?

## SUGGESTIONS FOR FURTHER READING

BLAISDELL, DONALD C. *International Organization.* New York: The Ronald Press, 1966.

BLOOMFIELD, LINCOLN P. *The United Nations and U. S. Foreign Policy: A New Look at the National Interest.* Boston: Little, Brown, 1960.

BRIERLY, J. A. *The Law of Nations: An Introduction to the International Law of Peace,* edited by Sir Humphrey Waldock. 6th ed. New York: Oxford University Press, 1963.

CLAUDE, INIS L., JR. *Swords into Plowshares: the Problems and Progress of International Organization.* 3rd ed., rev. New York: Random House, 1964.

COX, ARTHUR M. *Prospects for Peacekeeping.* Washington, D.C.: The Brookings Institution, 1967.

COYLE, DAVID CUSHMAN. *The United Nations and How It Works.* New ed., New York: Columbia University Press, 1965.

FALK, RICHARD A. AND WOLFRAM F. HANRIEDER. *International Law Organization: an Introductory Reader.* Philadelphia: J. B. Lippincott, 1968.

GOODSPEED, STEPHEN S. *The Nature and Function of International Organization.* 2nd ed. New York: Oxford University Press, 1967.

GROSS, ERNEST A. *The United Nations: Structure for Peace.* New York: Published for the Council on Foreign Relations by Harper & Row, 1962.

JACOB, PHILIP E. AND ALEXINE L. ATHERTON. *The Dynamics of International Organization: The Making of World Order.* Homewood, Illinois: The Dorsey Press, 1965.

KAY, DAVID A. (ed.). *The United Nations Political System.* New York: John Wiley & Sons, 1967.

NICHOLAS, H. G. *The United Nations as a Political Institution.* 3rd ed. London: Oxford University Press, 1967.

NYE, JOSEPH S., JR. *International Regionalism: Readings.* Boston: Little, Brown, 1968.

STOESSINGER, JOHN G. *The United Nations and the Superpowers: United States-Soviet Interaction at the United Nations.* New York: Random House, 1965.

VANDENBOSCH, AMRY AND WILLARD N. HOGAN. *Toward World Order.* New York: McGraw-Hill, 1963.

WATERS, MAURICE. *The United Nations: International Organization and Administration.* New York: The Macmillan Company, 1967.

# APPENDICES

A. *Charter of the United Nations*
B. *Test Ban Treaty*
C. *Non-Proliferation of Nuclear Weapons Treaty*

# Charter of the United Nations*

## We the peoples of the United Nations determined

to save succeeding generations from the scourge of war, which twice in our lifetime has brought untold sorrow to mankind, and
to reaffirm faith in fundamental human rights, in the dignity and worth of the human person, in the equal rights of men and women and of nations large and small, and
to establish conditions under which justice and respect for the obligations arising from treaties and other sources of international law can be maintained, and
to promote social progress and better standards of life in larger freedom,

## And for these ends

to practice tolerance and live together in peace with one another as good neighbors, and
to unite our strength to maintain international peace and security, and
to ensure, by the acceptance of principles and the institution of methods, that armed force shall not be used, save in the common interest, and
to employ international machinery for the promotion of the economic and social advancement of all peoples,

## Have resolved to combine our efforts to accomplish these aims.

Accordingly, our respective Governments, through representatives assembled in the City of San Francisco, who have exhibited their full powers found to be in good and due form, have agreed to the present Charter of the United Nations and do hereby establish an international organization to be known as the United Nations.

* Signed at the United Nations Conference on International Organization, San Francisco, California, June 26, 1945. Department of State Publication 2353, Conference Series 74.

CHAPTER I:   PURPOSES AND PRINCIPLES

## Article 1

The Purposes of the United Nations are:

1. To maintain international peace and security, and to that end: to take effective collective measures for the prevention and removal of threats to the peace, and for the suppression of acts of aggression or other breaches of the peace, and to bring about by peaceful means, and in conformity with the principles of justice and international law, adjustment or settlement of international disputes or situations which might lead to a breach of the peace;

2. To develop friendly relations among nations based on respect for the principle of equal rights and self-determination of peoples, and to take other appropriate measures to strengthen universal peace;

3. To achieve international cooperation in solving international problems of an economic, social, cultural, or humanitarian character, and in promoting and encouraging respect for human rights and for fundamental freedoms for all without distinction as to race, sex, language, or religion; and

4. To be a center for harmonizing the actions of nations in the attainment of these common ends.

## Article 2

The Organization and its Members, in pursuit of the Purposes stated in Article 1, shall act in accordance with the following Principles.

1. The Organization is based on the principle of the sovereign equality of all its Members.

2. All Members, in order to ensure to all of them the rights and benefits resulting from membership, shall fulfill in good faith the obligations assumed by them in accordance with the present Charter.

3. All Members shall settle their international disputes by peaceful means in such a manner that international peace and security, and justice, are not endangered.

4. All Members shall refrain in their international relations from the threat or use of force against the territorial integrity or political independence of any state, or in any other manner inconsistent with the Purposes of the United Nations.

5. All Members shall give the United Nations every assistance in any action it takes in accordance with the present Charter, and shall refrain from giving assistance to any state against which the United Nations is taking preventive or enforcement action.

6. The Organization shall ensure that states which are not Members of the United Nations act in accordance with these Principles so far as may be necessary for the maintenance of international peace and security.

7. Nothing contained in the present Charter shall authorize the United Nations to intervene in matters which are essentially within the domestic

jurisdiction of any state or shall require the Members to submit such matters to settlement under the present Charter; but this principle shall not prejudice the application of enforcement measures under Chapter VII.

## Chapter II: Membership

### Article 3

The original Members of the United Nations shall be the states which, having participated in the United Nations Conference on International Organization at San Francisco, or having previously signed the Declaration by United Nations of January 1, 1942, sign the present Charter and ratify it in accordance with Article 110.

### Article 4

1. Membership in the United Nations is open to all other peace-loving states which accept the obligations contained in the present Charter and, in the judgment of the Organization, are able and willing to carry out these obligations.

2. The admission of any such state to membership in the United Nations will be effected by a decision of the General Assembly upon the recommendation of the Security Council.

### Article 5

A Member of the United Nations against which preventive or enforcement action has been taken by the Security Council may be suspended from the exercise of the rights and privileges of membership by the General Assembly upon the recommendation of the Security Council. The exercise of these rights and privileges may be restored by the Security Council.

### Article 6

A Member of the United Nations which has persistently violated the Principles contained in the present Charter may be expelled from the Organization by the General Assembly upon the recommendation of the Security Council.

## Chapter III: Organs

### Article 7

1. There are established as the principal organs of the United Nations a General Assembly, a Security Council, an Economic and Social Council, a Trusteeship Council, an International Court of Justice, and a Secretariat.

2. Such subsidiary organs as may be found necessary may be established in accordance with the present Charter.

## Article 8

The United Nations shall place no restrictions on the eligibility of men and women to participate in any capacity and under conditions of equality in its principal and subsidiary organs.

### CHAPTER IV: THE GENERAL ASSEMBLY

#### COMPOSITION

## Article 9

1. The General Assembly shall consist of all the Members of the United Nations.

2. Each Member shall have not more than five representatives in the General Assembly.

#### FUNCTIONS AND POWERS

## Article 10

The General Assembly may discuss any questions or any matters within the scope of the present Charter or relating to the powers and functions of any organs provided for in the present Charter, and except as provided in Article 12, may make recommendations to the Members of the United Nations or to the Security Council or to both on any such questions or matters.

## Article 11

1. The General Assembly may consider the general principles of cooperation in the maintenance of international peace and security, including the principles governing disarmament and the regulation of armaments, and may make recommendations with regard to such principles to the Members or to the Security Council or to both.

2. The General Assembly may discuss any questions relating to the maintenance of international peace and security brought before it by any Member of the United Nations, or by the Security Council, or by a state which is not a Member of the United Nations in accordance with Article 35, paragraph 2, and, except as provided in Article 12, may make recommendations with regard to any such questions to the state or states concerned or to the Security Council or to both. Any such question on which action is necessary shall be referred to the Security Council by the General Assembly either before or after discussion.

3. The General Assembly may call the attention of the Security Council to situations which are likely to endanger international peace and security.

4. The powers of the General Assembly set forth in this Article shall not limit the general scope of Article 10.

## Article 12

1. While the Security Council is exercising in respect of any dispute or situation the functions assigned to it in the present Charter, the General As-

sembly shall not make any recommendation with regard to that dispute or situation unless the Security Council so requests.

2. The Secretary-General, with the consent of the Security Council, shall notify the General Assembly at each session of any matters relative to the maintenance of international peace and security which are being dealt with by the Security Council and shall similarly notify the General Assembly, or the Members of the United Nations if the General Assembly is not in session, immediately the Security Council ceases to deal with such matters.

## Article 13

1. The General Assembly shall initiate studies and make recommendations for the purpose of:

a. promoting international cooperation in the political field and encouraging the progressive development of international law and its codification;

b. promoting international cooperation in the economic, social, cultural, educational, and health fields, and assisting in the realization of human rights and fundamental freedoms for all without distinction as to race, sex, language, or religion.

2. The further responsibilities, functions, and powers of the General Assembly with respect to matters mentioned in paragraph 1 (b) above are set forth in Chapters IX and X.

## Article 14

Subject to the provisions of Article 12, the General Assembly may recommend measures for the peaceful adjustment of any situation, regardless of origin, which it deems likely to impair the general welfare or friendly relations among nations, including situations resulting from a violation of the provisions of the present Charter setting forth the Purposes and Principles of the United Nations.

## Article 15

1. The General Assembly shall receive and consider annual and special reports from the Security Council; these reports shall include an account of the measures that the Security Council has decided upon or taken to maintain international peace and security.

2. The General Assembly shall receive and consider reports from the other organs of the United Nations.

## Article 16

The General Assembly shall perform such functions with respect to the international trusteeship system as are assigned to it under Chapters XII and XIII, including the approval of the trusteeship agreements for areas not designated as strategic.

## Article 17

1. The General Assembly shall consider and approve the budget of the Organization.

2.   The expenses of the Organization shall be borne by the Members as apportioned by the General Assembly.

3.   The General Assembly shall consider and approve any financial and budgetary arrangements with specialized agencies referred to in Article 57 and shall examine the administrative budgets of such specialized agencies with a view to making recommendations to the agencies concerned.

VOTING

*Article 18*

1.   Each member of the General Assembly shall have one vote.

2.   Decisions of the General Assembly on important questions shall be made by a two-thirds majority of the members present and voting. These questions shall include: recommendations with respect to the maintenance of international peace and security, the election of the non-permanent members of the Security Council, the election of the members of the Economic and Social Council, the election of members of the Trusteeship Council in accordance with paragraph 1 (c) of Article 86, the admission of new Members to the United Nations, the suspension of the rights and privileges of membership, the expulsion of Members, questions relating to the operation of the trusteeship system, and budgetary questions.

3.   Decisions on other questions, including the determination of additional categories of questions to be decided by a two-thirds majority, shall be made by a majority of the members present and voting.

*Article 19*

A Member of the United Nations which is in arrears in the payment of its financial contributions to the Organization shall have no vote in the General Assembly if the amount of its arrears equals or exceeds the amount of the contributions due from it for the preceding two full years. The General Assembly may, nevertheless, permit such a Member to vote if it is satisfied that the failure to pay is due to conditions beyond the control of the Member.

PROCEDURE

*Article 20*

The General Assembly shall meet in regular annual sessions and in such special sessions as occasion may require. Special sessions shall be convoked by the Secretary-General at the request of the Security Council or of a majority of the Members of the United Nations.

*Article 21*

The General Assembly shall adopt its own rules of procedure. It shall elect its President for each session.

*Article 22*

The General Assembly may establish such subsidiary organs as it deems necessary for the performance of its functions.

CHAPTER V: THE SECURITY COUNCIL

COMPOSITION

*Article 23*

1. The Security Council shall consist of eleven Members of the United Nations. The Republic of China, France, the Union of Soviet Socialist Republics, the United Kingdom of Great Britain and Northern Ireland, and the United States of America shall be permanent members of the Security Council. The General Assembly shall elect six other Members of the United Nations to be non-permanent members of the Security Council, due regard being specially paid, in the first instance, to the contribution of Members of the United Nations to the maintenance of international peace and security and to the other purposes of the Organization, and also to equitable geographical distribution.

2. The non-permanent members of the Security Council shall be elected for a term of two years. In the first election of the non-permanent members, however, three shall be chosen for a term of one year. A retiring member shall not be eligible for immediate re-election.

3. Each member of the Security Council shall have one representative.

FUNCTIONS AND POWERS

*Article 24*

1. In order to ensure prompt and effective action by the United Nations, its Members confer on the Security Council primary responsibility for the maintenance of international peace and security, and agree that in carrying out its duties under this responsibility the Security Council acts on their behalf.

2. In discharging these duties the Security Council shall act in accordance with the Purposes and Principles of the United Nations. The specific powers granted to the Security Council for the discharge of these duties are laid down in Chapters VI, VII, VIII, and XII.

3. The Security Council shall submit annual and, when necessary, special reports to the General Assembly for its consideration.

*Article 25*

The Members of the United Nations agree to accept and carry out the decisions of the Security Council in accordance with the present Charter.

*Article 26*

In order to promote the establishment and maintenance of international peace and security with the least diversion for armaments of the world's human and economic resources, the Security Council shall be responsible for formulating, with the assistance of the Military Staff Committee referred to in Article 47, plans to be submitted to the Members of the United Nations for the establishment of a system for the regulation of armaments.

VOTING

## Article 27

1. Each member of the Security Council shall have one vote.
2. Decisions of the Security Council on procedural matters shall be made by an affirmative vote of seven members.
3. Decisions of the Security Council on all other matters shall be made by an affirmative vote of seven members including the concurring votes of the permanent members; provided that, in decisions under Chapter VI, and under paragraph 3 of Article 52, a party to a dispute shall abstain from voting.

PROCEDURE

## Article 28

1. The Security Council shall be so organized as to be able to function continuously. Each member of the Security Council shall for this purpose be represented at all times at the seat of the Organization.
2. The Security Council shall hold periodic meetings at which each of its members may, if it so desires, be represented by a member of the government or by some other specially designated representative.
3. The Security Council may hold meetings at such places other than the seat of the Organization as in its judgment will best facilitate its work.

## Article 29

The Security Council may establish such subsidiary organs as it deems necessary for the performance of its functions.

## Article 30

The Security Council shall adopt its own rules of procedure, including the method of selecting its President.

## Article 31

Any Member of the United Nations which is not a member of the Security Council may participate, without vote, in the discussion of any question brought before the Security Council whenever the latter considers that the interests of that Member are specially affected.

## Article 32

Any Member of the United Nations which is not a member of the Security Council or any state which is not a Member of the United Nations, if it is a party to a dispute under consideration by the Security Council, shall be invited to participate, without vote, in the discussion relating to the dispute. The Security Council shall lay down such conditions as it deems just for the participation of a state which is not a Member of the United Nations.

## CHAPTER VI: PACIFIC SETTLEMENT OF DISPUTES

### Article 33

1. The parties to any dispute, the continuance of which is likely to endanger the maintenance of international peace and security, shall, first of all, seek a solution by negotiation, enquiry, mediation, conciliation, arbitration, judicial settlement, resort to regional agencies or arrangements, or other peaceful means of their own choice.

2. The Security Council shall, when it deems necessary, call upon the parties to settle their dispute by such means.

### Article 34

The Security Council may investigate any dispute, or any situation which might lead to international friction or give rise to a dispute, in order to determine whether the continuance of the dispute or situation is likely to endanger the maintenance of international peace and security.

### Article 35

1. Any Member of the United Nations may bring any dispute, or any situation of the nature referred to in Article 34, to the attention of the Security Council or of the General Assembly.

2. A state which is not a Member of the United Nations may bring to the attention of the Security Council or of the General Assembly any dispute to which it is a party if it accepts in advance, for the purposes of the dispute, the obligations of pacific settlement provided in the present Charter.

3. The proceedings of the General Assembly in respect of matters brought to its attention under this Article will be subject to the provisions of Articles 11 and 12.

### Article 36

1. The Security Council may, at any stage of a dispute of the nature referred to in Article 33 or of a situation of like nature, recommend appropriate procedures or methods of adjustment.

2. The Security Council should take into consideration any procedures for the settlement of the dispute which have already been adopted by the parties.

3. In making recommendations under this Article the Security Council should also take into consideration that legal disputes should as a general rule be referred by the parties to the International Court of Justice in accordance with the provisions of the Statute of the Court.

### Article 37

1. Should the parties to a dispute of the nature referred to in Article 33 fail to settle it by the means indicated in that Article, they shall refer it to the Security Council.

2. If the Security Council deems that the continuance of the dispute is in fact likely to endanger the maintenance of international peace and security, it shall decide whether to take action under Article 36 or to recommend such terms of settlement as it may consider appropriate.

### Article 38

Without prejudice to the provisions of Articles 33 to 37, the Security Council may, if all the parties to any dispute so request, make recommendations to the parties with a view to a pacific settlement of the dispute.

### CHAPTER VII: ACTION WITH RESPECT TO THE PEACE, BREACHES OF THE PEACE, AND ACTS OF AGGRESSION

### Article 39

The Security Council shall determine the existence of any threat to the peace, breach of the peace, or any act of aggression and shall make recommendations, or decide what measures shall be taken in accordance with Articles 41 and 42, to maintain or restore international peace and security.

### Article 40

In order to prevent an aggravation of the situation, the Security Council may, before making the recommendations or deciding upon the measures provided for in Article 39, call upon the parties concerned to comply with such provisional measures as it deems necessary or desirable. Such provisional measures shall be without prejudice to the rights, claims, or position of the parties concerned. The Security Council shall duly take account of failure to comply with such provisional measures.

### Article 41

The Security Council may decide what measures not involving the use of armed force are to be employed to give effect to its decisions, and it may call upon the Members of the United Nations to apply such measures. These may include complete or partial interruption of economic relations and of rail, sea, air, postal, telegraphic, radio, and other means of communication, and the severance of diplomatic relations.

### Article 42

Should the Security Council consider that measures provided for in Article 41 would be inadequate or have proved to be inadequate, it may take such action by air, sea, or land forces as may be necessary to maintain or restore international peace and security. Such action may include demonstrations, blockade, and other operations by air, sea, or land forces of Members of the United Nations.

## Article 43

1. All Members of the United Nations, in order to contribute to the maintenance of international peace and security, undertake to make available to the Security Council, on its call and in accordance with a special agreement or agreements, armed forces, assistance, and facilities, including rights of passage, necessary for the purpose of maintaining international peace and security.

2. Such Agreement or agreements shall govern the numbers and types of forces, their degree of readiness and general location, and the nature of the facilities and assistance to be provided.

3. The agreement or agreements shall be negotiated as soon as possible on the initiative of the Security Council. They shall be concluded between the Security Council and Members or between the Security Council and groups of Members and shall be subject to ratification by the signatory states in accordance with their respective constitutional processes.

## Article 44

When the Security Council has decided to use force it shall, before calling upon a Member not represented on it to provide armed forces in fulfillment of the obligations assumed under Article 43, invite that Member, if the Member so desires, to participate in the decisions of the Security Council concerning the employment of contingents of that Member's armed forces.

## Article 45

In order to enable the United Nations to take urgent military measures, Members shall hold immediately available national air-force contingents for combined international enforcement action. The strength and degree of readiness of these contingents and plans for their combined action shall be determined, within the limits laid down in the special agreement or agreements referred to in Article 43, by the Security Council with the assistance of the Military Staff Committee.

## Article 46

Plans for the application of armed force shall be made by the Security Council with the assistance of the Military Staff Committee.

## Article 47

1. There shall be established a Military Staff Committee to advise and assist the Security Council on all questions relating to the Security Council's military requirement for the maintenance of international peace and security, the employment and command of forces placed at its disposal, the regulation of armaments, and possible disarmament.

2. The Military Staff Committee shall consist of the Chiefs of Staff of the permanent members of the Security Council or their representatives. Any Member of the United Nations not permanently represented on the Committee shall be invited by the Committee to be associated with it when the efficient

discharge of the Committee's responsibilities requires the participation of that Member in its work.

3. The Military Staff Committee shall be responsible under the Security Council for the strategic direction of any armed forces placed at the disposal of the Security Council. Questions relating to the command of such forces shall be worked out subsequently.

4. The Military Staff Committee, with the authorization of the Security Council and after consultation with appropriate regional agencies, may establish regional subcommittees.

## Article 48

1. The action required to carry out the decisions of the Security Council for the maintenance of international peace and security shall be taken by all the Members of the United Nations or by some of them, as the Security Council may determine.

2. Such decisions shall be carried out by the Members of the United Nations directly and through their action in the appropriate international agencies of which they are members.

## Article 49

The Members of the United Nations shall join in affording mutual assistance in carrying out the measures decided upon by the Security Council.

## Article 50

If preventive or enforcement measures against any state are taken by the Security Council, any other state, whether a Member of the United Nations or not, which finds itself confronted with special economic problems arising from the carrying out of those measures shall have the right to consult the Security Council with regard to a solution of those problems.

## Article 51

Nothing in the present Charter shall impair the inherent right of individual or collective self-defense if an armed attack occurs against a Member of the United Nations, until the Security Council has taken the measures necessary to maintain international peace and security. Measures taken by Members in the exercise of this right of self-defense shall be immediately reported to the Security Council and shall not in any way affect the authority and responsibility of the Security Council under the present Charter to take at any time such action as it deems necessary in order to maintain or restore international peace and security.

CHAPTER VIII: REGIONAL ARRANGEMENTS

## Article 52

1. Nothing in the present Charter precludes the existence of regional arrangements or agencies for dealing with such matters relating to the main-

tenance of international peace and security as are appropriate for regional action, provided that such arrangements or agencies and their activities are consistent with the Purposes and Principles of the United Nations.

2. The Members of the United Nations entering into such arrangements or constituting such agencies shall make every effort to achieve pacific settlement of local disputes through such regional arrangements or by such regional agencies before referring them to the Security Council.

3. The Security Council shall encourage the development of pacific settlement of local disputes through such regional arrangements or by such regional agencies either on the initiative of the states concerned or by reference from the Security Council.

4. This Article in no way impairs the application of Articles 34 and 35.

*Article 53*

1. The Security Council shall, where appropriate, utilize such regional arrangements or agencies for enforcement action under its authority. But no enforcement action shall be taken under regional arrangements or by regional agencies without the authorization of the Security Council, with the exception of measures against any enemy state, as defined in paragraph 2 of this Article, provided for pursuant to Article 107 or in regional arrangements directed against renewal of aggressive policy on the part of any such state, until such time as the Organization may, on request of the Governments concerned, be charged with the responsibility for preventing further aggression by such a state.

2. The term enemy state as used in paragraph 1 of this Article applies to any state which during the Second World War has been an enemy of any signatory of the present Charter.

*Article 54*

The Security Council shall at all times be kept fully informed of activities undertaken or in contemplation under regional arrangements or by regional agencies for the maintenance of international peace and security.

CHAPTER IX:   INTERNATIONAL ECONOMIC AND SOCIAL COOPERATION

*Article 55*

With a view to the creation of conditions of stability and well-being which are necessary for peaceful and friendly relations among nations based on respect for the principle of equal rights and self-determination of peoples, the United Nations shall promote:

    a.   higher standards of living, full employment, and conditions of economic and social progress and development;

    b.   solutions of international economic, social, health, and related problems; and international cultural and educational cooperation; and

    c.   universal respect for, and observance of, human rights and fundamental freedoms for all without distinction as to race, sex, language, or religion.

## Article 56

All Members pledge themselves to take joint and separate action in cooperation with the Organization for the achievement of the purposes set forth in Article 55.

## Article 57

1. The various specialized agencies, established by intergovernmental agreement and having wide international responsibilities, as defined in their basic instruments, in economic, social, cultural, educational, health, and related fields, shall be brought into relationship with the United Nations in accordance with the provisions of Article 63.

2. Such agencies thus brought into relationship with the United Nations are hereinafter referred to as specialized agencies.

## Article 58

The Organization shall make recommendations for the coordination of the policies and activities of the specialized agencies.

## Article 59

The Organization shall, where appropriate, initiate negotiations among the states concerned for the creation of any new specialized agencies required for the accomplishment of the purposes set forth in Article 55.

## Article 60

Responsibility for the discharge of the functions of the Organization set forth in this Chapter shall be vested in the General Assembly and, under the authority of the General Assembly, in the Economic and Social Council, which shall have for this purpose the powers set forth in Chapter X.

## CHAPTER X: THE ECONOMIC AND SOCIAL COUNCIL

### COMPOSITION

## Article 61

1. The Economic and Social Council shall consist of eighteen Members of the United Nations elected by the General Assembly.

2. Subject to the provisions of paragraph 3, six members of the Economic and Social Council shall be elected each year for a term of three years. A retiring member shall be eligible for immediate re-election.

3. At the first election, eighteen members of the Economic and Social Council shall be chosen. The term of office of six members so chosen shall expire at the end of one year, and of six other members at the end of two years, in accordance with arrangements made by the General Assembly.

4. Each member of the Economic and Social Council shall have one representative.

FUNCTIONS AND POWERS

*Article 62*

1. The Economic and Social Council may make or initiate studies and reports with respect to international economic, social, cultural, educational, health, and related matters and may make recommendations with respect to any such matters to the General Assembly, to the Members of the United Nations, and to the specialized agencies concerned.

2. It may make recommendations for the purpose of promoting respect for, and observance of, human rights and fundamental freedoms for all.

3. It may prepare draft conventions for submission to the General Assembly, with respect to matters falling within its competence.

4. It may call, in accordance with the rules prescribed by the United Nations, international conferences on matters falling within its competence.

*Article 63*

1. The Economic and Social Council may enter into agreements with any of the agencies referred to in Article 57, defining the terms on which the agency concerned shall be brought into relationship with the United Nations. Such agreements shall be subject to approval by the General Assembly.

2. It may coordinate the activities of the specialized agencies through consultation with and recommendations to such agencies and through recommendations to the General Assembly and to the Members of the United Nations.

*Article 64*

1. The Economic and Social Council may take appropriate steps to obtain regular reports from the specialized agencies. It may make arrangements with the Members of the United Nations and with the specialized agencies to obtain reports on the steps taken to give effect to its own recommendations and to recommendations on matters falling within its competence made by the General Assembly.

2. It may communicate its observations on these reports to the General Assembly.

*Article 65*

The Economic and Social Council may furnish information to the Security Council and shall assist the Security Council upon its request.

*Article 66*

1. The Economic and Social Council shall perform such functions as fall within its competence in connection with the carrying out of the recommendations of the General Assembly.

2. It may, with the approval of the General Assembly, perform services at the request of Members of the United Nations and at the request of specialized agencies.

3. It shall perform such other functions as are specified elsewhere in the present Charter or as may be assigned to it by the General Assembly.

VOTING

*Article 67*

1. Each member of the Economic and Social Council shall have one vote.
2. Decisions of the Economic and Social Council shall be made by a majority of the members present and voting.

PROCEDURE

*Article 68*

The Economic and Social Council shall set up commissions in economic and social fields and for the promotion of human rights, and such other commissions as may be required for the performance of its functions.

*Article 69*

The Economic and Social Council shall invite any Member of the United Nations to participate, without vote, in its deliberations on any matter of particular concern to that Member.

*Article 70*

The Economic and Social Council may make arrangements for representatives of the specialized agencies to participate, without vote, in its deliberations and in those of the commissions established by it, and for its representatives to participate in the deliberations of the specialized agencies.

*Article 71*

The Economic and Social Council may make suitable arrangements for consultation with non-governmental organizations which are concerned with matters within its competence. Such arrangements may be made with international organizations and, where appropriate, with national organizations after consultation with the Member of the United Nations concerned.

*Article 72*

1. The Economic and Social Council shall adopt its own rules of procedure, including the method of selecting its President.
2. The Economic and Social Council shall meet as required in accordance with its rules, which shall include provision for the convening of meetings on the request of a majority of its members.

CHAPTER XI: DECLARATION REGARDING NON-SELF-GOVERNING TERRITORIES

*Article 73*

Members of the United Nations which have or assume responsibilities for the administration of territories whose peoples have not yet attained a full measure of self-government recognize the principle that the interests of the inhabitants of these territories are paramount, and accept as a sacred trust the obligation to promote to the utmost, within the system of international peace and security established by the present Charter, the well-being of the inhabitants of these territories, and, to this end:

a.  to ensure, with due respect for the culture of the peoples concerned, their political, economic, social, and educational advancement, their just treatment, and their protection against abuses;

b.  to develop self-government, to take due account of the political aspirations of the peoples, and to assist them in the progressive development of their free political institutions, according to the particular circumstances of each territory and its peoples and their varying stages of advancement;

c.  to further international peace and security;

d.  to promote constructive measures of development, to encourage research, and to cooperate with one another and, when and where appropriate, with specialized international bodies with a view to the practical achievement of the social, economic, and scientific purposes set forth in this Article; and

e.  to transmit regularly to the Secretary-General for information purposes subject to such limitation as security and constitutional considerations may require, statistical and other information of a technical nature relating to economic, social, and educational conditions in the territories for which they are respectively responsible other than those territories to which Chapters XII and XIII apply.

## Article 74

Members of the United Nations also agree that their policy in respect of the territories to which this Chapter applies, no less than in respect of their metropolitan areas, must be based on the general principle of good-neighborliness due account being taken of the interests and well-being of the rest of the world, in social, economic, and commercial matters.

### CHAPTER XII:  INTERNATIONAL TRUSTEESHIP SYSTEM

## Article 75

The United Nations shall establish under its authority an international trusteeship system for the administration and supervision of such territories as may be placed thereunder by subsequent individual agreements. These territories are hereinafter referred to as trust territories.

## Article 76

The basic objectives of the trusteeship system, in accordance with the Purposes of the United Nations laid down in Article 1 of the present Charter, shall be:

a.  to further international peace and security;

b.  to promote the political, economic, social, and educational advance-

ment of the inhabitants of the trust territories, and their progressive development towards self-government or independence as may be appropriate to the
particular circumstances of each territory and its peoples and the freely expressed wishes of the peoples concerned, and as may be provided by the terms
of each trusteeship agreement;

    c.  to encourage respect for human rights and for fundamental freedoms
for all without distinction as to race, sex, language, or religion, and to encourage recognition of the interdependence of the peoples of the world; and

    d.  to ensure equal treatment in social, economic, and commercial mat-
ters for all Members of the United Nations and their nationals, and also equal
treatment for the latter in the administration of justice, without prejudice to
the attainment of the foregoing objectives and subject to the provisions of
Article 80.

## Article 77

    1.  The trusteeship system shall apply to such territories in the following
categories as may be placed thereunder by means of trusteeship agreements:

    a.  territories now held under mandate;

    b.  territories which may be detached from enemy states as a result of
the Second World War; and

    c.  territories voluntarily placed under the system by states responsible
for their administration.

    2.  It will be a matter for subsequent agreement as to which territories
in the foregoing categories will be brought under the trusteeship system and
upon what terms.

## Article 78

The trusteeship system shall not apply to territories which have become
Members of the United Nations, relationship among which shall be based on
respect for the principle of sovereign equality.

## Article 79

The terms of trusteeship for each territory to be placed under the trusteeship system, including any alteration or amendment, shall be agreed upon by
the states directly concerned, including the mandatory power in the case of
territories held under mandate by a Member of the United Nations, and shall
be approved as provided for in Articles 83 and 85.

## Article 80

    1.  Except as may be agreed upon in individual trusteeship agreements,
made under Articles 77, 79, and 81, placing each territory under the trusteeship
system, and until such agreements have been concluded, nothing in this Chapter shall be construed in or of itself to alter in any manner the rights whatsoever of any states or any peoples of the terms of existing international instruments to which Members of the United Nations may respectively be parties.

    2.  Paragraph 1 of this Article shall not be interpreted as giving grounds

for delay or postponement of the negotiation and conclusion of agreements for placing mandated and other territories under the trusteeship system as provided for in Article 77.

## Article 81

The trusteeship agreement shall in each case include the terms under which the trust territory will be administered and designate the authority which will exercise the administration of the trust territory. Such authority, hereinafter called the administering authority, may be one or more states or the Organization itself.

## Article 82

There may be designated, in any trusteeship agreement, a strategic area or areas which may include part or all of the trust territory to which the agreement applies, without prejudice to any special agreement or agreements made under Article 43.

## Article 83

1. All functions of the United Nations relating to strategic areas, including the approval of the terms of the trusteeship agreements and of their alteration or amendment, shall be exercised by the Security Council.
2. The basic objectives set forth in Article 76 shall be applicable to the people of each strategic area.
3. The Security Council shall, subject to the provisions of the trusteeship agreements and without prejudice to security considerations, avail itself of the assistance of the Trusteeship Council to perform those functions of the United Nations under the trusteeship system relating to political, economic, social, and educational matters in the strategic areas.

## Article 84

It shall be the duty of the administering authority to ensure that the trust territory shall play its part in the maintenance of international peace and security. To this end the administering authority may make use of volunteer forces, facilities, and assistance from the trust territory in carrying out the obligations towards the Security Council undertaken in this regard by the administering authority, as well as for local defense and the maintenance of law and order within the trust territory.

## Article 85

1. The functions of the United Nations with regard to trusteeship agreements for all areas not designated as strategic, including the approval of the terms of the trusteeship agreements and of their alteration or amendment, shall be exercised by the General Assembly.
2. The Trusteeship Council, operating under the authority of the General Assembly, shall assist the General Assembly in carrying out these functions.

## Chapter XIII: The Trusteeship Council

### COMPOSITION

*Article 86*

1. The Trusteeship Council shall consist of the following Members of the United Nations:

    a. those Members administering trust territories;

    b. such of those Members mentioned by name in Article 23 as are not administering trust territories; and

    c. as many other Members elected for three-year terms by the General Assembly as may be necessary to ensure that the total number of members of the Trusteeship Council is equally divided between those Members of the United Nations which administer trust territories and those which do not.

2. Each member of the Trusteeship Council shall designate one specially qualified person to represent it therein.

### FUNCTIONS AND POWERS

*Article 87*

The General Assembly and, under its authority, the Trusteeship Council, in carrying out their functions, may:

    a. consider reports submitted by the administering authority;

    b. accept petitions and examine them in consultation with the administering authority;

    c. provide for periodic visits to the respective trust territories at times agreed upon with the administering authority; and

    d. take these and other actions in conformity with the terms of the trusteeship agreements.

*Article 88*

The Trusteeship Council shall formulate a questionnaire on the political, economic, social, and educational advancement of the inhabitants of each trust territory, and the administering authority for each trust territory within the competence of the General Assembly shall make an annual report to the General Assembly upon the basis of such questionnaire.

### VOTING

*Article 89*

1. Each member of the Trusteeship Council shall have one vote.

2. Decisions of the Trusteeship Council shall be made by a majority of the members present and voting.

### PROCEDURE

*Article 90*

1. The Trusteeship Council shall adopt its own rules of procedure, including the method of selecting its President.

2. The Trusteeship Council shall meet as required in accordance with its rules, which shall include provision for the convening of meetings on the request of a majority of its members.

### Article 91

The Trusteeship Council shall, when appropriate, avail itself of the assistance of the Economic and Social Council and of the specialized agencies in regard to matters with which they are respectively concerned.

## CHAPTER XIV: THE INTERNATIONAL COURT OF JUSTICE

### Article 92

The International Court of Justice shall be the principal judicial organ of the United Nations. It shall function in accordance with the annexed Statute, which is based upon the Statute of the Permanent Court of International Justice and forms an integral part of the present Charter.

### Article 93

1. All Members of the United Nations are *ipso facto* parties to the Statute of the International Court of Justice.

2. A state which is not a Member of the United Nations may become a party to the Statute of the International Court of Justice on conditions to be determined in each case by the General Assembly upon the recommendation of the Security Council.

### Article 94

1. Each Member of the United Nations undertakes to comply with the decision of the International Court of Justice in any case to which it is a party.

2. If any party to a case fails to perform the obligations incumbent upon it under a judgment rendered by the Court, the other party may have recourse to the Security Council, which may, if it deems necessary, make recommendations or decide upon measures to be taken to give effect to the judgment.

### Article 95

Nothing in the present Charter shall prevent Members of the United Nations from entrusting the solution of their differences to other tribunals by virtue of agreements already in existence or which may be concluded in the future.

### Article 96

1. The General Assembly or the Security Council may request the International Court of Justice to give an advisory opinion on any legal question.

2. Other organs of the United Nations and specialized agencies, which may at any time be so authorized by the General Assembly, may also request advisory opinions of the Court on legal questions arising within the scope of their activities.

Chapter XV:   The Secretariat

*Article 97*

The Secretariat shall comprise a Secretary-General and such staff as the Organization may require. The Secretary-General shall be appointed by the General Assembly upon the recommendation of the Security Council. He shall be the chief administrative officer of the Organization.

*Article 98*

The Secretary-General shall act in that capacity in all meetings of the General Assembly, of the Security Council, of the Economic and Social Council, and of the Trusteeship Council, and shall perform such other functions as are entrusted to him by these organs. The Secretary-General shall make an annual report to the General Assembly on the work of the Organization.

*Article 99*

The Secretary-General may bring to the attention of the Security Council any matter which in his opinion may threaten the maintenance of international peace and security.

*Article 100*

1. In the performance of their duties the Secretary-General and the staff shall not seek or receive instructions from any government or from any other authority external to the Organization. They shall refrain from any action which might reflect on their position as international officials responsible only to the Organization.

2. Each Member of the United Nations undertakes to respect the exclusively international character of the responsibilities of the Secretary-General and the staff and not to seek to influence them in the discharge of their responsibilities.

*Article 101*

1. The staff shall be appointed by the Secretary-General under regulations established by the General Assembly.

2. Appropriate staffs shall be permanently assigned to the Economic and Social Council, the Trusteeship Council, and, as required, to other organs of the United Nations. These staffs shall form a part of the Secretariat.

3. The paramount consideration in the employment of the staff and in the determination of the conditions of service shall be the necessity of securing the highest standards of efficiency, competence, and integrity. Due regard shall be paid to the importance of recruiting the staff on as wide a geographical basis as possible.

## CHAPTER XVI: MISCELLANEOUS PROVISIONS

### Article 102

1. Every treaty and every international agreement entered into by any Member of the United Nations after the present Charter comes into force shall as soon as possible be registered with the Secretariat and published by it.

2. No party to any such treaty or international agreement which has not been registered in accordance with the provisions of paragraph 1 of this Article may invoke that treaty or agreement before any organ of the United Nations.

### Article 103

In the event of a conflict between the obligations of the Members of the United Nations under the present Charter and their obligations under any other international agreement, their obligations under the present Charter shall prevail.

### Article 104

The Organization shall enjoy in the territory of each of its Members such legal capacity as may be necessary for the exercise of its functions and the fulfillment of its purposes.

### Article 105

1. The Organization shall enjoy in the territory of each of its Members such privileges and immunities as are necessary for the fulfillment of its purposes.

2. Representatives of the Members of the United Nations and officials of the Organization shall similarly enjoy such privileges and immunities as are necessary for the independent exercise of their functions in connection with the Organization.

3. The General Assembly may make recommendations with a view to determining the details of the application of paragraphs 1 and 2 of this Article or may propose conventions to the Members of the United Nations for this purpose.

## CHAPTER XVII: TRANSITIONAL SECURITY ARRANGEMENTS

### Article 106

Pending the coming into force of such special agreements referred to in Article 43 as in the opinion of the Security Council enable it to begin the exercise of its responsibilities under Article 42, the parties to the Four-Nation Declaration, signed at Moscow, October 30, 1943, and France, shall, in accordance with the provisions of paragraph 5 of that Declaration, consult with one another and as occasion requires with other Members of the United Nations with a view to such joint action on behalf of the Organization as may be necessary for the purpose of maintaining international peace and security.

## *Article 107*

Nothing in the present Charter shall invalidate or preclude action, in relation to any state which during the Second World War has been an enemy of any signatory to the present Charter, taken or authorized as a result of that war by the Governments having responsibility for such action.

## CHAPTER XVIII: AMENDMENTS

### *Article 108*

Amendments to the present Charter shall come into force for all Members of the United Nations when they have been adopted by a vote of two thirds of the members of the General Assembly and ratified in accordance with their respective constitutional processes by two thirds of the Members of the United Nations, including all the permanent members of the Security Council.

### *Article 109*

1. A General Conference of the Members of the United Nations for the purpose of reviewing the present Charter may be held at a date and place to be fixed by a two-thirds vote of the members of the General Assembly and by a vote of any seven members of the Security Council. Each member of the United Nations shall have one vote in the conference.

2. Any alteration of the present Charter recommended by a two-thirds vote of the conference shall take effect when ratified in accordance with their respective constitutional processes by two-thirds of the Members of the United Nations including all the permanent members of the Security Council.

3. If such a conference has not been held before the tenth annual session of the General Assembly following the coming into force of the present Charter, the proposal to call such a conference shall be placed on the agenda of that session of the General Assembly, and the conference shall be held if so decided by a majority vote of the members of the General Assembly and by a vote of any seven members of the Security Council.

## CHAPTER XIX: RATIFICATION AND SIGNATURE

### *Article 110*

1. The present Charter shall be ratified by the signatory states in accordance with their respective constitutional processes.

2. The ratification shall be deposited with the Government of the United States of America, which shall notify all the signatory states of each deposit as well as the Security-General of the Organization when he has been appointed.

3. The present Charter shall come into force upon the deposit of ratifications by the Republic of China, France, the Union of Soviet Socialist Republics, the United Kingdom of Great Britain and Northern Ireland, and the United States of America, and by a majority of the other signatory states. A protocol of the ratifications deposited shall thereupon be drawn up by the Government of the United States of America which shall communicate copies thereof to all the signatory states.

4. The states signatory to the present Charter which ratify it after it has come into force will become original Members of the United Nations on the date of the deposit of their respective ratifications.

*Article 111*

The present Charter, of which the Chinese, French, Russian, English, and Spanish texts are equally authentic, shall remain deposited in the archives of the Government of the United States of America. Duly certified copies thereof shall be transmitted by that Government to the Governments of the other signatory states.

IN FAITH WHEREOF the representatives of the Governments of the United Nations have signed the present Charter.

DONE at the city of San Francisco the twenty-sixth day of June, one thousand-nine hundred and forty-five.

---

*Protocol of Entry into Force of the Amendments to Articles 23, 27 and 61 of the Charter of the United Nations Adopted by the General Assembly Resolutions 1991 A and B (XVIII) of 17 December 1963*

---

WHEREAS Article 108 of the Charter of the United Nations provides as follows:

*Article 108*

Amendments to the present Charter shall come into force for all Members of the United Nations when they have been adopted by a vote of two thirds of the members of the General Assembly and ratified in accordance with their respective constitutional processes by two thirds of the Members of the United Nations, including all the permanent members of the Security Council.

WHEREAS the General Assembly of the United Nations adopted on 17 December 1963, in accordance with the said Article 108, the amendments to

Articles 23, 27 and 61 of the Charter of the United Nations as set forth in resolutions 1991 A and B (XVIII),

WHEREAS the requirements of the said Article 108 with respect to the ratification of the above-mentioned amendments were fulfilled by 31 August 1965, as shown in the Annex to this Protocol, and the said amendments entered into force on that day for all Members of the United Nations.

AND WHEREAS the text of Articles 23, 27 and 61 of the Charter of the United Nations as amended reads as follows:

## Article 23

1. The Security Council shall consist of fifteen Members of the United Nations. The Republic of China, France, the Union of Soviet Socialist Republics, the United Kingdom of Great Britain and Northern Ireland, and the United States of America shall be permanent members of the Security Council. The General Assembly shall elect ten other Members of the United Nations to be non-permanent members of the Security Council, due regard being specially paid, in the first instance to the contributions of Members of the United Nations to the maintenance of international peace and security and to the other purposes of the Organization, and also to equitable geographical distribution.

2. The non-permanent members of the Security Council shall be elected for a term of two years. In the first election of the non-permanent members after the increase of the membership of the Security Council from eleven to fifteen, two of the four additional members shall be chosen for a term of one year. A retiring member shall not be eligible for immediate re-election.

3. Each member of the Security Council shall have one representative.

## Article 27

1. Each member of the Security Council shall have one vote.

2. Decisions of the Security Council on procedural matters shall be made by an affirmative vote of nine members.

3. Decisions of the Security Council on all other matters shall be made by an affirmative vote of nine members including the concurring votes of the permanent members; provided that, in decisions under Chapter VI, and under paragraph 3 of Article 52, a party to a dispute shall abstain from voting.

## Article 61

1. The Economic and Social Council shall consist of twenty-seven Members of the United Nations elected by the General Assembly.

2. Subject to the provisions of paragraph 3, nine members of the Economic and Social Council shall be elected each year for a term of three years. A retiring member shall be eligible for immediate re-election.

3. At the first election after the increase in the membership of the Economic and Social Council from eighteen to twenty-seven members, in addition to the members elected in place of the six members whose term of office expires at the end of that year, nine additional members shall be elected. Of

these nine additional members, the term of office of three members so elected shall expire at the end of one year, and of three other members at the end of two years, in accordance with arrangements made by the General Assembly.

4. Each member of the Economic and Social Council shall have one representative.

Now, THEREFORE, I, U THANT, Secretary-General of the United Nations, sign this Protocol in two original copies in the Chinese, English, French, Russian and Spanish languages, of which one shall be deposited in the archives of the Secretariat of the United Nations and the other transmitted to the Government of the United States of America as the depository of the Charter of the United Nations. Copies of this Protocol shall be communicated to all Members of the United Nations.

DONE at the headquarters of the United Nations, New York, thirty-first day of August, one thousand nine hundred and sixty-five.

---

APPENDIX B

## *Test Ban Treaty*

---

### TREATY

banning nuclear weapon tests in the atmosphere, in outer space and under water.

The Governments of the United States of America, the United Kingdom of Great Britain and Northern Ireland, and the Union of Soviet Socialist Republics, hereinafter referred to as the "Original Parties",

Proclaiming as their principal aim the speediest possible achievement of an agreement on general and complete disarmament under strict international control in accordance with the objectives of the United Nations which would put an end to the armaments race and eliminate the incentive to the production and testing of all kinds of weapons, including nuclear weapons,

Seeking to achieve the discontinuance of all test explosions of nuclear weapons for all time, determined to continue negotiations to this end, and desiring to put an end to the contamination of man's environment by radio-active substances,

Have agreed as follows:

SOURCE: *The Department of State Bulletin*, XLIX (August 12, 1963), 239–240.

## Article I

1. Each of the Parties to this Treaty undertakes to prohibit, to prevent, and not to carry out any nuclear weapon test explosion, or any other nuclear explosion, at any place under its jurisdiction or control:

(a) in the atmosphere; beyond its limits, including outer space; or underwater, including territorial waters or high seas; or

(b) in any other environment if such explosion causes radioactive debris to be present outside the territorial limits of the State under whose jurisdiction or control such explosion is conducted. It is understood in this connection that the provisions of this subparagraph are without prejudice to the conclusion of a treaty resulting in the permanent banning of all nuclear test explosions, including all such explosions underground, the conclusion of which, as the Parties have stated in the Preamble to this Treaty, they seek to achieve.

2. Each of the Parties to this Treaty undertakes furthermore to refrain from causing, encouraging, or in any way participating in, the carrying out of any nuclear weapon test explosion, or any other nuclear explosion, anywhere which would take place in any of the environments described, or have the effect referred to, in paragraph 1 of this Article.

## Article II

1. Any Party may propose amendments to this Treaty. The text of any proposed amendment shall be submitted to the Depositary Governments which shall circulate it to all Parties to this Treaty. Thereafter, if requested to do so by one-third or more of the Parties, the Depositary Governments shall convene a conference, to which they shall invite all the Parties, to consider such amendment.

2. Any amendment to this Treaty must be approved by a majority of the votes of all the Parties to this Treaty, including the votes of all of the Original Parties. The amendment shall enter into force for all Parties upon the deposit of instruments of ratification by a majority of all the Parties, including the instruments of ratification of all the Original Parties.

## Article III

1. This Treaty shall be open to all States for signature. Any State which does not sign this Treaty before its entry into force in accordance with paragraph 3 of this Article may accede to it at any time.

2. This Treaty shall be subject to ratification by signatory States. Instruments of ratification and instruments of accession shall be deposited with the Governments of the Original Parties—the United States of America, the United Kingdom of Great Britain and Northern Ireland, and the Union of Soviet Socialist Republics—which are hereby designated the Depositary Governments.

3. This Treaty shall enter into force after its ratification by all the Original Parties and the deposit of their instruments of ratification.

4. For States whose instruments of ratification or accession are deposited

subsequent to the entry into force of this Treaty, it shall enter into force on the date of the deposit of their instruments of ratification or accession.

5. The Depositary Governments shall promptly inform all signatory and acceding States of the date of each signature, the date of deposit of each instrument of ratification of and accession to this Treaty, the date of its entry into force, and the date of receipt of any requests for conferences or other notices.

6. This Treaty shall be registered by the Depositary Governments pursuant to Article 102 of the Charter of the United Nations.

## Article IV

This Treaty shall be of unlimited duration.

Each Party shall in exercising its national sovereignty have the right to withdraw from the Treaty if it decides that extraordinary events, related to the subject matter of this Treaty, have jeopardized the supreme interests of its country. It shall give notice of such withdrawal to all other Parties to the Treaty three months in advance.

## Article V

This Treaty, of which the English and Russian texts are equally authentic, shall be deposited in the archives of the Depositary Governments. Duly certified copies of this Treaty shall be transmitted by the Depositary Governments to the Governments of the signatory and acceding States.

IN WITNESS WHEREOF the undersigned, duly authorized, have signed this Treaty.

DONE in triplicate at the city of Moscow the fifth day of August, one thousand nine hundred and sixty-three.

For the Government of the United States of America

For the Government of the United Kingdom of Great Britain and Northern Ireland

For the Government of the Union of Soviet Socialist Republics

## Non-Proliferation of Nuclear Weapons Treaty

TEXT OF DRAFT TREATY ON THE NON-PROLIFERATION
OF NUCLEAR WEAPONS SUBMITTED BY
THE UNITED STATES AND THE SOVIET UNION
TO THE EIGHTEEN-NATION COMMITTEE ON DISARMAMENT
ON MARCH 11, 1968*

The States concluding this Treaty, hereinafter referred to as the "Parties to the Treaty",

Considering the devastation that would be visited upon all mankind by a nuclear war and the consequent need to make every effort to avert the danger of such a war and to take measures to safeguard the security of peoples,

Believing that the proliferation of nuclear weapons would seriously enhance the danger of nuclear war,

In conformity with resolutions of the United Nations General Assembly calling for the conclusion of an agreement on the prevention of wider dissemination of nuclear weapons,

Undertaking to cooperate in facilitating the application of International Atomic Energy Agency safeguards on peaceful nuclear activities,

Expressing their support for research, development and other efforts to further the application, within the framework of the International Atomic Energy Agency safeguards system, of the principle of safeguarding effectively the flow of source and special fissionable materials by use of instruments and other techniques at certain strategic points,

Affirming the principle that the benefits of peaceful applications of nuclear technology, including any technological by-products which may be derived by nuclear-weapon States from the development of nuclear explosive devices, should be available for peaceful purposes to all Parties to the Treaty, whether nuclear weapon or non-nuclear-weapon States,

Convinced that in furtherance of this principle, all Parties to this Treaty are entitled to participate in the fullest possible exchange of scientific informa-

* Submitted to the U.N. General Assembly on Mar. 14 as annex I to the report of the Conference of the Eighteen-Nation Committee on Disarmament (U.N. doc. A/7072).

tion for, and to contribute alone or in cooperation with other States to, the further development of the applications of atomic energy for peaceful purposes,

Declaring their intention to achieve at the earliest possible date the cessation of the nuclear arms race,

Urging the cooperation of all States in the attainment of this objective,

Recalling the determination expressed by the Parties to the Partial Test Ban Treaty of 1963 in its Preamble to seek to achieve the discontinuance of all test explosions of nuclear weapons for all time and to continue negotiations to this end,

Desiring to further the easing of international tension and the strengthening of trust between States in order to facilitate the cessation of the manufacture of nuclear weapons, the liquidation of all their existing stockpiles, and the elimination from national arsenals of nuclear weapons and the means of their delivery pursuant to a treaty on general and complete disarmament under strict and effective international control,

Have agreed as follows:

## Article I

Each nuclear-weapon State Party to this Treaty undertakes not to transfer to any recipient whatsoever nuclear weapons or other nuclear explosive devices or control over such weapons or explosive devices directly, or indirectly: and not in any way to assist, encourage, or induce any non-nuclear-weapon State to manufacture or otherwise acquire nuclear weapons or other nuclear explosive devices, or control over such weapons or explosive devices.

## Article II

Each non-nuclear-weapon State Party to this Treaty undertakes not to receive the transfer from any transferor whatsoever of nuclear weapons or other nuclear explosive devices or of control over such weapons or explosive devices directly, or indirectly; not to manufacture or otherwise acquire nuclear weapons or other nuclear explosive devices; and not to seek or receive any assistance in the manufacture of nuclear weapons or other nuclear explosive devices.

## Article III

1. Each non-nuclear-weapon State Party to the Treaty undertakes to accept safeguards, as set forth in an agreement to be negotiated and concluded with the International Atomic Energy Agency in accordance with the Statute of the International Atomic Energy Agency and the Agency's safeguards system, for the exclusive purpose of verification of the fulfillment of its obligations assumed under this Treaty with a view to preventing diversion of nuclear energy from peaceful uses to nuclear weapons or other nuclear explosive devices. Procedures for the safeguards required by this Article shall be followed with respect to source or special fissionable material whether it is being produced, processed or used in any principal nuclear facility or is outside any such facility. The safeguards required by this Article shall be applied on all source

or special fissionable material in all peaceful nuclear activities within the territory of such State, under its jurisdiction, or carried out under its control anywhere.

2. Each State Party to the Treaty undertakes not to provide: (a) source or special fissionable material, or (b) equipment or material especially designed or prepared for the processing, use or production of special fissionable material, to any non-nuclear-weapon State for peaceful purposes, unless the source or special fissionable material shall be subject to the safeguards required by this Article.

3. The safeguards required by this Article shall be implemented in a manner designed to comply with Article IV of this Treaty, and to avoid hampering the economic or technological development of the Parties or international cooperation in the field of peaceful nuclear activities, including the international exchange of nuclear material and equipment for the processing, use or production of nuclear material for peaceful purposes in accordance with the provisions of this Article and the principle of safeguarding set forth in the Preamble.

4. Non-nuclear-weapon States Party to the Treaty shall conclude agreements with the International Atomic Energy Agency to meet the requirements of this Article either individually or together with other States in accordance with the Statute of the International Atomic Energy Agency. Negotiation of such agreements shall commence within 180 days from the original entry into force of this Treaty. For States depositing their instruments of ratification after the 180-day period, negotiation of such agreements shall commence not later than the date of such deposit. Such agreements shall enter into force not later than eighteen months after the date of initiation of negotiations.

## Article IV

1. Nothing in this Treaty shall be interpreted as affecting the inalienable right of all the Parties to the Treaty to develop research, production and use of nuclear energy for peaceful purposes without discrimination and in conformity with Articles I and II of this Treaty.

2. All the Parties to the Treaty have the right to participate in the fullest possible exchange of scientific and technological information for the peaceful uses of nuclear energy. Parties to the Treaty in a position to do so shall also cooperate in contributing alone or together with other States or international organizations to the further development of the applications of nuclear energy for peaceful purposes, especially in the territories of non-nuclear-weapon States Party to the Treaty.

## Article V

Each Party to this Treaty undertakes to cooperate to insure that potential benefits from any peaceful applications of nuclear explosions will be made available through appropriate international procedures to non-nuclear-weapon States Party to this Treaty on a non-discriminatory basis and that the charge to such Parties for the explosive devices used will be as low as possible and exclude any charge for research and development. It is understood that non-nuclear-weapon States Party to this Treaty so desiring may, pursuant to a special agreement or agreements, obtain any such benefits on a bilateral basis or through an appropriate international body with adequate representation of non-nuclear-weapon States.

## Article VI

Each of the Parties to this Treaty undertakes to pursue negotiations in good faith on effective measures relating to cessation of the nuclear arms race at an early date and to nuclear disarmament, and on a treaty on general and complete disarmament under strict and effective international control.

## Article VII

Nothing in this Treaty affects the right of any group of States to conclude regional treaties in order to assure the total absence of nuclear weapons in their respective territories.

## Article VIII

1. Any Party to this Treaty may propose amendments to this Treaty. The text of any proposed amendment shall be submitted to the Depositary Governments which shall circulate it to all Parties to the Treaty. Thereupon, if requested to do so by one-third or more of the Parties to the Treaty, the Depositary Governments shall convene a conference, to which they shall invite all the Parties to the Treaty, to consider such an amendment.

2. Any amendment to this Treaty must be approved by a majority of the votes of all the Parties to the Treaty, including the votes of all nuclear-weapon States Party to this Treaty and all other Parties which, on the date the amendment is circulated, are members of the Board of Governors of the International Atomic Energy Agency. The amendment shall enter into force for each Party that deposits its instrument of ratification of the amendment upon the deposit of instruments of ratification by a majority of all the Parties, including the instruments of ratification of all nuclear-weapon States Party to this Treaty and all other Parties which, on the date the amendment is circulated, are members of the Board of Governors of the International Atomic Energy Agency. Thereafter, it shall enter into force for any other Party upon the deposit of its instrument of ratification of the amendment.

3. Five years after the entry into force of this Treaty, a conference of Parties to the Treaty shall be held in Geneva, Switzerland, in order to review the operation of this Treaty with a view to assuring that the purposes of the Preamble and the provisions of the Treaty are being realized. At intervals of five years thereafter, a majority of the Parties to the Treaty may obtain, by submitting a proposal to this effect to the Depositary Governments, the convening of further conferences with the same objective of reviewing the operation of the Treaty.

## Article IX

1. This Treaty shall be open to all States for signature. Any State which does not sign the Treaty before its entry into force in accordance with paragraph 3 of this Article may accede to it at any time.

2. This treaty shall be subject to ratification by signatory States. Instruments of ratification and instruments of accession shall be deposited with the Governments of _____, which are hereby designated the Depositary Governments.

3. This Treaty shall enter into force after its ratification by all nuclear-weapon States signatory to this Treaty, and 40 other States signatory to this Treaty and the deposit of their instruments of ratification. For the purposes of this Treaty, a nuclear-weapon State is one which has manufactured and exploded a nuclear weapon or other nuclear explosive device prior to January 1, 1967.

4. For States whose instruments of ratification or accession are deposited subsequent to the entry into force of this Treaty, it shall enter into force on the date of the deposit of their instruments of ratification or accession.

5. The Depositary Governments shall promptly inform all signatory and acceding States of the date of each signature, the date of deposit of each instrument of ratification or of accession, the date of the entry into force of this Treaty, and the date of receipt of any requests for convening a conference or other notices.

6. This Treaty shall be registered by the Depositary Governments pursuant to Article 102 of the Charter of the United Nations.

## Article X

1. Each Party shall in exercising its national sovereignty have the right to withdraw from the Treaty if it decides that extraordinary events, related to the subject matter of this Treaty, have jeopardized the supreme interests of its country. It shall give notice of such withdrawal to all other Parties to the Treaty and to the United Nations Security Council three months in advance. Such notice shall include a statement of the extraordinary events it regards as having jeopardized its supreme interests.

2. Twenty-five years after the entry into force of the Treaty, a Conference shall be convened to decide whether the Treaty shall continue in force indefinitely, or shall be extended for an additional fixed period or periods. This decision shall be taken by a majority of the Parties to the Treaty.

## Article XI

This Treaty, the English, Russian, French, Spanish and Chinese texts of which are equally authentic, shall be deposited in the archives of the Depositary Governments. Duly certified copies of this Treaty shall be transmitted by the Depositary Governments to the Governments of the signatory and acceding States.

IN WITNESS WHEREOF the undersigned, duly authorized, have signed this Treaty.

DONE *in* _____ at _____ this _____ of _____.